297 Murray Close/TriStar Pictures, Inc./PhotoFest; 315 Giraudon/Art Resource, NY; 329 file photo; 357 Courtesy of Nancy Schutt; 363 David Young-Wolff/Photo Edit; 375 National Museum of American Art, Washington, DC/Art Resource, NY; 391 Collection of the Artist; 411 Phyllis Kind Gallery, New York/Chicago; 423 Allan Landau; 427 Calvin and Hobbes. © 1986 Watterson, reproduced with permission of Universal Press Syndicate; 435 Robert Miller Gallery, New York; 451 National Museum of American Art, Smithsonian Institution/Art Resource, Bequest of Henry Ward Ranger through the National Academy of Design; 461 Courtesy Frumkin/Adams Galler, New York; 485 The Phillips Collection, Washington, DC; 493 Evans-Tibbs Collection, Washington, DC; 524-525 Archivo Iconográfico, SA/CORBIS; 527 Allan Landau; 528 Cathy Ferris; 534 From The World Book Encyclopedia. Copyright © 1992 World Book, Inc. By permission of World Book, Inc.; 535 Hammond Incorporated, Maplewood, NJ, photo by Allan Landau; 537 Courtesy of Macmillan Publishing; 542 (l) Bob Daemmrich/The Image Works, (c) E. R. Degginger/Earth Scenes, (r) Bob Daemmrich/Stock Boston; 546 Ralph J. Brunke; 551 Neal Mishler/Natural Selection; 555 (t) Bettmann/CORBIS, (b) Vernon Doucette/Stock Boston; 546 through 564 (gears) VCG/FPG; 569 Ralph J. Brunke; 571 Mark Burnett/Stock Boston; 572 Allan Landau; 581 (t) UPI/Bettmann/CORBIS, (bl) Bill Gallery/Stock Boston, (br) NASA; 584 Allan Landau; 619 GARFIELD © Paws, Inc. Reprinted with permission of UNIVERSAL PRESS SYNDICATE. All rights reserved; 621 624 Allan Landau; 631 Excerpt from LISTEN, BUDDY by Helen Lester. Text © 1995 by Helen Lester. Illustrations © 1995 by Lynn Munsinger. Reprinted by permission of Houghton Mifflin Company. All rights reserved; 632 The Boston Globe; 634 (t) Photofest, (b) Movie Still Archive; 639 Stephen Simpson/FPG; 646 Jeffrey Muir Hamilton/Liaison; 650 file photo.

ACKNOWLEDGMENTS

Text

Unit One "This is Just to Say" by William Carlos Williams, from *Collected Poems: 1909-1939, vol. I.* Copyright 1938 by New Directions Publishing Corporation. Reprinted by permission of New Directions Publishing Corp.

From *The Invisible Thread* by Yoshiko Uchida. Copyright 1991 by Yoshiko Uchida. Courtesy of the Bancroft Library, University of California, Berkeley.

Unit Two From "The Empire Builder" by Curtis Katz. Reprinted by permission.

From *Coast to Coast* by Betsy Byars. Copyright 1992 by Betsy Byars. Used by permission of Delacorte Press, a division of Random House Inc.

Unit Three From "Attacking the Nunataks" by John Boulanger. *International Wildlife*, November/December 1993. Reprinted with permission.

From *Julie of the Wolves* by Jean Craighead George. Copyright 1972 by Jean Craighead George. Reprinted by permission of HarperCollins Publishers, Inc.

From *Morning Girl* by Michael Dorris. Copyright 1992 by Michael Dorris. Published by Hyperion Books for Children.

Unit Four From *W.E.B. DuBois: A Biography* by Virginia Hamilton. Copyright © 1992 by Virginia Hamilton. Reprinted by permission of Arnold Adoff.

"The Jacket" by Gary Soto, is reprinted by permission from the publisher of *Small Faces* (Houston: Arte Publico Press—University of Houston, 1992).

Unit Five From "How Does Michael Fly?" by Julie Sheet. Copyrighted Chicago Tribune Company. All rights reserved. Used with permission, 1990.

From "Bathing Elephants" from *Keepers and Creatures at the National Zoo* by Peggy Thomson. Copyright 1988 by Peggy Thomson. Reprinted by permission of the author.

Unit Six From "A Popular Little Planet" by Douglas Anderson. Copywrited © 1992 Children's Television Workshop. Reprinted by permission.

"Thanking the Birds" by Joseph Bruchac, from *Keepers of the Earth: Native American Stories and Environmental Activities for Children* by Michael Caduto and Joseph Bruchac. Fulcrum Publishing, 350 Indiana St., #350, Golden, CO 80401. 303-277-1623. Reprinted by permission.

Photo

Cover KS Studio; **vi** Copyright © The Detroit Institute of Arts, City of Detroit Purchase; **vii** (t)Photodisc, Inc., (b)Ralph J. Brunke; **viii** (l)© Time, Inc., (r)Movie Still Archive; **ix** Edition Leipzig, Germany. Courtesy of the Library of the Academy of Sciences of St. Petersburg, Russia; **x** (t)From the Collection of the Portland Art Museum, (b)Courtesy of Carmen Garza; **xi** © DC Comics, Inc; **xii** Art Wise; **xiii** © DC Comics, Inc; **xiv** ©1983 Andy Warhol/Ronald Feldman Fine Arts, courtesy Ronald Feldman Arts, NY; **xvi** Robert Miller Gallery, New York; **xvii** Collection of Lois Mailou Jones; **xviii** Courtesy of Nancy Schütz; **xx** Ralph J. Brunke; **xxiii** Photodisc, Inc.; **xxiv** Scala/Art Resource, NY; **xxv** Art Wise; **xxvii** Los Angeles County Museum of Art, gift of Mrs. Homer Kripke; **xviii** xxix file photo; **xxxii-1** Philadelphia Museum of Art/CORBIS; **2-3** Jim Sugar Photo/CORBIS; **4** Art Wise; **8 through 14** Ralph J. Brunke; **16** Ralph A. Deinhold/Animals Animals; **18** Ralph J. Brunke; **21** Nathaniel Bruns; **23** Erich Lessing/Art Resource, NY; **24** Bob Daemmrich/Stock Boston; **27** Seth Resnick/Stock Boston; **30** *Farmhouse and Chestnut Trees at Jas-de-Bouffan,* c. 1885. Paul Cezanne (1839-1906). Oil on canvas, 36x29 inches. F. 1969.38.2.P The Norton Simon Museum; **32** Copyright © 1980, Helen Oji. Collection of Prudential Insurance Co., Newark, NJ; **35** Jim Sugar Photo/CORBIS; **36-37** Mike Dwyer/ Stock Boston/PictureQuest; **42** Allan Landau; **46 48 50 54** Ralph J. Brunke; **57** Courtesy of Tina Dunkley; **58 59** Ralph J. Brunke; **60** Historical Pictures/Stock Montage; **65** Private collection, photo courtesy of Joshua Baer & Company, Sante Fe, NM; **66** Steven Frame/Stock Boston; **67** Ralph J. Brunke; **70** Allan Landau; **72 74** Ralph J. Brunke; **78** FPG; **81** FPG; **83** Giraudon/Art Resource, NY. Copyright © 1992 ARS, New York/ADAGP, Paris; **84** Scala/Art Resource, NY; **88** Mike Dwyer/Stock Boston/PictureQuest; **100-101** Pal Hermansen/Tony Dwyer/Stock Boston/PictureQuest; **102** John Boulanger; **106** Lawrence Migdale/Stock Boston; **107** Matthew McVay/Stock Boston; **110** Ralph J. Brunke; **111** Janice Fried; **113** Edition Leipzig, Germany. Courtesy of the Library of the Academy of Sciences of St. Petersburg, Russia; **114** Thomas R. Fletcher/ Stock Boston; **115 116** Allan Landau; **117** Tony Shafrazi Gallery, New York. Collection Mr. & Mrs. K. Scharf; **118** Culver Pictures; **121** Salander-O'Reilly Galleries; **122** Jose Carrillo/Stock Boston; **126** Allan Landau; **127** Ralph J. Brunke; **128** Allan Landau; **130** Myrleen Ferguson/PhotoEdit; **133** Stephen Frisch/Stock Boston; **135** Giraudon/Art Resource, NY. Copyright © 1992 ARS, New York/SPADEM, Paris; **138** Scala/Art Resource, NY; **141** Pal Hermansen/Tony Stone Images; **142-143** Alan Detrick/ Photo Researchers; **148** Allan Landau; **152** (t)Frans Lanting/Minden Pictures, (b)From the Collection of the Portland Art Museum, photo by Edward S. Curtis; **156** Bill Aron/PhotoEdit; **157** Calvin and Hobbes. Copyright © 1992 Watterson. Reprinted with permission of Universal Press Syndicate. All rights reserved; **159** Scala/Art Resource, New York; **160** Charles Palek/Animals Animals; **164 166** UPI/Bettmann/CORBIS; **168** Tony Freeman/ PhotoEdit; **173** Acervo Patrimonial de la Secretario de Haciende y Credito Publico, Mexico, D.F.; **174** Courtesy of Carmen Garza; **179** Alan Detrick/ Photo Researchers; **180-181** Staffan Widstrand/CORBIS; **182** Allan Landau; **186** Peter L. Chapman/Stock Boston; **187** Allan Landau; **190** © DC Comics, Inc; **194** © AFP; **197** Los Angeles County Museum of Art, gift of Mrs. Homer Kripke; **202** Janice Fried/ Tony Stone Images; **204** Allan Landau; **206** Diane Graham-Henry/Tony Stone Images; **209** Tony Stone Images; **213** ©1983 Andy Warhol/Ronald Feldman Fine Arts, New York; **215** Staffan Widstrand/CORBIS; **216-217** Jim Brandenburg/Minden Pictures; **222 223 224** Art Wise; **225** © Jasper Johns/VAGA, New York 1992. Collection Albright-Knox Art Gallery, Buffalo, NY; **228** (t)Mike Okoniewski/The Image Works, (b)Myrleen Ferguson/PhotoEdit; **230-231 232** Allan Landau; **234** Art Wise; **241** David Young-Wolf/PhotoEdit; **243** Courtesy Elaine Horwitch Galleries, Scottsdale, Arizona; **247** Jim Brandenburg/ Minden Pictures; **248-249** Randy Faris/CORBIS; **294-295** SuperStock;

Teacher Wraparound Edition

GLENCOE

Writer's Choice

Grammar and Composition
Grade 6

McGraw Hill Glencoe

New York, New York   Columbus, Ohio   Chicago, Illinois   Peoria, Illinois   Woodland Hills, California

ACKNOWLEDGMENTS

Grateful acknowledgment is given authors, publishers, photographers, museums, and agents for permission to reprint the following copyrighted material. Every effort has been made to determine copyright owners. In case of any omissions, the Publisher will be pleased to make suitable acknowledgments in future editions.

Acknowledgments continued on page 703.

 The **Facing the Blank Page** feature in this book was prepared in collaboration with the writers and editors of *TIME*.

6+1 Trait® is a registered trademark of Northwest Regional Educational Laboratory, which does not endorse this product.

 **Glencoe McGraw-Hill**

The **McGraw·Hill** Companies

PRINTED IN THE UNITED STATES OF AMERICA

Send all inquiries to:
GLENCOE/MCGRAW-HILL
8787 Orion Place
Columbus, OH 43240-4027

ISBN 0-07-829814-8
(Student Edition)
ISBN 0-07-829807-5
(Teacher Wraparound Edition)

2 3 4 5 6 7 8 9 10 071/043 09 08 07 06 05

Contents

Teacher Wraparound Edition

Welcome to *Writer's Choice*

Congratulations! By opening this book, you've taken an important step toward helping your students become **better writers and communicators**. The pages that follow help you see at a glance the features of the *Writer's Choice* Student Edition, the Teacher Wraparound Edition, and the program's additional resources.

The Benefits of *Writer's Choice*

- An integrated approach to language arts
- Concise lessons that target key skills
- Diverse contexts and frequent writing opportunities
- Real-world writing examples from both students and published authors
- Systematic teaching and practice of grammar concepts

Quick Reference

- An easy-to-use Writing and Research Handbook
- A teacher edition with point-of-use convenience and built-in flexibility
- Program resources that expand your teaching options

Plus, Improved Test Performance

The **Taking Tests** unit of *Writer's Choice* gives students the strategies and the practice they need to become better test-takers. Working through the **Standardized Test Practice** pages will help students become comfortable with the format and the types of items they will typically face on standardized tests.

Targeted Writing Instruction, Modeling, and Practice

In **Part 1: Composition**, students will learn how to apply the writing process to various modes of writing. Grammar and other language arts skills are integrated into each lesson.

Real Writers at Work

A four-page **Writing in the Real World** case study launches each composition unit. This **behind-the-scenes glimpse of the writing process** offers students a model of good writing practices.

Targeted visuals provide access to writing skills for students who learn best visually.

Real-life examples offer models for students and answers to the difficult question "When am I ever going to use this?"

The **writing process,** as practiced by professional writers, presents a clear map for working through a piece of writing.

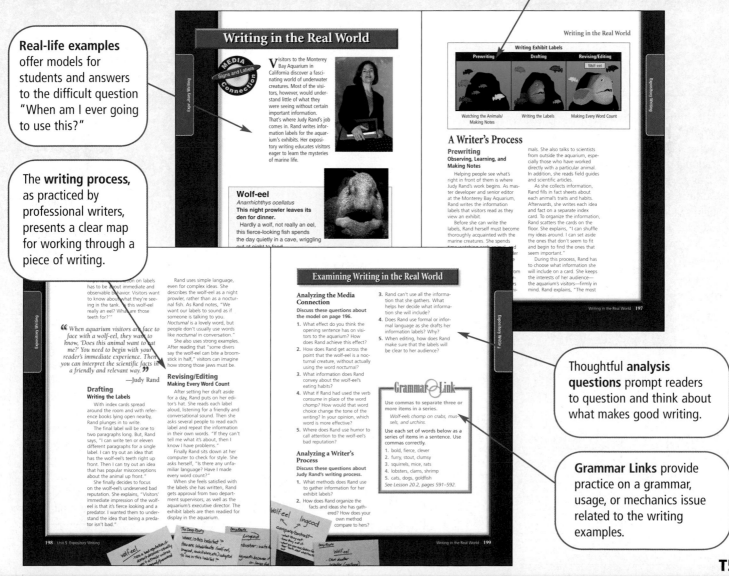

Thoughtful **analysis questions** prompt readers to question and think about what makes good writing.

Grammar Links provide practice on a grammar, usage, or mechanics issue related to the writing examples.

AT A GLANCE

Focused Four-Page Lessons

You won't find long-winded writing about writing in *Writer's Choice*. Literature models, student models, and instructional visuals combine to **show rather than just tell.**

Illustrations, graphs, and charts make information visual and easy to grasp. Also, fine art in many styles and from many cultures inspires writing and discussion.

Journal Writing activities midway through each lesson prompt students to "write to learn."

Literature Models supply students with models for good writing. Thoughtful callouts prompt students to analyze how published authors use the strategies being taught in the lesson.

Student models illustrate how student writers put into practice the lessons being taught.

Writing Activities provide prompts and rubrics related to the lesson. Grammar Links provide practice; other activities show alternative ways of working with the topic.

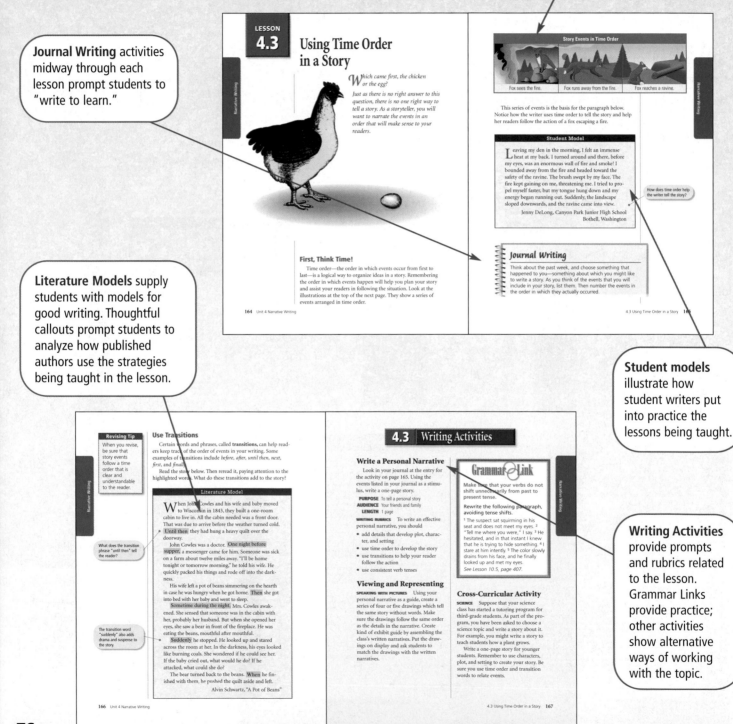

Scaffolded Instruction of the Writing Process

For each mode of writing, the **Writing Process in Action** pages walk students through the recursive steps of prewriting, drafting, revising, editing, and publishing a piece of writing.

The Reading/Writing Connection

Literature Models by contemporary authors mirror the mode of writing taught in each unit. Discussion questions and a related writing activity follow each selection.

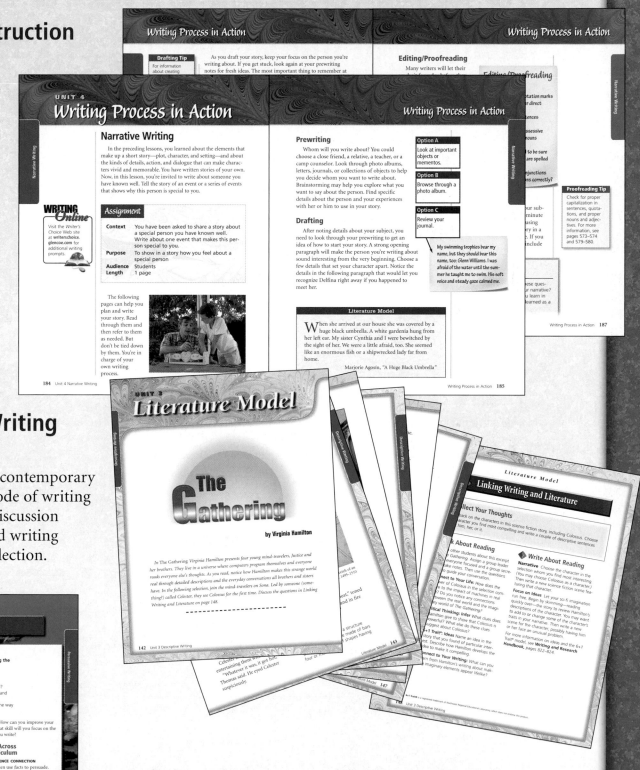

Authentic Assessment of Writing Skills

Unit Review questions, activities, and portfolio selections give you the opportunity to assess students' knowledge and skills.

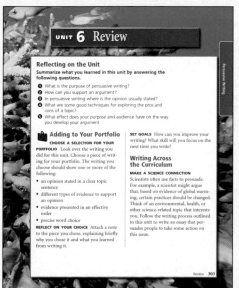

Systematic Grammar Instruction with Extensive Practice

Based on a define-explain-model approach and strongly supported with extensive practice-and-apply exercises, **Part 2: Grammar, Usage, and Mechanics** provides the solid foundation your students need.

Short Targeted Lessons

Each Part 2 lesson focuses on a single grammar, usage, or mechanics concept with **clear, direct teaching** and exercises for practice.

> **Exercises** give students the chance to practice what they've learned.

> A **definition** or **rule** clearly states the concept being taught.

> **Examples,** often in graphic form, illustrate the concept.

> **Elaboration** further explains and refines the concept.

12.6 Adverbs

■ An **adverb** is a word that modifies, or describes, a verb, an adjective, or another adverb.

What Adverbs Modify

Verbs	The Inca worked **carefully** on their buildings.
Adverbs	The Inca left their ancient cities **quite** suddenly.
Adjectives	Machu Picchu is a **very** large ruin in Peru.

When modifying a verb, an adverb may describe *how* or *in what manner* the action is done. It may describe *when* or *how often* an action is done. Also, it may describe *where* or *in what direction* an action was done.

Ways Adverbs Modify Verbs

How?	Machu Picchu sits **silently** in the Andes.
When?	Many scientists **now** explore this city.
Where?	Scientists dig **there** for facts about the Inca.

Many adverbs are formed by adding *-ly* to adjectives. However, not all words that end in *-ly* are adverbs. The words *friendly, lively, kindly,* and *lonely* are usually adjectives. Similarly, not all adverbs end in *-ly*.

Adverbs not Ending in -ly

afterward	often	there	hard
sometimes	soon	everywhere	long
later	here	fast	straight

12.6 Adverbs **461**

Exercise 11 Identifying Adverbs

For each of the following sentences, write the adverb and then write the word it modifies.

1. Hiram Bingham searched diligently for the lost Incan cities.
2. Bingham and his aides looked everywhere in western South America.
3. They traveled slowly through thick jungles.
4. Slowly they crossed rushing rivers.
5. The explorers cautiously carried their own food and supplies.
6. Bingham and his searchers carefully climbed the steep mountainsides.
7. They carefully studied the legends.
8. The Urubamba River snaked below.
9. The lost city of Machu Picchu lay above.
10. Once many people came to the Incan city.
11. Now the Peruvian jungle growth covered Machu Picchu.
12. The mist lifted briefly over the walled city.
13. The city's emptiness affected them greatly.
14. They felt strongly the passage of centuries.
15. Bingham's group worked hard at their task of discovery.
16. The Inca's irrigation system carried water efficiently.
17. They constructed their houses solidly.
18. The Inca were apparently skilled in agriculture.
19. They were plentifully supplied with water.
20. The people worked skillfully with metals, pottery, and wool.

Exercise 12 Using Adverbs

Write an adverb to modify the underlined word in each sentence.

1. People <u>think</u> of television as a recent invention.
2. Experimental broadcasts <u>began</u> in 1928.
3. The quality of the broadcasts was not <u>good</u>.
4. Two <u>important</u> inventions came after 1930.
5. Philo T. Farnsworth <u>patented</u> a scanning cathode ray tube in 1930.
6. Kate Smith <u>sang</u> on one of the first scheduled broadcasts.
7. By the early 1940s, twenty-three TV stations were <u>operating</u>.
8. TV <u>grew</u> after the lifting of wartime restrictions.
9. By 1949 more than a million families <u>had bought</u> TV sets.
10. Ten years later the number <u>had multiplied</u> to 50 million.

462 Unit 12 Adjectives and Adverbs

Adjectives and Adverbs

Comprehensive Grammar Assessment

Grammar Reviews at the end of each unit allow you to assess students' learning in a comprehensive and meaningful way.

A **Literature Model** shows students how a published author handles concepts that have been covered in the unit.

Exercises assess students' understanding of the concepts taught in the unit.

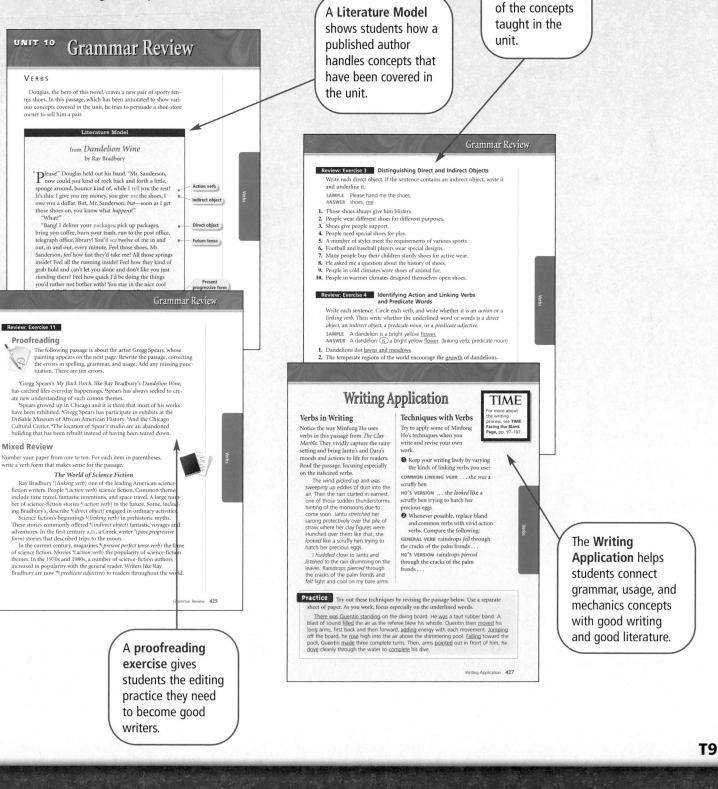

A **proofreading exercise** gives students the editing practice they need to become good writers.

The **Writing Application** helps students connect grammar, usage, and mechanics concepts with good writing and good literature.

A "Tool Kit" of Real-World Skills

Part 3: Resources and Skills provides instruction, examples, and practice in research, vocabulary, spelling, study skills, test-taking, listening and speaking, viewing and representing, and using electronic resources.

Clear Instruction

Easy-to-read text and graphics connect students' interests with what they need to know.

Helpful Examples

Examples, often in graphic form, illustrate and expand upon instruction.

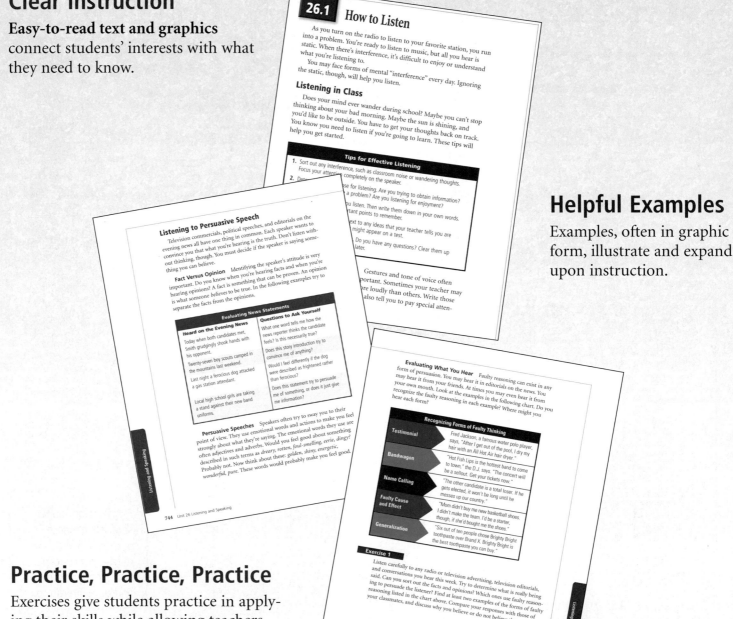

26.1 How to Listen

As you turn on the radio to listen to your favorite station, you run into a problem. You're ready to listen to music, but all you hear is static. When there's interference, it's difficult to enjoy or understand what you're listening to.

You may face forms of mental "interference" every day. Ignoring the static, though, will help you listen.

Listening in Class

Does your mind ever wander during school? Maybe you can't stop thinking about your bad morning. Maybe the sun is shining, and you'd like to be outside. You have to get your thoughts back on track. You know you need to listen if you're going to learn. These tips will help you get started.

Tips for Effective Listening

1. Sort out any interference, such as classroom noise or wandering thoughts. Focus your attention completely on the speaker.

2. Det... ...se for listening. Are you trying to obtain information? ...a problem? Are you listening for enjoyment?
...u listen. Then write them down in your own words. ...tant points to remember.
...ext to any ideas that your teacher tells you are ...might appear on a test.
Do you have any questions? Clear them up ...later.

Gestures and tone of voice often ...ortant. Sometimes your teacher may ...re loudly than others. Write those ...also tell you to pay special atten-

Listening to Persuasive Speech

Television commercials, political speeches, and editorials on the evening news all have one thing in common. Each speaker wants to convince you that what you're hearing is the truth. Don't listen without thinking, though. You must decide if the speaker is saying something you can believe.

Fact Versus Opinion Identifying the speaker's attitude is very important. Do you know when you're hearing facts and when you're hearing opinions? A fact is something that can be proven. An opinion is what someone *believes* to be true. In the following examples try to separate the facts from the opinions.

Evaluating News Statements

Heard on the Evening News	Questions to Ask Yourself
Today when both candidates met, Smith grudgingly shook hands with his opponent.	What one word tells me how the news reporter thinks the candidate feels? Is this necessarily true?
Twenty-seven boy scouts camped in the mountains last weekend.	Does this story introduction try to convince me of anything?
Last night a ferocious dog attacked a gas station attendant.	Would I feel differently if the dog were described as frightened rather than ferocious?
Local high school girls are taking a stand against their new band uniforms.	Does this statement try to persuade me of something, or does it just give me information?

Persuasive Speeches Speakers often try to sway you to their point of view. They use emotional words and actions to make you feel strongly about what they're saying. The emotional words they use are often adjectives and adverbs. Would you feel good about something described in such terms as *dreary, rotten, foul-smelling, eerie, dingy*? Probably not. Now think about these: *golden, shiny, energetic, wonderful, pure*. These words would probably make you feel good.

744 Unit 26 Listening and Speaking

Listening and Speaking

Evaluating What You Hear Faulty reasoning can exist in any form of persuasion. You may hear it in editorials on the news. You may hear it from your friends. At times you may even hear it from your own mouth. Look at the examples in the following chart. Do you recognize the faulty reasoning in each example? Where might you hear each form?

Recognizing Forms of Faulty Thinking

Testimonial	Fred Jackson, a famous water polo player, says, "After I get out of the pool, I dry my hair with an All Hot Air hair dryer."
Bandwagon	"Hot Fish Lips is the hottest band to come to town," the D.J. says. "The concert will be a sellout. Get your tickets now."
Name Calling	"The other candidate is a total loser. If he gets elected, it won't be long until he messes up our country."
Faulty Cause and Effect	"Mom didn't buy me new basketball shoes. I didn't make the team. I'd be a starter, though, if she'd bought me the shoes."
Generalization	"Six out of ten people chose Brighty Bright toothpaste over Brand X. Brighty Bright is the best toothpaste you can buy."

Exercise 1

Listen carefully to any radio or television advertising, television editorials, and conversations you hear this week. Try to determine what is really being said. Can you sort out the facts and opinions? Which ones are trying to persuade the listener? Find at least two examples of the forms of faulty reasoning listed in the chart above. Compare your responses with those of your classmates, and discuss why you believe or do not believe the messages.

26.1 How to Listen 747

Listening and Speaking

Practice, Practice, Practice

Exercises give students practice in applying their skills while allowing teachers to assess students' understanding of the subject.

T10

Taking Standardized Tests

While the entire *Writer's Choice* program has been designed to help students gain the skills and knowledge they need to achieve on standardized tests, the **Taking Tests** unit in particular helps students prepare for these tests.

Effective Test Preparation

The unit begins with **proven test-taking strategies** and an explanation of the types of items and formats most commonly used in standardized tests.

Extensive Test Practice

Exercises that mimic the format and content of standardized writing tests provide students with practice in answering items on sentence structure, usage, and mechanics.

Special Features: Enrichment and Remediation

Writer's Choice has many outstanding features to support and extend students' learning. From real-world advice to real-time remediation, these features **maximize students' potential.**

Writing Advice from the Pros

TIME Facing the Blank Page shows how professional writers and editors at **TIME magazine** practice each stage of the writing process. Thoughtful discussion questions, relevant writing assignments, and questions prompting students to think about their own writing conclude each section.

Prewriting

Getting Started: Finding Story Ideas

Generating good ideas for stories is as important—and can take as much time—as writing and editing the articles themselves. You may be assigned topics to write about; sometimes TIME writers get assignments, too. But just as often, writers are expected to come up with their own subjects and develop an interesting angle for a story.

Staff Writer and TV critic James Poniewozik tells how he gets started:

"Ideas for stories come from anything that surprises you. If you're watching a lot of television—for example, all the new pilots for the fall season—you might start noticing trends."

You might say, 'Gee, it seems that every other show has a voice-over on it, with characters talking directly to the camera.' You ask yourself, 'What does that mean? Is it a good thing or is it a bad thing? Is it a storytelling crutch, a way for writers to communicate characters' feelings without doing it through action and dialogue?' And so there's a story idea there—something that strikes you as a topic worth exploring.

The ideas part is pretty tough. I think one of the best ways to generate ideas is to talk to other people about things you're interested in. I've had a lot of story ideas that I didn't know were story ideas until I talked about them. I'll mention something in a conversation to others and they'll say, 'Oh, that sounds like it would make a topic for a story,' and I'll suddenly realize, 'Yes, it would!' Of course, I may have thought about the subject a half-dozen times before, but it never occurred to me to write about it."

Janice Simpson, Senior Editor:

"If something is interesting to you as a writer or reporter—if something piques your curiosity and you want to know more about it—then probably there are other people who do, too. So I think we start there. What interests you? What catches your attention?"

James Poniewozik: Write about what surprises you.

Another way to find story ideas is to work with your fellow writers. At TIME, the writers in each section hold "story meetings" to share news and ideas. Michael Lemonick, Senior Writer at TIME, discusses the collaborative process.

Michael Lemonick: Brainstorm with others.

Michael Lemonick writes for TIME's Science section:

"Our group holds brainstorm sessions once a week, where we share ideas with each other. I keep my eyes and ears open all the time—with radio, TV news, friends, scientific journals, more specialized magazines, and local newspapers. Mostly I want to know what regular people are interested in or worried about.

Once the idea is there, we consult with each other about sources. Then the editor sends out a query to correspondents, and we start to shape the story we want. For example, with our cover story on microbes, we had heard a report about a new strain of drug-resistant tuberculosis, but someone then brought up another point. Working together, we came up with a concept for a big story: war against diseases. We all communicate with each other verbally, within staff meetings, by phone, and we get further ideas from correspondents in the bureaus.

After I'm assigned a story, I read everything I can find that's been printed to get a sense of the subject. I also conduct some of the interviews, along with the correspondents."

TIME LEXICON

Query: a message sent from TIME's New York office to correspondents in the field asking them to gather information and conduct interviews for a proposed story.

LEARNING FROM THE WRITERS

DISCUSSION
1. What benefits of working collaboratively do both James Poniewozik and Michael Lemonick point out?
2. Do you prefer working by yourself, in pairs, or in groups? List the pros and cons of each method.

TRY IT OUT
1. Have a class brainstorming session to come up with ideas for your next writing project. Try working in pairs or small groups. See Lesson 2.2,

"Prewriting: Finding and Exploring a Topic."
2. Finding story ideas close to home. Using James Poniewozik's notion that story ideas come from anything that surprises you or from thoughts you've had over and over, think through a regular day at home or school. What routine event or daily observation might lend itself to a piece of writing? Have you found yourself telling anyone the same story or making the same comment day after day?

Choose one as the basis of a story for the school newspaper or a piece of creative writing.

HOW I WRITE
1. Look back over some of the writing you've done recently. Where did you get the idea for each piece? Do you see a pattern, or do you find writing ideas in a variety of ways?
2. Using Janice Simpson's advice, brainstorm a list of things you're interested in. Which ones might you want to develop in writing?

100 TIME Facing the Blank Page

TIME Facing the Blank Page **101**

7.7 Incorrect Use of Commas

Problem 1

Missing commas in a series of three or more items

com   We visited the museum, the zoo, and the aquarium.
com   Sam drove down the block, around the corner, and into the parking lot.

SOLUTION Use commas to separate three or more items in a series.

We visited the museum, the zoo, and the aquarium.
Sam drove down the block, around the corner, and into the parking lot.

Problem 2

Missing commas with direct quotations

com   "Biology class," said Ms. Blas, "meets tomorrow."
com   "Let's rake the leaves," said Ben, "before we leave."

SOLUTION The first part of an interrupted quotation ends with a comma, followed by quotation marks. The interrupting words are also followed by a comma.

"Biology class," said Ms. Blas, "meets tomorrow."
"Let's rake the leaves," said Ben, "before we leave."

Problem 3

Missing commas with nonessential appositives

com   Our house, a split-level, was painted last year.
com   My bicycle, a black ten-speed, was shipped to Alaska.

SOLUTION Determine whether the appositive is truly essential to the meaning of the sentence. If it is not essential, set off the appositive with commas.

Our house, a split-level, was painted last year.
My bicycle, a black ten-speed, was shipped to Alaska.

If you need more help with commas, turn to Lessons 20.2–20.4, pages 591–596.

320   Unit 7 Troubleshooter

Unit 7.7 Incorrect Use of Commas   321

Fixes for Common Errors

Teachers see certain errors again and again in student writing. **Troubleshooter** offers solutions to the most common of these errors, including fragments, run-ons, and lack of subject-verb agreement.

Writing for Work

Lessons on topics such as writing a business letter, conducting interviews, and creating multimedia presentations introduce students to the specialized skills of **Business and Technical Writing.**

Fun Facts About Language

Wordworks takes a humorous look at how we use and misuse our language. Unique one-page lessons give students an enjoyable way to study words and language development.

Easy-to-Reference Writing Guide

The **Writing and Research Handbook** provides tips for writing good sentences, paragraphs, and compositions; instruction on using the 6+1 Trait® model; and tools to help students conduct and document research.

Business Letters

Types of Business Letters

There are several types of business letters. You can use the formal business letter format to express your opinion; to request information or order a product; to make a complaint and describe a problem with a product or service; or to apply for a job, an award, or a scholarship.

When you write a business letter, keep your purpose in mind. Be brief. Don't include unnecessary information. Limit your letter to one page or less, if possible. A busy person is more likely to read your letter if it is brief.

A business letter is formal. Use polite language but a friendly tone. Avoid wordy language. For example, say "Thank you for your help" rather than "Thank you for your kind assistance in this matter."

TYPES OF BUSINESS LETTERS

Opinion Letter	Request Letter	Complaint Letter	Application Letter
State the issue briefly.	State your request briefly and clearly.	Be polite.	Write to a specific person.
State your opinion in the first sentence or two.	Make your request specific and reasonable.	Identify the product or service clearly.	Describe the job or program for which you're applying.
Support your opinion with reasons, facts, and examples.	Include all necessary information.	Describe the problem briefly and accurately.	List your qualifications.
Summarize your main points and offer a	Include your phone number or a self-addressed,	Request a specific solution.	Explain briefly why you're the best person for the position or the award.
		Keep a copy of your letter until your complaint has been resolved.	Request an application form or an interview.

Modified Block Style In modified block style, the heading, the closing, your signature, and your typed name begin at the center of the paper. Paragraphs may be indented-five spaces on a typewriter or half an inch on a computer—or not indented. If paragraphs are indented, there is no need to place a line space between them. The following letter is in modified block style with paragraphs indented.

```
                              708 Mount Vernon Rd.      (Heading)
                              Greenleaf, ME  10908
                              February 12, 2001

Mr. Bruce Chung, Manager              (Inside Address)
Greenleaf Department of Recreation
304 S. Main St.
Greenleaf, ME  10908

Dear Mr. Chung:    (Salutation)
     I understand that next month (March) you will be
arranging the schedule for the city softball fields for
spring and summer. Please schedule some time for kids
who are not part of any organized league.
     There are many kids in our community who do not    (Body)
belong to a league but who love to play softball. The
parents of these kids pay taxes that are used for city
recreation as do the parents of the kids in the leagues.
     I suggest reserving diamonds 4 and 6 on
Wednesdays from 2:30 p.m. to 5 p.m. This would not
interfere with evening or weekend games.

                              Yours truly,    (Closing)

                              Megan Payson    (Name and Signature)
                              Megan Payson
```

The Parts of a Business Letter

A business letter has six parts.

Heading
- your street address
- your city, state, and ZIP code
- the date

Inside Address
- the name of the person to whom you're writing

- the title of the person to whom you're writing (Place a comma after the name and write a short title on the same line. Use a separate line for a long title without a comma after the person's name.)
- the name of the business or organization
- the street address
- the city, state, and ZIP code

Business and Technical Writing **331**

Wordworks

DOES THIS MAKE ¢

Have you ever played the picture game in picture to represent a word? Your teamma word by looking at your drawing. The g all words are easy to draw or guess.

What if you always had to use picture something in common with people livin writing systems were first developing. P the earliest forms of writing—before a pictographic writing, a picture of a tre "tree" and a picture of the sun would There are limitations to pictographic Try creating a simple picture to me "thinking" or "dizzy." You'll soon isn't always worth a thousand w

As pictographic writing deve ther, people used pictures to r sounds of words. For example pictographs today, a picture could mean "sun" or "son

A picture could also be just one syllable of a word of a key to stand for the lucky would be one exa

A picture that repr word or phrase is call of rebuses was a big systems. The rebus

---

Wordworks

CAN YOU PICK A FLOUR?

"How is bread made?"

"I know that!" Alice cried eagerly. "You take some flour—"

"Where do you pick the flower?" the White Queen asked. "In a garden, or in the hedges?"

"Well, it isn't picked at all," Alice explained: "it's ground—"

"How many acres of ground?" said the White Queen.

In this passage from *Through the Looking Glass,* Lewis Carroll plays with homophones, words having the same sounds but different meanings.

Most of today's homophones didn't always sound alike. *Bear* and *bare* began as English words with the same meanings as today—a bear was an animal, and bare meant "uncovered." However, hundreds of years ago bear and bare didn't sound the same at all. The word bear, spelled *bera,* had two syllables. The word bare, spelled *bær,* had the vowel sound of the *a* in bat. Gradually, the pronunciations grew closer until the words became homophones.

Grate, which was borrowed from French originally had the same meaning as it does today, "a metal lattice to cover a window or fire." The English word great, which originally meant "thick" or "coarse," had two syllables. Later, the second syllable was lost, so that today we have another pair of homophones .

Challenge

"Cinderella opened a photo shop and waited for her prints to come." Think of another silly joke that depends upon homophones. Better yet, make one up.

ACTIVITY

Get It Together

Give the homophones for each pair of clues.

1. a story; what a dog wags
2. it stops your bike; a crack in a vase
3. bread before baking; female deer
4. a dark time; a medieval warrior
5. animal feet; a short rest

WRITING AND RESEARCH HANDBOOK

What are the basic tools for building strong sentences, paragraphs, compositions, and research papers? You'll find them in this handbook—an easy-to-use "tool kit" for writers like you. Check out the helpful explanations, examples, and tips as you complete your writing assignments.

Writing Good Sentences

A sentence is a group of words that expresses a complete thought. Every sentence has a subject and a predicate.

Using Various Types of Sentences

How you craft a sentence—as a statement, question, command, or exclamation—depends on the job you want the sentence to do.

Type	Job It Does	Ways to Use It
Declarative	Makes a statement	Report information *October is National Pizza Month.*
Interrogative	Asks a question	Make your readers curious *Why is pizza so popular?*
Imperative	Gives a command or makes a request	Tell how to do something *Spread the toppings on the pizza dough.*
Exclamatory	Expresses strong feeling	Emphasize a startling fact *Every second, Americans eat about 350 slices of pizza!*

Varying Sentence Structure and Length

Many sentences in a row that look and sound alike can be boring. Vary your sentence openers to make your writing interesting.

- **Start a sentence with an adjective or an adverb.**
  Suddenly the sky turned dark.
- **Start a sentence with a phrase.**
  Like a fireworks show, lightning streaked across the sky.
- **Start a sentence with a clause.**
  As the thunderstorm began, people ran for cover.

Many short sentences in a row make writing sound choppy and ull. To make your writing sound pleasing, vary the sentence length.

short sentences into longer ones.
oes are also called twisters. They are spinning clouds. The ds are funnel shaped.
does, also called twisters, are spinning funnel-shaped clouds.

te shorter sentences with longer sentences.
ado winds are powerful. They can hurl cows into the air, tear ees from their roots, and turn cars upside down.

Parallelism

allelism is the use of a pair or a series of words, phrases, or ces that have the same grammatical structure. Use parallelism tention to the items in the series and to create unity in writing.

Parallel	Gymnasts are strong, flexible, and move gracefully.	
lel	Gymnasts are strong, flexible, and graceful.	
Parallel	Do warm-up exercises to prevent sports injuries and for stretching your muscles.	
llel	Do warm-up exercises to prevent sports injuries and to stretch your muscles.	
ot Parallel	Stand on one leg, bend the other leg, and you should pull your heel.	
Parallel	Stand on one leg, bend the other leg, and pull your heel.	

Revising Wordy Sentences

Revise wordy sentences to make every word count.

- **Cut needless words.**
  Wordy — We need to have bike lanes in streets due to the fact that people like to ride their bikes to work and school, and it's not safe otherwise.
  Concise — We need bike lanes in streets so that people can safely ride to work and school.
- **Rewrite sentences opening with the word there.**
  Wordy — There are many kids riding their bikes in the street.
  Concise — Many kids ride their bikes in the street.
- **Change verbs in passive voice to active voice.**
  Wordy — Bikes are also ridden by grown-ups who want to keep fit.
  Concise — Grown-ups who want to keep fit also ride bikes.

Writing and Research Handbook **817**

A Teacher Wraparound Edition with Point-of-Use Convenience

The **Teacher Wraparound Edition** accommodates a diversity of teachers and learners with an easy-to-use format. Each lesson plan has four parts: Focus, Teach, Assess, and Close. The margins offer additional information and strategies to help you meet the varied needs of your students.

Teach provides varied strategies for customizing the lesson and addressing the needs of basic, average, and advanced learners.

Focus sets clear objectives for learning writing, thinking, listening, and speaking skills. It also provides a daily language activity and motivating activity to jump-start your lesson.

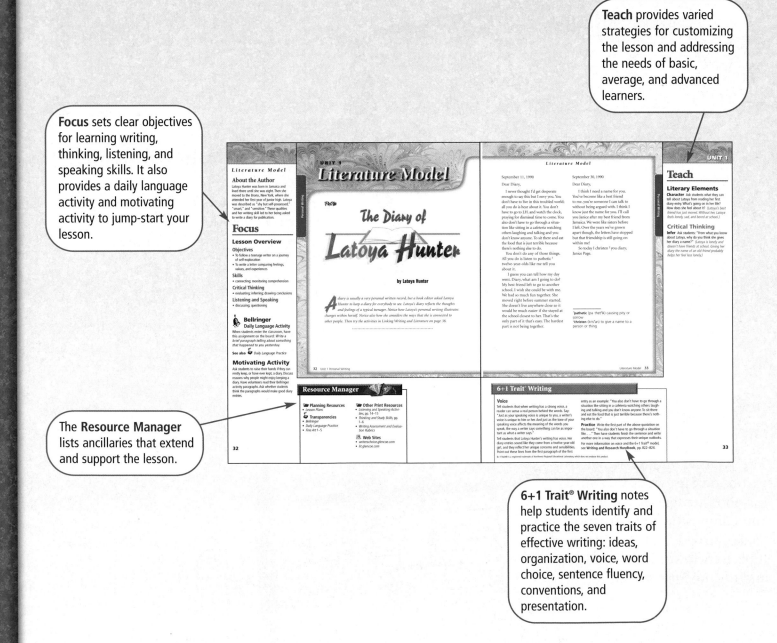

The **Resource Manager** lists ancillaries that extend and support the lesson.

6+1 Trait® Writing notes help students identify and practice the seven traits of effective writing: ideas, organization, voice, word choice, sentence fluency, conventions, and presentation.

A **Two-Minute Skill Drill** provides quick skill practice and challenges students to actively apply lesson concepts.

Bottom-channel notes support critical thinking, cooperative learning, cultural diversity, cross-curricular connections, fine art, technology, and civic literacy. They provide help to English language learners and less-proficient readers and offer enrichment and extension ideas for advanced students.

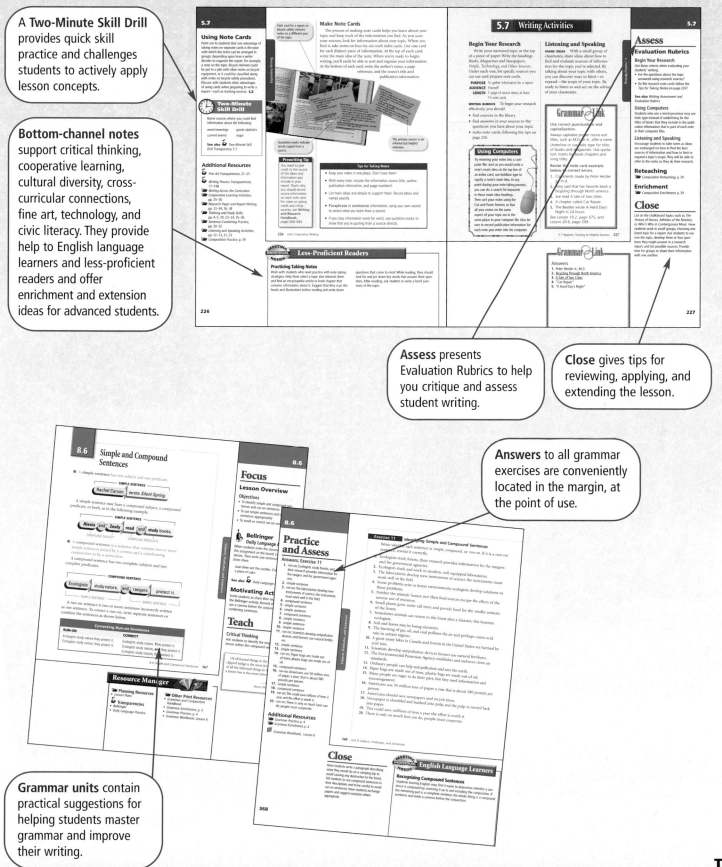

Assess presents Evaluation Rubrics to help you critique and assess student writing.

Close gives tips for reviewing, applying, and extending the lesson.

Answers to all grammar exercises are conveniently located in the margin, at the point of use.

Grammar units contain practical suggestions for helping students master grammar and improve their writing.

Program Resources That Expand Your Teaching Options

Writer's Choice and its ancillary resources deliver **comprehensive, research-based language arts instruction.** Whatever your teaching style or students' learning needs may be, there are program resources that are right for you.

Timesaving Teacher Resources

- TeacherWorks CD-ROM
- Testmaker: ExamView Pro CD-ROM
- Presentation Plus! CD-ROM
- Lesson Plans (print version)
- Block Scheduling Guide
- Teaching Transparencies: Writing Process, Bellringer Activities, Daily Language, Fine Art, and Two-Minute Skill Drill

- Spanish Resources Binder
- Vocabulary Power Puzzlemaker software

Glencoe Exclusive!
TeacherWorks™
All-In-One Planner and Resource Center

Glencoe Teacher Edition
Writer's Choice
Grammar and Composition

- Interactive Teacher Edition
- Interactive Lesson Planner with Calendar
- Point and Click Access Teaching Resources

All-in-One Teacher Support

Writing

Composition Reteaching

Composition Practice

Composition Enrichment

GLENCOE Writer's Choice
Grammar and Composition

Grade 7

- Composition Reteaching, Composition Practice, and Composition Enrichment
- Research Paper and Report Writing
- Style and Documentation Sourcebook for Writers
- Business and Technical Writing Activities
- Sentence-Combining Practice
- Writing Across the Curriculum
- Writing in the Real World
- Revising with Style blackline masters

For Basic, Average, and Advanced Learners

GLENCOE LANGUAGE ARTS
Revising with Style
Windows/Macintosh Software
Middle School

Glencoe Language Arts
TECHNOLOGY

Provides interactive exercises for
- Revising and combining sentences for effectiveness, parallelism and variety
- Building cohesive, well-organized paragraphs
- Proofreading and correcting common writing errors

Technology

- StudentWorks CD-ROM
- Revising with Style CD-ROM
- Writer's Assistant CD-ROM
- Sentence Diagramming CD-ROM
- Interactive Grammar and Language Workbook CD-ROM
- Language Arts PASS CD-ROM

- TIME Facing the Blank Page video
- Mindjogger Videoquizzes
- Guide to Using the Internet and Other Electronic Resources
- TechConnect Online
- Writer's Choice Online Edition: **www.mhln.com**

- Writer's Choice Web site: **www.writerschoice.glencoe.com**
- Glencoe Literature Web site: **www.lit.glencoe.com**

Assessment

- Tests with Answer Keys and Rubrics
- Taking Standardized Tests
- Writing Assessment and Evaluation Rubrics
- Testmaker: ExamView Pro CD-ROM

- Interactive Tutor: Self-Assessment CD-ROM
- ITBS Preparation and Practice Workbook
- SAT-9 Preparation and Practice Workbook
- TerraNova Preparation and Practice Workbook

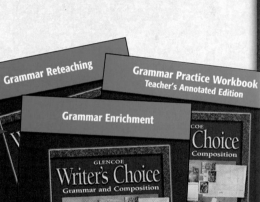

Integrated Language Arts

- inTIME magazine
- Humanities Across TIME
- Listening and Speaking Activities
- Viewing and Representing Activities

- Glencoe Literature Library
- Thinking and Study Skills
- Cooperative Learning Activities

Nonfiction Reading and Writing

Grammar

Differentiated Instruction

- Grammar Reteaching, Grammar Practice, and Grammar Enrichment
- Grammar and Language Workbook
- Grammar and Composition Handbook

- Grammar Practice Workbook
- Sentence Diagraming blackline masters

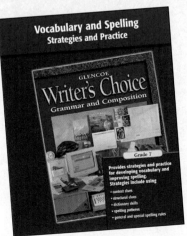

Vocabulary and Spelling

- Vocabulary and Spelling Strategies and Practice
- Spelling Power
- Vocabulary Power

Dinah Zike's FOLDABLES™ for *Writer's Choice*

Only *Writer's Choice* gives you the power of FOLDABLES™! *Dinah Zike's FOLDABLES™ for* **Writer's Choice** shows students how to use three-dimensional interactive graphic organizers to **organize** information, **review** concepts, and **assess** their knowledge.

Integrating Writing, Grammar, and Other Language Skills

The **Weekly Planner** saves you time by suggesting one way to **organize** the lessons in *Writer's Choice* into a yearlong course of instruction. Research suggests that students learn best when the language arts are **integrated.** The Weekly Planner is color coded to show you how to meaningfully integrate

Part 1 Composition

Part 2 Grammar, Usage, and Mechanics

Part 3 Resources and Skills

Differentiated Homework Options

The Weekly Planner lists several key grammar and composition resources you can use as homework for learners of different levels:

- **Reteaching** for basic learners
- **Practice** for average learners
- **Enrichment** for advanced learners

Key resources for improving language and thinking skills for learners of all levels appear under **Mixed Abilities.**

Assessment Opportunities

Tests with Answer Key and Rubrics (also available as *Testmaker* software) provides you with **Pretests** and **Mastery Tests** to gauge your students' progress in a unit. For selected composition units, the resource provides three tests:

- **Choice A** ⎫ writing tests you can use as
- **Choice B** ⎭ either pretests or mastery tests
- **Composition Objective Test** multiple-choice mastery test

Customized Lesson Plans

Keep in mind that this Weekly Planner is only a suggestion. *Writer's Choice* helps you adjust lesson plans to your instructional needs in several ways.

- The Teacher Wraparound Edition lists additional resources at point of use and in Resource Manager boxes.
- The *Lessons Plans* book cites activities relevant to each lesson.
- The *TeacherWorks*™ **CD-ROM** helps you customize your own lesson plans in a calendar format.

T18

	Lessons	Key Resources
WEEK 1 Personal Writing & Subjects, Predicates, and Sentences	**Part 1 Composition** **Unit 1 Personal Writing** Unit 1 Writing in the Real World, pp. 4–7 1.1 Writing as Self-Expression, pp. 8–11 1.2 Writing with Confidence, pp. 12–15 **Part 2 Grammar, Usage, and Mechanics** **Unit 8 Subjects, Predicates, and Sentences** 8.1 Kinds of Sentences, pp. 297–298 8.2 Sentences and Sentence Fragments, pp. 299–300	**Differentiated Homework Options** **Reteaching** *Composition Reteaching*, pp. 1–2 *Grammar Reteaching*, pp. 1–2 **Practice** *Composition Practice*, pp. 1–2 *Grammar Practice Workbook*, p. 1 **Enrichment** *Composition Enrichment*, pp. 1–2 *Grammar Enrichment*, p. 1 **Mixed Abilities** *Grammar and Language Workbook*, Lessons 1–2, 6 *Vocabulary and Spelling Strategies and Practice*, p. 1 **Assessment** *Tests with Answer Key and Rubrics*, pp. 1–2, 33–34 *Testmaker: ExamView Pro* CD-ROM
WEEK 2 Personal Writing & Subjects, Predicates, and Sentences	**Part 1 Composition** 1.3 Making Personal Connections, pp. 16–19 1.4 Responding to a Poem, pp. 20–23 Unit 1 Writing Process in Action, pp. 24–27 **Part 2 Grammar, Usage, and Mechanics** 8.3 Subjects and Predicates, pp. 301–302 8.4 Finding Subjects, pp. 303–304	**Classroom Activities** **Nonfiction Reading and Writing** *inTIME*, pp. 20–21 **Technology** *Revising with Style* CD-ROM *Writer's Assistant* CD-ROM **Differentiated Homework Options** **Reteaching** *Composition Reteaching*, pp. 3–4, 7 *Grammar Reteaching*, pp. 3–4 **Practice** *Composition Practice*, pp. 3–4, 7 *Grammar Practice Workbook*, pp. 2–3 **Enrichment** *Composition Enrichment*, pp. 3–4, 7 *Grammar Enrichment*, pp. 2–3 **Mixed Abilities** *Grammar and Language Workbook*, Lessons 3–4, 30
WEEK 3 Personal Writing & Subjects, Predicates and Sentence	**Part 1 Composition** Unit 1 Literature Model, pp. 28–34 Unit 1 Review, p. 35 **Part 2 Grammar, Usage, and Mechanics** 8.5 Compound Subjects and Compound Predicates, pp. 305–306 8.6 Simple, Compound, and Complex Sentences, pp. 307–308 Unit 8 Grammar Review, pp. 309–317	**Differentiated Homework Options** **Reteaching** *Grammar Reteaching*, pp. 4–6 **Practice** *Grammar Practice Workbook*, pp. 4–5 **Enrichment** *Grammar Enrichment*, pp. 4–5 **Mixed Abilities** *Grammar and Language Workbook*, Lessons 5–7; Unit 1 Review; Cumulative Review: Unit 1 *Vocabulary and Spelling Strategies and Practice*, p. 7 **Assessment** *Tests with Answer Key and Rubrics*, pp. 3–4, 35–36 *Testmaker: ExamView Pro* CD-ROM

	Lessons	Key Resources
WEEK 4 Study Skills	**Part 3 Resources and Skills** **Unit 23 Study Skills** 23.1 Exploring a Book, pp. 569–570 23.2 Planning Your Study, pp. 571–572 23.3 Using a Study Method, pp. 573–575 23.4 Notes and Outlines, pp. 576–578 23.5 Using Graphic Aids, pp. 579–582	**Classroom Activities** *inTIME,* p. 26 **Differentiated Homework Options** **Mixed Abilities** *Thinking and Study Skills,* pp. 30–32, 35–40 **Assessment** *Tests with Answer Key and Rubrics,* pp. 93–96 *Testmaker: ExamView Pro* CD-ROM
WEEK 5 The Writing Process & Nouns	**Part 1 Composition** **Unit 2 The Writing Process** Unit 2 Writing in the Real World, pp. 38–41 2.1 Exploring the Writing Process, pp. 42–45 2.2 Prewriting: Finding a Topic, pp. 46–49 2.3 Prewriting: Ordering Ideas, pp. 50–53 **Part 2 Grammar, Usage, and Mechanics** **Unit 9 Nouns** 9.1 Compound and Proper Nouns, pp. 319–320 9.2 Singular and Plural Nouns, pp. 321–322	**Differentiated Homework Options** **Reteaching** *Composition Reteaching,* pp. 8–10 *Grammar Reteaching,* pp. 7–8 **Practice** *Composition Practice,* pp. 8–10 *Grammar Practice Workbook,* pp. 6–7 **Enrichment** *Composition Enrichment,* pp. 8–10 *Grammar Enrichment,* pp. 6–7 **Mixed Abilities** *Grammar and Language Workbook,* Lessons 9–10 *Vocabulary and Spelling Strategies and Practice,* p. 2 **Assessment** *Tests with Answer Key and Rubrics,* pp. 5–6, 37–38 *Testmaker: ExamView Pro* CD-ROM
WEEK 6 The Writing Process & Nouns	**Part 1 Composition** 2.4 Drafting: Getting It Down on Paper, pp. 54–57 2.5 Revising: Reviewing Your Ideas, pp. 58–61 **Part 2 Grammar, Usage, and Mechanics** 9.3 Possessive Nouns, pp. 323–324 Unit 9 Grammar Review, pp. 325–331	**Differentiated Homework Options** **Reteaching** *Composition Reteaching,* pp. 11–12 *Grammar Reteaching,* p. 9 **Practice** *Composition Practice,* pp. 11–12 *Grammar Practice Workbook,* p. 8 **Enrichment** *Composition Enrichment,* pp. 11–12 *Grammar Enrichment,* p. 8 **Mixed Abilities** *Grammar and Language Workbook,* Lesson 11; Unit 2 Review; Cumulative Review: Units 1–2 **Assessment** *Tests with Answer Key and Rubrics,* pp. 39–40 *Testmaker: ExamView Pro* CD-ROM

	Lessons	Key Resources
WEEK 7 The Writing Process & Verbs	**Part 1 Composition** 2.6 Revising: Getting Paragraphs into Shape, pp. 62–65 2.7 Revising: Achieving Sentence Fluency, pp. 66–69 2.8 Editing/Proofreading: Checking Details, pp. 70–73 2.9 Presenting/Publishing: Sharing Your Work, pp. 74–77 **Part 2 Grammar, Usage, and Mechanics** **Unit 10 Verbs** 10.1 Action Verbs and Direct Objects, pp. 333–334 10.2 Indirect Objects, pp. 335–336 10.3 Linking Verbs and Predicate Words, pp. 337–338 10.4 Present, Past, and Future Tenses, pp. 339–340 10.5 Main Verbs and Helping Verbs, pp. 341–342 10.6 Present and Past Progressive Forms, pp. 343–344 10.7 Perfect Tenses, pp. 345–346	**Differentiated Homework Options** **Reteaching** *Composition Reteaching,* pp. 13–16 *Grammar Reteaching,* pp. 10–11, 13–16 **Practice** *Composition Practice,* pp. 13–16 *Grammar Practice Workbook,* pp. 9–14 **Enrichment** *Composition Enrichment,* pp. 13–16 *Grammar Enrichment,* pp. 9–15 **Mixed Abilities** *Grammar and Language Workbook,* Lessons 12–13, 15, 17–20
WEEK 8 The Writing Process & Verbs	**Part 1 Composition** Unit 2 Writing Process in Action, pp. 78–81 Unit 2 Literature Model, pp. 82–87 Unit 2 Review, p. 88 **Part 2 Grammar, Usage, and Mechanics** 10.8 Irregular Verbs, pp. 347–348 10.9 More Irregular Verbs, pp. 349–350 Unit 10 Grammar Review, pp. 351–359	**Classroom Activities** **Technology** *Revising with Style* CD-ROM *Writer's Assistant* CD-ROM **Differentiated Homework Options** **Reteaching** *Composition Reteaching,* p. 19 *Grammar Reteaching,* p. 17 **Practice** *Composition Practice,* p. 19 *Grammar Practice Workbook,* p. 15 **Enrichment** *Composition Enrichment,* p. 19 *Grammar Enrichment,* p. 16 **Mixed Abilities** *Grammar and Language Workbook,* Lessons 21–24, 58–62, 98–105; Unit 3 Review; Cumulative Review: Units 1–3 *Vocabulary and Spelling Strategies and Practice,* p. 8 **Assessment** *Tests with Answer Key and Rubrics,* pp. 7–8, 43–44 *Testmaker: ExamView Pro* CD-ROM
WEEK 9 Vocabulary and Spelling	**Part 3 Resources and Skills** **Unit 22 Vocabulary and Spelling** 22.1 Borrowed Words, pp. 542–543 22.2 Clues to Word Meanings, pp. 544–545 Wordworks: Words Borrowed from the French, p. 546 22.3 Using Word Parts, pp. 547–550 Wordworks: Word Origins, p. 551 22.4 Synonyms and Antonyms, pp. 552–553 Wordworks: Homographs, p. 554 22.5 Words That Sound Alike, pp. 555–556 22.6 Spelling Rules I, pp. 557–560 22.7 Spelling Rules II, pp. 561–563 Wordworks: Coded Language, p. 564 22.8 Problem Words, pp. 565–567	**Classroom Activities** **Nonfiction Reading and Writing** *inTIME, pp. 22–23* **Differentiated Homework Options** **Mixed Abilities** *Vocabulary and Spelling Strategies and Practice,* pp. 13–16, 21–34, 41–52 **Assessment** *Tests with Answer Key and Rubrics,* pp. 89–92 *Testmaker: ExamView Pro* CD-ROM

	Lessons	Key Resources

WEEK 10
 	
TIME Facing the Blank Page, Descriptive Writing, & Pronouns
	Part 1 Composition
	TIME **Facing the Blank Page,** pp. 89–99
	Unit 3 Descriptive Writing
	  Unit 3 Writing in the Real World, pp. 102–105
	  3.1 Painting a Picture With Words, pp. 106–109
	
	Part 2 Grammar, Usage, and Mechanics
	Unit 11 Pronouns
	  11.1 Personal Pronouns, pp. 361–362
	  11.2 Using Pronouns Correctly, pp. 363–364
	  11.3 Pronouns and Antecedents, pp. 365–366
		Classroom Activities
		Nonfiction Reading and Writing
		  Facing the Blank Page VHS video
		  inTIME, p. 17
		Differentiated Homework Options
		Reteaching
		  Composition Reteaching, p. 20
		  Grammar Reteaching, pp. 18–20
		Practice
		  Composition Practice, p. 20
		  Grammar Practice Workbook, pp. 16–17
		  Grammar and Language Workbook, Lessons 25–27
		  Vocabulary and Spelling Strategies and Practice, p. 3
		Enrichment
		  Composition Enrichment, p. 20
		  Grammar Enrichment, pp. 17–18
		Mixed Abilities
		  Grammar and Language Workbook, Lessons 25–27
		  Vocabulary and Spelling Strategies and Practice, p. 3
		Assessment
		  Tests with Answer Key and Rubrics, pp. 9–10, 45–46
		  Testmaker: ExamView Pro CD-ROM

WEEK 11
 	
Descriptive Writing & Pronouns
	Part 1 Composition
	  3.2 Observing and Taking Notes, pp. 110–113
	  3.3 Elaborating: Focusing on the Details, pp. 114–117
	  3.4 Ordering Descriptive Details, pp. 118–121
	
	Part 2 Grammar, Usage, and Mechanics
	  11.4 Possessive Pronouns, pp. 367–368
	  11.5 Indefinite Pronouns, pp. 369–370
	  Unit 11 Grammar Review, pp. 371–377
		Differentiated Homework Options
		Reteaching
		  Composition Reteaching, pp. 21–23
		  Grammar Reteaching, p. 21
		Practice
		  Composition Practice, pp. 21–23
		  Grammar Practice Workbook, pp. 18–19
		Enrichment
		  Composition Enrichment, pp. 21–23
		  Grammar Enrichment, pp. 19–20
		Mixed Abilities
		  Grammar and Language Workbook, Lessons 28–29; Unit 4
		    Review; Cumulative Review: Units 1–4
		Assessment
		  Tests with Answer Key and Rubrics, pp. 47–48
		  Testmaker: ExamView Pro CD-ROM

WEEK 12
 	
Descriptive Writing & Adjectives
	Part 1 Composition
	  3.5 Describing a Place, pp. 122–125
	  3.6 Getting to Know a New Place, pp. 126–129
	  Unit 3 Writing Process in Action, pp. 130–133
	
	Part 2 Grammar, Usage, and Mechanics
	Unit 12 Adjectives
	  12.1 Adjectives and Proper Adjectives, pp. 379–380
	  12.2 Articles and Demonstratives, pp. 381–382
		Classroom Activities
		Nonfiction Reading and Writing
		  inTIME, pp. 2, 16
		Technology
		  Revising with Style CD-ROM
		  Writer's Assistant CD-ROM
		Differentiated Homework Options
		Reteaching
		  Composition Reteaching, pp. 24–25
		  Grammar Reteaching, pp. 22–23
		Practice
		  Composition Practice, pp. 24–25
		  Grammar Practice Workbook, pp. 21–22
		Enrichment
		  Composition Enrichment, pp. 24–25
		  Grammar Enrichment, pp. 21–22
		Mixed Abilities
		  Grammar and Language Workbook, Lessons 30–31

	Lessons	Key Resources
WEEK 12 *continued*		**Assessment** *Tests with Answer Key and Rubrics,* pp. 11–12, 49–50 *Testmaker: ExamView Pro* CD-ROM
WEEK 13 Descriptive Writing & Adjectives	**Part 1 Composition** Unit 3 Literature Model, pp. 134–140 Unit 3 Review, p. 141 **Part 2 Grammar, Usage, and Mechanics** 12.3 Adjectives That Compare, pp. 383–384 12.4 Special Adjectives That Compare, pp. 385–386 Unit 12 Grammar Review, pp. 387–393	**Differentiated Homework Options** **Reteaching** *Grammar Reteaching,* p. 22 **Practice** *Grammar Practice Workbook,* pp. 23–24 **Enrichment** *Grammar Enrichment,* pp. 23–24 **Mixed Abilities** *Grammar and Language Workbook,* Lessons 32–33; Unit 5 Review; Cumulative Review: Units 1–5 *Vocabulary and Spelling Strategies and Practice,* p. 9 **Assessment** *Tests with Answer Key and Rubrics,* pp. 11–12, 51–52 *Testmaker: ExamView Pro* CD-ROM
WEEK 14 Library and Reference Resources	**Part 3 Resources and Skills** **Unit 21 Library and Reference Resources** 21.1 Using a Library, pp. 527–529 21.2 How Books Are Organized, pp. 530–531 21.3 How to Find a Book, pp. 532–533 21.4 Using References, pp. 534–535 21.5 Using a Dictionary, pp. 536–538 21.6 Understanding a Dictionary Entry, pp. 539–540	**Differentiated Homework Options** **Mixed Abilities** *Thinking and Study Skills,* pp. 23–29 *Vocabulary and Spelling Strategies and Practice,* pp. 35–40 **Assessment** *Tests with Answer Key and Rubrics,* pp. 85–88 *Testmaker: ExamView Pro* CD-ROM
WEEK 15 Narrative Writing & Adverbs	**Part 1 Composition** **Unit 4 Narrative Writing** Unit 4 Writing in the Real World, pp. 144–147 4.1 Developing a Real-Life Story, pp. 148–151 4.2 Keeping a Story Organized, pp. 152–155 4.3 Writing Dialogue, pp. 156–159 **Part 2 Grammar, Usage, and Mechanics** **Unit 13 Adverbs** 13.1 Adverbs Modifying Verbs, pp. 395–396 13.2 Adverbs Modifying Adjectives and Adverbs, pp. 397–398 13.3 Adverbs That Compare, pp. 399–400	**Classroom Activities** **Nonfiction Reading and Writing** *inTIME,* p. 10 **Differentiated Homework Options** **Reteaching** *Composition Reteaching,* pp. 29–31 *Grammar Reteaching,* pp. 25–26 **Practice** *Composition Practice,* pp. 29–31 *Grammar Practice Workbook,* pp. 23–25 **Enrichment** *Composition Enrichment,* pp. 29–31 *Grammar Enrichment,* pp. 25–26 **Mixed Abilities** *Grammar and Language Workbook,* Lessons 34–37 *Vocabulary and Spelling Strategies and Practice,* p. 4 **Assessment** *Tests with Answer Key and Rubrics,* pp. 13–14, 53–54 *Testmaker: ExamView Pro* CD-ROM

	Lessons	Key Resources

WEEK 16

Narrative Writing & Adverbs

Part 1 Composition
4.4 Writing About an Event, pp. 160–163
4.5 Responding to a Biography, pp. 164–167

Part 2 Grammar, Usage, and Mechanics
13.4 Telling Adjectives and Adverbs Apart, pp. 401–402
13.5 Avoiding Double Negatives, pp. 403–404
Unit 13 Grammar Review, pp. 405–413

Differentiated Homework Options
Reteaching
Composition Reteaching, pp. 32–33
Grammar Reteaching, pp. 27–28
Practice
Grammar Practice Workbook, pp. 26–27
Enrichment
Composition Enrichment, pp. 32–33
Grammar Enrichment, pp. 27–28
Mixed Abilities
Grammar and Language Workbook, Lessons 38–40; Unit 6 Review; Cumulative Review: Units 1–6

Assessment
Tests with Answer Key and Rubrics, pp. 55–56
Testmaker: ExamView Pro CD-ROM

WEEK 17

Narrative Writing & Prepositions, Conjunctions, and Interjections

Part 1 Composition
Unit 4 Writing Process in Action, pp. 168–171

Part 2 Grammar, Usage, and Mechanics
Unit 14 Prepositions, Conjunctions, and Interjections
14.1 Prepositions, pp. 415–416
14.2 Prepositional Phrases, pp. 417–418
14.3 Pronouns After Prepositions, pp. 419–420
14.4 Prepositional Phrases as Adjectives and Adverbs, pp. 421–422
14.5 Telling Prepositions and Adverbs Apart, pp. 423–424

Classroom Activities
Technology
Revising with Style CD-ROM
Writer's Assistant CD-ROM

Differentiated Homework Options
Reteaching
Composition Reteaching, p. 36
Grammar Reteaching, pp. 29–31
Practice
Composition Practice, p. 36
Grammar Practice Workbook, pp. 28–31
Enrichment
Composition Enrichment, p. 36
Grammar Enrichment, pp. 29–31
Mixed Abilities
Grammar and Language Workbook, Lessons 41–45

Assessment
Tests with Answer Key and Rubrics, pp. 57–58
Testmaker: ExamView Pro CD-ROM

WEEK 18

Narrative Writing & Prepositions, Conjunctions, and Interjections

Part 1 Composition
Unit 4 Literature Model, pp. 172–178
Unit 4 Review, p. 179

Part 2 Grammar, Usage, and Mechanics
14.6 Conjunctions, pp. 425–426
14.7 Interjections, pp. 427–428
Unit 14 Grammar Review, pp. 429–437

Differentiated Homework Options
Reteaching
Grammar Reteaching, pp. 32–33
Practice
Grammar Practice Workbook, p. 32
Enrichment
Grammar Enrichment, p. 32
Mixed Abilities
Grammar and Language Workbook, Lessons 46–47; Unit 17 Review; Cumulative Review: Units 1–17
Vocabulary and Spelling Strategies and Practice, p. 10
Assessment
Tests with Answer Key and Rubrics, pp. 15–16, 59–60
Testmaker: ExamView Pro CD-ROM

Lessons	Key Resources

WEEK 19
Electronic Resources

Part 3 Resources and Skills
Unit 27 Electronic Resources
27.1 The Internet, pp. 645–646
27.2 Getting on the Internet, pp. 647–650
27.3 Evaluating Internet Sources, pp. 651–653
27.4 Using E-Mail, pp. 654–655
27.5 Other Electronic Resources, pp. 656–657

Classroom Activities
Technology
Guide to Using the Internet and Other Electronic Sources
Assessment
Tests with Answer Key and Rubrics, pp. 109–112
Testmaker: ExamView Pro CD-ROM

WEEK 20
Expository Writing & Subject-Verb Agreement

Part 1 Composition
Unit 5 Expository Writing
Unit 5 Writing in the Real World, pp. 182–185
5.1 Writing to Help Others Understand, pp. 186–189
5.2 Comparing and Contrasting Two Things, pp. 190–193

Part 2 Grammar, Usage, and Mechanics
Unit 15 Subject-Verb Agreement
15.1 Making Subjects and Verbs Agree, pp. 439–440
15.2 Problems with Locating the Subject, pp. 441–442
15.3 Agreement with Compound Subjects, pp. 443–444

Classroom Activities
Nonfiction Reading and Writing
inTIME, pp. 14–15
Differentiated Homework Options
Reteaching
Composition Reteaching, pp. 37–38
Grammar Reteaching, pp. 34–36
Practice
Composition Practice, pp. 37–38
Grammar Practice Workbook, pp. 33–35
Enrichment
Composition Enrichment, pp. 37–38
Grammar Enrichment, pp. 33–35
Mixed Abilities
Grammar and Language Workbook, Lessons 48, 50–51
Vocabulary and Spelling Strategies and Practice, p. 5

Assessment
Tests with Answer Key and Rubrics, pp. 17–18, 61–62
Testmaker: ExamView Pro CD-ROM

WEEK 21
Expository Writing & Subject-Verb Agreement

Part 1 Composition
5.3 Explaining How to Do Something, pp. 194–197
5.4 Writing a Report, pp. 198–201
5.5 Writing a Book Report, pp. 202–205

Part 2 Grammar, Usage, and Mechanics
Unit 15 Grammar Review, pp. 445–453

Classroom Activities
Nonfiction Reading and Writing
inTIME, pp. 3–5, 12–13
Differentiated Homework Options
Reteaching
Composition Reteaching, pp. 39–41
Practice
Composition Practice, pp. 39–41
Enrichment
Composition Enrichment, pp. 39–41
Mixed Abilities
Grammar and Language Workbook, Lesson 49; Unit 8 Review; Cumulative Review: Units 1–8

Assessment
Tests with Answer Key and Rubrics, pp. 63–64
Testmaker: ExamView Pro CD-ROM

WEEK 22
Expository Writing & Glossary of Special Usage Problems

Part 1 Composition
Unit 5 Writing Process in Action, pp. 206–209

Part 2 Grammar, Usage, and Mechanics
Unit 16 Glossary of Special Usage Problems
16.1 Using Troublesome Words I, pp. 455–456
16.2 Using Troublesome Words II, pp. 457–458

Classroom Activities
Technology
Revising with Style CD-ROM
Writer's Assistant CD-ROM
Differentiated Homework Options
Reteaching
Composition Reteaching, p. 44
Grammar Reteaching, p. 37
Practice
Composition Practice, p. 44
Grammar Practice Workbook, p. 36

	Lessons	Key Resources
WEEK 22 *continued*		**Enrichment** *Composition Enrichment,* p. 44 *Grammar Enrichment,* p. 36 **Mixed Abilities** *Grammar and Language Workbook,* Lessons 58–62 **Assessment** *Tests with Answer Key and Rubrics,* pp. 65–66 *Testmaker: ExamView Pro* CD-ROM
WEEK 23 Expository Writing & Glossary of Special Usage Problems	**Part 1 Composition** Unit 5 Literature Model, pp. 210–214 Unit 5 Review, p. 215 **Part 2 Grammar, Usage, and Mechanics** Unit 16 Grammar Review, pp. 459–463	**Differentiated Homework Options** **Mixed Abilities** *Grammar and Language Workbook,* Unit 10 Review; Cumulative Review: Units 1–10 *Vocabulary and Spelling Strategies and Practice,* p. 11 **Assessment** *Tests with Answer Key and Rubrics,* pp. 19–20, 67–68 *Testmaker: ExamView Pro* CD-ROM
WEEK 24 Listening and Speaking	**Part 3 Resources and Skills** **Unit 25 Listening and Speaking** 25.1 Listening, pp. 617–620 25.2 Informal Speaking, pp. 621–623 25.3 How to Give an Oral Report, pp. 624–627	**Classroom Activities** **Nonfiction Reading and Writing** *inTIME,* pp. 18–19 **Cooperative Learning** *Listening and Speaking Activities,* pp. 6–11, 17–18 **Differentiated Homework Options** **Mixed Abilities** *Thinking and Study Skills,* pp. 33–34 **Assessment** *Tests with Answer Key and Rubrics,* pp. 101–104 *Testmaker: ExamView Pro* CD-ROM
WEEK 25 Persuasive Writing & Diagraming Sentences	**Part 1 Composition** **Unit 6 Persuasive Writing** Unit 6 Writing in the Real World, pp. 218–221 6.1 Taking a Stand, pp. 222–225 6.2 Stating a Position, pp. 226–229 **Part 2 Grammar, Usage, and Mechanics** **Unit 17 Diagraming Sentences** 17.1 Diagraming Simple Subjects and Simple Predicates, p. 465 17.2 Diagraming the Four Kinds of Sentences, p. 466 17.3 Diagraming Direct and Indirect Objects, p. 467	**Classroom Activities** **Nonfiction Reading and Writing** *inTIME,* pp. 6–9, 27, 30–32 **Technology** *Sentence Diagraming* CD-ROM **Differentiated Homework Options** **Reteaching** *Composition Reteaching,* pp. 45–46 **Practice** *Composition Practice,* pp. 45–46 **Enrichment** *Composition Enrichment,* pp. 45–46 **Mixed Abilities** *Grammar and Language Workbook,* Lessons 52–54 *Thinking and Study Skills,* pp. 3–7 *Vocabulary and Spelling Strategies and Practice,* p. 6 **Assessment** *Tests with Answer Key and Rubrics,* pp. 21–22, 69–70 *Testmaker: ExamView Pro* CD-ROM

Lessons	Key Resources

WEEK 26
 	
Persuasive Writing & Diagraming Sentences
	Part 1 Composition
	  6.3 Using Facts and Opinions, pp. 230–233
	  6.4 Writing a TV Review, pp. 234–237
	  Unit 6 Writing Process in Action, pp. 238–241
	
	Part 2 Grammar, Usage, and Mechanics
	  17.4 Diagraming Adjectives and Adverbs, p. 468
	  17.5 Diagraming Predicate Nouns and Predicate Adjectives, p. 469
		Classroom Activities
		Nonfiction Reading and Writing
		  inTIME, pp. 11, 29
		Technology
		  Revising with Style CD-ROM
		  Sentence Diagraming CD-ROM
		  Writer's Assistant CD-ROM
		
		Differentiated Homework Options
		Reteaching
		  Composition Reteaching, pp. 47–48
		Practice
		  Composition Practice, pp. 47–48, 51
		Enrichment
		  Composition Enrichment, pp. 47–48, 51
		Mixed Abilities
		  Grammar and Language Workbook, Lesson 55

WEEK 27
 	
Persuasive Writing & Diagraming Sentences
	Part 1 Composition
	  Unit 6 Literature Model, pp. 242–246
	  Unit 6 Review, p. 247
	
	Part 2 Grammar, Usage, and Mechanics
	  17.6 Diagraming Prepositional Phrases, p. 470
	  17.7 Diagraming Compound Sentence Parts, p. 471
		Classroom Activities
		Technology
		  Sentence Diagraming CD-ROM
		
		Differentiated Homework Options
		Mixed Abilities
		  Grammar and Language Workbook, Lessons 56–57; Unit 9 Review; Cumulative Review: Units 1–9
		  Vocabulary and Spelling Strategies and Practice, p. 12
		
		Assessment
		  Tests with Answer Key and Rubrics, pp. 23–24, 71–72
		  Testmaker: ExamView Pro CD-ROM

WEEK 28
 	
Viewing and Representing
	Part 3 Resources and Skills
	Unit 26 Viewing and Representing
	  26.1 Interpreting Visual Messages, pp. 629–634
	  26.2 Analyzing Media Messages, pp. 635–639
	  26.3 Producing Media Messages, pp. 640–643
		Classroom Activities
		Cooperative Learning
		  Viewing and Representing Activities
		
		Assessment
		  Tests with Answer Key and Rubrics, pp. 107–110
		  Testmaker: ExamView Pro CD-ROM

WEEK 29
 	
Troubleshooter & Capitalization
	Part 1 Composition
	Unit 7 Troubleshooter
	  7.1 Sentence Fragment, pp. 250–251
	  7.2 Run-on Sentence, pp. 252–253
	  7.3 Lack of Subject-Verb Agreement, pp. 254–255
	
	Part 2 Grammar, Usage, and Mechanics
	Unit 18 Capitalization
	  18.1 Capitalizing Sentences, Quotations, and Salutations, pp. 473–474
	  18.2 Capitalizing Names and Titles of People, pp. 475–476
	  18.3 Capitalizing Names of Places, pp. 477–478
		Differentiated Homework Options
		Reteaching
		  Grammar Reteaching, pp. 39–40
		Practice
		  Grammar Practice Workbook, pp. 38–39
		Enrichment
		  Grammar Enrichment, pp. 38–39
		Mixed Abilities
		  Grammar and Language Workbook, Lessons 6–7, 48
		
		Assessment
		  Tests with Answer Key and Rubrics, pp. 25–26, 73–74
		  Testmaker: ExamView Pro CD-ROM

	Lessons	Key Resources
WEEK 30 Troubleshooter & Capitalization	**Part 1 Composition** 7.4 Incorrect Verb Tense or Form, pp. 256–257 7.5 Incorrect Use of Pronouns, pp. 258–259 7.6 Incorrect Use of Adjectives, pp. 260–261 7.7 Incorrect Use of Commas, pp. 262–263 7.8 Incorrect Use of Apostrophes, pp. 264–265 7.9 Incorrect Capitalization, pp. 266–267 **Part 2 Grammar, Usage, and Mechanics** 18.4 Capitalizing Other Proper Nouns and Adjectives, pp. 479–480 Unit 18 Grammar Review, pp. 481–487	**Differentiated Homework Options** **Reteaching** *Grammar Reteaching,* p. 41 **Practice** *Grammar Practice Workbook,* p. 40 **Enrichment** *Grammar Enrichment,* p. 40 **Mixed Abilities** *Grammar and Language Workbook,* Lessons 16, 25–27, 32–33, 63–70, 72, 80, Unit 11 Review; Cumulative Review: Units 1–11 **Assessment** *Tests with Answer Key and Rubrics,* pp. 27–28, 75–76 *Testmaker: ExamView Pro* CD-ROM
WEEK 31 Taking Tests	**Part 3 Resources and Skills** **Unit 24 Taking Tests** 24.1 Tips for Test Taking, pp. 584–585 24.2 Test Items, pp. 586–587 24.3 Standardized Tests, pp. 588–590 24.4 Standardized Test Practice, pp. 591–615	**Classroom Activities** **Assessment Practice** *Taking Standardized Tests* **Differentiated Homework Options** **Mixed Abilities** *Thinking and Study Skills,* pp. 41–42 **Assessment** *Tests with Answer Key and Rubrics,* pp. 97–100 *Testmaker: ExamView Pro* CD-ROM
WEEK 32 Business and Technical Writing & Punctuation	**Part 1 Composition** **Business and Technical Writing** Business Letters, pp. 269–273 **Part 2 Grammar, Usage, and Mechanics** **Unit 19 Punctuation** 19.1 Using the Period and Other End Marks, pp. 489–490 19.2 Using Commas I, pp. 491–492 19.3 Using Commas II, pp. 493–494 19.4 Using Commas III, pp. 495–496	**Classroom Activities** **Nonfiction Reading and Writing** *inTIME,* pp. 33 **Technology** *Writer's Assistant* CD-ROM **Differentiated Homework Options** **Reteaching** *Grammar Reteaching,* pp. 42–45 **Practice** *Grammar Practice Workbook,* pp. 41–44, 46–47 **Enrichment** *Grammar Enrichment,* pp. 41, 43–47 **Mixed Abilities** *Business and Technical Writing Activities,* pp. 1–7 *Grammar and Language Workbook,* Lessons 71–74 **Assessment** *Tests with Answer Key and Rubrics,* pp. 29–30, 77–78 *Testmaker: ExamView Pro* CD-ROM
WEEK 33 Business and Technical Writing & Punctuation	**Part 1 Composition** Memos, pp. 274–277 Application Forms, pp. 278–281 **Part 2 Grammar, Usage, and Mechanics** 19.5 Using Semicolons and Colons, pp. 497–498 19.6 Using Quotation Marks and Italics, pp. 499–500 19.7 Using Apostrophes and Hyphens, pp. 501–502 19.8 Using Abbreviations, pp. 503–504 19.9 Writing Numbers, pp. 505–506 Unit 19 Grammar Review, pp. 507–515	**Differentiated Homework Options** **Reteaching** *Grammar Reteaching,* pp. 46–52 **Practice** *Grammar Practice Workbook,* pp. 48–52 **Enrichment** *Grammar Enrichment,* pp. 48–52 **Mixed Abilities** *Business and Technical Writing Activities,* pp. 8–14 *Grammar and Language Workbook,* Lessons 75–85; Unit 12 Review; Cumulative Review: Units 1–12 **Assessment** *Tests with Answer Key and Rubrics,* pp. 79–80 *Testmaker: ExamView Pro* CD-ROM

	Lessons	Key Resources
WEEK 34 Business and Technical Writing & Sentence Combining	**Part 1 Composition** Instructions, pp. 282–285 Incident Reports, pp. 286–289 **Part 2 Grammar, Usage, and Mechanics** **Unit 20 Sentence Combining** 20.1 Compound Sentences, pp. 517–518 20.2 Compound Elements, pp. 519–520	**Differentiated Homework Options** **Mixed Abilities** *Business and Technical Writing Activities,* pp. 15–19 *Grammar and Language Workbook,* Lessons 4–5 **Assessment** *Tests with Answer Key and Rubrics,* pp. 81–82 *Testmaker: ExamView Pro* CD-ROM
WEEK 35 Business and Technical Writing & Sentence Combining	**Part 1 Composition** Multimedia Presentations, pp. 290–293 **Part 2 Grammar, Usage, and Mechanics** 20.3 Prepositional Phrases, pp. 521–522 Unit 20 Mixed Review, p. 523	**Differentiated Homework Options** **Mixed Abilities** *Business and Technical Writing Activities,* pp. 20–22 *Grammar and Language Workbook,* Lesson 42 **Assessment** *Tests with Answer Key and Rubrics,* pp. 31–32, 83–84 *Testmaker: ExamView Pro* CD-ROM

The Middle School Concept

Philip M. Anderson

Professor and Acting Dean of Education and Executive Officer of Urban Education Ph.D. Program, Queens College, City University of New York

How Do Middle School Students Learn?

To reach middle school students, we as teachers have to know what makes them special. Noisier and livelier than elementary school students, yet unready for the abstract, academic model of high school, middle school students pursue knowledge about their world with a zest rarely seen at lower or higher grades.

Surveys of young adolescents report the following concerns:

- developing a personal identity
- dealing with questions encompassing morals and values
- securing a place of status in their peer group
- sorting out the maze of adult expectations
- anticipating their future lives (Paul S. George, et al., *The Middle School—and Beyond,* ASCD, 1992).

Meeting these developmental needs helps motivate middle school students, ensures their interest in activities and outcomes, and creates a productive learning environment that is at once rewarding for them and satisfying for us.

A program of instruction for middle school students should meet their individuated developmental needs *and* foster learning. Programs that do both typically feature these essential elements:

Middle school students learn best through active involvement.

Interdisciplinary curriculum Middle school students wish to measure themselves against their new interpretations and perceptions of the world. Students learn content best through central, cross-curricular themes (or problems) drawn from their own experience.

Cooperative Learning Activities Studies of cooperative learning in the middle school report higher achievement levels, greater use of high-level thinking, and increased self-esteem. Cooperative learning models—typically involving heterogeneous groups of students working toward a common goal—also encourage students to value interdependence and collaboration.

Integration of Skills Middle school students do not learn useful skills well in isolation. They seek a connected world view and need help seeing relationships between ideas and actions. Activities connecting reading, writing, speaking, listening, and viewing are more likely to help students learn skills and content.

Middle school students learn best through active involvement. They need time to read, write, and explore. Sure, "active involvement" means some noise and disorder, but that noise and disorder is the sound and look of learning.

Writer's Choice Delivers!

- Writing assignments that cover a variety of curriculum areas
- *Writing Across the Curriculum* and *Research Paper and Report Writing* blackline masters that provide practical help for writing in content areas
- Media Connections and TIME Facing the Blank Page that connect the world of writing with the world of everyday experience
- Cooperative learning activities with clear, step-by-step guidance
- Listening and Speaking and Viewing and Representing activities
- Literature Models that connect reading and writing

Integrating the Language Arts

Denny Wolfe

Professor of English Education at Old Dominion University in Norfolk, Virginia; Director of the Tidewater Virginia Writing Project

Why Integrate the Language Arts?

As English teachers, we have a unique responsibility: to assist students in their growth toward language maturity. Specifically, we must help students read, write, speak, and listen capably and effectively. If we're successful, students learn to think critically and imaginatively.

Reading, writing, speaking, and listening are complementary processes. That is, growth in any one enhances growth in the others. During and after reading and writing, for example, the exchange of perceptions through further oral and written activities broadens and deepens students' understanding. A curriculum designed to help students achieve both *oracy* (speaking and listening competence) and *literacy* (reading and writing competence) fosters total language growth.

> *Making language work for students is like making cars work for drivers.*

Think of learning how to drive. Competent drivers manage a variety of tasks simultaneously—steering, using the brake, paying attention to road signs. Cars won't work for drivers unless they learn to perform these tasks in concert. Making language work for students is like making cars work for drivers. To become truly competent readers,writers, listeners, and speakers, students must recognize that all language processes are interdependent, more meaningful when used together. We as teachers must lead them to this recognition.

How Can We Integrate the Language Arts?

We can help students integrate skills by drawing together two worlds: the world of literature (fiction and nonfiction) and the world of students' experience.

Activities such as the following accomplish this objective:

- Discuss a topic (such as sunsets) in general terms before writing something specific about it (such as a memorable experience students associate with a particular sunset)
- Read or listen to a literary or informational text about the topic (such as a poem about sunsets or an article explaining why the sun appears to change color)
- Relate the text to their own experience in discussion or journal writing as a precursor to fuller reflections in a formal piece of writing or oral presentation (such as an analysis of the poem or a report on puzzling natural phenomena)

When students engage in experiences that integrate reading, writing, speaking, and listening, they gain a sense of the wholeness of English. They develop a sense of community as they talk together, share perceptions from their reading, and respond to each other's writing. In short, they grow toward full language maturity and become better, more imaginative thinkers.

Writer's Choice Delivers!

- Cooperative Learning—reading, writing, speaking, listening, and thinking toward common goals
- Writing Applications, Grammar Links, and Troubleshooter solutions that integrate composition and grammar
- Listening and Speaking Activities that integrate listening and speaking with composition lessons
- Annotated Literature Models that take the mystery out of writing well
- Literature-based Grammar Reviews

Cultural Diversity

Arnold Webb

Senior Research Associate, Research for Better Schools, Philadelphia, Pennsylvania

What Is Cultural Diversity?

Cultural diversity is one of those terms that we educators tend to believe we all use in the same way.

But what educators consider to be meaningful cultural diversity in our classrooms ranges from fostering a common culture to celebrating different cultures. Hard-core adherents to each of these views believe strongly that their approach is the only viable way to channel the dynamic cultural and ethnic mix in our classrooms into areas that support and strengthen our democratic society.

But as Asa Hilliard reminds us, we do not need "to choose between (cultural) commonality and uniqueness." In truth, both are essential. We must provide an environment in which children can understand the world around them and their place in that society as citizens and upholders of democratic precepts and ideals. We cannot do this, however, without empowering all children to recognize and value their individual worth. For many

children, that empowerment can occur only when their educational environment provides opportunities for them to appreciate how their heritage contributes to their land of origin and to the American dream.

How Do We Strike the Right Balance?

How do we teachers strike a balance between providing youngsters with a positive sense of self-worth through pride in their cultural heritage and engendering appreciation of our unique shared culture as Americans? We might begin by responding candidly to these questions:

- What do I know about the culture of my students?
- How is this knowledge utilized in my planning and teaching?
- Does the curriculum I teach reflect the truths of a pluralistic society? In what ways?
- What opportunities are provided in my classroom for children to know, understand, and relate to classmates from other backgrounds and cultures?
- What skills are my students learning that enable them to contribute positively to our society?

Whatever our answers, in the final analysis, we teachers must be responsive to the needs and exigencies of our changing society. For example, the 2000 Census reveals that one of every four Americans is a person of color. Cultural and ethnic diversity is endemic. We can shy away from its impact to our detriment, or we can build upon its strengths to our and our students' benefit.

Writer's Choice Delivers!

- Student Advisory Board-approved instruction that reflects the needs and interests of a variety of students
- Cultural Diversity and Civic Literacy annotations in the Teacher Wraparound Edition
- Media Connections that exemplify a variety of social roles and contributions
- Student Models, Literature Models, photographs, and fine art that reflect cultural variety and the truths of a pluralistic society

Differentiated Instruction

Beverly Ann Chin

Professor of English and Director of the English Teaching Program, University of Montana; Director of the Montana Writing Project

How Can We Teach Writing to Students with Different Abilities?

Our students bring a wide variety of experiences, attitudes, learning styles, cultures, and languages to our classrooms. The diversity of abilities is most apparent when we teach writing. Many students learn English as a second language or speak standard English as a second dialect. We may have some students who seem unable to put their ideas on paper, while other students view themselves as writers and initiate their own writing.

> *We can teach writing to students with different abilities when we create learning environments that immerse students in reading, writing, speaking, listening, and viewing.*

We can teach writing to students with different abilities when we create learning environments that immerse students in reading, writing, speaking, listening, and viewing. By placing our students at the center of the curriculum, we engage them as active learners and language learners. We can meet our students' varying needs, interests, and abilities if we respect their languages and implement flexible teaching strategies.

Here are some guidelines for teaching writing to students with different abilities.

1. Provide activities leveled to the various ability ranges of students.
2. Vary the instruction and management of writing workshops by structuring small-group, partnership, and individual writing activities.
3. Provide frequent opportunities for students to write, read, and reflect.
4. Emphasize fluency and quality of ideas before correctness by teaching grammar, usage, and mechanics in the context of students' writing.
5. Foster students' roles as members of our learning community by encouraging them to present and publish their writing.
6. Evaluate writing process as well as progress through portfolios, observations, anecdotal records, and student conferences.
7. Help students understand the connections between oral and written language.
8. Appreciate the diversity of students by enabling them to discover their individual and social identities through meaningful language activities.

Writer's Choice Delivers!

- Short, manageable lessons to meet specific writing needs and goals
- Wide variety of writing prompts with different degrees of guidance
- Journal writing and portfolio keeping
- Activities labeled L1, L2, or L3 for basic, average, and advanced learners
- Alternative strategies for English language learners
- Writing conferences and peer responses
- Listening and Speaking and cooperative learning activities
- Practice, Reteaching, and Enrichment workbooks to meet individual needs

Writing Across the Curriculum

Beverly Ann Chin

What Is Writing Across the Curriculum?

Writing across the curriculum integrates subject-area instruction with writing instruction. When students write about specific subject area concepts, they use writing as a means for discovering what they know, what they want to know, and what they've learned. Through writing, we help students engage in higher-level thinking skills of application, analysis, synthesis, and evaluation. We also encourage students to reflect on their feelings and progress as learners in the subject area.

> *Writing across the curriculum integrates subject area instruction with writing instruction.*

What Strategies Work Well?

When we use the following writing-across-the-curriculum strategies in our teaching, students become better learners and better communicators in the different subject areas.

Writer's Choice Delivers!

- Writing assignments that cover a range of subject areas and that clearly identify purpose, audience, and real-world context
- TIME Facing the Blank Page and Writing in the Real World that explore and model how today's professionals write in the world of work
- *Writing Across the Curriculum* and *Research Paper and Report Writing* blackline masters that provide practical help for writing in the content areas
- Guided Practice, Independent Practice, and Cross-Curricular activities that engage students
- Journal Writing activities that occur in every composition lesson

1. Invite students to write journal entries about any subject area. For example, in science, students record notes analyzing the data from an ongoing science experiment. In social studies, students chart the ways different television stations report local news events during a one-week period. By routinely making journal entries, students document their growth as thinkers. The journal is also a place where students can do prewriting or drafting of an idea for a piece of writing.

2. Assign types of real-world writing. Writing assignments that incorporate a clear purpose and audience motivate students to write. Helping students to see themselves in different roles gives them the opportunity to experiment with different voices. For example, in an art writing assignment, students can imagine they are museum curators writing a promotional brochure about a new exhibit. In a social studies unit on the California gold rush, students can imagine they are Chinese immigrants writing letters home about life in the mining camps.

When we engage our students in writing across the curriculum, we motivate students to explore subject-area knowledge as well as provide them with a powerful tool for lifelong learning.

Journal Writing

Charleen Silva Delfino

English Curriculum Coordinator, East Side Union High School-District, San Jose, California; Codirector of the San Jose Area Writing Project

Journals—What Are They?

When I first began teaching high school, journals sounded more like diaries. Students were given little structure or purpose in writing and were encouraged to write for an assigned amount of time—even if what they wrote was gibberish. Today journal writing is very different.

- Students have a specific purpose for their journals. The purpose varies, but it is always present in my planning and in my students' writing.
- The *main* audience is always the writer himself or herself.
- The focus is on content and not on form. Consistent use of journals helps students develop fluency.

Why Use Journals?

It is impossible for students to fail journal writing. Knowing this helps students become more confident as writers and learners, more confident to generate and validate ideas and beliefs. Journals enable students to explore ideas for a formal paper and to record impressions and reconstruct memories for personal writings. Journals enable students to use prior knowledge and experiences as they respond to a piece of literature. Students may keep a double entry journal, recording words, phrases, or sentences that impress them on one side of a page and then asking questions, responding, or debating these ideas on the opposite side of the page. I often use journals to review previously learned materials and to check the effectiveness of a lesson. For example, I might ask students to identify the most interesting or important thing learned in the previous lesson. In this manner, I can check for understanding as quickly as I can correct an objective test, and I also get a better picture of my students as learners.

How Should We Respond to Student Journals?

I never correct journal writing. However, I think it is important to respond to journals, and I vary the way I do this.

- I write a journal entry of my own to the whole class, sharing viewpoints I learned from the students.
- I use highlighters to identify key ideas in student journals that I found interesting, amusing, or challenging.

Using journals in my classroom has helped me establish a supportive learning atmosphere where students as writers are trusting and open and willing to take risks.

Writer's Choice Delivers!

- A unit devoted to Personal Writing, with lessons on journal writing
- A Journal Writing prompt halfway through each composition lesson
- Writing Process in Action features that include journal writing as a means for students to reflect on their writing experiences

Portfolios

Bonnie S. Sunstein

Associate Professor of English and Education, College of Education, University of Iowa

What Are Portfolios?

Once the exclusive hallmark of artists, musicians, heads of state, and financiers, portfolios can now be found in colorful and energetic varieties in schools and colleges across the country. The word *portfolio* derives from the Latin *portare* (to carry) and *fogli* (leaves or sheets of paper). With homage to their heritage, all portfolios "carry" representative "leaves" of paper for the display of their owners' work. Some portfolios hold samples of students' *best* work. Deciding what's best becomes a negotiation between a teacher and a student in which both consider what is important in writing.

> **P**ortfolios help us evaluate where we've been, assess where we are, and project where we want to go next.

How Can Portfolios Help Students, Teachers, and Schools?

Portfolios help us evaluate where we've been, assess where we are, and project where we want to go next. They facilitate evaluation and assessment for students, teachers, and schools.

Writer's Choice Delivers!

- Portfolio and Reflecting ideas at the end of every composition unit
- Writing Portfolios for collecting student work
- writing activities that point the way at each stage of the writing process
- Rubrics for Self-evaluation with every Writing Process in Action
- Unit Reviews that help students ask the right questions about their work

- A collection of writing over time can offer **students** insights as they write reflectively about their own learning. They provide opportunities for metacognition as students think about their own thinking and document it. Students become authorities in judging what is good or bad about their work.
- Portfolios enable **teachers** to include students in the evaluation process. In addition, a teacher's own portfolio can include written reflections on the time devoted to students and to personal literacy.
- With portfolios, **whole classes** can view progress over time and make more informed decisions about curriculum coverage.
- For **school systems,** large-scale use of portfolios can offer new information and raise questions that have never been asked before.

Portfolios are not simply writing folders redone; they are documented collections of literary decisions made at certain times by certain people. They reflect our philosophies of reflection, evaluation, and learning. Portfolio keeping is decision making, and making decisions involves asking tough questions—of teachers and students—about their values in writing and reading.

Vision, Values, and Assessment

Jacqueline Jones Royster

Professor of English and Associate Dean of the College of Humanities, Ohio State University

What Should Our Perspective on Assessment Be?

In this age of high-stakes testing, it is difficult to avoid a strong focus on test preparation. At a time like this, it is extremely important that we clarify our vision and values as they pertain to effective teaching and learning and begin a meaningful discussion of what, why, how, and when to measure. With a clarification of vision and values, we turn away from ourselves as failure detectives and language-use police. Objectives for learning take a rightful place as the linchpins for teaching and translate reflexively into measures of learning and achievement.

> *Assessment is critical throughout the learning process, not just at the end of it.*

Assessment is critical *throughout* the learning process, not just at the end of it. We need to think well beyond ordinary techniques of testing and evaluation. In determining learning quality, we are drawn to a need for multiple measures, both quantitative and qualitative, and alternative mechanisms. The imperative is twofold:

1. to clarify a fully developed picture of students' abilities and their capacity to activate and maximize learning

2. to select a range of mechanisms that reaffirm the values in learning that we seek to engender and also mirror both the ways we teach and the ways our students learn

What Is the Role of Portfolios?

One strategy for addressing this twofold imperative is a portfolio system. Portfolios invite a consideration of multi-ple measures, interpretations, and reading over time and across tasks and purposes, thus becoming the embodiment of learning and pedagogy, so that the emphasis is on learning rather than on assessment.

Portfolios also provide opportunities for teachers and students to engage in the type of talk and reflection that maximizes the capacity for assessment to filter itself more productively through-out the learning process.

The challenge is to reconceive testing and evaluation as a multidimen-sional measurement of learning and achievement. The push is to defuse the adversarial nature of the testing relationship so that teachers are in a position to identify, reaffirm, and reward growth, development, and achievement.

Writer's Choice Delivers!

- *Teacher's Guide to Writing Assessment,* with additional models and guidelines for assessment.
- student checklists and teacher rubrics for writing activities
- Reflection and Portfolio activities within each Part 1 Unit Review
- comprehensive Grammar Reviews to end each Part 2 unit
- strategies and practice in taking tests
- an array of objective and holistic tests
- composition tests with criteria for the student's self-evaluation
- Pretests and Mastery Tests for assessing Grammar, Usage, and Mechanics
- tests available as *Testmaker* software

Technology

Barbara King-Shaver

*Supervisor of English, South Brunswick High School, Monmouth Junction, New Jersey;
Adjunct Faculty Member, Rutgers University Graduate School of Education*

How Does Technology Aid in the Writing Process?

In an era of word processors, e-mail and instant messaging, and near-universal access to the Internet in public schools (U.S. Department of Education, National Center for Education Statistics, "Internet Access in U.S. Public Schools and Classrooms: 1994–2002," 2003), students have never had so many tools at their disposal for becoming better writers. At each stage of the writing process, these technologies greatly accelerate and extend what students had been able to do with pen and paper and a library card.

> *Students have never had so many tools at their disposal for becoming better writers.*

Prewriting Students who freewrite using a word processor have less tendency to stop and edit what they have written, so they develop fluency and generate ideas more quickly. Students who use Internet search engines to find information can quickly explore potential topics for writing. E-mail and instant messaging allow students to brainstorm outside the classroom.

Drafting With a word processor, the ease with which students can later revise frees them from having to correct mistakes while drafting.

Revising The cut, copy, and paste functions of a word processor let students remove or rearrange whole sentences or paragraphs in one or two simple steps. Students can easily share their work with teachers and peers, either by printing out copies or by sending e-mail attachments. Teachers and peers can use editing tools to indicate where revisions are needed.

Editing and Proofreading Word processors contain editing tools such as spelling and grammar checkers. Online, students can find dictionaries, thesauri, grammar references, and style guides that will help them identify errors.

Publishing and Presenting Students using word processors can print out clean, presentable copies of their writing. Teachers can post student work on classroom Web pages to increase students' potential audience.

How Does Technology Aid Assessment?

Technology makes assessment more efficient. Since results of computer-based tests can be instantaneous, teachers can tell right away whether to review lessons or to move ahead. A typical computer-based test may also include features that allow teachers to monitor students' progress more easily.

Writer's Choice Delivers!

- Using Computers notes and Technology Tips
- writing prompts and online support at writerschoice.glencoe.com
- reteaching and practice with *Writer's Assistant* CD-ROM
- interactive exercises with *Revising with Style* CD-ROM
- pretests, posttests, and the option to customize with *Testmaker: ExamView Pro* CD-ROM
- online instruction in technology and language arts skills with *TechCONNECT*

Writing and Thinking

Philip M. Anderson

Professor and Acting Dean of Education and Executive Officer of Urban Education Ph.D. Program, Queens College, City University of New York

How Can Writing Develop Thinking?

The connections between writing and thinking are not well established in schools. Allan Glatthorn's analysis of thinking-skills programs found most rely on oral language, some ignoring written language altogether. Similarly, many "writing across the curriculum" programs give scant attention to thinking skills, instead restricting instruction solely to formal aspects of the term paper or to note-taking techniques for lectures (Frances Link, ed., *Essays on the Intellect*, ASCD, 1985).

Research conducted on thinking indicates that cognitive processes must be taught, since they do not arise instinctively nor do they come from social experience. Writing represents an important means for teaching thinking, since it involves **personal, active,** and **integrative** cognitive processes. But cognitive structures underlying writing need to be made explicit, allowing for a reciprocal relationship between growth in thinking and growth in writing.

How Can Thinking Be Taught During the Writing Process?

Many students perceive school writing as "knowledge telling"; they write all they know about a subject and stop. They expend little effort in expanding, analyzing, or reformulating that knowledge. However, teachers can help students master these higher-order thinking skills by emphasizing thinking throughout the recursive writing process. The following strategies and activities will help.

- **Journal Writing** Journal writing provides a means for uncovering and examining tacit knowledge, because students are encouraged to draw upon their **personal** experience.

- **Using Graphics** Graphic aids, such as Venn diagrams, stimulate students' thinking at the prewriting stage and provide **active** direction during the composition process.
- **Scaffolding** With the **integrative** strategy of scaffolding, teachers and students collaborate on tasks that students may have difficulty accomplishing on their own, especially those tasks that involve making meaning and organizing thought processes.

Good scaffolding of writing instruction includes the following steps.

1. Explain to students the goals of the assignment and the purpose of composition.
2. Hold conferences with students during the writing process.
3. Encourage peer and teacher/student dialogues during the revision process.

Process models of composing combined with cognitive-process instruction will result in students who can think clearly, independently, and effectively.

Writer's Choice Delivers!

- clearly defined writing assignments
- opportunities for peer conferencing
- Journal Writing activities in each composition lesson
- graphic organizers to aid prewriting
- a writing objective, as well as critical thinking and listening and speaking skills, identified in the Teacher Wraparound Edition
- *Thinking and Study Skills* blackline masters

Cooperative Learning

Charleen Silva Delfino

English Curriculum Coordinator, East Side Union High School District, San Jose, California; Codirector of the San Jose Area Writing Project

Why Cooperative Learning?

Walking down the hallway, I heard voices coming out of Mrs. Kennett's classroom. I knew that the noise I heard was the sound of eager students energetically discussing their friends' writing. Entering the room, I watched young writers asking questions, making suggestions, trying different options. When was the last time I had seen young people this engaged in the process of writing? Writing, especially in schools, is often a lonely enterprise entered into without great enthusiasm.

These students, representing many cultures, worked in groups of four responding to historical fiction they had written.

Their stories were to be published in a class anthology about the immigrant experience. These students were engaged in a *practical* cooperative learning activity. They had a real audience and a real purpose for their writing. They had something to say because they cared about their own writing and they cared about the writing of the members of their group.

With cooperative learning, students are actively involved in their instruction; they are not passive participants in the learning process. Students need to be trained in a variety of ways to provide feedback to each other about their writing. Then, in small group activities, students are more willing to participate and risk. If the group is constructed well, each student has a part and a contribution to make. The different learning styles and abilities of each student can be addressed.

What Makes Cooperative Learning Groups Work?

Careful planning is essential. I have developed four rules that have made cooperative learning more successful for me:

1. Give clear directions.
2. Model with the whole class whatever you expect the students to do in their small groups.
3. Have students responsible for something concrete when they are finished.
4. Vary the purpose and the activity of cooperative learning groups.

What is important is that learning be student-centered and that each student take an active role, making decisions and staying involved in the learning process.

Writer's Choice Delivers!

- cooperative learning activities such as responding to literature, responding to fine art, group problem-solving, and researching for group writing
- peer response and peer editing
- writing conferences within Writing Process in Action lessons
- additional optional cooperative activities in the Teacher Wraparound Edition

Teaching Grammar and Usage

Mark Lester

Professor of English Emeritus, Eastern Washington University; formerly Chair of the Department of English as a Second Language, University of Hawaii

Why Do We Teach Grammar?

All native speakers of a language have a vast intuitive knowledge of the rules of their language. However, this knowledge is so deeply below the level of conscious awareness that native speakers cannot easily talk or even consciously think about how their own language works.

The study of grammar in school gives students the concepts and terms necessary for talking and thinking about language. A conscious knowledge of grammatical concepts and terms is also necessary for students to compare and contrast their use of language with other people's use of language and to explore alternative ways of expressing their own ideas.

> *Good grammar programs constantly connect grammar to usage problems in the students' own writing.*

How Can We Teach Grammar Effectively?

Research shows us that teaching grammar terminology exclusively is ineffectual. Grammar terminology is abstract and loaded with hidden assumptions. Robert deBeaugrande compared grammar terminology to a ladder with the bottom rungs cut out—if you don't already know the concept underlying the terminology, the terminology itself will be of little use to you. In order to grasp grammar terminology, students first need numerous examples and extensive practice sessions to grasp the concepts underlying the terms.

One technique that helps students grasp grammatical concepts is sentence combining. Sentence combining shows students how sentences with multiple phrases and clauses are built from underlying simple sentences.

Sentence combining also allows students to compare and evaluate the grammatical and stylistic effect of different ways of combining the same simple sentences.

How Can We Teach Usage Effectively?

Usage is the way that we use grammar. Grammar provides a vocabulary that students and teachers need in order to talk about usage problems. For example, talking to a student about the subject-verb agreement errors in the student's paper would be very difficult if the student did not know what the terms *subject* and *verb* meant.

Good grammar programs constantly connect grammar to usage problems in the students' own writing. Probably the most effective way of dealing with usage problems is to collect examples of the error from the students' own papers. Then have students discuss the error, focusing on what the error is and how it can be corrected. Finally, back up the discussion with relevant exercises on grammar and usage.

Writer's Choice Delivers!
- manageable two-page grammar lessons
- visual/verbals that convey grammar concepts graphically
- Writing Process Grammar Tips in composition units
- Grammar Reviews to integrate grammar, writing, and literature
- **Troubleshooter,** a self-help guide to grammar, usage, and mechanics
- alternative strategies for students of all ability levels in the Teacher Wraparound Edition

Improving Writing and Other Skills with Foldables™

by Dinah Zike, M.Ed., Creator of Foldables™

Foldables™, *my three-dimensional interactive graphic organizers, have been shown by teachers and students to enhance students' comprehension by tapping into kinesthetic learning abilities. Students fold paper, cut tabs, write, and manipulate what they have made in order to* **organize** *information;* **review** *skills, concepts, and strategies; and* **assess** *their knowledge.*

Using Dinah Zike's Foldables™ in Writing and English/Language Arts Classes

Glencoe/McGraw-Hill shares my vision that Foldables can play an important role in students' learning. The regular use of these manipulatives will help students to master essential writing and other English/language arts skills by

- focusing on the **steps of the writing process** and on the specific requirements of various types of writing

- recognizing and classifying **parts of speech** and other **grammatical structures**

- building **vocabulary**

- developing **research skills** and **listening and speaking skills**

Using Foldables Makes Learning Easy and Enjoyable

Anyone who has paper, scissors, and maybe a stapler or some glue can use **Foldables** in the classroom. Just follow the illustrated step-by-step directions. These directions have been tested with teachers and students to make sure that they are easy to use and simple to understand for both students and teachers. Look at the sample below (and try it yourself!). On the following reproducible pages (T43–T48), you'll find additional Foldables that you can use with lessons from *Writer's Choice*.

Learning Objective: to recognize and classify types of nouns

On this Foldable you can list all the nouns in a set of sentences and identify them according to type.

Step 1. Place a sheet of paper in front of you so that the long side is at the top. Fold the paper in half from side to side.

Step 2. Then fold it in half from side to side again, making four columns.

Step 3. Fold down about an inch at the top of the paper.

Step 4. Unfold the paper and draw lines along the folds. In the section at the top of each column, write the labels *Common, Proper, Concrete,* and *Abstract.*

Step 5. As you read each sentence, list the nouns in the correct column. Remember that some nouns can be placed in more than one column.

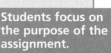
Students focus on the purpose of the assignment.

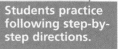
Students practice following step-by-step directions.

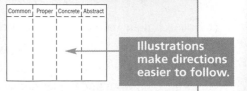
Illustrations make directions easier to follow.

Common	Proper	Concrete	Abstract

Compare-and-Contrast Writing

Learning objective: to prepare for compare-and-contrast writing by identifying similarities and differences between two subjects

FOLDABLES™
Graphic Organizers
Use the following Foldable to help you generate ideas for a piece of writing in which you compare and contrast two subjects.

Step 1. Place a sheet of paper in front of you so that the long side is at the top. Fold the paper in half from top to bottom.

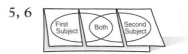

Step 2. Fold the paper into thirds.

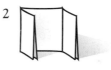

Step 3. Unfold the last fold and draw ovals, making sure that the ovals overlap in the middle section.

Step 4. Cut through the top layer of paper along the fold lines. This will make three tabs.

Step 5. On the left tab, write a label for the first subject being compared and contrasted. On the right tab, write a label for the second subject. Write the label **Both** in the middle tab where the ovals overlap.

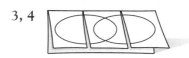

Step 6. Under the left tab, jot down characteristics that are unique to the first subject. Under the right tab, jot down characteristics that are unique to the second subject. Under the middle tab, jot down characteristics that the two subjects share.

You may use this Foldable with writing in a variety of genres—including descriptive writing, expository writing, and persuasive writing—as long as your writing activity involves comparing and contrasting two subjects. The subjects may be persons, places, things, events, ideas, qualities—almost anything that you want to compare.

Persuasive Writing

Learning objective: to develop support for a claim in persuasive writing

 As you work on a piece of persuasive writing, use the following Foldable to help you track the kinds of evidence you use for support.

Step 1. Stack three sheets of paper with the top edges about an inch apart. Be sure to keep the edges straight.

Step 2. Fold up the bottom edges of the paper to form six tabs, five of which will be the same size.

Step 3. When the top five tabs are the same size, crease the fold to hold the tabs in place and staple the sheets together along the crease.

Step 4. Turn the sheets so that the stapled edge is at the top. On the top tab, write the claim you wish to make. Label the five remaining tabs *Facts, Statistics, Examples/Incidents, Opinions,* and *Reasons.*

Step 5. Take notes on your Foldable as you collect evidence to support your claim. Under each tab, write down at least two pieces of evidence of the kind labeled on the tab.

Step 6. Mark with an asterisk (*) what you think are the most persuasive pieces of evidence. Be sure to include them as support for your claim in your first draft.

1
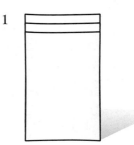

2

3, 4, 5, 6
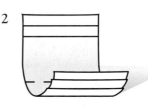

By changing the labels, you can adapt this simple Foldable for several other types of writing. For example, you can use this Foldable to help you write a personal narrative about an event in your life. Just write your name on the top tab. Then change the remaining tabs to read *What?, Where?, When?, Why?,* and *How?* Record your answers to these questions under the tabs. Then refer to your answers as you prepare an outline for your narrative.

Research Paper Writing

Learning objective: to generate and answer questions for research

FOLDABLES™
Graphic Organizers

As you work on a research paper, use the following Foldable to help you identify what you know, what you might want to know, and what you learned about your research topic.

Step 1. Place a sheet of paper in front of you so that the long side is at the top. Fold the top of the paper down, stopping about an inch from the bottom.

1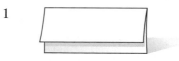

Step 2. Fold the paper into thirds from side to side as shown.

2

Step 3. Unfold the paper. Then, along both folds, cut the top layer only. This will make three tabs.

3

Step 4. Write the title of your research topic along the bottom of the page. Label the tabs **Know, Want to Know,** and **Learned.**

Step 5. Before you begin your research, write what you already know about the topic under the left tab and what you want to know under the middle tab.

4, 5, 6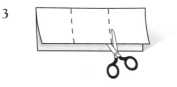

Step 6. As you find information on your research topic, jot down notes in your own words about what you learned under the right tab. Then use your notes to guide your writing of your research paper.

By changing the labels, you can adapt this simple Foldable for several other types of writing. For example, you can use this Foldable to help you write persuasively, as in an editorial. Just write the topic along the bottom of the page. Then change the tab labels to read (from left to right) **My Opinion, Supporting Facts,** and **Reasons.**

Kinds of Sentences

Learning objective: to understand and write four types of sentences

 To help you review the four types of sentences, use the following Foldable.

Step 1. Draw a mark at the midpoint of a sheet of paper along the long side. Then fold the top and bottom edges in to touch the midpoint.

Step 2. Fold the paper in half from side to side.

Step 3. Turn the paper vertically. Unfold it and cut along the inside fold lines to form four tabs.

Step 4. Label the tabs **Simple, Compound, Complex,** and **Compound-Complex.**

Step 5. Under each tab, write a definition of the type of sentence and write an example of that type of sentence.

By changing the labels on the tabs, you can use this Foldable with lessons from *Writer's Choice* as follows:
- to classify four kinds of sentences according to whether they are declarative, imperative, exclamatory, or interrogative
- to review compound nouns, possessive nouns, collective nouns, and appositives
- to identify action verbs, linking verbs, transitive verbs, and intransitive verbs

1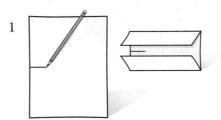

2

3

4, 5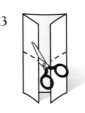

Building Vocabulary

Learning objective: to expand vocabulary by recording new words

 Use the following Foldable for recording new words that you come across as you read or listen.

Step 1. Place a sheet of paper in front of you with the long side at the top.

Step 2. Fold the top of the paper down and the bottom up to divide the paper into thirds.

Step 3. Turn the paper vertically, unfold, and label the columns **Word, Root,** and **Prefixes/Suffixes.**

Step 4. Fill in the chart for each new word you come across during the day. (Keep in mind that not every new word you come across will have all of the parts.)

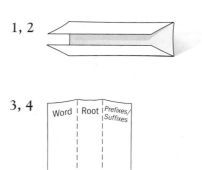

Check your understanding of the words by using them in original sentences that you write on the back of the chart or on a separate sheet of paper.

Facts and Opinions

Learning objective: to identify facts and opinions in writing or in oral presentations

 Use this Foldable to help you to read and listen critically.

Step 1. Place a piece of paper in front of you with the long side at the top. Fold the paper in half from top to bottom.

Step 2. Turn the paper and fold down one inch from the top.

Step 3. Unfold the paper and draw a line along the one-inch fold. Label the left column **Facts** and the right column **Opinions.**

Step 4. As you read or listen to a speech or a radio commercial, write the facts in the column labeled **Facts** and the opinions in the column labeled **Opinions.**

By changing the labels, you can adapt this Foldable for several other uses. For example, you might use it to list the **Pros** and **Cons** of an argument.

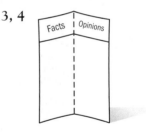

GLENCOE

Writer's Choice

Grammar and Composition
Grade 6

Mc Graw Hill **Glencoe**

New York, New York   Columbus, Ohio   Chicago, Illinois   Peoria, Illinois   Woodland Hills, California

ACKNOWLEDGMENTS

Grateful acknowledgment is given authors, publishers, photographers, museums, and agents for permission to reprint the following copyrighted material. Every effort has been made to determine copyright owners. In case of any omissions, the Publisher will be pleased to make suitable acknowledgments in future editions.

Acknowledgments continued on page 703.

 The **Facing the Blank Page** feature in this book was prepared in collaboration with the writers and editors of *TIME*.

6+1 Trait® is a registered trademark of Northwest Regional Educational Laboratory, which does not endorse this product.

The McGraw·Hill Companies

PRINTED IN THE UNITED STATES OF AMERICA

Send all inquiries to:
GLENCOE/MCGRAW-HILL
8787 Orion Place
Columbus, OH 43240-4027

ISBN 0-07-829814-8
(Student Edition)
ISBN 0-07-829807-5
(Teacher Wraparound Edition)

3 4 5 6 7 8 9 10 071/043 09 08 07 06 05

PROGRAM CONSULTANTS

Mark Lester is Professor of English Emeritus at Eastern Washington University. He formerly served as Chair of the Department of English as a Second Language, University of Hawaii. He is the author of *Grammar and Usage in the Classroom* (Allyn & Bacon, 2000) and of numerous other professional books and articles.

Sharon O'Neal is Associate Professor at the College of Education, Texas State University–San Marcos, where she teaches courses in reading instruction. She formerly served as Director of Reading and Language Arts of the Texas Education Agency and has authored, and contributed to, numerous articles and books on reading instruction and teacher education.

Jacqueline Jones Royster is Professor of English and Associate Dean of the College of Humanities at Ohio State University. She is also on the faculty at the Bread Loaf School of English at Middlebury College in Middlebury, Vermont. In addition to the teaching of writing, Dr. Royster's professional interests include the rhetorical history of African American women and the social and cultural implications of literate practices.

Jeffrey Wilhelm, a middle and high school English teacher for thirteen years, is currently Associate Professor of English Education at Boise State University, where he specializes in adolescent literacy, with research interests in struggling readers and writers. He has been a National Writing Project site director for the past eight years. He has written eleven books on literacy education and numerous articles and chapters. He has won the NCTE Promising Research Award for *You Gotta BE the Book* and the Russell Award for Distinguished Research for *Reading Don't Fix No Chevys.*

Denny Wolfe, a former high school English teacher and department chair, is Professor of English Education, Director of the Tidewater Virginia Writing Project, and Director of the Center for Urban Education at Old Dominion University in Norfolk, Virginia. Author of more than seventy-five articles and books on teaching English, Dr. Wolfe is a frequent consultant to schools and colleges on the teaching of English language arts.

BOOK OVERVIEW

v

CONTENTS

Part 1 Composition

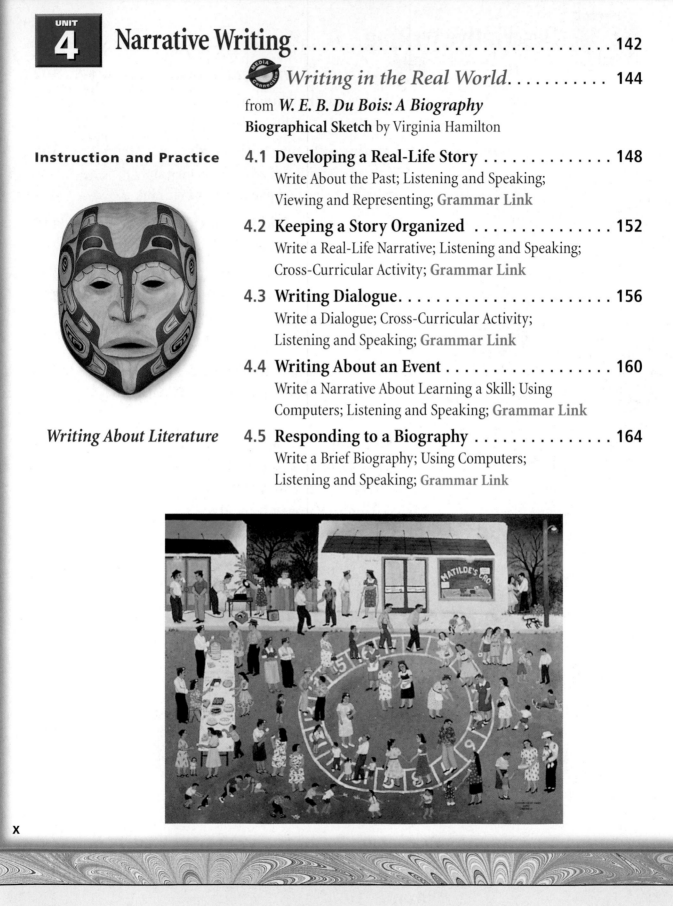

xiii

Part 2 Grammar, Usage, and Mechanics

Part 3 | Resources and Skills

UNIT 23 Study Skills 568

Instruction and Practice

xxiii

Reference Section *Fast answers to questions about writing, research, and language*

LITERATURE MODELS

Composition Models

Each literature selection is an extended example of the mode of writing taught in the unit.

Skill Models

Excerpts from outstanding works of fiction and nonfiction exemplify specific writing skills.

LITERATURE MODELS

FINE ART

Fine art—paintings, drawings, photos, and sculpture—is used to teach as well as to stimulate writing ideas.

GLENCOE

Writer's Choice

Grammar and Composition

Welcome to Writer's Choice!

Your writing and your choices are what this book is all about. Take a few minutes to get to know each of the book's four main parts: Composition; Grammar, Usage, and Mechanics; Resources and Skills; and the Writing and Research Handbook.

Part 1

Composition

How do you become a better writer? By writing! Four-page lessons give you the strategies you need to improve your writing skills. Each lesson focuses on a specific writing problem or task. The lessons offer clear instruction, show models of effective writing, and—most importantly—provide a variety of writing activities for you to practice what you've learned.

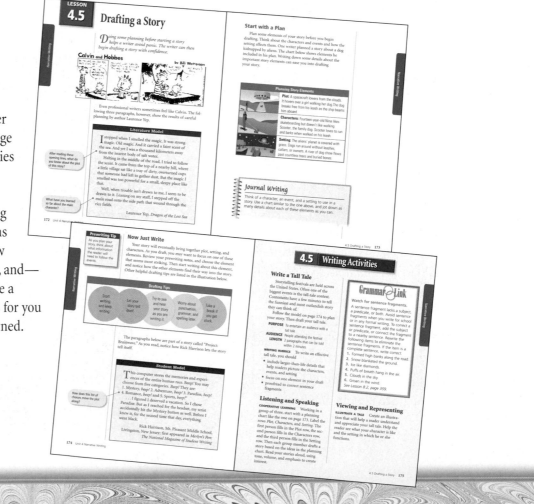

Part 2

Grammar, Usage, and Mechanics

Short focused lessons make learning grammar easy. Rules and definitions teach you the basics, while examples and literature models show you how the concepts are used in real-life writing.

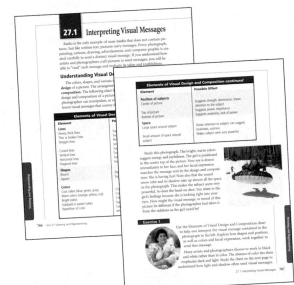

Part 3

Resources and Skills

Would you like to improve your study skills, learn how to give a speech, or get better at taking tests? The lessons in this part give you the skills you need to do all these things and more. Each lesson is complete, concise, and easy to use.

WRITING AND RESEARCH HANDBOOK

This user-friendly handbook gives explanations, examples, and tips to help you write strong sentences, paragraphs, compositions, and research papers. Use it whenever you get stuck!

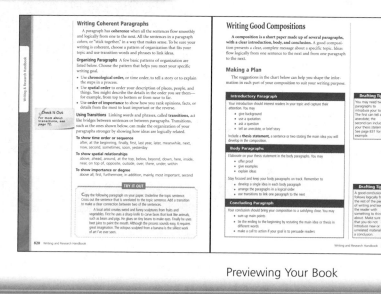

Composition

Objectives

The units in Part 1 guide students in their development toward becoming effective, confident writers. In these units, students will be asked

- To compose in a variety of forms
- To write for a variety of purposes and audiences
- To compose using a recursive writing process
- To draw on technology in the process of writing
- To write clearly, legibly, and effectively, using the conventions and mechanics of English
- To use writing as a tool for research and inquiry and to compile and represent information using available technology
- To analyze the writing strategies of others
- To work collaboratively to analyze and evaluate their own writing and that of their peers

Viewing the Art

Marsden Hartley was born in Lewiston, Maine in 1877. He studied at the Cleveland School of Art and in New York and Europe. Some of Hartley's work was influenced by a brief residence in New Mexico, but he is probably best known for his paintings of the coast and the people of his native state. Hartley died in 1943.

Interpret and Analyze Use the following questions for discussion:

- What adjectives do you think Hartley might have used to describe this scene?
- What kind of story does this picture remind you of?

"There was plenty of rain-water in the hollows of soft stones...."

—Louis Untermeyer, "The Dog of Pompeii"

Resource Manager

Use the following resources to customize your teaching of the units in Part 1.

Planning Resources
- *Lesson Plans*
- *Block Scheduling*

Transparencies
- *Bellringer*
- *Daily Language Practice*
- *Fine Art*
- *Two-Minute Skill Drill*
- *Writing Process*

Other Print Resources
- *Business and Technical Writing*
- *Composition Enrichment*

- *Composition Practice*
- *Composition Reteaching*
- *Cooperative Learning Activities*
- *Dinah Zike's Foldables™ for Writer's Choice*
- *Glencoe Literature Library*
- *Grammar Handbook*
- *Grammar Workbook*
- *Guide to Using the Internet and Other Electronic Resources*

PART 1

Composition

*Hurricane Island,
Final Haven, Maine,
by Marsden Hartley.
1942*

Discussing the Quotation

Invite students to point out what they notice in the painting. (rock or stones, water) Ask how these two different substances—stone and water—are alike and different. (water is fluid, moving; stone is hard, ungiving) Have the quotation read aloud and ask students what they picture when they think of "the hollows of soft stones." Why might the author have chosen these words?

In "The Dog of Pompeii" (*Glencoe Literature: The Reader's Choice,* Course 1, page 546), the water in the "hollows of soft stones" is a source of life for the main character and his dog. Does the role of water and stone change in the course of the story? Encourage students to read the selection and to share their ideas.

Writing Prompt Have students list qualities of rock and water, beginning with how each looks and feels. Ask students to write descriptions of Marsden Hartley's painting, using some or all of the qualities they have listed.

1

* *inTime*
* *Listening and Speaking Activities*
* *Research Paper and Report Writing*
* *Sentence-Combining Practice*
* *Spelling Power*
* *Taking Standardized Tests*
* *Tests with Answer Key and Rubrics*
* *Thinking and Study Skills*
* *Vocabulary Power*
* *Writing Across the Curriculum*

* *Writing Assessment & Evaluation Rubrics*
* *Writing in the Real World*

Video
* *Facing the Blank Page*
* *MindJogger Videoquizzes*

Software
* *Interactive Grammar Workbook*
* *Presentation Plus!*

* *Revising with Style*
* *Testmaker*
* *Vocabulary Power Puzzlemaker*
* *Writer's Assistant*

Web Sites
* *writerschoice.glencoe.com*
* *lit.glencoe.com*
* *TechCONNECT*

UNIT 1

Personal Writing

Viewing the Art

Traveling can provide a quiet time—a time for thinking, reading, or personal writing. Students might imagine what these travelers are seeing through the window, what they are thinking about the cities or towns through which they are moving. Do they compare the imagined lives of people they will never meet with their own lives?

Interpret and Analyze Use the following questions for discussion.

1. What mood do you think this picture presents? How does the photographer's use of silhouettes rather than details evoke that mood?
2. Imagine that you were viewing the people in this picture in a video or film rather than in a still photograph. Explain how your response might be different.

Discussing the Quotation

Read the quotation aloud. Discuss in what circumstances a person might make such a statement. What feeling does it present?

Writing Prompt Use the photograph or a personal experience to describe what a quiet, thought-filled traveler might be thinking and wondering about. Let students know that they can learn more about Zitkala-Ša and her experiences by reading "The Land of Red Apples." The selection is included in Course 1 of *Glencoe Literature: The Reader's Choice*, pp. 54–59.

> "I sat perfectly still, with my eyes downcast, daring only now and then to shoot long glances around me."

—Zitkala-Ša, "The Land of Red Apples"

2

Resource Manager

Planning Resources
- *Lesson Plans*
- *Block Scheduling*

Transparencies
- *Bellringer*
- *Daily Language Practice*
- *Fine Art*

- *Two-Minute Skill Drill*
- *Writing Process*

Other Print Resources
- *Composition Enrichment*
- *Composition Practice*
- *Composition Reteaching*
- *Cooperative Learning Activities*

- *Glencoe Literature Library*
- *Grammar and Composition Handbook*
- *Grammar Workbook*
- *Listening and Speaking Activities*
- *Tests with Answer Key and Rubrics*
- *Thinking and Study Skills*
- *Writing Across the Curriculum*

Personal Writing

Objectives

- To explore personal writing
- To learn prewriting techniques
- To develop an understanding of oneself through writing
- To recognize and use various types of personal writing, such as letters, journals, and poetry

✔ ASSESSMENT OPTIONS

📂 *Tests with Answer Key and Rubrics*
Unit 1 Choice A Test, p. 1
Unit 1 Choice B Test, p. 2
Unit 1 Composition Objective Test, pp. 3–4

💾 *Testmaker*
Unit 1 Choice A Test
Unit 1 Choice B Test
Unit 1 Composition Objective Test

You may wish to administer either the Unit 1 Choice A Test or the Unit 1 Choice B Test as a pretest.

Key to Ability Levels

L1 Level 1 activities are within the basic ability range of students.

L2 Level 2 activities are within the ability range of average students.

L3 Level 3 activities are more challenging activities.

- *Writing Assessment and Evaluation Rubrics*
- *Writing in the Real World*

📼 **Video**
- *MindJogger Videoquizzes*

💾 **Software**
- *Presentation Plus!*
- *Revising with Style*
- *Testmaker*
- *Writer's Assistant*

🖥 **Web Sites**
- *writerschoice.glencoe.com*
- *lit.glencoe.com*

Focus

Lesson Overview

Objectives
- To explore how personal writing can be used to relate events from one's life
- To analyze personal writing

Skills
- analyzing; discussing

Critical Thinking
- recalling; visualizing; evaluating; defining and clarifying

Listening and Speaking
- discussing; questioning

Bellringer
Daily Language Activity

When students enter the classroom, have this assignment on the board: *Write four sentences about four trips you have made. The trips might be to distant or nearby places.*

Grammar Link to the Bellringer

Ask students to consider how much a reader would learn from their sentences. Have they created clear pictures? Ask them to underline the nouns in their sentences and try to replace them with more specific nouns.

See also *Daily Language Practice*

Motivating Activity

Invite students to reexamine their four sentences and decide which trip they would most like to write about.

Personal Writing

Writing in the Real World

In the summer of 1990, Bill Pinkney set out on an adventure that few would ever dream of taking: a solo round-the-world voyage in a sailboat. The excerpts below are from a personal journal that Pinkney kept for most of his remarkable, 32,000-mile trip.

Round-the-World Voyage

by Bill Pinkney

Wednesday, January 15   48° 51′ S 161° 57′ W
Gray overcast morning but near midday the sky cleared completely. I lowered the main sail and set about restrapping the headboard. I had to climb on the boom and straddle it like a horse, with my feet in the lowered sails. I was able to keep my balance and perform the task. It was a challenge because the swell was at least 3 meters. The task completed I felt a great sense of achievement. That problem could have degenerated into a real disaster if left to fester.

Friday, February 7   52° 56′ S   85° 42′ W
I sat in my cocoon (my bunk) and went through all the photos I have on board. The sights and memories made an otherwise grey day a warm and joyful time. It is difficult sometimes to grasp the full scope of the experiences, places and people that have filled my life over the last five to six years.

Resource Manager

Planning Resources
- *Lesson Plans*

Transparencies
- *Bellringer*
- *Daily Language Practice*
- *Writing Process 1–10*

Other Print Resources
- *Cooperative Learning Activities*
- *Thinking and Study Skills,* pp. 3, 5, 20, 22
- *Writing Assessment and Evaluation Rubrics*
- *Writing in the Real World,* pp. 1–4

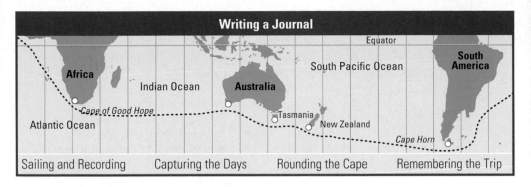

Writing a Journal

Equator

South Pacific Ocean

Africa

Indian Ocean

Australia

South America

Cape of Good Hope

Atlantic Ocean

Tasmania

New Zealand

Cape Horn

Sailing and Recording | Capturing the Days | Rounding the Cape | Remembering the Trip

A Writer's Process

Prewriting
Sailing and Recording

Former Chicago businessman Bill Pinkney set sail from Boston on August 5, 1990. Traveling southeastward, he rode the winds to Bermuda and Brazil. After crossing the Atlantic to the Cape of Good Hope, South Africa, he headed to Cape Leeuwin, Australia, and South East Cape, Tasmania. From there Pinkney slipped around South West Cape, New Zealand. Across the Pacific was Pinkney's final goal—Cape Horn. Rounding Cape Horn is one of the most dangerous feats a solo sailor can perform. Once he rounded the Cape, Pinkney sprinted home, arriving twenty-two months after he began.

What was it like to sail this route all alone? "There was no such thing as a typical day,"

Pinkney said. Good weather or bad, Pinkney rarely became bored. He spent hours fixing sails, cooking, reading, and navigating. He also taped videos for friends, family, and students in Chicago and Boston, who were tracking his voyage. Just as important, Pinkney kept a daily account of the trip.

Between Boston and Tasmania, Pinkney recorded most of his experiences on videotape. But in Tasmania, a friend gave him "a very fancy diary book." From Tasmania onward, it was in this book that Pinkney wrote his daily journal entries.

Drafting
Capturing the Days

After leaving Tasmania, Pinkney hit a string of rough days. Still a month from Cape Horn, he had rough weather

Have students preview the title and introduction to the Media Connection on page 4. Discuss reasons people may have for various types of personal writing. Why might an explorer, for instance, keep a journal? Have students read the journal entries.

Discussion Prompts

- Have you ever read a book or magazine article that told about personal experiences? Did it describe the author's feelings rather than just recite facts?
- Have you ever received a letter from a friend who was on vacation? Did it make the place vivid to you? Did it express your friend's reactions?
- If you were recording a sailing adventure as Pinkney did, what could you show on a videotape that you couldn't tell in writing? What could you tell in a journal entry that you couldn't show on videotape?
- How would a daily journal create a more accurate picture of an adventure than a journal that recorded only exciting moments?

Personal Writing

Writing in the Real World

Science

Invite interested students to find out more about how sailors communicate over long distances while at sea (by radio satellite). Some students might look for information at the library and then share their findings with the class. Other students might wish to find out more about how sailors determine their position with the help of radar and loran. Have them look up *radar* and *loran* in the dictionary to learn how these words were coined. (*ra*dio *d*etecting *a*nd *r*anging; *lo*ng *ra*nge *n*avigation)

5

Writing in the Real World

Teach

Discussion Prompts

Stimulate a discussion of the Writing in the Real World journal excerpts. You may want to invite students to talk about

- whether they would prefer to take a long trip by land, sea, or air, and what types of experiences they would hope to have
- what books they would want to read on a long solo journey, and what music they would listen to
- whether they would keep a daily journal, write letters, or choose some other form of personal writing, and what sorts of experiences they would record
- how they might wish to make use of their personal writing when the journey was over

Additional Resources

Writing Process Transparencies 1–10
Writing in the Real World, pp. 1–4
Cooperative Learning Activities, pp. 1–6
Thinking and Study Skills, pp. 2–3

---

and tense moments with the boat. He wrote about many of these moments in his journal. He usually wrote at the navigation station—the nerve center of the boat.

Pinkney began each journal entry by recording the date as well as the latitude and longitude of his location. Then he wrote about his daily adventures. Sometimes, Pinkney says, he drew pictures "of events that happened on a regular basis." These included sightings of whales, dolphins, and ships.

As January eased into February, Pinkney neared Cape Horn, and conditions began to improve. On February 13, Pinkney's dream came true. That night, in pitch blackness, he rounded Cape Horn.

"The anticipation of getting to the Cape was great," recalled Pinkney. "I had in my mind exactly when I was going to arrive. But the weather was getting bad, and my radar went out. I wanted to pass close enough to be able to see the light; it's only visible for about five or six miles. But, because I lost my radar, I couldn't figure my distance, so I kept a general track in an area that would keep me well off. If I wasn't careful, the weather would have blown me up on the Cape."

Pinkney didn't see the Cape Horn light, but he did glimpse the Cape the next morning. "I was exhilarated," Pinkney recalled. "I had completed my mission—I had passed all five capes."

Later Pinkney entered the moment in his journal. "The dream is fulfilled," he wrote. "Not without pain, fear, depression, and anger. But also with love, faith, determination, and humor. I only caught a glimpse of the great 'Rock,' but it will stay in my mind forever."

Presenting
Remembering the Trip

Sailing swiftly north from Cape Horn, Pinkney finished his trip about four months later. He arrived in Chicago to a home-town welcome in June 1992. Pinkney was the first African American to sail solo around the five capes.

"When I started this trip, the object was to finish, and there were days when I would have liked to quit. But I knew that I owed it to myself to stick to my commitment, because once I had done it, no one could ever take the accomplishment away from me."

Thanks to his journal, Pinkney would never lose his life's greatest adventure. "Every time you read your journal you get to do the good things all over again," Pinkney said.

Cooperative Learning

Sharing Likes and Dislikes

Divide the class into small groups. Ask the groups to discuss what they think they would like and dislike about traveling around the world alone in a sailboat. Students should take turns sharing their thoughts. Groups can complete a pair of lists, one of "likes" and one of "dislikes," which they can refer to as they write a pretend letter to Bill Pinkney. Ask volunteers to read their group's letter aloud to the class.

Examining Writing in the Real World

Analyzing the Media Connection

Discuss these questions about the journal entries on page 4.

1. Why do you think Pinkney starts his journal entries by giving the date and his location at sea?
2. Why do you think Pinkney mentions the weather in both of his journal entries?
3. What kind of factual information does Pinkney record? Why do you suppose he includes this information?
4. What feelings does Pinkney express in his journal entries? Why do you think he writes about his feelings in his journal?
5. What things could Pinkney record more effectively in a personal journal than in a videotape?

Analyzing A Writer's Process

Discuss these questions about Bill Pinkney's writing process.

1. What two methods did Pinkney use to record his experiences during his long voyage? Why did he record them?
2. Where on the boat did Pinkney usually go to write in his journal? In what ways might it help a person to keep a journal-writing routine?

3. In his journal, Pinkney recorded both ordinary days as well as high points. What was the advantage of describing both?
4. Why do you think Pinkney didn't revise or edit his journal?
5. What value does Pinkney say the journal is to him now that his trip is over?

Pinkney uses specific nouns to create clear pictures. In this example, he specifies what kind of sail (the main sail) and what part of the boat he adjusted (the headboard).

*I lowered the **main sail** and set about restrapping the **headboard.***

In each sentence below, replace two nouns or pronouns with more specific nouns. (You may need to make other changes too.)

1. They went to the museum in a vehicle.
2. Plants lined the way to the building.
3. Inside, a woman helped them find places.
4. The adults liked an exhibit on weather.
5. The others liked the exhibits about animals the best.

See Lesson 9.1, page 319.

Writing in the Real World

Assess

Analyzing the Media Connection

1. Dates and locations at sea help readers grasp the scope of his journey.
2. Weather at sea can determine the success or failure of a voyage.
3. Pinkney gives details of work and circumstances vital to his journey and unfamiliar to most readers.
4. Pinkney mentions a sense of achievement and pleasure as he recalls people and experiences in his past. His memories are clearly important to him as he finds himself far from human companionship.
5. Recollections, in particular, are more effective in journal form.

Analyzing a Writer's Process

1. Pinkney used videotape as well as a personal diary to record his experiences. He kept these records to document a unique journey, and in order to share his experience with others, particularly with students.
2. He usually wrote at the navigation station. Many writers of journals find that writing in the same place each day encourages them to write regularly.
3. Even a journey around the world will have ordinary days. These provide contrast to the days that bring high points or the low points in which he and his boat are threatened by high seas or storms.
4. Pinkney's journal is an accurate on-the-spot response to a rare experience. Keeping it in its original form maintains the excitement of the actual journey.
5. Pinkney states that he will never lose his life's greatest adventure and that he gets "to do the good things all over again" each time he reads it.

Reteaching

Encourage students to discuss the challenges in these journal entries.

Enrichment

Invite students to trace Pinkney's route on the map on page 5, naming the continent in which each cape is located.

Grammar Link

Answers

Answers will vary, but samples are given below.
1. Our class went to the Science Museum in a school bus.
2. Tulips lined the sidewalk to the planetarium.
3. Inside, a guide pointed out to students several interesting exhibits.
4. Ms. Jackson liked the exhibit on weather.
5. Students preferred the polar exhibit.

Close

Have students discuss how they could use a journal to record an imaginary journey of their choosing.

Focus

Lesson Overview

Objectives

- To recognize writing as a way to express, discover, and reflect on ideas
- To use freewriting to start the writing process

Skills

- using freewriting to explore ideas; expressing oneself

Critical Thinking

- relating personal feelings; generating new information

Listening and Speaking

- discussing

🔔 Bellringer
Daily Language Activity

When students enter the classroom, have this assignment on the board: *List three activities that fit your idea of adventure, and list three feelings that you associate with each of activity. Examples:*

ski jumping—skill, thrill, fear;

reading fiction—understanding,

escape, emotion

Grammar Link to the Bellringer

Ask students to substitute pronouns for nouns in the second sentence: *Joseph tried ski jumping for the first time last winter. Joseph loved ski jumping.*

✍ **See also** *Daily Language Practice*

Motivating Activity

Students may find that their ideas of adventure vary greatly. Tell them that, as with other activities they engage in, writing is a way of showing who they are.

Personal Writing

Writing as Self-Expression

Your personal writing expresses the real you. Through personal writing, you can look at yourself, share your feelings with others, or explore your ideas.

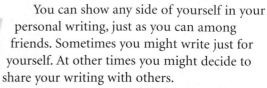

You can show any side of yourself in your personal writing, just as you can among friends. Sometimes you might write just for yourself. At other times you might decide to share your writing with others.

Personal writing can also be a way to look at yourself on paper. As the model below shows, novelist Terry McMillan discovered that writing a poem could cheer her up.

Literature Model

I did not sit down and say, "I'm going to write a poem about this." It was more like magic. I didn't even know I was writing a poem until I had written it. Afterward, I felt lighter, as if something had happened to lessen the pain. And when I read this "thing" I was shocked because I didn't know where the words came from. I was scared, to say the least, about what I had just experienced, because I didn't understand what had happened.

Terry McMillan, *Breaking Ice*

Resource Manager

Planning Resources
- *Lesson Plans*

📋 Transparencies
- *Bellringer*
- *Daily Language Practice*
- *Fine Art 1–5*
- *Two-Minute Skill Drill*
- *Writing Process 1–10*

📁 Other Print Resources
- *Composition Enrichment*, p. 1
- *Composition Practice*, p. 1
- *Composition Reteaching*, p. 1
- *Cooperative Learning Activities*
- *Listening and Speaking Activities*, pp. 14–15
- *Thinking and Study Skills*, pp. 3–5

- *Writing Across the Curriculum*
- *Writing Assessment and Evaluation Rubrics*

Write to Express Your Point of View

Sometimes personal writing can sound like talking to your best friend. When you write about your own experiences, ideas, and interests, just let your ideas come out naturally, as they do in a conversation. Here's one example.

How does Angie make her writing sound friendly?

What details does Angie use to create lively pictures for Sara?

AQUARIUM

Dear Sara,
Wow! My dad took me to see the aquarium today. One of the fish tanks there was so huge it could probably hold a whale. The best part was when a scuba diver fed the tropical fish. They glowed like neon lights—electric blue, lime green, and dazzling gold. The colors were amazing.
— Angie

ADDRESS

Like spending a night in the woods, personal writing can be an adventure. It can be a way of exploring the world around you. Best of all, writing can help you explore your own thoughts and feelings.

Teach

Using the Model
Note for students that in the Literature Model on page 8, Terry McMillan honestly expresses her feelings. She says that her writing made her feel both "scared" and "shocked." Nevertheless, she made a discovery—that writing could make her feel better, too. **L2**

Finding Your Voice
Call students' attention to the personal quality of the letter on page 9. Angie creates lively pictures by using vivid modifiers—"electric blue," "lime green," "dazzling gold." The use of "Wow!" and the inclusion of personal feelings makes her writing sound friendly. **L1**

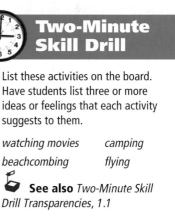

Two-Minute Skill Drill

List these activities on the board. Have students list three or more ideas or feelings that each activity suggests to them.

watching movies   *camping*

beachcombing   *flying*

See also *Two-Minute Skill Drill Transparencies, 1.1*

Journal Writing Tip

Identifying Topics Encourage students to identify the part of their writing that they personally find the most interesting. Remind them that that part is likely to interest other readers, too.

Teach

Using the Model

In the model on page 10, a student uses a favorite topic—volcanoes—to get him started freewriting. He is interested in the physical aspects of volcanoes as well as in the folklore surrounding them. Tell students that by exploring topics of personal interest, they'll find they have more to say. **L2**

Getting Started

If students have difficulty thinking of a topic, remind them that freewriting lets them get their thoughts down on paper in whatever order they occur. If students get stuck, urge them to keep writing—even if they repeat themselves or write things that do not seem interesting. Assure them that one idea can lead to another and another until a good topic presents itself. **L1**

Additional Resources

For personal **writing prompts**, see *Fine Art Transparencies* 1–5.

Daily Language Practice

Writing Process Transparencies 1–10
Writing Across the Curriculum
Cooperative Learning Activities, pp. 1–6
Listening and Speaking Activities, pp. 14–15
Thinking and Study Skills, pp. 3, 5–6
Composition Practice, p. 1

Personal Writing

TIME

For more about exploring ideas, see **TIME Facing the Blank Page,** page 92.

Freewrite to Explore Ideas

One of the easiest ways to express yourself in writing is through freewriting. When you freewrite, you explore your thoughts on paper. You don't have to worry about punctuation, spelling, or even making sense. You just start writing—and keep writing, nonstop, for a few minutes. See where your thoughts lead you.

Ideas for freewriting can come from almost anywhere—games, movies, people, or your favorite activity after school. Take a look at the student model to the right. Can you tell what got this student started freewriting?

Learning about volcanoes is one of my favorite things to do. Volcanoes are fiery, explosive, large, dangerous, and rocky. They can easily erupt. They are located in hot climates. Volcanoes have legends. The people who live near the volcanoes have superstitions about them. The lava is like slime we made in chemistry.

Gaurav Gahin Lake Tw

Journal Writing

Think back on something that happened to you today. Freewrite about it for five minutes. When you finish, look back over your writing. What ideas from your freewriting could you write more about?

MEETING INDIVIDUAL NEEDS

English Language Learners

Using Two Languages

Suggest that students who find writing in English difficult switch to their native language for a word or two if they get stuck during freewriting. Once they have found an interesting focus for their writing, encourage them to use English. Remind them that they do not need to worry about correct spelling or punctuation until they have finished the exercise. Then they can work with the teacher or another student to revise and edit the piece.

Write a Personal Response

Look through this book to find a painting that has people in it. What activities do you see the people doing? Freewrite for five minutes about whatever comes into your mind when you look at the painting.

PURPOSE To express personal thoughts and feelings

AUDIENCE Yourself

LENGTH Write for five minutes

WRITING RUBRICS To freewrite effectively, you should

- write what you see
- write what you think and feel
- use words that create specific images

Cross-Curricular Activity

GEOGRAPHY Pick a place on the globe that you've visited or would like to visit. Do some research on that place. Write a postcard or letter to a friend; describe your real or imaginary adventures there. Try to give a specific feeling of what the place is like.

Listening and Speaking

What is your favorite place in your own community? Tell your classmates about that place and why you like it. If you wish, you can write out what you plan to say before you give your presentation.

Grammar Link

Replace nouns with the correct forms of pronouns in your writing.

*The best part was . . . the tropical fish. **They** [the fish] glowed . . . .*

Rewrite the sentences below, replacing the underlined words with pronouns.

1. <u>Jeff and I</u> went to the aquarium.
2. We looked at <u>the tropical fish</u>.
3. <u>The fish</u> were in huge tanks.
4. <u>Jeff</u> has his own tropical fish.
5. The fish were a present to <u>Jeff</u>.

See Lesson 11.1, page 361, and Lesson 11.2, page 363.

Assess

Evaluation Rubrics

Write a Personal Response

Use these criteria when evaluating your students' writing.

- Does the student's writing clearly relate to the painting?
- Does the student's writing create specific images?
- Does the student's writing give evidence of sustained freewriting for a five-minute period?

See also *Writing Assessment and Evaluation Rubrics.*

Cross-Curricular Activity: Geography

Consider the following as you evaluate each student's work.

- Are imagined or real personal observations and experiences included?
- Does the writing give a feeling of what the place is like?

Listening and Speaking

Make sure students participate effectively in the discussion, giving classmates a "feel" of their favorite places.

Reteaching

📁 *Composition Reteaching*, p. 1

Enrichment

📁 *Composition Enrichment*, p. 1

📇 *Fine Art Transparencies* 1–5

Close

Have students share and evaluate the postcards and letters they wrote for the Cross-Curricular Activity. Have the class evaluate whether the post cards and letters give a good picture of their writers and whether they make the place sound interesting.

Grammar Link

Answers
1. *We* went to the aquarium.
2. We looked at *them*.
3. *They* were in huge tanks.
4. *He* has his own tropical fish.
5. The fish were a present to *him*.

Focus

Lesson Overview

Objectives

- To use a journal to express ideas and personal feelings
- To improve study skills by using a learning log

Skills

- keeping a journal; expressing ideas in writing

Critical Thinking

- defining and clarifying; decision-making

Listening and Speaking

- discussing, listening to oral reading

Bellringer
Daily Language Activity

When students enter the classroom, have this assignment on the board: *List three good reasons why a person might want to keep a journal.*

Grammar Link to the Bellringer

Ask students to write sentences ranking their three reasons for keeping a journal. Which reason is good, which is better, and which is best?

See also *Daily Language Practice*

Motivating Activity

Ask students if they have ever kept a journal. Encourage them to discuss the reasons they gave in the Bellringer for keeping journals. Explain that various kinds of journals are kept for different purposes. What most journals have in common is that they explore and record personal experiences, thoughts, and feelings.

Personal Writing

Writing with Confidence

A personal journal is meant just for you. You may choose to share it, however. Journal writing doesn't need to be formal. What is important is putting your thoughts on paper.

Like anything else you learn to do, writing seems more natural the more you do it. The more you write, the more confident you'll feel.

One way to build your writing confidence is to keep a personal journal. A journal is usually a notebook or a binder in which you write regularly. It is a place for you to write whatever you want. Look at the journal below. What kinds of things does this writer put in a journal?

Lights Make Rare Showing

The northern lights made a rare late-summer showing as reports came in from across the state about the various colors that filled the sky.

"It looked like a glowing rainbow smeared everywhere," said one motorist, who had pulled his car to the side of the road to watch.

Called au...
scientists...
may be...
Norther...
Green...
the m...
colors...
often...

> October 5
> Last night the sky was better than any video game. My sister Tracy and I sat outside and watched the northern lights. Mom said the northern lights are caused by invisible little particles that the sun shoots out. She said that when the particles hit the earth's atmosphere, they glow. I hope I always remember what that ~~looked~~ glow looked like and how good it was to drink hot apple cider under the sky.

Resource Manager

Planning Resources
- *Lesson Plans*

Transparencies
- *Bellringer*
- *Daily Language Practice*
- *Fine Art 1–5*
- *Two-Minute Skill Drill*
- *Writing Process 1–10*

📁 Other Print Resources
- *Composition Enrichment*, p. 2
- *Composition Practice*, p. 2
- *Composition Reteaching*, p. 2
- *Cooperative Learning Activities*, pp. 1–6
- *Listening and Speaking Activities*, pp. 14–15

- *Thinking and Study Skills*, pp. 3, 4, 9
- *Writing Across the Curriculum*
- *Writing Assessment and Evaluation Rubrics*

Keep a Journal

Your journal is a place where you can take risks with your writing. You might jot down notes about daily events, write poems, or just doodle. You might use your journal to collect things like photos, newspaper clippings, or ticket stubs. You can write about new and different ideas, personal feelings, and special memories. Sometimes you might invite others to share your thoughts and feelings. Here are a few suggestions on keeping a journal:

- Use a notebook or binder that you enjoy writing in.
- Write regularly, even if only for 10 minutes a day.
- Date each entry. Dates can help you find specific entries later.
- Write about whatever you want. Your journal is a place to think freely. Nobody is going to grade you on what you say or how you say it.

Journal Writing

Write down some ideas for things you could write about in a personal journal. They could be an activity you take part in, an experience you have had, or an idea you're thinking about. Remember, you can write about anything that is important to you.

Teach

Using the Model

Ask students what may have prompted the journal entry on page 12. How does the writer reveal what made the experience special? Introduce the idea that students can make use of past journal entries when gathering ideas for new projects. **L2**

Using Images

Students more comfortable with images than words may prefer to keep a scrapbook in which they draw and collect items of personal interest. They might then include brief captions for each item. **L1**

Two-Minute Skill Drill

List these events on the board. Have students write which they would use to record each: travel journal, personal journal, or learning log.

birthday party   *music lessons*

train trip   *history class*

See also *Two-Minute Skill Drill Transparencies, 1.2*

Journal Writing Tip

Journal Options Remind students that journals can be used in many ways: To record daily events, reactions to a class, or thoughts about personal relationships; even to play with words, write stories, poems, or song lyrics.

Teach

Keeping a Daily Journal

If students find it difficult to write in their journals consistently, suggest that they carry a pocket-sized notebook with them throughout the day, so they can jot down ideas as they occur. Or they could set aside a specific time for writing each day, such as during a free period or before bed. Suggest that they set a goal of writing for three minutes a day for the first week, six minutes for the next, working up to writing for ten minutes a day. **L2**

Beginning a Learning Log

Invite students to select a school subject—perhaps the one that interests them most or one they find difficult—and begin a learning log, keeping it for two weeks or for the length of time that a particular topic is being taught. Then they can consider whether the learning log was useful enough that they wish to continue using it. **L3**

Additional Resources

For personal **writing prompts,** *see Fine Art Transparencies 1–5.*

Daily Language Practice

Writing Process Transparencies 1–10

Writing Across the Curriculum

Cooperative Learning Activities, pp. 1–6

Thinking and Study Skills, pp. 2, 5

Listening and Speaking Activities, pp. 14–15

Composition Practice, p. 2

Personal Writing

Use a Journal to Help You Study

You can use a type of journal called a learning log to help you study. A learning log is a place to write about what you are studying. It's just for you; no one else will read it.

Learning Log	
Purpose	**Entry**
Summarize.	After Herbert Hoover won the 1928 election, there were signs of economic problems. In 1929, the stock market crashed, marking the beginning of the Great Depression.
Highlight main ideas.	During this time, Americans were going too deeply into debt.
Define problems.	I still don't understand how the economy and the stock market are related.
Ask questions.	Why didn't anyone see the signs and do something before the market crashed?

> What did you mean when you wrote, "Last night the sky was better than any video game"?

> I was trying to describe what it felt like to watch the northern lights. The way the colors flickered across the sky, it seemed to be raining fire.

MEETING INDIVIDUAL NEEDS · English Language Learners

Talking About Writing

Students whose first language is not English may benefit from talking about their writing with a friend. Some students might feel more comfortable paired with a student of similar linguistic background. Others might benefit more from talking with a classmate fluent in English.

1.2 Writing Activities

Write a Journal Entry

Think about all of the things that happened to you yesterday. Write a journal entry for that day. It might be an entry for a personal journal or a learning log entry.

PURPOSE To explore ideas through journal writing

AUDIENCE Yourself

LENGTH 2–4 paragraphs

WRITING RUBRICS To write an effective journal entry, you should

- write the date for the journal entry
- write about whatever you want
- use your own words

Using Computers

You may wish to keep your personal journal or your learning log on a computer. Many computer programs allow you to set up secured files. You can open secured files only with a secret password. Putting your journal entries in a secured file saves them "for your eyes only."

Viewing and Representing

Pick one of your own journal entries that you especially like. Find an image in a magazine that would make a good illustration for this entry. Show that image to your classmates and explain how the image matches your entry.

Grammar Link

Use forms of *good* correctly in your writing.

Use *good, better,* or *best* to complete each sentence below.

1. Our soccer team is having a _____ year.
2. Of the three players, Jan is the _____ goalie.
3. I am quite _____ at defense.
4. Les is _____ than I am at long kicks.
5. The coach thinks we will do _____ than we did last season.
6. Saturday we play the _____ team in the league.
7. We hope to play _____ than we did last week.
8. Rosa is our _____ scorer.
9. Mr. Chen does a _____ job coaching the team.
10. We hope to end up with the _____ record in the league.

See Lesson 12.3, page 383, and Lesson 12.4, page 385.

1.2 Writing with Confidence **15**

Assess

Evaluation Rubrics

Write a Journal Entry

Use these criteria when evaluating your students' writing.

- Does the entry reveal reactions, thoughts, memories, or experiences?
- Does the entry experiment with a personal writing style, perhaps including images or scrapbook items?
- Does the entry include a date?

See also *Writing Assessment and Evaluation Rubrics*.

Using Computers

Encourage students to choose passwords that will not be easily guessed but that they will not forget. Help them understand how to set up a secured file.

Viewing and Representing

Students should explain to classmates how the images selected relate to the journal entries.

Reteaching

📁 *Composition Reteaching,* p. 2

Enrichment

📁 *Composition Enrichment,* p. 2

Close

Invite volunteers to share their journal entries with the class. Have the class discuss the entries. Did they get any new ideas about journal writing? Did the students who shared their entries benefit from the feedback?

Grammar Link

Answers

1. good	**6.** best
2. best	**7.** better
3. good	**8.** best
4. better	**9.** good
5. better	**10.** best

Using Other Comparatives Other common modifiers have irregular comparative forms.

bad	worse	worst
many	more	most

Have students practice using these words in sentences.

Focus

Lesson Overview

Objectives
- To compare verbal and written communication
- To write a friendly letter

Skills
- expressing thoughts and feelings; writing the five main parts of a friendly letter

Critical Thinking
- relating thoughts and feelings

Listening and Speaking
- discussing

Bellringer
Daily Language Activity

When students enter the classroom, have this assignment on the board: *Compare talking on the telephone to writing a letter to a friend. Write a short paragraph about why people might write letters and why people might use the telephone.*

Grammar Link to the Bellringer

Have students look over their paragraphs for correct capitalization and punctuation.

See also *Daily Language Practice*

Motivating Activity

Ask students if they have ever received a friendly letter. Discuss why people write letters, and why some people choose to communicate by letter instead of telephone. Ask students whether they would rather receive a letter or a phone call from a friend. Tell students that writing a letter, like writing in a journal, is a means of self-expression.

LESSON

1.3

Personal Writing

Making Personal Connections

When you write a personal letter, you make a connection. You can tell what you are doing or share your thoughts and feelings. Whether you write a short note or a long letter, what you write should sound like you.

A personal letter is like a gift that lasts a long time. You can hold, reread, and keep a letter. It's not like a telephone call, where the words are gone when you hang up.

In the model below a boy is writing to share his delight about getting a new dog. The boy's name is Carl Davis III, and he's a character in a book by Rosa Guy.

Literature Model

Spots belongs to me! I'm bringing him home! You'll love him. Never in your life have you seen a dog so devoted, so intelligent. How lucky I am. To be seeing my mother, my father, my friend Selena, soon, and to have my very own dog, and to be able to visit Grandma whenever I wish. . . . My life just keeps opening and opening and opening. What a wonderful life.

Rosa Guy
The Ups and Downs of Carl Davis III

Resource Manager

Planning Resources
- *Lesson Plans*

Transparencies
- *Bellringer*
- *Daily Language Practice*
- *Fine Art 1–5*
- *Two-Minute Skill Drill*
- *Writing Process 1–10*

📁 Other Print Resources
- *Composition Enrichment,* p. 3
- *Composition Practice,* p. 3
- *Composition Reteaching,* p. 3
- *Listening and Speaking Activities,* pp. 14–15
- *Thinking and Study Skills,* pp. 7, 9
- *Writing Across the Curriculum*

- *Writing Assessment and Evaluation Rubrics*

Write to Keep in Touch

The writing you send to friends and family can take many forms. You can send thank-you letters, get-well cards, or notes of apology. You can talk about things that interest you. You can ask questions. You can tell your experiences, thoughts, and feelings. Writing a letter is a special way to let other people know what you're doing. Also, if you send a letter, you might get one in return.

Read what one writer included in a letter to his grandfather.

> Dear Grandpa,
>
> Are you ready for a surprise? I just started saxophone lessons. I'm going to play you a song when I come visit. Right now my cheeks hurt from practicing so much. Sometimes the only sound I can make is a honk. It sounds like a weird bird. Unfortunately, it's really loud, but I'm working on that. I can't wait to see you.
>
> Marvin

How does Marvin make his letter sound like a conversation?

What kinds of things does Marvin talk about that make his letter friendly?

Journal Writing

Think of a friend to whom you could write a letter. List some activities that both you and your friend enjoy. List some things that you've done lately that you'd like to share with your friend.

Teach

Using the Model

Tell students that Carl Davis has been away from his parents and is about to join them. Ask students what feelings the writer expresses about his new dog (excitement, pride, sense of good luck). Carl also feels lucky and happy about being reunited with friends and family. Point out that people often write letters to share important experiences with friends and family. **L2**

Writing a Note

Before they try writing a letter, give students a chance to write a simple note for a birthday, thank you, or get-well card addressed to someone they know. Students may create an illustrated card first. Suggest that they include at least three sentences in their note. **L1**

Two-Minute Skill Drill

Have students list the five main parts of a friendly letter and briefly explain each.

See also *Two-Minute Skill Drill Transparencies, 1.3*

Journal Writing Tip

Gather Information Students might prefer simply to list the activities they have in common with a friend. Students might title their list by writing "Activities my friend and I enjoy."

Teach

Writing a Closing

Invite students to list as many different closings for a personal letter as they can. Encourage them to be inventive. Then have them name a real or imaginary person they might write a letter to using each closing. For example, they might use *Respectfully* on a letter to a favorite teacher and *Later, Dude* on a short note to a friend. **L3**

Additional Resources

For personal **writing prompts**, see *Fine Art Transparencies* 1–5.

Daily Language Practice

Writing Process Transparencies 1–10

Writing Across the Curriculum, pp. 1–6

Cooperative Learning Activities, pp. 1–6

Thinking and Study Skills, pp. 2, 5

Listening and Speaking Activities, pp. 14–15

Composition Practice, p. 3

Personal Writing

Write a Friendly Letter

Getting a letter is like getting a surprise package. It's fun to find out what's inside. Whatever the letter says, it will probably have five main parts: the heading, the greeting, the body, the closing, and the signature.

Look at the letter below. At the top is the heading, which includes the date and usually the writer's address. Next you'll see the greeting, a way of saying hello. Then comes the body, where the writer tells whatever he or she wants to say. Finally, the writer says good-by with a closing such as *Your friend, Love,* or *Sincerely,* and then signs his or her name. No matter what a letter looks like, it's the thoughts and feelings that go into it that are the most important.

Heading

Greeting

Body

Closing

Signature

18 Unit 1 Personal Writing

MEETING INDIVIDUAL NEEDS English Language Learners

Writing a Short Note

Students acquiring English may benefit from working with a partner to prepare a short note. Have students first explain orally what they want to say. Then have them write a draft. Ask students to share this with a partner to correct errors and to determine if the note is clear and says what the student intended it to say.

Write a Friendly Letter

Write a brief letter to a friend or relative about something that has happened to you recently.

PURPOSE To share thoughts and feelings

AUDIENCE A friend or relative

LENGTH 2–3 paragraphs

WRITING RUBRICS To write an effective friendly letter, you should

- clearly describe what happened and your feelings about it
- include the five main parts of a friendly letter

Listening and Speaking

Find an issue that you feel strongly about. Write down all of your feelings on the issue and give a speech about it.

Using Computers

You might compose your letter on a computer. After you write the letter, reread and change it until it suits you. If your computer has a spell checker, use it to find any misspellings. Then print out the letter.

Grammar Link

Use clear punctuation and capitalization in letters.

Look at each section of the letter from Marvin's grandfather. Then correct the capitalization and punctuation in the friendly letter below. The letter contains 11 errors.

> 621 Norton avenue
> portland OR 97216
> September 18 2001
> Dear aunt Lisa
> I have just found out that we are going to Boulder, colorado, during the winter vacation. Father says I can bring my best friend, Sung. She will be good company raul will be in school and can't come with us. Maybe we can visit you. Will you be home then. I'll send more details as soon as we're sure of our plans.
>
> Love
> Maria

See Lesson 8.6, page 307; 18.1, page 473; Lesson 18.3, page 477; Lesson 19.1, page 489; Lesson 19.3, page 493; and Lesson 19.4, page 495.

Spelling Hints

As you revise your friendly letter, remember that if a word ends with a silent *e* and you want to add a suffix that begins with a vowel (such as *-ing*) you drop the *e*. Examples: *write/writing; hope/hoping.*

Personal Writing

1.3 Making Personal Connections **19**

Assess

Evaluation Rubrics

Write a Friendly Letter

Use these criteria when evaluating your students' writing.

- Does the student's letter include the five main parts of a friendly letter?
- Does the student's letter give detail about the writer's experience?
- Does the student's letter include feelings and reactions?

See also *Writing Assessment and Evaluation Rubrics.*

Listening and Speaking

Distribute newspapers to the class to help students find issues they feel strongly about. Have students practice giving their speeches in small groups to practice their rate, volume, pitch, and tone.

Using Computers

Make sure students know how to use the spell checker on their word processor. You might also want to explain cut and paste features to your students.

Reteaching

📁 *Composition Reteaching,* p. 3

Enrichment

📁 *Composition Enrichment,* p. 3

✏ *Fine Art Transparencies* 1–5

Close

Initiate a discussion about the different kinds of letters people write. Remind students that not every letter has to be about a momentous event. People often write about little events that happen during a typical day.

Grammar Link

Answers

1. Avenue
2. Portland
3. Portland, OR
4. September 18,
5. Aunt
6. Lisa,
7. Colorado
8. company.
9. Raul
10. then?
11. Love,

Capitalization and Punctuation After students have corrected the capitalization and punctuation errors in the Grammar Link, have them check their own letters for errors.

Focus

Lesson Overview

Objectives
- To learn about ways to respond to a poem
- To write a poem using vivid adjectives

Skills
- using specific adjectives

Critical Thinking
- analyzing; contrasting; comparing

Listening and Speaking
- discussing

🔔 Bellringer
Daily Language Activity

When students enter the classroom, have this assignment on the board: *List the names of five poems or songs with words that you know and like.*

Grammar Link to the Bellringer

Have students think about the songs or poems they listed in the Bellringer. Have them identify any specific adjectives used in the song lyrics or poems.

📝 **See also** *Daily Language Practice*

Motivating Activity

Encourage students to tell what they like about the poems or songs they listed. Some students may have written their own poems or songs. Ask them if they think this type of writing is easier or more difficult than other kinds of writing. Explain that writing a poem, like journal writing, is a means of self-expression.

Personal Writing

LESSON 1.4

WRITING ABOUT LITERATURE

Responding to a Poem

*P*oems are a way of sharing experiences and feelings. You can read poems, and you can write them. All you need is an idea or feeling to get started.

William Carlos Williams wrote the poem below. In addition to being a poet, he was a doctor. Frequently, he turned everyday experiences into poems.

Literature Model

This Is Just to Say

I have eaten
the plums
that were in
the icebox

and which
you were probably
saving
for breakfast

Forgive me
they were delicious
so sweet
and so cold

William Carlos Williams

Jot down your thoughts about the poem. How would you feel if you received it? Did it make you think of eating plums? What did it make you want to do?

Resource Manager

Planning Resources
- *Lesson Plans*

📝 **Transparencies**
- *Bellringer*
- *Daily Language Practice*
- *Fine Art 1–5*
- *Two-Minute Skill Drill*
- *Writing Process 1–10*

📁 **Other Print Resources**
- *Composition Enrichment, p. 4*
- *Composition Practice, p. 4*
- *Composition Reteaching, p. 4*
- *Cooperative Learning Activities, pp. 1–6*
- *Listening and Speaking Activities, pp. 14–15*

- *Thinking and Study Skills, pp. 5, 22*
- *Writing Across the Curriculum*
- *Writing Assessment and Evaluation Rubrics*

Start with a Poem

One way of responding to a poem is to write. You might write your ideas about the poem in your journal or learning log. In the journal entry below, one student tells how Williams's poem made her feel.

> When I read the poem, I felt like I had actually taken some plums that weren't mine out of the icebox. I have never done that, but I could almost feel what it was like to take something out of the icebox.
>
> Once I stole one of my brother's cookies. He hadn't seen me, but he was so little that I felt bad. I apologized and he said he understood.
>
> Jenny Jeep, O'Plaine Elementary School
> Gurnee, Illinois

Another way to respond to a poem is to draw a picture. The student who drew this was inspired by the poet's description of the plums.

Journal Writing

Reread the notes you jotted down after reading "This Is Just to Say." Think about how you would respond. Would you write something, or would you draw a picture? Write or draw your response.

Teach

Using the Model

Students having difficulty relating their own experiences to the poem might benefit from some prompts. Ask students if they have ever apologized for something; lost an item borrowed without permission; or tasted a sweet and delicious fruit. Questions like these can help students focus on an image or experience to use in their responses. **L2**

Cooperative Learning

After students have responded to "This Is Just to Say," have them form groups. Each student in a group should share a response to the poem. Others should listen actively, and then comment or ask questions about the writer's response. **L1**

Two-Minute Skill Drill

List these nouns on the board and have students choose an adjective to describe each.

plums	snow
breakfast	mountain
cookie	dogs

See also *Two-Minute Skill Drill Transparencies, 1.4*

Journal Writing Tip

Responses to the Poem Remind students they can respond to any part of the poem that strikes them—a certain image, a line of words, the overall idea, or just the way the poem sounds.

Cultural Connections

Sharing Poetry

Suggest that students share poetry about everyday experiences. Challenge students to find poems from different regions around the world. Encourage them to read their special poems to the class. Invite students to compare the experiences that are described in the poems and, if possible, to evaluate similarities and differences among various cultures.

Teach

Using the Models
Like the poem on page 20, both students' poems are about feeling sorry. Both students used Williams's poem as a "jumping-off" point for their own writing. Have students jot down responses as they read. That way any creative ideas prompted by the reading will not slip away. Point out that reading poems, and reading in general, is a good way for students to get their creative juices flowing. **L2**

Responding with a Poem
Set aside a period for students to read and discuss poems they have found outside of class. Suggest that they bring in shorter poems so everyone can have a chance to read and respond. Have students respond to these poems by writing a poem of their own in their journals. **L3**

Additional Resources

For personal **writing prompts**, see *Fine Art Transparencies* 1–5.

Daily Language Practice

Writing Process Transparencies 1–10
Writing Across the Curriculum
Cooperative Learning Activities, pp. 1–6
Thinking and Study Skills, pp. 5, 22
Listening and Speaking Activities, pp. 14–15
Composition Practice, p. 4

Personal Writing

Respond with a Poem

Another good way to respond to a poem is to write a poem of your own. You might write about the same idea as in the poem you read. You could also write about a different idea.

Read the two poems below. What idea in Williams's poem do you think Shayne Bell is responding to? What different idea is Kim Myers writing about? What similarities or differences can you find between Kim's and Shayne's responses?

> Can you tell how these two poems are similar?

> How does Shayne help her readers to understand what the plums taste like?

I'm Sorry

I didn't mean
    to make you mad.
I didn't mean
    to hurt you.

I was just angry
    that was all.
I said some things
    I didn't mean.

Please forgive me.
    Let's not fight.
The fight was not important.
    Kim Myers,
    Westfield School,
    Winthrop Harbor, Illinois

For what I have done,
I will go out and find
the best plums in town.
I will even grow the plums
    that will be as sweet as candy,
that will be sweeter and more delicious.
There will be enough for you to have
at least 10 a day for a year,
to tell you I'm so sorry I ate your plums.
    Shayne Bell,
    Wauconda Junior High,
    Wauconda, Illinois

> Poets often divide poems into sections called stanzas. Kim's poem has three stanzas, just like the poem on page 20.

22 Unit 1 Personal Writing

MEETING INDIVIDUAL NEEDS English Language Learners

Reading and Writing Poetry
Students acquiring English will probably find the poem by Kim Myers easier to read. The shorter lines, use of repetition, and simple vocabulary and sentence structure make it a more accessible model. Have students look for words that are repeated within the poem. Note that the repeated use of *I* to start four of the lines underscores the writer's feeling of being sorry. As students write their own poems, point out that a graceful poem may use very simple words and have a simple structure.

1.4 Writing Activities

Write a Poem

Reread the poem by Kim Myers on page 22.

Then write your own poem in response to Myers's poem.

PURPOSE To respond to a poem with a poem of your own

AUDIENCE Students your age

LENGTH 10 or more lines

WRITING RUBRICS To write an effective poetic response to Myers's poem, you should

- make notes on your ideas about the poem
- make notes on how the poem makes you feel

Cross-Curricular Activity

ARCHITECTURE Observe a house or building near where you live. Take notes

Pieter Brueghel the Elder, *Hunters in the Snow*, 1565

Personal Writing

Grammar Link

Use specific adjectives to create strong, clear images.

In one of her poems, Kim Myers uses the specific adjectives *sweet* and *delicious.*

Add at least one specific adjective to each sentence below.

1. I ate an orange yesterday.
2. I found it in a basket on the table.
3. I peeled the skin.
4. I chewed up each section.
5. Then I wiped my hands and face.

See Lesson 12.1, page 379.

on it, going into as much detail as possible. Is the building inviting? Or is it unappealing? Later, turn your notes into a two-paragraph description, using concrete facts to support your opinion.

Viewing and Representing

Everybody's interpretation of art is different. Choose a painting in this book. What do you think is happening in the painting? Describe the work in two paragraphs, supporting your interpretation with details and examples.

Assess

Evaluation Rubrics

Write a Poem

Use these criteria when evaluating your students' writing.

- Does the poem respond to some aspect of Myers's poem?
- Does the poem include specific details based on Myers's poem?
- Does the poem reflect the writer's personal thoughts and feelings?

See also *Writing Assessment and Evaluation Rubrics.*

Cross-Curricular Activity: Architecture

Ask students to hand in their notes with their descriptions. Did students take effective notes about several features of the house? Did they include personal reactions to the house? Did they include specific adjectives in their descriptions? Did students organize their notes effectively to write their descriptions?

Viewing and Representing

Make sure students' paragraphs relate closely to the painting they chose to describe. Did they overlook any important details?

Reteaching

📁 *Composition Reteaching,* p. 4

Enrichment

📁 *Composition Enrichment,* p. 4

📦 *Fine Art Transparencies* 1–5

Close

Invite students to read the two student poems aloud. Discuss similarities between the poems as well as differences.

Grammar Link

Answers

Answers will vary, but some suggestions are given below.

1. I ate a juicy orange yesterday.
2. I found it in a woven basket . . . .
3. I peeled the fragrant skin.
4. I chewed up each sweet section.
5. Then I wiped my sticky hands . . . .

Viewing the Art

Pieter Bruegel the Elder, *Hunters in the Snow,* 1565
Bruegel was a close observer of nature. He captures the winter twilight in the gray-green sky and the dark tones of the trees and figures in this 46-by-64-inch painting that hangs in the Kunsthistorisches Museum, Vienna, Austria.

Writing Process in Action

Focus

Lesson Overview

Objectives
- To write a personal essay
- To proofread the work of other writers, and to respond to peer feedback

Skills
- using the five stages of the writing process: prewriting, drafting, revising, editing/proofreading, and publishing/presenting

Critical Thinking
- recalling; main idea; summarizing

Listening and Speaking
- discussing; note taking

Bellringer
Daily Language Activity

When students enter the classroom, have this assignment on the board: *Write a few sentences about the most interesting place you have ever visited.*

Grammar Link to the Bellringer

Have students add specific adjectives to describe the nouns they wrote for the Bellringer.

See also *Daily Language Practice*

Motivating Activity

Point out that special experiences and new places often go together, as in Yoshiko Uchida's account of visiting a farm for the first time on student page 28. Many students, however, may also remember special experiences they've had at home, at school, or in their community.

Personal Writing

Personal Writing

In preceding lessons you've learned about various kinds of personal writing. You've expressed your own ideas and feelings in journal entries and personal letters. You've also had the chance to write your responses to poems. Now it's time to make use of what you've learned. In this lesson you're invited to write about a day that became special in your life.

Assignment

Context

You have decided to submit your writing to *Up, Up, and Away.* This is a magazine that publishes student writing about special days, new experiences, or new feelings.

Purpose

To write a brief account of a special day or event in your life

Audience

The readers of *Up, Up, and Away,* ages 10–15

Length

1 page

WRITING Online

Visit the *Writer's Choice* Web site at **writerschoice.glencoe.com** for additional writing prompts.

The following pages can help you plan and write your account. Read through them and then refer to them as you need to. Don't feel limited by them, however. You are in charge of your own writing process.

24   Unit 1 Personal Writing

Resource Manager

Planning Resources
- *Lesson Plans*

Transparencies
- *Bellringer*
- *Daily Language Practice*
- *Writing Process 1–10*

Other Print Resources
- *Composition Enrichment,* p. 7
- *Composition Practice,* p. 7
- *Composition Reteaching,* p. 7
- *Grammar Workbook,* Lesson 30
- *Writing Assessment and Evaluation Rubrics*

Software
- *Writer's Assistant*

Web Sites
- *writerschoice.glencoe.com*
- *lit.glencoe.com*

Writing Process in Action

Personal Writing

Prewriting

Sometimes keying in on a few single words can help you focus your prewriting thoughts. For example, think of the words *usually, often,* and *always.* Those are words that describe every-day events. Now think of words like *once, seldom,* and *never.* Such words can help you identify the special day or experience that will make a good writing topic. The options graphic at the right will help you with these early, important steps.

Look at page 10 for suggestions on freewriting. Your goal is to choose a topic that fits the assignment and has meaning for you.

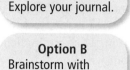

Option A
Explore your journal.

Option B
Brainstorm with a friend.

Option C
Freewrite for ideas.

> The first time I ever went camping real camping in real woods, far away from streets and sidewalks. All the sounds were new. The intense, black night. What would sleep be like under the stars?

Drafting

As you go over your prewriting notes, think about the specific words and images that will make your readers aware of the special nature of your topic. For example, Yoshiko Uchida writes of riding through vineyards on her first visit to a farm—a wondrous experience for a city girl. Notice the language she uses to give the sense of discovering a new world.

Literature Model

I could hear crickets singing and frogs croaking and all the other gentle night sounds of the country. I felt as though I were in another more immense, never-ending world, and wished I could keep riding forever to the ends of the earth.

Yoshiko Uchida, *The Invisible Thread*

Teach

Prewriting

Developing Ideas for Personal Writing

Students preparing to freewrite may benefit from writing prompts. Offer some categories to help them focus their thoughts (the first time I—, the only time I—, the best time I had—, and so forth). Mention that these categories are just starting points, and that they should feel free to follow an idea wherever it leads them. **L2**

Drafting

Adding Details

Uchida is aware of the singing crickets and other night sounds as she lies under the star-filled sky. These soft sounds provide a gentle music for the scene. Challenge students to list how sound played a part in their special day. Point out that they may wish to use details about music or musical sounds, as Uchida did, to give readers a sense of their experience. **L3**

Teach

Revising

Peer Editing

Students can work in writing conferences with peer editors before they revise their writing. You may duplicate the Peer Response forms in *Writing Assessment and Evaluation Rubrics*. Suggest that peer editors discuss these questions: What did you like best about the writing? Were enough details provided? **L2**

Editing/Proofreading

Peer Editing

After students have edited their own work, have them edit another student's writing. Remind them to refer to the Editing/Proofreading Checklist on student page 27. **L2**

Publishing/Presenting

Before students present their personal writing, discuss how they can prepare their papers for publication. Emphasize the importance of a neatly written final draft.

Additional Resources

Writing Process Transparencies 1–10
Composition Practice, p. 7

Grammar Workbook, Lesson 30

Personal Writing

Drafting Tip

For help with getting a flow of your ideas down on paper, see Lesson 2.4, pages 54–57.

Revising Tip

For help with revising your writing, see Lesson 2.5, pages 58–61.

Question A
Is my writing clear?

Question B
Does the writing sound like me?

Question C
Have I made effective use of details?

You can bring the same kind of amazement to your own writing if you keep your experience and feelings focused. What made this day important to you?

When you're ready to start your draft, take a deep breath and relax. The most important thing about drafting is to get your ideas down on paper. You can always change things later.

Revising

To begin revising, read over your draft to make sure that what you have written fits your purpose and your audience. Then have a **writing conference.** Read your draft to a partner or small group. Use your audience's reactions to help you evaluate your work.

The darkness in the forest was ~~amazing~~ awesome. Stars blinked brightly overhead. My aunt and uncle kidded me about and getting lost like some city kid wandering off too far from the camp.

I didn't think I would like the freeze-dried food we had brought along. It was some kind of stew, made by mixing water and these foil envelopes of powder. My uncle cooked it over a portable gas stove. You can't make a fire at this national park. and it looked kind of gross

---

Enrichment and Extension

Follow-up Ideas

- Set aside time for students to celebrate the conclusion of their writing projects. Encourage them to share their finished pieces.
- Collect the finished pieces and illustrate, bind, and display the work.

Extending Personal Writing

Brainstorm with students ways they can use personal writing in other subject areas:
- a personal log of science experiments
- a journal of past experiences to be included in a time capsule

Editing/Proofreading

At the editing stage you put the finishing touches on your writing. A careful editing job shows your readers that you care about your work and don't want any errors to distract them from your ideas.

The checklist at the right will help you edit your writing. Usually writers **proofread** for only one kind of error at a time. Using this method means that you will read through your work several times, looking for only one kind of error each time.

Publishing/Presenting

Maybe your class wants to make its own special edition of *Up, Up, and Away.* This would give you the chance to have other students read your writing. Likewise, you would have the chance to see how other students tackled this assignment.

Of course, you may not feel ready to share your work with anyone other than your teacher. That's OK. There is some risk involved in sharing with a wider audience. You decide what's best for you.

Editing/Proofreading Checklist

1. Have I used **specific nouns and adjectives** to create good images?
2. Have I used **pronouns correctly?**
3. Have I used **forms of "good"** correctly?
4. Are all sentences complete?
5. Have I used **standard spelling, capitalization, and punctuation?**

Personal Writing

Proofreading Tip

For proofreading symbols, see page 72.

Journal Writing

Reflect on your writing process experience. Answer these questions in your journal: What do you like best about the personal account you wrote? What was the hardest part of writing it? What did you learn in your writing conference? What new things have you learned as a writer?

Assess

Evaluation Rubrics

Use the following questions to evaluate students' finished writing.

- Do prewriting notes explore a memorable personal experience?
- Does the draft build on the prewriting notes?
- Does it clearly communicate why the day or event was memorable to the student?
- Does it provide vivid details about the experience?
- Has the student ordered the account in a way that is easy to follow?
- Is the revision an improvement of the draft?
- Does the revision include language that is natural to the writer?
- Does the piece adhere to spelling and punctuation rules?
- Has the student used the questions on page 27 to edit his or her writing?

See also *Writing Assessment and Evaluation Rubrics.*

Reteaching
📁 *Composition Reteaching,* p. 7

Enrichment
📁 *Composition Enrichment,* p. 7

Close

Ask students: What did you learn about yourself from the assignment? Have you changed the way you see your everyday experiences?

Listening and Speaking

Creating Dialogue

Tell students they may wish to incorporate dialogue into their accounts to help convey how they were feeling during their special experiences. Suggest that students try reading their dialogue aloud with a partner. Does the dialogue sound natural? Tell students that dialogue can convey personal feelings and capture the unique details of an experience.

Personal Writing

About the Author

Yoshiko Uchida, the daughter of Japanese parents, was born and grew up in California. *The Invisible Thread* is a memoir of her early life up to the time she completed her education and found her first job.

Focus

Lesson Overview

Objectives

- To analyze a published story as a model for personal writing
- To participate in a group discussion about a literature model
- To write a personal narrative about a first-time experience

Skills

- monitoring comprehension, summarizing

Critical Thinking

- drawing conclusions, inferring

Listening and Speaking

- discussing

Bellringer
Daily Language Activity

When students enter the classroom, have this assignment on the board: *Write a few sentences about a place you visited for the first time.*

See also *Daily Language Practice*

Motivating Activity

Ask students to think of a time when they left their everyday surroundings and went to a totally different kind of place. What new sights did they see? What new experiences did they have? How did the place and their experiences make them feel?

Yoshiko Uchida
from

The Invisible Thread

In her autobiography, The Invisible Thread, *Yoshiko Uchida focuses on the personal discoveries she made about people and places while growing up. As this passage opens, Uchida and her family are driving off for their first visit to a farm. As you read, note the personal details that the author uses to make her writing clear and appealing to her readers. Then try the activities in Linking Writing and Literature on page 34.*

As we turned off the main highway, it seemed as though we were driving through a vast ocean of vineyards[1] that spread out on both sides of the dusty road. Before long we could see the Okubo waterpump windmill sprouting up among the grapevines.

"There it is!" Keiko shouted. "There's the Okubo farm!"

She reminded Papa of his earlier promise and convinced him there was nothing on the deserted road that she could possibly hit. Papa knew he would never hear the end of it if he didn't give her a chance, so he stopped the car.

---

1 **vineyards** (vin′ yərdz) fields planted with grapevines

28 Unit 1 Personal Writing

Resource Manager

Planning Resources
- *Lesson Plans*

Transparencies
- *Bellringer*
- *Daily Language Practice*
- *Fine Art 1–5*

Other Print Resources
- *Listening and Speaking Activities,* pp. 14–15
- *Thinking and Study Skills,* p. 3
- *Writing Assessment and Evaluation Rubrics*

Web Sites
- *writerschoice.glencoe.com*
- *lit.glencoe.com*

Literature Model

Keiko was in heaven as Papa let her slide over behind the wheel. But poor Mama was clutching my arm again.

"Careful, Kei Chan," she cautioned. "Be careful."

Keiko started slowly, like a tired turtle. But by the time she made the final turn toward the farm, she was feeling confident and picking up a little speed.

"Honk the horn to let them know we're here," Papa said.

> **66** *. . . Keiko not only honked the horn, but simultaneously crashed into Jick's dog house. . . .* **99**

At which point Keiko not only honked the horn, but simultaneously[2] crashed into Jick's dog house, knocked it over on its side, and stopped just inches short of the walnut tree.

"Look out, for heaven's sake," we all shouted. "Look out!"

Jick barked furiously at the sudden assault[3] on his territory, and the chickens scrambled in every direction,

___

2 **simultaneously** (sī′ məl tā′ nē əs lē) occurring at the same time
3 **assault** (ə sôlt′) a violent attack

screeching and cackling as though the end of the world had come.

The startled Okubos rushed from their house, blinking in the sun, surveying with alarm what only moments before had been their peaceful yard.

"We're here!" Keiko shouted, as if they needed to be told. "We're here!"

Because the Okubos' two grown daughters had already left home, they welcomed my sister and me as though we were their grandchildren, and we called them Oji San (uncle) and Oba San (auntie).

Oji San gave us a quick tour of the farm. He showed us how to pump water from the well and put our heads down to gulp the cold water that came gushing out. He pointed to the outhouse, saying, "I guess you've never used one of those before." We certainly hadn't. Whenever I had to use it, I held my breath and got out as fast as I could.

He also let us look for eggs in the henhouse, and took us to the barn where we staggered about in the hayloft, trying to pitch hay with forks that were bigger than we were.

He saved the best for last, taking us to a fenced enclosure where two dusty mules ambled over to greet us.

"Meet Tom and Jerry," he said. Then pulling some scraggly weeds by the fence, he told us to feed them to the mules.

Literature Model **29**

Personal Writing

Teach

Active Reading Strategies

Monitor Comprehension Tell students that when they *monitor comprehension,* they think about whether they understand what they are reading. Ask: "Where is the family at the start of the story, and where are they headed?" *(They are on a deserted road and are headed for the Okubo farm.)*

6+1 Trait® Writing

Word Choice Ask: "Which groups of words in the beginning paragraphs of the excerpt suggest the wide open spaces of farm country?" *(a vast ocean of vineyards that spread out on both sides of the dusty road, the Okubo water pump windmill sprouting up among the grapevines, nothing on the deserted road)*

Active Reading Strategies

Monitor Comprehension

Explain to students that it is a good idea to pause occasionally as they read to think about whether they understand the meaning of the text. Suggest that they try the following strategies to monitor their comprehension:

• Ask yourself questions about the main ideas, characters, and events.
• If you can't answer one of your questions, try rereading

more slowly, skimming what you have read, or reading ahead.
• Ask your teacher or a classmate for help.

Practice Have students write two questions about the events taking place on pages 28 and 29. Have students take turns asking their classmates to answer the questions.

Teach

Literary Element

Point of View Tell students that *point of view* refers to the person telling the story. With a first-person point of view, the narrator is a character in the story. The narrator sees things as that person sees them. A first-person narrator refers to himself or herself with the pronouns *I* or *me*. With a third-person point of view, the narrator is not a character in the story. Ask students to identify the narrator in this excerpt and to determine whether the story is told from the first- or third-person point of view. *(The narrator is Keiko's sister. The story is told from the first-person point of view.)*

Personal Writing

Literature Model

Paul Cézanne, *Farmhouse and Chestnut Trees at Jas-de-Bouffan*, c. 1885

Viewing the Art

Paul Cézanne, *Farmhouse and Chestnut Trees at Jas-de-Bouffan*, c. 1885
In this painting, French artist Paul Cézanne (1839–1906) celebrates the beauty of a simple scene. This oil painting, measuring 36 by 29 inches, is in the Norton Simon Museum.

I thrust some weeds at them and the mules grabbed them hungrily, showing their enormous yellow teeth. They seemed friendly enough, but I was rather glad they were on the other side of the fence.

"They like you," Oji San said. "Maybe they'll do something nice for you later on."

"Like what, Oji San?"

Oji San just grinned and smashed his felt hat down over his forehead. "You'll see," he said. "Wait and see."

Sitting on mats spread out under the walnut tree, we had a wonderful picnic supper of soy-drenched chicken and corn grilled over an out-door pit. There were rice balls, too, sprinkled with black sesame[4] seeds that looked like tiny ants.

Oji San waited until the sun had dipped down behind the dusty grapevines and a soft dusky haze settled in the air. Then he announced he was taking us all on a moonlight ride through the vineyards. It was more than we'd ever hoped for.

Keiko took her usual place up front by Oji San, hoping for a brief chance at the reins. Mama and Papa chatted quietly with Oba San, and I lay stretched out in back, looking up at the enormous night sky.

There seemed to be millions and billions of stars up there. More than I'd ever imagined existed in the

> **"It was as though the entire sky had dropped closer to earth to spread out its full glory. . . ."**

universe. They seemed brighter and closer than they were in Berkeley. It was as though the entire sky had dropped closer to earth to spread out its full glory right there in front of me.

I listened to the slow *clop-clop* of the mules as they plodded through the fields, probably wondering why they were pulling a wagonload of people in the dark, instead of hauling boxes of grapes to the shed under the hot, dry sun.

I could hear crickets singing and frogs croaking and all the other gentle night sounds of the country. I felt as though I were in another more immense,[5] never-ending world, and wished I could keep riding forever to the ends of the earth.

When we got back to the farm, it was time for an outdoor Japanese bath. Oji San built a fire under a

---

4 **sesame** (ses' ə mē) an Asian plant whose seeds are used for food and oil
5 **immense** (i mens') without limits; vast

Literature Model **31**

Personal Writing

Teach

Critical Thinking
Draw Conclusions Explain to students that when they *draw a conclusion*, they use a number of pieces of known information to make a general statement about people, places, or events. Ask students to use information from the selection to determine the relationship between the narrator's family and the Okubos. Ask: "What evidence points to that conclusion?" *(The Okubos are close friends, but probably not relatives, of the narrator's family. They invite the narrator's family to visit their farm, they treat the narrator and her sister like grandchildren, and the two girls call the Okubos uncle and auntie.)*

Critical Thinking
Infer Tell students that when they *infer*, they use their own experience to guess at what the author doesn't come right out and say. Ask students to infer the characteristics of Oji San and to back up their descriptions with details from the story. *(He is kind, generous, and considerate. He takes the time to show the girls how to drink from the well, he lets them look for eggs in the hen house, and he takes them on a moonlight ride.)*

Critical Thinking
Infer The narrator says, "Keiko took her usual place up front." Ask students what they can infer about Keiko from this and other details in the excerpt. *(In the car, Keiko sits up front because she wants to drive. She does the same in the cart, hoping to be able to take the reins. Clearly, she likes to take control and try new things. She shows little fear.)*

6+1 Trait® Writing

Conventions
Tell students that all languages have certain conventions, or rules about correct use of the language. Grammar, usage, spelling, punctuation, and capitalization are all important conventions of written English. English is easy to read and understand when all writers follow the same conventions. When writers follow the conventions of English, it is easier for readers to understand text.

Practice Direct students' attention to the way dialogue is punctuated in the excerpt. Explain that quotation marks signal the words of a speaker. Commas are used to separate spoken words from such identifying phrases as "he said." Also point out that a new paragraph signals a change in speakers. Have students write a brief conversation between two or three people, using the conventions of punctuation and paragraphing.

6+1 Trait® is a registered trademark of Northwest Regional Educational Laboratory, which does not endorse this product.

Active Reading Strategies

Monitor Comprehension Point out to students that on this page Oba San calls out to "Kei Chan" and "Yo Chan" that their bath is ready. Students should recognize *Kei* as a shortened version of *Keiko,* but they may mistakenly think that *Chan* is a last name. Actually, it's an affectionate suffix added to the names of the two young girls, comparable to the respectful *san* that the girls add to the words *Oji* and *Oba* (uncle and aunt). Ask students to use whatever information they have to identify the narrator of the selection. (If necessary, remind students this is an autobiographical piece.) *(The narrator is the author, Yoshiko Uchida, familiarly called Yo Chan by her elders.)*

Personal Writing

Literature Model

square tin tub filled with water, banking[6] the fire when the water was hot and inserting a wooden float so

we wouldn't burn our feet or backsides when we got in.

Oba San hung some sheets on ropes strung around the tub and called out, "*Sah, ofuro!* Come, Kei Chan, Yo Chan. The bath is ready. You girls go first."

Mama gave us careful instructions about proper bathing procedures.

---

6 banking (bangk' ing) partially covering a fire with ashes so that it will burn more slowly and for a longer period of time

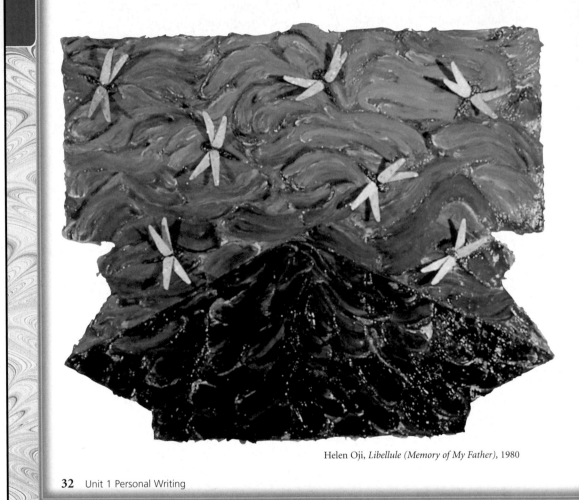

Helen Oji, *Libellule (Memory of My Father),* 1980

Viewing the Art

Helen Oji, Libellule *(Memory of My Father)* 1980
In this piece, Helen Oji expresses aspects of her Japanese heritage. She used acrylics, rhoplex, and glitter on a kimono-shaped paper canvas. The work measures 60 by 72 inches, and is in the collection of the Prudential Insurance Company.

Literature Model

"Wash and rinse yourselves outside before you get into the tub," she reminded us. "And keep the water clean."

" As always, Keiko was fearless. "

When we were ready to climb in, I saw steam rising from the water and was afraid I'd be boiled alive. "You go first," I told my sister.

As always, Keiko was fearless. She jumped right in and sank down in the steaming water up to her neck.

"Ooooooh, this feels wonderful!" she said.

I quickly squeezed in next to her, and we let the warm water gurgle up to our chins.

Keiko looked up at the glorious night sky and sighed, "I could stay here forever."

Personal Writing

Active Reading Strategies

Summarize At the end of the excerpt, Keiko says, "I could stay here forever." Ask students to summarize the reasons she feels the way she does. *(She is impressed by the comfort of an outdoor Japanese bath, the gentle sounds of the country evening, the vastness of the night sky, and the feeling of closeness to family and friends.)*

Additional Resources

*For personal **writing prompts**, see Fine Art Transparencies 1–5.*

Listening and Speaking Activities, pp. 14–15

Thinking and Study Skills, pp. 3

Critical Thinking

Infer

Explain to students that inferring involves using reason, experience, and clues from the text to make an educated guess about what a writer does not come right out and say. Paying attention to descriptions, dialogue, events, and relationships in a piece of writing are all good ways to infer meaning.

Practice Ask students what they can infer about Mama from her instructions to the girls about bathing. *(She understands and respects custom and good manners, and she wants to teach those qualities to her daughters.)*

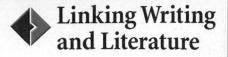

Linking Writing and Literature

Assess

Evaluation Rubrics

◆ Talk About Reading

Possible responses to the questions:

1. Answers will vary, but students will likely remember special highlights.
2. Keiko is a take-charge girl who enjoys being in control. (She wants to drive the car.) She is not perfect. (She drives into the dog house.)
3. The author uses quotation marks to signal dialogue. A new paragraph signals a change in speaker.
4. The use of dialogue enables the author to show the characters in action rather than just tell the reader about them.

◆ Write About Reading

The personal narrative should do the following:

• include interesting details to introduce the setting and characters
• organize events logically
• use dialogue effectively
• include a satisfying conclusion

Close

Ask students to write a friendly letter to a character in *The Invisible Thread*. They may even want to write about a special personal experience.

Personal Writing

Literature Model

◆ Linking Writing and Literature

◆ Collect Your Thoughts

Keiko and her sister had never visited a farm before. How do they react? What do they find to be most interesting or memorable? Jot some ideas in your notebook.

◆ Talk About Reading

Discuss the excerpt from *The Invisible Thread* with a group of your classmates. Select one person to lead the discussion and another to take notes. Use the following questions to focus the discussion.

1. **Connect to Your Life** Think about the first time you went someplace special you had never been to before—for example, an art museum or a wild animal park. What do you remember seeing, thinking, and doing that made the visit memorable? Make some notes in your journal about the experience and what it meant to you.

2. **Critical Thinking: Infer** What do you learn about Keiko's character while the family is driving to the farm? How do you know?

3. **6+1 Trait®: Conventions** The excerpt includes a lot of dialogue. What punctuation does the author use to signal dialogue? How do you know when the speaker has changed?

4. **Connect to Your Writing** How does the author's use of dialogue make the characters seem more real?

◆ Write About Reading

Personal Narrative Write a personal narrative describing the first time you and others went to a memorable place. Explain what you found there that made the visit so special. Include dialogue in your narrative.

Focus on Conventions Use appropriate grammar, usage, and mechanics (spelling and punctuation) as you write. Pay special attention to the way you punctuate dialogue in your narrative.

For more information on writing conventions and the 6+1 Trait® model, see **Writing and Research Handbook,** pages 682–684.

6+1 Trait® is a registered trademark of Northwest Regional Educational Laboratory, which does not endorse this product.

Cultural Connections

History

When Japan bombed Pearl Harbor in 1941, Uchida was a senior at the University of California. In the aftermath of the attack she and her family, along with some 120,000 Japanese Americans, were sent to live in internment camps in the West. These camps, which were similar to prisons, have now been formally condemned by the United States Congress for violating the civil rights of Japanese Americans.

UNIT 1 Review

Reflecting on the Unit

Summarize what you learned in this unit by answering the following questions.

❶ What are some ways to express your ideas and feelings through personal writing?

❷ How does writing in a personal journal build confidence in your writing skills?

❸ How can a learning log help you make sense of what you study?

❹ What are some important things to remember about writing a friendly letter?

❺ How can you express personal feelings in response to a poem?

📎 Adding to Your Portfolio

Choose a selection for your portfolio.

Look over the personal writing you did during this unit. Select a completed piece of writing to put into your portfolio. The piece you choose should show some or all of the following characteristics:

- grows out of a freewriting idea
- records your personal ideas, experiences, or feelings
- uses specific words that create clear images for your reader
- sounds like you

REFLECT ON YOUR CHOICE. Attach a note to the piece you chose, explaining briefly why you chose it and what you learned from writing it.

SET GOALS. How can you improve your writing?

What skill will you focus on the next time you write?

Writing Across the Curriculum

MAKE A MATHEMATICS CONNECTION. Write down some of your ideas and feelings about mathematics. What do you like most about math? What do you dislike or find difficult? What kinds of math materials do you like to use? What skill or concept would you enjoy teaching to a younger child?

Review **35**

Personal Writing

Review

Reflecting on the Unit

You may have students respond to Reflecting on the Unit in writing or through discussion.

Writing Across the Curriculum

To help students organize their ideas and feelings about mathematics, you might lead them in a discussion about their mathematics experiences.

Adding to Your Portfolio

Suggest that students select writing samples that reflect who they are and what they care about. These samples might include writing that contains personal thoughts, feelings, and experiences. Mention that students need not share any parts of their journals that they consider private.

Portfolio Evaluation

If you grade the portfolio selections, you may want to award two marks—one each for content and form. Explain your assessment criteria before students make their selections. Commend

- experimentation with creative prewriting techniques
- clear, concise writing in which the main idea, audience, and purpose are evident
- successful revisions
- work that shows a flair for language

✔ ASSESSMENT OPTIONS

📁 *Tests with Answer Key and Rubrics*
Unit 1 Choice A Test, p. 1
Unit 1 Choice B Test, p. 2
Unit 1 Composition Objective Test, pp. 3–4

💾 *Testmaker*
Unit 1 Choice A Test
Unit 1 Choice B Test
Unit 1 Composition Objective Test

You may wish to administer one of these tests as a mastery test.

📼 *MindJogger Videoquizzes*

The Writing Process

Modern technology usually works so smoothly that we may give it little thought. But someone first figured out each invention, and someone must understand the functioning of the invention in order to fix anything that breaks or wears out.

Interpret and Analyze Use the following questions for discussion.

1. What auto parts do you recognize? What process does this picture show? What might the photographer's focus on this particular area of a car suggest?

2. Imagine that you are watching a friend, relative, or neighbor peering under the hood of a car. What might your first question be as you try to follow the process of fixing the car?

Discussing the Quotation

Read the quotation aloud. Discuss in what circumstances a person might act in such a way. What is the character interpreting, and how is he doing it? How can being aware of how things work together help a mechanic– and a writer? Encourage students to read "The Circuit" in *Glencoe Literature: The Reader's Choice*, Course 1, page 5.

Writing Prompt Characterizing the people in a narrative is part of a story-writer's process. Use the quotation on these pages to discover something about the character who "listened to the motor." Write your thoughts about that character and discuss your conclusions with a classmate.

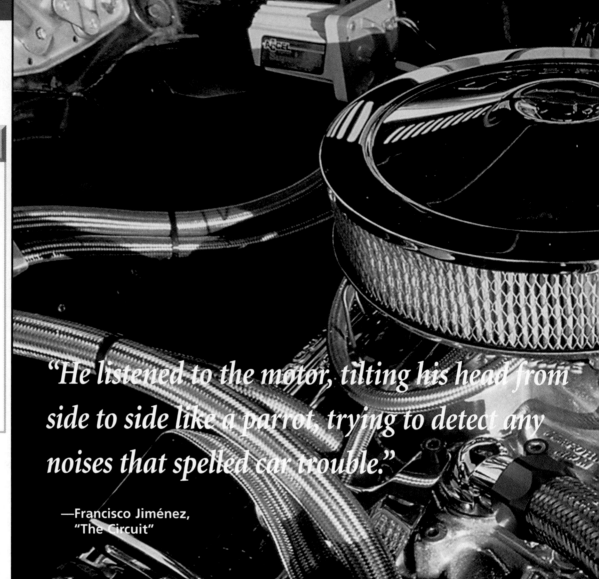

"He listened to the motor, tilting his head from side to side like a parrot, trying to detect any noises that spelled car trouble."

—Francisco Jiménez,
"The Circuit"

36

Planning Resources
- *Lesson Plans*
- *Block Scheduling*

Transparencies
- *Bellringer*
- *Daily Language Practice*
- *Fine Art*

- *Two-Minute Skill Drill*
- *Writing Process*

Other Print Resources
- *Composition Enrichment*
- *Composition Practice*
- *Composition Reteaching*
- *Cooperative Learning Activities*

- *Glencoe Literature Library*
- *Grammar and Composition Handbook*
- *Grammar Workbook*
- *Listening and Speaking Activities*
- *Sentence-Combining Practice*
- *Spelling Power*
- *Tests with Answer Key and Rubrics*

UNIT 2 The Writing Process

Objectives

- To understand ordering ideas and structuring paragraphs
- To develop an understanding of the five stages of the writing process
- To apply the five stages of the writing process to personal writing
- To practice polishing a piece of writing

✔ ASSESSMENT OPTIONS

Tests with Answer Key and Rubrics
Unit 2 Choice A Test, p. 5
Unit 2 Choice B Test, p. 6
Unit 2 Composition Objective Test,
pp. 7–8

Testmaker
Unit 2 Choice A Test
Unit 2 Choice B Test
Unit 2 Composition Objective Test

You may wish to administer either the Unit 2 Choice A Test or the Unit 2 Choice B Test as a pretest.

Key to Ability Levels

L1 Level 1 activities are within the basic ability range of students.

L2 Level 2 activities are within the ability range of average students.

L3 Level 3 activities are more challenging activities.

- *Thinking and Study Skills*
- *Vocabulary and Spelling Strategies and Practice*
- *Writing Across the Curriculum*
- *Writing Assessment and Evaluation Rubrics*
- *Writing in the Real World Video*

Video
- *MindJogger Videoquizzes*

Software
- *Presentation Plus!*
- *Revising with Style*
- *Testmaker*
- *Writer's Assistant*

Web Sites
- *writerschoice.glencoe.com*
- *lit.glencoe.com*

Focus

Lesson Overview

Objectives

- To explore ways in which the writing process may be used to select and define a topic, and to collect and organize information
- To analyze a writer's process

Skills

- understanding the role of direct quotations; becoming aware of audience; defining a topic

Critical Thinking

- analyzing; making generalizations

Listening and Speaking

- discussing

🔔 Bellringer
Daily Language Activity

When students enter the classroom, have this assignment on the board: *Write a paragraph describing a place that might be of interest to a person traveling through your community for the first time.*

Grammar Link to the Bellringer

Encourage students to check their paragraphs to make sure that they contain only complete sentences. How can they tell when a sentence is complete?

👆 **See also** *Daily Language Practice*

Motivating Activity

Ask students to imagine they are visiting their community for the first time. What kind of information about the area might they want or need to know?

Writing in the Real World

Curtis Katz has always loved trains. Today, his lifelong hobby is part of his job as a coach attendant for Amtrak. As he rides the *Empire Builder,* a train that makes the six-day journey from Chicago to Spokane, Katz tells passengers about the land they see outside the train windows. He has even written a guide for other attendants, so they too can share this information with their riders. The excerpt below is part of an announcement that Katz makes as the *Empire Builder* glides by the Bear Paw Mountains in Montana.

from *The Empire Builder: Scenic and Historic Announcements*

By Curtis Katz

The long trek took its toll on the Nez Percé people, and October of 1877 found them huddled in the mountains you see to the south, with winter weather setting in. By that time the Indians had outdistanced the pursuing General Howard, and Chief Joseph hoped to lead his people over the border into Canada for a rendezvous with Chief Sitting Bull, hardly two days' journey away. But while the Indians regrouped, General Howard sent a telegram to Colonel Nelson Miles, who was stationed to the east of the Indians' location.

Colonel Miles intercepted the Nez Percé in the Bear Paw Mountains. There ensued a fierce three-day battle, at the end of which Chief Joseph, realizing the hopelessness of his situation, surrendered to Colonel Miles. In his speech of surrender, Chief Joseph uttered his most famous quote, "From where the sun now stands, I will fight no more. . . ."

38 · Unit 2 The Writing Process

Resource Manager

Planning Resources
- *Lesson Plans*

👆 Transparencies
- *Bellringer*
- *Daily Language Practice*
- *Writing Process* 1–10

📂 Other Print Resources
- *Cooperative Learning Activities,* pp. 7–12
- *Thinking and Study Skills,* pp. 1, 8, 11, 22
- *Writing Assessment and Evaluation Rubrics*
- *Writing in the Real World,* pp. 5–8

A Writer's Process

Prewriting
Collecting the Ideas

Finding information about the *Empire Builder* route was no problem for Katz. First he collected information from members of the train crew. Carrying a small notebook on all his trips, Katz took notes from conductors and brake operators who lived along the route. He also recorded stories that he heard from passengers.

In addition, Katz did research in books. When he had an overnight stop, he went to used-book shops looking for stories and biographies about people and places in the area. "One thing led to another," he explained. "I'd pick up an out-of-print book. That book contained lists of other books."

Katz also researched facts in railroad magazines, such as *Trains.* As Katz read books and conducted interviews, he recorded the information in his notebook. Eventually, Katz had material on subjects ranging from train robberies to mountain climbing.

Drafting
Writing the Guide

During the week-long breaks between trips, Katz wrote almost constantly. Surrounded by boxes of historical documents, his toy trains, and shelves full of books, he found it easy to get involved in the material. He discovered that in many cases, he had several versions of the same story. So one of the first things he had to do was decide which version to use. Katz explains that he had "to make judgment calls. . . . Sometimes I included several versions."

Katz also had to choose a pattern of organization. He decided to organize his manuscript to follow his route from west to east. Passengers who take the train east to west hear the manuscript in reverse. "I did it kind of straight ahead—from one end of the route to the other," Katz explained. "I wrote each section in the order in which it occurred. It's not like a short story where you write from the middle out. This was strictly written by the way the railroad ran."

As he was drafting, Katz found that he needed to do some additional research to fill in missing facts. He also checked statistics, such as dates and mountain heights.

The drafting process took several weeks. Meanwhile, Katz continued to gather new information during the six-day train trips. To his route folder, he clipped notes and newspaper articles that people gave him.

The Writing Process

Teach

Reading Media

Have students preview the title and focus of the Media Connection. Explain that Curtis Katz prepared his travel announcements by applying the writing process to information about an Amtrak train route in the western United States. Invite students to read the article.

Discussion Prompts

Invite students to discuss various types of writing and the processes that might have produced them. Examples to consider might include the following:

- a descriptive essay
- a newspaper or magazine article
- a book report
- a travel guide
- a biography

Applying Ideas

- How might you make a "judgment call" when sources of information appear to conflict?
- When you find more information than you can possibly use in a writing project, how do you decide which information to include and which to set aside?

Connections Across the Curriculum

History

Railroads changed life in the West forever. They diminished isolation, brought consumer goods and new immigrants to the land, and enabled farmers and ranchers to send their products to markets in the East. Railroads also brought problems. They were often built at the expense of migrant laborers and contributed to the destruction of native cultures and the degradation of natural environments. Invite students to discuss the impact of railroads on the West.

Teach

Discussion Prompts

- How might a writer decide the order in which information is arranged and presented?
- How might statistics make writing more interesting and informative?

Evaluating Ideas

Stimulate a discussion of the Media Connection. You may want to invite students to talk about

- sources of information Mr. Katz used to prepare his travel announcements
- the use of peer reviewers in preparing manuscripts
- the importance of grammar in the writing process

Additional Resources

Writing Process Transparencies, 1–10

Writing in the Real World, pp. 5–8

Cooperative Learning Activities, pp. 7–12

Thinking and Study Skills, pp. 1, 8, 11, 22

Vocabulary and Spelling Strategies and Practice, p. 2

The Writing Process

Revising
Putting the Guide in Final Form

Katz wrote the original manuscript by hand. Then he typed it. He used the typed version to revise, cutting and pasting the manuscript in the order he wanted. Then he combined the typewritten sections with new inserts.

Katz kept his audience in mind as he revised. Since other coach attendants would be learning the announcements, the guide needed to be easy to read. Katz says, "I tried . . . to make things grammatically correct. When you're speaking conversationally, you use phrases. This wouldn't do in a written version."

❝ *Passengers apparently enjoy being informed about the country that they are passing through. . . . I imagine they find these announcements entertaining and educational, and perhaps such announcements give them a sense of place when in unfamiliar territory.* ❞
—*Curtis Katz*

Editing/Proofreading
Polishing the Manuscript

After retyping all of this material, Katz reread the manuscript. He made corrections in red ink and noted additions in black ink. "Even in the proofreading process," says Katz, "new information came to hand. I couldn't resist adding it."

While proofreading, Katz checked for broad generalizations. He corrected them by adding specific details. Finally, he asked his wife to read the edited manuscript. "She asked me, 'Do you really want to say it that way?'" Katz used his wife's feedback to clarify any parts of the manuscript that were fuzzy or awkward.

Publishing/Presenting
Using the Guide

Katz's manuscript was distributed to his fellow coach attendants. In a cover letter, he encouraged them to have fun with the announcements: "Passengers can always tell the difference between someone reading over the [loudspeaker] and someone speaking ." He also encouraged them to "embellish with your own style and material."

Katz has never stopped working on the guide, continuing to gather stories and update announcements. In his office is a photocopy of the "completed" manuscript. Throughout it, Katz has clipped notes for a later edition.

Visual Thinking

Using Photographs in Writing

Because photographs often recall the story of a place as well as words do, writers use photographs as note-taking tools. Have students bring in photographs of places they have visited. They can freewrite about a photo for five minutes and use their notes to write a travel announcement.

Examining Writing in the Real World

Analyzing the Media Connection

Discuss these questions about the guide excerpt on page 38.

1. What is the topic of the excerpt from Katz's guide? Why might it interest riders of the *Empire Builder*?

2. What date does Katz mention in the excerpt? What names of historical figures does he provide? Why do you think Katz uses these concrete details?

3. What quotation does Katz use in the excerpt? Explain why you think he used the speaker's exact words, rather than paraphrasing or describing them.

4. What distances and directions does Katz provide in the excerpt? Why might a passenger aboard the train be interested in them?

5. Imagine that you are a passenger on the *Empire Builder.* How would information from the excerpt enhance your trip?

Analyzing a Writer's Process

Discuss these questions about Curtis Katz's writing process.

1. Describe the things Katz did to gather information for his guide. How is your own process of exploring an idea and gathering

material like Katz's? How is it different?

2. Did Katz always know exactly what kind of information he was looking for while doing his research? Explain your answer.

3. Did Katz stop researching information when the prewriting stage was done? Why or why not?

4. What kinds of things did Katz surround himself with as he wrote? How did they affect him?

5. What did Katz check for while editing his manuscript? Who helped him in this process? How?

Use complete sentences in your writing.

Revise each fragment below so that it is a complete sentence.

1. the Lincoln Memorial in Washington, D.C.
2. statue of Abraham Lincoln
3. is a popular tourist attraction
4. the words from the Gettysburg Address
5. the beautiful white building

See Lesson 8.2, page 299.

Grammar Link

Answers

Answers will vary. Some suggestions follow.

1. We visited the Lincoln Memorial in Washington, D.C.
2. Using our new cameras, my sister and I photographed the statue of Abraham Lincoln.
3. Washington is a popular tourist attraction.
4. I read the words from the Gettysburg Address.
5. Rows of red flowers grew in front of the beautiful white building.

Enrichment

Have students interview subjects and create their own travel brochures. Remind them to accurately record the comments of the people they interview.

Close

Ask students to discuss the writing process. Which part of the process do they think is most important? Why?

Assess

Analyzing the Media Connection

1. Katz's topic is the history of Chief Joseph and the Nez Percé people. Riders of the *Empire Builder* travel through the country where the Nez Percé people live.

2. He mentions October, 1877, and names Chief Joseph, Chief Sitting Bull, General Howard, and Colonel Miles. These details strengthen his narrative.

3. "From where the sun now stands, I will fight no more . . ." by Chief Joseph. The words are powerful and direct.

4. He mentions south and east, the border into Canada, and two days journey to emphasize distances and locations, which would be of interest to a traveler.

5. Students may suggest they would better appreciate the region through which they were passing.

Analyzing a Writer's Process

1. Katz did research in old books and railroad magazines, conducted interviews, and recorded the information. Students should recognize that most informative writing requires research.

2. Katz knew what type of information he wanted but recorded many related facts and differing versions. He stated that he had "to make judgment calls."

3. He continued to gather information to fill in missing facts as he traveled.

4. He surrounded himself with historical documents, toy trains, and shelves full of books. These items helped him get involved in his work.

5. Katz checked for generalizations and added specific details. His wife and possibly his passengers helped him.

Reteaching

Invite students to read tourist brochures. How might the writers of these brochures have used the writing process?

Focus

Lesson Overview

Objectives

- To recognize the stages of the writing process
- To become aware of one's own writing process

Skills

- selecting a topic; organizing information; drafting and revising

Critical Thinking

- analyzing; using a model

Listening and Speaking

- evaluating; questioning; discussing

 **Bellringer**
Daily Language Activity

When students enter the classroom, have this assignment on the board: *If you had to write a report about a favorite family recipe, what writing process would you follow? List the steps you would follow to write such a report.*

Grammar Link to the Bellringer

Ask students how many of them included checking punctuation as a part of their writing process. Why is checking punctuation important?

See also *Daily Language Practice*

Motivating Activity

Invite students to discuss difficulties they have had writing reports or other documents. Explain that this lesson will provide them with a process that can make writing easier.

The Writing Process

Exploring the Writing Process

T he writing process has five stages: prewriting, drafting, revising, editing/proofreading, and publishing/presenting. Follow this process to create a finished piece of writing.

Maya, a reporter for her school newspaper, was stuck for a topic. While visiting her friend Bernard, Maya watched him cook a pot of gumbo for dinner. She thought that cooking was a topic that might interest other students. She pulled out her notebook and began taking notes.

Resource Manager

Planning Resources
- *Lesson Plans*

Transparencies
- *Bellringer*
- *Daily Language Practice*
- *Fine Art 6–10*
- *Two-Minute Skill Drill*
- *Writing Process 1–10*

Other Print Resources
- *Composition Enrichment,* p. 8
- *Composition Practice,* p. 8
- *Composition Reteaching,* p. 8
- *Cooperative Learning Activities,* pp. 7–12
- *Listening and Speaking Activities,* pp. 6-7, 10–13
- *Thinking and Study Skills,* pp. 2, 5

- *Vocabulary and Spelling Strategies and Practice,* pp. 35–52
- *Writing Across the Curriculum*
- *Writing Assessment and Evaluation Rubrics*

As soon as Maya got an idea and started taking notes, she had begun the prewriting stage of the writing process.

Begin with Ideas

Most writers take their work through all five of the stages you'll read about here. They often go through some stages more than once. Knowing about each of these stages will be helpful in completing your writing assignment.

PREWRITING Prewriting begins the moment you start to collect ideas. During this stage, writers explore ideas for writing topics. Look at the prewriting notes Maya made as she watched Bernard. Some of her notes are sentence fragments. Notice that she wrote what Bernard did and what she thought. Sometimes she wrote down words Bernard used.

DRAFTING Drafting involves developing your prewriting notes into connected sentences and paragraphs. During this stage, writers try new ideas and make connections. Sometimes they make some discoveries or even decide to change their topic. That's just part of the adventure of writing.

> *Lots of stages in making gumbo.*
> *Bernard put chicken and sausage into the gumbo. Is there a meatless version?*
> *Whew! Those peppers even smell hot!*
> *Okra—what does it taste like?*
> *Bernard says that in Bantu, an African language, the word for okra is gumbo. Maybe there's a story idea in that.*

Journal Writing

What is your family's favorite recipe that has been handed down through the years? What is special about this recipe or food? Jot down ways to turn answers to these questions into a writing topic.

The Writing Process

Teach

Using a Writing Process Checklist

Students may find the five stages of the writing process intimidating. To help eliminate such fears and make students more comfortable with the process, ask them to create a five-column chart for the five stages. Encourage students to use the chart when they write, making a check mark in the appropriate column as they complete each stage. **L2**

Generating a Topic

Ask students to imagine that they are going to write a report about a hobby. Encourage them to spend ten minutes writing down ideas for the report. When students have finished, invite volunteers to read their lists of ideas. Help students focus their ideas into writing topics. **L2**

Two-Minute Skill Drill

Have students write as many ideas as they can think of for a written presentation entitled "The Musician I Admire Most."

See also *Two-Minute Skill Drill Transparencies, 2.1*

Journal Writing Tip

Generating Topics When students write about family recipes, remind them to consider not only their own experiences and preferences but those of other family members.

Teach

Revising a Manuscript

Invite students to work in pairs, exchanging draft copies and marking potential revisions. Help students to work through the comments their revision partners made, deciding which comments to incorporate in their final manuscripts. **L1**

Using Different Presentation Formats

Encourage students to explore alternative methods for publishing and presenting their work. They might use computer technologies such as electronic mail or a disk to send their final manuscript to distant readers. The students might also augment a verbal presentation with video images or recorded audio effects. **L3**

Additional Resources

For **writing prompts** for using the writing process, see *Fine Art Transparencies* 6–10.

Daily Language Practice

Writing Process Transparencies, 1–10

Writing Across the Curriculum

Cooperative Learning Activities, pp. 7–12

Thinking and Study Skills, pp. 2, 5

Listening and Speaking Activities, pp. 6–7, 10–13

Vocabulary and Spelling Strategies and Practice, pp. 35–52

Composition Practice, p. 8

The Writing Process

Follow Through

After getting your ideas on paper, you need to make sure they are clear. Look at the follow-through stages.

REVISING The goal of revising is to make your writing clearer and more interesting to your audience. To revise, add or delete information where needed. Read your writing aloud to others to get their reactions. Check to see that sentences and paragraphs fit together.

EDITING/PROOFREADING The object of editing and proofreading is to correct errors in spelling, grammar, and punctuation. To edit, read your draft, watching for mistakes. Use proofreading symbols to mark changes on your draft.

PUBLISHING/PRESENTING Publishing/presenting includes everything from turning work in to your teacher to publishing a class book.

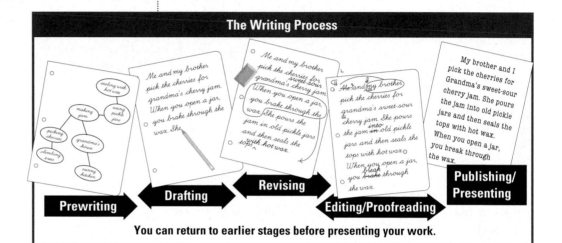

The Writing Process

Prewriting → Drafting → Revising → Editing/Proofreading → Publishing/Presenting

You can return to earlier stages before presenting your work.

MEETING INDIVIDUAL NEEDS

English Language Learners

Understanding the Writing Process

Students whose first language is not English can better understand the idea of *process* by thinking about the process of learning English. Students probably began learning the language by learning single words or phrases and slowly working these words into simple sentences. Then students worked step by step, increasing the complexity of their sentences as they became more familiar with the language.

Write About Your Writing Process

Follow the writing process to write your own paragraph. Describe how you write now and what you might try in the future. For help in organizing your thoughts and for more information on the 6+1 Trait® model, see **Writing and Research Handbook,** pages 679–683.

PURPOSE To describe your own writing process

AUDIENCE Yourself

LENGTH 1 paragraph

WRITING RUBRICS To explore your writing process, you should

- prewrite by making a list of what you do when you write. Organize your list.
- draft a paragraph. Begin with a general statement about what you do when you write.
- revise your paragraph after hearing a peer's comments
- edit and proofread your work

Using Computers

Use a computer to list ideas about your own writing process. Create a table with five columns: one for prewriting, one for drafting, one for revising, one for editing/ proofreading, and one for publishing/ presenting.

Grammar Link

Use correct punctuation at the ends of sentences.

Write each sentence below, ending it with the correct punctuation mark.

1. Have you read the book *The Lion King*
2. How scary parts of it are
3. The book came out after the movie
4. Read me the end of the story
5. Which character did you like best

See Lesson 19.1, page 489.

Listening and Speaking

BRAINSTORMING In a small group, each group member should offer a tip for prewriting. Repeat the process for drafting, revising, editing/proofreading and publishing/presenting. Take notes on helpful ideas. Discuss the writing process. What works for you? How can you help each other with this process?

The Writing Process

Assess

Evaluation Rubrics

Write About Your Writing Process

Use these criteria when evaluating your students' writing:
- Did students use the writing process to write their paragraphs?
- Were students' present and future writing processes detailed?
- Are paragraphs accurate in grammar, usage, and mechanics?

See also *Writing Assessment and Evaluation Rubrics.*

Using Computers

If students are trying this option for the first time, make sure they know how to create the chart or table format.

Listening and Speaking

Make sure students summarize the main ideas of their discussions in their notes and that they demonstrate the ability to make appropriate statements to communicate agreement or disagreement with others' ideas. Encourage students to use these notes for future writing projects.

Reteaching

📁 *Composition Reteaching,* p. 8

Enrichment

📁 *Composition Enrichment,* p. 8

🎨 *Fine Art Transparencies* 6–10

Close

Invite students to create sets of written guidelines to the writing process that they can use in future writing. You may wish to review students' individual guidelines to make sure they are accurate.

Grammar Link

Answers

1. ? **2.** ! **3.** . **4.** . **5.** ?

Using Correct Punctuation Suggest that students reread the paragraphs they wrote describing their own writing process. Did they vary the type of sentences they used? Would their paragraphs be more lively if they did? Remind students as they revise to check for correct punctuation.

Focus

Lesson Overview

Objectives

- To frame questions to generate topics for writing projects
- To use graphic organizers to organize ideas for topics

Skills

- listing writing ideas; using clusters

Critical Thinking

- categorizing; classifying; generating new information

Listening and Speaking

- discussing; questioning

🔔 Bellringer
Daily Language Activity

When students enter the classroom, have this assignment on the board: *Imagine that you are writing an article for a student newspaper. You can pick any topic you want, but the article has to be of interest to ninth graders. Write a paragraph explaining how you would pick a topic.*

Grammar Link to the Bellringer

Invite students to list any possessive nouns in their Bellringer paragraphs. Help them to correct any punctuation errors in the possessive nouns.

See also *Daily Language Practice*

Motivating Activity

Invite students to discuss problems they have had in coming up with interesting writing topics. What techniques might they suggest for students having difficulty choosing a topic?

The Writing Process

LESSON
2.2

Prewriting: Finding a Topic

Prewriting techniques can help you explore ideas and pinpoint possible topics that will interest readers. These techniques include listing, questioning, and clustering.

Think About a Topic

Sometimes it is difficult to nail down a topic that interests you. Once you do, you still need to know that your topic will be of interest to your readers.

Before Maya went to Bernard's house, she had struggled to find the right topic for her article. She needed a topic that would catch and hold the attention of her readers. She also wanted a topic she cared about. When people write about topics that truly interest them, that interest energizes the writing. This energy can be felt by the audience.

After her visit with Bernard, Maya knew she was close to pinning down her writing topic. She enjoys cooking, and she thought that others might be interested, too. However, she was not sure. She decided that she needed to do some research to find out if her audience would be as interested in cooking as she was.

Resource Manager

Planning Resources
- *Lesson Plans*

📖 Transparencies
- *Bellringer*
- *Daily Language Practice*
- *Fine Art 6–10*
- *Two-Minute Skill Drill*
- *Writing Process 1–10*

📁 Other Print Resources
- *Composition Enrichment*, p. 9
- *Composition Practice*, p. 9
- *Composition Reteaching*, p. 9
- *Cooperative Learning Activities*, pp. 7–12
- *Listening and Speaking Activities*, pp. 6–7, 10–13
- *Thinking and Study Skills*, pp. 1, 4–5, 7–8, 34–37

- *Vocabulary and Spelling Strategies and Practice*, pp. 35–52
- *Writing Across the Curriculum*
- *Writing Assessment and Evaluation Rubrics*

Ask Questions

Prewriting techniques can help you explore topics that will interest both you and your readers. Maya combined questioning and listing in her prewriting. She asked herself the following questions:

- What do my friends like to learn about?
- What articles have appeared lately in the school newspaper?
- What things have I done recently?

Maya then took those three questions and made a list to answer each one. Read her notes.

The Writing Process

What do my friends like to learn about?
Plants/ animals/ ecology
Other countries
Unusual sports and games
Cooking
People in history
TV and movie sta

What articles have appeared lately in the school newspape
School art show
Interview with the school principal
Plans for fund-raisin carnival
Results of Mr. Chana family-history project

What things have I done recently?
Taught my brother how to dive
Got an A on my science report
Made angel food cake from scratch
Watched Sharon draw a cartoon strip

Journal Writing

Use Maya's lists as an example. Write three questions of your own. Create a list of ideas below each question. Then decide which three ideas might interest you most. Why would you want to write about these ideas? Answer this question in your journal.

Teach

Using Visuals

Have visual learners generate writing ideas by looking through photo albums and magazines. Help them to group pictures with similar ideas. Students can then jot down ideas about one group of photos. Guide them to develop the ideas into a topic. **L2**

Recording Discussions

Suggest that students use a tape recorder to find a writing topic. Help pairs of students record a discussion about personal interests. In an interview-type format, one partner might ask: What do you care about most? What do you like to read about? What are your friends interested in? Students can then listen to the tape, using these questions and answers to find writing topics. **L1**

Two-Minute Skill Drill

Invite students to write a quick cluster around one of the following words:

science   art   music
sports   computers

See also *Two-Minute Skill Drill Transparencies, 2.2*

Journal Writing Tip

Answering Questions Remind students that a good way to start searching for a writing topic is to think about things they know or do well.

Teach

Finding Topics

Ask students to give you examples of some objects or actions they saw on the way to school today. List these examples on the board. Then circle five of them. Ask the class to think of as many writing topics as possible for each circled item. Help students to see that writing topics are all around them. **L2**

Using Clusters

Once students have decided on topics, they can use clusters to explore the topics. Encourage them to take their clusters out as far as they can, including as much detail as they like. They can use words, phrases, or sentences to explore and expand their ideas. Point out that the more details they include, the more information they'll have to draw from when they write. **L3**

Additional Resources

For prewriting ideas, see Fine Art Transparencies *6–10.*

Daily Language Practice

Writing Process Transparencies, 1–10

Writing Across the Curriculum

Cooperative Learning Activities, pp. 7–12

Thinking and Study Skills, pp. 1, 4–5, 7–8, 34–37

Listening and Speaking Activities, pp. 6–7, 10–13

Vocabulary and Spelling Strategies and Practice, pp. 35–52

Composition Practice, p. 9

The Writing Process

Use Cluster Diagrams

When Maya studied her lists, she noticed that some ideas fit together. A few involved collecting things. Others were about her friends' interests. Seeing these connections made Maya decide to write about her friends' hobbies.

Maya further explored her topic, using another prewriting technique called clustering. She began by writing "My Friends' Hobbies" in the center of a piece of paper. Then she drew a circle around the words. As Maya focused on that idea, details popped into her mind. Even though she knew she might not use all the ideas, she wrote them down anyway. She circled each idea, and drew lines to show where the details came from and how they were related.

As her cluster grew, Maya felt more confident about her topic.

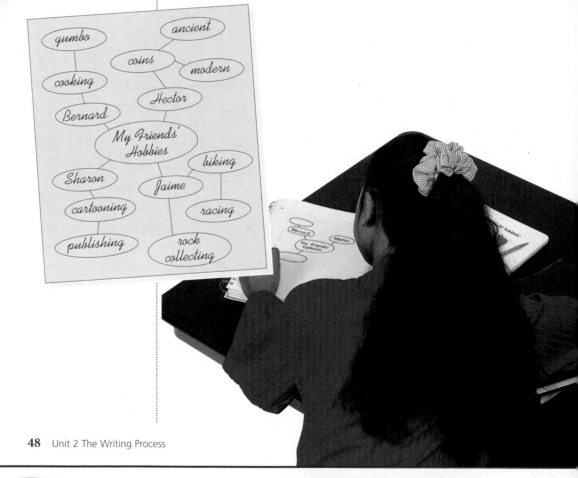

MEETING INDIVIDUAL NEEDS
English Language Learners

Using Translation Partners

Encourage students to use topic exploration as a way to practice and expand their English vocabulary. Remind students that they need not be concerned with grammatically correct construction when listing or clustering. Encourage them to write as many of their ideas as possible in English. They can then consult dictionaries or work with other students who are learning English to find English translations for their remaining ideas.

Explore a Topic

Review the three lists you created for this lesson's Journal Writing. Choose one of your journal ideas that really interests you. Apply prewriting techniques to explore the idea fully. Later in this unit you will develop the topic into a finished piece of writing.

PURPOSE To apply prewriting techniques

AUDIENCE Yourself

LENGTH Lists of varying lengths and a diagram

WRITING RUBRICS To develop a topic, you should

- ask yourself questions about your idea
- use clustering to explore your idea and collect details
- think about why the topic interests you and how you can interest your readers

Using Computers

Consider using a computer drawing program to create your idea cluster. Use the Copy and Paste functions to add circles to your cluster.

Grammar Link

Use possessive nouns correctly in your writing.

Possessive nouns describe ownership and are written with apostrophes.

Mr. Chan's *project, or* **my friends'** *hobbies*

Rewrite each sentence, using the correct possessive form of the noun in parentheses.

1. (Sally) hobby is swimming.
2. Sally swims on (Westville) swimming team.
3. Several of her (friends) hobbies also include swimming.
4. Her swim (team) colors are red and blue.
5. Sally's two swim (caps) colors are also red and blue.

See Lesson 9.3, page 323.

Listening and Speaking

COOPERATIVE LEARNING With a small group, choose a topic that interests you. Together, create a cluster diagram to explore the idea and add details to the diagram. Group members should each contribute at least two ideas.

The Writing Process

Assess

Evaluation Rubrics

Explore a Topic

Use these criteria when evaluating your students' writing:

- Are details and ideas related to the topic?
- Is clustering used appropriately, including circles and lines linking related ideas?

See also *Writing Assessment and Evaluation Rubrics.*

Using Computers

Make sure students know how to use a computer drawing program. If students don't have access to a such a program, have them design a chart to organize their ideas.

Listening and Speaking

Make sure each group member contributes at least two ideas that are included on the cluster diagram.

Reteaching

📁 *Composition Reteaching,* p. 9

Enrichment

📁 *Composition Enrichment,* p. 9

🖐 *Fine Art Transparencies* 6–10

Close

Invite students to explain in their own words how techniques such as questioning, listing, and clustering can help them to decide on a writing topic. What tips would they offer other students working to choose a topic?

Grammar Link

Answers

1. Sally's   **2.** Westville's   **3.** friends'

4. team's   **5.** caps'

Using Possessive Nouns Invite students to make a list of objects that they saw on the way to school or can see in the classroom. Help them to write possessive forms of the nouns: for example, *Tom's book, Ms. Chan's briefcase, Ellen's cat,* or *Adrienne's bicycle.*

Focus

Lesson Overview

Objectives

- To identify the purpose and audience for a piece of writing
- To use questions to a plan an essay

Skills

- formulating questions; ordering information

Critical Thinking

- defining and clarifying; categorizing; classifying

Listening and Speaking

- discussing; questioning

🔔 Bellringer
Daily Language Activity

When students enter the classroom, have this assignment on the board: *Write brief directions for how to make a cheese, lettuce, and tomato sandwich. Include the gathering of all ingredients and equipment in your directions.*

Grammar Link to the Bellringer

Have students reread directions for making their sandwiches and find phrases that include a past participle, such as "after you have added" or "when you have sliced."

📖 See also *Daily Language Practice*

Motivating Activity

Have several volunteers read their directions. Which directions are most effective? Why?

The Writing Process

Prewriting: Ordering Ideas

𝒫 rewriting notes are much like a collection of baseball cards. These notes need to be ordered so that your readers will understand your message.

Organize Your Ideas

When you write, you can order your ideas in a variety of ways. Knowing your purpose for writing can help you decide what order to use. Most writing has one of four purposes.

- To tell an experience or story
- To describe how something or someone looks or acts
- To explain how something works or how to do something
- To persuade someone of something

Sometimes, one way of organizing works better than others for a certain purpose. For example, if you want to tell a story, you usually put events in the order in which they happened. If you want to convince someone of something, you might put your strongest argument last.

The passage on the opposite page tells about a boy and his mother walking down the street. They're exploring the town where they've just moved. Think about how the author organizes his details so that readers can picture what this town is like.

50 Unit 2 The Writing Process

Resource Manager

Planning Resources
- *Lesson Plans*

📖 Transparencies
- *Bellringer*
- *Daily Language Practice*
- *Fine Art 6–10*
- *Two-Minute Skill Drill*
- *Writing Process 1–10*

📁 Other Print Resources
- *Composition Enrichment*, p. 10
- *Composition Practice*, p. 10
- *Composition Reteaching*, p. 10
- *Cooperative Learning Activities*, pp. 7–12
- *Listening and Speaking Activities*, pp. 6–7, 10–13

- *Thinking and Study Skills*, pp. 2–4, 9, 20–21
- *Vocabulary and Spelling Strategies and Practice*, pp. 35–52
- *Writing Across the Curriculum*
- *Writing Assessment and Evaluation Rubrics*

Literature Model

The first building we had seen when we turned the corner onto State Street was the church. Then we had come to a large house, followed by several stores. Some of the doors were closed, but one was open. There were men inside, talking. The whole next block was one long building. I stared up at all the windows.

David Kherdian, *Root River Run*

How do "first," "then," "followed by," and "next" help you know the order of details?

The Writing Process

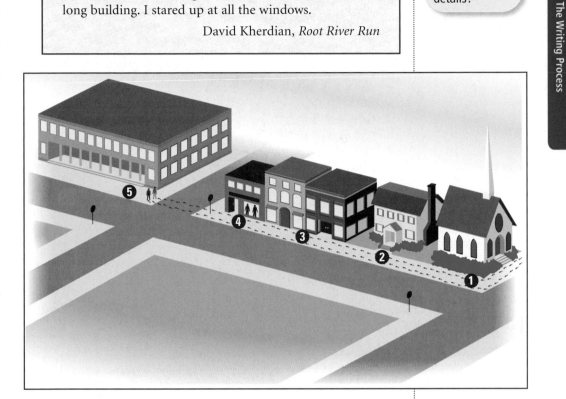

Journal Writing

Look through your journal for an entry that tells a story, describes something, explains something, or persuades someone. Is there a writing purpose you haven't tried yet in your journal? If so, make a list of possible topics for that writing purpose.

Teach

Using the Model

The author describes the buildings in the order in which he passed by them. Encourage volunteers to discuss possible orders they might use to describe the buildings on their own street. Would they start with their house, or would they first describe a playground or a school? **L2**

Ordering a Story

Remind students that in stories the narrator often starts in the middle of the action and moves back and forth in time. Ask students why this type of ordering might be more interesting than sequential order. **L3**

Two-Minute Skill Drill

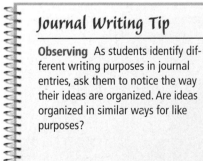

Ask students to write down the steps they took traveling to school that morning. Have them use the following words in their explanations:

| first | before | finally |
| next | then | |

See also *Two-Minute Skill Drill Transparencies, 2.3*

Journal Writing Tip

Observing As students identify different writing purposes in journal entries, ask them to notice the way their ideas are organized. Are ideas organized in similar ways for like purposes?

Teach

Ordering from Clusters

Suggest an idea and help the class to create a cluster on the chalkboard. Then break the class into small groups. Each group should create a list from one of the branches of the cluster, with each person in the group suggesting an item. The group should then order details in the way they would appear in a piece of writing. Groups should present their lists to the class and compare results with the other groups. **L2**

Sorting Ideas

Students may find ordering ideas easier if they first sort the ideas into the categories "more important" and "less important" Help students to sort ideas from their clusters into these two categories. Then work with them to sort their ideas from these categories into a final order. **L1**

Additional Resources

For **writing prompts**, see *Fine Art Transparencies* 6–10.

Daily Language Practice

Writing Process Transparencies, 1–10

Writing Across the Curriculum

Cooperative Learning Activities, pp. 7–12

Thinking and Study Skills, pp. 2–4, 9, 20–21

Listening and Speaking Activities, pp. 6–7, 10–13

Vocabulary and Spelling Strategies and Practice, pp. 35–52

Composition Practice, p. 10

The Writing Process

Sketch a Plan

Maya looked back at her cluster diagram. Then she chose some of the details and added information to them. To organize her ideas, she made a list. Maya thought about her readers and her purpose for writing. Because she wanted to draw her readers into her article, she reordered her ideas in a way she thought would appeal to the readers. Below, you can see how Maya used her list to order her ideas.

To grab her readers' attention right away, Maya put what she thought was the most interesting hobby first.

This detail sounds interesting. Why didn't Maya list it with a number?

Topic: Hobbies of classmates

5 Cooking with Bernard Gumbo is the Bantu word for okra

1 Jaime and his racing bike

2 Sharon-cartoonist for the school paper

4 Hector's amazing coin collection

Ancient and modern coins

3 Sharon's sketchbook

MEETING INDIVIDUAL NEEDS — English Language Learners

Ordering By Example

Help students to understand the concept of ordering ideas by providing them with examples of well-ordered ideas in published writing. Articles that explain a process, computer manuals, and short stories are good sources of examples. Have students read carefully and take notes to record the order of ideas. Then have them discuss how ordered ideas helped make the writing understandable or enjoyable. Encourage students to apply what they have learned about order to their own work.

Write an Ordered List

Review the cluster diagram that you prepared for your writing topic. Use it to help plan the contents and the structure of your piece of writing.

PURPOSE To order details for writing
AUDIENCE Yourself
LENGTH 1 page

WRITING RUBRICS To plan and structure your writing, you should

- choose details from a cluster diagram and list them
- add information about each detail
- organize the detailed list in the order you think will appeal to your readers

Cross-Curricular Activity

SOCIAL STUDIES Make a cluster diagram to explore a topic from your social studies class. Organize the details that you know about the topic. Check your textbook and other sources for additional details about your topic.

Grammar Link

Use past participles correctly in writing.

Past participles must be used with helping verbs.

*The first building we **had** seen . . .*

Rewrite each sentence below using the past participle form of the verb in parentheses.

1. Mr. Akito has (sketch) the scene with charcoal.
2. Earlier he had (make) a watercolor painting.
3. Our art teacher had (tell) us about the artist earlier.
4. We have (look) at much art.
5. What have you (like) best so far?

See Lesson 10.5, page 341.

Viewing and Representing

PLANNING Choose a work of art from this book. Make a cluster diagram with the artwork's title in the circle. Add details to your diagram about what you see. Who or what is in the artwork? What colors does the artist use? How does the work make you feel and why? Number the details in a logical order. Use this order to write a paragraph about the piece of art.

The Writing Process

Assess

Evaluation Rubrics

Write an Ordered List

Use these criteria when evaluating your students' writing:

- Does the list use details from the cluster diagram?
- Does it add information about each detail?
- Does it present ideas in a logical order?

See also *Writing Assessment and Evaluation Rubrics.*

Cross-Curricular Activity: Social Studies

Make sure that the main topic is written in the center of each cluster diagram and that a reasonable number of details are listed.

Viewing and Representing

Make sure that students' paragraphs consist of vivid details that are presented in logical order.

Reteaching

📁 *Composition Reteaching*, p. 10

Enrichment

📁 *Composition Enrichment*, p. 10

🖼 *Fine Art Transparencies* 6–10

Close

Have students work together to agree on general guidelines for ordering ideas in writing. Remind them that their rules may vary depending upon the type of writing.

Grammar Link

Answers

1. has sketched
2. had made
3. had told
4. have looked
5. have you liked

Focus

Lesson Overview

Objectives
- To organize ideas into paragraphs
- To complete a first draft

Skills
- developing details; organizing information; analyzing prewriting notes and ideas

Critical Thinking
- analyzing; organizing; defining and clarifying; evaluating; elaborating

Listening and Speaking
- discussing

🔔 Bellringer
Daily Language Activity

When students enter the classroom, have this assignment on the board: *Write three questions related to the following statements: Catamount is another name for a mountain lion. Mountain lions live in the United States. They are hunters.*

Grammar Link to the Bellringer

Ask students what kind of sentences are written on the board for the Bellringer activity. (declarative) Then ask them what kind of sentences are the questions they wrote. (interrogative) Have students think of two other sentence types. (exclamatory, imperative) Can they give examples of these?

📝 **See also** *Daily Language Practice*

Motivating Activity

Lead a discussion comparing a first draft to a play rehearsal. Ask students if a rehearsal has to be perfect. Why not?

The Writing Process

LESSON 2.4

Drafting: Getting It Down on Paper

*D*uring drafting, you turn ideas into sentences and paragraphs. When you draft, you just let the words flow. Later you can look for mistakes in grammar or spelling.

Maya couldn't wait to put her prewriting ideas into a first draft. She spread out her latest list, her cluster diagram, and the writing supplies she might need. Then she started to work. Maya thought about some different ways she could organize. She also thought about some things she could say that would make her readers interested right away.

54   Unit 2 The Writing Process

Resource Manager

Planning Resources
- *Lesson Plans*

📝 **Transparencies**
- *Bellringer*
- *Daily Language Practice*
- *Fine Art* 6–10
- *Two-Minute Skill Drill*
- *Writing Process* 1–10

📂 **Other Print Resources**
- *Composition Enrichment,* p. 11
- *Composition Practice,* p. 11
- *Composition Reteaching,* p. 11
- *Cooperative Learning Activities,* pp. 7–12
- *Listening and Speaking Activities,* pp. 6–7, 10–13
- *Thinking and Study Skills,* pp. 7–13

- *Vocabulary and Spelling Strategies and Practice,* pp. 35–52
- *Writing Across the Curriculum*
- *Writing Assessment and Evaluation Rubrics*

Start the Draft

The act of writing can make you think in new ways. When you begin to write, you may discover new ideas to add to your writing. You may also find that having prewriting notes can help you remember your original ideas and plan.

Maya made those same discoveries as she began to draft her article. Her cluster diagram and numbered list reminded her of the basics. She thought of ways to catch her audience's interest, and she talked to her friends about possibilities. Here's her introduction and part of her second paragraph.

> *It's time for a Wilson Elementary Wildcats Quiz! Who has attended bike-racing camp in Colorado? Who has boxes full of money in his closet? Whose gumbo can really make your mouth water? Whose name do you see in every edition of the school newspaper? They're all fellow Wildcats, students with some amazing hobbies.*
>
> *Take Jaime Sanchez, for example. He's been part of a local bike-racing club for two years.*

Which details do you recognize from Maya's cluster diagram and numbered list?

How does Maya make her readers want to go on reading the article?

Journal Writing

Look through your journal. Pick out two or three different types of topics. What might be an interesting introduction for each topic? Write your ideas in your journal.

Teach

Using the Model

Ask students what Maya did to catch her readers' interest at the beginning of her article. Point out that Maya has incorporated several details from her prewriting notes. Ask students to think of some other ways that Maya might have captured the attention of her readers. **L2**

Organizing Ideas

Students with learning disabilities might have trouble translating prewriting ideas into a structured paragraph form. These students may have more success if they try first to sketch each idea on a separate piece of paper. Tell students to arrange and rearrange the drawings until they are satisfied with the order of ideas. Then they can write a sentence for each drawing, using these sentences as the foundation for their draft. **L1**

Two-Minute Skill Drill

Ask students to write four kinds of sentences—declarative, exclamatory, interrogative, and imperative—including the word *window* in each.

See also *Two-Minute Skill Drill Transparencies, 2.4*

Journal Writing Tip

Identifying Relationships and Patterns Remind students that when they review prewriting notes, they should look for related ideas.

Teach

Thinking Critically

Ask students to share a piece of recorded music that features their favorite musical instrument. Tell them to refer to specific parts of the music that feature their favorite instrument. Ask them, *Why does your instrument sound better in this music than another instrument would?* **L2**

Discussing Writing Approaches

Tell students that every writer has a way to get started writing. Toni Morrison revealed, "I always know the ending; that's where I start." Ernest Hemingway said, "I rise at first light and I start by rereading and editing everything I have written to the point I left off." Ask students to list advantages and disadvantages of each approach. Which method would they prefer? **L3**

Additional Resources

For **writing prompts** for writing a draft, *see Fine Art Transparencies 6–10.*

Daily Language Practice

Writing Process Transparencies 1–10

Writing Across the Curriculum

Cooperative Learning Activities, pp. 7–12

Thinking and Study Skills, pp. 7–13

Listening and Speaking Activities, pp. 6–7, 10–13

Vocabulary and Spelling Strategies and Practice, pp. 35–52

Composition Practice, p. 11

The Writing Process

Get Unstuck . . .

Maya got stuck on her introduction. She wasn't sure how to make it interesting. Two things helped. Maya had read that author Betsy Byars often begins writing in the middle of a story idea. So Maya began her draft by writing about Jaime and Sharon. As she wrote, she began to see how she might introduce them.

Maya also talked to her friend Stefan about her article. "Well, nothing makes me as curious as a question does," he told her. His comment helped Maya think of a way to draft her introduction. Maya's draft shows that she wrote her introduction, using the advice from her friend. Most of the introduction, is made up of questions that the rest of her draft will answer.

Sometimes it's hard to keep ideas flowing onto the paper. One or more of the following suggestions may help.

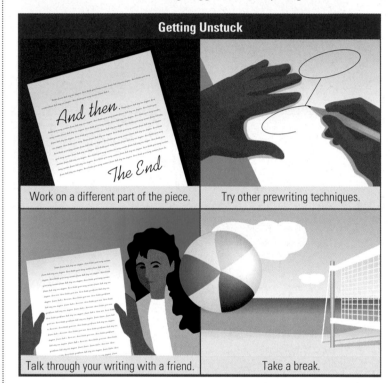

Getting Unstuck

Work on a different part of the piece.

Try other prewriting techniques.

Talk through your writing with a friend.

Take a break.

MEETING INDIVIDUAL NEEDS — English Language Learners

Choosing Words

To help students with a limited English vocabulary get started, give them several sentence starters to use in opening sentences. Some examples are *The most interesting/exciting/surprising thing about my new school/neighborhood is* _____ and *One of my favorite activities is* _____ *because it allows me to* _____ . Explain that students can use these sentence starters in their first drafts. Later, when they revise, they can rewrite the sentences in their own words.

Write a Draft

Review the ordered list you prepared about your topic. Use the list to write the first draft of your article or story. For more information on drafting, see **Writing and Research Handbook,** page 681.

PURPOSE To write a first draft
AUDIENCE Yourself
LENGTH 2–3 paragraphs

WRITING RUBRICS To write a draft, you should

- begin by writing an introduction that will catch your readers' attention
- write from your notes and add to them
- if you get stuck, talk with a friend or try a prewriting technique

Cross-Curricular Activity

ART Write about your responses to the

Grammar Link

Use different kinds of sentences when you write.

Revise each sentence, writing it in the sentence type indicated in parentheses.

1. We will miss the bus. (interrogative)
2. Is everyone ready? (declarative)
3. We would like to go to the zoo. (exclamatory)
4. Will you please wait for me? (imperative)
5. Was this my favorite trip! (declarative)

See Lesson 8.1, page 297.

picture. What does it remind you of? How does it make you feel?

Viewing and Representing

SPELLING Make a list of words that describe the girls' actions in *Double Dutch Series: Keeping Time.* Exchange papers with a partner and check each other's spelling.

The Writing Process

Tina Dunkley, *Double Dutch Series: Keeping Time,* 1987

Assess

Evaluation Rubrics

Write a Draft

Use these criteria when evaluating your students' writing:

- Did students develop details by questioning, listing, or clustering?
- Did students incorporate details from prewriting into a draft?
- Did students arrange details in an order that makes sense?
- Did students keep the purpose and audience in mind?

See also *Writing Assessment and Evaluation Rubrics.*

Cross-Curricular Activity: Art

Evaluate students' writing on the following elements: including personal responses; using specific details from the picture to clarify or explain.

Viewing and Representing

Have students use dictionaries to check the spelling of partners' words.

Reteaching

📁 *Composition Reteaching,* p. 11

Enrichment

📁 *Composition Enrichment,* p. 11

📦 *Fine Art Transparencies* 6–10

Close

Ask students what they would do if they got stuck while writing a draft. Remind them of the recursiveness of the writing process.

Grammar Link

Answers

1. Will we miss the bus?
2. Everyone is ready.
3. Would we like to go to the zoo!
4. Please wait for me. (!)
5. This was my favorite trip.

Viewing the Art

Tina Dunkley, *Double Dutch Series: Keeping Time,* 1987
This picture is batik on silk, 18-by-24 inches. Batik is a process of dying cloth. Wax is applied to the parts of the fabric not to be dyed. After the cloth is dipped in dye and dried, it is dipped in boiling water to remove the wax.

Focus

Lesson Overview

Objectives

- To organize paragraphs by adding, deleting, and combining text
- To produce a cohesive, coherent draft

Skills

- ordering sentences; using transition words; making subjects and verbs agree

Critical Thinking

- analyzing; relating; visualizing; defining and clarifying

Listening and Speaking

- discussing; speaking to a group

Bellringer

Daily Language Activity

When students enter the classroom, have this assignment on the board: *Write two sentences that you think would be good beginnings for two pieces of writing.*

Grammar Link to the Bellringer

Ask students to rewrite the sentences they wrote for the Bellringer, beginning each sentence with either *Here* or *There*. Then ask students to underline the verb in each sentence.

See also *Daily Language Practice*

Motivating Activity

Ask students to imagine they are watching a movie. The first scene shows a family traveling to Mars. The spaceship breaks down and the family is stranded in space. Next the scene shifts to children playing in a park. How might the audience feel? Why must a piece of writing, like a movie, stick to one main idea?

The Writing Process

LESSON 2.6

Revising: Getting Paragraphs into Shape

After you have revised your draft, look closely at each paragraph. Be sure each one expresses the main idea in a way that is clear to the reader.

Ask yourself these questions about each paragraph: Does it have a main topic? Does each sentence relate to the topic? Are the sentences in a sensible order? Without realizing it, you think about these questions when you read. When a paragraph is off track or unclear, you notice. The paragraph is difficult to understand. In the model below, how does the writer keep his idea on track?

topic sentence
supporting idea
supporting idea
supporting idea

Which sentence tells what this paragraph is about?

How do the other sentences help make the main idea easy to understand?

Literature Model

You will want several layers of clothing for backpacking. One reason for this is that temperatures can rise or drop several degrees in just a few minutes, particularly in thin mountain air. Stepping from sunlight into shadow can bring a drop of twenty degrees or more. Another reason is that [backpacking] is hard work. Your body will be hot as you hike, but when you stop you will cool off fast.

Richard B. Lyttle
The Complete Beginner's Guide to Backpacking

Resource Manager

Planning Resources
- *Lesson Plans*

Transparencies
- *Bellringer*
- *Daily Language Practice*
- *Fine Art* 6–10
- *Two-Minute Skill Drill*
- *Writing Process* 1–10

Other Print Resources
- *Composition Enrichment*, p. 13
- *Composition Practice*, p. 13
- *Composition Reteaching*, p. 13
- *Cooperative Learning Activities*, pp. 7–12
- *Listening and Speaking Activities*, p. 6–7, 10–13

- *Thinking and Study Skills*, pp. 7–9, 13
- *Vocabulary and Spelling Strategies and Practice*, pp. 35–52
- *Writing Across the Curriculum*
- *Writing Assessment and Evaluation Rubrics*

Recognize a Paragraph's Shape

Every sentence in a paragraph should have a reason for being there. In Lyttle's paragraph, the main idea is expressed in a topic sentence. Some paragraphs begin with a topic sentence. Others build to a topic sentence that comes at the end.

In a paragraph, all the sentences should work together to develop the main idea in a clear, coherent, way. Lyttle's paragraph on page 62 *begins* with a topic sentence. Other sentences flow from the idea in the topic sentence. Vicki McVey's paragraph below *ends* with a topic sentence. Notice how the topic sentence ties together the sentences that lead to it.

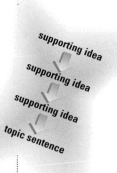

supporting idea

supporting idea

supporting idea

topic sentence

The Writing Process

Literature Model

The Pacific Ocean covers almost one third of the earth . . . and there are people who live on tiny islands in the middle of it. They can't see anything from horizon to horizon except water, and yet they set out in canoes for other tiny islands, . . . and get there. These are among the most amazing wayfinders of all time.

Vicki McVey, *The Sierra Club Wayfinding Book*

What do you learn about the people described in this paragraph?

Which sentence is the topic sentence?

Journal Writing

Read a few paragraphs in a library book or textbook, and answer these questions in your journal: Is there a topic sentence that tells the main idea in each paragraph? Where does the topic sentence appear? What do these answers tell you about writing paragraphs?

Teach

Using the Model

Emphasize that the topic sentence in the model on page 63 comes at the end of the paragraph. Ask students the purpose of the first two sentences in the paragraph. (They offer supporting details.) Is this type of paragraph structure effective? Why or why not? **L2**

Constructing a Paragraph

Find a well-constructed paragraph that has a topic sentence with a clearly stated main idea. Write the paragraph, starting each sentence on a new line. Then copy the paragraph, and cut the copies into separate sentences. Ask students to pair up with another student. Give all but the topic sentence to each pair of students. Ask them to construct a paragraph and then write a topic sentence that states the main idea. **L2**

Two-Minute Skill Drill

Ask students to write a verb for each of the following sentences.

There _____ ducks.

Here _____ John.

There _____ a cloud.

Here _____ Tina and Lydia.

See also *Two-Minute Skill Drill Transparencies, 2.6*

Journal Writing Tip

Topic Sentences For those paragraphs in library books with no topic sentences, ask students to write an appropriate main idea topic sentence. You may want to advise students to avoid fiction, which may contain dialogue.

Teach

Thinking Visually

Explain that a transition word is like a bridge that connects ideas. Ask students to summarize the message of the graphic on this page. Ask students if they think the drawing is effective. Encourage students to draw other images to show the idea of a word or phrase linking two ideas. **L1**

Writing Stories

Students might enjoy writing their own stories based on the weaving shown on page 65. Encourage them to research the geography and people of the Navajo reservation where Shiprock is located. When they have finished their stories, they should use the comments and suggestions of peer reviewers to help them revise. Students may share stories. **L3**

Additional Resources

For **writing prompts**, see *Fine Art Transparencies* 6–10.

Daily Language Practice

Writing Process Transparencies, 1–10
Writing Across the Curriculum
Cooperative Learning Activities, pp. 7–12
Thinking and Study Skills, pp. 7–9, 13
Listening and Speaking Activities, pp. 6–7, 10–13
Vocabulary and Spelling Strategies and Practice, pp. 35–52
Composition Practice, p. 13

The Writing Process

Shape Up Your Paragraphs

A strong paragraph has a clear main idea even if it does not have a topic sentence. These guidelines can help you find ways to make each paragraph you write stronger. Maya used them to make a few more changes on her draft.

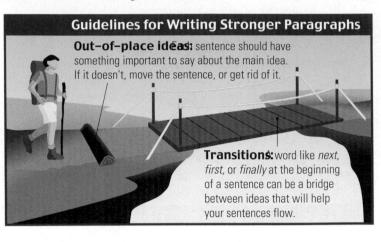

Guidelines for Writing Stronger Paragraphs

Out-of-place ideas: Each sentence should have something important to say about the main idea. If it doesn't, move the sentence, or get rid of it.

Transitions: A word like *next*, *first*, or *finally* at the beginning of a sentence can be a bridge between ideas that will help your sentences flow.

Maya switched the two sentences. She thought the second sentence would work better at the beginning of the paragraph.

Review the guidelines above. Why did Maya take out these two sentences?

Why did Maya change these two sentences?

SOS stands for Sharon Olivia Sanders. Someday you might see the initials SOS in your favorite comic strip. Sharon loves cartooning. She has been drawing pictures since she was three. ~~She has her own room, which used to belong to her brother. He's away at college now.~~ Sharon can draw animals and spaceships. She can draw anything else you can imagine. Sharon makes cartooning look easy.

MEETING INDIVIDUAL NEEDS — English Language Learners

Choosing Words

Students learning English may benefit from extra practice in using transition words. Write the following words on the board: *first, next, then, after, finally*. Model writing a simple paragraph in which each sentence starts with one of these words. The paragraph should describe a simple process, such as running a VCR. Next have students work in pairs to write their own paragraphs, beginning each sentence with a transition word. They can begin by verbalizing the steps in the process in their first language.

Use Strong Paragraphs

Study your draft again. Make each paragraph stronger.

PURPOSE To strengthen paragraphs

AUDIENCE Yourself

LENGTH 2–4 paragraphs

WRITING RUBRICS To make paragraphs stronger, you should

- be sure that each paragraph is about one main idea
- take out any sentence that does not relate to the main idea
- put the ideas in a sensible order
- use transition words

Artist unknown, Navajo, Shiprock rug, c. 1930

Cross-Curricular Activity

ART Look at the photo of a Navajo rug. Write a strong paragraph about what the weaver may have wanted to show. Express your main idea in a topic sentence and support it with details.

Make subjects and verbs agree in sentences with *there.*

Find the subject of each sentence below. Then write the correct form of the verb in parentheses.

1. There (is/are) a new skating rink at the mall.
2. There (is/are) many kids from our class who are good skaters.
3. There (has been/have been) times when the rink was not crowded.

See Lesson 15.2, page 441.

Viewing and Representing

COOPERATIVE LEARNING Find an image in this or another textbook that expresses something about technology in our world. In a small group, share your images. Then discuss how the artist used colors, shapes, figures, or designs.

The Writing Process

Assess

Evaluation Rubrics

Use Strong Paragraphs

Use these criteria when evaluating your students' writing.
- Does each sentence contain a detail that relates to the main idea?
- Do sentences have transition words?
- Do the ideas flow?

See also *Writing Assessment and Evaluation Rubrics.*

Cross-Curricular Activity: Art

Evaluate the paragraph on the following: a topic sentence that clearly states the main idea; details from the art to support the main idea. Have students orally share their ideas and insights.

Viewing and Representing

Make sure each student participates effectively in his or her small group discussion.

Reteaching

📁 *Composition Reteaching,* p. 13

Enrichment

📁 *Composition Enrichment,* p. 13

🎨 *Fine Art Transparencies 6–10*

Close

Write an idea for a topic sentence on the board, such as *Yesterday was the most wonderful day of my life.* Then ask for volunteers to think of sentences that give supporting details. Encourage students to use transition words.

Grammar Link

Answers
1. skating rink; is
2. kids; are
3. times; have been

Viewing the Art

Artist unknown, Navajo, *Shiprock rug,* c. 1930

This rug of hand-spun wool, woven by an unknown Navajo weaver in the 1930s, depicts Shiprock, a geological formation located on a Navajo reservation in northern New Mexico. The 55-by-34-inch rug hangs in a private collection.

Focus

Lesson Overview

Objectives
- To combine sentences to produce cohesive paragraphs
- To vary sentence length and structure to make writing more lively

Skills
- combining sentences; varying sentence beginnings; using connecting words

Critical Thinking
- evaluating; patterning

Listening and Speaking
- discussing; speaking to a group

🔔 Bellringer
Daily Language Activity

When students enter the classroom, have this assignment on the board: *Combine any two of these sentences to make an interesting new sentence:*
The dog barked. The waves rolled in. The sun shone. I found my towel.

Grammar Link to the Bellringer

Have students look at the new sentence they wrote for the Bellringer and underline the word or words they used to combine the original sentences.

📝 **See also** *Daily Language Practice*

Motivating Activity

Write the following sentences on the board, and then read them aloud: *The wind blew through the trees. The leaves fell to the ground. The children played in the park.* Ask students how the sentences sound. Help them recognize that their similar construction makes these sentences sound boring together.

The Writing Process

LESSON 2.7

Revising: Achieving Sentence Fluency

Varying, or changing, the length of sentences can make your writing lively and a pleasure to read. When sentences are the same length, the writing sounds all the same and can be very boring.

In the model below, Marjorie Kinnan Rawlings describes a flock of whooping cranes that seem to be doing a strange dance. Read the paragraph aloud. Does the paragraph have sentence fluency? In other words, do the sentences flow smoothly from one to the other? Think about how sentence length affects the way the sentence sounds.

> Would this sentence sound different if it were written as three sentences?

Literature Model

Two stood apart, erect and white, making a strange music that was part cry and part singing. The rhythm was irregular, like the dance. The other birds were in a circle. In the heart of the circle, several moved counter-clock-wise. The musicians made their music. The dancers raised their wings and lifted their feet, first one and then the other. They sunk their heads deep in their snowy breasts, lifted them and sunk again. They moved soundlessly, part awkwardness, part grace. The dance was solemn. Wings fluttered, rising and falling like out-stretched arms.

Marjorie Kinnan Rawlings, *The Yearling*

Resource Manager

Planning Resources
- *Lesson Plans*

📝 **Transparencies**
- *Bellringer*
- *Daily Language Practice*
- *Fine Art 6–10*
- *Two-Minute Skill Drill*
- *Writing Process 1–10*

📁 Other Print Resources
- *Composition Enrichment*, p. 14
- *Composition Practice*, p. 14
- *Composition Reteaching*, p. 14
- *Cooperative Learning Activities*, pp. 7–12
- *Listening and Speaking Activities*, p. 6–7, 10–13
- *Sentence-Combining Practice*

- *Thinking and Study Skills*, pp. 9, 11, 38
- *Vocabulary and Spelling Strategies and Practice*, pp. 35–52
- *Writing Across the Curriculum*
- *Writing Assessment and Evaluation Rubrics*

Write Notes to Yourself

As Maya wrote about her friend Hector Huang, she heard long and short sentences working together to create a pleasing pattern. Maya wanted to be sure that readers would hear this pattern, too.

With her readers in mind, Maya made a plan. She wrote some comments on her draft and put it aside for a day. Read what Maya wrote, and think about how a plan like Maya's might work for you.

> Do you agree with Maya's question? How could you avoid repeating these words?

Should I use this word twice?

Too many "Hector's coins" Don't get boring

My friend Hector enjoys biking and canoeing. For his favorite hobby, though, he can stay indoors. You see, Hector is a numismatist. A numismatist is a coin collector. Some of Hector's coins are made of copper. The rest of Hector's coins are made of nickel. They Hector's coins flash white and gold in sunlight. Hector began his collection three years ago when his grandmother gave him a buffalo nickel.

Journal Writing

Choose a paragraph you wrote in a story or an article some time ago, and read it aloud. Listen to the sound of your sentences. Think of ways to improve the sound without changing the meaning of your ideas. In your journal, experiment with different ways of revising your paragraph.

Teach

Using the Model
Ask students to rewrite the first sentence in the literature model on page 66 to make three or four separate sentences. Ask for volunteers to read their new sentences aloud, then discuss with students how these new sentences sound. Point out that breaking up the first sentence makes the prose sound choppy and dull. **L2**

Using the Model
Encourage students to explain whether or not Maya should repeat the word *numismatist*. Point out that Maya might revise to produce the following sentence: "You see, Hector is a numismatist, a coin collector." Ask students for other suggestions for ways to revise the sentence. **L2**

Two-Minute Skill Drill

Write these two sentences on the board and have students combine them using a connecting word or conjunction.

I love the sunshine. I don't like getting a sunburn.

See also *Two-Minute Skill Drill Transparencies, 2.6*

Journal Writing Tip

Defining and Clarifying Problems
Tell students that they can act as their own reviewers and write comments to themselves in the margin of the original paragraph.

Teach

Revising Paragraphs

Encourage students to try reading their sentences into a tape recorder. Point out that when they play back the tape, they should listen carefully for short, choppy sentences and repeated words. Students can revise their paragraphs and record their revisions, listening to them to make sure the revisions improve the sound but do not change the meaning. **L1**

Discussing Repetition

Tell students that occasionally repetition can be an effective tool—for example, in a political speech. Ask students why this might be, and encourage them to suggest other times when repetition might help a piece of writing. **L3**

Additional Resources

- For **writing prompts**, see *Fine Art Transparencies*, 6–10.
- *Daily Language Practice*
- *Writing Process Transparencies*, 1–10
- *Writing Across the Curriculum*
- *Cooperative Learning Activities*, pp. 7–12
- *Thinking and Study Skills*, pp. 9, 11, 38
- *Sentence-Combining Practice*
- *Listening and Speaking Activities*, pp. 6–7, 10–13
- *Vocabulary and Spelling Strategies and Practice*, pp. 35–52
- *Composition Practice*, p. 14

The Writing Process

Think About Each Sentence

Maya noticed that her sentences were boring when certain words were repeated again and again. She studied her sentences and decided that she could make her writing smooth by combining some sentences. The point of sentence combining is to join sentences without changing the basic meaning. Combining should help the writing flow more smoothly and sound better.

Another way to make writing more interesting is to vary the beginnings of sentences. Writing also sounds boring if every sentence begins with *I* or *The*. Look at the chart below. How did Maya use these hints to change her writing?

Hints for Sentence Combining
1. Take out repeated words.
2. Use connecting words, such as *and, but,* and *or.*
3. Vary sentence beginnings.

Notice that changing the repeated words does not change the meaning of the paragraph.

Should I use this word twice?

Too many "Hector's coins" Don't get boring

How does using a connecting word here make the sentence easier to read?

My friend Hector enjoys biking and canoeing. For his favorite hobby, though, he can stay indoors. You see, Hector is a numismatist. A numismatist is a coin collector. Some of Hector's coins are made of copper. The rest of Hector's coins are made of nickel. They Hector's coins flash white and gold in sunlight. Hector began his collection three years ago when his grandmother gave him a buffalo nickel.

English Language Learners

MEETING INDIVIDUAL NEEDS

Varying Sentence Length and Structure

Since English sentences might have a less-than-smooth sound for students who are learning English, these students may not be able to distinguish between the dull, choppy sound of many short sentences and the smooth, rhythmic sound created by a variety of sentence lengths. For these students you may want to focus on both correct sentence structure and variety in sentence length and structure.

Smooth Out Paragraphs

Improve your draft by revising the sentences within each paragraph.

PURPOSE To improve paragraphs by revising sentences

AUDIENCE Yourself

LENGTH 2–4 paragraphs

WRITING RUBRICS To make your writing more interesting, you should

- vary the length of sentences by combining some of them
- avoid unnecessary repetition
- use connecting words, such as *and*, *but*, and *or*
- vary sentence beginnings

Using Computers

Use a word processing program to compose your paragraph. Write the paragraph's sentences in a list. Check for similar lengths, similar beginnings, and repetitions. Revise your sentences and re-form them into a paragraph.

Viewing and Representing

COOPERATIVE LEARNING Work in a small group to describe a painting in this book. Each member should write one sentence for a group paragraph. Then read your paragraph aloud and revise to improve its flow.

Combine sentences for smoother paragraphs.

Combine the following pairs of sentences by writing compound subjects or compound verbs. Use the conjunctions in parentheses to combine the sentences.

1. My town is not too big. My town is big enough for me. (but)
2. Colorado has a good baseball team. Cincinnati has a good baseball team. (and)
3. My family can go hiking in the mountains. We can go camping. (or)
4. I like to go to the museum. Ed likes to go to the museum. (and)
5. We ski in winter. We swim in summer. (and)

See Lesson 20.2, page 519.

The Writing Process

Assess

Evaluation Rubrics

Smooth Out Paragraphs

Use these criteria when evaluating your students' writing.
- Do the sentences flow smoothly?
- Is unnecessary repetition avoided?
- Is there a variety of sentence lengths?

See also *Writing Assessment and Evaluation Rubrics.*

Using Computers

You might want to show students how to use cut and paste features of their word processing program to help them form their paragraphs.

Viewing and Representing

Evaluate each paragraph on the following: avoidance of unnecessary repetition; variety of sentence lengths; specific details about the painting.

Reteaching

📁 *Composition Reteaching*, p. 14

Enrichment

📁 *Composition Enrichment*, p. 14

🎨 *Fine Art Transparencies* 6–10

Close

Tell students that varying sentence patterns is very important when writing poetry, too. Ask students to write short poems of three to six lines about anything they like. Tell them to pick a sentence structure pattern to use before they begin, such as short-long-short.

Answers

1. My town is not too big, but it is big enough for me.
2. Colorado and Cincinnati have good baseball teams.
3. My family can go hiking or camping in the mountains.
4. My friend and I like to go to the museum.
5. We ski in winter and swim in summer.

Focus

Lesson Overview

Objectives

- To identify and revise grammatical and mechanical errors in writing
- To produce an error-free final draft

Skills

- editing; proofreading

Critical Thinking

- establishing and evaluating criteria; making decisions

Listening and Speaking

- discussing; note taking; listening accurately

Bellringer
Daily Language Activity

When students enter the classroom, have this assignment on the board: *Rewrite this sentence correctly.*

johns father took us to a basketball game we seen famous players and eat popcorn.

Grammar Link to the Bellringer

Make a list of the types of errors that you found in the Bellringer.

See also *Daily Language Practice*

Motivating Activity

Write a paragraph on the board that includes eight of the more common proofreading mistakes (misspelled words, missing punctuation, incorrect capitalization, incorrect possessives and contractions, wrong verb tense, sentence fragments, run-on sentences, and incorrect pronouns). Have students revise the paragraph in small groups.

The Writing Process

Editing/Proofreading: Checking Details

Your writing is not finished until you edit and proofread it. Final checking shows the pride you take in your work.

Checklist

- Check tire pressure
- Oil chain
- Check brakes
- Adjust seat

Maya's friends Jaime and Marta take their biking seriously. Maya watched Jaime and Marta tune up their bikes before a race. Marta showed Maya the checklist they were using. Marta explained that using a checklist gives them confidence during the race. They know they have checked everything and can concentrate on performing well. Maya was surprised. She uses a writing checklist for the same reason.

Resource Manager

Planning Resources
- *Lesson Plans*

Transparencies
- *Bellringer*
- *Daily Language Practice*
- *Fine Art* 6–10
- *Two-Minute Skill Drill*
- *Writing Process* 1–10

Other Print Resources
- *Composition Enrichment*, p. 15
- *Composition Practice*, p. 15
- *Composition Reteaching*, p. 15
- *Cooperative Learning Activities*, pp. 7–12
- *Listening and Speaking Activities*, p. 6–7, 10–13

- *Thinking and Study Skills*, pp. 20–21, 38
- *Vocabulary and Spelling Strategies and Practice*, pp. 35–52
- *Writing Across the Curriculum*
- *Writing Assessment and Evaluation Rubrics*

Polish Your Work

To make sure your sentences are clear, you need to edit your draft. Look for mistakes that might have slipped in. Think about the questions in the checklist on the right. You might want to read the draft one time for each question.

Look at Maya's second paragraph. She used the checklist to edit her draft. For each question she read through her work once. That way, she was more likely to catch errors. Maya will correct errors not covered by this checklist in a later reading.

Editing/Proofreading Checklist

1. Do I have sentence fragments?
2. Do I have any run-on sentences?
3. Have I used correct punctuation and capitalization?
4. Are my verb forms and tenses correct?

The Writing Process

Take Jaime Sánchez for example. He and his sister Marta ~~loves~~ *love* biking. *They both have been* Part of a local bike-racing club for too years. They've even ~~winned~~ *won* some amateur races. This spring, though, Jaime wanted to learn more about racing ~~they~~ *His club* sent him to a four-day racing camp sponsored by the United states Cycling Federation. This was JAime's first trip to Colorado.

Why did Maya change this sentence? Which question on Maya's list covers the problem?

There's more than one way to handle this run-on sentence. How else might you revise it?

Journal Writing

Have you made certain writing mistakes in your papers? In your journal, list questions that can help you catch these mistakes. For more help, see the checklist on page 72.

Teach

Using the Model

Maya formed two sentences to revise a run-on. Maya might have revised the run-on sentence this way: *Because Jaime wanted to learn more about racing, his club sent him to a four-day racing camp.* **L2**

Using Fragments Deliberately

Students who read extensively may point out that some writers deliberately use fragments and run-on sentences in their work. Explain that writers occasionally do this for effect or to achieve a certain style. Suggest that students bring in published works that contain fragments and run-on sentences. Discuss the effects that fragments and run-ons have on the selections. **L3**

Two-Minute Skill Drill

Have students write this sentence correctly: *I went over to Jordan's house and together, we made cookies.* Ask students what question on the checklist on page 71 covers this type of error.

See also *Two-Minute Skill Drill Transparencies, 2.8*

Journal Writing Tip

Write an Editing Checklist Students should look for mistakes that they are likely to repeat. Reviewing writing assignments that have been returned with teacher comments may help.

Teach

Recognizing Fragments

Some students may need examples of fragments and run-on sentences in order to recognize them in their own writing. Provide review sheets with lists of fragments and run-on sentences. After students have checked their papers for fragments and run-ons, ask them if they would like partners who have mastered these concepts to check their papers. **L2**

Using Proofreading Symbols

Some students may find proofreading symbols confusing. Explain that each symbol in the proofreading chart is a kind of shorthand used to edit writing. Ask students why these symbols might have been developed. Write a few sentences with mistakes on the board. Have students use proofreading symbols to revise the text and, in the margin, write out what each symbol tells them to do. **L1**

Additional Resources

 For **writing prompts**, see *Fine Art Transparencies*, 6–10.

Daily Language Practice

Writing Process Transparencies, 1–10
Cooperative Learning Activities, pp. 7–12
Thinking and Study Skills, pp. 20–21, 38
Listening and Speaking Activities, pp. 6–7, 10–13
Vocabulary and Spelling Strategies and Practice, pp. 35–52
Composition Practice, p. 15

The Writing Process

Use Proofreading Symbols

If you've traveled—by bike, by car, or on foot—you've seen road signs. Some road signs use words to communicate, but many others use pictures. Look at the picture on the left. What does the symbol on the sign tell you?

In a similar way, you can use signs when you edit. The chart below shows a few proofreading symbols. Use these symbols as you edit your writing. Study both parts of the chart. Then see how Maya used the checklist and the symbols to edit part of her draft.

Proofreading	
Symbols	**Checklist**
∧ insert	**1.** Does each sentence have the right punctuation?
✗ delete	**2.** Are all words spelled correctly?
⊙ period	**3.** Are possessives and contractions written correctly?
∧ comma	**4.** Are capital letters used as needed?
≡ capital letter	
/ lower-case letter	

Take Jaime Sánchez∧for example. He and his sister Marta love biking. They both have been part of a local bike-racing club for ~~too~~ *two* years. They've even won some amateur races. This spring, though, Jaime wanted to learn more about racing⊙His club sent him to a four-day racing camp sponsored by the United ≡states Cycling Federation. This was J/Aime's first trip to Colorado.

MEETING INDIVIDUAL NEEDS

English Language Learners

Using Proofreading Marks

Once students understand how to use proofreading marks, they may find the symbols to be an effective way to identify errors. Have students work with partners to correct each other's writing using proofreading marks. Once they have applied symbols to their errors, encourage students to verbally explain the mistakes and their corrections to each other.

Edit Your Draft

Review your completed draft. This is the time to put it into finished form. Read it through again, making any changes you want. Then edit carefully, checking for errors.

PURPOSE To apply editing techniques
AUDIENCE Yourself
LENGTH 2–4 paragraphs

WRITING RUBRICS To edit your draft, you should

- make sure forms of verbs and pronouns are correct
- look for mistakes in punctuation, capitalization, and spelling
- look for extra words or words that have been left out
- check for fragments and run-on sentences

Using Computers

Use the grammar checker or spelling checker to check your draft. It's always a good idea to have an extra set of eyes (even electronic ones) looking at your work. Still, the program will not catch everything. Make sure that you edit the draft yourself too.

Grammar Link

Avoid fragments and run-on sentences in your writing.

Edit and rewrite to correct the following sentences. For examples of fragments and run-ons, see Maya's draft on page 71.

1. Lee collects pictures of her favorite singers she has a large collection.
2. She even has some old pictures. Of the Beatles.
3. She goes to many concerts sometimes she gets autographs of the stars.
4. She has lots of pictures in her room it looks great.
5. Lee also has a good collection of tapes. From rock to hip-hop.

See Unit 7 Troubleshooter; and Lessons 8.2, page 299; and 8.6, page 307.

Listening and Speaking

COOPERATIVE LEARNING In a small group, share your ideas about ways that the computer can help you prewrite, draft, revise, edit, and present your work. Use the computer to make a table summarizing your ideas. Post the table in your classroom.

Assess

Evaluation Rubrics

Edit Your Draft

Use these criteria when evaluating your students' writing:
- Did the student use proofreading symbols correctly?
- Did the student find his or her errors and mark them accurately?

See also *Writing Assessment and Evaluation Rubrics.*

Using Computers

If students are using spelling or grammar checkers for the first time, make sure they know how to access these features.

Listening and Speaking

Make sure each student participates effectively in his or her discussion. Students' tables should include suggestions for each of the five stages of writing.

Reteaching

📁 *Composition Reteaching,* p. 15

Enrichment

📁 *Composition Enrichment,* p. 15

Close

Stress to students that, like professional writers, they must edit and proofread any writing they intend others to read. Ask students what message it sends to readers when a piece of writing contains errors. Have students create two sets of proofreading checklists like the ones in the lesson, one to keep at school and one to keep at home.

Grammar Link

Answers

Answers may vary.
1. Lee collects pictures of her favorite singers. She has a large collection.
2. She even has some old pictures of the Beatles.
3. She goes to many concerts. Sometimes, she gets stars' autographs.
4. She has lots of pictures in her room. It looks great.
5. Lee also has a good collection of tapes, from rock to hip-hop.

Fixing Run-ons Correct this run-on: *Lee's parents think Lee's music is too loud Lee says the volume is fine.* (Answer: *. . . loud. Lee says . . .*)

Focus

Lesson Overview

Objectives

- To explore ways to present student work
- To prepare a final copy of student work for publication

Skills

- planning a presentation

Critical Thinking

- classifying; elaborating

Listening and Speaking

- discussing; evaluating

🔔 Bellringer
Daily Language Activity

When students enter the classroom, have this assignment on the board: *List three ways you can share your piece of writing with others.*

Grammar Link to the Bellringer

Have students rewrite their Bellringer response as a single sentence, inserting commas in the list of ways to share their writing.

See also *Daily Language Practice*

Motivating Activity

Ask students to think of all the ways they have shared writing with other people. What other ways can they think of that they haven't tried? Encourage students to commit to a new mode of presentation for their next piece of writing.

LESSON

2.9

Publishing/Presenting: Sharing Your Work

There are several ways to share your writing. Keep in mind, however, that some writing is private and not meant to be shared.

Maya chose to share her writing in the school newspaper. When she saw her article in print, she was very proud. She ran into her homeroom waving *The Wilson Chronicle*. Her friends were excited to see it, but Maya was the most excited of all.

74   Unit 2 The Writing Process

Resource Manager

Planning Resources
- *Lesson Plans*

📖 Transparencies
- *Bellringer*
- *Daily Language Practice*
- *Fine Art 6–10*
- *Two-Minute Skill Drill*
- *Writing Process 1–10*

📁 Other Print Resources
- *Composition Enrichment,* p. 16
- *Composition Practice,* p. 16
- *Composition Reteaching,* p. 16
- *Cooperative Learning Activities,* pp. 7–12
- *Listening and Speaking Activities,* pp. 6–7, 10–13

- *Thinking and Study Skills,* pp. 1, 14, 20
- *Vocabulary and Spelling Strategies and Practice,* pp. 35–52
- *Writing Across the Curriculum*
- *Writing Assessment and Evaluation Rubrics*

Plan Your Publishing or Presentation

You can present your writing in many different ways. Each way of presenting requires a different kind of final copy. Your teacher might want your name, the date, and the paper's title in the upper-right corner of your paper. A school newspaper might require that the final copy be typed with your name at the end.

No matter what the specific requirements are, any final copy should be clean and readable. The chart below offers some suggestions about presenting certain types of writing.

Oral Presentation
Almost anything you write can be shared aloud. Consider holding a group reading or using background music in your presentation.

Class Book
Collect copies of classmates' finished writing in a class book. You can keep it in class to enjoy, or you can donate it to the school library.

Newspaper
Items about local people and events are important parts of newspaper writing.

Literary Magazines
Literary magazines such as *Stone Soup* and *Cricket* publish poems and stories by students.

Journal Writing

In your journal, brainstorm ideas about different ways you might present your finished piece of writing. Which would be the most fun? The most exciting? How would you like to have your piece illustrated?

Teach

Cooperative Learning

Students can work together to produce a "Guide to Successful Presenting" booklet. Students can brainstorm a list of guidelines to help writers who want to share their stories, poems, and articles. Tips might cover such points as where to send articles, how to present a neat paper, and how to give an effective speech. **L2**

Getting Published

Encourage interested students to research the submission guidelines for different magazines and newspapers that publish the writing of young people, such as *Stone Soup, Cricket, New Moon,* and local newspapers. Then encourage students to polish an appropriate piece of writing and submit it for publication. **L3**

Two-Minute Skill Drill

Ask students where the best place to present a piece of writing about how to raise puppies would be: in a cooking magazine, in a speech to an animal protection organization, or in a literary magazine.

See also *Two-Minute Skill Drill Transparencies, 2.9*

Journal Writing Tip

Ways to Present As students brainstorm new and different ways for presenting, remind them to make sure that their ideas are appropriate for the piece and audience.

75

Teach

Presenting Creatively

The opportunity to present their work as part of a group may stimulate less motivated writers to share their writing with others. Many of these students may be able to suggest unique and interesting ways for the class to present its work, such as in a booklet of class quotes or humorous class stories. **L2**

Presenting Visually

Those students who are more skilled at communicating through visual images than through writing have several options for their presentations. For example, they can present their ideas in a cartoon strip with simple captions; through film, if they have access to a video camera; or through a series of photographs that tell a story. **L2**

Additional Resources

For **writing prompts**, see *Fine Art Transparencies* 6–10.

Daily Language Practice

Writing Process Transparencies, 1–10

Cooperative Learning Activities, pp. 7–12

Thinking and Study Skills, pp. 7, 9, 17, 21

Listening and Speaking Activities, pp. 6–7, 10–13

Vocabulary and Spelling Strategies and Practice, pp. 35–52

Composition Practice, p. 16

The Writing Process

Prepare the Final Copy

Read this part of Maya's article as it appeared in *The Wilson Chronicle*. You can trace some ideas back to Maya's prewriting notes. Other ideas came up along the way.

THE WILSON CHRONICL

WILDCATS' HOBBIES ARE AMAZ

by Maya Gonzales

It's time for a Wilson Elementary Wildcats Quiz. Who has attended bike-racing camp in Colorado? Who has boxes of money in his closet? Whose gumbo can make you feel like you're in Louisiana? Whose name do you see in every edition of this paper? They're all fellow Wildcats, students with some amazing hobbies.

Take Jaime Sánchez, for example. He and his sister Marta love biking. They both have been part of a local bike-racing club for two years. This spring Jaime wanted to learn even more about racing. His club sent him to a four-day racing camp sponsored by the United States Cycling Federation. "I never thought racing camp would be so super," Jaime

says. "I found some new friends there, and I learned a lot about being a better racer!"

SOS, who draws "Wildcat World" for this newspaper, also likes to learn. SOS stands for Sharon Olivia Sanders. Sharon loves cartooning. She has been drawing pictures since she was three. She can draw animals, spaceships, or anything else you can imagine. Sharon makes cartooning look easy, but she works really hard at it. She has sketchbooks filled with cartoon ideas. Two pages, for example, show a horse running, jumping, sticking its head out a stable door, and winking. Sharon's favorite subjects, however, are people. She says, "I learn by studying people's faces and watching them move. I think that's

why my cartoons a realistic as well as funny."

Hector Huang enjoys biking and canoeing, but fo favorite hobby h can stay indoors You see, Hecto numismatist, a collector. Hect began his colle three years ago

> Note that Maya stayed with the order of details she considered while prewriting. (See page 52.)

> How has Maya changed this sentence? Why do you think she made this change?

English Language Learners

Contributing with Pictures

Students might feel more confident about contributing to the class "Guide to Successful Presenting" booklet (see Teach—Cooperative Learning, page 75) if they are encouraged to use pictures. Some students might want to work with a partner and provide illustrations for their partner's tips. Others might write their own tips on presenting by making a cartoon strip. They can represent the tips in a series of drawings and add captions beneath each panel.

Present Your Work

Now that your writing is complete, decide how you will present it and to whom.

PURPOSE To present a finished piece of writing

AUDIENCE Your choice

LENGTH 2–4 paragraphs

WRITING RUBRICS To present your writing, you should

- find out the requirements for the form of presentation you have chosen
- be sure your work is prepared properly
- present your work in the way you have chosen

Viewing and Representing

COOPERATIVE LEARNING In a small group, think about how you can start your own class book. Would it be illustrated? By whom? What kinds of writing would it have? How many pieces of writing would it include? Who would gather the writing? Who would make sure that it is legible? Pick two or three people to write up the group's ideas and suggestions. Then present them to the class.

Grammar Link

Use commas correctly in your writing.

*Sharon's favorite subjects, **however,** are people.*

Revise each sentence below, using commas to set off interrupters.

1. Maya's hobby as you can imagine is writing stories.
2. Not all of her stories however have been published.
3. Her favorite topics of course are people.
4. Several of her stories in fact tell about members of her family.
5. One story as you may know tells about her brother's trip to Chicago.

See Lesson 19.2, page 491.

Using Computers

After completing the Grammar Link, try typing the sentences into the computer. Use the grammar-check feature to check your work.

The Writing Process

Assess

Evaluation Rubrics

Present Your Work

Use these criteria when evaluating your students' writing.

- presentation modes chosen are appropriate to the style and subject of their writing
- final copy is prepared with requirements of presentation form in mind
- writing is presented to an audience

See also *Writing Assessment and Evaluation Rubrics*.

Viewing and Representing

Assess your students' ideas for a class booklet by evaluating their suggestions for its layout, content, production, and distribution.

Using Computers

Make sure students know how to access the grammar-check feature of the word processor they use.

Reteaching

📁 *Composition Reteaching,* p. 16

Enrichment

📁 *Composition Enrichment,* p. 16

Close

Engage students in a reflection on the writing process. Have students compare the final copy of their writing to their prewriting notes. How did their ideas change? What do students think were some of the best ideas for presentations?

Grammar Link

Answers

1. Maya's hobby, as you can imagine, is writing stories.
2. Not all of her stories, however, have been published.
3. Her favorite topics, of course, are people.
4. Several of her stories, in fact, tell about members of her family.
5. One story, as you may know, tells about her brother's trip to Chicago.

Using Commas in Quotations Point out Maya's use of commas in direct quotations. Have students rewrite the following sentence, inserting commas as needed. "I had fun writing the article" Maya said "and it was exciting to see it in print!" ("I had fun writing the article," Maya said, "and it was exciting to see it in print!")

Focus

Lesson Overview

Objectives

- To research an activity from the past
- To complete and present an essay about an activity from the past

Skills

- prewriting, drafting, revising, editing/proofreading, and publishing/presenting

Critical Thinking

- synthesizing

Listening and Speaking

- interviewing; observing; note taking

Bellringer
Daily Language Activity

When students enter the classroom, have this assignment on the board: *List some customary activities or pastimes that people seldom do anymore. You may have seen these customs in movies or heard of them from an older relative.*

Grammar Link to the Bellringer

Have students check for sentence fragments in their lists. Point out that we often use fragments when we take notes. Now have students rewrite their ideas in complete sentences.

See also *Daily Language Practice*

Motivating Activity

Ask students why people often enjoy reading, hearing, and watching stories about the past.

The Writing Process

The Writing Process

In previous lessons you've learned about writers' tasks during each stage of the writing process. Now you will practice more of what you've learned: prewriting, drafting, revising, editing/ proofreading, and publishing/presenting. You will also practice using the techniques used in Maya's article.

Assignment

Context

You are going to send a piece of writing to a student publication called *The Way Things Were,* which publishes stories about pastimes or forgotten activities from earlier times.

Purpose

To remember for others a lost activity

Audience

Student readers of *The Way Things Were*

Length

1 page

Visit the *Writer's Choice* Web site at **writerschoice.glencoe.com** for additional writing prompts.

The pages that follow offer step-by-step advice on how to approach this assignment. You don't have to remember it all. Read through the pages before you start. Then refer to each stage if you need help while you work on your assignment.

Resource Manager

Planning Resources
- *Lesson Plans*

Transparencies
- *Bellringer*
- *Daily Language Practice*
- *Writing Process* 1–10

📁 Other Print Resources
- *Composition Enrichment,* p. 19
- *Composition Practice,* p. 19
- *Composition Reteaching,* p. 19
- *Grammar Workbook,* Lessons 98–105
- *Thinking and Study Skills,* pp. 3, 5, 23–24, 34–35

- *Writing Assessment and Evaluation Rubrics*

💾 Software
- *Writer's Assistant*

🖥 Web Sites
- *writerschoice.glencoe.com*
- *lit.glencoe.com*

Writing Process in Action

Prewriting

What do machines do today that people did by hand a century ago? What was life like before micro-wave ovens, computers, and video games? Do you know anyone who has milked a cow or made soap?

Use one of the options at the right or an idea of your own to begin exploring a topic. You can develop your topic by freewriting.

Look at pages 46–53 for help with other kinds of prewriting.

Option A
Visit a living-history museum.

Option B
Read old maga-zines in the library.

Option C
Talk to older people.

> Great-grandmother Watkins grew her own vegetables in a garden. Since many vegetables ripened at the same time of year, she had to preserve them so that the family would have vegetables all year.

Drafting

While you review your freewriting notes, think about how you can make the activity you're describing clear and interesting to your readers. Notice how author Betsy Byars uses questions and answers to explain a process.

Drafting Tip

To review ideas for getting "unstuck" when your drafting runs into a snag, see the chart on page 56 of Lesson 2.4.

Literature Model

He moved around the plane. "Look under the cowl. . . . Check the oil—the gas. The gas cap's up here."

"What's that wire sticking out of it?"

Pop unscrewed the cap. "That's the gas gauge. See, there's a cork on the end. The cork floats on the gas, and as the gas goes down, so does the cork and the wire."

Betsy Byars, *Coast to Coast*

Teach

Prewriting

Choosing a Topic

If students have trouble finding a topic, point out that many writers have made a career of writing how-to articles and books. There are how-to explanations available for almost every conceivable activity, from making a paper bag mask to building an airplane. Encourage students to look through newspapers, magazines, and how-to books in the library to get ideas for a writing topic. **L2**

Drafting

Developing Interview Questions

Some students may have difficulty creating a list of interview questions that lead to a clear explanation rather than just a yes or no answer. Question words such as *who, what, when, where, why,* and *how* can help students form questions that require detailed answers. Students can practice asking questions with a partner, who will make up answers. Students should rephrase their questions until they are clear and precise. They can then use this prepared list of questions when they interview their subjects. **L2**

Teach

Revising

Peer Editing

Suggest that peer editors respond to the following questions: Does the piece have a strong opening? Does the writer use vivid language? Is the explanation of the activity clear? Are there grammar and spelling errors?

You may want to duplicate the Peer Response forms in the *Writing Assessment and Evaluation Rubrics* for use in writing conferences. **L2**

Editing/Proofreading

Peer Editing

After students have edited their own work, have them edit another student's writing. Remind them to refer to the Editing Checklist on page 81. **L2**

Publishing/Presenting

Before students present their descriptive writing, discuss how to prepare their papers for publication. Emphasize the importance of the final draft and that it must be neatly done.

Additional Resources

Writing Process Transparencies, 1–10

Thinking and Study Skills, pp. 3, 5, 23–24, 34–35

Composition Practice, p. 19

Grammar Workbook, Lessons 98–105

The Writing Process

You can also use a question-and-answer format as you write your draft. Write out a few important questions that can be asked about your topic. What types of things would student readers of *The Way Things Were* ask about your topic? Respond to the questions with answers that help describe your topic. Use these questions as you complete your draft.

Revising

To begin revising, read over your draft to make sure that what you have written fits your purpose and audience. Then have a **writing conference.** Read your draft to a partner or a small group. Use your audience's reactions to help you evaluate your work.

Question A
Will readers understand what I'm writing about?

Question B
Have I varied the length of my sentences?

Question C
Are my paragraphs well constructed?

> I always thought of pickles as something that came in a jar, but my great-grandmother Watkins used to pickle almost everything in her garden. *Whether* She pickled watermelon rind, summer squash, onions, cauliflower, carrots, and green beans, ~~as well as~~ *or* cucumbers. ~~The process for all of these was very similar.~~ *she used a similar process.* First, She had to gather and clean the vegetables. To clean the vegetables, she *first* washed and *then* examined each one. Then she removed bruises and spots with a paring knife.

Enrichment and Extension

Follow-up Ideas

Set aside time for students to celebrate the conclusion of their writing projects. Encourage them to share their finished pieces with the whole class or in small groups.

Extending Explanation of a Process

Brainstorm with students ways they can use their expertise in writing to explain a process in other subject areas, such as describing the process of an election in the United States.

You can also set your writing aside for a day or two before you make revisions. Then you can read your work as a reader would. The questions in the boxes below can help both you and the listeners in your writing conference.

Editing/Proofreading

You've worked hard to decide what you want to say and how to say it well. You want your final draft to be free of errors. During the editing stage, you can get rid of any mistakes that distract readers from your ideas. The editing checklist at the right will help you catch errors. When you find one, mark it with the appropriate **proofreading** symbol. Read your work one time for each type of error. Use a dictionary and the Grammar, Usage, and Mechanics section of this book for additional help.

Publishing/Presenting

Make sure your explanation is legibly written or typed on clean white paper before submitting it to *The Way Things Were*. To help readers understand your subject, draw your own diagrams, or include clipped or photocopied illustrations.

If you have the opportunity to make an oral presentation, think about how you could demonstrate the activity in your writing. Use objects related to your subject, or simply act out the process.

> ### Editing/Proofreading Checklist
>
> - Have I used the proper forms of verbs and pronouns?
> - Do I have any sentence fragments or run-on sentences?
> - Are my spelling, punctuation, and usage correct?

The Writing Process

> ### Proofreading Tip
>
> For proofreading symbols, see page 72 or 267.

Journal Writing

Reflect on your writing process experience. Answer these questions in your journal: What do you like best about your writing? What was the hardest part of writing it? What did you learn in your writing conference? What new thing have you learned as a writer?

Evaluation Rubrics

Use the following questions to evaluate students' finished writing.
- Does the article fulfill a clear purpose, centering on an outdated pastime?
- Does the article present the steps of an explanation in a clear and logical order?
- Does the writer address a specific audience?
- Does the writer use vivid language to create interest?
- Does the writer use grammar, usage, and mechanics correctly?

See also *Writing Assessment and Evaluation Rubrics*.

Journal Writing Tip

Reflecting on the Writing Process Suggest that students look back at their prewriting notes, their drafts and revisions, and their notes from peer conferencing in order to answer the questions.

Reteaching
📁 *Composition Reteaching*, p. 19

Enrichment
📁 *Composition Enrichment*, p. 19

Close

Ask students to consider what they've learned about people from the past. Discuss how the assignment has changed the way students look at their activities.

About the Author

Betsy Byars (1928–) was born and grew up in Charlotte, North Carolina. She began writing for children when her own children were small. Byars gets her story ideas from things that happen around her, from events of her children's lives, and from newspaper and magazine articles. In *Coast to Coast,* Byars draws on her own interest in flying. She won the Newbery Award for *The Summer of the Swans* in 1971.

Focus

Lesson Overview

Objectives

- To analyze a selection as a model for lively writing
- To share responses to a story in an informal discussion
- To write a journal entry

Skills

- monitoring comprehension; sequencing

Critical Thinking

- drawing conclusions

Listening and Speaking

- discussing

Bellringer
Daily Language Activity

When students enter the classroom, have this assignment on the board: *Write down several topics that you know enough about to use in a story.*

See also *Daily Language Practice*

Motivating Activity

Ask students if they have ever flown in a plane. What kind of experience was it?

Literature Model

The Writing Process

BETSY BYARS
from
Coast to Coast

Coast to Coast *tells the story of thirteen-year-old Birch, her retired grandfather, Pop, and what happens when Birch suggests that they fly his 1940 airplane cross-country. As you read, think about how the author gets and keeps her readers' attention. After reading, try the activities in Linking Writing and Literature on page 87.*

"I do. I want to do something. I can't explain it. I have to do something. And here is this perfectly good airplane." His jaws moved, chewing on the idea.

"What I meant about getting old, Pop, was that it's not getting pain in your joints or bad teeth. It's, like, not wanting to have fun."

Her grandfather got busy. He emptied the bucket and put the wet towels inside. "Help me push the plane back in the hangar. I'm tired of talking about my age."

"Yes, but it's my turn to pick. Remember? I picked being named for a tree, you picked flying in the war, now I pick this. I want to talk about you."

"Birch, the airplane is sold."

"You haven't got the money yet."

"I don't want to take any chances."

Resource Manager

Planning Resources
- *Lesson Plans*

Transparencies
- *Bellringer*
- *Daily Language Practice*
- *Fine Art 6–10*

📂 Other Print Resources
- *Listening and Speaking Activities,* pp. 12, 23
- *Thinking and Study Skills,* pp. 3, 5, 9, 22
- *Vocabulary and Spelling Strategies and Practice,* p. 8
- *Writing Assessment and Evaluation Rubrics*

💻 Web Sites
- *writerschoice.glencoe.com*
- *lit.glencoe.com*

Literature Model

"See? Don't take any chances—that's exactly what getting old is. Don't step on the grass. Don't go out of the yard!"

"That's enough. I mean it."

Birch was silent for a moment. Then in a different voice, as if she were taking up a new topic, she said, "You never have taken me up."

Her grandfather glanced at the sky. Beneath her eyeshade, Birch's eyes narrowed. She knew she had him now.

> **❝**Birch was silent for a moment. Then in a different voice, as if she were taking up a new topic, she said, ❛You never have taken me up.❜**❞**

"I really want to go!" As she said it, she realized it was true. She needed to get away from this world, and this was the way to do it. "What are we waiting for?"

"I don't guess it would hurt to fly to the beach and back."

"Then get in! Let's go!"

"Don't get in too big a hurry." Her

---

1 **aileron** (ā′ lə ron′) movable part on the back of an airplane wing

Robert Delaunay, *Homage to Blériot*, c. 1913–1914

grandfather smiled. It was his first real smile of the afternoon.

Birch followed him around the plane. "What are you doing?"

"Well, right now, I'm doing a preflight inspection. I check the tires, the control surfaces, move them for freedom and cable looseness." He raised the aileron[1] and looked at the cable underneath. "I check the tail wheel springs . . . the stabilizer trim . . ."

"Does everybody do this? Or are you just extra careful?"

"There used to be a saying. 'Kick the tire. Twang the wire. Light the fire and let her go.' Nowadays a pilot checks everything—the prop for nicks, the cowling pins for security . . ." He

Literature Model **83**

Active Reading Strategies

Monitor Comprehension Ask students how Birch defines "getting old." *(not wanting to have fun; not taking any chances or risks; staying put)*

Critical Thinking

Draw Conclusions Ask: "Why are Birch and Pop arguing? What does each want?" *(They're arguing about the plane. Birch wants Pop to keep it so he can continue to have adventures; Pop wants to sell it so he will be able to do other things.)*

Viewing the Art

Robert Delaunay, *Homage to Blériot*, c. 1913–1914
In this collage, Robert Delaunay honors French aviator Louis Blériot, the first person to fly across the English Channel. Delaunay's 98$\frac{1}{4}$-by-99-inch collage on canvas is on display in the Kunstmuseum in Basel, Switzerland.

The Writing Process

Literature Model

Henri Rousseau, *View of the Bridge at Sèvres,* 1908

moved around the plane. "Look under the cowl—birds are very fond of building nests under cowls. Check the oil—the gas. The gas cap's up here."

"What's that wire sticking out of it?"

Pop unscrewed the cap. "That's the gas gauge. See, there's a cork on the end. The cork floats on the gas, and as the gas goes down, so does the cork and the wire."

Pop reached in the cabin and removed a clear plastic tube from the seat pocket. He drained some gas into the tube, checked it and threw it out. "Good! No water got in the gas from our wash job."

"How do you know, Pop?"

"Water's heavier than gas, so it would be on the bottom. And they look different."

84 Unit 2 The Writing Process

Viewing the Art

Henri Rousseau, *View of the Bridge at Sèvres,* **1908**
Henri Rousseau's $31\frac{1}{2}$-by-39-inch oil painting *View of the Bridge at Sèvres* is on view at the Pushkin Museum in Moscow. This painting depicts an idyllic country scene at odds with the technological advances of the time.

Literature Model

"So can I get in now?" He nodded, and Birch stepped to the right side of the plane. "Do I sit in the front or back?"

"The pilot sits in the back."

"But how do you see the instruments?"

"I can see all I have to. Put your foot on the tire, not on the strut and . . ."

Birch pulled herself in and fastened the seat belt. "This is the first time I've been in a little airplane. Pop, your instruments are ancient."

"They're 1940, same as the plane." Her grandfather leaned into the cockpit. "This is the altimeter—it tells you how high you are. I'm setting that to the altitude of the field—it's about sea level so I set it on zero. Carburetor heat—off. Switch—off."

He moved the stick back and forth while looking at the tail, then from side to side while watching the wing. "Put your heels on the brake pedals."

"Oh, we both have brake pedals?"

"Yes, it's dual control."

She looked down at the pedals and positioned her feet so that her heels were on the smaller ones.

"I'm going to swing the prop to start the engine."

"You mean, like, it's going to start and I'm going to be sitting in here by myself with the engine going?"

Pop opened the throttle a half inch.

"Look at my feet, Pop, and make sure they're on the brakes."

"I did."

"Because I do not want to take off by myself. I saw that in an Abbott and Costello movie."

"This is the gas primer." Pop pulled out a knob and slowly pushed it back in. Then he stepped to the front of the plane and gave the prop a few turns. Birch listened to the clicks and watched the tip of the prop over the cowling.

> **“** Pop leaned in and pushed the throttle back. The propeller turned slowly at idle, almost invisible against the blue sky. **”**

"Now turn that overhead ignition switch on for me."

"This?"

"Right, and yell 'Contact' just before you do."

"Incidentally, I'm terrified. Contact!"

"Brakes?"

"Brakes!" she yelled, pressing her heels harder.

Pop came around and stood by the cabin. He reached forward with his

Literature Model **85**

The Writing Process

6+1 Trait® Writing

Sentence Fluency

Explain to students that the term *sentence fluency* relates to the rhythm and flow of words on the page. Sentence fluency can be achieved by varying the length and style of sentences and by using transitional words and phrases to connect ideas. Remind students that in the excerpt from *Coast to Coast*, Byars uses unusual sentence structures— sentence fragments and run-on sentences, for example— to make the action come to life for the reader.

Practice Ask students to imitate Byars's unusual sentence structure in a brief description of some exciting event. Their descriptions may include dialogue when appropriate.

6+1 Trait® is a registered trademark of Northwest Regional Educational Laboratory, which does not endorse this product.

Active Reading Strategies

Sequencing To make sure students understand the process of the preflight check, ask them to list in order the steps involved.

(Sample answer:
1. check the tires
2. check the control surfaces
3. check the tail wheel springs
4. check the stabilizer trim
5. look under the cowl
6. check the oil and gas
7. set the altimeter)

Critical Thinking

Draw Conclusions Ask: "Why do you think Pop doesn't want Birch's mom to know about their flight?" *(She may think Pop is too old to be flying airplanes. He doesn't want to risk her disapproval.)*

Additional Resources

Fine Art Transparencies, 6–10
Listening and Speaking Activities,
    pp. 12, 23
Thinking and Study Skills,
    pp. 3, 5, 9, 22
Vocabulary and Spelling Strategies and
    Practice, p. 8

Literature Model

The Writing Process

right hand and gave the prop a quick downward pull. The engine caught. Pop leaned in and pushed the throttle back. The propeller turned slowly at idle, almost invisible against the blue sky.

Then he climbed in. "I got the brakes now," he yelled above the noise of the engine.

Birch took her feet off the pedals. "I feel a lot better with you in here."

The plane started forward. Following the yellow line on the pavement, they moved from the ramp down the taxiway and stopped just short of the runway.

"I'm revving up the engine now to check the magnetos[2] and carburetor heat."

"Check everything!"

He leaned forward. "Belt tight?"

"You bet. Let's go!"

"Birch?"

"What, Pop?"

"Let's don't say anything about this to your mom."

"Of course not! It's a secret mission." She put one hand on the window. "Aren't you going to close this?"

"We can close it later if you get too much wind."

"No, I like it open! Let's go!" And Birch's heart raced as Pop turned the J-3 onto runway nine.

---

2 magnetos (mag nē′ tōz) small machines composed of magnets that provide the electric spark to make an engine start

---

Active Reading Strategies

Clarify

Explain to students that *to clarify* means "to make clear." Sometimes a section of text may be confusing because of the number of details or the difficulty of the vocabulary. List on the board some methods that students can use to clarify a passage.

- Reread the section slowly.
- Write the text in your own words.
- Look up the definitions of unknown words.
- Read ahead.

Practice: Have students identify a section of the selection that is unclear to them. Direct them to clarify the text by rereading, reading ahead, and/or looking up words. Then ask them to write the section in their own words.

Linking Writing and Literature

◆ Collect Your Thoughts

Think about Birch, Pop, and the J-3. What does the airplane represent for Pop? For Birch? Why does Birch want Pop to keep the airplane? Explore your thoughts in your notebook.

◆ Talk About Reading

Discuss the excerpt from *Coast to Coast* with a group. Choose one student to lead the discussion and another to take notes. Use the following questions to guide your discussion.

1. **Connect to Your Life** Think about a special relationship you have with an elderly person—a relative, perhaps, or a neighbor. What makes the relationship good for both of you? What do the two of you share?

2. **Critical Thinking: Evaluate** Compare and contrast Birch and Pop. How are they similar? In what ways do they differ? Do their personalities complement each other?

3. **6+1 Trait®: Sentence Fluency** During the preflight check, Pop and Birch often speak in brief, clipped sentences—sometimes just a single word. Explain why these types of sentences are appropriate to the action in the story.

4. **Connect to Your Writing** What type of organization does Byars use to describe starting the airplane? Why is this organization appropriate to what's happening in the story?

6+1 Trait® is a registered trademark of Northwest Regional Educational Laboratory, which does not endorse this product.

◆ Write About Reading

Journal Entry Write an entry in your journal that describes a special relationship you have with a person much older than you. Reflect on how this person became a part of your life and the admirable qualities the person possesses. Also, think about what it is about you that this person appreciates.

Focus on Sentence Fluency A journal entry is informal, personal writing, but it can still contain sentence fluency. Try to vary sentence length and style and use transitional words to connect ideas.

For more information on sentence fluency and the 6+1 Trait® model, see **Writing and Research Handbook,** pp. 682–684.

◆ Linking Writing and Literature

Assess

Evaluation Rubrics

◆ Talk About Reading

Possible responses to the questions:

1. Answers will vary, but responses should acknowledge the role each individual plays in the relationship.

2. Birch is opinionated, brash, and adventurous. Pop is also adventurous but much less brash. Experience has taught him to be cautious. Most students will agree that the two personalities are a good match.

3. They convey the way people actually speak—especially when checking items on a list.

4. Time order. It's appropriate because she is describing a process.

◆ Write About Reading

The journal entry should do the following:
- introduce the reader to the older person in the relationship
- clearly describe what the two have in common
- explain why the relationship is special to both
- contain sentence fluency

Close

Have students write the steps for performing a simple activity as if they were explaining it to a younger student. As students share their steps, have the class suggest improvements.

Enrichment and Extension

What Happens Next?

Challenge students to draft a scene in which they have a conversation with Birch after she returns from her flight to the beach with her grandfather. Students can use specialized or informal language in the conversation to make the scene more realistic. Then ask students to read the draft of their scenes aloud to the class. Students should offer suggestions for revising the scene.

Review

Reflecting on the Unit
You may have students respond to Reflecting on the Unit in writing or through discussion.

Writing Across the Curriculum
To help students make a science connection, you may wish to guide a session in which students try to think of creative recreational uses for technology.

Adding to Your Portfolio
Ask students to consider the writing they have included in their portfolios. Students should write a short summary explaining how they used the writing process for each piece they have included. Students can then refer to these explanations for help with future projects.

Portfolio Evaluation
If you grade the portfolio selections, you may want to award two marks—one each for content and form. Explain your assessment criteria before students make their selections. Commend
- experimentation with creative prewriting techniques
- clear, concise writing in which the main idea, audience, and purpose are evident
- successful revisions
- work that shows a flair for language

✔ ASSESSMENT OPTIONS

📁 *Tests with Answer Key and Rubrics*
Unit 2 Choice A Test, p. 5
Unit 2 Choice B Test, p. 6

💾 *Testmaker*
Unit 2 Choice A Test
Unit 2 Choice B Test
Unit 2 Composition Objective Test

You may wish to administer one of these tests as a mastery test.

📼 *Mindjogger Videoquizzes*

The Writing Process

UNIT 2 Review

Reflecting on the Unit
Summarize what you learned in this unit by answering the following questions.

❶ What are the five steps of the writing process?
❷ What are the important elements of each step?
❸ What are some specific strategies you can use as you move through each step?

👜 Adding to Your Portfolio

CHOOSE A SELECTION FOR YOUR PORTFOLIO Look over the writing you did for this unit. Select a favorite piece for your portfolio. The writing you choose should show some or all of the following:

- ideas developed from prewriting
- a sensible organization of ideas
- a clear main idea supported by detail sentences
- interesting and varied sentences
- careful editing and proofreading
- neat, legible handwriting

REFLECT ON YOUR CHOICE Attach a note to the piece you chose, explaining briefly why you chose it and what you learned from writing it.

SET GOALS How can you improve your writing? What skill will you focus on the next time you write?

Writing Across the Curriculum

MAKE A SCIENCE CONNECTION Describe a game or hobby you like. To do that, first use prewriting techniques to come up with an activity that uses technology or requires some up-to-the-minute information.

Draft a paragraph explaining how to do the activity, including your reason for writing about this activity. Revise, edit, and proofread your work. Decide how you would like to present it.

TIME

Facing the Blank Page

Inside the writing process with TIME writers and editors

89

Focus

Lesson Overview

Objectives

- To apply strategies used by professional writers to all stages of the writing process
- To use writing to reflect upon the ideas of others
- To use resources for help during the writing process
- To generate ideas for writing by using prewriting strategies
- To develop ideas through the use of the drafting process
- To revise writing based on peer and self-directed evaluation
- To edit writing for specific purposes and for clarity and conciseness
- To use available technology to support aspects of creating, revising, editing, and publishing texts

🔔 Bellringer
Daily Language Activity

When students come into the classroom, have this assignment on the board: *List some ways you come up with ideas when you are given a writing assignment.*

Motivating Activity

Have students share their lists of strategies for getting started writing. (These might include freewriting, brainstorming, listing, and outlining.) Encourage students to discuss their favorite prewriting strategies and to explain why some strategies tend to work better for them than others. Point out that there is no single right way to get started—individual preferences often dictate which strategy one uses. But also note that students should continue to try different approaches. Young writers may find that an approach they usually avoid is helpful for a particular writing project.

Resource Manager

Planning Resources
- *Lesson Plans*

📑 Transparencies
- *Writing Process*

📂 Other Print Resources
- *Composition Enrichment*
- *Composition Practice*
- *Composition Reteaching*

- *Grammar and Composition Handbook*
- *Guide to Using the Internet and Other Electronic Resources*
- *Writing Assessment and Evaluation Rubrics*

💾 Video
- *Facing the Blank Page*

💾 Software
- *Presentation Plus!*
- *Revising with Style*

🖥 Web Sites
- *writerschoice.glencoe.com*
- *lit.glencoe.com*

Teach

Generating Ideas

Review with your class the prewriting strategies discussed in Lesson 2.2 (free-writing, brainstorming, and clustering). Give students a general subject, such as "animals," and have them use each type of prewriting to generate a story idea for their class newspaper.

Assess

Evaluation Rubrics

Talk About It

Ask students to elaborate upon each item in the list by giving examples of how one might gather ideas using the strategy. Extend the discussion by asking students whether certain prewriting strategies lend themselves better to certain writing forms, such as essays, posters, letters, stories, poems, and so on.

Try It Out

1. Students' stories should
   - be adapted from a newspaper or magazine story
   - present information in a style and a voice appropriate for a sixth-grade audience
2. Students' brainstorming sessions should
   - generate ideas for future writing projects
   - exhibit cooperation and respect among group members

Prewriting
Generating Ideas

Martha Pickerill, Assistant Managing Editor of TIME FOR KIDS.

Where do ideas for stories come from? Martha Pickerill explains how it works at TIME FOR KIDS, TIME's "kid-sister" publication:

❝We're fortunate that our first stop is TIME magazine. We have access to all of TIME's reporting and photos, and sometimes their graphics people will help us out, too. It's not always the case that what TIME is doing in any week is appropriate or is the best cover story for kids, who are our readers. So sometimes we'll take a story that's been quite small in TIME and turn it into a cover story.❞

Pickerill recalls a story idea the TIME FOR KIDS (TFK) staff developed on its own because it was such a good fit for TFK's reading audience:

❝The story was actually suggested by a parent of a boy involved in Boundless Playgrounds, an organization that develops playgrounds for kids who are in wheelchairs or otherwise physically disabled. It started with a short e-mail from the boy's father, who had seen our magazine. So we contacted the organization and did some more legwork.

The interesting thing is that these playgrounds are built so that able-bodied kids can use them, too. A lot of the ideas came from kids who had tried to use playgrounds and couldn't because of their physical limitations. And so they came up with a better idea, and they convinced somebody to build it. It was a perfect story for us, because kids really made a difference in what was going on in their world. It showed kids being powerful.❞

LEARNING FROM THE EDITOR

DISCUSSION
What are your sources for writing ideas? (Possibilities include your imagination, brainstorming with friends and family members, newspapers, magazines, TV, and radio.) Make a class list.

TRY IT OUT
1. Start small. Look through a newspaper or magazine to identify a small story that could be expanded for a sixth-grade reading audience. Research and write the story!

2. Brainstorm with the class. Try working with a partner or with a small group to generate ideas for future writing projects.

Civic Literacy

Persuading Others to Take Action Ask students to use their writing skills to persuade others to make the playgrounds in their own community accessible to children of all abilities. Have students choose a writing form they feel would be most appropriate to their purpose—persuading others to take action to improve the community. For example, they might choose to write a letter to the editor of a local paper inviting citizens to form a local chapter of Boundless Playgrounds. They might write an editorial for their student paper calling for a student action committee to make local school playgrounds accessible. Or they might write a letter to the chairperson of Boundless Playgrounds asking for help. Allow students to follow through if they wish by mailing their letters and submitting their work.

The Value of Outlining

MARIO RUIZ FOR TIME

Jill Smolowe:
Following a road map.

Jill Smolowe, now an Associate Editor at *People* magazine, was a Senior Writer at TIME from 1994 to 1996. She prepares to write a story by carefully outlining her ideas and supporting information. Her method, she admits, is not for everyone—but it's highly effective in helping her meet deadlines!

Jill Smolowe:

❝The way I work is very personal. Since I often write lengthy stories and I often write them on deadline, I really need to know where I'm going before I start. If I just leap in and don't have a road map, then I may veer off and find myself not knowing where the story is going.

So I outline very carefully. I literally take the line count I'm given, and I estimate 20 lines per paragraph. Then I list the number of paragraphs. I literally think through every paragraph: what is the theme I'm going to tackle? Which anecdotes and which information will I be inclined to use? As I actually write the story, that may shift, but at least when I sit down to write, I have a road map. These outlines are very much like the ones I learned to do in school, and they do serve the function of keeping me on a path as I'm writing. With deadlines, that's very, very important. ❞

> **OUTLINING TIP**
>
> "I don't do a formal outline, but I know where the ideas are going to fall. And figuring out how to order my ideas helps me see what may be the best way to start a story."
> —**Martha Pickerill**

LEARNING FROM THE WRITER

TALK ABOUT IT
1. Smolowe compares writing to taking a trip and sees a parallel between an outline and a road map. How do you see writing? Explore the comparison further. How can you be creative while following a route? How can you learn along the way? Is there more than one road to a given destination?

2. How do you organize your ideas before you begin a piece of writing? As a class, share and compare styles of outlining or organizing ideas for various writing purposes.

TRY IT OUT
Outline backwards. Take a piece of writing you finished recently and, whether or not you made an outline for it before you began, make an outline *from* it now.

LOOK IT OVER
Does this new outline reflect what you originally wanted to say? If not, how should you revise your writing so that it conveys your message?

Teach

Technology Tip

Outlining Many word processing programs include an outlining feature that enables you to create an outline and a skeleton "draft" at the same time. If you revise your outline, the draft changes along with it.

⬦ Cross-reference: Outlining

For instruction and practice in outlining, refer students to Lesson 2.3, pp. 50–53.

Practice and Assess

Evaluation Rubrics

Talk About It

1. Students' discussion should explore Smolowe's comparison of an outline and a road map. Students should voice their opinions about the validity of the comparison and share ideas that spring from the comparison, such as whether an outline allows one to be creative and whether there might be other ways to plan and structure writing.

2. Students should compare their outlining styles and other prewriting activities with those of their classmates. As an extension, ask students to list any new ideas they gained about prewriting from the discussion.

Try It Out

Students should
- outline a recent piece of writing
- use the outline to evaluate the development and organization of the piece
- decide what revisions they would like to make to the piece based upon the outline

---

Writing in the Real World

Writing to an Editor

The father of a boy involved in Boundless Playgrounds e-mailed Martha Pickerell the idea for her story. Ask students to think about something or someone from their own lives—an event, local organization, or person— that could serve as the basis for a good story. Ask them to send a letter or e-mail to the editor of a newspaper or magazine describing the story idea and its appeal to the periodical's target audience.

Teach

Technology Tip

Encourage students to word process first drafts. Copy and paste functions make it easy for writers to try different patterns of organization.

Assess

Evaluation Rubrics

Talk About It

1. During discussion, students should point out similarities between drafting a piece of writing and constructing a chair. The comparison suggests that Gibbs views writing as a craft, believes that ideas must be fully supported, organizes her ideas carefully, considers her purpose and audience throughout the writing process, and values feedback and collaborative writing.
2. Students should voice their opinions about the validity of the comparison and generate new similes that clarify a stage of the writing process or the process as a whole.

Try It Out

Students should
- select a recent piece of their own writing
- use the "well-built chair test" to evaluate the organization and the development of the piece
- decide whether to revise the piece by adding specific details

⮂ Cross-reference: Drafting

For instruction and practice in drafting and writing topic sentences, refer students to Lessons 2.4–2.6, pp. 54–65.

Drafting

Getting Organized

Nancy Gibbs, Senior Editor at TIME, shares a way to think about writing that one of her mentors taught her as a young journalist:

Nancy Gibbs: Building the chair.

DIANA WALKER FOR TIME

❝Organization is the first thing you have to learn, and in some ways, it's the hardest, because everything follows from there. One of the editors who was teaching me the craft a long time ago used to liken writing a story to building a chair. The craftsmanship is basic: the chair has to stand up. It has to support weight. Ideally, it should be comfortable. Even better, it ought to be nice to look at. But at the most basic level, it

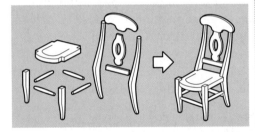

has to be structurally sound. It needs four legs, and a seat that won't fall through, and a back that won't collapse. From there, you can decide what kind of chair it's going to be, and how it might be carved, decorated, and upholstered.

I really believe in collaborative writing. You send a paragraph to someone and say, 'Does this work? Am I making the point?' Words and imagery may be one person's strength, while clarity and structure may be another's. If writing is like building a chair, here at TIME we hand the chair to one another.❞

LEARNING FROM THE WRITER

TALK ABOUT IT
1. When Gibbs likens writing a story to building a chair, she uses a *simile,* a figure of speech that points out what is similar about two seemingly unlike things. What does her use of this comparison suggest about the way she writes?

2. In what ways is the comparison of writing a story to building a chair appropriate or inappropriate?

TRY IT OUT
Create your own simile. It can be for writing in general or for one part of the writing process.

LOOK IT OVER
Analyze a piece of your writing. Does it hold up under the "well-built chair test"? Is it structurally sound, with a good beginning, middle, and end? Is it "upholstered" with enough details? What could you revise to make it "a better chair"?

Cooperative Learning

Peer Editing

Nancy Gibbs says, "If writing is like building a chair, here at TIME we hand the chair to one another." Have students practice what Gibbs preaches by applying the "well-built chair test" to one another's writing. Pair students and ask them to evaluate the organization and the development of their partner's writing. Encourage partners to offer each other specific suggestions for revision. Allow students time to make revisions.

Approaching the First Draft

James Poniewozik, a Staff Writer at TIME, starts a writing project by "thinking" on paper. Writing a first draft shows him what he wants to say in the final piece. He describes his process this way:

Writing as thinking

❝Some people believe that before you begin to write, you should pretty much know exactly what you want to say—and I think the opposite is true. There's a famous quote from the writer E. M. Forster: 'How do I know what I think until I see what I say?' I think that's really true. Writing is not just getting down a completely formed thought that you have in your head. Writing is actually a process of thinking in itself.❞

Starting to write

❝What I'll generally do to start off is to write out sections of a piece: things that I definitely want to get in. I'll write a paragraph here and a paragraph there. As I start writing them, it'll seem to make sense: I see how the paragraphs should be organized, and then I'll sense the flow of the piece.❞

First drafts: Topic sentences

❝It's important that you remember that it is just a first draft, and that you'll need to go back and revise. When you start writing, it's good to concentrate on the idea of having topic sentences for individual paragraphs. It does help focus you. By the time you're done, it may have changed, but at least it gives you a strong focus point to start from.❞

Poniewozik's notes: An order emerges.

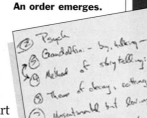

LEARNING FROM THE WRITER

TALK ABOUT IT
1. Explore the idea that writing is thinking on paper. What did E. M. Forster mean when he asked, "How do I know what I think until I see what I say?"

2. Summarize the steps that James Poniewozik takes in the process of writing an article. How are your drafting steps like or unlike his?

TRY IT OUT
Think on paper. Select one of the topics for writing that the class listed during the brainstorming session and try working on it the way Poniewozik does. Write down the ideas you want to get in and develop them into paragraphs in any order. Next put the paragraphs in an order that makes sense. Connect them with writing that helps each paragraph's main idea flow smoothly into the next. You now have a first draft!

LOOK IT OVER
How well did Poniewozik's method work for you? Read each paragraph to see that it has a topic sentence with a clearly stated main idea and that all of the other sentences develop that idea. Rewrite paragraphs that need help.

TIME Facing the Blank Page **95**

Enrichment and Extension

Learning from Authors

What do other professional writers have to say about the writing process? Challenge students to use library resources or the Internet to investigate how their favorite authors go about writing. Have students share favorite author quotations and tips in brief oral reports.

Teach

Topic Sentences

Remind students that a topic sentence may fall at the beginning or at the end of a paragraph, depending upon the effect the writer hopes to achieve. Have students write two paragraphs—one with a topic sentence at the beginning and one that ends with the topic sentence—and discuss how placement of the topic sentence affects meaning.

Assess

Evaluation Rubrics

Talk About It

1. During discussion, students should share their interpretations of the Forster quotation (e.g., Forster meant that writing helped him clarify what he thought by making his abstract thoughts concrete). Encourage students to explain whether they share Forster's view of writing and why.

2. During the drafting stage, James Poniewozik writes sections of the story, focuses his ideas by writing clear topic sentences, and decides how to organize the story by looking at the natural flow of ideas. Unlike Forster and Poniewozik, inexperienced writers often force themselves to write "in order": introduction and main idea first, body next, conclusion last. Discuss the disadvantages of this approach; then have students compare and contrast their drafting process with Poniewozik's.

Try It Out

Students should complete the following steps in the order presented.
- Jot down the points they want to make.
- Develop the points into paragraphs, without regard for the overall structure of the piece.
- Identify the natural flow of ideas and decide how to sequence the paragraphs.
- Connect the paragraphs by providing context and transitions.
- Evaluate the effectiveness of the steps.

Look It Over

Students should
- select a recent piece of their own writing
- check to see whether each paragraph contains a topic sentence
- add or revise topic sentences as needed

Teach

Technology Tip

Revising Most word processing programs have a revising function that allows editors to mark revisons without deleting the original first draft. Encourage students to practice using this revising function and to make use of any other online editing functions included in their word processing program.

Assess

Evaluation Rubrics

Talk About It

In their discussion, students should share their lists of hobbies and explain why they classified each hobby as an art or a craft. Through discussion, students should clarify what they think Janice Simpson means when she classifies magazine editing as a craft rather than an art (e.g., For Simpson, editing is a craft because editors refine and revise rather than create). Students should explain whether they agree with Simpson's view of the editing process and why.

Try It Out

Students' job descriptions should
- clearly describe the peer editor's role
- list the specific responsibilities of a peer editor

Look It Over

Students should
- describe whom they turn to when they need an editor and why
- analyze how they react to editors' suggestions

Revising

The Role of the Editor

Janice Simpson, Senior Editor at TIME, describes her role:

"The biggest trick of editing is to make someone else's words sound their best, not to substitute your own words. It's a collaborative effort, because you're working very intimately. Writing is an act of creation. I don't think what we do is an art form; it's a craft, but it's a very fine craft. When writers create something, they put a piece of themselves into it. So when you're editing, like it or not, you're commenting on that person. And in the editing process, what you're doing is looking at their story and saying, 'Let me figure out what it was you wanted to say. Not what I wanted to say, what you wanted to say.'"

An editor is the first audience for a piece of writing.
Senior Editor Bill Saporito:

"The real job of the editor is to be the stand-in for the reader. You've got to decide what you think the reader is most interested in, and you also have to make the story readable if it's not in that shape when it comes in.

You want to make sure that a story is organized properly, that it's not too long or too short. Were all the important questions answered? Did the reporter and the writer do the job that you sent them to do? If not, how do you change it? Do you send it back for a rewrite, do it yourself, or simply ask for more information?

Sometimes you simply ask the writer questions: 'Is this right? Have you asked about this? What about these aspects?'"

Janice Simpson: Making writers' words sound their best.

LEARNING FROM THE EDITOR

TALK ABOUT IT
List your hobbies or interests. Which would you classify as crafts? Which do you think of as art forms? What does Simpson mean when she says that the editing process is a craft, not an art form? What is your view of the process?

TRY IT OUT
Define the editor's role. As peer editor for other students, what should your role be? Draft a job description.

LOOK IT OVER
Who edits your writing—classmates, friends, family? Which group's approach works best for you, and why?

Listening and Speaking

Giving Constructive Criticism

To be effective peer editors, students must learn how to give constructive criticism. Point out that professional editors generally follow these guidelines: adopt a positive or neutral tone, criticize the writing rather than the author, and be prepared to explain why a particular revision is needed. Using these guidelines, model how to give constructive criticism. Then have students exchange papers, evaluate each other's work, and practice providing constructive criticism.

Knowing Your Audience

Nelida Cutler is the senior editor at TIME FOR KIDS. "A good editor enhances the work of a good writer by making changes that improve the story," says Cutler. When Cutler edits TFK articles, she asks herself the following:

- **Is the information accurate?**
- **Does the story make sense?**
- **Did the writer choose the best words and phrases for the intended audience?**
- **Are the spelling and grammar correct?**

WRITING TIP

Advice for aspiring writers:

Practice all kinds of writing: stories, book reports, letters, journal writing.

Read stories and articles carefully. Look for important facts and details. Think about why an author started a story the way he or she did.

Look up new words in the dictionary. Use new words in your everyday life and in your writing.

—**Nelida Cutler**

LEARNING FROM THE EDITOR

Cutler helps adapt stories from the World Report Edition of TFK for the younger News Scoop Edition.

WORLD REPORT EDITION

Fun for All

In elementary school, Hannah Kristan's least favorite part of the day was recess. "I never got to do anything except sit there," she recalls.

Hannah, 12, was born with spina bifida (*spy*-na *biff*-eh-dah), a condition that kept her spine from forming completely. She uses a wheelchair. For kids in wheelchairs, most playgrounds are terrible places to play. Wheelchairs can sink in the parks' soft surfaces, and chairs won't fit on the equipment.

Three years ago, Hannah heard about the Hasbro National Resource Center for Boundless Playgrounds, a group that creates playgrounds for children of all abilities.

NEWS SCOOP EDITION

A Dream Comes True

When Hannah Kristan was in elementary school, her least favorite part of the day was recess. "I never got to do anything except sit there," she recalls.

Hannah, 12, was born with a disease that kept the bones in her back from forming properly. She uses a wheelchair. For kids in wheelchairs, most playground equipment is off limits.

In 1996 Hannah heard about Boundless Playgrounds. The group, formed by a toy company, creates special playgrounds for children of all abilities.

TALK ABOUT IT
Compare the TFK articles. How do their language and their details differ? Which lines did Cutler change?

TRY IT OUT
Revise a section of a piece of your writing. Rewrite it for a younger audience—perhaps a younger friend or sibling. What changes will you have to make? As you draft and revise the new version of your writing, use the TFK articles above as guides.

TIME Facing the Blank Page **97**

Unity and Coherence

Use the selections from *Time for Kids* to teach a minilesson on unity and coherence. Review the use of transitions discussed in Lesson 2.7, pp. 66–69, and how to check details discussed in Lesson 2.8, pp. 70–73. Explain that when all paragraphs work together and are directly related to the main idea, a piece has unity. When there are clear and logical links between paragraphs, a piece has coherence. At the next writing opportunity, have students revise their drafts for unity and coherence to ensure that each idea is relevant and leads logically and smoothly into the next.

Assess

Evaluation Guidelines

Talk About It

In their discussion, students should note that the editors simplified the language of the *News Scoop Edition* to make it suitable for younger readers. The editors also used shorter sentences and fewer details. The editors changed all the lines except the direct quotation. Extend the discussion by asking students why the editors might have included the direct quotation in both versions of the story. (*Sample answer:* The quotation adds interest and is expressed in simple language.)

Try It Out

In their revisions, students should
- use vocabulary and sentence structure appropriate for younger readers
- attempt to capture younger readers' interest

Critical Thinking

Connecting Reading and Writing

In her list of tips for aspiring writers and editors, Nelida Cutler points out the vital connection between reading and writing. Distribute copies of a *Time for Kids* article (available online) or another appropriate sample of nonfiction to your class. Together, analyze why the author starts the story the way that he or she does, what the purpose of the story is, and how the author supports the main ideas of the article. If students were to give a letter grade to the story, what would it be? Why?

Teach

Technology Tip

Editing and Proofreading Most word processing programs have a spell-check function. Remind students to use the function during the editing and proofreading stage of the writing process, but warn them that even the best spell-checkers are not capable of finding all spelling errors. Students must still proofread carefully.

Internet Connection

Many students will use online resources for their writing. The following sites teach students how to evaluate information found on the Web and how to cite that information if it is used in a report: Evaluating Internet Resources (http://library.lib.binghamton.edu/search/evaluation.html), Citing Internet and Other Electronic Resources (http://library.lib.binghamton.edu/search/citing.html), and A Style Sheet for Citing Internet Sources (http://www.cas.usf.edu/english/walker/mla.html).

Assess

Evaluation Rubrics

Talk About It

In their discussion, students should note common incorrect usages, such as "I feel badly," "between you and I," and misuse of the adverb *hopefully*. Encourage students to voice their opinions about the importance of following rules in spoken and written language and support their opinions with concrete reasons. You might extend the discussion by asking students how the occasion for communicating and the audience might affect language use. For example, do students follow standard rules of usage when speaking informally with friends? Why or why not?

Try It Out

Students' proofreading should
- demonstrate an understanding of major rules of grammar and usage
- be expressed in standard proofreaders' marks

Editing and Proofreading

Copy Editing

Once a TIME story has been written and edited, it needs to be copy-edited and proofread before the final version is printed in the magazine. Copy editors read a story to make sure every word is correct, using a set of symbols to mark up an article.

Judy Paul is TIME's Deputy Copy Chief:
"Our mandate is plain: we're responsible for checking spelling, basic grammar, and TIME style. TIME style is the way TIME does something differently from the dictionary or other publications. "

Judy's department receives letters from TIME readers who pay close attention to the language in the magazine:
"We have always gotten lots of reader mail about style and usage. It's something that interests people, and the letters show that people care. I think the tendency in society is to say that how we speak is not important; you only need to make yourself understood. But people care a lot more than that. They want writing to be elegant and correct. "

WRITING TIP

Language in Action: Adjectives and Verbs

"Many younger writers think a lot of adjectives will dress up their writing. But too many adjectives can clutter a piece of writing. On the other hand, verbs are great. The right verb makes all the difference. If you say, 'John walked into the room,' you get a sense that somebody came into the room. But try: 'John raced into the room.' Or: 'John sauntered into the room.' He's still coming into the room, but each of those verbs gives you a different feeling, a different sense of who that person is and what his attitude is."

—Janice Simpson, Senior Editor

LEARNING FROM THE EDITOR

TALK ABOUT IT
Like Paul's letter writers, point out some examples of incorrect usage that you have seen and heard. On the board, list each example along with its correct form. What is the importance of following rules of usage in spoken language? In written language?

TRY IT OUT
Use proofreading power. Trade papers with a partner and use the checklist and the basic proofreading symbols in Lesson 2.8 as you proofread each other's work. How do your marked-up pages compare with this page from TIME's copy desk?

Exploring Language

Using Descriptive Verbs

In the writing tip, Janice Simpson demonstrates how descriptive verbs can clarify and enliven a piece of writing. Challenge your class to generate a list of at least ten verbs that describe how someone might walk. Insert each verb into the sample sentence *John walked into the room,* and have students discuss how the verb affects their perceptions of John.

Publishing and Presenting

Like TIME, TIME FOR KIDS solicits feedback by asking readers to write or e-mail the magazine with comments. Then the editors publish letters in a section called "Kids Talk Back!" Here are some letters received by TFK.

Kids Talk Back!

Dear TFK,
In my neighborhood we lost 26 trees because of Hurricane Floyd ["A Monster Hurricane," 9/24]. I covered the hurricane for my science journal, and I found out that some of the trees that died were 90 years old, the same age as my grandmother.
—Alexander Chris,
Baltimore, MD

Dear TFK,
Maybe if everyone greeted each other like the Maori tribe, with a *hongi* (pressing noses) ["A Warm Welcome," 9/24], we would be a nicer society. What a different way to say hello!
—Kelsie Alexander,
Madison, AL

Kids Talk Back!

Dear TFK,
I think that kids' sports ["Sports Overload?", 11/5] are getting too competitive, and some coaches are so worried about winning that they take all the fun out of it for us kids.
—Kari Bjerke,
Waukesha, WI

Dear TFK,
It's great that people are taking the time to make playgrounds for handicapped kids ["Fun for All," 11/5]. I know someone in a wheelchair, and she hates to go to playgrounds because she can't get up on the swings. There should be more playgrounds like these.
—Courtney Roche,
Enfield, CT

LEARNING FROM THE WRITERS

TALK ABOUT IT
The writers of the letters above in "Kids Talk Back!" comment on articles in TFK by sharing personal opinions and experiences. For what reasons did these kids decide to "talk back" to TFK? Reread the letters and try to determine each writer's purpose.

TRY IT OUT
1. Write a letter to the editor. Respond to something you have read in a magazine or newspaper or take a stand on a topic that interests you. For suggestions on how to make your point as clearly as possible, read Lesson 6.1, "Taking a Stand," in the unit on persuasive writing. For tips on punctuating letters correctly, see Lessons 18.1, 19.3, and 19.5.
2. Write a letter to a friend. Lesson 1.3, "Making Personal Connections," offers advice on writing friendly letters. After reading the lesson, write a letter to a friend or a family member with whom you have not been in touch in a while.

Assess

Evaluation Rubrics

Talk About It
In their discussion, students should try to determine the purpose of each sample letter to the editor. Purposes might include the following: to offer feedback, to persuade, to practice writing for a specific audience, or to get published.

Try It Out
1. Students' letters to the editor should
- respond to the text or take a stand on an issue of the student's choice
- demonstrate an understanding of basic persuasive appeals
- be punctuated correctly
2. Students' letters should
- incorporate the advice from Lesson 1.3
- be addressed to someone with whom the student has been out of touch

Close

If possible, invite a professional writer working in your community to your class to share his or her insights and advice on the writing process.

Writing in the Real World

Internet Connection Encourage your students to submit their writing to online magazines and other sites for young writers. Some fun sites that accept young writers' work are: Word Dance (**http://www.word dance.com/**), Global Wave (**http://www.cs.bilkent.edu.tr/~david/derya/ gw/gw21/index.html**), Young People's Press Online (**http://www .ypp.net/**), and The Young Writer's Club (**http://www.cs.bilkent.edu.tr/ ~david/derya/ywc.html**). You should review these sites to be sure their content is appropriate for your class.

Descriptive Writing

Ask students to examine the photograph and to identify the elements of weather they notice.

Interpret and Analyze Use the following questions for discussion:

1. What sort of story might a writer place in this type of setting? How would the setting determine some of the story elements?

2. Imagine a film or video that contained this scene. What weather elements might a film director focus on (such as the sound of the wind, a single tree blowing)? How might this help with telling the story?

Discussing the Quotation

After having the quotation read aloud, ask students what kind of wind they picture, based on its description. Ask how the photograph may add to their understanding of the meaning of the words. Encourage students to learn more about the quotation's meaning by reading Julius Lester's "Why Dogs Are Tame" in *Glencoe Literature: The Reader's Choice,* Course 1, page 119.

Writing Prompt Suggest that students work with partners or small groups to create an introduction to a short story set in a place like that shown in the photograph. What situations can they imagine for their characters, who must deal with such powerful wind and weather? Invite volunteers to share their story introductions with the class.

"The wind had carried knives and cut through everything standing in its path."

—Julius Lester, "Why Dogs Are Tame"

100

Planning Resources
- *Lesson Plans*
- *Block Scheduling*

Transparencies
- *Bellringer*
- *Daily Language Practice*
- *Fine Art*

- *Two-Minute Skill Drill*
- *Writing Process*

Other Print Resources
- *Composition Enrichment*
- *Composition Practice*
- *Composition Reteaching*
- *Cooperative Learning Activities*

- *Glencoe Literature Library*
- *Grammar and Composition Handbook*
- *Grammar Workbook*
- *Sentence-Combining Practice*
- *Tests with Answer Key and Rubrics*
- *Thinking and Study Skills*
- *Writing Across the Curriculum*

Descriptive Writing

Objectives

- To understand that descriptive writing is often based on observation
- To take notes based on observations
- To focus on first impressions and details in preparing to write descriptively
- To order details in order to help readers visualize based on a description
- To create word pictures that include details based on sensory perceptions
- To compose vivid, well-organzied descriptions

✔ ASSESSMENT OPTIONS

📁 *Tests with Answer Key and Rubrics*
Unit 3 Choice A Test, p. 9
Unit 3 Choice B Test, p. 10
Unit 3 Composition Objective Test, pp. 11–12

💾 *Testmaker*
Unit 3 Choice A Test
Unit 3 Choice B Test
Unit 3 Composition Objective Test

You may wish to administer either the Unit 3 Choice A Test or the Unit 3 Choice B Test as a pretest.

Key to Ability Levels

L1 Level 1 activities are within the basic ability range of students.

L2 Level 2 activities are within the ability range of average students.

L3 Level 3 activities are more challenging activities.

- *Writing Assessment and Evaluation Rubrics*
- *Writing in the Real World*

📼 **Video**
- *MindJogger Videoquizzes*

💾 **Software**
- *Presentation Plus!*
- *Revising with Style*
- *Testmaker*
- *Writer's Assistant*

🖥 **Web Sites**
- *writerschoice.glencoe.com*
- *lit.glencoe.com*

Focus

Lesson Overview

Objectives

- To identify ways in which a naturalist uses description
- To examine the effective use of descriptive detail

Skills

- analyzing; noting descriptive details

Critical Thinking

- comparing; visualizing

Listening and Speaking

- discussing

Bellringer
Daily Language Activity

When students enter the classroom, have this assignment on the board: *Use sentences to list five ways you could learn about a distant place you have never been to but would like to learn more about.*

Grammar Link to the Bellringer

Have students identify the subjects and verbs in the writing they did in the Bellringer activity. Do the subjects and verbs agree in number?

See also *Daily Language Practice*

Motivating Activity

Ask students to describe an animal or object that they have observed in the natural world. Point out that good naturalists write two kinds of descriptions—precise, in-depth ones that assume background knowledge for people familiar with the subject, and more basic ones for people who may be unfamiliar with the subject. For example, ask students how they would describe a thunderstorm to someone who knows what one is and to someone who has never experienced one.

Descriptive Writing

Writing in the Real World

MEDIA Connection
Magazine Article

Descriptions bring colorful images to many forms of writing—even scientific articles! In the following excerpt, scientist John Boulanger paints pictures for readers of a scene in the far northern Yukon. What was Boulanger doing there? He and six other scientists were investigating life on nunataks (nun' ə taks')—small islands in a sea of ice. The nunataks are home to all kinds of livings things. The scientists were hoping especially to find pikas—stocky little animals reported to live on some of the most remote nunataks. In this excerpt, Boulanger describes the moment he discovered his first one.

from "Attacking the Nunataks," *International Wildlife*

by John Boulanger

I quietly wait for the sun to rise and rouse any pikas from their boulder homes. About 30 minutes later, an animal with a gray coat and white underside peers up at me from a boulder 10 meters (about 11 yds.) away. Yahoo!! Here at last is a collared pika, a member of the rabbit family that more closely resembles a large mouse.

The animal sniffs curiously at me. For the next 20 minutes I watch as it sizes me up. It stares at me for a few seconds at a time, disappearing now and then with a characteristic chirp under a boulder. In between staring bouts, it clips some grass and scampers back to safety.

Resource Manager

Planning Resources
- *Lesson Plans*

Transparencies
- *Bellringer*
- *Daily Language Practice*
- *Writing Process* 11-13B

Other Print Resources
- *Cooperative Learning Activities,* pp. 13-18
- *Thinking and Study Skills,* pp. 3-9
- *Writing Assessment and Evaluation Rubrics*
- *Writing in the Real World,* pp. 9-12

Pikas spend the short growing season harvesting grass and other plant material. They stash it in hay piles under the boulders to keep as food for the long winter.

I wonder why these pikas are so jumpy in such an isolated location. My question gets a quick answer when a new visitor appears, a short-tailed weasel, perhaps looking for a pika breakfast. The newcomer moves continuously over and between the boulders like a snake.

A weasel is a formidable predator for a pika. About the same girth as its prey, this hunter can go anywhere a pika can. Unexpectedly, the weasel runs up to me, obviously curious. Then fear overcomes curiosity, and it flees to a nearby meadow.

I observe other activity in this meadow. Insects bounce around in the multicolored array of alpine flowers. Water pipits and snow buntings fly erratically searching for insects in the luxuriant meadows. Golden eagles soar above, looking for inattentive ground squirrels whose chirps fill the air.

A Writer's Process

Prewriting
Observing a World

Boulanger, along with the six other scientists on the mission, would spend two months in the icy Yukon investigating life on the nunataks. All of that time would be part of the prewriting process for Boulanger. Although his main mission there was to gather facts as a scientist, he also was recording information for an article in the magazine *International Wildlife*. Doing these jobs meant carefully observing the strange, cold world. Taking good notes of his observations was an equally important task.

Even as he was taking notes, Boulanger thought about how he could convey the world in front of him to his readers. "I was always trying to figure out ways that I could describe being up there to someone who had never been there before," Boulanger says. "For example, in one area we came to a place where gigantic glacial streams were running on either side of us." How would Boulanger describe the roaring streams? Could he compare them to something familiar? "Finally, it struck me that these streams were like water slides at an amusement park," he says.

Boulanger looked for visual details as he sat on nunataks, watching the animals. When he spotted a pika, for instance, he noted its color, texture, size—details that would help him write a vivid word picture.

He also recorded other sensory details, such as the sounds of the animals and the feel of the ice and slush.

Reading Media
Have students preview the title and focus of the Media Connection. Explain to students that Boulanger is a naturalist who described in detail a part of the world not often seen. Have students read the Media Connection.

Discussion Prompts
- Have you ever read an article in a magazine or newspaper about a place you have never been to before? Did the writer make you feel as if you were really there? How does a writer accomplish this?
- If you were visiting a city in another part of the country or the world and writing a postcard to a friend back home, what kinds of things would you describe to your friend?

Teach

Discussion Prompts

- Describe the process Boulanger used to take notes and to write his descriptions.
- Why did Boulanger compare feelings from the intense sun with feelings of being "in a gigantic frying pan"? What technique has Boulanger used to create this word picture? (comparison, imagery) Is it effective?
- What other writing topics might require a great deal of note taking before starting on the drafting process?
- Did Boulanger consider his audience while writing his article? How would his audience influence what he wrote?

Additional Resources

Writing Process Transparencies, 11–13B

Writing in the Real World, pp. 9–12

Cooperative Learning Activities, pp. 13–18

Thinking and Study Skills, pp. 3–9

To be sure his notes were safe, Boulanger used a special reporter's notebook. It was made of paper that could get wet and not fall apart. Boulanger wrote with a pencil so his notes wouldn't blur if they fell into snow.

Boulanger wrote whenever something caught his eye. Usually, the team was moving and Boulanger had to dash off impressions. "I didn't pay that much attention to grammar," he says. "I'd just quickly spill my mind out and then use the notes later to remember."

Sometimes, he had time to write a full description. Confronted with the icy, roaring "water slides," Boulanger stopped and wrote. "That moment was so intense, I sat down and took ten or fifteen minutes to really try to describe it," he says.

At 8:00 or 9:00 P.M., after a full day of work, Boulanger often crawled into his sleeping bag and expanded his notes. In the far north at that time of year, the sun doesn't set until midnight. Even at 9:00 P.M., it's still light and often warm enough to write. Some of Boulanger's longest entries were made at these quiet times.

Drafting
Writing the Article

Faced with so many amazing sights, Boulanger wrote more

than 200 pages of notes. Rich in detail, they formed the basis of his science article.

Before starting to draft, Boulanger developed a plan for his article. After opening with a description of his thrilling plane ride into the wilds, he explained what the scientific team had set out to do. From there, Boulanger wrote his article like a field journal. He entered a date and then described the day's discoveries and listed his questions. The reader would learn along with the team.

When drafting descriptions, Boulanger continued to search for comparisons that would relate this alien icebound world to something more familiar. Besides conveying information, his comparisons helped readers visualize scenes in a fresh, imaginative way. For example, to describe the intense sunlight, Boulanger wrote: "The sun is intensely bright, and its fiery reflection on the snow makes me feel as if I am in a gigantic frying pan."

One of the hardest parts of writing was choosing what to write about. Boulanger had to boil down two months of notes into a short magazine article. "You have to be very selective," he explains. "I chose things I thought were interesting. That way, readers can live the experience with me, feel like they're there, too."

Civic Literacy

Protecting the Environment

Naturalists are aware that their work can interfere with nature. Most of them go out of their way to minimize their impact on the environment. If your students wish to prepare articles about something they can observe in nature, encourage them to make sure they infringe as little as possible on the areas that they are observing.

Examining Writing in the Real World

Analyzing the Media Connection

Discuss these questions about the article excerpt on pages 102–103.

1. To what other animals does Boulanger compare a pika and a weasel? Why do you think he makes these comparisons?

2. What visual details does he provide about various animals' color, size, or appearance?

3. In the second paragraph, what picture of the pika do the details draw?

4. Boulanger says that the pika "peers up at me." Find other examples where he uses vivid verbs.

5. In the last paragraph point out three descriptive adjectives or adverbs and tell how they enhance the word picture.

Analyzing a Writer's Process

Discuss these questions about John Boulanger's writing process.

1. How and when did Boulanger take notes?

2. How does Boulanger's style of notetaking compare to yours?

3. Why did he use familiar comparisons to describe life on the nunataks?

4. Why was turning his notes into an article a challenging task for Boulanger?

 Grammar Link

Make sure the subject and verb in a sentence agree, even when a phrase comes between them.

*The **variety** of plants and animals **is** amazing.*

Write the following sentences. In each one, underline the subject once and the verb twice. If they agree, write *correct.* If they do not agree, correct the verb.

1. The team of scientists skis across glaciers.

2. The nunataks, small islands in a sea of ice, is home to many living things.

3. John Boulanger, with other biologists, travel by plane to Mt. Logan.

4. Gigantic streams of glacial water is on either side of us.

5. A weasel in the pika colony hopes to catch his breakfast.

See Lesson 15.1, page 439.

Writing in the Real World

Assess

Analyzing the Media Connection

Possible responses include

1. He compares a pika to a rabbit and a mouse.

2. Pika: gray coat, white underside, jumpy; weasel: short-tailed, same girth as its prey; pipits and snow buntings: erratic fliers; eagles: soaring; ground squirrels: inattentive

3. The pika is a small, vulnerable, jumpy animal that is curious but cautious. It eats grass and moves quickly.

4. Other vivid verbs include: *sniffs; clips; scampers; stash; flees: bounce; soar.*

5. Descriptive adjectives and adverbs include *multicolored, alpine, erratically, luxuriant, inattentive.* Specific descriptive details bring the picture to life.

Analyzing a Writer's Process

1. He took notes in a special waterproof reporter's notebook. He wrote his impressions during the day and expanded on his notes in the evening.

2. Students may state that his system takes more time and relies more on observation than does theirs.

3. Familiar comparisons help readers picture what he sees and experience in some way what he experiences.

4. His notes were extensive. He had to select experiences that were interesting and that would fit within the format of a short article.

Reteaching

As a group, create a list of places students want to read about.

Enrichment

Challenge students to write about why a natural object or area is valuable to the environment.

Grammar Link

Answers
1. team skis correct
2. ninataks are
3. Boulanger travels
4. streams are
5. weasel hopes correct

Checking Subject-Verb Agreement Write the following verbs on the board: *survive, discover, collect, observe,* and *search.* Have students use either the singular or plural form of each of the verbs in a sentence about the Media Connection. When they are finished, have them exchange papers with a partner, who will revise the sentences, making the singular verbs plural and the plural verbs singular.

LESSON
3.1

Focus

Lesson Overview

Objectives

- To produce a piece of descriptive writing
- To use language that is clear and effective
- To develop vocabulary through the use of a thesaurus

Skills

- using colorful, effective language in written and oral descriptions

Critical Thinking

- evaluating words and phrases for their effect

Listening and Speaking

- taking notes on others' oral descriptions

🔔 Bellringer
Daily Language Activity

When students enter the classroom, have this assignment on the board: *Write at least three sentences describing how a real or fictional person looks and acts. Try to make that individual come to life for your readers.*

Grammar Link to the Bellringer

Ask students to identify any possessive pronouns in their descriptions in the Bellringer. If their descriptions contain possessive nouns, have students replace the nouns with pronouns.

📖 **See also** *Daily Language Practice*

Motivating Activity

Invite volunteers to read their descriptions aloud. Have others identify the words or phrases that best help listeners picture the person being described. Discuss why the descriptions are effective.

Descriptive Writing (sidebar)

LESSON 3.1 — Painting a Picture with Words

An effective written description is one that presents a clear picture to your reader. An interesting description attracts the reader. Descriptions can present broad views or close-ups.

Good descriptive writing can take a reader anywhere. In the excerpt below, writer Jean Craighead George takes you to the Arctic. She describes the world of Miyax, an Inuit girl.

> The writer sets the scene for the action by describing the sky and the landscape first.

> Which precise details help you see what Miyax sees?

Literature Model

Miyax pushed back the hood of her sealskin parka and looked at the Arctic sun. It was a yellow disc in a lime-green sky, the colors of six o'clock in the evening and the time when the wolves awoke. Quietly she put down her cooking pot and crept to the top of a dome-shaped frost heave, one of the many earth buckles that rise and fall in the crackling cold of the Arctic winter. Lying on her stomach, she looked across a vast lawn of grass and moss and focused her attention on the wolves she had come upon two sleeps ago.

Jean Craighead George
Julie of the Wolves

106 Unit 3 Descriptive Writing

Resource Manager

Planning Resources
- *Lesson Plans*

📖 **Transparencies**
- *Bellringer*
- *Daily Language Practice*
- *Fine Art* 11–15
- *Two-Minute Skill Drill*
- *Writing Process* 11–13B

📁 Other Print Resources
- *Composition Enrichment*, p. 20
- *Composition Practice*, p. 20
- *Composition Reteaching*, p. 20
- *Cooperative Learning Activities,* pp. 13–18
- *Thinking and Study Skills*, pp. 3, 9, 12, 20, 22
- *Writing Across the Curriculum*

- *Writing Assessment and Evaluation Rubrics*

Zoom In

Like George, you can use descriptive writing to help your reader see what you see, hear what you hear, and feel what you feel. In the paragraph below, George continues her description. Notice how she zooms in closer to the scene.

Which details help bring you closer to the wolf?

Literature Model

Amaroq [one of the wolves] glanced at his paw and slowly turned his head her way without lifting his eyes. He licked his shoulder. A few matted hairs sprang apart and twinkled individually. Then his eyes sped to each of the three adult wolves that made up his pack and finally to the five pups who were sleeping in a fuzzy mass near the den entrance. The great wolf's eyes softened at the sight of the little wolves, then quickly hardened into brittle yellow jewels as he scanned the flat tundra [plain].

Jean Craighead George
Julie of the Wolves

Compare the two paragraphs from *Julie of the Wolves*. In the first, George sets the overall scene. In the second, she moves in closer. She draws the reader into the wolf's world. She lets the reader see the wolf's emotions through its eyes.

Journal Writing

Having read the two descriptions from *Julie of the Wolves*, make a word picture of the scene. To start, list the descriptive details that made the scene clear to you. If you wish, draw a sketch of the scene.

Teach

Using the Model

Jean Craighead George's vivid imagery describing the Arctic environment and wolves ("yellow disc in a lime-green sky," "dome-shaped frost heave") not only takes readers to the scene, it also places them with Miyax in her earnest observation of the wolves. Discuss why observation is so important to Miyax. (Information about a person's surroundings could be important for survival in such a challenging environment.) **L2**

Two-Minute Skill Drill

Have students choose one of the ideas below and then write vivid words and phrases that could be used to describe that idea.

• *busy playground*
• *active animal indoors or outdoors*
• *harsh weather or environment*

See also *Two-Minute Skill Drill Transparencies, 3.1*

Journal Writing Tip

Word Pictures After students complete their journal entries, ask them whether they discovered descriptive details that they missed on the first reading.

Teach

Teaching from the Art

Call students attention to the art. Have them discuss details they would add if the art were to be expanded into a four-page guide book. **L1**

Using a Thesaurus

Students can expand the list of vivid words they made during the two-minute drill on page 107 by looking up some of their words in a thesaurus. For example, if they listed *run* for active animal, they might find words like *dash* and *race*. **L1**

Using Metaphors

Write the last sentence in the model on page 107 on the board. Ask students to identify the metaphor in the sentence. ("The great wolf's eyes…quickly hardened into brittle, yellow jewels… .") Assign students to write one or two sentences using metaphors. For example, the wolf's fatherly attention to his family could be expressed by the metaphor "Amaroq was a sentry on duty as he kept watch over his cubs." **L3**

Additional Resources

📖 For descriptive **writing prompts**, *see Fine Art Transparencies* 11–15.

📖 *Daily Language Practice*

📖 *Writing Process Transparencies,* 11–13B

📁 *Writing Across the Curriculum*

📁 *Cooperative Learning Activities,* pp. 13–18

📁 *Thinking and Study Skills,* pp. 3, 9, 12, 20, 22

📁 *Composition Practice,* p. 20

Descriptive Writing

Vocabulary Tip

When you get ready to describe something, close your eyes and picture it. Then list words and phrases that tell how it looks, feels, smells, sounds, or tastes.

Ideas for Descriptive Writing

Books aren't the only place where descriptions are used. In fact, you probably use descriptions every day. For example, when you tell a friend about a new movie, you probably use description. When you take notes on a field trip, you probably use description for that, too.

Maybe you've taken a trip to the zoo. Did you notice the descriptive writing all around you? Signs at the zoo describe the animals. Posters describe new attractions. Advertisements describe food for sale. What examples of descriptive writing can you find in the illustration below?

Descriptive Writing

New at Zoo **Baby Spotted Owl!**

Fresh Hot Roasted Nuts

From China's Bamboo Forests

The **Giant Panda…**

Zoo Guide

The Polar Bear lives along the frozen shores of the icy Arctic Ocean. Adult Polar Bears weigh about 1,000 pounds.

MEETING INDIVIDUAL NEEDS — English Language Learners

Choosing Words

Encourage students who have difficulty writing in English first to sketch a place they wish to describe. The setting can be a real or imaginary place. Urge them to include at least two elements in the sketch that show how the place looks or feels. (For example, a bright sun and drooping plants could illustrate a hot setting. A moon and shadowed trees could illustrate a dark, mysterious one.) Students can then "translate" their sketches into English words step by step.

Descriptive Writing

Write a Description of a Wolf

Write a description of a wolf for a group of younger students. Imagine that your description will prepare them to see this animal at the zoo. Look at the photo on page 107 or at other pictures of wolves. Ask yourself: How big is the wolf? What does it remind me of? What color is its coat? What color are its eyes?

PURPOSE To describe an animal
AUDIENCE Younger students
LENGTH 1–2 paragraphs

WRITING RUBRICS To write a description, you should

- look at or think about what you want to describe
- list details about what you see or remember
- use your list to write your description

Listening and Speaking

COOPERATIVE LEARNING In a small group, take turns orally describing places that are familiar to you. For example, you might describe a specific place in or near your school. Describe these places without naming them. As each person tells about his or her place, other group members should write down the details that provide the best clues about what the place is and then identify it.

Using Computers

Look at your list of descriptive details from the Journal Writing activity on page 107. On the computer, write each descriptive detail in a new way.

Grammar Link

Use possessive pronouns to show ownership of something.

Notice how Jean Craighead George uses possessive pronouns in the models on pages 106 and 107.

Replace each underlined word or group of words with a possessive pronoun.

1. <u>Miyax's</u> attention was focused on the wolves.
2. <u>The wolf's and Miyax's</u> eyes met.
3. <u>The wolf's</u> eyes glittered in the light.
4. Three other adult wolves and five pups made up <u>the wolf's</u> pack.
5. <u>Jean Craighead George's</u> book *Julie of the Wolves* is an award-winner.

See Lesson 11.4, page 367.

3.1 Painting a Picture with Words **109**

Assess

Evaluation Rubrics

Write a Description of a Wolf

When evaluating students' descriptive passages look for

- a clear topic sentence
- effective use of sensory images
- use of specific and significant details
- attention to details that will be interesting and clear to younger readers

See also *Writing Assessment and Evaluation Rubrics.*

Listening and Speaking

Each description should

- include specific clues about a selected site
- provide details that help students picture the place

Reteaching

📁 *Composition Reteaching,* p. 20

Enrichment

📁 *Composition Enrichment,* p. 20

Close

Invite students to share their favorite descriptions from this lesson and say why they chose them.

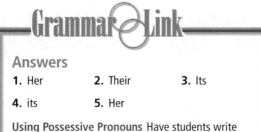

Grammar Link

Answers

1. Her   2. Their   3. Its

4. its   5. Her

Using Possessive Pronouns Have students write five sentences with at least one possessive noun in each sentence. Pairs of students can exchange sentences and convert their partner's possessive nouns into possessive pronouns.

Focus

Lesson Overview

Objectives
- To identify information that will serve as a source of ideas for a description
- To take accurate and relevant notes

Skills
- observing events; using sensory experiences; using vivid language to describe events

Critical Thinking
- analyzing; comparing

Listening and Speaking
- discussing; note taking

Bellringer
Daily Language Activity

When students enter the classroom, have this assignment on the board: *Write down the name of a favorite movie. Jot down at least three reasons why you like it so much.*

Grammar Link to the Bellringer

Have students circle any action verbs they used in the Bellringer activity.

See also *Daily Language Practice*

Descriptive Writing

Observing and Taking Notes

*S*ensory details call up realistic images of taste, sound, smell, touch, and sight. These details can add richness to your descriptions of everyday things.

In the model below, Maya Angelou describes a picnic she remembers from her childhood. Notice the sensory details Angelou uses to help readers picture the scene.

Literature Model

The summer picnic gave ladies a chance to show off their baking hands. On the barbecue pit, chickens and spareribs sputtered in their own fat and a sauce whose recipe was guarded in the family. . . . Pound cakes sagged with their buttery weight and small children could no more resist licking the icings than their mothers could avoid slapping the sticky fingers. . . . On one corner of the clearing a gospel group was rehearsing. Their harmony, packed as tight as sardines, floated over the music of the county singers and melted into the songs of the small children's ring games.

Maya Angelou, *I Know Why the Caged Bird Sings*

> The writer uses parallelism to aid her description.

Grammar Tip

For more information on parallelism, see **Writing and Research Handbook,** page 678.

Resource Manager

Planning Resources
- *Lesson Plans*

Transparencies
- *Bellringer*
- *Daily Language Practice*
- *Fine Art* 11-15
- *Two-Minute Skill Drill*
- *Writing Process* 11-13B

Other Print Resources
- *Composition Enrichment*, p. 21
- *Composition Practice*, p. 21
- *Composition Reteaching*, p. 21
- *Cooperative Learning Activities*, pp. 13-18
- *Thinking and Study Skills*, pp. 3, 6, 34-37
- *Writing Across the Curriculum*

- *Writing Assessment and Evaluation Rubrics*

Angelou brings her description of the picnic to life by including details that help you see, hear, feel, taste, and smell the picnic. In your own descriptive writing, you can do the same thing. Just learn to pay attention to your senses.

Notice What's Around You

Whenever you see, hear, smell, taste, or touch, you learn something about the world around you. Look at the picture on this page. Then look at the list of sensory descriptive words alongside the picture. Which things in the picture relate to each sensory word?

Hot

Colorful

Sweet

Smoky

Musical

Journal Writing

Recall one of your favorite places. Which senses do you use most when you're there? Make a list of details that you see, hear, touch, taste, and smell. Then circle the details that best describe your place.

Descriptive Writing

Teach

Using the Model

Maya Angelou's description comes from her mental notes of a picnic she attended. In just a few sentences, she uses dense layers of sensory details to re-create the scene for the reader. Have students make lists of the sensory details that Angelou uses. As they find the details, they should write them in categories of sight, sound, feeling, taste, and smell. **L2**

Listing Details

If some students find it difficult to describe situations or places, tell them to try to imagine themselves at the picnic pictured on this page. Encourage them to write a list of different sensory details they would experience if they were there. After they finish their list, they can use it to write a detailed paragraph. **L1**

Two-Minute Skill Drill

Write the following situations on the board. Have students make up an interesting sensory detail for each.

a picnic on the beach

riding a crowded bus

a ride at a carnival

See also *Two-Minute Skill Drill Transparencies, 3.2*

Journal Writing Tip

Comparing and Contrasting
Ask students to consider why they have chosen a certain place as their favorite. Does their choice have anything to do with their sensory experiences at that place? How is their favorite place different from others they might have chosen?

Teach

Describing Work Situations

Challenge students to think of an interesting occupation in which note taking is important. Ask students: What kinds of details would a crime detective write in his or her notes? A reporter at a sports event? An insurance agent touring an area devastated by a hurricane? Have students pick an occupation and imagine a situation in which they'd take notes. With their detailed list, they then can write a page or two about the situation. **L3**

Additional Resources

- For for descriptive **writing prompts**, see *Fine Art Transparencies* 11–15.
- *Daily Language Practice*
- *Writing Process Transparencies* 11–13B
- *Writing Across the Curriculum*
- *Cooperative Learning Activities*, pp. 13–18
- *Thinking and Study Skills*, pp. 3, 6, 34–37
- *Composition Practice*, p. 21
- *Composition Reteaching*, p. 21
- *Composition Enrichment*, p. 21

Descriptive Writing

Vocabulary Tip

If you can't find just the right word when revising, turn to a thesaurus. A thesaurus is a reference book that groups together words with similar meanings.

Take Notes

Exploring the world around you can be an adventure. Make careful notes about important experiences. Taking notes can help you remember your experiences and share them with others later.

When you take notes on an experience, don't worry about grammar, spelling, or punctuation. Just ask yourself what you see, hear, touch, taste, and smell. Then jot down whatever details will help you remember the experience.

Later, when you prepare to write a draft, reread your notes. Keep in mind that you don't have to use all the details you gathered. Choose those details that create the strongest impression of the experience. If you're describing a concert, for example, you might focus on sights and sounds. If you're describing a holiday dinner, you might concentrate on smells and tastes.

> A hot, sticky day. We played touch football. The ball felt hard and the laces felt like large mountains on a globe. Afterward I got a hamburger well done. The hard, burnt, top layer was crunchy, but the inside was soft. I chewed slowly, closing my eyes. I heard the wind blow through the trees. I smelled hamburger and it reminded me of summer. Then there was a water fight. The water felt so good, my clothing molding to my body like a second layer of skin.
>
> Laura Makinen
> St. Clement School
> Chicago, IL

BLOCK PARTY

MEETING INDIVIDUAL NEEDS

English Language Learners

Writing from Dictated Notes

Students learning English may have trouble using English to describe the different senses. Encourage them to communicate their sensory details orally to English-speaking students, who can jot down notes for them. For instance, students learning English can describe the food pictured on this page—the taste, feel, smell, and appearance. Then they can write a paragraph using the notes taken from their oral descriptions.

Write a Description of Living Things

Study the scene in this painting. If it were real, what would you see and smell? What do the flowers, caterpillars, and moths look like? Write a description that other students might use to identify the plant and insects shown.

PURPOSE To make a scene recognizable to others

AUDIENCE Other students

LENGTH 1–2 paragraphs

WRITING RUBRICS To write a strong description, you should

- use sensory details—tell how something looks, sounds, smells, tastes, or feels
- take notes on what you notice
- include the most effective details in your draft

Maria Sibylla Merian, *Coral Bean Tree and Saturniid,* c. 1700

Listening and Speaking

Observe a subject in nature. You might choose a dandelion, a spider, a rock, or whatever interests you. Take field notes—careful notes based on what you observe. Use your five senses to gather details. Afterward, use your notes to describe what you saw to a partner.

Cross-Curricular Activity

SCIENCE The saturniid moth, shown in the picture, is also called the giant silkworm moth. Read about it in the encyclopedia. Then write a descriptive paragraph about it.

Grammar Link

Use action verbs to make your descriptive writing come to life.

Notice the variety of action verbs Angelou uses in the model on page 110. Replace the blank in each sentence below with an action verb.

1. The boys _____ through the woods looking for tracks.
2. The children _____ the fried chicken.
3. Marley _____ her guitar for us.
4. Birds _____ in the surrounding trees.
5. We _____ at the dog's antics.

See Lesson 10.1, page 333.

Descriptive Writing

Assess

Evaluation Rubrics

Write a Description of a Scene

When evaluating students' descriptions, look for

- use of sensory details
- use of notes
- selection of most effective details for a written description of a scene to be recognizable by others

See also *Writing Assessment and Evaluation Rubrics.*

Listening and Speaking

Each description should include details based on the use of the five senses.

Cross-Curricular Activity: Science

Paragraphs should include description and make use of details from a reference source.

Reteaching

📁 *Composition Reteaching,* p. 21

Enrichment

📁 *Composition Enrichment,* p. 21

📦 *Fine Art Transparencies* 11–15

Close

Have students discuss using sensory details to describe. Ask students which senses they prefer to write about the most. Which help create the clearest picture?

Grammar Link

Answers

Answers will vary. Samples follow.
1. crept 2. devoured 3. strummed
4. chirped 5. giggled

Action Verbs After students have chosen action verbs, write the first sentence on the board. Make a list of student verbs and discuss them. Continue with the rest of the sentences.

Viewing the Art

Maria Sibylla Merian, *Coral Bean Tree and Saturniid,* c. 1700

Maria Sibylla Merian (1647–1717) also wrote books on natural science, often with original copperplate illustrations.

Interpret and Analyze Ask students how *Coral Bean Tree and Saturniid* differs from illustrations in modern science books.

Focus

Lesson Overview

Objectives
- To observe and record details
- To recreate observations and impressions in writing
- To use vivid modifiers in writing

Skills
- observing objects; identifying details; using vivid adjectives

Critical Thinking
- analyzing

Listening and Speaking
- informal speaking; evaluating

🔔 Bellringer
Daily Language Activity

When students enter the classroom, have this assignment on the board: *Write a short description of a car that you admire.*

Grammar Link to the Bellringer

Invite students to share with the class any parts of their description that include a series of items or characteristics. Did they include commas to punctuate their description? Invite a volunteer to write on the board part of a description that includes a series. Help the volunteer to use commas to punctuate the description properly.

See also *Daily Language Practice*

Motivating Activity

Invite students to discuss a time when they've wanted to describe a place, a person, or an object to someone but had difficulty doing so. Why was it so hard to give a good description?

Descriptive Writing

Elaborating: Focusing on the Details

*W*ith strong descriptions, you can help your readers see what you see. Use details that create that effect.

In the model below, Ian Fleming describes a wonderful car—a magical *Paragon Panther*—that has just been fixed up to look like new. Notice the details Fleming includes.

> What details does the writer use to show readers that the car was flashy?

Literature Model

Every detail gleamed and glinted with new paint and polished chrome down to the snarling mouth of the big boa-constrictor horn. . . . from the rows and rows of gleaming knobs on the dashboard to the brand-new, dark-red leather upholstery; from the cream-colored collapsible roof to the fine new tires; from the glistening silver of the huge exhaust pipes snaking away from holes in the bright green hood to the glittering license plates that said GEN II.

Ian Fleming,
Chitty Chitty Bang Bang

Fleming elaborates on his description by focusing only on the details showing that the car looked new. By including these details and leaving out others, he presents a clear picture of the car.

114 Unit 3 Descriptive Writing

Resource Manager

Planning Resources
- *Lesson Plans*

📋 Transparencies
- *Bellringer*
- *Daily Language Practice*
- *Fine Art* 11-15
- *Two-Minute Skill Drill*
- *Writing Process* 11-13B

📁 Other Print Resources
- *Composition Enrichment,* p. 22
- *Composition Practice,* p. 22
- *Composition Reteaching,* p. 22
- *Cooperative Learning Activities,* pp. 13-18
- *Thinking and Study Skills,* pp. 3, 5, 7, 9, 15, 17, 19
- *Writing Across the Curriculum*

- *Writing Assessment and Evaluation Rubrics*

Pay Attention to First Impressions

Even an ordinary car has details that you can put into a description. All you have to do is look closely. Start with your first impressions—your first thoughts upon noticing something. In the notes on the right are the first impressions one writer had of the car shown on this page.

You might try thinking about your own first impressions as you walk down a street. What are the first things you notice? What details stick in your mind after you get home?

shiny

glare of sun's reflection

canary yellow

boxy shape

fat, black tires

loud

Descriptive Writing

Journal Writing

Find three familiar objects in your classroom. Write your first impressions of them. What are your first thoughts on noticing each one? Then elaborate, writing three or four additional details you notice about each object.

Teach

Comparing First Impressions

Show students an object. Then ask them to close their eyes. What details can they remember about the object? Have them open their eyes and re-examine the object. Which details are still in their mind from their first impression? Students can compare observations and discuss why they chose the details they did. **L2**

Two-Minute Skill Drill

Ask students to list five words that describe a dog, cat, or other pet they have known.

See also *Two-Minute Skill Drill Transparencies, 3.3*

Journal Writing Tip

Elaborating Ask students whether any of the details they have written describe something new they noticed about the object. Why do they think they noticed this new detail? Point out that concentration can increase their powers of observation.

Teach

Practicing Observation

Encourage students to use their descriptive skills to create a written advertising brochure. They might describe a type of car, a pair of sneakers, a restaurant meal, or another item in their brochure. Remind students that the words in their brochures should both describe the object and entice customers to buy it. **L3**

Additional Resources

✎ For descriptive **writing prompts**, see *Fine Art Transparencies* 11–15.

✎ *Daily Language Practice*

✎ *Writing Process Transparencies* 11–13B
📁 *Writing Across the Curriculum*
📁 *Cooperative Learning Activities,* pp. 13–18
📁 *Thinking and Study Skills,* pp. 3, 5, 7, 9, 15, 17, 19
📁 *Composition Practice,* p. 22
📁 *Composition Reteaching,* p. 22
📁 *Composition Enrichment,* p. 22

Descriptive Writing

Grammar Tip
Details listed in a series of three or more items require commas to separate them. For more information, see Lesson 19.2, page 491.

Take a Closer Look

After noting your first impressions, start gathering details. One way is to identify the small things that help create each impression. For example, your first impression of a car might be "shiny." You might take a closer look and notice the polished chrome, freshly waxed paint, and gleaming hubcaps. All these details create the impression of "shiny."

Another way of gathering details is to reexamine your subject. Check for details you might have overlooked. Try to use all your senses. Maybe you forgot to describe the roar of the engine or the smell of the exhaust. Maybe you didn't notice how warm the hood was in the sun.

MEETING INDIVIDUAL NEEDS English Language Learners

Describing Accurately

Invite students to observe an object. Next, ask them to write as much of a description as they can, first using English words and then words from their primary language. Then help them to complete their description in English, pointing out English meanings for their primary-language words when possible. You may wish to have students make a list of the new descriptive words they have learned along with the meanings of these words.

Descriptive Writing

Kenny Scharf, *Stellaradiola*, 1985

Write a Description of Art

Above is a photo of a detailed piece of art. Examine the picture carefully. Describe the piece as if you were writing an article for your school newspaper.

PURPOSE To convey an impression by using details

AUDIENCE Readers of your school paper

LENGTH 2–3 paragraphs

WRITING RUBRICS To use details effectively in a description, you should

- start with one of your first impressions
- elaborate, adding specific details
- use details that help the reader visualize what you are describing

Viewing and Representing

COOPERATIVE LEARNING In a small group, discuss the artwork. What does its title, *Stellaradiola*, mean? What is the art piece about? How did the artist show his ideas? What do you think the artist wants you to feel or understand?

Cross-Curricular Activity

GEOGRAPHY Landmarks are natural or man-made objects. They help people know where they are. Pick an object you see on your way to school. Describe the object carefully so that a new student could use it as a landmark for finding the school.

Use commas to separate items in a series.

A comma usually precedes *and* when three separate details are listed. An example is

polished chrome, freshly waxed paint, and gleaming hubcaps.

Add commas in the following sentences. Write *correct* if a sentence needs no commas.

1. The art was humorous colorful and unique.
2. The front grill, headlight trim, and bumper were made of chrome.
3. The book is concise well written and informative.
4. The moth was grey soft and furry.
5. The car tires were old fat and ugly.

See Lesson 19.2, page 491.

Assess

Evaluation Rubrics

Write a Description of Art

When evaluating students' descriptions, look for

- details that are specific
- details that help readers visualize the piece of art

See also *Writing Assessment and Evaluation Rubrics.*

Viewing and Representing

Students should share their impressions and interpretations of the art, citing specific details of the art.

Cross-Curricular Activity: Geography

Descriptions should be clear and include details that will enable another person to identify the place being described.

Reteaching

📁 *Composition Reteaching*, p. 22

Enrichment

📁 *Composition Enrichment*, p. 22

🎨 *Fine Art Transparencies* 11–15

Close

Invite students to discuss improvements in their descriptive skills. Ask them to suggest tips for writing good descriptions.

Answers

1. The art was humorous, colorful, and unique.
2. correct
3. The book is concise, well written, and informative.
4. The moth was gray, soft, and furry.
5. The car tires were old, fat, and ugly.

Viewing the Art

Kenny Scharf, *Stellaradiola*, 1985
Kenny Scharf's pop-surrealist *Stellaradiola* consists of acrylic paint, jewels, plastic toys, and mirror figurines on a radio. Its dimensions are 16 by 29 by 7 inches. It is in the collection of Mr. and Mrs. K. Scharf.

Focus

Lesson Overview

Objectives
- To identify appropriate details
- To sequence details for descriptive writing

Skills
- observing details; ordering details; using transition words

Critical Thinking
- relating; visualizing

Listening and Speaking
- discussing; evaluating

🔔 Bellringer
Daily Language Activity

When students enter the classroom, have this assignment on the board: *Write a short description of this classroom.*

Grammar Link to the Bellringer

Ask volunteers to look for prepositional phrases such as *at the front, in the middle, on the right,* or *at the back* in their descriptions. How do these phrases make the descriptions easier to understand?

📕 **See also** *Daily Language Practice*

Motivating Activity

Ask students to discuss the image of their classroom that a stranger might have after reading their description. Invite students to discuss times in which people have described something to them and the object or place turned out to be much different from the description.

Descriptive Writing

Ordering Descriptive Details

If details are presented in a sensible order, readers get a picture in their minds. Transition words help make the picture sharper.

In the model below, Freeman Hubbard orders details in his description of a circus parade in the early 1900s. Notice that Hubbard gives details in the order of their appearance in the parade. This makes it easy for readers to picture the scene.

Literature Model

The street was alive with noise as the first four lovely ladies on horseback, trumpets lifted to their lips, came into sight. They were always lithe and lovely, and the plumes they wore danced as their horses pranced. Then came the band, in red uniforms with gold braid, riding on a gilded band wagon that was sometimes drawn by as many as forty horses. The band never stopped playing: the big bass drum thumped steadily, the trumpets shrilled and blared, the cymbals flashed in the sun. Behind the band came great floats.

Freeman Hubbard, *Great Days of the Circus*

Resource Manager

Planning Resources
- *Lesson Plans*

📕 **Transparencies**
- *Bellringer*
- *Daily Language Practice*
- *Fine Art* 11-15
- *Two-Minute Skill Drill*
- *Writing Process* 11-13B

📂 Other Print Resources
- *Composition Enrichment*, p. 23
- *Composition Practice*, p. 23
- *Composition Reteaching*, p. 23
- *Cooperative Learning Activities*, pp. 13-18
- *Thinking and Study Skills*, pp. 3, 11, 17
- *Writing Across the Curriculum*

- *Writing Assessment and Evaluation Rubrics*

Decide Where to Start

To order your own descriptive details, you might imagine your eye is a video camera lens. First, pick a starting point. Then pick a way to move your eye's camera across your subject. One way is to start at the front and move toward the back. Another way is to start at one side and move toward the other side. The order you use should be one that makes sense to your reader.

Front to Back

At the front of the parade came the women on horseback. After them the band rode in on a wagon. The great floats rolled in behind the band.

Left to Right

On the left a tall blonde rider pranced on horseback. To the right came another rider draped with a banner. Two riders waving at the crowd were at the far right.

Journal Writing

Describe your classroom, using two different ordering methods. Compare the results. Which order makes more sense? Why?

Drafting Tip

When you're drafting a description, make a quick sketch of the scene. The sketch can help you decide how to order your details.

Teach

Using Transitions

Freeman Hubbard gives readers a direct view, as if he were standing off to the side at the front, holding a movie camera to capture the players moving past him. Help students pick out phrases and sentences, such as "First four lovely ladies on horseback came into sight," "Then came the band," and "Behind the band came great floats." Point out that these phrases give clues to the arrangement and movement of the scene. **L2**

Two-Minute Skill Drill

Invite students to arrange the following objects on their desks and write a description of the arrangement:

a pencil, an eraser, a book, and a paper clip

See also *Two-Minute Skill Drill Transparencies, 3.4*

Journal Writing Tip

Identifying Spatial Relationships Invite students to describe the classroom or another area from several different vantage points.

Teach

Experimenting with Order

Students may benefit by using transition words orally before writing them. Let some students take turns standing in various arrangements while other students describe these arrangements orally, for example "Anne is standing in back of Jerome," "Lorenzo is to the right of Susan," "Aaron and Kira are standing next to the door." **L2**

Additional Resources

For descriptive **writing prompts**, see *Fine Art Transparencies* 11–15.

Daily Language Practice

Writing Process Transparencies 11–13B
Writing Across the Curriculum
Cooperative Learning Activities, pp. 13–18
Thinking and Study Skills, pp. 3, 11, 17
Composition Practice, p. 23

Descriptive Writing

Grammar Tip

Prepositional phrases, such as *in the middle,* can also tell position. For information about using commas with prepositional phrases, see Lesson 19.2, page 491.

Use Transitions

Words and phrases such as *after, on the left,* and *to her right* are called transitions. They show how the details in the descriptions are related. Transitions make the descriptions on page 119 easier to follow. Below is another example. Notice how the description changes when just the transition words are changed.

> In back of the floats marched the drum major.

> In front of the floats marched the drum major.

Transitions are powerful tools. Without them, you just have a list of details—not a description. Transition words can turn the details into vivid images. The chart below shows some additional transitions you can use.

Transitions		
in back of	beside	first
in front of	above	last
to the left of	below	then
to the right of	next	after

MEETING INDIVIDUAL NEEDS — English Language Learners

Listing Transition Words

Students learning English may find it helpful to prepare a list of common transition words that they can refer to as they write. Have students work with more fluent partners to develop two columns entitled *Spatial Transitions* and *Sequence Transitions.* Have students review lists of prepositions for words to include in each list, such as

beside and *to the left.* Then have students look in this or another book for other examples of transitional phrases to write in their journals along with any necessary definitions, context, or sketches that will help them recall the meaning of the English word or phrase.

Descriptive Writing

Describe a Scene

The painting on this page shows a farm. How could you describe it? Start by listing the details. Use your list to write your description.

PURPOSE To order details in a description
AUDIENCE Yourself, later
LENGTH 1–2 paragraphs

WRITING RUBRICS To organize the details in a description, you can

• begin with the details that are at the front

• end with the details that are at the back

• use transitions to tell where objects are located

Louisa Matthiasdottir, *Sheep in Blue Landscape,* 1991

Using Computers

Use a drawing software program to create a graphic organizer. In the graphic organizer, list the details that describe the farm scene. Number the details in the order in which you will use them.

Listening and Speaking

COOPERATIVE LEARNING Write a brief description of an object or place. Then read your description aloud to a small group. Group members should draw a picture of what they hear. Discuss whether it was easy or difficult to draw the object or place and tell why.

Grammar Link

Use prepositional phrases to show location.

Add a prepositional phrase to each sentence to show location.

1. The farm _____ belonged to the Kinsmans.
2. The barn _____ was painted red.
3. The cows stood calmly _____.

See Lesson 14.2, page 417.

3.4 Ordering Descriptive Details **121**

Assess

Evaluation Rubrics

Describe a Scene

When evaluating students' descriptions of scenes, look for

• use of spatial organization from closest to farthest away

• details that add to the clarity of the description

• transition words

See also *Writing Assessment and Evaluation Rubrics.*

Listening and Speaking

Each written response should use details to identify an object or place and may use logical order to present details.

Reteaching

📁 *Composition Reteaching,* p. 23

Enrichment

📁 *Composition Enrichment,* p. 23

📦 *Fine Art Transparencies* 11–15

Close

Encourage students to create a brochure for a recreational or commercial area of their community. The brochure can include a photograph or drawing of the area along with an ordered description. When students are finished with their brochures, invite them to compare their written descriptions. Why did the students choose the perspective they did? What could they do to make their descriptions of the area more accurate?

Grammar Link

Answers

Answers will vary, but some suggestions are given below.

1. on the hill
2. beside the house
3. under the tree

Viewing the Art

Louisa Matthiasdottir, *Sheep in Blue Landscape,* 1991

The rich colors in *Sheep in Blue Landscape* help re-create the serene Icelandic landscape of Louisa Matthiasdottir's birth. This 14-by-21-inch oil-on-canvas painting is held by the Salander-O'Reilly Gallery.

Interpret and Analyze Discuss the effect of the artist's use of the color blue.

Focus

Lesson Overview

Objectives
• To use sensory details based on observation
• To use details to write a description

Skills
• choosing descriptive details; using common and proper adjectives

Critical Thinking
• observing details; visualizing a place; identifying relationships and patterns

Listening and Speaking
• discussing

Bellringer
Daily Language Activity

When students enter the classroom, have this assignment on the board: *List five places you have seen in the last week.*

Grammar Link to the Bellringer

Have students add an adjective to describe each of the places on their lists.

👆 **See also** *Daily Language Practice*

Motivating Activity

The place Eric Garcia describes in the student model is a famous one—the Sierra Nevada mountains. Any place, though, qualifies as a subject for descriptive writing because it is the writer's perceptions that make it memorable to readers. Ask students to name places about which they could write. What are the most memorable details about these places?

Descriptive Writing

LESSON
3.5

Describing a Place

By using sensory details, writers are able to share images and experiences with their readers.

In the model below, Eric Garcia describes a place like the one shown in the photo. Notice how the details help you experience the place as if you were there, too.

> What details does Eric include to appeal to the senses other than sight?

> Details and word choice such as "clean air" and grass "soft like a waterbed" help create the impression of a pleasant and peaceful place.

Student Model

I am up in the Sierra Nevada mountains. I breathe clean air and smell the pine trees. I lie on grass, soft like a waterbed, high green trees around me blocking the sun. The forest animals are all around me making chirping noises. I feed birds and squirrels while I'm on the ground. They seem so peaceful when I am feeding them. When I feed them, they tickle my funny bone.

Eric Garcia, Emperor School
San Gabriel, California

122 Unit 3 Descriptive Writing

Resource Manager

Planning Resources
• *Lesson Plans*

👆 **Transparencies**
• *Bellringer*
• *Daily Language Practice*
• *Fine Art* 11-15
• *Two-Minute Skill Drill*
• *Writing Process* 11-13B

📁 **Other Print Resources**
• *Composition Enrichment,* p. 24
• *Composition Practice,* p. 24
• *Composition Reteaching,* p. 24
• *Cooperative Learning Activities,* pp. 13-18
• *Thinking and Study Skills,* pp. 3, 9, 11, 20, 22
• *Writing Across the Curriculum*

• *Writing Assessment and Evaluation Rubrics*

Explore a Place

Choose a special place to write about. When you describe your own special place, include specific details as Eric did. Without details, readers might think your place is like the picture below—dark and uninteresting. To fill in the details, ask yourself questions.

Vocabulary Tip

Specific nouns and adjectives can help make your description more precise. For more information about adjectives, see Lesson 12.1, page 379.

Questions	Answers
Q. What do I see?	**A.** A crane, some wading birds, jungle trees, and rapids
Q. What do they look like?	**A.** The crane is white. The flock of birds is scarlet. The jungle trees are dark green. The rapids make a waterfall.
Q. What sounds do I hear?	**A.** Water roaring over rocks

Journal Writing

Pick a place that you can observe and describe it. Ask yourself questions to generate details. List the details, and then underline the ones that show your place most clearly.

Teach

Choosing Details

Students who feel uncertain about which impressions or details to choose may benefit from limiting the task. Ask them to think of a place and to list as many details as they can. From the list, have them choose one or two *sight* details. Next, have them choose one or two *sound* details. After choosing the details, they can write sentences describing what they see and hear.

Two-Minute Skill Drill

List these nouns on the board and have students write descriptive adjectives for each.

garage	*meadow*
park	*library*
hilltop	*attic*

See also *Two-Minute Skill Drill Transparencies, 3.5*

Journal Writing Tip

Evaluating Ideas Point out that generating questions and answers is only a first step in creating a vivid description. Good writers choose only the best details for their writing purpose.

Teach

Using the Model

Armstrong Sperry's place description contrasts sharply with that of the previous writer. Mystery and drama replace the peaceful mood in the mountain scene. Encourage students to look at the model and write down specific words and phrases they could use to write about places. **L2**

Descriptive Language

In the Literature Model, point out the simile (comparison of unlike objects using *like* or *as*) "boiled like a witch's cauldron." Ask students what the simile adds to their picture of the scene. Encourage students to use literary devices such as similes in their own descriptive writing. **L3**

Writing for Radio

News reporters for radio or newspapers have to describe a scene more precisely than reporters on television, because a reading or listening audience cannot see a scene as television viewers do. Encourage students to watch a news story on television and to take notes on the setting of the story. Then tell them to write a one- or two-paragraph description that they would hear on the radio or read in the newspaper. **L2**

Additional Resources

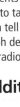

For descriptive **writing prompts**, see *Fine Art Transparencies* 11–15.

Daily Language Practice

Writing Process Transparencies 11–13B
Writing Across the Curriculum
Cooperative Learning Activities, pp. 13–18
Thinking and Study Skills, pp. 3, 9, 11, 20, 22
Composition Practice, p. 24

Descriptive Writing

Describe the Scene

Once you've selected your details, use them to write a draft. What order should you use? Questions like the ones shown below can help you decide.

- Which details go together?

- Where are they located?

- Can you link the details with transitions?

- The rapids are on the right, between the rocks.

- The white crane is rising from the rocks.

- The flock of birds is flying through the dark green jungle.

As you draft your description, think about ways to draw your readers in. You might start by choosing one strong impression of your place. Then choose only those details that help create that impression vividly for your readers. In the model below, the writer describes a jungle river valley.

Presenting Tip

Read your description to a friend. What questions does he or she have about it?

What words help you picture the location of the details?

Words like "witch's cauldron," "heavy wings," "scarlet," and "dark green" create a feeling of mystery and drama.

Literature Model

As the jungle valley broadened, the river became an archipelago [group] of islets [small islands]. To the right a gorge opened up, with rapids cascading between sheer walls of rock. The water boiled like a witch's cauldron. . . . From the rocks a white crane rose on heavy wings; a flock of ibis [tall wading birds] fled in a wedge formation, scarlet against a backdrop of dark green.

Armstrong Sperry, *Thunder Country*

 English Language Learners

Getting the Picture

Students learning English may benefit from the following exercise. Supply students with a picture or photograph of a place. Have students identify and label as many things in the picture as they can. Then have students think of adjectives to describe the items they have labeled. Encourage students to think about what they might see, hear, or feel if they were to visit the place. Students can then write sentences to describe the place in the picture.

3.5 | Writing Activities

Describe a Place

Pick a place that's special, such as a neighborhood basketball court or a quiet corner of the library. Observe your place closely or just think about it. Then write a description of it for a student magazine called *Special Places*.

Try to elaborate by using all the details that make your place special to you. Ask yourself: What colors do I see? What do I smell? What do I hear?

PURPOSE To describe a favorite place accurately
AUDIENCE Readers of a student magazine
LENGTH 2–3 paragraphs

WRITING RUBRICS To use details effectively in a description, you should

- decide which details go together
- order the details to present a clear picture
- use transitions to link ideas

Using Computers

Some word processing programs have a built-in electronic thesaurus. You might use the electronic thesaurus to help you choose interesting nouns and verbs. By carefully choosing your words, you can make your place description more vivid.

Grammar Link

Use adjectives to create clear pictures for readers.

Specific adjectives help to make descriptions vivid and precise. Notice the adjectives Armstrong Sperry uses to modify nouns in the model on page 124.

Add at least one adjective to each sentence below to make the statement clearer and more interesting.

1. The bird flew over the river.
2. The man wrote in his notebook.
3. We hiked on the trails.
4. The air nipped at our noses.
5. The wolf watched over the pups in the den.

See Lesson 12.1, page 379.

Viewing and Representing

In a small group, create a collage of special places. Use pictures from magazines, photographs, or drawings. Each person should tell about the places he or she selected. You may want to choose a picture in the collage as a special place to describe for the writing assignment.

Descriptive Writing

Assess

Evaluation Rubrics

Describe a Place

When evaluating students' descriptions of a place, look for
- carefully organized details
- details in effective order
- appropriate transitions
- awareness of audience

See also *Writing Assessment and Evaluation Rubrics.*

Viewing and Representing

Students' collages should show illustrations from magazines, and possibly photographs and drawings. All students in a group should have contributed.

Reteaching

Composition Reteaching, p. 24

Enrichment

Composition Enrichment, p. 24

Fine Art Transparencies 11–15

Close

Have students read their descriptions aloud to partners. Ask the partners if they could picture the place in their minds based on the description. Discuss in what ways the writing is helpful.

Grammar Link

Answers
Answers will vary, but some suggestions are given below.
1. red-plumed
2. studious
3. rocky
4. frosty
5. wary

Descriptive Adjectives After students have finished, write the first sentence on the board. Underline the nouns and beneath them write students' adjectives. Have students rewrite the sentence using adjectives from the list. Discuss why one adjective may be more descriptive than another. Continue with the other sentences.

Focus

Lesson Overview

Objectives
- To respond to descriptive language used in literature
- To create a descriptive product

Skills
- responding to a description; using details; capitalizing proper nouns

Critical Thinking
- visualizing details; elaborating on an emotional response

Listening and Speaking
- discussing; informal speaking; questioning

Bellringer
Daily Language Activity

When students enter the classroom, have this assignment on the board: *List five places that you would like to visit some day.*

Grammar Link to the Bellringer

Have students check their lists for correct capitalization of proper nouns.

See also *Daily Language Practice*

Motivating Activity

Tell students to freewrite for five minutes, describing the school cafeteria. Ask half the class to describe the negative characteristics of the cafeteria and the other half to describe the positive ones. Then have each side trade papers and write a response to what they read.

Descriptive Writing

WRITING ABOUT LITERATURE

Getting to Know a New Place

*D*escriptive writing can create strong feelings in a reader. Specific details help to set a mood.

Descriptive writing can also bring out new feelings. In the model below, a young city girl finds herself in the woods for the first time. Think about your own feelings as you read Nicholasa Mohr's description.

> Details like "sweet fragrance" and "warm sunlight" create a soft, dreamy feeling.

> How does Nilda feel about this place?

Literature Model

*T*he sun came through the leaves, stems, and petals, streaming down like rows of bright ribbons landing on the dark green earth. . . . Nilda walked over to the flowers and touched them. Inhaling the sweet fragrance, she felt slightly dizzy, almost reeling. She sat down on the dark earth and felt the sun on her face, slipping down her body and over to the shrubs covered with roses. The bright sash of warm sunlight enveloped her and the flowers; she was part of them; they were part of her.

Nicholasa Mohr, *Nilda*

Reading Mohr's description, you might have thought about the warm sun. You might have thought about being dizzy or happy. When you read something, there's no right or wrong way to feel. The same piece of writing can bring out different responses in different people.

Resource Manager

Planning Resources
- *Lesson Plans*

Transparencies
- *Bellringer*
- *Daily Language Practice*
- *Fine Art* 11-15
- *Two-Minute Skill Drill*
- *Writing Process* 11-13B

📂 Other Print Resources
- *Composition Enrichment,* p. 25
- *Composition Practice,* p. 25
- *Composition Reteaching,* p. 25
- *Cooperative Learning Activities,* pp. 13-18
- *Thinking and Study Skills,* p. 9, 12, 22
- *Writing Across the Curriculum*

- *Writing Assessment and Evaluation Rubrics*

Respond to a Description

One way to respond to a place description is with a creative project of your own. To begin, you might choose a place that the description makes you think of.

Once you've chosen your place, you might take some photos of it. With photos you can focus on details that create the feeling of your place. Here two students show photos from their trip to Bandelier National Monument in New Mexico.

Another way to describe your place is by making a map of it and drawing in the details. Below, the students show Bandelier National Monument in a homemade map.

Jenny and Katie Bresee,
George Washington Carver School,
San Francisco, California

Journal Writing

List the most memorable details in the model on page 126. What did they make you think or feel? Write your response in your journal.

Descriptive Writing

Teach

Using the Model

If students have trouble thinking of a place in response to the literature model, let them work with partners so they can first talk about the place. A listener might be able to ask questions that will help the student think of more descriptive details. Then when the student has talked about the place, he or she will find it easier to describe. **L2**

Two-Minute Skill Drill

Write these names on the board. Have students write them, capitalizing them correctly.

new jersey   belgium

eiffel tower   el salvador

lake erie   salt lake city

See also Two-Minute Skill Drill Transparencies, 3.6

Journal Writing Tip

Picturing It Encourage students to think about a place or an experience they have had that the Literature Model reminded them of. Tell students that it is easier to write about thoughts and feelings if they have a place in mind that they can picture.

Teach

Teaching From the Art

If students are creating a brochure about a local place, encourage them to interview people who live or work there, or other students who may have visited there. They can gather information or impressions which will make their brochure more interesting. Encourage students to discuss the effectiveness of the art on the page and to suggest other art they might like to add. **L2**

Additional Resources

For descriptive **writing prompts**, see *Fine Art Transparencies* 11–15.

Daily Language Practice

Writing Process Transparencies 11–13B
Writing Across the Curriculum
Cooperative Learning Activities, pp. 13–18
Thinking and Study Skills, pp. 9, 12, 22
Composition Practice, p. 25

Proofreading Tip
Names of places are proper nouns and always start with capital letters. For more information about proper nouns, see Lesson 9.1, page 319.

Do a Double Take

You can create a travel brochure by adding captions to your photos and map. Travel brochures describe places that people might like to visit. To create your own brochure, concentrate on the details of your place. Which ones might interest other people? Here is Jenny and Katie's travel brochure for Bandelier National Monument.

travel brochure

When you enter Bandelier National Monument it's a whole other world. It's like going back in time. There are cliff dwellings, ruins, rivers, streams, and even a bat cave.

When early humans came to Bandelier, they found that the small caves that dotted the cliff face made excellent homes. Inside the caves, the air is musty and cool like air conditioning.

The creek that runs through Bandelier is the Rito de los Frijoles. Lots of plants and animals depend on the water from the creek. You can see skunks, rabbits, mice, birds, bats, deer, coyotes a mountain lions come to dr at the Rito de los Frijoles.

Trail
Road
Rito de los Frijoles
Rio Grande
Cliff Dwellings
Valley Ruin

MEETING INDIVIDUAL NEEDS

English Language Learners

Writing Names of Places

For their travel brochures, students may want to choose a place from their country of origin to describe. Point out that sometimes places and names do not have English translations. Have students write their descriptions with out worrying about the translations. When they have finished writing, have them circle the words or phrases they are not sure of and look them up in a dictionary or atlas.

Write a Travel Brochure

Create your own travel brochure. The purpose of the brochure is to get people to visit the place that is described. Plan to include at least two photos, drawings, or maps in your brochure. Then describe your place in writing.

PURPOSE To create a travel brochure
AUDIENCE Vacationers
LENGTH 3–4 paragraphs

WRITING RUBRICS To write a description of a place for a travel brochure, you should

- freewrite to think of a place to describe
- list details that tell what's special about the place
- include your own feelings about the place
- choose facts that will interest your readers

Using Computers

Some word processing programs offer a page-layout option. Using this option can help make your travel brochure look like the real thing. With page layout, you can design and view your brochure on screen. You can decide where to put text and captions and where to leave space for photos and maps. Then, after you print, you can put the photos and maps in the blank spaces.

Grammar Link

Capitalize proper nouns.

The names of specific people and places are proper nouns, which always begin with a capital letter. Note the proper nouns Jenny and Katie Bresee used in their travel brochure on page 128.

Write the sentences below. Then revise them, adding capital letters as necessary.

1. The island of puerto rico is near Florida.
2. The island's capital city is san juan.
3. The island is part of a group called the west indies.
4. Puerto rico is bounded on the north by the atlantic ocean.
5. To the south lies the caribbean sea.

See Lesson 9.1, page 319.

Listening and Speaking

PRESENTING Take turns reading your travel brochures in a small group. Tell about your map and pictures. Read your captions. Other group members should take notes. They should jot down words that make the place easy to picture and that create images that stay in their minds. After each reading, share ideas about your descriptions.

Descriptive Writing

Assess

Evaluation Rubrics

Write a Travel Brochure

When evaluating students' travel brochures, look for

- use of descriptive details
- emotional response to the place being described
- use of interesting facts
- clarity of description
- effective use of graphics

See also *Writing Assessment and Evaluation Rubrics.*

Listening and Speaking

Evaluate listening students' skills at identifying each speaker's use of details.

Reteaching

📁 *Composition Reteaching,* p. 25

Enrichment

📁 *Composition Enrichment,* p. 25

🖼 *Fine Art Transparencies* 11–15

Close

Discuss how descriptive writing can bring about an emotional response in readers. Have students exchange travel brochures and write a response to the descriptive writing.

Grammar Link

Answers

1. Puerto Rico
2. San Juan
3. West Indies
4. Puerto Rico, Atlantic Ocean
5. Caribbean Sea

Proper Nouns Have each student make a list of common nouns that refer to places, such as *river, stadium,* and *canyon.* Students can then switch papers and next to each common noun write a proper noun such as *Hudson River, Astrodome,* and *Grand Canyon.*

Focus

Lesson Overview

Objective

- To use writing process skills to write a detailed description

Skills

- using the five stages of the writing process: prewriting, drafting, revising, editing/proofreading, and publishing/presenting

Critical Thinking

- recalling; choosing sensory details; visualizing

Listening and Speaking

- discussing

🔔 Bellringer
Daily Language Activity

When students enter the classroom, have this assignment on the board: *Think back to your earliest possible memory. What do you remember? Write several sentences and include specific details.*

Grammar Link to the Bellringer

Have students underline the descriptive words they used in the Bellringer activity. Could they replace any of them with more vivid words?

📝 **See also** *Daily Language Practice*

Descriptive Writing

Descriptive Writing

In the preceding lessons, you've learned how to paint pictures with words. You've also had the chance to use details as you wrote descriptions of places, animals, and things. Now it's time to put together what you learned. In this lesson, you will describe something memorable in your life.

Assignment

Context

An artist friend wants you to write a description of something memorable in your life. Afterward, your friend plans to paint a detailed picture based on your description.

Purpose

To inspire an artist with a memorable description

Audience

An artist

Length

1 page

WRITING *Online*

Visit the *Writer's Choice* Web site at **writerschoice. glencoe.com** for additional writing prompts.

The following pages can help you plan and write your description. Read through them. Then refer to them as you need to, but don't be tied down by them. Remember that you're in charge of your own writing process.

Resource Manager

Planning Resources
- *Lesson Plans*

📝 **Transparencies**
- *Bellringer*
- *Daily Language Practice*
- *Writing Process* 11-13B

📂 **Other Print Resources**
- *Composition Enrichment*, p. 25
- *Composition Practice*, p. 25
- *Composition Reteaching*, p. 25
- *Grammar Workbook, Lesson* 93
- *Thinking and Study Skills*, pp. 9, 12, 22
- *Writing Assessment and Evaluation Rubrics*

💾 **Software**
- *Writer's Assistant*

🖥 **Web Sites**
- *writerschoice.glencoe.com*
- *lit.glencoe.com*

Writing Process in Action

Prewriting

You know so many people, places, and things. How do you choose a subject to describe? You might try exploring the possibilities through prewriting. The options on this page suggests several methods of prewriting. You can freewrite, as the writer has in the example here. You can also build a cluster of details or brainstorm for a list of impressions. You can even try combining approaches.

Option A
Make a cluster of details.

Option B
Brainstorm for a list of impressions.

Option C
Freewrite for ideas.

> My grandmother cooks my favorite spaghetti sauce. It smells of peppers and garlic. Her blue apron gets all stained. She walks in soft shoes that make flopping sounds. The kitchen is hot from the stove.

As you explore through prewriting, remind yourself to use all five senses. Try to discover specific details for each sense. Think about the small details that make things special.

Now that you've chosen a subject, think about what details an artist would need to paint it. What order of details would be easiest to follow? What impressions do you want to give your reader?

Remember that there's no right or wrong prewriting strategy to use. Stick with whatever works best for you.

Drafting

While you draft, think about turning your prewriting into a clear, detailed description. Don't worry about your grammar, spelling, and punctuation at this point. Just let your ideas flow in an order that makes sense to you now. Try to make your reader understand what it's like to be there, up close to your subject. In the following model, Michael Dorris vividly describes a young girl's sense of wonder as she discovers the details of her own face reflected in her father's eyes.

TIME

For more about generating ideas for details, see **TIME Facing the Blank Page,** page 90.

Drafting Tip

For more information about gathering and recording effective details, see Lessons 3.2–3.3, pages 110–117.

Teach

Prewriting

Developing Ideas for Descriptive Writing

Remind students to consider an ordinary event when looking for a memorable experience to write about, like the example of the grandmother's spaghetti sauce on the notebook on page 131. A memorable experience might take only a few minutes or might be part of a series of events. What is important is that the experience is vivid in the writer's mind, as if it occurred just yesterday. **L2**

Choosing a Subject

Suggest students look through family photos or photos from magazines, choose photos they are in or that they can imagine they are in, and list the details. Then they can write descriptions using their lists. **L1**

Additional Resources

📂 *Thinking and Study Skills,* pp. 3, 5, 12

Drafting

Deciding What to Include

Students may have difficulty choosing what to emphasize and what to omit from their descriptions. Encourage them to focus on what made this experience memorable for them and how they can best describe it so that readers can experience it themselves. **L2**

Teach

Revising

Peer Editing

Students can work in writing conferences with peer editors before they revise their work. Suggest that peer editors answer these questions.

- Does the writer use a variety of sensory details?
- Does the writer use descriptive words to recall memories?
- Are transitions used appropriately?
- Does the writing help me to experience what the writer experienced? **L2**

Editing/Proofreading

Peer Editing

After students have edited their own work, have them edit another student's writing. Remind them to refer to the Editing/Proofreading Checklist on student page 133. **L2**

Publishing/Presenting

Before students present their descriptive writing, discuss how to prepare their papers for publication. Emphasize the importance of the final draft and that it must be neatly done.

Additional Resources

Writing Process Transparencies 11–13B

Thinking and Study Skills, pp. 3, 5, 12

Composition Practice, p. 29

Grammar Workbook, Lessons 98-105

Descriptive Writing

Literature Model

I leaned forward, stared into the dark brown circles, and it was like diving into the deepest pools. Suddenly I saw two tiny girls looking back. Their faces were clear, their brows straight as canoes, and their chins as narrow and clean as lemons. As I watched, their mouths grew wide. They were pretty.

Michael Dorris, *Morning Girl*

Revising Tip

For more information about ordering details and using transitions, see Lesson 3.4, pages 118–121.

Question A
Have I used all my senses?

Question B
Are my details vivid?

Question C
Have I made effective use of transitions?

Revising

To begin revising, read over your draft to make sure that what you've written fits your purpose and audience. Then have a writing conference. Read your draft to a partner or small group. Use your audience's reactions to help you evaluate your work.

> i like hiding under the kitchen table while
>   Beneath the table
> my grandmother cooks spaghetti, I can smell
>   simmering
> the garlic and green peppers ~~cooking~~ and watch
>   r
> my grandmother stiring the sauce. Her apron
>   red
> always gets covered with these tiny spatters.
> She doesn't mind, though. She's too busy testing
>   padding   soft
> the noodles or ~~going to~~ the sink in her house
> slippers.

Enrichment and Extension

Producing Descriptive Writing

Students may appreciate suggestions for other opportunities to produce descriptive writing:

- Have students look through an art history book for fine art representing a moment in history. Encourage them to write a descriptive paragraph of the event based on the artist's depiction.

- Brainstorm with students ways they can use their expertise in descriptive writing: the most memorable person I ever met; a natural wonder; the funniest thing that ever happened to me.

Editing/Proofreading

Now's the time to check for the standard conventions—grammar, spelling, and mechanics. At this stage you'll add the finishing touches to the word picture you've painted.

To go with your description, you might also draw a picture. By sketching the same details you used in your writing, you can make your images even easier to imagine.

Use the checklist at the right to help you during proofreading. It's best to focus on one question at a time.

Publishing/Presenting

This is the moment you've worked toward—sharing the description you wrote for your artist friend. As you've probably discovered, writing can be a very satisfying way to describe the world around you. By writing, you can tell others about all the special details you notice every day.

Editing/Proofreading Checklist

- Have I used descriptive adjectives and action verbs?
- Do my transitions help the reader?
- Do my subjects and verbs agree?
- Have I used proper punctuation and capitalization?
- Is every word spelled correctly?

Proofreading Tip

For proofreading symbols, see page 72 or 267. The computer can help you proofread. Use its spelling checker and grammar checker features.

Journal Writing

Reflect on your writing process experience. Answer these questions in your journal: What do you like best about your description? What was the hardest part of writing it? What did you learn in your writing conference? What new thing have you learned as a writer?

Assess

Evaluation Rubrics

Use the following questions to evaluate the students' finished writing. Make sure that

- all five senses are used in describing the scene
- details are carefully described
- transitions clearly show the order of the details
- careful attention is given to grammar, spelling, and mechanics
- an artist could paint a scene that comes close to the written description

See also *Writing Assessment and Evaluation Rubrics.*

Reteaching
📁 *Composition Reteaching,* p. 29

Enrichment
📁 *Composition Enrichment,* p. 29

Journal Writing Tip

Using Sensory Details Students may want to ask themselves whether they have used all five senses to develop their descriptions. Would their words inspire an artist?

Close

Have students write a paragraph explaining what they think is the most important stage in the writing process and why they feel this way.

Cultural Connections

History

People's memories have been used to reconstruct the history of many groups that have been ignored by history texts. These groups include former enslaved persons, immigrants, Appalachian women, Native Americans, and so forth. Students may wish to read some oral history anthologies, such as the Foxfire series, or the many and varied works for young people by Milton Meltzer.

Literature Model

Literature Model

About the Author

Michael Dorris (1945–1999) was born in Washington state. His father was a Modoc. The Modoc are a Native American people who live in the Pacific Northwest. Dorris wrote largely about the lives and concerns of Native Americans in books for young readers such as *Guests* and *Sees Behind Trees.* He taught in the Department of Native American Studies at Dartmouth College.

Focus

Lesson Overview

Objectives

• To examine a professional writer's use of descriptive detail
• To analyze a writer's description of characters
• To write a personal essay that describes self

Skills

• monitoring comprehension, summarizing, predicting

Critical Thinking

• interpreting

Listening and Speaking

• discussing

🔔 Bellringer
Daily Language Activity

When students enter the classroom, have this assignment on the board: *Pretend you are writing to someone you have never met. In a few sentences, describe what you look like.*

✍ **See also** *Daily Language Practice*

Motivating Activity

Ask students to consider how much of their description in the Bellringer is based on what they see in a mirror. Have them imagine themselves in a time before mirrors existed. How might they determine what they look like?

• Michael Dorris •

from

MORNING GIRL

Award-winning author Michael Dorris describes the world of Morning Girl— the Bahamas in 1492, shortly before Columbus's arrival. In this excerpt from the novel, Morning Girl seeks her family's help in learning what her own face looks like. As you read, pay special attention to Dorris's descriptions and the impressions and images they create. Then try the activities in Linking Writing and Literature on page 140.

The water is never still enough. Just when I can almost see my face, when my eyes and my nose and my mouth are about to settle into a picture I can remember, a fish rises for air or a leaf drops to the surface of the pond or Star Boy tosses a pebble into my reflection and I break into shining pieces. It makes no sense to him that I'm curious about what people see when they look at me.

"They see *you*," he said, as if that answered my question. We were searching for ripe fruit on the trees behind our house.

"But what *is* me?" I asked him. "I wouldn't recognize myself unless I

134 Unit 3 Descriptive Writing

Resource Manager

Planning Resources
• *Lesson Plans*

✍ **Transparencies**
• *Bellringer*
• *Daily Language Practice*
• *Fine Art 11–15*

📁 **Other Print Resources**
• *Thinking and Study Skills*, pp. 3, 5, 6, 12
• *Writing Assessment and Evaluation Rubrics*

💻 **Web Sites**
• *writerschoice.glencoe.com*
• *lit.glencoe.com*

Literature Model

Pablo Picasso, *Études*, 1920

Literature Model **135**

Active Reading Strategies

Monitor Comprehension Ask students how Morning Girl is trying to see her face as the story begins on page 134. *(She is trying to look at her reflection on the surface of a pond.)* Ask: "Why doesn't she just look in a mirror?" *(The story takes place in the Bahamas in 1492. There were no mirrors there at that time.)*

Critical Thinking

Interpret Ask students what Star Boy means when he tells his sister, "They see you." *(He means they see the same person he sees when he looks at his sister.)*

Viewing the Art

Pablo Picasso, *Études*, 1920
Many people consider Pablo Picasso to be the greatest painter of the 1900s. One reason for this evaluation is that he constantly developed his art in response to the world's changing conditions. Picasso is also famous for his sculpture, drawings, graphics, and ceramics.

Active Reading Strategies

Summarize Explain to students that when they summarize what they read, they restate, briefly and in their own words, the most important ideas or events of a piece of writing. Ask students to summarize how Morning Girl compares her face to that of her mother. *(They compare chins, lips, eyebrows, noses, and ears.)*

Descriptive Writing

Literature Model

was sitting on the bottom of a quiet pool, looking up at me looking down."

"You are . . . *you*." He lost his patience and walked away to find his friend Red Feathers.

But what did "you" mean? I knew my hands very well. I study them when I trim my nails with the rough edge of a broken shell, making them smooth and flat. I could spread my fingers and press them into wet sand to see the shape they leave. Once I tried to do that with my head, but all I got was a big shallow hole and dirty hair.

I knew the front of my body, the bottoms of my feet. I knew the color of my arms—tan as the inside of a yam after the air has dried it—and if I stretched my tongue I could see its pink tip.

"Tell me about my face," I asked Mother one day when we were walking along the beach.

She stopped, turned to me in confusion. "What *about* your face?"

"Is it long and wrinkled, like Grandmother's, or round as a coconut, like Star Boy's? Are my eyes wise like yours or ready to laugh like Father's? Are my teeth as crooked as the trunks of palm trees?"

Mother cocked her head to the side and made lines in her forehead. "I don't think I've ever looked at you that way," she said. "To me you've

always been yourself, different from anyone else."

"But I want to *know*," I begged her.

> ❝ *'Tell me about my face,' I asked Mother one day . . .* ❞

Mother nodded. "I remember that feeling. Try this."

She took my hand and guided it to my neck. "Touch," she told me. "Very softly. No, close your eyes and think with your fingers. Now compare." She placed my other hand on her face, the face I know better than any other.

I traced the line of her chin. Mine was smaller, pointier. I followed her lips with one thumb, my own with the other. Hers seemed fuller.

"Your mouth is wider," I cried, unhappy with myself.

"That's because I'm smiling, Morning Girl."

And suddenly my mouth was wide, too, and my cheeks were hills on either side.

Next I found the lashes of our eyes, then moved above them. Even without watching I could see the curved shape of Mother's dark brows. They made her look surprised at everything, surprised and delighted.

"Mine are straight," I said.

136 Unit 3 Descriptive Writing

Critical Thinking

Interpret

Tell students that interpreting is a way of using their own understanding of the world to discover meaning in a text and that discovering meaning is crucial to understanding. Encourage students to ask themselves questions about the text, such as "How can I use my knowledge of myself and of the world to figure out what the author is really saying here?" and "What larger idea might this passage be about?"

Practice Ask students to think about Star Boy's pronouncement, "You are . . . *you*." What is he trying to tell his sister? *(that everyone is an individual, a unique person)*

Literature Model

Paul Gauguin, *Tahitian Women*, or *On the Beach*, 1891

Descriptive Writing

"Like your grandfather's."

He had always looked tired. I liked surprised better.

"Now, here." Mother cupped my fingers around the tip of my nose. I could feel the breath rush in and out of my nostrils. I could smell the fruit I had picked with Star Boy.

Finally we moved to the ears, and in the dark they were as delicate and complicated as the inside of a spiral[1] shell, but soft.

"Our ears are the same," I told Mother, and she felt with her own hand, testing and probing every part.

"You're right." She sounded as pleased as I was.

I opened my eyes and memorized her ears. At least *that* part I would now recognize.

---

1 **spiral** (spī'rəl) curving, winding

Literature Model **137**

Viewing the Art

Paul Gauguin, *Tahitian Women, or On the Beach*, 1891
Born in France, Paul Gauguin traveled to the South Pacific, settling in Tahiti, where he produced colorful canvases of the people and the environment. The style in which he painted is called *synthetism,* which emphasized simple forms and used vivid colors. Both elements are part of the quiet scene in this painting done in 1891, which measures 27 by 35 1/2 inches and hangs in the Louvre in Paris, France.

6+1 Trait® Writing

Voice Direct students' attention to the figurative language Morning Girl uses to describe herself when her mother asks, "Do you know Morning Girl any better?" Ask: "How does the language Morning Girl uses reflect her personality?" (*She is frustrated sometimes and is insecure about how she appears to the rest of the world. Still, the language also reveals that she has a sense of humor.*)

Active Reading Strategies

Summarize Ask students to summarize what happens when Morning Girl encounters her father fixing his fishing lance. (*Morning Girl wonders why people find it strange that she wants to know how she looks. Her father tells her to look into his eyes, where she sees herself reflected. She sees that she is pretty, and her father says that her reflection will always be in his eyes.*)

Descriptive Writing

Literature Model

"Did this help you?" she asked me. "Do you know Morning Girl any better?"

"Oh yes," I said. "She has a chin like a starfish and brows like white clouds on the horizon. Her nose works. Her cheeks swell into mountains when she smiles. The only thing right about her is her ears."

> **"** *Do you know Morning Girl any better?* **"**

Mother covered her mouth, the way she does when she laughs and doesn't want anyone to stare. "That's my Morning Girl," she said. "That's her exactly."

The next day, as I was getting up and Star Boy was about to go to sleep on his mat, I leaned close to him.

"What does my chin look like?" I demanded.

He blinked, frowned, made his eyes small while he decided. "A starfish," he finally said.

I was very worried until I saw he was making a joke.

"I heard Mother telling Father," he confessed when I pinched him. "But

---

2 juts out (jutz out) sticks out

I don't know." He rubbed his arm, showed me where I had made it turn red. "To me it looks like the end of the rock that juts out[2] into the ocean near the north end of the island. The one they call 'The Giant Digging Stick.'"

"You don't have to be curious about *your* face," I whispered. "All you have to do is wait for a jellyfish to float on shore and get stranded when the tide leaves. Sometimes I see one and I think it's you, buried in the sand up to your neck."

When I went outside, Father was sitting on a log fixing a shark's tooth to use as a hook at the end of his fishing lance.

"Who is this?" he asked the lance. "Who is this with my wife's ears stuck onto the side of her head?"

> **"** *Why should my own face be a secret from me?* **"**

"You laugh at me, too," I said. "But why is it so strange to want to know what everyone else already knows? Why should my own face be a secret from me?"

"There *is* a way," Father said kindly, and motioned me to stand beside him. He knelt down so that we would

---

Compare and Contrast

Comparing Selections

Finding how literature selections are alike and different will deepen students' understanding of the selections. Compare and contrast the excerpts from *Morning Girl* and *Coast to Coast* (pp. 82–86) by saying: "Young girls are the main characters in both selections, and both girls want something. The two girls differ in what they want. Morning Girl wants to know how she looks to other people. Birch wants to get her grandfather to take her in his airplane."

Practice Ask students to write a paragraph identifying other similarities and differences between *Morning Girl* and *Coast to Coast*. (*Examples:* Morning Girl *takes place in 1492 and has a first-person narrator.* Coast to Coast *is set in the near present and has a third-person narrator.* Morning Girl *seeks help from her parents; Birch needs her grandfather's help. Birch wants "to get away from this world."* Morning Girl *is satisfied with her world.*)

be the same size. "Look into my eyes," he told me. "What do you see?"

I leaned forward, stared into the dark brown circles, and it was like diving into the deepest pools. Suddenly I saw two tiny girls looking back. Their faces were clear, their brows straight as canoes, and their chins as narrow and clean as lemons.

As I watched, their mouths grew wide. They were pretty.

"Who are they?" I couldn't take my eyes off those strange new faces. "Who are these pretty girls who live inside your head?"

"They are the answer to your question," Father said. "And they are always here when you need to find them."

Active Reading Strategies

Predict Ask: "Will Morning Girl meet the challenges of life successfully? Why?" *(Sample response: Yes. This excerpt shows her to be a determined girl developing a positive self-image and a strong sense of self-worth. Also, she is being taught life's lessons by sensitive, wise parents.)*

Additional Resources

For descriptive **writing prompts**, see *Fine Art Transparencies* 11–15.

Thinking and Study Skills, pp. 3, 5, 6, 12

6+1 Trait® Writing

Voice

Tell students that *voice* is the presence of the writer in the language he or she uses. Every writer has a unique, distinctive voice, or style of writing. Voice can be conveyed through the words the writer uses and the way they are structured in sentences. In works of fiction, like the excerpt from *Morning Girl*, voice is often found in the speech patterns of the characters.

Practice Ask students to write two brief descriptions of someone or something. Tell them to try projecting a clearly different voice in each description by modifying word choice, sentence structure, and overall style.

6+1 Trait® is a registered trademark of Northwest Regional Educational Laboratory, which does not endorse this product.

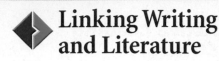

Linking Writing and Literature

Assess

Evaluation Rubrics

◆ Talk About Reading

Possible responses to the questions:

1. Answers will vary, but most students will understand that physical features are just one aspect of a person's complete self.
2. He is telling Morning Girl she can see herself reflected literally in his eyes and figuratively in his love for her.
3. Mother and Father are older and wiser than Morning Girl and Star Boy. This is signaled by their calm, patient speech— a contrast to the insistent, impetuous speech of their daughter and son.
4. It is through this conversation that Morning Girl learns that she is much more than just what she looks like. Students should understand that the conversation allows the writer to show the reader the main idea rather than just telling the reader about it.

◆ Write About Reading

The personal essay should do the following:
- introduce the reader to the person being described
- include vivid details
- include descriptive nouns and modifiers
- communicate a clear, coherent impression

Close

Have students write a brief physical description of a person, using some of the techniques used in *Morning Girl*. Ask volunteers to share their writing.

Literature Model

Descriptive Writing

Linking Writing and Literature

◆ Collect Your Thoughts

Think about Morning Girl's desire to know what she looks like. Do you think she's just being vain, or is she expressing some deeper desire? In your journal, jot down some thoughts about Morning Girl's quest.

◆ Talk About Reading

Discuss the excerpt from *Morning Girl* with a small group. Ask one person to lead the group's discussion and another to take notes. Use the following question to guide you.

1. **Connect to Your Life** Unlike Morning Girl, you can see yourself in mirrors, photographs, videos, and so on. But is the person you *see* the person you *are?* Why?

2. **Critical Thinking: Interpret** Morning Girl asks, "Who are these pretty girls who live inside your head?" What does her father mean when he replies, "They are the answer to your question, and they are always here when you need to find them."

3. **6+1 Trait®: Voice** How does the author's voice change when Morning Girl's mother or father is speaking? What signals this change?

4. **Connect to Your Writing** Why is Morning Girl's conversation with her father important to the main idea of the excerpt? What lesson does this teach you about your own writing?

◆ Write About Reading

Personal Essay Like Morning Girl, everyone wonders at some time or another who they really are and how other people see them. In a personal essay, describe who you are. How do you see yourself? How do others—your family, teachers, friends, new acquaintances—see you? Draw a picture of yourself with words.

Focus on Voice. Voice is the authentic self of the writer or a character expressed through words. As you write about who you are, choose language and sentence structures that express your true voice.

For more information on voice and the 6+1 Trait® model, see **Writing and Research Handbook,** pages 682–684.

6+1 Trait® is a registered trademark of Northwest Regional Educational Laboratory, which does not endorse this product.

140 Unit 3 Descriptive Writing

🌐 Cultural Connections

History

The home of Morning Girl and Star Boy is the present-day island of San Salvador, the landing site of Columbus's first voyage. Morning Girl and her family are Arawak, a people who lived on many Caribbean islands and along the Amazon in South America. The Caribbean Arawaks were destroyed by disease and slavery after the exploration of the Americas. The only remaining Arawaks live in Brazil, along the Xingu River.

UNIT 3 Review

Reflecting on the Unit

Summarize what you learned in this unit by answering the following questions.

❶ What are some strategies for observing and noting details before you write?

❷ What kinds of details can help give the reader a vivid picture?

❸ How can you organize the details of your writing so that they have a clear order?

❹ How can you draw readers in and help them share your experiences and feelings?

Adding to Your Portfolio

CHOOSE A SELECTION FOR YOUR PORTFOLIO Look over the descriptive writing you did for this unit. Choose one completed piece for your portfolio. The piece you choose should show some or all of the following:

- a general impression, followed by details that create that impression
- descriptive details gathered by using all the senses
- a logical way of ordering of details that is clear to the reader
- transitions that are used to connect details

REFLECT ON YOUR CHOICE Attach a note to the piece you chose, explaining briefly why you chose it and what you learned from writing it.

SET GOALS How can you improve your writing? What skill will you focus on the next time you write?

Writing Across the Curriculum

MAKE AN ART CONNECTION Find a photograph of an outdoor scene in the country, and compare it with the painting on page 121. Study details such as light and shadow, shapes, and color. Then describe both the painting and the photograph, and tell how each one makes you feel.

Review **141**

Review

Reflecting on the Unit

You may have students respond to Reflecting on the Unit in writing or through discussion.

Writing Across the Curriculum

Remind students that making notes of first impressions and observing carefully help in gathering details. Point out that adding sensory details makes descriptive writing more interesting.

Adding to Your Portfolio

Encourage students to keep the checklist from this page to use whenever they complete descriptive writing activities. Tell them they can apply the checklist to previously written works in order to improve them. Finally, encourage students to have friends or relatives read their descriptive pieces to see whether there is anything still unclear about the descriptions.

Portfolio Evaluation

If you grade the individual portfolio selections, you may want to award two marks—one each for content and form. Explain your assessment criteria before students make their selections. Commend

- experimentation with creative prewriting techniques
- clear, concise writing in which the main idea, audience, and purpose are evident
- successful revisions
- work that shows a flair for language

✔ ASSESSMENT OPTIONS

📁 *Tests with Answer Key and Rubrics*
Unit 3 Choice A Test, p. 9
Unit 3 Choice B Test, p. 10
Unit 3 Composition Objective Test,
    pp. 11-12

💾 *Testmaker*
Unit 3 Choice A Test
Unit 3 Choice B Test
Unit 3 Composition Objective Test

You may wish to administer one of these tests as a mastery test.

📺 *Mindjogger Videoquizzes*

Narrative Writing

Viewing the Art

A photograph of yellow roses may convey freshness and abundance. The sunlight dappling the roses may suggest the warmth and energy of spring or summer.

Interpret and Analyze Use the following questions for discussion:

- How might a rose bush surprise you? When might it not suggest "freshness and abundance"?

- What kind of story might come from an encounter with yellow roses?

Discussing the Quotation

John Gardner creates a mood of vitality and surprise in the quotation from his short story "Dragon, Dragon." Students can find the entire story in Course 1 of *Glencoe Literature: The Reader's Choice,* beginning on page 640. Before referring students to the story, ask what they picture after reading the quotation. How does reading about such a fantastic occurrence affect them? Are they interested in learning more about such peculiar circumstances?

Writing Prompt Have students imitate the playful and amusing sound of Gardner's writing as they narrate a quick succession of events that occurred at a sporting or social event. Encourage them to use a friendly, engaging tone in their writing.

> "*Suddenly, to everyone's surprise, the queen turned into a rosebush.*"

—John Gardner, "Dragon, Dragon"

142

Resource Manager

Planning Resources
- *Lesson Plans*
- *Block Scheduling*

📖 Transparencies
- *Bellringer*
- *Daily Language Practice*
- *Fine Art*

- *Two-Minute Skill Drill*
- *Writing Process*

📁 Other Print Resources
- *Composition Enrichment*
- *Composition Practice*
- *Composition Reteaching*
- *Cooperative Learning Activities*

- *Glencoe Literature Library*
- *Grammar and Composition Handbook*
- *Grammar Workbook*
- *Listening and Speaking Activities*
- *Research Paper and Report Writing*
- *Sentence-Combining Practice*
- *Tests with Answer Key and Rubrics*

Narrative Writing

143

Objectives

- To analyze published examples and to use them as a model for writing
- To learn about elements of real-life story-telling and to create a narrative using real-life occurrences
- To identify and use time order and transition words to help narrative flow
- To gain an understanding of dialogue and to use dialogue to enhance a narrative
- To learn about and master details of narrative writing

✔ ASSESSMENT OPTIONS

📁 *Tests with Answer Key and Rubrics*
Unit 4 Choice A Test, p.13
Unit 4 Choice B Test, p. 14
Unit 4 Composition Objective Test, pp. 15–16

💾 *Testmaker*
Unit 4 Choice A Test
Unit 4 Choice B Test
Unit 4 Composition Objective Test

You may wish to administer either the Unit 4 Choice A Test or the Unit 4 Choice B Test as a pretest.

Key to Ability Levels

L1 Level 1 activities are within the basic ability range of students.

L2 Level 2 activities are within the ability range of average students.

L3 Level 3 activities are more challenging activities.

- *Thinking and Study Skills*
- *Writing Across the Curriculum*
- *Writing Assessment and Evaluation Rubrics*
- *Writing in the Real World*

📼Video
- *MindJogger Videoquizzes*

💾 Software
- *Presentation Plus!*
- *Revising with Style*
- *Testmaker*
- *Writer's Assistant*

🖥Web Sites
- *writerschoice.glencoe.com*
- *lit.glencoe.com*

Focus

Lesson Overview

Objectives
- To explore how narrative writing can tell the story of a person's life
- To recognize characteristics of good narrative writing

Skills
- identifying details about a person; using quotations correctly

Critical Thinking
- synthesizing; identifying the main idea; recalling; summarizing; making inferences

Listening and Speaking
- discussing; interviewing; questioning

🔔 Bellringer
Daily Language Activity

When students come into the classroom, have this assignment on the board: *List five to ten people you admire. (They can be people you know personally or only know about; they can be people who are living or historical figures.)*

Grammar Link to the Bellringer

Remind students that certain words are always capitalized—names, for example. Ask students what other words require capitalization. Point out that the first word in a complete quotation is capitalized.

👆 **See also** *Daily Language Practice*

Motivating Activity

Have each student contribute one name from his or her list for the Bellringer assignment, and write the names on the board. Then call on volunteers to state briefly why they admire the person they named. Try to get students to refer to specific details when describing what they admire about the person.

Narrative Writing (sidebar tab)

Writing in the Real World

MEDIA Connection
Biography

A good biography satisfies our natural curiosity about the lives of other people. A biography may be short, such as a personality profile in a newspaper or a magazine. Or, it may be book-length, such as Virginia Hamilton's biography of W. E. B. Du Bois, a great civil rights leader and educator. The following excerpt opens Hamilton's Du Bois biography.

from W. E. B. Du Bois: A Biography

By Virginia Hamilton

Dr. William Edward Burghardt Du Bois lay dying in the city of Accra, Ghana, on the coast of West Africa. He was the black man who, with obvious love, had called all black people "my people." The age-old fight for equality waged by blacks everywhere had been "his" battle for more than half a century, and winning it would have been the greatest achievement of his life. For years William Du Bois had led "his" people in their protest struggle for liberty; now he lay dying far away from America, the country of his birth.

Life flickered and flamed, then faltered, in the ninety-five-year-old Dr. Du Bois. He had moments of consciousness throughout the solemn evening, and he was told that all was well in America. Back home it was the eve of a monumental gathering. Blacks and whites by the thousands were preparing to march on Washington, D.C., the next day. Every step they took would lead them closer to the freedom of which the Doctor had dreamed. Every song they sang would speak of justice, which he had worked so hard to make a reality.

Twenty minutes before midnight, on August 27, 1963, Dr. W. E. B. Du Bois died. The following day nearly half a million Americans carried out the largest protest demonstration ever seen in the United States. In the songs and slogans of the thousands on the move was the courageous spirit for which the Doctor had strived in the past.

144 Unit 4 Narrative Writing

Resource Manager

Planning Resources
- *Lesson Plans*

👆 Transparencies
- *Bellringer*
- *Daily Language Practice*
- *Writing Process* 14–16B

📁 Other Print Resources
- *Cooperative Learning Activities,* pp. 19–24
- *Thinking and Study Skills,* p. 9
- *Writing Assessment and Evaluation Rubrics*
- *Writing in the Real World,* pp. 13–16

A Writer's Process

Prewriting
Building a Story

Choosing the subject for her biography was not difficult for Virginia Hamilton. Her interest in Dr. Du Bois had sprouted many years earlier. Her father often read stories aloud that were written by Du Bois. Hamilton recalls, "I didn't know the significance of it at the time. I just knew that Du Bois was someone my father greatly admired." Later, as a young woman, Hamilton heard Du Bois speak in her hometown of Yellow Springs, Ohio. His eloquence impressed her, and the interest in her future biographical subject grew.

Hamilton published *W. E. B. Du Bois: A Biography* in 1972. Researching and writing about Du Bois's long life—he lived to be ninety-five—took Hamilton about five years. By the end of the research phase, Hamilton had collected a huge number of facts. Now she needed to "find the story." She recalls, "The material itself began to speak to me for him."

Organizing the information was a big task, but Hamilton tried to keep it simple. She started with the most basic information—what she calls "the bare bones." Hamilton explains, "You've got all this material, all these facts, when you do a biography. All the dates in the world! And you say, 'How am I going to do this?' Well, the way you do it is you start with the beginning. You start with, this man was born, or this man died, and you go from there."

Drafting
Making It Real

A biography is a narrative that makes a real person come alive through words. Like any other narrative, a biography must tell an engaging story. Hamilton is very much aware of this. "I'm strongly plot-oriented," she says. "I try to represent original ideas—and good stories."

To advance the plot, Hamilton quotes her subject as much as possible. She knows that readers want to hear the person's own words. Hamilton believes strongly that biographers should quote their subjects' actual words, not invent their own dialogue.

In addition to using actual quotations, Hamilton uses concrete details about her subject's life. For example, Hamilton found information about young Du Bois's packing for school that she included in the biography. The

Teach

Reading Media
Have students preview the Media Connection by reading the heads and subheads throughout. Point out that "the story" referred to is about a real life. Ask how a life is like a story. Then direct students to read the Media Connection.

Discussion Prompts
- How important is research in telling the story of a real person's life?
- Do you think using made-up dialogue in a biography is a good idea? Why, or in what cases?
- How can a writer keep a biography interesting?

Cultural Connections

Understanding an Author's Motivation

Hamilton has written two biographies. The other was about singer and actor Paul Robeson (1891–1976), who sang opera as well as American spirituals. Hamilton's interest in Robeson, like her interest in Du Bois, grew out of her family circumstances. Her family was musical, and like Robeson, believed that people should stand up for their beliefs. Ask students to think of public figures their parents or other family members admire. Have students discuss what is admired about these people and whether students share the feelings of admiration expressed by members of their families.

Teach

Prompts for Discussion

Invite students to talk about

- starting points for biographies—at what point in Du Bois's life did Hamilton begin the narrative? Did her choice make the narrative more or less interesting? Why? How did Hamilton make the opening dramatic?
- the idea of a life as a story—if someone is still alive, how should the story end?
- what makes a life story worth reading about—is it more than events or achievements?

Additional Resources

- *Writing Process Transparencies, 14–16B*
- *Writing in the Real World, pp. 13–16*
- *Cooperative Learning Activities, pp. 19–24*
- *Thinking and Study Skills, p. 9*

Narrative Writing

Writing in the Real World

details seemed real to her, and she hoped they would bring Du Bois alive to her readers as well.

Revising
Shaping the Story

Writing a biography can become complicated. All the facts and quotations can tangle the thread of the narrative. A biographer's task is to shape the material into a clear and understandable story. During the revision process, parts often need to be cut or rearranged. Hamilton explains, "All that information can't go into one, small biography. So you have to pick and choose."

To keep the story interesting, a biographer can present events in a way that creates suspense. For example, Hamilton began her Du Bois biography with his death in Africa rather than chronologically with his birth in America.

She presented events out of sequence because she wanted readers to wonder why Du Bois was dying far from his home. She wanted them to question why huge crowds came the next day to a rally in Washington, D.C. Beginning with the end of her subject's life allowed Hamilton to open the story dramatically and build suspense. In the first three paragraphs, readers can sense the impact of Du Bois's life on others.

Editing
Finishing Touches

As she shaped the story of Du Bois's life, Hamilton focused on her writing style, or voice, including word choice, sentence length, and figures of speech. She kept the narrative simple. The story itself "demanded I write it as simply as I could," she notes, "and introduce to people this person whom they probably would have a hard time believing had existed."

Civic Literacy

Discussing *Crisis*

At Fisk University, W.E.B. Du Bois wrote that trained leadership was necessary if African Americans were to reach full equality with whites. Du Bois studied history and sociology. He earned an undergraduate degree at Fisk and advanced degrees at Harvard. His articles and

editorials in *Crisis,* which he edited for 24 years, persuaded both African Americans and whites to work toward ending racial discrimination. Explain that *Crisis* was the publication of the NAACP. Why do students suppose that title was chosen?

Examining Writing in the Real World

Analyzing the Media Connection

Discuss these questions about the model on page 144.

1. Why do you think Hamilton mentions both Africa and America?

2. Writers use *alliteration*—the repetition of initial consonants—to flavor their language. Find one example of alliteration in Hamilton's writing and explain its effect.

3. What is Hamilton's opinion of Du Bois? What words and phrases helped you identify the author's feelings about her subject?

4. Based on the opening, what do you think the excerpt's theme is?

5. What major events from Du Bois's life does the excerpt present?

Analyzing a Writer's Process

Discuss these questions about Virginia Hamilton's writing process.

1. How did Hamilton choose the subject for her biography?

2. What details did Hamilton include to make her subject come to life?

3. Why does Hamilton believe in quoting the subject's own words?

4. Do you agree with Hamilton's claim that the biographer must identify with the subject in a personal way? Why or why not?

5. What must a biographer do with all the information she or he collects? Explain.

Virginia Hamilton uses actual quotations to advance the plot and describe the characters.

> *"I want to go to Harvard," Du Bois said, "because it is the oldest and largest and most widely known college."*

Correctly punctuate and capitalize each direct quotation.

1. in 1888, Du Bois graduated from Fisk, said Cass.

2. did you know Marley asked he was the first African American to earn a PhD.?

3. "he believed college-educated African Americans should lead the fight against discrimination, said Ms. Bean.

4. Kate noted, "the narrative begins by describing Dr. Du Bois's death.

5. David added, "what a dramatic beginning!

See Lesson 18.1, page 473.

Assess

Analyzing the Media Connection

1. Hamilton mentions them to show Du Bois's strong connection to both places.

2. Possible answers: "Life flickered and flamed, then faltered..." "Every song they sang would speak of justice...." These add drama and emphasis to the narrative.

3. She admires and respects him. Possible answers include: "with obvious love"; led "his" people in their protest struggle; "he had worked so hard to make [freedom] a reality"; "courageous spirit."

4. The excerpt's theme is Du Bois's fight for equality and the changes he helped bring about.

5. The excerpt presents his long fight for equality and his death.

Analyzing a Writer's Process

1. She chose her subject based on her father's admiration of Du Bois, which led to her own interest in Du Bois's life and work. She also heard Du Bois speak.

2. She mentioned that Du Bois was dying far from his birth country, for example.

3. She believes in quoting the subjects' own words so that readers can "hear" the subjects speak.

4. Answers will vary.

5. Biographers must shape the information into an engaging story.

Reteaching

Ask students to write three questions about Du Bois that they would like answered in a biography.

Enrichment

Have students discuss ways in which a person's autobiography and biography might differ.

Close

Invite students to write a brief biographical anecdote about an adult they know. Allow time to share stories in class.

Answers

Capitalized words in each sentence are as follows:
1. "In . . . Cass."
2. "Did . . . know," Mary asked, "he . . . PhD?"
3. "He . . . discrimination," said . . .
4. Kate noted, "The . . . death."
5. David added, "What . . . beginning!"

More Practice with Quotations Have pairs interview one another for a thumbnail biography and take notes. Have each student write a paragraph about the interview, including correctly punctuated quotations.

Note

Students may find inspiration in *Extraordinary Black Americans: From Colonial to Contemporary Times,* Susan Altman; *The First Women Who Spoke Out,* Nancy Smiler Levinson; or *Great Lives: Sports,* George Sullivan.

Focus

Lesson Overview

Objectives
- To learn about the qualities of a good narrative
- To create a narrative using real-life occurrences

Skills
- capturing the reader's attention; finding the right idea

Critical Thinking
- evaluating

Listening and Speaking
- discussing

🔔 Bellringer
Daily Language Activity

When students enter the classroom, have this assignment on the board: *Write down three events in your life, small or big, that you think would make interesting stories. Use complete sentences.*

Grammar Link to the Bellringer

Ask students to look at their responses to the Bellringer and identify the tense of each verb.

See also *Daily Language Practice*

Motivating Activity

Students will be interested in hearing you tell a brief story about an incident in your own life. This could be anything: taking a trip, hosting an unusual house guest, or having some type of mishap. Humor often helps capture students' interest. After telling your story, invite students to share similar stories about their own lives.

LESSON
4.1

TIME

For more about story ideas, see **TIME Facing the Blank Page,** page 92.

Developing a Real-Life Story

A real-life story tells about actual events that happen to real people. A well-written real-life narrative, like good fiction, should hold the reader's attention by presenting interesting characters in a carefully thought-out setting and plot.

You can find stories in books, on television, and in films. What about the true stories in your own mind? You also have fascinating real-life stories to tell.

Stories can be as different as the people who tell them. No two storytellers have exactly the same background or outlook. Think of a hundred people having the same experience, such as attending a sporting event or watching a parade. Each of them would probably tell about the experience in a different way.

148 Unit 4 Narrative Writing

Resource Manager

Planning Resources
- *Lesson Plans*

📝 Transparencies
- *Bellringer*
- *Daily Language Practice*
- *Fine Art 16–20*
- *Two-Minute Skill Drill*
- *Writing Process 14–16B*

📁 Other Print Resources
- *Composition Enrichment,* p. 29
- *Composition Practice,* p. 29
- *Composition Reteaching,* p. 29
- *Cooperative Learning Activities,* pp. 19–24
- *Listening and Speaking Activities,* p. 23

- *Thinking and Study Skills,* pp. 3, 5, 13, 22
- *Writing Across the Curriculum*
- *Writing Assessment and Evaluation Rubrics*

Capture the Reader's Attention

A narrative is a story that answers the question *What happened?* Before you begin a narrative, decide why someone might read the story. Then think about *who* will read it.

Above all, a good narrative must capture a reader's attention from the very beginning. Strong opening paragraphs make the reader want to continue. Read the beginning of the story below.

Grammar Tip

When you edit your draft of a narrative, make sure that all verb tenses are used correctly. For more information, see Lessons 10.4–10.7, pages 339–346.

Literature Model

"**O**wen! Time to go!"
I was spying down from behind the crest of the sand dune back of the house. Our car looked like an upside-down bug, a bug with spindly legs waving frantically in the air. Fishing rods were sticking out the back window, my bike was hanging off the rear, and the roof rack was piled with more junk than we had brought. It was the end of summer. Labor Day. Two o'clock in the afternoon. Time to go home.

But not me. I was going to stay.

"Owen! *Time to go!*"

My parents stood there, helpless, not knowing where to even begin to look for me.

Avi, A Place Called Ugly

> How does the writer grab your attention and make you want to read on?

All well-written stories have the same elements. Good stories tell about characters who are involved in some sort of action in a certain place, and the events are presented in a clear order.

Journal Writing

You have stories to tell about experiences you've had. In your journal, jot down an idea for a story. Note the characters, place, and action for your story.

Teach

Using the Model

Ask students to reread the passage from *A Place Called Ugly*. Remind them that this selection is taken from the very beginning of the book. Ask them to tell about the incident in their own words. What is the setting? Who is there? Why would they want to read on? **L2**

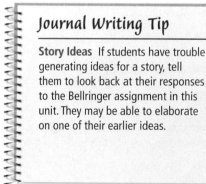

Two-Minute Skill Drill

Have students rewrite this opening sentence of a story, adding vivid words to make it more attention-getting:

Blanca was sitting on her porch one summer afternoon, waiting for the mail carrier.

See also *Two-Minute Skill Drill Transparencies,* 4.1

Journal Writing Tip

Story Ideas If students have trouble generating ideas for a story, tell them to look back at their responses to the Bellringer assignment in this unit. They may be able to elaborate on one of their earlier ideas.

Teach

Generating Ideas

On the board list the following approaches to generating ideas for narrative writing: brainstorming, listing, reading journal entries, and looking at pictures. Ask volunteers to explain how each approach works. Have students choose a technique they have not yet tried and use it to come up with a topic for a real-life narrative. Then call on volunteers to describe to the class how the activity helped them make a selection. **L2**

Recalling Events

Ask students to imagine that a friend or relative who has been away for a long time will telephone soon. So that they will remember important events to tell this person, students will make notes in advance of the imaginary call. Then have students form pairs to share their notes and role-play their phone conversations. **L1**

Additional Resources

For *narrative* **writing prompts,** see *Fine Art Transparencies* 16–20.

Daily Language Practice

Writing Process Transparencies, 14–16b

Writing Across the Curriculum
Cooperative Learning Activities, 19–24
Thinking and Study Skills, pp. 3, 5, 13, 22
Listening and Speaking Activities, p. 23
Composition Practice, p. 29

(sidebar) Narrative Writing

Find the Right Idea

Real-life stories may come from successes or failures in the lives of real people. They may come from accidents or struggles. Sometimes you'll find that ideas for real-life stories come easily. Other times you may find that you can't come up with an idea at all. When this happens, you may want to try a few different strategies. Reread some of your journal entries, or make a list of places, events, or people you know. Browse through a family scrapbook. Look at the ideas below.

Moving into our new house

Ben comes home from the hospital

Our friend Loo Wang from China

Building the doghouse

Listing
1. Important dates in history
2. People I admire
3. Fun vacations
4. Exciting events I have taken part in
5. Things that make me lau[gh]

Journal Entry
Today Mom and Ben and I went for a ride in a helicopter. At first, Ben was afraid of flying in something so small. Mom and I had to let him sit between us. Then, as soon as we got up in the air, he had to sit by the

Enrichment and Extension

Choosing Words

If some students are unsure of what real-life event to write about, suggest that they write about their experiences learning a new language or living in a new place.

Pairs of students can work together to come up with adjectives that describe their feelings and bring their narratives to life.

Write About the Past

Think of an important event in your life that you could describe to a friend. Think about what you want to tell about it and how. To prepare for writing, list some sentences or phrases with beginnings such as *I saw, I remember,* and *I felt.*

PURPOSE To record a real-life experience
AUDIENCE A friend
LENGTH 3–4 paragraphs

WRITING RUBRICS To write an effective real-life narrative, you should

- use your list to help you compose
- establish characters, a place, and action
- include interesting details
- create interest with your first paragraph

Listening and Speaking

COOPERATIVE LEARNING Think of your favorite school experience from a past year. Write a brief narrative about this experience. Working in a small group, read your narratives to one another. Revise your own narrative based on what the group said was unclear or uninteresting. Assemble all the narratives into a booklet.

Viewing and Representing

MAKE A POSTER Create a poster that illustrates the school experience you

Use consistent verb tenses when you write.

Notice the consistent use of verb tense in this sentence from the model (all refer to a time in the past):

*Fishing rods **were sticking** out the back window, my bike **was hanging** off the rear, and the roof rack **was piled** with more junk. . . .*

Rewrite each sentence below to make the verb tenses consistent.

1. On our vacation last year, my family and I visited Denver, and we see the capitol.
2. At camp I will learn to canoe; it was fun.
3. The game ended in a tie, and everyone in the stands will cheer for the teams.
4. My family move to San Diego at the end of the year, and my mom bought a business.
5. When I got home from school, my dog ran happily and jumped with joy.

See Lessons 10.4–10.7, pages 339–346.

wrote about. Display the posters in your classroom and see whether students can match your poster with your narrative.

4.1 Developing a Real-Life Story **151**

Narrative Writing

Assess

Evaluation Rubrics

Write About the Past

Use these criteria when evaluating your students' writing. Does the writing

- present characters, a place, and action?
- include interesting details about the characters and setting?
- capture the reader's attention in the opening paragraph?

See also *Writing Assessment and Evaluation Rubrics.*

Listening and Speaking

Ask group members to evaluate each other's narratives. Do the narratives grab and hold the reader's attention? If students chose to collect their group's narratives in a booklet, does the final product reflect the combined efforts of all group members?

Viewing and Representing

Students' posters should show creative effort. Monitor students' understanding of the assignment and have them seek clarification as needed.

Reteaching

📁 *Composition Reteaching,* p. 29

Enrichment

📁 *Composition Enrichment,* p. 29

Close

Ask students to name some of their favorite story plots from books, films, or television. What made these stories favorites? Draw students into a discussion of which plots or portions of plots could have come from real-life experiences.

Answers

1. . . . and we saw the capitol.
2. At camp I will learn to canoe; it will be fun.
3. The game ended in a tie, and everyone in the stands cheered for the teams.
4. My family moved . . . mom bought . . .
5. Correct

Focus

Lesson Overview

Objectives
- To learn how to use time order to organize a narrative
- To select and sequence events in a narrative using time order

Skills
- sorting through detail; putting events in order

Critical Thinking
- evaluating; comparing

Listening and Speaking
- discussing; informal speaking

Bellringer
Daily Language Activity

When students enter the classroom, have this assignment on the board: *Imagine that you want to write a narrative about a surprise birthday party. Write down a detail that happens before the party, at the moment of surprise, and during the party.*

Grammar Link to the Bellringer

Have students rewrite one of their details using the comparative form of an adjective.

See also *Daily Language Practice*

Motivating Activity

Ask students if they have ever watched a television program with the sound turned off. Have them discuss how they were able to follow the story (background, sequence of events, facial expressions, clothing, etc.). Point out that creating a "wordless story" (for example, a dance, a painting, mime, or a picture book) can be a valid way of preparing for writing a narrative based on personal experience. Let students know that oral stories passed on through generations are also good sources for story-writing ideas.

Narrative Writing

LESSON 4.2
Keeping a Story Organized

To tell a story that is clear, the events and details need to be arranged in a logical order. Many stories can even be told without words.

Rhythmic drumbeats, beautifully dressed dancers, colorful masks, tall totem poles, carved house fronts—these are the props of the Kwakiutl storytellers. The Kwakiutl peoples of the northwestern coast of North America tell stories as a part of their everyday lives. They may use art, dancing, chanting, or the beating of drums. A new baby or a wedding may call for celebration with stories from nature. Often these storytellers use no words, yet the people understand their tales. The storyteller gives important details and events in an understandable order.

How would you tell a story without using words? Make a list of the ways you would try.

Glen Rabena, *Mosquito Mask* (in a Native American style), n.d.

Edward S. Curtis, *Masked Kwakiutl Dancers*, c. 1915

152 Unit 4 Narrative Writing

Resource Manager

Planning Resources
- *Lesson Plans*

Transparencies
- *Bellringer*
- *Daily Language Practice*
- *Fine Art 16-20*
- *Two-Minute Skill Drill*
- *Writing Process 14-16B*

Other Print Resources
- *Composition Enrichment*, p. 30
- *Composition Practice*, p. 30
- *Composition Reteaching*, p. 30
- *Cooperative Learning Activities*
- *Listening and Speaking Activities*, p. 23

- *Thinking and Study Skills*, pp. 3, 5, 11, 34
- *Writing Across the Curriculum*
- *Writing Assessment and Evaluation Rubrics*

Sort Through the Details

When you write a story, you use words. Like the Kwakiutl storytellers, you should choose your details carefully. You also need to organize the details in a way that's clear to your readers.

When you begin to draft your narrative, you may find that you have too many details to tell. Choose only the details that are essential to your story. If you do this, your readers won't get confused by ideas that don't really matter. Sometimes you may have to cut out some details in order to keep the most important details clear. Look at the following notes, taken by a student preparing to write a short narrative. Which three notes do you think would be the strongest parts of a narrative called "My Paper Route"?

Revising Tip

When you are ready to revise, have a partner read your draft. Ask if you have left out any important details or if the order of the details is confusing.

· Narrative Writing

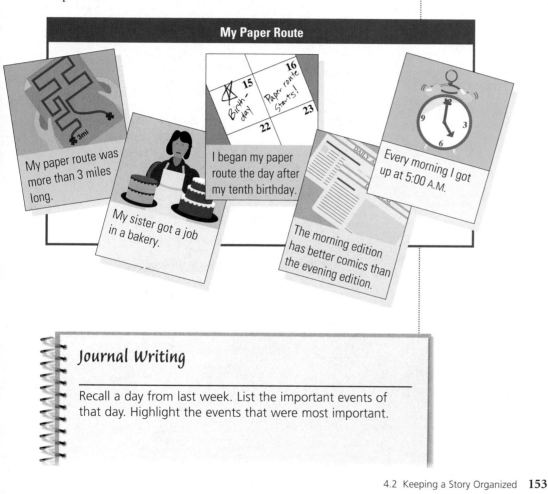

My Paper Route

My paper route was more than 3 miles long.

My sister got a job in a bakery.

I began my paper route the day after my tenth birthday.

The morning edition has better comics than the evening edition.

Every morning I got up at 5:00 A.M.

Journal Writing

Recall a day from last week. List the important events of that day. Highlight the events that were most important.

Teach

Evaluating Details

To help students evaluate the notes on the student page, have volunteers read the notes aloud. Ask students what they think the main idea of the narrative is. After determining that the main idea is "My Paper Route," ask students to explain whether they think each note is strongly, somewhat, or not at all related to the main idea. If other students disagree with an evaluation, ask them to explain their reasoning. **L1**

Two-Minute Skill Drill

Write on the board this narrative about a trip to the dentist. Ask: *Which detail is the most important? Which is least important?*

I read a magazine in the waiting room. The dentist told me I needed braces. The office smelled like toothpaste.

See also *Two-Minute Skill Drill Transparencies, 4.2*

Journal Writing Tip

Comparing To determine if an event on a given day was significant, students might ask themselves questions such as the following: Did the event change my mood? Did the event relate to one of my special interests? Did the event reveal some aspect of my personality? A yes answer probably means the idea would be a good one to include in students' writing.

Teach

Using the Model

Ask students to select the time order words and phrases that help readers follow the story: *The first day, On the third day, Every morning, For the first few weeks, After a few weeks.* Also, point out to students that the story was probably not created directly from the five notes on page 154. Instead, the writer probably added and deleted notes before writing a first draft, then revised the draft one or more times. **L2**

Using Time Order

For students who have difficulty with chronology, talk about and show some examples of time order, such as their daily school schedules, calendars, or bus schedules. Help students discuss their schedules, using words such as *first* or *next*. To help them organize their narratives, suggest they write each event in their narrative on a separate index card and then line up the cards in the correct order. Tell students to write transition words at the top of the cards to connect the events. **L1**

Additional Resources

- For narrative **writing prompts**, see *Fine Art Transparencies* 16–20.
- *Daily Language Practice*
- *Writing Process Transparencies,* 14–16B
- *Writing Across the Curriculum*
- *Cooperative Learning Activities,* pp. 19–24
- *Thinking and Study Skills,* pp. 3, 5, 11, 34
- *Listening and Speaking Activities,* p. 23
- *Composition Practice,* p. 30

Narrative Writing

Drafting Tip

Write each part of the event as a separate sentence. You can decide later how you want to combine the details.

Organize Events

After you've chosen the important events for your narrative, you need to place them in some particular order. Time order is an effective way to organize your story. When using time order, you tell what happened first, second, and so on. You may use words like *then* or *next.* These words will help your readers follow your story.

The writer of the real-life story below uses three of the statements shown on page 153. Notice the other details the writer adds to fill out the story.

I began my paper route the day after my tenth birthday.

> I began my paper route the day after my tenth birthday. The first day was the worst. A man from the newspaper office came with me. He and I walked more than 3 miles and delivered 423 papers. On the third day, I went out all by myself.
>
> Every morning I got up at five o'clock. Then I rode my bike down to the drop-off point to pick up my papers. For the first few weeks, I didn't think I would ever finish. I felt so tired, and my feet hurt. My route, you see, was more than 3 miles long. After a few weeks, though, it didn't seem so bad. Sometimes, especially on nice mornings, I actually liked it.

Every morning I got up at 5:00 A.M.

My paper route was more than 3 miles long.

MEETING INDIVIDUAL NEEDS — English Language Learners

Using Images to Organize

Students whose first language is not English may have difficulty with time order words. Students might benefit from first organizing their personal narrative as a series of drawings. After representing each event and detail in order, they can write appropriate time order words in their first language and then in English next to the images. The pictures and vocabulary reminders can serve as an outline when students write their narratives.

Write a Real-life Narrative

A magazine called *Challenge* is looking for narratives about exciting experiences. Think about an exciting experience you have had and write a narrative, arranging details to build interest and suspense.

PURPOSE To organize details to write about a real experience

AUDIENCE The editors of *Challenge*

LENGTH 3–4 paragraphs

WRITING RUBRICS To use details effectively in a narrative, you should

- choose the details that are most important to your story
- arrange the details to make your story clear and dramatic
- proofread to check grammar and spelling

Listening and Speaking

TELLING A STORY Turn your narrative about an exciting experience into a story that you tell orally. Deliver it first to a group of three or four classmates. Ask them for comments and suggestions to make your story more interesting and exciting. Rehearse it several times and then present it for the entire class as part of a storytelling series that might be spread over the school term.

Use the comparative forms of *bad* correctly.

When you compare two things, use *worse*. Use *worst* to compare three or more things.

The first day was the **worst.**

Complete each sentence below with the correct form of *bad*.

1. Is Janice's cold _____ than Bill's?
2. Of all the suggestions, that one is the _____ .
3. Was the accident a _____ one?
4. That is the _____ idea of all.
5. My handwriting is _____ than yours.

See Lesson 12.4, page 385.

Cross-Curricular Activity

MUSIC Find a piece of music on a CD or cassette that tells a story. It might be a version of an old ballad or a modern folk or country song. Write a brief narrative of the story line in the song. Then, meet with a small group and play your musical selections for each other. Discuss what the music adds to the story in terms of the song's meaning and the feelings it evokes.

Assess

Evaluation Rubrics

Write a Real-life Narrative

Use these criteria when evaluating your students' writing. Did the writer

- choose details that are important to understanding his or her story?
- put the details in an order that makes sense?
- proofread the finished product?

See also *Writing Assessment and Evaluation Rubrics*.

Listening and Speaking

Monitor groups to encourage storytellers and to model giving constructive comments.

Cross-Curricular Activity

Students' writing should
- tell the story described in the music
- explain what the music adds to the meaning of the story

Reteaching

Composition Reteaching, p. 30

Enrichment

Composition Enrichment, p. 30

Fine Art Transparencies, 16–20

Close

An exercise in nonverbal storytelling may be a great way to bring together students. Give individual students instructions for pantomiming a simple story or concept. Ask the other students to guess what this individual is trying to convey without words. It may be an opportunity for students who are learning English to share their first languages.

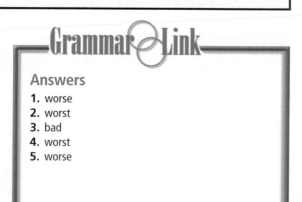

Answers
1. worse
2. worst
3. bad
4. worst
5. worse

Focus

Lesson Overview

Objectives

- To gain an understanding of the use of dialogue in a narrative
- To use dialogue to enhance a narrative and to punctuate dialogue correctly

Skills

- identifying the speaker; writing a dialogue; listening

Critical Thinking

- organizing; clarifying; evaluating writing

Listening and Speaking

- listening to conversations; tape-recording a story

Bellringer
Daily Language Activity

When students enter the classroom, have this assignment on the board: *Write down at least three sentences from a conversation you had this morning.*

Grammar Link to the Bellringer

Ask students if they used quotation marks when writing what they said. Have volunteers write their sentences, using quotation marks, on the board.

See also *Daily Language Practice*

Motivating Activity

Invite volunteers to relate their dialogues from the Bellringer activity. Remind students to say the exact words of both speakers as they remember them and to speak with the appropriate feelings. Point out that people often use fragments, slang, and shortened words in their everyday speech. Suggest students consider including dialogue in their narratives to make them more realistic and interesting.

Narrative Writing

LESSON 4.3

Writing Dialogue

Dialogue is the words spoken by the characters in a story. Well-written dialogue can help bring characters and events to life. What characters say, and how they say it, tells a lot about them.

Dialogue can help make a story lifelike and exciting. Read the passage below. Think about the message the dialogue gives about the characters.

The writer tells about Uncle Nachum in the first paragraph. In the dialogue he shows the character in action.

You don't have to use a short phrase to identify speakers each time they speak if the identity of the speaker is clear.

Literature Model

Uncle Nachum had a joke or witty remark for every occasion, telling them in his hoarse voice and enjoying what he said with a hearty laugh. . . . As I watched him at his tricks, he would throw me one of his clever questions, such as, "How many ends does a stick have?"

"Two!" I answered.

"And half a stick?"

"One!" I loudly declared.

And then Uncle Nachum would rock with great, thundering laughter. How did that short body come by such a tremendous laugh? When he laughed it seemed the walls laughed too.

Benjamin Tene, *In the Shade of the Chestnut Tree*

Resource Manager

Planning Resources
- *Lesson Plans*

Transparencies
- *Bellringer*
- *Daily Language Practice*
- *Fine Art* 16–20
- *Two-Minute Skill Drill*
- *Writing Process* 14–16B

Other Print Resources
- *Composition Enrichment,* p. 31
- *Composition Practice,* p. 31
- *Composition Reteaching,* p. 31
- *Cooperative Learning Activities,* pp. 19–24
- *Listening and Speaking Activities,* p. 23

- *Thinking and Study Skills,* pp. 3, 5, 34
- *Writing Across the Curriculum*
- *Writing Assessment and Evaluation Rubrics*

Identify the Speaker

When you write a dialogue, you need to help your readers keep track of who is speaking. Show which words a character speaks by putting quotation marks around the words. Also, tell who is speaking by using a phrase such as *she said*. When a different character begins to speak, start a new paragraph.

Now look at how this conversation can be written as dialogue.

"Tommy told a funny story at school today. I almost died!" said Calvin.

"Tell it to me," said Hobbes.

"Well, actually the story itself wasn't so funny. It was the *way* he told it."

"How did he tell it?" asked Hobbes.

"He was drinking milk and when he laughed, it came up his nose!"

Tips for Writing Dialogue	
Here's How	**Here's Why**
Use quotation marks before and after the speaker's exact words.	To show which words the character actually spoke
Use phrases with a word such as *said*. Start a new line each time a different character speaks.	To let the reader know who is speaking To make the dialogue easier to follow

Journal Writing

Recall a recent conversation you had with a friend. Practice dialogue by recording the conversation in your journal. Be careful to make clear who is saying what.

Teach

Using the Model

Point out that the use of dialogue helps give Uncle Nachum's questions more impact and makes the passage more interesting. To demonstrate, first read the passage without the dialogue, rewording it slightly. Then have a student read aloud the dialogue as written. Ask students why they think dialogue makes the passage better. **L2**

Understanding Dialogue

Select a short narrative with a lot of dialogue. Have students take turns reading the narrator's part and the characters' parts. Then ask students what difficulties they had, such as keeping the characters straight or distinguishing narration from dialogue. Ask them what they learned from listening to one another read. **L1**

Two-Minute Skill Drill

Write these phrases on the board. Have students choose an appropriate adverb to complete each phrase.

she said _____

he shouted _____

Tina asked _____

she remarked _____

See also *Two-Minute Skill Drill Transparencies,* 4.3

Journal Writing Tip

Using Vivid Words Ask students to name some synonyms for the word *said,* such as *whispered, yelled,* or *mumbled.* Point out that using these vivid words can help give additional information about a speaker's mood and personality.

Teach

Using the Model

Point out that the narrative on the left describes Ralph as "just a little kid." Guide students to see that the narrative on the right <u>shows</u> that Ralph is young by letting the reader in on what Ralph thinks and feels through what he says and how he says it. Next, direct students' attention back to the narrative on the left. How does it describe Meg? How does the narrative on the right describe her? **L2**

Applying and Extending

Invite students to find passages of dialogue from a book or a magazine article. Have students meet in small groups to read their passages aloud. Before reading, students should describe the setting and action. Afterwards, have the students who are listening describe what they have learned about the characters from the dialogue. **L3**

Additional Resources

📇 For dialogue **writing prompts**, see *Fine Art Transparencies* 16–20.

📇 *Daily Language Practice*

📇 *Writing Process Transparencies,* 14–16B

📁 *Writing Across the Curriculum*
📁 *Cooperative Learning Activities,* pp. 19–24
📁 *Thinking and Study Skills,* pp. 3, 5, 34
📁 *Listening and Speaking Activities,* p. 23
📁 *Composition Practice,* p. 31

Narrative Writing

Presenting Tip

After you write a story with dialogue, tape-record the story with different people reading the words of the characters.

Listen Carefully

Paying attention to conversations is one of the best ways to get to know people. In your narrative writing, the words your characters say can help readers get to know them, too.

Two short narratives are shown below. The first one does not use dialogue; the second one does. See how dialogue shows the personalities of the two characters in the second narrative. What is one example of how dialogue helps you get to know Meg and Ralph?

Vocabulary Tip

When you draft dialogue, you can use adverbs in your identifying phrases to tell how a person is speaking. For more information about adverbs, see Lessons 13.1 and 13.2, pages 395–398.

Last summer I almost got lost in the woods. My sister Meg and my little brother Ralph were with me. Meg is nine and has a pretty wild imagination. Ralph is just a little kid.

Our family was camping at Lake McGee. The first day we hiked the trail to the overlook. Everything went fine until we came to some big trees that had fallen over the trail. We walked around them. On the other side, though, we couldn't see the trail! We retraced our steps, but we still couldn't find the trail!

The writer uses the adverbs "softly" and "excitedly" in these identifying phrases.

"Well, I think we may be lost," I announced.

"L-l-lost?" Ralph said softly, grabbing my hand.

"Well, not <u>really</u> lost, kiddo. Just lost for a minute," I said, trying to reassure him—and myself. "Let me think. What color were those trail blazes?"

"Maybe wolves will find us, and we'll become wolf children and live in the woods forever!" said Meg excitedly. Ralph began to whimper.

"You're not helping, Meg. Now, let's try to think. Which way is the trail?"

MEETING INDIVIDUAL NEEDS — Less Proficient Readers

Choosing Words

Students may need extra help in writing and identifying descriptive phrases in dialogue. First, write the following line on the board: *"Go home, Spot!" she said.* Ask students to name vivid verbs they could use instead of *said.* Then provide students with a picture of two people talking.

Have students work in pairs to write dialogue for the two characters. Encourage them to use different verbs to show how the characters are speaking. Have them use a thesaurus if appropriate. Encourage students to read their dialogues aloud.

Write a Dialogue

Write a conversation between two characters of different ages, backgrounds, or personalities.

PURPOSE To use dialogue for characterization
AUDIENCE Your class
LENGTH At least 8 lines of dialogue

WRITING RUBRICS To write effective dialogue, you should

- use dialogue that reveals character
- use phrases that identify speakers
- indent and punctuate correctly to indicate clearly who is speaking

Cross-Curricular Activity

ART Study the Edvard Munch painting. What might these women be saying? Describe the painting by writing a short narrative that includes dialogue.

Edvard Munch, *Women on a Bridge*, c. 1903

Grammar Link

Use quotation marks before and after a direct quotation.

To make dialogue clear, use quotation marks around the words a character says.

"It may rain," Sue said.

Write the following sentences, adding quotation marks to mark the beginning and end of dialogue.

1. Maria said, It's pouring. Where did this rain come from?
2. Let's run under that awning! yelled Kiko.
3. Maria yelled back, We may have to swim there!
4. I'm not moving, said Seth as he sat in a puddle.
5. Oh no, said Maria, Seth is soaked to the bone!

See Lesson 19.6, page 499.

Listening and Speaking

DRAMATIC READINGS Working in groups of three or four, look through a literature book for examples of dialogue that reveal information about the characters and their personalities. In your group, develop a dramatic reading of the passage and present it to the class. Have someone in the group provide the appropriate sound effects.

Narrative Writing

Assess

Evaluation Rubrics

Write a Dialogue

Use these criteria when evaluating your students' writing. Does the writing

- show what each character is like?
- include identifying phrases to show who is speaking?
- use quotation marks and other punctuation correctly?
- include line breaks to show changes in speakers?

See also *Writing Assessment and Evaluation Rubrics.*

Cross-Curricular Activity: Art

Evaluate the students' narratives based on the following:
- clarity in showing who is speaking
- awareness of time and place presented in the painting
- creativity in imagining what the women might be saying

Listening and Speaking

Have students monitor their understanding of the assignment and seek clarification as needed.

Reteaching

📁 *Composition Reteaching, p. 31*

Enrichment

📁 *Composition Enrichment, p. 31*

📖 *Fine Art Transparencies 16–20*

Close

Have students work in pairs, reading their dialogues aloud to each other. Partners can tell whether the dialogues clearly showed who said what. They can then discuss what each character seems like and why.

Grammar Link

Answers

1. Maria said, "It's pouring. Where did this rain come from?"
2. "Let's run under that awning," yelled Kiko.
3. Maria yelled back, "We may have to swim there!"
4. "I'm not moving," said Seth as he sat in a puddle.
5. "Oh no," said Maria, "Seth is soaked to the bone!"

Viewing the Art

Edvard Munch, *Women on a Bridge*, c. 1903
This oil-on-canvas painting, from the Munch Museum in Oslo, Norway, is not typical of Edvard Munch's work. The Norwegian painter and print-maker (1863–1944) usually chose more somber themes of love and death.

Focus

Lesson Overview

Objectives

- To learn how to select details, describe feelings and events, and come to a conclusion when writing a narrative
- To consider purpose and audience when composing a narrative

Skills

- setting a purpose; choosing important details; writing a conclusion

Critical Thinking

- recalling an event; evaluating information; drawing a conclusion

Listening and Speaking

- telling a story

🔔 Bellringer
Daily Language Activity

When students enter the classroom, have this assignment on the board: *List three interesting or important events from your life.*

Grammar Link to the Bellringer

Ask students to write one sentence to describe each event, using a conjunction (*and, or,* or *but*) in each sentence.

✒ **See also** *Daily Language Practice*

Motivating Activity

Ask students to recall an encounter with an animal other than a pet. They might think of animals in the wild, at a park, at a zoo, or on a farm. Let them freewrite for five minutes about the incident. Then guide them in a discussion of what they wrote, encouraging them to explain what made the encounter interesting or unusual and how they felt at the time. Tell students that such an experience might be turned into an interesting narrative.

Narrative Writing

LESSON 4.4

Writing About an Event

Real-life narratives often grow out of special experiences in a writer's life. The writer usually finds a way to tell readers how the experience was special.

Here's how one student wrote about a camping trip. Look for the ways she tells that this was a special event, and notice how she brings her story to a conclusion.

> The writer begins her story by telling you that this was a real experience.

Student Model

It was during our most recent camping trip, in Yellowstone, that I had my first real bear experience. We'd finished dinner so we hung our leftover roast beef in a tree out of reach of any hungry bears, played three rounds of Boggle, and went to sleep.

In the middle of the night I woke up with an urgent need for the bathroom. I had just popped my head out of the tent when I saw someone reaching for our roast beef . . . . He looked a little larger than my father, but who else could it be? I looked back into our tent and there was my father peacefully snoring. . . . I realized what it was—a bear!!! I zipped up the tent flap very, very slowly (all needs for the bathroom instantly cured) and crawled back into my sleeping bag.

Rebecca Bardach, Berkeley, California
First appeared in *Cricket*

Resource Manager

Planning Resources
- *Lesson Plans*

📓 **Transparencies**
- *Bellringer*
- *Daily Language Practice*
- *Fine Art* 16–20
- *Two-Minute Skill Drill*
- *Writing Process* 14–16B

📁 Other Print Resources
- *Composition Enrichment,* p. 32
- *Composition Practice,* p. 32
- *Composition Reteaching,* p. 32
- *Cooperative Learning Activities,* pp. 19–24
- *Listening and Speaking Activities,* p. 23

- Thinking and Study Skills, pp. 3, 5, 11
- Writing Across the Curriculum
- Writing Assessment and Evaluation Rubrics

Make the Most of an Idea

Rebecca Bardach told her story because it was her first experience with a live bear. She gave some details about the camping trip to set the scene for her readers. Also, she let readers know she was frightened and unfamiliar with bears.

When you write about a real-life experience, think of the specific things that made it special to you. Make some notes about information you have that your audience may not have; these notes will help you realize what background you may need to give your readers. As you plan your story, use the three questions below to help you.

Prewriting Tip

To get started, imagine that you are telling your story to a friend on the telephone. Make a list of things you would tell your friend.

Narrative Writing

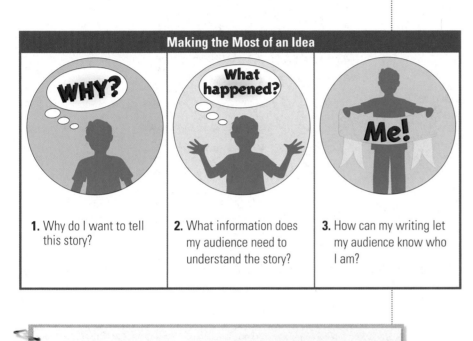

Making the Most of an Idea

1. Why do I want to tell this story?

2. What information does my audience need to understand the story?

3. How can my writing let my audience know who I am?

Journal Writing

Write a journal entry about a family event. What made this event special?

Teach

Using the Model

Point out that the first sentence in the model tells why the experience was important to the writer. Students may not be sure how to start their own drafts. Once students have chosen events to write about, ask them the following questions: *What made this event special to you? What made it memorable?* Suggest they use their answers to write the opening sentence of their draft. **L2**

Writing with Feeling

Rebecca uses three exclamation points to show her incredible surprise at discovering a wild bear. Tell students that there are other ways for writers to show amazement. Experienced writers carefully choose and arrange their words to convey the idea of surprise, instead of relying on exclamation points. Write the following line from the model, and ask students to rewrite it in a way that shows surprise without using exclamation points. *I realized what it was—a bear!!!* **L3**

Two-Minute Skill Drill

List these nouns on the board and have students write an adjective for each to make it more specific.

bear	*air*	*sky*
day	*house*	*water*

See also *Two-Minute Skill Drill Transparencies,* 4.4

Journal Writing Tip

Setting the Scene Point out that vivid details of sight, sound, and smell can help readers visualize a scene.

Teach

Using the Model

Copy the model text on the board, including revisions. Elicit students' comments and suggestions for further—or better—changes. When you and your students have finished, ask them to compare the version on the board to the original text from this page. Do they like the new version better? Why or why not? **L2**

Discussing Conclusions

Ask students to suggest reasons why a good conclusion is important to a narrative. Tell students that sometimes it's hard to figure out how to conclude a narrative. Guide students to suggest different ways to conclude a real-life narrative, such as telling what they did, what they felt, what they learned, or what someone else did. **L1**

Additional Resources

- For narrative **writing prompts**, see *Fine Art Transparencies* 16–20.

- *Daily Language Practice*

- *Writing Process Transparencies,* 14–16B
- *Writing Across the Curriculum*
- *Cooperative Learning Activities,* pp. 19–24
- *Thinking and Study Skills,* pp. 3, 5, 11
- *Listening and Speaking Activities,* p. 23
- *Composition Practice,* p. 32

Narrative Writing

Grammar Tip

Proofread your narrative for spelling and punctuation. For information about punctuation of dialogue, see Lesson 19.6, page 499.

Finish the Job

Every well-written narrative has a conclusion. One type of conclusion sums up the story and reflects on what happened.

The conclusion should give your audience the feeling that the story is complete. You might conclude with phrases like these: *I learned that . . .* or *From then on, I knew . . .* or *Ever since this experience, I have felt . . .*

Read this draft of a young writer's story. Notice how the writer revised the draft using the questions on page 161.

The writer left out an important detail. Readers need to know that she made many copies of the announcement.

To complete the story, the writer needs to tell how she felt about finding the kitten's owner.

I am really excited about the ways that a computer has changed my life. It even helped me find a lost pet's owner.

When the kitten first showed up at our back door, I wanted to keep it. I knew, though, that it belonged to someone else.

Then I got an idea. I could use the computer at school to find the kitten's owner. I typed up an announcement with a description of the kitten and my address and phone number. Then I added a graphic of a cat at the top.

I printed thirty copies of the announcement on orange paper.

After school I put a copy of the announcement on the porch of every house on my street. At 7:30 that night, I was petting the kitten when the phone rang. "Yes, she's right here, and she's fine," I told the voice on the phone.

When I hung up the phone, I had a good feeling inside.

MEETING INDIVIDUAL NEEDS — English Language Learners

Communicating Experience

Ask students from different countries to write about an experience they had while in their native country, while coming to the United States, or after they had arrived in the United States. Encourage students to work with an English-proficient partner or to use a thesaurus or a dictionary if necessary. Invite students to share their stories with the rest of the class.

Write a Narrative About Learning a Skill

Learning a skill often takes hard work. Draft a narrative about a skill, such as swimming or riding a bike, you had difficulty learning. Write your narrative for a younger person who is having trouble mastering the skill.

As you plan your draft, list details about what helped you learn and what you learned about yourself from the experience.

PURPOSE To share a real-life experience
AUDIENCE A younger person
LENGTH 3–4 paragraphs

WRITING RUBRICS To write a narrative about what you learned from mastering a skill, you should

- include essential information
- reveal how you felt
- build to a conclusion
- proofread to avoid run-on sentences

Using Computers

The line-spacing function on your word processor can help when you plan to have a peer review your work. Double-space your draft to make it easier to read. Also, leave wide margins around your text. These changes will give your partner plenty of room to write comments.

Avoid run-on sentences.

A run-on sentence is two or more sentences incorrectly written as one.

Correct each run-on below. To do so, you may write separate sentences. You may also combine the sentences with a comma and a conjunction (*and, or,* or *but)* or with a semicolon.

1. Helen Keller's life is an inspiration she worked tirelessly for the visually and hearing impaired.
2. John F. Kennedy was president in the 1960s, he started the Peace Corps.
3. Harriet Tubman was born a slave she escaped and led 300 other enslaved people out of slavery.
4. I didn't think I'd ever be able to do it I finally learned to ski.

See Lesson 8.6, page 307.

Listening and Speaking

COOPERATIVE LEARNING With a partner, exchange your skill narratives and have each partner proofread the other's paper. Then have your partner read your paper aloud, while you take notes about ways to make it clearer or more dramatic.

Narrative Writing

Assess

Evaluation Rubrics

Write a Narrative About Learning a Skill

Use these criteria when evaluating your students' writing. Each student's writing should

- reflect the personality and feelings of the writer
- present a story about perseverance
- have a conclusion
- include important details
- use conjunctions correctly

See also *Writing Assessment and Evaluation Rubrics.*

Using Computers

Students should have double-spaced their drafts and left wide margins.

Listening and Speaking

Emphasize to students that narratives should be dynamic and clear. Reading aloud and listening are valuable ways to monitor the flow of a narrative.

Reteaching

📁 *Composition Reteaching*, p. 32

Enrichment

📁 *Composition Enrichment*, p. 32

Close

Have students share narratives with the class. Then have them offer each other suggestions and feedback on the following points:

- Was there enough information in the narrative?
- Did the writer let the audience know how he or she was feeling?
- Was the conclusion strong?

Grammar Link

Answers

Answers will vary. One suggeston is given below.
1. Helen … inspiration; she … impaired.
Correcting Run-on Sentences After students have corrected their sentences, write them on the board. Ask volunteers to write their corrections underneath. Then ask whether anyone corrected the sentences differently. Have volunteers write their corrections under the first ones.

Focus

Lesson Overview

Objectives
- To identify ways to respond to a biography in writing
- To construct an effective written response to a biography

Skills
- writing in a journal; writing a biographical article

Critical Thinking
- summarizing; analyzing

Listening and Speaking
- role-playing an interview

Bellringer
Daily Language Activity

When students enter the classroom, have this assignment on the board: *Think of a person you would like to learn more about. If you could meet this person, what questions would you ask him or her?*

Grammar Link to the Bellringer

Have students underline the verbs in the questions they wrote. Discuss verb tense, with the focus on the past tense.

See also *Daily Language Practice*

Motivating Activity

Ask students to think of people whose biographies they have read. Do they enjoy stories about real people? Point out that most biographies do more than give information about a person's accomplishments. They often tell about making difficult decisions, adjusting to changes, and overcoming hardships. Point out that these stories often inspire readers and give them ideas they can use in their own lives.

Narrative Writing

LESSON 4.5

WRITING ABOUT LITERATURE
Responding to a Biography

Reading biographies lets you learn about other people. In addition, your personal response to a biography may lead to other discoveries—about yourself and the world around you.

Rosa Parks is often called the mother of the civil rights movement in America. Her years of brave work began on a bus in Montgomery, Alabama. The following passage about the beginning of her 50-year struggle is from *Rosa Parks: The Movement Organizes* by Kai Friese.

Every day when the bus she caught to or from work arrived, Mrs. Parks and the other black passengers would enter through the front doors and buy a ticket from the driver. Then they would get off the bus, enter through the rear doors, and look for a seat at the back of the vehicle. The front half of the bus was

reserved for whites, and blacks couldn't set foot in it. If the white section was filled, blacks were expected to give their seats to white passengers.

Rosa Parks was finding it more and more difficult to accept this kind of treatment. She would argue with bus drivers who told her to give up her seat, and she would march straight through the front section of the bus after paying her fare.

One day in 1943, she was thrown off a bus by a driver named James F. Blake for refusing to use the rear door. Blake told her that if she thought she was too important to go to the back door, she should stay off his bus. Many drivers learned to recognize Rosa Parks, with her hair in a braided bun, and her wire spectacles. If they saw her standing alone at a stop, they would often drive right past her.

22

23

Resource Manager

Planning Resources
- *Lesson Plans*

Transparencies
- *Bellringer*
- *Daily Language Practice*
- *Fine Art* 16–20
- *Two-Minute Skill Drill*
- *Writing Process* 14–16A

Other Print Resources
- *Composition Enrichment,* p. 33
- *Composition Practice,* p. 33
- *Composition Reteaching,* p. 33
- *Cooperative Learning Activities,* pp. 19–24
- *Listening and Speaking Activities,* p. 23

- *Thinking and Study Skills,* pp. 9, 23-24, 35, 37
- *Writing Across the Curriculum*
- *Writing Assessment and Evaluation Rubrics*

Learn About Others

A biography is one kind of real-life narrative. It's the story of a person's life, written by someone else. The person being written about is the subject of the biography.

When you read a biography, you learn about a person's life and accomplishments. You learn about the events that affected the person's life. You may also learn, as in the story of Rosa Parks, how the subject of a biography affected history. Look at what the student writer of the model below learned from reading *Rosa Parks: The Movement Organizes*.

Prewriting Tip

To help you recall information as you read a biography, jot down notes about the details that impress you.

Student Model

Rosa Parks was a brave black woman who believed in herself. When she saw how unfairly blacks were treated by white people in Montgomery, she decided to fight back. She didn't fight with violence but with the "weapon of protest." One day she refused to give up her seat on a bus to a white person, so she was arrested. She had always obeyed this rule before, but this time she was tired of being pushed around.

Even though her arrest was a small matter, it started a big movement. First came the boycott of buses and businesses. Then came the protests and sit-ins. Then came the civil rights movement. Rosa Parks showed everyone how much power you can have if you believe in yourself.

Timmy Baltz, Hufford School, Joliet, Illinois

Journal Writing

Recall a biography you have read in a book, magazine, or newspaper, or one you have seen on film. Write in your journal what you thought about this biography.

Teach

Changing Point of View

Invite students to project themselves into the situation described in the passage on page 165. Have them write about the event from the point of view of Rosa Parks. As they board the bus or wait at the bus stop, what do they see? What are they thinking? Remind students to use the pronoun *I* when they write from the point of view of the subject. **L2**

Using the Model

Ask students to think about how they might feel if people started to avoid them or make their lives difficult because they had taken a stand on an issue that was important to them. Ask students to share current examples of people being treated in this manner. **L2**

Two-Minute Skill Drill

List these verbs on the board. Have students write the past tense of each verb and then orally provide examples of them in sentences.

talk	*walk*	*dance*
learn	*collect*	*visit*

See also *Two-Minute Skill Drill Transparencies*, 4.5

Journal Writing Tip

Recording Thoughts About a Biography Encourage students to focus on what they learned from the biography. Did the person have to overcome difficulties? How do the students feel about what the person accomplished?

Teach

Comparing Biographies

Small groups of students might be interested in discussing different biographies of the same person. Suggest that everyone in the group read about the same incident or period in the subject's life. Each person should then share what he or she learned about the subject along with his or her personal feelings and thoughts about the subject. Encourage students to see that biographies can present the same information differently. **L2**

Writing a Letter

Have students each write a letter to the author of a biography that he or she particularly enjoyed. What did they like most about the biography? What did they learn by reading it? Do they have any questions to ask the author? **L3**

Additional Resources

For narrative **writing prompts**, see *Fine Art Transparencies* 16–20.

Daily Language Practice

Writing Process Transparencies, 14–16B

Writing Across the Curriculum

Cooperative Learning Activities, pp. 19–24

Thinking and Study Skills, pp. 9, 23–24, 35, 37

Composition Practice, p. 33

Listening and Speaking Activities, p. 23

Narrative Writing

Grammar Tip

As you revise your writing, make sure not to shift your verb tenses without a reason. For help with verb tenses, see Lessons 10.4–10.9, pages 339–350.

Respond in Different Ways

When you read a biography, you may be surprised. You may laugh. You may even cry. Probably more than anything else, you'll learn things you never expected to learn.

A good biography may prompt you to respond. You might tell a friend about it. You may respond in writing. The list below tells different ways you can respond to a biography.

Ways to Respond to a Biography

1. Write an account of an event as if the subject of the biography is describing it.
2. Write a journal entry for one day in the person's life.
3. Compare the way the person reacted to an event to the way you would have reacted to the same event.
4. Write an imaginary interview with the person, using questions similar to those below.

An Interview with Rosa Parks

Why did you decide not to give up your seat that day?

Do you mean that you had not stood up for your rights before this time?

Were you afraid of what might happen to you?

Mashi Fisher, Evanston, Illinois

MEETING INDIVIDUAL NEEDS   English Language Learners

Understanding Special Words

Students with limited English vocabulary may not be familiar with the words *boycott, sit-in,* and *protest.* Define these terms with the class, giving examples.

If students are very new to the United States, you may also want to provide a brief background on the civil rights movement.

4.5 | Writing Activities

Write a Brief Biography

Read a biography or a short biographical article about an athlete, musician, or movie star. Then imagine that you have spent a day with the person. Write an account of what you did with this person. Tell where you went and what you talked about.

PURPOSE To respond to a biography
AUDIENCE Yourself
LENGTH 3–4 paragraphs

WRITING RUBRICS To write an effective biography, you should

- use information you learned from your reading
- relate that information to your own experience
- use appropriate verb tenses

Using Computers

With three or four classmates, choose a public figure who, like Rosa Parks, might be a good role model. Use the Internet to find more information on the figure and then have each person write questions he or she would like to ask the subject.

Listening and Speaking

COOPERATIVE LEARNING In your group, take turns role-playing the subject while the others ask questions. Use the

Grammar Link

Don't overuse the present tense of verbs in your writing.

Write the correct form of the verb in parentheses to complete each sentence.

1. Rosa Parks's life has (inspire) many young African Americans.
2. When Parks (refuse) to give up her seat, she made history.
3. I have (learn) how to play the clarinet this year.
4. I (practice) every day.
5. Our top player (pitch) a perfect game last night.
6. He had (pitch) another perfect game earlier this season.
7. It (snow) last night.
8. It has (snow) twice this winter.
9. Last year, it had (snow) more by this date.
10. I have (like) snow since I was a little kid.

See Lessons 10.4, 10.5, and 10.7, pages 339–342 and 345–346.

information from your Internet search to help you answer the questions. Record your questions and answers as a group response to the biography.

Assess

Evaluation Rubrics

Write a Brief Biography

Use these criteria when evaluating your students' writing. Verify that the student's biography

- reflects an understanding of the biography's subject and his or her accomplishments or contributions
- expresses the student's thoughts about the subject
- reveals a personal response to something the subject has said or done

See also *Writing Assessment and Evaluation Rubrics.*

Using Computers

Make sure that students understand how to use the Internet for research.

Listening and Speaking

Encourage students to monitor their understanding of the assignment and to seek clarification as needed.

Reteaching

📁 *Composition Reteaching,* p. 33

Enrichment

📁 *Composition Enrichment,* p. 33

📧 *Fine Art Transparencies* 16–20

Close

Initiate a discussion about other ways students might respond in writing to the biography of Rosa Parks. They might write a play, compose a protest song, or write a letter about civil rights and send it to a government leader.

Grammar Link

Answers

1. inspired
2. refused
3. learned
4. practiced
   or
   practice
5. pitched
6. pitched
7. snowed
8. snowed
9. snowed
10. liked

Using the Past Tense Have students write sentences about a biographical subject of their choice. Their sentences should include past tense verbs, either alone or with the helping verb *has, have,* or *had.*

Focus

Lesson Overview

Objectives

- To develop a narrative about an important real-life experience
- To use the stages of the writing process to create and present a finished piece

Skills

- using the five stages of the writing process: prewriting, drafting, revising, editing/proofreading and publishing/ presenting; using a cluster diagram; writing dialogue

Critical Thinking

- recalling; analyzing; evaluating; synthesizing

Listening and Speaking

- discussing; reading aloud; telling a story

Bellringer
Daily Language Activity

When students enter the classroom, have this assignment on the board: *List your three favorite pieces of clothing. After each one, write a sentence that tells why you like it.*

Grammar Link to the Bellringer

Ask students to rewrite the sentences they wrote for the Bellringer as dialogue. Put this example on the board: *"This coat is the most colorful coat I've ever seen," I said.* Remind students to use quotation marks and speaker words.

See also *Daily Language Practice*

Motivating Activity

Have students describe how they feel when they wear one of the articles of clothing described in the Bellringer. What special significance does it have for them?

Narrative Writing

Narrative Writing

In the preceding lessons, you've learned about turning real-life experiences into good stories. You've practiced elaborating with details in chronological order and writing dialogue that shows what characters are like. You've also had the chance to learn how to write a brief biography. Now it's time to put together everything you've learned. In this lesson, you will tell the story of how a piece of clothing affected your life.

WRITING Online

Visit the *Writer's Choice* Web site at **writerschoice. glencoe.com** for additional writing prompts.

Assignment

Context

You want to submit a real-life narrative to a make-believe publication called *Wore Stories*. Your story will focus on how a piece of clothing affected your life.

Purpose

To retell a past experience through a narrative

Audience

Student readers of *Wore Stories*

Length

1 page

The next few pages can help you plan and write your story. Read through them and then refer to them as you need to. Don't be tied down by them, however. Remember, you're in charge of your own writing process.

Resource Manager

Planning Resources
- *Lesson Plans*

Transparencies
- *Bellringer*
- *Daily Language Practice*
- *Writing Process* 14–16B

Other Print Resources
- *Composition Enrichment*, p. 36
- *Composition Practice*, p. 36
- *Composition Reteaching*, p. 36
- *Grammar Workbook, Lesson* 78
- *Thinking and Study Skills*, p. 15, 19
- *Writing Assessment and Evaluation Rubrics*

Software
- *Writer's Assistant*

Web Sites
- *writerschoice.glencoe.com*
- *lit.glencoe.com*

Writing Process in Action

Prewriting

Prewrite to explore your thoughts about an old piece of clothing. How did you get it? How did you feel about wearing it? What happened to you while wearing it? The graphic to the right offers options to help you recall your thoughts and feelings.

Option A
Use a cluster diagram.

Option B
Review your journal.

Option C
Freewrite about a topic.

I always felt great in my too-big red shirt. I got it as a gift. It was soft and had white shiny buttons, and I wore it whenever I wanted to feel ready for my day. Why do I remember it so well?

Pages 8–11 offer more tips on freewriting. Your goal is to gather details and experiences to use in your real-life narrative.

Drafting

As you look over the prewriting notes you made, think about how you want to begin your real-life narrative. The opening paragraph should capture and hold readers' attention from the very beginning. For example, notice how Gary Soto begins his narrative.

> **Drafting Tip**
>
> For help with developing your opening, see Lesson 4.1, pages 148–151.

Literature Model

My clothes have failed me. I remember the green coat that I wore in fifth and sixth grades when you either danced like a champ or pressed yourself against a greasy wall, bitter as a penny toward the happy couples.

Gary Soto, "The Jacket"

Soto begins by telling the reader that his clothes have let him down. Then he introduces a specific piece of clothing (his

Teach

Prewriting

Using a Cluster Diagram

Students may benefit from using a cluster diagram to help them gather details about their story ideas. Suggest they freewrite first and then use details from what they have written to begin building the diagram. Encourage them to add more details, listing whatever comes to mind that relates to the main idea. Remind them that in the process they may uncover other writing ideas they will want to make note of for future use. **L2**

Developing Ideas

Some students may feel more comfortable tape-recording their ideas. Have students think about a piece of clothing that is important to them. Then have them talk about it to a friend while tape-recording the conversation. Tell students to ask each other questions about what they don't understand or want to know more about. When students are finished, have them listen to their tapes and write down any interesting ideas. **L1**

Drafting

Getting Started

Tell students that if they get stuck and can't think of a strong opening paragraph, they can start in the middle of their narrative— or even at the end! After they have some of their ideas on paper, it might be easier to think of a good beginning. Remind students to describe the setting and any characters in their narratives. **L2**

Teach

Revising

Peer Editing

Students can work in writing conferences with peer editors before they revise their writing. You may want to duplicate the Peer Response forms in *Writing Assessment and Evaluation Rubrics.* Suggest that peer editors respond to the following questions: What effect did the clothing have on the writer's life? What details are the most effective? **L2**

Editing/Proofreading

Peer Editing

After students have edited their own work, have them edit another student's writing. Remind them to refer to the Editing/Proofreading Checklist on the student page. **L2**

Publishing/Presenting

Before students present their narrative writing, discuss how to prepare their papers for publication. Emphasize the importance of the final draft and that it must be legible and neat.

Additional Resources

Writing Process Transparencies, 14–16B

Thinking and Study Skills, pp. 15, 19

Composition Practice, p. 36

Grammar Workbook, Lessons 78

Narrative Writing

Grammar Tip

If you need help revising dialogue, see Lesson 4.3, pages 156–159.

jacket) that he wore during a certain period of time (fifth and sixth grade).

How will you begin your narrative? Perhaps you'll start by describing the piece of clothing. The choice is up to you.

Revising

To begin revising, read over your draft to make sure that what you have written fits your purpose and your audience. Then have a **writing conference.** Read your draft to a partner or a small group. Use your audience's reactions to help you evaluate your work so far. The following questions can help you and your listeners.

Question A

Does my first sentence grab readers' attention?

Question B

Have I included all the important information?

Question C

Are the events in an order that makes sense?

My Aunt Jane shouted, "Surprise!"
She held out a red shirt. It was a gift that I instantly loved, even though I could tell it was to big.
Just wearing it, though, made me feel bigger older.
That night I wore the huge shirt to dinner, where my parents let me sit at the head of the table.
When I reached for my napkin, my sleeve knocked over a glass of water. The shirt's puffy sleeves hung down almost into my food. A dark area spread across the tablecloth. My shirt was wet, too.

Journal Writing Tip

Remembering Details Tell students that one important, but sometimes difficult, aspect of writing a narrative is remembering details. Ask students what the writing of their narratives helped them to remember.

Enrichment and Extension

Follow-up Ideas

- Encourage students to illustrate their narratives, either with drawings or with photographs. Bind students' finished work into a class book.
- Have a story circle in which students take turns telling their stories.

Extending Narrative Writing

- Explore opportunities for extending narrative writing beyond the classroom, such as creating a newsletter for teenagers in which they share real-life narratives about important or interesting experiences.

Editing/Proofreading

You've worked hard to write your real-life narrative. You want your readers to focus on what you've written. You don't want to distract them with any mistakes. Pay attention to capitalization, punctuation, and spelling. Make sure your writing is legible and neat. You can find more specific **proofreading** help on pages 70–73.

Publishing/Presenting

Before writing your final copy, you may want to have a family member or friend read your narrative. She or he may have some suggestions that will help. Maybe you'd rather not share your story with anyone except your teacher.

You could include a photograph or a drawing of yourself wearing the piece of clothing. That would help your reader picture the events in your narrative even more clearly.

Editing/Proofreading Checklist

- Have I used correct and varied verb forms?
- Are my sentences complete?
- Is it clear who's talking in my dialogue?
- Have I used quotation marks and other forms of punctuation correctly?

Proofreading Tip

For proofreading symbols, see page 72.

Journal Writing

Reflect on your writing process experience. Answer these questions in your journal. What do you like best about your narrative? What was the hardest part of writing it? What did you learn from your writing conference? What new thing have you learned as a writer?

Assess

Evaluation Rubrics

Use the following questions to evaluate students' finished writing.
- Does the opening of the narrative draw the reader into the story?
- Does the narrative include important details and information?
- Are events in an order that makes sense?
- Is dialogue used effectively? Is it clear who's talking?
- Are verbs used correctly?
- Are the sentences complete?
- Have quotation marks been used correctly?
- Has the edited narrative been checked for grammar, usage, spelling, and mechanics?
- Is the writing legible?

See also Writing Assessment and Evaluation Rubrics.

Reteaching
📁 *Composition Reteaching*, p. 36

Enrichment
📁 *Composition Enrichment*, p. 36

Close

Ask students what they enjoyed most about writing a real-life narrative. Did they like writing about an article of clothing? Why or why not? Ask students for other ideas, such as a scary moment, a memorable meal, or a family vacation. Write students' suggestions on the board. Tell them to remember these ideas the next time they want to write a real-life narrative.

Cultural Connections

Discussing Clothing

Point out that people sometimes wear clothing that reflects their cultural backgrounds. Ask students to give some examples (yarmulkes, turbans, saris, kimonos, kilts, dashikis, and so on). If students are personally familiar with such clothing, ask them to explain its significance and whether it is worn on special occasions or every day. Tell students they may wish to consider clothing items related to their cultural background as they generate ideas for their narrative.

About the Author

Gary Soto (1952–) teaches English and Chicano Studies at the University of California at Berkeley. Soto is a poet, novelist, short story writer, and essayist. The selection is from *Living up the Street* (1985), his award-winning memoir about growing up in a working-class family in Fresno.

Focus

Lesson Overview

Objectives

- To evaluate a literature selection that illustrates effective narrative writing
- To apply understanding of how writing a story can lead to self-discovery
- To write an autobiographical essay

Skills

- monitoring comprehension, interpreting, predicting, connecting, clarifying

Critical Thinking

- interpreting

Listening and Speaking

- discussing

🔔 Bellringer
Daily Language Activity

When students enter the classroom, have this assignment on the board: *Have you ever had a piece of clothing that made you feel a certain way when you wore it? Tell about it in a paragraph.*

See also 📖 *Daily Language Practice*

Motivating Activity

Tell students that in "The Jacket" Gary Soto describes part of his childhood during which he felt that nothing good would ever happen. Ask students if they have ever felt this way. Encourage them to write about this experience in their journals. Point out that even unhappy times offer an opportunity for self knowledge.

Literature Model

Gary Soto

THE JACKET

In this narrative, Gary Soto writes about a time when he felt the shame and anger of an outsider. He blames his experiences on an ugly jacket he had to wear. As you read the story, note how Soto uses descriptive details to help the reader understand the importance of this real-life experience. Then try the activities in Linking Writing and Literature on page 178.

My clothes have failed me. I remember the green coat that I wore in fifth and sixth grades when you either danced like a champ or pressed yourself against a greasy wall, bitter as a penny toward the happy couples.

When I needed a new jacket and my mother asked what kind I wanted, I described something like bikers wear: black leather and silver studs with enough belts to hold down a small town. We were in the kitchen, steam on the windows from her cooking. She listened so long while stirring dinner that I thought she understood for sure the kind I wanted. The next day when I got

---

Resource Manager

Planning Resources
- *Lesson Plans*

📖 **Transparencies**
- *Bellringer*
- *Daily Language Practice*
- *Fine Art 16–20*

📁 Other Print Resources
- *Listening and Speaking Activities*, p. 23
- *Thinking and Study Skills*, p. 9
- *Writing Assessment and Evaluation Rubrics*

💻 Web Sites
- *writerschoice.glencoe.com*
- *lit.glencoe.com*

Narrative Writing

Augustín Lazo, *Head,* 1940

home from school, I discovered draped on my bedpost a jacket the color of day-old guacamole. I threw my books on the bed and approached the jacket slowly, as if it were a stranger whose hand I had to shake. I touched the vinyl sleeve, the collar, and peeked at the mustard-colored lining.

Literature Model **173**

Teach

Critical Thinking

Interpret Ask students what two important points the narrator is making in the first paragraph. *(The narrator is signaling that the story will have something to do with clothing and that at this time in a person's life, the right clothes can mean the difference between happiness and despair.)*

Active Reading Strategies

Predict Ask: "How do you think the narrator will feel about his new jacket? What makes you think so." *(Sample response: He will hate it. He asked for a biker jacket with black leather, silver studs, and lots of belts, but he got one "the color of day-old guacamole," with vinyl sleeves and a mustard-colored lining.)*

Viewing the Art

Augustín Lazo, *Head,* 1940
Cabeza—the title of the piece in Spanish—was painted with oil on celotex by Augustín Lazo (1896–1971) in 1940. It measures 19 by 15 1/2 inches, and hangs in the collection of La Secretaría de Hacienda y Crédito Público, Mexico.

Interpret and Analyze Use the following question for discussion:

• Compare and contrast the mood of the picture and the mood of the selection. Do the picture and the story have any elements in common?

6+1 Trait® Writing

Word Choice Soto refers to the jacket as "the ugly brother who tagged along wherever I went." Ask students to explain what this metaphor means. *(Like a pesky sibling, the jacket was a constant, unavoidable, and unwelcome presence in the narrator's life.)*

Narrative Writing

Literature Model

fence. Everybody saw me. Although they didn't say out loud, "Man, that's ugly," I heard a buzz-buzz of gossip and even laughter that I knew was meant for me.

And so I went, in my guacamole jacket. So embarrassed, so hurt, I couldn't even do my homework. I received Cs on quizzes, and forgot the state capitals and the rivers of South America, our friendly neighbor. Even the girls who had been friendly blew away like loose flowers to follow the boys in neat jackets.

> **❝** *And so I went, in my guacamole jacket.* **❞**

I wore that thing for three years until the sleeves grew short and my forearms stuck out like the necks of turtles. All during that time no love came to me—no little dark girl in a Sunday dress she wore on Monday. At lunchtime I stayed with the ugly boys who leaned against the chain-link fence and looked around with propellers of grass spinning in our mouths. We saw girls walk by alone, saw couples, hand in hand, their heads like bookends pressing air together. We saw them and spun our propellers so fast our faces were blurs.

I blame that jacket for those bad years. I blame my mother for her bad taste and her cheap ways. It was a sad time for the heart. With a friend I spent my sixth-grade year in a tree in the alley waiting for something good to happen to me in that jacket, which had become the ugly brother who tagged along wherever I went. And it was about that time that I began to grow. My chest puffed up with muscle and, strangely, a few more ribs. Even my hands, those fleshy hammers, showed bravely through the cuffs, the fingers already hardening for the coming fights. But that L-shaped rip on the left sleeve got bigger; bits of stuffing coughed out from its wound after a hard day of play. I finally taped it closed, but in rain or cold weather the tape peeled off like a scab and more stuffing fell out until that sleeve shriveled into a palsied arm. That winter the elbows began

> **❝** *I blame that jacket for those bad years.* **❞**

to crack and whole chunks of green began to fall off. I showed the cracks to my mother, who always seemed to be at the stove with steamed-up glasses, and she said that there were children in Mexico who would love

Compare and Contrast

Compare and Contrast

Tell students that examining how two people, situations, or ideas are alike and different can lead to a better understanding of each. Explain that the narrator in "The Jacket" and Morning Girl in the excerpt from *Morning Girl* (pp. 134–139) are both struggling with their identity—who they really are. Morning Girl seeks her identity in how she looks physically. The narrator in "The Jacket" seeks his in how cool (or uncool) his clothes are.

Practice Ask students to compare the protagonists in the two excerpts. Who is more successful in resolving the identity question? *(Both struggle with questions of identity. They are different in that Morning Girl can confide her fears in her mother, whereas the narrator in "The Jacket" cannot. When the selections end, Morning Girl answers her identity question, but the narrator in "The Jacket" is still struggling with the "ugly brother.")*

Literature Model

that jacket. I told her that this was America and yelled that Debbie, my sister, didn't have a jacket like mine. I ran outside, ready to cry, and climbed the tree by the alley to think bad thoughts and watch my breath puff white and disappear.

> **"** *. . . I went outside with my jacket across my arm.* **"**

But whole pieces still casually flew off my jacket when I played hard, read quietly, or took vicious spelling tests at school. When it became so spotted that my brother began to call me "camouflage," I flung it over the fence into the alley. Later, however, I swiped the jacket off the ground and went inside to drape it across my lap and mope.

I was called to dinner: steam silvered my mother's glasses as she said grace; my brother and sister with their heads bowed made ugly faces at their glasses of powdered milk. I gagged too, but eagerly ate big rips of buttered tortilla that held scooped up beans. Finished, I went outside with my jacket across my arm. It was a cold sky. The faces of clouds were piled up, hurting. I climbed the fence, jumping down with a grunt. I started up the alley and soon slipped into my jacket, that green ugly brother who breathed over my shoulder that day and ever since.

Narrative Writing

Teach

Literary Elements

Symbolism Ask: What did the jacket come to symbolize in the narrator's life? *(The jacket symbolizes everything that is bad and everything that has gone wrong in his life.)*

Additional Resources

Fine Art Transparencies, 16–20
Listening and Speaking Activities, p. 23
Thinking and Study Skills, p. 9

6+1 Trait® Writing

Word Choice

Tell students that effective word choice means using rich, colorful, and exact language that brings a piece of writing to life for the reader. Effective word choice can include strong verbs, precise modifiers, metaphors, and similes. In "The Jacket," Soto's lively language enables the reader to see and feel what the narrator does and thus to make a strong connection to the story.

Practice Remind students that a simile is a comparison using *like* or *as*. Ask students to locate several similes in "The Jacket" and then write several of their own to describe something with which they are familiar. *(Examples: danced like a champ, thin as a young tree, stared at the jacket like an enemy, arms feeling like braille from goose bumps, teeth chattered like a cup of crooked dice, their heads like bookends)*

6+1 Trait® is a registered trademark of Northwest Regional Educational Laboratory, which does not endorse this product.

Linking Writing and Literature

Assess

Evaluation Rubrics

◆ Talk About Reading

Possible answers to the questions:

1. Answers will vary, but most students will identify with the narrator's sense of despair, anger, and embarrassment at having to wear the jacket.

2. The narrator's mother is a frugal, practical woman who provides for her family, though not always in ways that they wish.

3. The narrator's words—*the color of day-old guacamole, vinyl sleeve, mustard-colored lining, ugly,* and *big*—make it easy for the reader to picture the jacket, and they show how much the narrator dislikes it.

4. The list may include, but not be limited to, the following: a likeable narrator, a narrator who shares my feelings, a situation that rings true and reminds me of my own life, believable characters, vivid and colorful language that helps me see what is being described. Students might suggest they can use these qualities in their own narrative or personal writing.

◆ Write About Reading

The autobiographical essay should do the following:

• quickly get the reader's attention
• relate an interesting experience from the student's life
• have a clear main idea
• include interesting, vivid language

Close

Ask students to recall a time when they felt embarrassed and imagined that everyone was laughing or looking at them. Have students write briefly in their journals about the incident and how they felt.

Literature Model

◆ Linking Writing and Literature

◆ Collect Your Thoughts

Think about "The Jacket," the excerpt from Gary Soto's memoir *Living Up the Street*. What do you think is the main idea of the excerpt? Make some notes that explain what the story is about.

◆ Talk About Reading

Discuss "The Jacket" with your classmates. Select one person to lead the discussion and another to take notes. Use the following questions to guide the discussion.

1. **Connect to Your Life** Have you ever found yourself in a situation similar to that of the narrator's? How did being in that situation make you feel? Did you experience any of the same emotions as the narrator?

2. **Critical Thinking: Draw Conclusions** Think about what the narrator's mother does and says. How would you describe her?

3. **6+1 Trait®: Word Choice** What words does Soto use to describe the jacket? How does his word choice help you to understand how he feels about it?

4. **Connect to Your Writing** What makes "The Jacket" interesting to read? What makes it seem realistic to you? Make a list of the qualities that make the excerpt enjoyable. Then discuss how you could create those qualities in your own writing.

◆ Write About Reading

Autobiographical Essay Write an auto-biographical essay in which you tell about an experience that affected you, like the new jacket affected the narrator of the excerpt. Explain what happened, how it made you feel, and why you felt that way.

Focus on Word Choice Think carefully about the words you choose to tell your story. Use precise action words, modifiers, and figurative language that paint clear and colorful images for your readers.

For more information on word choice and the 6+1 Trait® model, see **Writing and Research Handbook,** pages 682–684.

6+1 Trait® is a registered trademark of Northwest Regional Educational Laboratory, which does not endorse this product.

Narrative Writing

UNIT 4 Review

Reflecting on the Unit

Summarize what you learned in this unit by answering the following questions.

❶ What are the characteristics of a well-written real-life story?

❷ How can you keep a story clearly on track?

❸ What are the important things to remember when you write dialogue?

❹ How can you help your readers understand what was special about an event?

❺ In what ways might you learn from and respond to a biography?

🎒 Adding to Your Portfolio

CHOOSE A SELECTION FOR YOUR PORTFOLIO Look over the narrative writing you did during this unit. Select a completed piece of writing to put into your portfolio. The piece you choose should show some or all of the following:

- a beginning that makes the reader want to continue reading
- believable characters in a specific place, involved in clearly explained action
- realistic dialogue that gives details about the characters
- an order that helps the reader follow the action
- a conclusion that winds up the story

REFLECT ON YOUR CHOICE Attach a note to the piece you chose, explaining briefly why you chose it and what you learned from writing it.

SET GOALS How can you improve your writing? What skill will you focus on the next time you write?

Writing Across the Curriculum

MAKE A SOCIAL STUDIES CONNECTION Think about how someone from another culture or part of the world might react to your narrative about a piece of clothing. How might you meet this person? What questions might he or she ask? How might you need to change or add to your narrative? Write brief notes to respond to these questions.

Review **179**

Review

Reflecting on the Unit
You may have students respond to the summary questions in writing or through discussion.

Writing Across the Curriculum
Have students consider how clothing needs are different in various parts of the world. Encourage students to think about the other person's point of view.

Adding to Your Portfolio
To help students choose pieces for their portfolios, suggest that they review journal entries and biography responses as well as the real-life stories they have written. Since this unit emphasizes personal narratives, they may want one of the portfolio pieces they select to be about the experience or event that was most meaningful to them.

Portfolio Evaluation
If you grade the individual portfolio selections, you may want to award two marks—one each for content and form. Explain your assessment criteria before students make their selections. Commend

- experimentation with creative prewriting techniques
- clear, concise writing in which the main idea, audience, and purpose are evident
- successful revisions
- work that shows a flair for language

✔ ASSESSMENT OPTIONS

📁 *Tests with Answer Key and Rubrics*
Unit 4 Choice A Test, p. 13
Unit 4 Choice B Test, p. 14
Unit 4 Composition Objective Test, pp. 15–16

💾 *Testmaker*
Unit 4 Choice A Test
Unit 4 Choice B Test
Unit 4 Composition Objective Test

You may wish to administer one of these tests as a Mastery Test.

📼 *Mindjogger Videoquizzes*

Discussing the Quotation

Read aloud the quotation selected from Jean Craighead George's "Koko: Smart Signing Gorilla." Ask students how the photograph helps to represent or extend the quotation's meaning. Let students know that they can find out more about Jean Craighead George and "Koko: Smart Signing Gorilla" in *Glencoe Literature: The Reader's Choice,* Course 1, pp. 158–165.
Writing Prompt Make a list of questions that you would like to have answered about endangered species, gorillas, or The Gorilla Foundation.

"Koko is one of an endangered species. The foundation she inspired, The Gorilla Foundation, is dedicated to breeding gorillas in captivity."

—Jean Craighead George, "Koko: Smart Signing Gorilla".

Expository Writing

181

Objectives

- To understand and use the techniques of expository writing
- To organize details effectively
- To order information for presenting a step-by-step process
- To write reports such as book reports
- To use the stages of the writing process—prewriting, drafting, revising, editing/proofreading, and publishing/presenting—to create and present a finished piece of expository writing
- To evaluate one's own expository writing and the expository writing of others

✔ ASSESSMENT OPTIONS

📁 *Tests with Answer Key and Rubrics*
Unit 5 Choice A Test, p. 17
Unit 5 Choice B Test, p. 18
Unit 5 Composition Objective Test, pp. 19–20

💾 *Testmaker*
Unit 5 Choice A Test
Unit 5 Choice B Test
Unit 5 Composition Objective Test

You may wish to administer either the Unit 5 Choice A Test or the Unit 5 Choice B Test as a pretest.

Key to Ability Levels

L1 Level 1 activities are within the basic ability range of students.

L2 Level 2 activities are within the ability range of average students.

L3 Level 3 activities are more challenging activities.

- Thinking and Study Skills
- Writing Across the Curriculum
- Writing Assessment and Evaluation Rubrics
- Writing in the Real World

💾 **Software**
- *Presentation Plus!*
- *Revising with Style*
- *Testmaker*
- *Writer's Assistant*

🖥 **Web Sites**
- writerschoice.glencoe.com
- lit.glencoe.com

📼 **Video**
- MindJogger Videoquizzes

Focus

Lesson Overview

Objectives

- To explore a type of expository writing—newspaper articles
- To become aware of the role of research in preparing some expository writing
- To learn about the process of producing a newspaper article

Skills

- recalling; locating information; writing explanations

Critical Thinking

- analyzing; visualizing; synthesizing

Listening and Speaking

- discussing

Bellringer
Daily Language Activity

When students enter the classroom, have this assignment on the board: *List four subjects for magazine or newspaper articles that you think should be illustrated for best effect.*

Grammar Link to the Bellringer

Ask students what is wrong with the following sentence: *An illustrated article is more better than one that is all writing.* Remind them that *better* is the only comparative needed.

See also *Daily Language Practice*

Motivating Activity

Encourage students to skim through a current newspaper or magazine until a story catches their eye. Then ask them to discuss what it was about the story that grabbed their attention. (A headline, an illustration, a graphic, or a photograph may have piqued their interest.) Volunteers may wish to explain to the class why they found a particular headline or visual compelling.

Expository Writing

Writing in the Real World

MEDIA Connection
Newspaper Article

A significant number of articles in the press are expository—they explain what the public is curious about. In the article excerpted below, sports writer Julie Sheer of the *Chicago Tribune* tries to answer a critical question for hoops fans: "How *does* Michael Jordan fly?"

from "How Does Michael Fly?"

by Julie Sheer

No conversation about Michael Jordan is complete without references to hang time. So, what exactly is hang time? The velocity, or speed, a player has when he takes off, combined with the path his center of gravity follows on the way up, plus body manipulations along the way, fool us into thinking he's hanging in the air for an unusually long period of time. . . .

. . . So, how is it he's able to hit the heights he does? Michael's rocket-powered leaps are helped by long legs and a slender torso, which give him a higher center of gravity. However, it's the makeup of his muscles, mainly the quadriceps, calf muscles and gluteus, that gives him the power.

A good jumper will have muscles that store elastic energy and also a larger percentage of fast-twitch than slow-twitch fibers. . .

When it comes to technique, Jordan's flight patterns can't be duplicated. "I just make it up," he admits.

Resource Manager

Planning Resources
- Lesson Plans

Transparencies
- Bellringer
- Daily Language Practice
- Writing Process 17–19B

Other Print Resources
- Cooperative Learning Activities
- Thinking and Study Skills, pp. 8, 22, 39–40
- Writing Assessment and Evaluation Rubrics
- Writing in the Real World, pp. 17–20

A Writer's Process

Prewriting
Capturing an Idea

A newspaper staff is always on the lookout for good ideas. What are people curious about? What information would they like to have? Steve Cvengros, editor at the *Chicago Tribune*, knew he'd found a good story idea when he saw a headline in *USA Today.* "It only seems [Michael] Jordan floats longer. There's no such thing as defying gravity," the story said.

Cvengros brought the idea to his *Tribune* team—writer Julie Sheer and artist Dennis Odom. The three agreed to do the story as a graphic—drawings and words combined.

Writer Sheer went immediately to work. She had many questions: Why is Chicago Bulls star Michael Jordan able to jump so high? Can he really hang in the air? How does gravity affect his flight?

She found some answers in reference books, such as *Sport Science*, and in books on Jordan. She gathered more information by interviewing coaches and scientists on the phone.

Sheer and Odom also interviewed Jordan to get his point of view.

Little by little, Sheer and Odom started to get the picture.

They learned that Jordan has a great number of fast-twitch fibers in his leg muscles that act as springs to rocket him off the ground. In flight, Jordan's arm and leg movements make him look as if he's floating.

Drafting
Writing and Illustrating

Many expository articles have information that is best explained through graphics—charts, graphs, and pictures. In this case, the *Tribune* team agreed that they wanted a big painting of Jordan in the center of their full-page article.

Odom's first challenge was to do the painting. To find just the right pose, he studied thousands of photographs of Jordan in action. Then Odom went to work on the smaller illustrations.

Meanwhile Sheer began to write. To help organize her draft, Sheer needed to break down the information into topics. "I sat down at a computer and typed up some headlines," she said. These served as subheads that broke down the main topic of "flight" into smaller topics—"the muscle behind the magic" and "stages of a vertical jump."

The writing job was tough, Sheer said. "I had to pick out what was most important and

Expository Writing

Teach

Reading Media

Have students preview the title and focus of the Media Connection. Point out that an illustration may greatly enhance a newspaper article and can work to extend its meaning. Have students read the article.

Discussion Prompts

Discuss any expository writing with graphics that students have read. Use prompts such as the following:

- Have you ever read a description of a fish or other creature that included a labeled diagram?
- Have you ever read an illustrated explanation of a process such as how blood circulates or how a video game is played?
- At what tasks did the writer-illustrator team of Sheer and Odom work in the early stages of the project? (research, outlining)
- How much collaboration is necessary at the beginning of a shared project? Should the team members work separately at first?

Cultural Connections

Adapting Games

Tell students that although basketball was first popularized in the United States, by the latter half of the twentieth century it had become an international sport and an Olympic spectacle. When adopted by other countries, games such as basketball may be altered to suit the new playing community. Ask students if they know how any sports have been adapted to suit younger and smaller players. Do they know of sports that began elsewhere and are now popular in the United States? (Soccer is one example.) How have these sports changed?

Teach

Discussion Prompts

- What should you be looking for as you prepare to revise a first draft of expository writing? What did the editor, Cvengros, look for as he read Sheer's first draft?

- What special problems might come up as you prepare to revise an illustrated explanation? How did the writer-illustrator team organize the information about Michael Jordan?

Extending Ideas

Stimulate a general discussion of the Media Connection. You may want to invite students to talk about

- how they would go about becoming an expert on a subject for an article
- whether they would plan to include pictures or graphics
- how they would design their pages

Additional Resources

Writing Process Transparencies, 17–19B

Cooperative Learning Activities, pp. 25–30

Writing in the Real World, pp.17–20

Thinking and Study Skills, pp. 8, 22, 39–40

Expository Writing

boil it down so I understood it. Then I had to explain it so a reader could understand."

Revising
Designing the Page

When Sheer finished writing her draft, she gave it to Cvengros, the editor. He checked the draft for words used too often, facts without sources, and writing that had become so technical that it had lost its fun.

Odom finished his illustrations and turned his attention to drawing an outline of the finished page. He photocopied his painting of Jordan and pasted it in the center. Now the team was ready to fit the other pieces of art and copy onto the page.

How did the team organize the information to explain Jordan's skill? After several tries, they decided on two columns. The left column would explain the science of "hang time." The column on the right would explain the special features of Jordan's muscular system.

Editing/Proofreading
Fine-Tuning

With the pieces put together, the team was ready to fine-tune the page. They read the headlines and subheads. Were they clear? Were they fun? They saw that some ideas needed more space. Others had to be cut.

During the final checking, they made sure that the facts were printed correctly. Copy editors proofread for errors such as misspelled words and mistakes in grammar. The sports editor reviewed the final page too. "He's a real basketball nut, so he read every word," Sheer said.

Publishing
Going to Press

At last the page went to press. According to Cvengros, the big colorful graphic was a huge success. Jordan himself liked the page. "We had a special copy made for Michael," Cvengros said proudly.

Civic Literacy

Using Newspaper Graphics

Newspapers often combine graphics with text to educate local readers about a particular danger and what might be done to avoid it. For example, before a solar eclipse, many newspapers present a diagram showing how to make a safe viewing screen for the event. As flu season opens, newspapers often print charts showing symptoms, treatments, and danger signs. Ask students to find and explain additional examples from their own local papers.

Examining Writing in the Real World

Analyzing the Media Connection

Discuss these questions about the model on page 182.

1. What kinds of things does Sheer assume her audience knows about Michael Jordan? How can you tell?

2. What term does Sheer define in the excerpt? Why do you think she provides this definition?

3. What cause-and-effect explanation does Sheer give? Why is this information important?

4. Whom does Sheer quote in the article? In your opinion, how does the quote add or detract from the article's effect?

5. Would you describe Sheer's writing style as formal or informal? Support your answer with examples.

Analyzing a Writer's Process

Discuss these questions about Julie Sheer's writing process.

1. How did writer Julie Sheer gather information for her story?

2. Why did Sheer find writing the story difficult?

3. Describe Sheer's technique for organizing her draft. How does your organizational technique differ from Sheer's?

4. How did the *Tribune* team work together to design and review the page?

5. What did the team members check before sending the page to press?

Grammar Link

Avoid double comparisons when you write.

Never use *more* or *most* with adjectives or adverbs ending in *-er* or *-est.*

A good jumper will have . . . a larger percentage of fast-twitch . . . fibers.

Revise the sentences below, correcting the double comparisons.

1. Michael Jordan jumped more better than any other player.

2. On the court, Jordan was an even more greater performer than Julius Erving.

3. His center of gravity is more higher than that of most people.

4. Jordan had the most longest "hang time" of the Chicago Bulls.

5. Jordan is one of the most greatest players ever.

See Lesson 12.3, page 383, and Lesson 13.3, page 399.

Answers

1. Michael Jordan jumped better than any other player.

2. On the court, Jordan was an even greater performer than Julius Erving.

3. His center of gravity is higher than that of most people.

4. Jordan had the longest "hang time" of the Chicago Bulls.

5. Jordan is one of the greatest players ever.

Close

Have students discuss examples of expository writing with graphics they find in their textbooks.

Assess

Analyzing the Media Connection

1. Sheer assumes that the audience knows Michael Jordan as a basketball superstar known for his incredible, long-lasting jumps and leaps. She never identifies him as such.

2. Sheer defines *hang time;* it's the focus, or topic, of the article.

3. She explains the cause of hang time. This information supports the article's main idea.

4. Sheer quotes Michael Jordan. The student may suggest that the quote adds interest to the article by using the superstar's own words.

5. The writing style is informal. Answers will vary. Possible answers include: "So what exactly is hang time?" "So, how is it . . ."

Analyzing a Writer's Process

1. Sheer found information in reference books; in books on Jordan; and by interviewing coaches, scientists, and Jordan himself.

2. She had to explain difficult concepts to the reader.

3. Sheer created headlines (or subheads) to break down the topic. Students may suggest that they use outlines or index cards to organize their material.

4. The editor checked the draft's content; the illustrator created illustrations and outlined the page; copy editors proofread for errors; the sports editor checked sports facts.

5. The team made sure their facts were accurate, and they revised grammatical errors.

Reteaching

Remind students that if they create a graphic to go with a piece of writing, the words and artwork should reinforce each other.

Enrichment

Students might first conceive of an expository piece as a series of pictures. Then they can write a caption for each image as a first step toward completing a draft.

Focus

Lesson Overview

Objectives
- To recognize different kinds of expository writing
- To write a clear and concise explanation

Skills
- recognizing ways to inform and explain; writing an explanation

Critical Thinking
- identifying; defining and clarifying

Listening and Speaking
- discussing; explaining a process

Bellringer
Daily Language Activity

When students enter the classroom, have this assignment on the board: *Write three sentences explaining how to light a candle. Label your sentences Step 1, Step 2, and Step 3.*

Grammar Link to the Bellringer

Ask students to underline any pronouns in their Bellringer sentences. Is the referent of each pronoun clear?

✍ **See also** *Daily Language Practice*

Motivating Activity

To help students realize that they are already familiar with expository writing, encourage them to recall and discuss information they have learned through reading.

Teach

Using the Model

Point out that the writer uses time references to help explain the development of the oil lamp. These references place the invention in a time frame readers can understand. **L2**

Expository Writing

LESSON
5.1

Writing to Help Others Understand

Expository writing is writing that shares knowledge. It informs or explains, sometimes by defining, classifying, or giving directions.

> ### Literature Model
>
> Some 20,000 years ago, people realized that they could get light by burning oil, and the first lamps appeared. These lamps were hollowed-out rocks full of animal fat. Lamps with wicks of vegetable fibers were first made in about 1000 B.C. They had a simple channel to hold the wick; later, the wick was held in a spout.
>
> Lionel Bender, *Invention*

You may never have used an oil lamp. Having read this explanation, though, you know how and when lamps were invented. Bender has shared some knowledge on a subject you may not have known about.

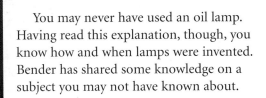

Resource Manager

Planning Resources
- Lesson Plans

✍ Transparencies
- Bellringer
- Daily Language Practice
- Fine Art 21–25
- Two-Minute Skill Drill
- Writing Process 17–19B

📂 Other Print Resources
- Composition Enrichment, p. 37
- Composition Practice, p. 37
- Composition Reteaching, p. 37
- Cooperative Learning Activities, pp. 26–30
- Listening and Speaking Activities, pp. 12–13, 21, 24

- Research Paper and Report Writing, pp. 32–38
- Sentence-Combining Practice, pp. 30–32
- Thinking and Study Skills, pp. 6–9, 12–13, 17–18, 20
- Writing Across the Curriculum
- Writing Assessment and Evaluation Rubrics

Learn from Expository Writing

Bender's paragraph is a good example of expository writing. It informs. It helps people learn about the world around them.

You can find expository writing in many places: textbooks, cookbooks, encyclopedias, newspapers, instruction manuals. No matter where you find it, expository writing is always meant to help people learn.

If you've ever jotted down directions for someone, you have already done some expository writing. You've helped someone learn how to get somewhere. Look at the following directions. How does the writer share knowledge with the reader?

TOP SECRET

Peter—
- Look out your window. See the mailbox on the corner? At 2:30 p.m. Sunday, go there.

- Next, walk three blocks down West Liberty Street. Then turn right onto Central.

- The third house on the left is my aunt's place. She said we could practice in her basement. I'll be waiting with my guitar, and we'll make that tape for your mom's surprise party.

Journal Writing

List some topics that you could explain to others. Choose one idea and write down three pieces of information about it.

Teach

Using the Model

In the example on the previous page, the writer gives step-by-step directions with clear and specific details. Point out that directions can become unclear when steps are missing, out of order, or incomplete. Call attention to the arrangement of these directions in short, easy-to-follow steps and the writer's use of visual details such as the mailbox, and the street name, which help orient the reader. **L2**

Making Inferences

Ask students to think about how new inventions often arise from people's specific needs. What specific need led to the invention of the oil lamp? (the need to have light after sunset) Point out that one invention is often made obsolete by another. What invention made the oil lamp obsolete in many parts of the world? (the electric lightbulb) **L1**

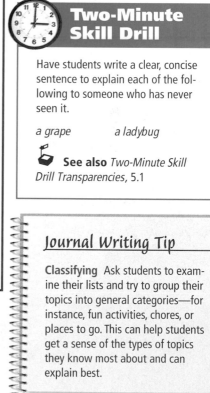

Two-Minute Skill Drill

Have students write a clear, concise sentence to explain each of the following to someone who has never seen it.

a grape   *a ladybug*

See also *Two-Minute Skill Drill Transparencies*, 5.1

Journal Writing Tip

Classifying Ask students to examine their lists and try to group their topics into general categories—for instance, fun activities, chores, or places to go. This can help students get a sense of the types of topics they know most about and can explain best.

Teach

Promoting Discussion

Discuss how a broad topic can be explored in a variety of ways. For the topic of astronomy, for instance, a student might define a star, explain the process by which the solar system formed, give instructions for focusing a telescope, compare two planets, or classify the different kinds of eclipses. Encourage students to identify how each topic is expository.

Rewriting for Clarity

Ask students if they have ever been frustrated by poorly written instructions. Suggest that they try rewriting such instructions to make them easier to follow. Remind students that sometimes a difficult step can be made easier by dividing it into smaller steps.

Additional Resources

For expository **writing prompts**, see *Fine Art Transparencies* 21–25.

Daily Language Practice

Writing Process Transparencies, 17–19B

Writing Across the Curriculum

Cooperative Learning Activities, pp. 26–30

Thinking and Study Skills, pp. 6–9, 12–13, 17–18, 20

Listening and Speaking Activities, pp. 12–13, 21, 24

Sentence-Combining Practice, pp. 30–32

Research Paper and Report Writing, pp. 32–38

Composition Practice, p. 37

Vocabulary Tip

When editing, check your spelling. Many foreign words such as *mbira* have unusual spellings. For more information on words borrowed from other languages, see Lesson 22.1, page 543.

Expository Writing

Inform and Explain in Different Ways

Directions, such as those on page 187, are one kind of expository writing. Other kinds of expository writing explain a process, provide a definition, compare and contrast two things, or divide things into groups. Read the two kinds of expository writing shown below.

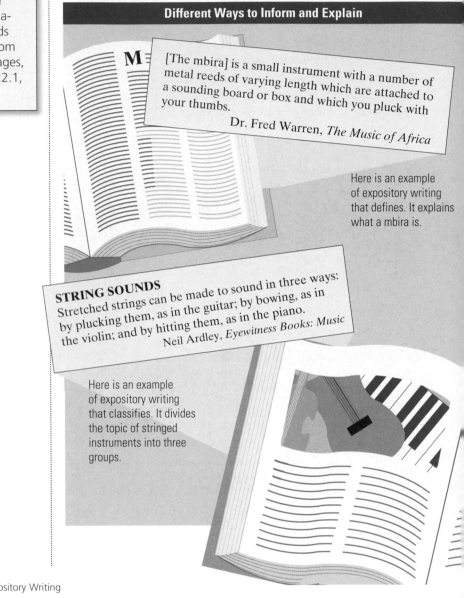

Different Ways to Inform and Explain

[The mbira] is a small instrument with a number of metal reeds of varying length which are attached to a sounding board or box and which you pluck with your thumbs.

Dr. Fred Warren, *The Music of Africa*

Here is an example of expository writing that defines. It explains what a mbira is.

STRING SOUNDS
Stretched strings can be made to sound in three ways: by plucking them, as in the guitar; by bowing, as in the violin; and by hitting them, as in the piano.

Neil Ardley, *Eyewitness Books: Music*

Here is an example of expository writing that classifies. It divides the topic of stringed instruments into three groups.

Less Proficient Readers

Understanding Directions

Invite students to discuss strategies for comprehending directions written in English. What strategies have been helpful to them in the past? Encourage students to discuss using photographs or other graphics, using a dictionary or context clues to define unfamiliar words, and breaking directions into smaller steps. You might wish to guide students through a complete set of directions using these strategies.

Expository Writing

Write an Explanation of a Game

Think about how to play a simple playground game. List the rules for playing. Then write an explanation of the game for a younger student who has never played it.

PURPOSE To teach a new game
AUDIENCE A younger student
LENGTH 1–2 paragraphs

WRITING RUBRICS To write an effective explanation of a game, you should

- define the game and its goal
- explain the steps in the game, from first to last
- print legibly for a young reader

Cross-Curricular Activity

HISTORY In a history book, find a paragraph that explains something, such as how the Constitution was adopted. Read the paragraph at least twice. Then, in your own words, write a summary of what the paragraph says.

Make a pronoun clearly refer to its antecedent.

. . . **people** realized that **they** could get light. . . .

Rewrite each sentence to make the meaning clear.

1. People have always invented things, and they have helped them learn more about the world.
2. Telescopes help us learn about the stars; they bring them into focus.
3. The inventor has a brother, and he helps him with his experiments.
4. They have many books about inventions in the school library.

See Lesson 11.3, page 365.

Viewing and Representing

ILLUSTRATING AN EXPLANATION To help a younger student understand your game, provide some drawings to explain its rules and action. Draw four or five pictures (stick figures will do) that would help a young student see how the game really works. Compare your writing with your drawings to make sure the drawings send the same message as the writing.

Assess

Evaluation Rubrics

Write an Explanation of a Game

Use these criteria when evaluating your students' writing.
- Did the student include a definition of the game and its goal?
- Did the student provide an explanation of the steps in order from first to last?

See also *Writing Assessment and Evaluating Rubrics.*

Cross-Curricular Activity: History

Use the following questions to assess each student's paragraph:
- Did the student explain the paragraph's main idea?
- Did the student write the explanation in his or her own words?

Viewing and Representing

Student illustrations should
- illustrate the rules of the game
- clarify written information

Reteaching

📁 *Composition Reteaching*, p. 37

Enrichment

📁 *Composition Enrichment*, p. 37

🖼 *Fine Art Transparencies* 21–25

Close

Ask students to take their journal entry from page 187 and expand it into a paragraph. Have them identify their paragraph as a definition, directions, classification, comparison, explanation of a process, or whatever type of expository writing it is.

Grammar Link

Answers

Answers may vary. Suggestions follow:
1. . . . and these things have helped them . . .
2. . . . because they bring the stars into focus.
3. . . . and his brother helps him with his experiments.
4. There are many books . . .

Focus

Lesson Overview

Objectives

- To learn how to note similarities and differences between two things
- To write comparison-contrast pieces

Skills

- organizing details; making a Venn diagram

Critical Thinking

- analyzing; comparing; contrasting

Listening and Speaking

- discussing; questioning; evaluating

🔔 Bellringer
Daily Language Activity

When students enter the classroom, have this assignment on the board: *List four ways cats and dogs are alike and four ways they are different.*

Grammar Link to the Bellringer

Ask students to pick the correct verb for this sentence: *Neither my cat nor the dogs next door (has, have) any use for squirrels.* Tell them that *have* is correct and that they will be practicing the rule that explains this.

🔖 **See also** *Daily Language Practice*

Motivating Activity

Encourage students to discuss two subjects that have meaning for them—two events (movies, holidays), two objects (video games, articles of clothing), or two people—comparing and contrasting by telling what they like and dislike about each subject.

Expository Writing

LESSON
5.2

Comparing and Contrasting Two Things

Comparison-contrast analysis is one kind of expository writing. When you compare two things, you explain how they are similar. When you contrast them, you explain how they differ.

VS.

Superman and Batman are two of the best-known comic book superheroes. They are alike in some ways but different in other ways. Which crime fighter has which powers? How are the superheroes' personal histories similar and different? To answer these questions, you might write a comparison-contrast piece.

190 Unit 5 Expository Writing

Resource Manager

Planning Resources
- Lesson Plans

🔖 Transparencies
- Bellringer
- Daily Language Practice
- Fine Art 21–25
- Two-Minute Skill Drill
- Writing Process 17–19B

📁 Other Print Resources
- Composition Enrichment, p. 38
- Composition Practice, p. 38
- Composition Reteaching, p. 38
- Cooperative Learning Activities, pp. 26–30
- Listening and Speaking Activities, pp. 12–13, 21, 24
- Research Paper and Report Writing, pp. 32–38

- Sentence-Combining Practice, pp. 30–32
- Thinking and Study Skills, pp. 6, 8–9, 11, 15
- Writing Across the Curriculum
- Writing Assessment and Evaluation Rubrics

Organize the Details

To compare and contrast in writing, you'll need to keep your details organized. The following methods can help you do that.

EXAMINE YOUR SUBJECTS A good way to begin your comparison-contrast piece is with a careful examination. First think about one subject, and list descriptive details that go with that subject. For example, you might note that Batman travels by car and wears a mask and a cape. Then make a list of the same kinds of details for Superman. How does he get around? What does he wear?

SORT WHAT YOU SEE Once you've listed some details, you can sort them for comparison and contrast. At this point, some writers use a Venn diagram like the one below. A Venn diagram is made of two ovals. Each oval contains the details of one of the subjects. Details that the two subjects have in common go where the ovals overlap.

Grammar Tip

When comparing and contrasting two people, use the comparative form of an adjective. When comparing and contrasting two actions, use the comparative form of an adverb. For more about comparative adjectives and adverbs, see Lessons 12.3 and 12.4, pages 383–386, and Lesson 13.3, page 393.

Expository Writing

Differences
• Shows his face
• Born on Krypton
• Travels by flying

Similarities
• Has a secret identity
• Wears a cape
• Helps people

Differences
• Wears a mask
• Born on Earth
• Travels by car (Batmobile)

Notice how the details for each superhero come from a look at the same points of concern: costume, method of travel, birthplace, mission, and identity.

Journal Writing

Pick your two favorite activities. List the details of each activity. Then put the details into a Venn diagram. What is similar and different about the two activities?

5.2

Teach

Making a Venn Diagram

When making a Venn diagram, some students may find it helpful to work with a partner. Suggest that each partner select a favorite activity. Students can then discuss the similarities and differences between the two activities, each noting the details of his or her activity in an oval—one half of a Venn diagram. Finally, partners can combine their individual ovals into a Venn diagram that contains details about both activities. **L2**

Using Visual Cues

Point out to students that they can begin to compare and contrast Superman and Batman just by examining the artwork. How are the two superheroes similar? (Both wear costumes with capes; both are muscular.) How are they different? (Batman wears a mask, Superman does not; Batman's symbol is a bat, Superman's symbol is a large red *S*; Batman wears gloves, Superman does not.) **L1**

Two-Minute Skill Drill

Have students write one term of comparison and one term of contrast for each of the following:

| happy | dark clouds |
| boots | courage |

See also *Two-Minute Skill Drill Transparencies,* 5.2

Journal Writing Tip

Analyzing Information Suggest that students delete all but the five or six most important details from their Venn diagrams. This can help make the diagrams manageable and readable.

Teach

Using the Model

Point out that the writer uses a separate paragraph for each subject. Words such as *like* and phrases such as *in some ways*, however, act as clues indicating the presence of a similarity or difference. Students may wish to refer to the Venn diagram to find the similarities and differences referred to in the model. **L2**

Making Connections

Point out that cultural icons often arise from distinct historical periods. The image of the coonskin-capped pioneer hero dates back to early westward expansion. Likewise, the Star Trek characters arose when outer space became "the final frontier."

Students might discuss other fictional or legendary figures and try to identify by world affairs, cultural movements, or any other historical reference points the specific historical period out of which they came. **L3**

Additional Resources

For ideas for comparison-contrast writing, see *Fine Art Transparencies* 21–25.

Daily Language Practice

Writing Process Transparencies, 17–19B

Writing Across the Curriculum

Cooperative Learning Activities, pp. 26–30

Research Paper and Report Writing, pp. 32–38

Thinking and Study Skills, pp. 6, 8–9, 11, 15

Sentence-Combining Practice, pp. 30–32

Listening and Speaking Activities, pp. 12–13, 21, 24

Composition Practice, p. 38

192

Expository Writing

Revising Tip

When revising a comparison-contrast piece, try making a separate paragraph for each subject you discuss. This will make the piece easier for your readers to follow. For more information about revising paragraphs, see Lesson 2.6, pages 62–65.

Take a look at the similarities and differences covered in this selection. Notice that they are the same ones shown in the Venn diagram on page 191.

TIME

For more about organizing a draft, see **TIME Facing the Blank Page,** page 94.

Write the First Draft

Now that you've made a Venn diagram, you're ready to write your draft. Details you pull from the middle of the Venn diagram are similarities. Details pulled from the outsides are differences. As you think about the order of presenting information, pull details from your diagram.

Notice how the following comparison-contrast piece is organized. First it tells about Superman. Then it tells about Batman. This kind of organization is called subject by subject. It's a way of showing clearly the similarities and differences between two subjects. It helps readers picture the subjects side by side.

Literature Model

The Great Depression was in its final years. World War II waited across the ocean in Europe. Out of this time came two of our earliest comic-book superheroes.

Superman appeared in 1938. When fighting crime, he flew through the air, wearing a caped costume to disguise his true identity. Today we know him as The Man of Steel, dedicated to helping others, an orphan from the planet Krypton.

In 1939 Batman was created. Like Superman, he was a caped hero with a secret identity and a mission to make the world a better place. In some ways, however, Batman was one of a kind. For instance, he was the first Earth-born superhero. He covered his face with a mask. And to get around, he drove a one-of-a-kind car called the Batmobile.

Today, the world is a different place with many different problems. Although times have changed, many of our superheroes have stayed with us. With luck there will always be superheroes to call on whenever we need one.

MEETING INDIVIDUAL NEEDS **English Language Learners**

Choosing Words

Students who are not native English speakers may have difficulty choosing characteristics to use in a Venn diagram. Suggest that these students work with a partner and follow the Batman-Superman model on page 191. You might suggest that students compare and contrast themselves and their partners. Have them label the overlapping oval *Friends* and the individual ovals with each person's name. Next, have each student enter her or his birthplace, goals, favorite outfits, preferred mode of travel, and so on.

Write a Comparison-Contrast Piece

Write to a good friend who has moved away. In your letter compare and contrast two things of interest to you both. For example, you might compare two athletes or a movie and a book.

PURPOSE To share information by comparing and contrasting

AUDIENCE A friend

LENGTH 2–3 paragraphs

WRITING RUBRICS To write a good comparison-contrast piece, you should

- list details about each subject
- create a Venn diagram
- organize details subject by subject
- write legibly in cursive or manuscript
- proofread to ensure correct grammar and punctuation

Using Computers

Find two Web sites that provide sports coverage and information. Write a brief report in which you compare and contrast the features of the sites. In your conclusion, you might answer questions such as the following: Which would be better for fans who want recent game results? Which would be better for fans who want background on games? Which covers a greater number of sports?

Grammar Link

Be sure verbs agree with compound subjects.

When two or more subject words are linked by *or* or *nor,* the verb agrees with the subject that is closer to it.

Complete each sentence below by writing the correct form of the verb in parentheses.

1. Neither the superheroes' costumes nor their mission (has, have) changed in fifty years.
2. Either powers or weaknesses (is, are) more important.
3. The Power Rangers or Batman (is, are) the most popular today.
4. Neither Superman nor the Power Rangers (drives, drive) an amazing car.
5. (Is, Are) superheroes or a real-life hero more important to you?

See Lesson 15.3, page 443.

Listening and Speaking

COOPERATIVE LEARNING In a small group, study and talk about two kinds of pets. Each group member should add details to a Venn diagram comparing and contrasting the two animals. Each should use the diagram to draft a short comparison-contrast piece.

Expository Writing

Assess

Evaluation Rubrics

Write a Comparison-Contrast Piece

Use these criteria when evaluating your students' writing. The assignment should show
- a Venn diagram with similarities and differences labeled
- a letter organized with details for each subject

See also *Writing Assessment and Evaluation Rubrics.*

Using Computers

Students' reports should show comparison and contrast of details found at two Web sites.

Listening and Speaking

Does each comparison-contrast piece accurately reflect details from the group's Venn diagram?

Reteaching

📁 *Composition Reteaching,* p. 38

Enrichment

📁 *Composition Enrichment,* p. 38

🖨 *Fine Art Transparencies 21–25*

Close

To reinforce the concept of diagraming, challenge the class to suggest images for Venn diagrams of any two subjects they have been comparing and contrasting. For example, a Venn diagram that compares and contrasts two novels might appear as the outline of two overlapping books.

Grammar Link

Answers
1. has
2. are
3. is
4. drive
5. Are

Focus

Lesson Overview

Objectives

- To understand the process of ordering information
- To write an explanation of how to do something

Skills

- breaking a process into steps; linking the steps clearly; writing an explanation

Critical Thinking

- analyzing; relating steps; clarifying

Listening and Speaking

- informal speaking; listening critically

Bellringer

Daily Language Activity

When students enter the classroom, have this assignment on the board: *Write a brief paragraph that explains how to take a photograph.*

Grammar Link to the Bellringer

Ask students to underline the verbs in their Bellringer paragraph. Have they used action verbs such as *pose* and *click,* or only vague verbs such as *do*?

See also *Daily Language Practice*

Motivating Activity

Ask students to imagine that for some reason they can no longer use a camera. How would they direct an assistant to take pictures for them? How would they explain the process?

You might also try an activity in which students try to explain to each other a simple task (for example, how to whistle or how to tie a bow).

Explaining How to Do Something

Expository writing is used to explain a process, step by step. Transition words help make the order of the steps clear for the reader.

Pictured above is French painter Henri Matisse (1869–1954), an important artist of modern times. His painting was known for its bright colors and unusual shapes. Late in his life, Matisse became physically unable to paint as he once had. He then took up a new form—the collage. With the help of an assistant, he pinned paper shapes together to create pictures.

Resource Manager

Planning Resources
- Lesson Plans

Transparencies
- Bellringer
- Daily Language Practice
- Fine Art 21–25
- Two-Minute Skill Drill
- Writing Process 17–19B

Other Print Resources
- Composition Enrichment, p. 39
- Composition Practice, p. 39
- Composition Reteaching, p. 39
- Cooperative Learning Activities, pp. 29–30
- Listening and Speaking Activities, pp. 12–13, 21, 24

- Research Paper and Report Writing, pp. 32–38
- Sentence-Combining Practice, pp. 30–32
- Thinking and Study Skills, pp. 1, 8–9, 11, 17
- Writing Across the Curriculum
- Writing Assessment and Evaluation Rubrics

If you were Matisse explaining your method to a new assistant, how would you make your instructions clear? Where would you start?

Break the Process into Steps

If you've ever used a recipe or built a model, you've probably followed a process step by step. Almost any job is easier if you approach it one step at a time.

Explaining how to make a collage is no exception. If you explain the process in steps, your reader will have an easier time understanding it. Be sure to include every step and to present steps in the right order. Explain with extra care any steps that might be confusing.

Revising Tip

When writing an explanation of a process, try picturing it slowly in your mind. This will help you include all the steps.

Expository Writing

Making a Collage

1. Gather your materials: paper, paints, brushes, scissors, pins, paste.

2. Paint the paper with whatever colors you want.

3. Cut the painted paper into shapes.

4. Pin or paste the shapes onto a large sheet of plain white paper.

Journal Writing

Think of a process you go through every day. List all the steps in the process. Circle any steps that you think are hard to understand. Make notes about ways to explain these steps.

5.3

Teach

Focusing on the Steps

Students may benefit by focusing on the imperative verbs in the directions for making a collage on this page. The verbs break the process into a series of actions. If students were to describe the steps in mounting a photograph, for example, they might make a list such as this one: (1) *Assemble* photograph, cardboard, glue, scissors; (2) *Cut* cardboard to size; (3) *Apply* glue to back of photograph; (4) *Press* photograph to cardboard until dry. **L2**

Trying It Out

After students have written a process explanation, encourage them to try following their own directions, doing only the steps they have written down. Were they able to complete the process successfully? **L1**

Two-Minute Skill Drill

Have students reorder the following steps, adding transitions and a "How to" title.

Throw the skin in the garbage. Strip the rest of the skin off and finish eating. Break off the hard stem at the top. Peel back the skin in strips part way down and eat the top part of the fruit.

See also *Two-Minute Skill Drill Transparencies*, 5.3

Journal Writing Tip

Defining and Clarifying Encourage students to check their explanations for steps that may be hard to follow. These steps may contain information better handled in two steps; they may be out of order or contain vague verbs such as *put* instead of exact verbs such as *pin* or *paste*.

Focus

Lesson Overview

Objectives

- To ask questions about a topic
- To conduct research and gather information
- To take notes and organize information
- To write a report

Skills

- choosing a topic; asking questions; gathering information; writing a report

Critical Thinking

- generating new information; summarizing; making inferences

Listening and Speaking

- analyzing; questioning; discussing; evaluating; presenting

Bellringer
Daily Language Activity

When students enter the classroom, have this assignment on the board: *Write possible titles for reports on three ocean-related topics.*

Grammar Link to the Bellringer

Ask students to underline the capital letters in their Bellringer titles. Did they remember to capitalize first and last words and all other important words?

See also *Daily Language Practice*

Motivating Activity

Ask students to decide which of their Bellringer titles identifies a topic that would be the right size for a one-page report. Introduce the idea that finding something that is the right size is as crucial to good report writing as it is to buying shoes.

198

Expository Writing

LESSON
5.4

Writing a Report

To write a report, choose a topic that interests you. Gather information from a variety of sources. Organize what you learn and present it in your own words to inform your readers.

As the diagram below illustrates, you need to choose a topic that is the right size. A topic that is too broad will have too much information for a short report. A narrow topic will not give you enough about which to write.

All About Sharks

The Truth About Shark Myths

Swimming Speed of Pacific Nurse Sharks

Gather Information

When you write a research report, you share what you know—and what you have learned—about your topic. Spend a few minutes jotting notes about what you think you know about your topic. What do you hope to find out? Make a list of questions that you'd like your research to answer. Let your questions guide your research, and write down new questions that come to you as you learn more about your topic.

Begin your research at the library. Encyclopedias and other reference works can give you some basic information about

198 Unit 5 Expository Writing

Resource Manager

Planning Resources
- Lesson Plans

Transparencies
- Bellringer
- Daily Language Practice
- Fine Art 21–25
- Two-Minute Skill Drill
- Writing Process 17–19B

Other Print Resources
- Composition Enrichment, p. 40
- Composition Practice, p. 40
- Composition Reteaching, p. 40
- Cooperative Learning Activities, pp. 26–30
- Listening and Speaking Activities, pp. 12–13, 21, 24
- Research Paper and Report Writing, pp. 32–38

- Sentence-Combining Practice, pp. 30–32
- Thinking and Study Skills, pp. 2, 4, 11, 13, 23–24, 35
- Writing Across the Curriculum
- Writing Assessment and Evaluation Rubrics

your topic and lead you to other sources. Be sure to look for books and magazine articles on your topic. You may also use CD-ROMs and the Internet to conduct research.

Once you've found a few sources on your topic, begin reading and taking notes. Put quotation marks around any information you copy from your sources word for word. But think about what you're reading and take notes using your own words when you can.

For every note, be sure to jot down a page reference and the title and author of the source as well as publication information. That way, you'll be able to properly give credit to your sources as you write. For information about exploring a variety of sources and giving credit as you write, see the Writing Research Papers section of the **Writing and Research Handbook,** pages 685–690. Study the sample source and note card below.

Shark Behavior
Eugenie Clark, "Sharks: Magnificent and Misunderstood," National Geographic,
August 1981.
When I read that Dr. Eugenie Clark thinks sharks normally don't bother people, it made me think I could go swimming in the ocean without being scared.

SHARKS

No creature on earth has a worse, and perhaps less deserved, reputation than the shark. During 26 years of research on sharks, I have found them to be normally unaggressive and even timid towards man.

Eugenie Clark,
"Sharks: Magnificent and Misunderstood"

Journal Writing

Think of a topic that you'd like to write a report about. In your journal, jot down a list of questions about your topic that you'd like your research to answer. Also note some ideas about the types of sources you might use to explore your topic.

Expository Writing

Editing Tip

Don't throw away your notes before your report is finished. As you edit, if you need to check a fact, you can look back at your notes.

Teach

Using the Model

Discuss with students the importance of documenting their sources when they conduct research. The note card includes both the title and author of the source. Without such attributions, students deprive authors and publishers of the recognition they deserve. Students who use an author's words and ideas without citing their source may also be guilty of plagiarism. Let students know your preference for their documenting of their sources. **L2**

Narrowing a Topic

Students having difficulty narrowing a topic may find the library's computer index helpful. You could point out that a student looking under a topic such as *Moon* might discover several subheads (narrower topics), including *charts, exploration, folklore,* and *influence on weather.* Mention that, on the computer screen, the main topic is usually highlighted and subheads appear below the main topic in alphabetical order. **L1**

Two-Minute Skill Drill

Suppose you had decided on *Tides* as a general topic for a research report. To help direct your research, list as many questions as you can about tides.

See also *Two-Minute Skill Drill Transparencies,* 5.4

Journal Writing Tip

Starting the Process Check to see that students' topics are neither too broad nor too narrow for a report. Also check to see that students will be able to find answers to their questions in the various sources they list. Remind students that videos, tape recordings, and other nonprint sources may hold the information they need.

Teach

Using the Model

Discuss with students how the introduction serves its purpose—stating the topic of the report and engaging the reader's attention.Then discuss how the conclusion shows what the writer has discovered—that people still have a lot to learn about sharks. Ask students whether the report makes them curious to learn more about sharks. **L2**

Applying and Extending

Point out that research skills are used in many different professions. Invite students to discuss how detectives, lawyers, teachers, architects, doctors, artists, writers, and actors all may find that doing research can help them in their work. Can students think of other occupations in which research skills would be useful? Stress that good research skills can be used in and out of school and in all walks of life. **L3**

Additional Resources

For ideas for report writing, see *Fine Art Transparencies* 21–25.

Daily Language Practice

Writing Process Transparencies, 17–19B

Writing Across the Curriculum
Cooperative Learning Activities, pp. 26–30
Research Paper and Report Writing, pp. 32–38
Composition Practice, p. 39
Thinking and Study Skills, pp. 2, 4, 13, 23–24, 35
Sentence-Combining Practice, pp. 30–32
Listening and Speaking Activities, pp. 12–13, 21, 24

Expository Writing

Write About What You've Learned

After taking notes, organize them so that you can write. You might begin by asking yourself, "What's the report about?" Your

answer can become the introduction to your report. As you write the body of your draft, answer this question: "What did I discover?" Finally, as you tie your paper together in the conclusion, think about what you learned. A good conclusion can include a summary of information

and leave your readers with a better understanding of your topic. Read the model below and notice the three main parts.

Model

In what way does the introduction do what it should do?

Most people are scared of sharks, but Dr. Eugenie Clark, a famous marine biologist, says that they shouldn't be. She and other scientists have done studies to prove that sharks aren't so scary. She published some of her findings in the *National Geographic* article "Sharks: Magnificent and Misunderstood" in August 1981.

The body of the report shows what information the writer discovered.

According to Clark, sharks don't just swim around, eating all the time. Some sharks go for weeks without eating. Basking sharks and whale sharks eat only plankton and small fish. Sharks typically do not bite people unless they feel threatened and need to protect themselves.

What does the conclusion say about what the writer learned?

After reading about Dr. Clark's adventures, I learned that people still have much to learn about sharks. It's good to learn more, though, because the new information lets us understand what's really true about sharks. Now I can swim without being scared.

200   Unit 5 Expository Writing

English Language Learners

Peer Reviewing Strategies

Students who are learning English should review each other's drafts and identify the introduction, the body, and the conclusion. Thoughtful reviewers whose first language is English should then read the drafts of the students learning English and give constructive comments. The reviewers might read passages aloud so that the writers can hear inaccuracies in the language and make revisions.

Write a Report

Review what you wrote for the Journal Writing activity on page 199 and continue working on your report. Find sources on your topic in the library and look for answers to your research questions as you read. Take notes, carefully recording the source of each piece of information. Organize your data in a logical order and write a report.

PURPOSE To present information about a topic of your choice

AUDIENCE Your classmates and teacher

LENGTH 3–5 paragraphs

WRITING RUBRICS To write an effective report, you should

- locate sources of information
- take notes on what you find
- organize the information into an introduction, a body, and a conclusion
- proofread for legibility and grammatical correctness

Using Computers

Desktop publishing software can give your report a professional look. Using desktop publishing, you can put text into columns and make a cover page. You can even provide space for pictures or diagrams to be scanned in or pasted on after printing.

When you take notes, capitalize the names of authors. Capitalize the first and last words and all other important words in a title.

Note how the writer of the report on sharks wrote the title and author of the source: *Eugenie Clark, "Sharks: Magnificent and Misunderstood."*

Write each name or title below, using capital letters as needed.

1. virginia morrell
2. "The really secret life of plants"
3. *Presidential curiosities: The complete book of U.S. presidents*
4. *the oregon trail*
5. "antarctica, the last continent"
6. esther forbes

See Lesson 18.2, page 475, and Lesson 18.4, page 479.

Listening and Speaking

PRESENTING Take turns reading your reports aloud in a small group. Prepare for your turn by practicing your oral reading. Speak slowly, clearly, and with appropriate expression and body language. Display any maps, graphs, or photos that enhance your report and help communicate your message.

Assess

Evaluation Rubrics

Write a Report

Use these criteria when evaluating your students' writing.

- Does their writing show that they have researched the topic?
- Have students included a clear introduction, body, and conclusion?
- Does their writing show attention to details and correction of grammatical and punctuation errors?

See also *Writing Assessment and Evaluation Rubrics.*

Listening and Speaking

Allow students time to practice their oral reading. Before students share their work in small groups, discuss with the class what it means to listen effectively and without distraction. Stress the importance of listening respectfully to the work of other students.

Reteaching

📂 *Composition Reteaching*, p. 40

Enrichment

📂 *Composition Enrichment*, p. 40

Close

Invite one or two volunteers to read their reports aloud for the entire class. The class can offer comments on the choice of a topic, the organization of the piece, and the usefulness of the information.

Answers

1. Virginia Morrell
2. "The Really Secret Life of Plants"
3. *Presidential Curiosities: The Complete Book of U.S. Presidents*
4. The Oregon Trail
5. "Antarctica, the Last Continent"
6. Esther Forbes

Capitalizing Other Words Remind students also to capitalize proper adjectives and geographic areas: the Roosevelt era; the Far East.

Teach

Using the Model

Remind students that a well-written book report can entice others to read the book. A report can suggest questions that only reading the book can answer. For example, after having read in the report on this page that Cassie and Little Man refused to use the ripped-up books, students might wonder: Do Cassie and her brother ever get good books? Does Mrs. Crocker realize she was wrong to punish the children? What other examples of racism do the children encounter? **L2**

Comparing Books

Some students may wish to compare the book they have chosen to review with another they have read. In this way they can combine the book report format with a comparison-contrast piece. They also might draw some conclusions about different genres. For example, having read two mystery books, a student might conclude that most mysteries contain a plot twist. **L3**

Additional Resources

For expository **writing prompts**, see *Fine Art Transparencies 21–25.*

Daily Language Practice

Writing Process Transparencies, 17–19B

Writing Across the Curriculum

Cooperative Learning Activities, pp. 26–30

Research Paper and Report Writing, pp. 32–38

Thinking and Study Skills, pp. 7, 13, 18, 20

Listening and Speaking Activities, pp. 12–13, 21, 24

Sentence-Combining Practice, pp. 30–32

Composition Practice, p. 39

Expository Writing

In this report, the writer gives the title of the book right at the beginning. Why do you think she gives it again near the end?

At the end Natalie gives her opinion of the book—a definite thumbs-up.

Tell Your Feelings

One of the most useful parts of a book report is your feelings about the book. Here's how one student felt after reading *Roll of Thunder, Hear My Cry.*

Title: *Roll of Thunder, Hear My Cry*

Author: Mildred D. Taylor

Main Characters: The main characters are a black family called the Logans. Cassie is the only girl. Stacey is the older boy. Little Man is the younger boy.

Setting: Rural Mississippi in 1933

Summary: The novel is about the prejudiced way blacks were still being treated after the end of slavery. One example is the first day of school, when Cassie's and Little Man's teacher, Mrs. Crocker, tells them that this year they will have the privilege of using books. Cassie and Little Man are overjoyed—until they receive the tattered books and find out they received them only because they were too ripped up for the white children. When Cassie and Little Man refuse to use the books, they get punished by Mrs. Crocker. Much to Mrs. Crocker's surprise, though, Cassie and Little Man's mother think they did the right thing.

What I Thought: *Roll of Thunder, Hear My Cry* really shows you the unfair way blacks were treated back then, and it's a funny story in some parts and sad in others. It makes you think of the book's title, which comes from a song that slaves once sang. The song tells people not to be defeated by their enemies. That's mostly what the book's about, and I would definitely recommend reading it.

Natalie Bogira, Chute Middle School, Evanston, Illinois

204   Unit 5 Expository Writing

MEETING INDIVIDUAL NEEDS | **English Language Learners**

Understanding the Parts of a Book Report

Have students who are still learning English pair with students who are fluent English speakers to review their book report drafts. Using the Parts of a Book Report graphic on page 203 as a checklist, the English-speaking students can model finding and labeling each part of their book reports. They should then assist their partners in identifying the required parts in their own reports. Have students prompt their partners to fill in any missing pieces.

Write a Book Report

Write a short report about a book you like for your school newspaper. Jot down your thoughts about the book. Then write the first draft.

PURPOSE To share your ideas about a book
AUDIENCE Readers of the school newspaper
LENGTH 3–4 paragraphs

WRITING RUBRICS To write an effective book report, you should

- include the title and author
- identify the main characters and the setting
- summarize the story
- explain your personal reactions

Using Computers

Find Web sites that contain book reviews. Find reviews of two or three of the books you've read recently. Compare and contrast your own views with those of the reviewers.

Listening and Speaking

COOPERATIVE LEARNING In a small group, prepare an oral book report. Note the book's title, author, characters, and setting. Agree on a plot summary. Then discuss different opinions of group members about the book to include in the report.

Make subjects and verbs agree.

When two or more subjects are joined by *and*, the verb is usually plural. Note the subject-verb agreement in this sentence.

> **Cassie Logan and her brother experience** *racial prejudice.*

For each sentence write the correct form of the verb in parentheses.

1. Courage and pride (are, is) what the Logan family possesses.
2. Both Cassie's mother and her father (understand, understands) the importance of the land.
3. Farming fields and a vast forest (cover, covers) their 400 acres.
4. Big Ma and Mama also (own, owns) part of the land.
5. The taxes and mortgage on the land (have, has) not been paid.
6. Papa and other farmers (leave, leaves) home looking for work.
7. Big Ma, who is in her sixties, and Mama (run, runs) the farm.
8. Stacey and Little Man (set, sets) off for school in threadbare clothes.
9. First-graders and fourth-graders (share, shares) a classroom.
10. Where (are, is) Miss Crocker and Miss Davis?

See Lesson 15.3, page 443.

5.5 Writing a Book Report **205**

Expository Writing

Assess

Evaluation Rubrics

Write a Book Report

Use these criteria when evaluating your students' writing.

- Does the report include the title and the author of the book?
- Does the report identify the main characters and setting?
- Does the report summarize the story?
- Does the report express the student's feelings about the book and support them with specific examples?
- Does the report contain enough information to familiarize someone with the book without giving away any surprises?

See also *Writing Assessment and Evaluation Rubrics.*

Listening and Speaking

Each group's oral report should
- reflect input from all members of the group
- show that the book was discussed and that more than one opinion was considered

Reteaching

📁 *Composition Reteaching,* p. 41

Enrichment

📁 *Composition Enrichment,* p. 41

Close

Ask a volunteer to read aloud a report on a favorite book that is not well known to the class. Encourage the class to make constructive comments afterward. Would they now be interested in reading this book?

Grammar Link

Answers

1. are	**6.** leave
2. understand	**7.** run
3. cover	**8.** set
4. own	**9.** share
5. have	**10.** are

Using *There is* and *There are* Tell students that when a sentence begins with the introductory word *There*, the verb must agree with the subject that follows. Examples:
1. There *is* lively and engaging *action* in this novel.
2. There *are* thirty *students* in this class.

Writing Process in Action

Focus

Lesson Overview

Objective

- To write a step-by-step explanation of a process

Skills

- using the five stages of the writing process: prewriting, drafting, revising, editing/proofreading and publishing/presenting

Critical Thinking

- analyzing; synthesizing; generating new information

Listening and Speaking

- discussing in small groups and as a class

🔔 Bellringer
Daily Language Activity

When students enter the classroom, have this assignment on the board: *List three things that you can do that your classmates or younger students might not be able to do.*

Grammar Link to the Bellringer

Ask students who "you" and "them" are in the following sentence: "I bet I'm the only student who knows how to make a birdhouse, but you can make them quite easily." Remind students to use pronouns that are consistent and precise in meaning.

✏️ **See also** *Daily Language Practice*

Motivating Activity

Ask students to share their responses to the Bellringer activity. Ask students whether they have ever tried to teach one of the skills on their list to a friend. What happened? What kinds of questions did they have to answer? Mention that explaining a process in writing requires the writer to anticipate readers' questions.

Expository Writing

In preceding lessons you learned about ways to share knowledge with others through expository writing. You also had a chance to do your own expository writing—to compare and contrast, give directions, and write a report. Now it is time for you to put together what you know. In this lesson you are invited to write a "how-to" explanation of a process.

Assignment

Context

The editors at *How To,* a magazine written by and for students wanting to share something they know, want you to write about a step-by-step process.

Purpose

To write an explanation of something you've learned to do

Audience

Student readers of *How To*

Length

1 page

WRITING Online

Visit the *Writer's Choice* Web site at **writerschoice. glencoe.com** for additional writing prompts.

The following pages can help you plan and write your explanation. Read through them and then refer to them as you need to. Don't feel limited by them. Remember that you're in charge of your own writing process.

Resource Manager

Planning Resources
- Lesson Plans

📠 **Transparencies**
- Bellringer
- Daily Language Practice
- Writing Process 17–19B

📁 **Other Print Resources**
- Composition Enrichment, p. 44
- Composition Practice, p. 44
- Composition Reteaching, p. 44
- Grammar Workbook, Lessons 98–105
- Sentence-Combining Practice, pp. 30–32
- Thinking and Study Skills, p. 4, 11, 14

- Writing Assessment and Evaluation Rubrics

💾 **Software**
- Writer's Assistant

🖥️ **Web Sites**
- writerschoice.glencoe.com
- lit.glencoe.com

Writing Process in Action

Prewriting

Whether telling how to bathe an elephant or make a sandwich, you must explain one step at a time to make it easier for a reader to follow along. These options can help you explore ways to begin your explanation.

You might visit the library to find more information. Remember to make notes about what you discover. If you're still stuck, try reviewing pages 198–200 for more ideas about research.

Option A
Try clustering to discover what steps go together.

Option B
Try drawing a picture of each step.

Option C
List everything you can recall about the process.

1. choose a stone
2. roll the stone
3. other players toss sticks
4. measure to see which stick is closest

Drafting

In your draft, try to include as much information as you can. Don't leave out anything your reader might need to know.

While you draft, think about ways to link the steps you listed in the prewriting stage. Consider combining or expanding steps. Note how much detail Peggy Thomson includes for one step in the process of bathing elephants at the zoo.

Vocabulary Tip

For a list of transition words you can use to link steps in a process, see Lesson 5.3, page 196.

Literature Model

Kathy pours out green oil soap from a bottle, letting it spread across the great gray expanses of skin and foaming it up with streamers from her hose. Now, with her ankus propped against the railings and her hose lying on the floor, she lights into a two-handed scrub job.

Peggy Thomson
Keepers and Creatures at the National Zoo

Teach

Prewriting

Developing Ideas for Expository Writing

Help students determine which information is vital to include in a step-by-step explanation of a process. Suggest that students focus on the process's end result. They should include anything they need to reach that result and can discard anything they do not need. As a test, students should consider each step in the process and imagine what would happen if it were left out. Could readers still complete the process? **L2**

Sharing a Culture

Encourage students of different cultural backgrounds to explain processes familiar to them but not to students of other cultural backgrounds. Students might consider explaining how to play a traditional game, make or play a simple musical instrument, or create a special holiday dish. **L2**

Drafting

Organizing Ideas

Help students to organize information and to prepare for revising as they draft. Suggest they do the following:

- Number each step of the process.
- Use the word *because* to explain something about each step: it will remind them to anticipate readers' questions of "why."
- Use a new paragraph for each step.
- Leave several line spaces between each paragraph so that later additions and corrections to the draft can be made more easily. **L1**

Teach

Revising

Students can work in writing conferences with peer editors before they revise their writing. You may want to duplicate the Peer Response forms in *Writing Assessment and Evaluation Rubrics.* Suggest that peer editors respond to the following questions: *Is any information missing? Which steps need more explanation? Are the steps in order?* **L2**

Editing/Proofreading

Peer Editing

After students have edited their own work, have them edit another student's writing. Remind them to refer to the Editing/Proofreading Checklist on page 209. **L2**

Publishing/Presenting

Before students present their expository writing, discuss how to prepare their papers for publication. Emphasize the importance of the final draft and that it must be neatly done.

Additional Resources

Writing Process Transparencies, 17–19B

Thinking and Study Skills, pp. 7, 13, 18, 20

Sentence-Combining Practice, pp. 30–32

Composition Practice, p. 39

Grammar Workbook, Lessons 98–105

Expository Writing

Revising Tip

When revising a "how-to" explanation, ask another person to follow your explanation. This will help you identify steps that are unclear or missing. For more help see Lesson 5.3, page 195.

Some steps can be explained simply. Others may be so complicated that a diagram or picture will give the clearest explanation. As you draft, try whatever method seems best.

Revising

To begin revising, read over your draft to make sure that what you have written fits the assignment, especially your purpose and your audience. Then have a **writing conference.** Read your draft to a partner or small group. Use your audience's reactions to help you evaluate your work so far. The questions below can help you and your listeners.

Question A
Have I included every step in the proper order?

Question B
Is each step stated clearly?

Question C
Have I linked my steps with transitions?

Chunkey, a game invented by *is*
Mississippians, is fun even today. These were
the
ancient Native Americans who lived in the
Mississippi River Valley. To play, you first need
round
to get a small stone. It should be a rounded
stone. Then one player rolls the stone. Other
the spot where
players stand aside and throw sticks at where
When the stone
they think the stone will stop rolling. After it
stops, you check to see which stick is the closest.
Whoever threw that stick is the winner.

Enrichment and Extension

Follow-up Ideas

- Suggest that students illustrate their process with photographs, drawings, or computer-generated art.
- Encourage students to contribute their writing to a "How to" anthology that can be kept in the school library.

Journal Writing Tip

Understanding Audience Ask students to decide whether their explanation was suited to their audience's interests, knowledge, and ability.

Editing/Proofreading

Following the steps of a process takes concentration. For that reason you'll want to **proofread** your draft for spelling, grammar, and punctuation errors. Such small mistakes might distract your audience.

The questions on the notepad can be your starting point. You also might share your draft with a friend or family member. Another person can often discover mistakes you have overlooked.

Publishing/Presenting

Before presenting your explanation, ask yourself if *How To* readers could complete the process, following only your steps. If the answer is yes, then you're ready to present your paper. The final copy may include diagrams or pictures that would make your explanation even easier to understand.

Editing/Proofreading Checklist

- Have I used action verbs that make sense?
- Have I used pronouns correctly?
- Do verbs agree with subjects?
- Have I checked the spelling of any words I'm unsure of?

Expository Writing

Proofreading Tip

For proofreading symbols, see page 72 or 267.

Grammar Tip

When editing your report, check that you have used pronouns correctly. If you need help with pronouns, refer to Lessons 11.1–11.5, pages 361–370.

Journal Writing

Reflect on your writing-process experience. Answer these questions in your journal: What do you like best about your explanation? What was the hardest part of writing it? What did you learn in your writing conference? What new things have you learned as a writer?

Writing Process in Action **209**

Evaluation Rubrics

Use the following questions to evaluate students' finished writing.

- Are all necessary steps in the process included?
- Is each step clearly stated?
- Are the steps appropriately ordered and linked with transitions?
- Does the explanation include pictures or diagrams to clarify difficult steps?
- Does the explanation include cautions that will prevent readers from making mistakes or being injured?
- Does the explanation provide readers with enough information to complete the process from start to finish?
- Is the writing correct in grammar, usage, and mechanics?

See also *Writing Assessment and Evaluation Rubrics*.

Reteaching
📂 *Composition Reteaching*, p. 44

Enrichment
📂 *Composition Enrichment*, p. 44

Close

Ask students to discuss the step-by-step explanations or processes that are easiest—and most difficult—for them to follow. Lead them to discuss what makes some instructions unsuccessful: The process is hard to visualize and is unsupported by pictures; the writer doesn't understand the reader's needs; the writer doesn't understand the process. Encourage students to add to the criteria for good instructions listed in this lesson.

Visual Thinking

Illustrating a Process

Some students may find it helpful to use illustrations to demonstrate the steps in their process. In describing how to use in-line skates, for instance, students might sketch the skates, the sidewalk or other skating area, correct movements for the skates, and so forth. Afterward, these illustrations could be cut out, ordered, and given captions. Captions could then be linked with transitions as a first step toward drafting, or in some cases captions could be fleshed out so they can serve as the instructions.

About the Author

Peggy Thomson is a journalist who lives close to the National Zoo in Washington, D.C. Her book is the result of months of work watching and talking to zookeepers.

Focus

Lesson Overview

Objectives

- To read a selection to examine and appreciate how a professional writer uses descriptive language, dialogue, and transition words to explain a step-by-step process
- To write an expository essay that explains a process

Skills

- monitoring comprehension; questioning

Critical Thinking

- inferring

Speaking and Listening

- discussing

Bellringer

Daily Language Activity

When students enter the classroom, have this assignment on the board: *List in order five things you do when washing a dog.*

See also *Daily Language Practice*

Motivating Activity

Ask students to name some of the responsibilities of a pet owner. Next, mention that some people, such as veterinarians, zoo keepers, and animal trainers, have jobs that consist entirely of caring for animals. Have students write a short paragraph about which of these jobs they think they might enjoy, and why.

UNIT 5

Literature Model

Expository Writing

Peggy Thomson

BATHING ELEPHANTS

In Keepers and Creatures at the National Zoo, *Peggy Thomson explains how zoo-keepers go about their everyday tasks as well as how they relate to the animals. Giving elephants a daily bath is one way keeper Kathy Wallace has earned the elephants' trust and respect. As you read this chapter from the book, try picturing each step in the bathing process Thomson describes. Then complete the activities in Linking Writing and Literature on page 214.*

"Okay, Biki! Okay, Shant! Wiggle your ears!" Kathy commands. "And keep them wiggling." During this wash-behind-the-ears time, the keeper runs her fingers over the thin skin at the back of the ears and pricks a bit at the stick-out veins with the point of her ankus,[1] hoping to prepare the animals for occasional needle pricks during checkups by a veterinarian.

Now she wants her animals down. Lying down is a vulnerable[2] position for them. It's only because of feeling

---

1 ankus (ang' kəs) a pointed stick with a hook, that is used for leading an elephant
2 vulnerable (vul' nər ə bəl) subject to physical injury

210 Unit 5 Expository Writing

Resource Manager

📁 **Planning Resources**
- *Lesson Plans*

📋 **Transparencies**
- *Bellringer*
- *Daily Language Practice*
- *Fine Art 21–25*

📁 **Other Print Resources**
- *Listening and Speaking Activities, pp. 21, 24*

- *Writing Assessment and Evaluation Rubrics*

💻 **Web Sites**
- *writerschoice.glencoe.com*
- *lit.glencoe.com*

Literature Model

safe with her that Ambika and Shanthi obey. They go to their knees. At commands of "Down!" they flop to one side. And here the scrub up of this pair begins.

Elephants are cursed with dry, old skin on their backs. It builds up in a way that's unsightly and probably itchy. The skin cracks and harbors infections down inside, so keepers have to scrub away day in, day out, to lift the dead stuff off. Today Kathy uses a scrub brush on Ambika and, because of her blisters, a sponge on Shanthi. For Nancy's worse case of dead skin on the back she has tools of a rougher sort—a cement block with a handle and the kind of scraper used to remove rust from car bodies.

At this point Kathy pours out green oil soap from a bottle, letting it spread across the great gray expanses of skin and foaming it up with streamers from her hose. Now, with her ankus propped against the railings and her hose lying on the floor, she lights into a two-handed scrub job. Steam rises all about, shifted by whuffling puffs of air from the elephants' trunks. The keeper works hard, talking to Ambika: "This place is beginning to smell like a beauty parlor," and to Shanthi: "All right, I see you squinching[3] up your eyes. It stings on your blisters, I bet it does." Whatever the discomfort, the young elephant lies still, her feet crossed, her trunk up, quietly feeling about her forehead, her ears, her back and on beyond to touch "Auntie" and twine briefly with "Auntie's" trunk.

Midway through the bath, keeper Kathy masterminds the shift of the two large bodies, the rocking back up onto the knees and the flop down again from left to right side. Along the way various scraped patches of skin receive smeary dabs of yellow salve. (Elephant keepers say they never order lemon meringue pie at restaurants. They've lost their appetite for it.) Sometimes, though not today, there's also an oiling for the wiry black bristles at the end of the tail.

Footwork, which comes last, is the most difficult part of the bath and the most crucial,[4] for feet must be sound to support an elephant's great weight. With the two bathers standing again, admired, praised, patted, hugged about the knees, Kathy asks for a "Foot up! Way up! Thank you!" A foot is presented, and she begins her careful look through all the cracks and fissures[5] of its pad for the presence of pebbles and other foreign matter.

---

3 **squinching** (skwinch′ ing) looking with the eyes partly closed
4 **crucial** (krōō′ shə l) very important
5 **fissures** (fish′ ərz) long, narrow, deep cracks

Literature Model **211**

Expository Writing

Teach

Active Reading Strategies

Question Ask students to suggest a question for each full paragraph on page 211 that will help them remember important information from that paragraph. *(Sample responses: Why do keepers have to scrub the elephants' skin every day? Why does Shanthi "squinch up" her eyes? Why do the elephants have to shift positions? Why is cleaning the elephants' feet crucial?)*

Critical Thinking

Infer Why don't the elephant keepers ever order lemon meringue pie at restaurants? *(Because it reminds them of the yellow salve they use on the elephants.)*

6+1 Trait® Writing

Organization

Explain to students that the way a piece of writing is organized is critical to reader understanding. Well-organized writing follows a logical pattern, it engages the reader, and it makes strong connections between ideas. Writing can be organized by using text structures such as sequence, compare and contrast, problem and solution, and cause and effect. Tell students that this selection is organized by sequence.

Practice To help students visualize the organization of the excerpt, have them create a chart or some other type of graphic organizer that shows each event in the order it happened.

6+1 Trait® is a registered trademark of Northwest Regional Educational Laboratory, which does not endorse this product.

6+1 Trait® Writing

Organization Ask students to explain the purpose of words and phrases like *which comes last, this morning,* and *by the time.* (*These words and phrases help the reader follow the steps of the bathing process.*)

Expository Writing

Literature Model

Over the microphone the narrator describes the foot, how its callousy pads wear down in the wild with the long hikes each day in search of food, but how in a zoo the pads, which grow quickly, need to be rasped[6] down or even carved away in slices; and how keepers then check the fresh, smooth surface for tiny holes, which tell them a pebble has entered and may be working its way upward with each step, to cripple the elephant painfully once it touches bone.

Watchers from the railing can't see the foot up close. They see the probings with the pick or with the point of the ankus. They see Kathy using both hands on a drawknife[7] to cut away a slice of leathery, rubbery pad and then another. (It doesn't hurt the elephant.) And they hear the thunk of the slice into her bucket.

This morning Kathy does only one of Shanthi's front feet. At that, it takes almost half an hour, for she has to work around tender bruises and to wind up with a nicely rounded shape to the pad. Her knife will need a sharpening before she next uses it on the other feet, this afternoon and tomorrow. She must also rasp down the nails, which get too little scuffing in zoo life to wear down properly.

Bath and foot-care time now flows into demonstration time

directed by the keeper team of Kathy and Morna out in the yard. Here people clap to see the elephants maneuver[8] on command, present a foot, balance on tiny stools, and move huge logs with their trunks. By the time Ambika and Shanthi take their bows, the keepers are beginning to wilt. There's an element of tension in the playful-looking baths they give and in the training shows—in just dealing with animals who could so easily pulverize[9] them if they chose to.

In the office, keepers Kathy and Morna speak of the awe they feel in the animals' trust of them and in the animals' forbearance,[10] *not* to hurt the keepers. They also speak of a kind of communication that goes on among the elephants, sometimes during bath time, more often first thing in the morning. "We're aware of it when we enter the building," says Morna. "We feel something. We feel it before we hear it, a kind of vibrating in the air,

---

6 **rasped** (raspt) scraped or rubbed
7 **drawknife** (drô′ nīf′) a knife with a handle at each end, used to shave surfaces
8 **maneuver** (mə nōō′ vər) to move or proceed skillfully toward a desired goal
9 **pulverize** (pul′ və rīz′) to break down or crush completely
10 **forbearance** (fôr bār′ əns) patience

Active Reading Strategies

Monitor Comprehension

Remind students that asking themselves questions as they read is an effective way to make sure they understand and remember what they are reading. If students find they don't know the answer to a question they have asked, they should go back to the text and reread until the answer becomes apparent.

Practice: Ask students working in groups to write six questions about the excerpt—one each beginning with the words *who, what, when, where, why,* and *how.* Have each group ask the students in another group to answer their questions to reinforce understanding of the excerpt.

like a cat's purring, only just beyond our hearing. Sometimes that rumbling seems to be a message to us. Like: It's good to see you. We're glad you're here."

Expository Writing

Andy Warhol, *Endangered Species: African Elephant*, 1983

Literature Model **213**

Teach

Literary Element

Dialogue Explain to students that writers often use dialogue to add interest or to draw attention to something in their work. Ask: "What does Thomson's use of dialogue add to her writing?" *(It shows the reader the caring relationship between the keepers and the elephants.)*

Additional Resources

Fine Art Transparencies, 21–25
Listening and Speaking Activities, pp. 21, 24

Viewing the Art

Andy Warhol, *Endangered Species: African Elephant*, 1983
Andy Warhol (1929–1987) was a leading figure in the pop art movement. This picture is a 38-by-38-inch silkscreen. It is currently housed at the Ronald Feldman Gallery in New York City.

Linking Writing and Literature

Assess

Evaluation Rubrics

◆ Talk About Reading

Possible answers to the questions:

1. Students should note that elephants have dry old skin that must be scrubbed away to avoid infections. Also, elephants in a zoo do not wear down their foot pads and nails as they would in the wild, so groomers must do this for them.

2. Elephants are even-tempered animals that seem to enjoy the company of and work well with humans.

3. She uses transitional words and phrases such as *during, now, at the command of "Down," at this point,* and *midway through the bath*.

4. Identify the process, organize the steps in proper sequence, use precise language, explain any specialized vocabulary, and use transitional words and phrases to signal new steps.

◆ Write About Reading

The expository essay should do the following:

• introduce the process as part of a larger story

• describe each step of the process clearly

• organize the steps of the process sequentially

• include transitional words and phrases to signal new steps in the process

• define any specialized vocabulary

Close

Point out that although many people think zoos are a means of preserving endangered animals, others believe zoos are cruel and exploitive places. Encourage students to discuss some of the pros and cons of taking animals out of their natural environment in order to protect them. Students might find it helpful to imagine themselves a zoo animal and then argue both sides.

Expository Writing

Literature Model

◆ Linking Writing and Literature

◆ Collect Your Thoughts

Think about what Peggy Thomson is describing in this chapter from her book. Make some notes that explain what she is describing *generally* and what she is describing *specifically*.

◆ Talk About Reading

Discuss the selection "Bathing Elephants" with your classmates. Select one person to lead the discussion and another to take notes. Use the following questions to guide the discussion.

1. **Connect to Your Life** What did you learn about the health requirements of elephants in a zoo?

2. **Critical Thinking: Draw Conclusions** After reading this excerpt, what conclusions can you draw about the temperament of elephants?

3. **6+1 Trait®: Organization** How does Thomson signal new steps in the process she is describing? What words and phrases does she use?

4. **Connect to Your Writing** When you write to describe a process, what are some things you can do to ensure that your description will be clear to the reader?

◆ Write About Reading

Expository Essay Write an expository essay in which you describe a process as Peggy Thomson did in "Bathing Elephants." Include your description as part of an interesting story, such as how you bathed your dog after she encountered a skunk or how you repaired a flat tire on your bike when you were a long way from home.

Focus on Organization Be sure to organize the steps in the process in correct order. Use appropriate words and phrases to signal new steps. If other people were involved in the process, use dialogue to make the story more interesting to your readers.

For more information on organization and the 6+1 Trait® model, see **Writing and Research Handbook,** pages 682–684.

6+1 Trait® is a registered trademark of Northwest Regional Educational Laboratory, which does not endorse this product.

214 Unit 5 Expository Writing

Cultural Diversity

Protecting Endangered Species

Sometimes an animal that is protected in one country is hunted and killed in another. Different nations rely on different animals for food and resources. Japan and Norway, for example, have ancient whaling traditions and have continued to hunt whales even after much of the world stopped whaling in the late twentieth century. The nations of the world continue to negotiate for the uniform protection of endangered animals around the globe.

UNIT 5 Review

Reflecting on the Unit

Summarize what you learned in this unit by answering the following questions.

❶ What are the different kinds of expository writing and the purpose of each?

❷ What prewriting methods can you use to organize information for a comparison-contrast essay?

❸ What strategies can help you write a clear explanation of a process?

❹ How do you gather information for a research report?

❺ What are the six main parts of a book report?

Adding to Your Portfolio

CHOOSE A SELECTION FOR YOUR PORTFOLIO Look over the expository writing you did for this unit. Choose a completed piece for your portfolio. The piece you select should show some or all of the following:

- for a comparison-contrast essay, details organized from a prewriting list, chart, drawings, or Venn diagram

- for a process explanation, steps presented in a clear order and with transitions to link them

- for a report, information gathered through research

- a clear introduction, body, and conclusion

REFLECT ON YOUR CHOICE Attach a note to the piece you chose, explaining briefly why you chose it and what you learned from writing it.

SET GOALS How can you improve your writing? What skill will you focus on the next time you write?

Writing Across the Curriculum

MAKE A HISTORY CONNECTION Scan your history textbook and identify two people to compare and contrast—perhaps two political leaders or two explorers. List details about each person and create a Venn diagram showing the similarities and differences. Organize your findings, and then draft a short comparison-contrast essay.

Review **215**

Review

Reflecting on the Unit

You may have students respond to Reflecting on the Unit in writing or through discussion.

Writing Across the Curriculum

Students may find it helpful to work with a partner as they complete their Venn diagrams. Remind students that creating a separate paragraph for each main idea makes their work easier to read.

Adding to Your Portfolio

Suggest that students work in pairs to select portfolio samples. Acting as peer reviewers, students can help their partners make their portfolio selections.

Portfolio Evaluation

If you grade the portfolio selections, you may want to award two marks—one each for content and form. Explain your assessment criteria before students make their selections. Commend

- experimentation with creative prewriting techniques
- clear, concise writing in which the main idea, audience, and purpose are evident
- successful revisions
- work that shows a flair for language

✔ **ASSESSMENT OPTIONS**

📂 *Tests with Answer Key and Rubrics*
Unit 5 Choice A Test, p. 17
Unit 5 Choice B Test, p. 18
Unit 5 Composition Objective Test, pp. 19–20

💾 *Testmaker*
Unit 5 Choice A Test
Unit 5 Choice B Test
Unit 5 Composition Objective Test

You may wish to administer one of these tests as a mastery test.

📼 *Mindjogger Videoquizzes*

Persuasive Writing

Viewing the Art

Some photographs use striking images or vivid colors to stir emotion in the viewer. Others use widely recognized symbols or surprising juxtapositions. The photograph shown here uses a wolf to evoke a mood and, possibly, to convey a message about the animal world.

Interpret and Analyze Use the following questions for discussion:

- What might be the meaning of this picture? Which elements of the picture help to convey its meaning?
- How do photographs influence and inform their viewers? Compare and contrast the power of photography with the power of writing.

Discussing the Quotation

This quotation by Sigurd Olson seeks to persuade readers of the urgency of wolves' survival. Encourage a discussion of Olson's message. How does he try to influence readers' opinions? Is he convincing? Have students explain their answers. To view the relationship between wolves and humans "through a wolf's eyes," encourage students to read the excerpt from *Brother Wolf* by Jim Brandenburg. It's in *Glencoe Literature: The Reader's Choice*, Course 1, page 116.

Writing Prompt Have students write a short essay about moments when they switched opinions about something. What convinced them to change their minds?

"Can wolves and humans coexist? The answer is clear: We can. The deeper truth is even clearer: We must."

—Sigurd Olson, *The Singing Wilderness*

216

Resource Manager

Planning Resources
- Lesson Plans
- Block Scheduling

Transparencies
- Bellringer
- Daily Language Practice
- Fine Art
- Two-Minute Skill Drill
- Writing Process

Other Print Resources
- Composition Enrichment
- Composition Practice
- Composition Reteaching
- Cooperative Learning Activities
- Glencoe Literature Library
- Grammar and Composition Handbook
- Grammar Workbook

- Listening and Speaking Activities
- Tests with Answer Key and Rubrics
- Thinking and Study Skills
- Writing Across the Curriculum
- Writing Assessment and Evaluation Rubrics
- Writing in the Real World

UNIT 6

Persuasive Writing

Objectives

- To gain a familiarity with the persuasive writing process and to craft effective persuasive pieces
- To learn about position statements and to support positions with evidence
- To identify target audiences and to write with audience in mind
- To identify facts and opinions and to use them in writing
- To understand published pieces such as television reviews and newspaper articles and to use them as models for writing

✔ ASSESSMENT OPTIONS

📁 *Tests with Answer Key and Rubrics*
Unit 6 Choice A Test, p. 21
Unit 6 Choice B Test, p. 22
Unit 4 Composition Objective Test, pp. 23–24

💾 *Testmaker*
Unit 6 Choice A Test
Unit 6 Choice B Test
Unit 6 Composition Objective Test

You may wish to administer either the Unit 6 Choice A Test or the Unit 6 Choice B Test as a pretest.

Key to Ability Levels

L1 Level 1 activities are within the basic ability range of students.

L2 Level 2 activities are within the ability range of average students.

L3 Level 3 activities are more challenging activities.

217

📺 Video
- MindJogger Videoquizzes

💾 Software
- Presentation Plus!
- Revising with Style
- Testmaker
- Writer's Assistant

🖥 Web Sites
- writerschoice.glencoe.com
- lit.glencoe.com

Focus

Lesson Overview

Objectives

• To learn about the process of creating an effective persuasive script
• To recognize the attributes of persuasive writing

Skills

• analyzing persuasive techniques, tone, structure; analyzing a writer's process

Critical Thinking

• synthesizing; interpreting; evaluating

Listening and Speaking

• discussing

🔔 Bellringer
Daily Language Activity

When students come into the classroom, have this assignment on the board: *Write an imaginary conversation between friends in which one tries to persuade the other to recycle paper.*

Grammar Link to the Bellringer

Have students check what they write for correct uses of commas with quotations.

See also *Daily Language Practice*

Motivating Activity

Ask students what they know about how television programs are produced. When television producers, or others, have an idea for a program, how do they go about creating it? (Possible steps include research, planning, writing a script, choosing the visuals, filming, and so on.)

Persuasive Writing

Writing in the Real World

MEDIA
Screenplay
Connection

When producers at Children's Television Workshop (CTW) decided to do a program on the way people devour the world's resources, they asked Douglas Anderson to write the script. Anderson set out to create a program that would persuade viewers of the need to save vital resources on the planet Earth. How many resources do people consume? In the excerpt that follows, Anderson finds a creative way to answer that question.

from "A Popular Little Planet"
by Douglas Anderson

A baby is born. One person more! That's wonderful. But now we'll need a lot more stuff, because the average American, over a lifetime, is gonna use resources, like:

• one hundred million gallons of water;
• three hundred bushels of apples;
• seven best friends;
• shirts;
• oil;
• underwear;
• paper;

• and 147 pairs of shoelaces.

And, if this person is anything like me, then he's gonna want even *more* stuff, like:

• three library cards;
• 35 hats;
• 4,000 comic books;
• two cats;
• three skateboards;
• a mountain of fries;
• seven cars;
• and a lifetime of stuff I can't even think of right now!

218 Unit 6 Persuasive Writing

Resource Manager

Planning Resources
• Lesson Plans

📑 Transparencies
• Bellringer
• Daily Language Practice
• Writing Process 20–22B

📁 Other Print Resources
• Cooperative Learning Activities, pp. 31–36
• Thinking and Study Skills, pp. 3, 5, 22, 38
• Writing Assessment and Evaluation Rubrics
• Writing in the Real World, pp. 21–24

And *that's* just for one person! Remember, 172 people are born on this planet every minute. And that's about 250,000 people born every day!

Do we *have* enough stuff?

A Writer's Process

Prewriting
Researching and Outlining

Work on the program began with careful research. As Anderson said, "You don't necessarily know your position on an issue before you start researching."

The staff at CTW helped Anderson learn more about the earth's resources and how people use them. Researcher Vivian Trakinski received information from the National Science Foundation. Scientist Edward Atkins suggested books and articles on resources for Anderson to read.

Anderson and the CTW staff learned that the human population has reached five billion and that it is using vital resources at an alarming rate. Gathering reliable information was important to Anderson. "In any kind of writing you have a responsibility to get the facts right. All the neat ideas for the show come out of this work."

Their research completed, the group then stated the program's position: To avoid running out of resources, people need to conserve and share.

Using this position and the facts uncovered in research, Anderson drafted an outline for the program.

"This is where you define the ideas you want to convey and the order in which you want to say them," he said. He shared the outline with Trakinski, Atkins, and the producer.

The group discussed the outline for "A Popular Little Planet," as the show would be called. They decided that the program would emphasize three major points: First, five billion people now live on the planet. Second, people gobble up resources. Sometimes they fight over resources because there aren't enough to go around. Third, there are ways people can help solve this problem. By sharing and conserving resources, people can make sure there is enough for everyone.

Persuasive Writing

Teach

Reading Media

Have students preview the title of the Media Connection. Discuss with them how television programs are able to influence people's opinions. Have students read the script.

Discussion Prompts

- Why is research important? How does research help to develop ideas for the program? Why does Anderson say, "All the neat ideas for the show come out of this [research] work"?

- Why might it be important to state a position before starting to write a persuasive piece? How does Anderson organize ideas, facts, and examples to back up his position?

- Have you ever seen an advertisement in a newspaper or magazine that made you want to go out and buy the product? What kind of words did the writers use?

Cultural Connections

Creating a Shared Culture

Because it reaches millions of viewers daily, television has become a powerful persuasive tool. Recent surveys show that United States households watch an average of seven hours of television a day. Discuss with students the role television plays in creating a shared culture. Remind students of the television coverage of a recent crisis during which people across the nation shared information and experienced many of the same emotional responses. This is one way television creates a shared culture.

Writing in the Real World

Teach

Discussion Prompts

- What kind of facts did Anderson use to explain his point? Were they effective? Did they make you stop and think?
- Why did Anderson try to use fun examples to make his point? Do you think a show like his would be entertaining?

Additional Resources

Persuasive Writing

Drafting
Writing the Script

Anderson now had to figure out how to use the resources of television to make his points. He said, "I knew I could use everything from music to cartoons and graphics."

Anderson had to think of ways to dramatize each point. How, for example, could he show the alarming amount of resources people use? Anderson wrote a scene in which Z, one of the actors, lists the things that belong to just one person. That scene, excerpted on page 218, ends with "Do we *have* enough stuff?"

To answer that question, in one scene Z and his partner, Stephanie, decide to make cookies and brownies. The problem? They each have only half the ingredients they need.

In the scene Stephanie and Z fight over the ingredients. "Then," Anderson said, "they realize that by sharing resources each person can have what he wants."

Anderson ended the segment with a real-life example of people and resources. He showed a film about water shortages in California, where 30 million people live. The point was clear: People must conserve water so that everyone will have enough.

Anderson thinks these scenes were persuasive for several reasons. First, they were energetic and entertaining. Just as important, ideas drew viewers in step by step. "Using fun examples, we built up to the point we wanted to make," he said.

Anderson believes that building a strong case is the way to convince people. He explains, "Rule number one in persuasive writing is that you have to know what you're talking about. Number two, telling people what to think doesn't work. Very often the most persuasive thing you can do is to set out the facts and let people develop their own ideas."

Revising/Presenting
Rewriting the Script

Anderson's draft went through many reviews and revisions at CTW. First, the producer checked to be sure the show would both entertain and persuade. Then the science adviser checked it for accuracy. CTW executives and students also reviewed the script. Anderson used everyone's comments to write a second draft, and after that he prepared a third version. Finally, several months later, after taping and editing were complete, "A Popular Little Planet" went on the air.

"There's no way of knowing for sure whether people started behaving differently," Anderson said. "But we did get a lot of mail, and the mail was wonderful."

Writing in the Real World

Social Studies

Relate the topic of the program to local problems in the use of resources. Encourage students to find out what the local problems are, why they exist, what the community is doing about them, and how students and their families can help. Some students might wish to formulate a main-idea statement for a piece of persuasive writing.

Examining Writing in the Real World

Analyzing the Media Connection

Discuss these questions about the script excerpt on page 218.

1. What is the main point that scriptwriter Douglas Anderson makes in the excerpt?

2. Why do you think Anderson lists the resources that just one person might use, instead of giving facts about global use of resources?

3. Why do you think Anderson includes such items as comic books and fries in his list?

4. Does Anderson write in a formal or informal tone? Support your answer with examples.

5. Why do you think Anderson ends by posing a question, not a statement about the planet's limited resources?

Analyzing a Writer's Process

Discuss these questions about Douglas Anderson's writing process.

1. What was the main goal of the program that Anderson wrote for CTW?

2. How did Anderson gather his information? How important does Anderson think research is to the final script?

3. What purpose did writing an outline serve for Anderson and his co-workers?

4. At what point did the group determine the program's position? What three points would the program emphasize?

5. After Anderson drafted the script, what kinds of review and revision did it go through?

Use commas to set off direct quotations.

"Then," Anderson said, "they realize that by sharing resources each person can have what he wants."

Write the following sentences, adding commas to set off the quotations.

1. "Our trash disposal is a big problem" said the mayor.

2. "We hope" she continued "that the recycling program will help."

3. A reporter asked "Will the recycling include magazines?"

4. "Not until next year" a council member answered.

5. "For details" the mayor added "read the brochure we are mailing to each home."

See Lesson 19.4, page 495.

Assess

Analyzing the Media Connection

1. The average American uses an enormous amount of resources over a lifetime.

2. A student may suggest that the situation is easier to grasp when just one person's use of resources is listed.

3. He includes such items to appeal to the interests of his young audience.

4. He writes in an informal tone, using language, such as "stuff," "gonna," and "mountains of fries."

5. He does this to encourage his audience to think about the situation.

Analyzing a Writer's Process

1. The program's main goal was to get viewers to think about how they use Earth's resources.

2. He read books and articles on resources. Anderson thinks that research helps a writers define his or her position on an issue and provides key ideas for the show.

3. It defined the ideas for the show and the order in which they would be presented.

4. They determined the position after doing the research. The program would emphasize the large world population, people's use of resources, and ways people can share and conserve resources.

5. It was checked by the producer to make sure it was entertaining and persuasive, by the science adviser for accuracy, and by CTW executives and students. Anderson used everyone's comments to revise his draft.

Reteaching

Review Anderson's words in column two on page 220. Stress the importance of giving people the facts they need to make judgments.

Enrichment

Encourage students to suggest ways of dramatizing global warming or other environmental issues.

Grammar Link

Answers

1. "... big problem," said the mayor.
2. "We hope," she continued, "that ..."
3. A reporter asked, "Will the ... "
4. "Not until next year," a council ...
5. "For details," the mayor added, "read the brochure we are mailing ... "

Using Commas Have students write dialogue for a one-minute TV message and check for correct use of commas to set off direct quotations.

Close

Ask students how Anderson dramatized the need to share resources. Then ask them to think of another way to dramatize the same point.

Note

For more information on conservation, refer students to publications such as *Audubon*, *Garbage*, or *Worldwatch*.

Focus

Lesson Overview

Objectives

- To gain an understanding of position statements and supporting evidence
- To write a position statement with two support statements

Skills

- stating a goal; selecting supporting evidence; avoiding sentence fragments

Critical Thinking

- analyzing; evaluating; comparing and contrasting

Listening and Speaking

- discussing

Bellringer
Daily Language Activity

When students enter the classroom, have this assignment on the board: *Write five sentences trying to persuade your parents to let you have a pet (or another pet).*

Grammar Link to the Bellringer

Have students check the sentences they have written for sentence fragments. Ask them to complete all sentence fragments.

See also *Daily Language Practice*

Motivating Activity

Ask students if they have ever approached a cat or a dog that they did not know. What did they do? How did the animal react? Discuss whether it is okay to pet a strange dog or cat. Have students jot down their ideas in a brief paragraph.

Persuasive Writing

Taking a Stand

One purpose of persuasive writing is to make readers think or feel a certain way about an idea or a product. Another purpose is to make readers take action. Sometimes it does both. What is the writer's goal in the model below?

Literature Model

Most dogs are very friendly once they get to know you. But, like people, dogs don't always want to be friends right away. They need time to get acquainted and decide that you're okay.

Don't make the mistake of trying to pet or hug a strange dog. You wouldn't like it if someone you didn't know ran up and hugged you. Most dogs don't like it either.

Dr. Ann Squire
101 Questions and Answers About Pets and People

> What does the writer tell you that might lead you to approach dogs carefully?

222 Unit 6 Persuasive Writing

Resource Manager

Planning Resources
- Lesson Plans

Transparencies
- Bellringer
- Daily Language Practice
- Fine Art 26-30
- Two-Minute Skill Drill
- Writing Process 20-22B

☛ Other Print Resources
- Composition Enrichment, p. 45
- Composition Practice, p. 45
- Composition Reteaching, p. 45
- Cooperative Learning Activities, pp. 31–36
- Listening and Speaking Activities, p. 22, 28

- Thinking and Study Skills, pp. 5–7, 9, 20
- Writing Across the Curriculum
- Writing Assessment and Evaluation Rubrics

What Does It Take to Convince You?

Often persuasive writing begins by stating the writer's goal. Then evidence—information to support that goal—follows. Some support statements will make you think ("The rain forest is disappearing at the rate of . . ."). Some support statements will make you feel a certain way ("You won't fit in unless you wear . . ."). Finally, there is usually a reminder of what the writer wants you to think or do.

As a reader, you need to think carefully about the support presented in persuasive writing. After all, the writer is trying to change your thoughts or actions. From the excerpt on page 222, do you agree with the support statement in the chart below?

Goal	Support
Do not hug or pet a strange dog.	Dogs don't always want to be friends right away.

Journal Writing

List in your journal three examples of persuasive writing you have read recently. Have any persuaded you to change your thoughts or actions? Write a brief paragraph explaining why or why not.

Teach

Using the Model

Ask students to identify the sentence that states the writer's main point. ("Don't make the mistake of trying to pet or hug a strange dog.") Ask what the writer says that might affect the way the students approach dogs. (The writer compares dogs to people in that neither necessarily want to be friendly right away.) **L2**

Identifying Persuasion

Ask students to identify examples of persuasive writing they come across every day (advertisements, billboards, posters, letters to the editor, editorial cartoons, reviews of movies or TV shows, political campaign speeches). Stress that the purpose of persuasive writing is to bring about change. Ask what kind of change the writer of each example hopes to bring about. (Students should identify changes in both thoughts and actions.) **L1**

Two-Minute Skill Drill

List these sentences on the board and have students choose the more persuasive sentence and explain why.

Wear Spikes air pump sneakers and you will fly to the basket.

Buy Spikes sneakers if you want to play basketball.

See also *Two-Minute Skill Drill Transparencies, 6.1*

Journal Writing Tip

Evaluating Ideas Encourage students to cite persuasive appeals that actually did persuade them. What made these appeals effective? Some students might also describe unsuccessful appeals, explaining why these didn't work.

Teach

Comparing and Contrasting

To highlight some persuasive appeals used in advertising, you might ask students to pick ads for two brands of the same type of product and compare and contrast the effectiveness of each, based on the students' own responses. Another useful comparison might be how the same product or kind of product is advertised in a magazine with a teenage audience and in a magazine with an adult audience. **L2**

Changing the Audience

Challenge students to identify ways in which the letter on this page might be rewritten to appeal to a different audience, such as the girl's grandmother. Discuss changes they might make in the choice of arguments or language. Encourage students to mention a few specific details they'd include to persuade their own grandmother, or another adult, to visit. **L3**

Additional Resources

📖 For persuasive **writing prompts,** see *Fine Art Transparencies*, 26–30.

📖 *Daily Language Practice*

📖 *Writing Process Transparencies,* 20–22B

📁 *Writing Across the Curriculum*

📁 *Cooperative Learning Activities,* pp. 31–36

📁 *Thinking and Study Skills,* pp. 5–7, 9, 20

📁 *Composition Practice,* p. 45

📁 *Listening and Speaking Activities,* pp. 22, 28

Persuasive Writing

How Often Do You Persuade?

Persuasive writing can take many forms, from a 500-page book to a few words on a billboard. It can even exist in friendly letters or cards.

Suppose that you want to persuade a friend who lives out of town to visit you during the summer. You might make up a package including posters, brochures, and articles about the attractions of your home town. You could present your best persuasive ideas in a letter like the one at the left. Read it to see where Rachel put her main idea and her support.

Dear Jenna,

Hi! How's life? I'm fine. I was just hit by a killer idea. Why don't you come to Iowa City for the July Fourth week? Doesn't that sound great?! Not only could we see fab fireworks, but the jazz festival is that weekend. You would love it. Tons of music and great people. They block off the streets and different kinds of food shops set up stands. From frozen yogurt to bar-be-que. It's great.

When we're not listening to music, there is a wonderful bead shop in this little row of second-story shops called the Hall Mall. Every kind of bead you could imagine. Of course we would have to get the world's best chocolate malts at this quaint little drug store.

I don't know if this sounds fun, but it is. Well, gotta motor. Think about my offer.

Love ya,
Rachel

Rachel Hardesty
Willowwind School
Iowa City, Iowa

Viewing and Representing

Getting the Message

Students will benefit from seeing visual examples of persuasive writing. Bring in magazine and newspaper ads, editorials, brochures, and other materials to display and discuss. Ask volunteers to bring in their own examples.

Work with students to identify the main persuasive messages in each example and the thoughts or actions they aim to change. Point out the evidence used in each example.

Create a Poster

Make a poster to convince students to wear safety equipment when biking or skateboarding. Use photos or drawings to reinforce your words.

PURPOSE To persuade others to use safety equipment

AUDIENCE Other students

LENGTH 1 page

WRITING RUBRICS To write a persuasive essay, you should

- state clearly your main goal
- give at least two support statements
- end with a reminder of what you want people to think or do

Jasper Johns. *Numbers in Color.* 1958–1959

Avoid sentence fragments in your writing.

A *fragment* is a group of words that does not present a complete thought and may lack a subject, a predicate, or both.

Revise each sentence fragment below to make a complete sentence. Write clearly and legibly, and check your spelling.

1. Tons of music and great people.
2. From frozen yogurt to barbeque.
3. Every kind of bead you could imagine.

See Lesson 8.2, page 299.

Cross-Curricular Activity

ART Study the reproduction of *Numbers in Color* on this page, and then state your opinion of it. Supply at least two support statements to back up your opinion.

Listening and Speaking

PRESENT A DEBATE Stage a debate about *Numbers in Color.* Take turns presenting your opinions and support statements to the class. Then encourage the class to evaluate the persuasiveness of the arguments presented.

Persuasive Writing

Assess

Evaluation Rubrics

Create a Poster

Use these criteria when evaluating your students' writing:
- A position statement is clearly stated.
- Support statements are based on facts or logical examples.
- The poster reflects the interests of the targeted audience (other students).

See also *Writing Assessment and Evaluation Rubrics.*

Cross-Curricular Activity: Art

Students' opinions may be positive or negative but should be supported with appropriate facts and examples.

Listening and Speaking

Make sure that each student contributes opinions and offers constructive criticism. Evaluate students' spoken messages in terms of content, credibility, and delivery.

Reteaching

📁 *Composition Reteaching*, p. 45

Enrichment

📁 *Composition Enrichment*, p. 45

📦 *Fine Art Transparencies* 26–30

Close

Have students write a persuasive letter based on an issue in their own lives, such as asking a parent for permission to attend an event or trying to persuade a teacher that video games can be educational. Encourage students to work with a peer reviewer. Students may wish to send off their letters to see if they really work!

Answers

Answers will vary, but some suggestions are given.
1. The party had tons of music . . .
2. The buffet had everything from . . .
3. . . . could imagine was in the store.

Viewing the Art

Jasper Johns, *Numbers in Color*, 1958–1959
Johns's patterns, brushstrokes, and colors allow viewers to see familiar objects in new and exciting ways. *Numbers in Color,* 66 1/2 by 49 1/2 inches, Albright Knox Art Gallery, Buffalo, New York.
Interpret and Analyze Use the following questions for discussion:
- What familiar objects can you see in this picture? How are they organized?
- What do you think is the meaning of the picture? Justify your answers.

Focus

Lesson Overview

Objectives
- To understand the importance of adapting persuasive writing to a target audience
- To present a position in an appealing way

Skills
- writing a letter; using reference sources; capitalizing proper nouns and adjectives

Critical Thinking
- evaluating; defining problems; identifying main ideas; using criteria

Listening and Speaking
- discussing; speaking persuasively

🔔 Bellringer
Daily Language Activity

When students enter the classroom, have this assignment on the board: *Think of an item you would like to sell. Write a brief paragraph telling how you would advertise it.*

Grammar Link to the Bellringer

Have students check their sentences for proper capitalization.

📖 **See also** *Daily Language Practice*

Motivating Activity

Have students write three persuasive slogans that could be used as advertisements for the items they wrote about in the Bellringer. Tell students to keep their audience in mind as they write the slogans. Ask students how the slogans might be changed if a different audience were targeted.

Persuasive Writing

Stating a Position

When you have a goal you really care about, the challenge is winning over your audience.

As you choose a goal for your persuasive piece, answer the questions in the chart below. If you can answer yes to each question, you've found a good topic.

Do I know enough about this topic?

Finding a Persuasive Writing Topic
• Do I know enough about this topic?
• Do I care about this topic?
• Do people disagree about this topic?

The students at one school have several ideas for projects. Some want to put in a juice machine to raise money for new computers. Some want to start a garden to grow vegetables for a food pantry. Some want to organize an ethnic festival to celebrate different cultures. If you were the student council representative to the school board, it would be your job to persuade the school board to adopt one of the ideas.

Do I care about this topic?

Do people disagree on this topic?

Resource Manager

Planning Resources
- Lesson Plans

📖 **Transparencies**
- Bellringer
- Daily Language Practice
- Fine Art 26–30
- Two-Minute Skill Drill
- Writing Process 20–22B

📁 Other Print Resources
- Composition Enrichment, p. 46
- Composition Practice, p. 46
- Composition Reteaching, p. 46
- Cooperative Learning Activities, pp. 31–36
- Listening and Speaking Activities, p. 22

- Thinking and Study Skills, pp. 1–2, 4–5, 13, 20
- Writing Across the Curriculum
- Writing Assessment and Evaluation Rubrics

Give Reasons

Why should people adopt your ideas? You need to provide convincing reasons.

The proposal written by last year's representative to the school board appears below. Notice the clear organization and persuasive sound of the letter.

Literature Model

Dear Ms. Perez and the school board:

For this year's student project, we would like to set up paper-recycling bins at key places around the school. This project will benefit the school in several ways. It will give students a chance to improve the environment by cutting down on waste. It will encourage students from all grades to work together to set up and run the recycling project. It will also help raise money we can use for future projects.

We would like to put a recycling bin in each classroom. A group of students will be chosen each week to collect the bins and set them out for pickup. A permanent group will oversee the project with Mr. Hansen, the science teacher. With your support, this project will be a success.

> Note that the first sentence is a statement of the main goal.

> What reasons does the student provide in support of the proposal? Are they convincing?

Grammar Tip

When you write a letter that speaks for a group or an organization, be sure to use the right pronouns. For more information on pronouns, see Lessons 11.1–11.5, pages 361–370.

Persuasive Writing

Journal Writing

Take two minutes to list as many persuasive-writing topics as you can. Circle those topics to which you can answer yes for all three of the questions on page 226. Why are some topics not circled? Change these enough so that you can circle them. Keep these topics for use in future projects.

Teach

Using the Model

Ask students to identify the main purpose of each paragraph. (The first paragraph states the main idea and presents three benefits of the project. The second paragraph explains how the project would work.) Ask students how this letter might change if it were being written to the students instead of to the school board. **L2**

Using a Visual

A visual might help students understand how evidence is used to support a main idea. Draw a triangular "roof" on the chalkboard, and write *Main Idea* on it. Below the roof, draw three supporting "pillars," writing *Evidence* on each one. Next, draw the same diagram on the board, without words, and invite volunteers to write the model's main idea and supporting details on its roof and pillars. Point out that just as pillars support a roof, pieces of evidence work together to support an opinion. **L1**

Two-Minute Skill Drill

Write this topic on the board and have students list three pieces of supporting evidence:

Support Paper Recycling!

☛ **See also** *Two-Minute Skill Drill Transparencies, 6.2*

Journal Writing Tip

Evaluating Ideas You might suggest that students use a prewriting technique, such as clustering or listing. This will help them to determine whether they know enough about a topic and to revise some of their topics for later use.

Teach

Using a Thesaurus

Ask students what special projects they'd like to have the school or the sixth-grade class undertake. Then have students explain how they'd go about trying to persuade the school board or principal to adopt their projects. (Include benefits to the school, to the community, and to students.) Ask the class to tell what reasons would be effective or ineffective, helping them identify those that might be especially appealing to their targeted audience. **L2**

Choosing Words

Ask small groups of students to choose a school policy they would like to see changed. Ask them to propose a change, such as giving students a say in planning the lunch menus. Each group should identify the types of people they might need to persuade (parents, teachers, school board members, fellow students) and discuss what points would appeal to each audience. Then each team member should choose one of these audiences and write a letter proposing the policy change. **L3**

Additional Resources

- For persuasive **writing prompts,** see *Fine Art Transparencies* 26–30.
- *Daily Language Practice*
- *Writing Process Transparencies,* 20–22B
- *Writing Across the Curriculum*
- *Cooperative Learning Activities,* pp. 31–36
- *Thinking and Study Skills,* pp. 1–2, 4–5, 13, 20
- *Listening and Speaking Activities,* pp. 22, 28
- *Composition Practice,* p. 46

Persuasive Writing

Presenting Tip

Choose the form that best presents your argument. Will you send a letter or face your audience in person? The form of presentation may affect how you state your ideas.

Consider Your Audience

Whenever you try to convince someone of something, you need to keep your audience in mind. For example, imagine that you're trying to get your family to plan a day of activities in the city. You might spark your sister's interest by telling her about the great restaurants. Your mom might take more interest in the museums. The street performers might appeal more to your brother.

Different people have different interests and different levels of knowledge. Choose reasons that appeal to your audience. One student's goal was to argue for the ethnic festival. She sent a letter to the school board and another letter to the students. Her goal was the same in both letters, but at least one of her reasons was different. Why?

An ethnic festival will build pride and help students understand cultures different from their own.

The reason presented to the school board focuses on what the festival will teach students. The reason statement for students focuses on how much fun the festival will be.

An ethnic festival will give us a chance to enjoy sharing many different foods and customs.

228 Unit 6 Persuasive Writing

Writing in the Real World

Examining Advertisements

Supply students with a stack of magazines. Have students search through the magazines to find examples of persuasive writing in the advertisements. Work with students to find the main idea or position statement and identify the supporting evidence. Point out that sometimes ads rely on visual information rather than writing. Ask students how the illustrations can be persuasive.

Write a Proposal

Choose a project that your sixth-grade class might do in the school or in the community. Explain your idea in a written proposal to your teacher or the school principal.

PURPOSE To practice persuading an adult audience

AUDIENCE Your teacher or principal

LENGTH 2–4 paragraphs

WRITING RUBRICS To write a persuasive proposal, you should

- state your goal clearly
- follow it with supporting reasons that will appeal to your audience

Using Computers

E-mail Using an attachment function, e-mail your proposal to a friend or relative for his or her evaluation. Use the comments you get back to help you revise your work.

Grammar Link

Capitalize proper nouns and adjectives.

Capitalize the names of languages, countries, and nationalities in the list. You will need to capitalize 10 words.

1. haitian, chinese, and italian food
2. art from mexico
3. tapes of irish, israeli, and russian music
4. jewelry from india and greece
5. a cuban band

See Lesson 18.4, page 479.

Viewing and Representing

TRAVEL DISPLAY Find some attractive pictures of your town or neighborhood in a magazine, book, or brochure. With a partner, make a display on a poster or a bulletin board and write a few paragraphs telling other students your age why you think they would enjoy coming to visit your area. Invite classmates to comment on your display.

Persuasive Writing

Assess

Evaluation Rubrics

Write a Proposal

Use these criteria when evaluating your students' writing:

- Is the main idea or position presented clearly?
- Do the supporting reasons reflect an awareness of the needs and interests of the stated audience (teacher or principal)?

See also *Writing Assessment and Evaluation Rubrics.*

Viewing and Representing

Displays should be attractive and appealing. Paragraphs should include convincing reasons to visit.

Reteaching

📁 *Composition Reteaching,* p. 46

Enrichment

📁 *Composition Enrichment,* p. 46

🎨 *Fine Art Transparencies* 26–30

Close

Discuss how ordinary citizens might use persuasive writing to make changes in their communities. (They might write letters to the editor and to their legislators, write pamphlets or fliers to distribute to neighbors, or create posters to display.)

6.2 Stating a Position **229**

Grammar Link

Answers

1. Haitian, Chinese, and Italian food
2. art from Mexico
3. tapes of Irish, Israeli, and Russian music
4. jewelry from India and Greece
5. a Cuban band

Using Facts and Opinions

*W*hat kinds of evidence will you use to support your goal and your reasons?

Persuasive Writing

Focus

Lesson Overview

Objectives

- To learn how to differentiate between facts and opinion as supporting evidence
- To use facts and opinions to support a position

Skills

- gathering evidence; organizing facts and opinions

Critical Thinking

- classifying facts and opinions; ordering

Listening and Speaking

- discussing

🔔 Bellringer
Daily Language Activity

When students enter the classroom, have this assignment on the board: *Write a sentence that lists at least three animals that would make unusual pets.*

Grammar Link to the Bellringer

Remind students that items in a series must have commas to separate them. Have students check the sentences they wrote for commas within a series.

See also *Daily Language Practice*

Motivating Activity

Ask students: *Have you ever had a pet snake or any other unusual pet? Would you recommend that pet to a friend? Why or why not?* Then have students jot down their ideas for possible class pets. Discuss their ideas, including the reasons students give. You might make a chart, writing each suggestion as a heading near the top of the chalkboard and listing pieces of supporting evidence under each heading.

Each year Mrs. Van's class chooses a class pet. Her students write persuasive papers, arguing for their choice. What pet would you argue for? What evidence could you present to prove your point?

Literature Model

Ever since a snake tempted Eve with an apple in the Garden of Eden, snakes have been considered evil, hateful, and repulsive creatures. However, most snakes are harmless and helpful. They kill rats and other rodents that destroy crops and invade our homes. Many kinds make fascinating, even beautiful pets. They are not slimy. Their scaly skin feels like dry leather. They don't make a sound, they are odorless, and you don't have to feed them every day.

Leda and Rhoda Blumberg
Lovebirds, Lizards, and Llamas: Strange and Exotic Pets

What evidence do the writers use to suggest that snakes can make good pets?

230 Unit 6 Persuasive Writing

Resource Manager

Planning Resources
- Lesson Plans

Transparencies
- Bellringer
- Daily Language Practice
- Fine Art 26–30
- Two-Minute Skill Drill
- Writing Process 20–22B

📂 Other Print Resources
- Composition Enrichment, p. 47
- Composition Practice, p. 47
- Composition Reteaching, p. 47
- Cooperative Learning Activities, pp. 31–36
- Listening and Speaking Activities, pp. 22, 28

- Thinking and Study Skills, pp. 3, 10, 13, 14, 17–19
- Writing Across the Curriculum
- Writing Assessment and Evaluation Rubrics

Gather the Evidence

You believe that a snake would be the perfect class pet. How can you persuade your classmates and your teacher? Persuading people to change their attitudes or to take action requires evidence. Evidence comes in two forms: facts and opinions.

FACTS Facts are statements that can be proved. For example, the statement "They are not slimy" is a fact. You could prove it by touching a snake or by reading about snakes.

Revising Tip

As you gather evidence, write down the source of each fact or opinion you intend to use.

Sources of Facts		Sources of Opinions	
Observations	Books and Magazines	Experts	Experiences

OPINIONS An opinion is a personal belief or feeling. It can't be proved. The authors of the excerpt on page 230 think that snakes make fascinating pets. Because the authors are experts, you would probably believe them. The opinions of experts can be powerful evidence. Personal experience can also be good evidence. A person who has a lot of experience is often considered an expert.

Journal Writing

Select a persuasive article from a newspaper or magazine, and identify the goal. Save the article in your journal. Make notes in your journal about how facts and opinions support the goal. Make sure your writing is legible.

6.3 Using Facts and Opinions **231**

Listening and Speaking

Determining Fact and Opinion

Let students know that it is sometimes difficult to separate facts from opinions while listening to a speaker. The emotions of the speaker, the expressions on the speaker's face, and the speaker's gestures all work together to convince listeners of the speaker's message. It is important to concentrate on the speaker's words. Determine whether the speaker is supporting his or her ideas with facts and whether the information being presented is valid and reliable.

Teach

Using the Model

Have students explain what evidence the writer uses to prove that snakes make good pets. (Most snakes are harmless, and they don't make noise, don't smell, and don't need to be fed every day.) Invite students to add any other reasons they think of. (the educational value of observing a snake closely) **L2**

Comparing Results

Students form teams of four, each student working with a partner. Each team creates a main idea statement about a pet they'd like to have in the classroom. Each partner pair makes a list of evidence supporting the main-idea statement. Encourage students to think of examples for each type of evidence shown in the chart on this page. Have students compare their results with those of the other partner pair in their team. **L2**

Two-Minute Skill Drill

Write the following on the board and ask students to write whether each is a fact or an opinion:

Some snakes are 30 feet long.

Snakes are fun to watch.

See also *Two-Minute Skill Drill Transparencies, 6.3*

Journal Writing Tip

Evaluating ideas Encourage students to assess the effectiveness of each fact and opinion they find in their article. Suggest that they list evidence in order, from most convincing to least convincing.

231

Teach

Identifying Fact and Opinion

Put the headings *Fact* and *Opinion* on the board. Read through the model and point out each piece of evidence to students. Work with them to decide if it is a fact (snakes are quiet, clean, do not cause allergies, eat worms, and are inexpensive to feed) or an opinion (snakes are fascinating, easy to feed, and more educational than a common pet). **L1**

Changing the Audience

Ask students to revise the model as if they were trying to convince fellow students rather than the teacher. What order might be most effective for the pieces of evidence? (They might draw readers in by talking about how unusual and intriguing certain snakes are.) What other persuasive statements could they make? (They might give interesting information about snakes, such as their great variety; about 2,700 kinds exist.) **L3**

Additional Resources

For persuasive **writing prompts,** see *Fine Art Transparencies* 26–30.

Daily Language Practice

Writing Process Transparencies, 20–22B

Writing Across the Curriculum

Cooperative Learning Activities, pp. 31–36

Thinking and Study Skills, pp. 3, 10, 13, 14, 17–19

Listening and Speaking Activities, pp. 22, 28

Composition Practice, p. 47

Persuasive Writing

Revising Tip

If you use others' opinions in persuasive writing, check while revising to make sure you say whose opinions they are.

What evidence does the writer use to support the goal statement? Are word choices precise?

Because this was written for Ms. Van, the writer decided to start with what the students would learn from a snake.

Organize Your Argument

After you gather your evidence, review it piece by piece. Which evidence is the strongest or most convincing? Sometimes you might want to put the strongest piece of evidence first in your paper. Other times you might want to save it until the end. Decide which order of evidence best supports your goal.

Make a list of your evidence in the order that seems most persuasive. Use this list to draft your persuasive argument. Of course, you may change the order of the evidence during revision. Notice the revisions of this draft about pet snakes.

In choosing a class pet, we could pick no *finer* ~~better~~ animal than a snake. Experts point out that snakes are quiet, clean, and easy to care for. They aren't slimy, and they make fascinating pets.

The smaller kinds, which we are most likely to get, *eat* ~~feed on~~ worms. So they would be easy and inexpensive to feed. Also, people don't have allergies to snakes as they do to dogs, cats, and birds.

Snakes behave very differently from more common pets. We would learn more about the animal world by adopting a snake than we would by choosing a pet we know well.

Enrichment and Extension

Expressing Opinions

To help students distinguish between facts and opinions, tell them that opinions are usually based on what people think and feel. Opinions often begin with words such as, *I think, I believe,* or *I feel.* Show students some pictures of snakes. Have students make up sentences telling what they think, believe, or feel about snakes. Explain that facts are information that can be found in books or from observing. Facts can be proven; you know they are true.

Write a Persuasive Letter

Television shows are canceled all the time. Sometimes even a popular TV show goes off the air. If many people write or call the network, sometimes the show returns. What if your favorite show had just been canceled? Write a letter to the president of the network to persuade him or her to bring back the show.

PURPOSE To keep your favorite TV program from being canceled

AUDIENCE A network executive

LENGTH 2–3 paragraphs

WRITING RUBRICS To write a persuasive letter, you should

- make your point clear in a goal statement
- use facts or opinions as evidence
- organize your evidence to appeal to your audience

Cross-Curricular Activity

COOPERATIVE LEARNING In a small group, plan a campaign to persuade fellow students to support a community project. For example, you could suggest setting up donation boxes for homeless people or forming an after-school club to work on community environmental issues. Agree on the goal you wish to pursue. List evidence—facts and opinions—to support your position. Have two people

Grammar Link

Use commas to separate three or more items in a series.

Snakes have been considered evil, hateful, and repulsive.

Add commas as needed in the sentences below.

1. Let's find a good project for the fourth fifth and sixth graders.
2. We could plant flowers shrubs and trees around the building.
3. Students could sweep rake and trim on a regular schedule.

See Lesson 19.2, page 491.

plan ways to present your proposal while others think of slogans and attention-getting phrases that present your evidence.

Listening and Speaking

DISCUSSING PETS Together with students from various cultural backgrounds, make a presentation to the class in which each of you talks about the most common pets in your own culture. Where appropriate, give the names for these pets in languages other than English. Take part in a class discussion of differences and similarities regarding the importance of pets within cultures.

Grammar Link

Answers

1. fourth, fifth, and sixth graders
2. flowers, shrubs, and trees
3. sweep, rake, and trim

Separating Items in a Long Series Have students add one or two more items to each sentence. Remind students to be careful of where the conjunction is placed as they add the items and place the commas.

Persuasive Writing

Assess

Evaluation Rubrics

Write a Persuasive Letter

Use these criteria when evaluating your students' writing:

- Does the letter begin by stating the main idea?
- Does the letter include both facts and opinions?
- Is evidence ordered in a way that reflects awareness of the audience?

See also *Writing Assessment and Evaluation Rubrics.*

Cross-Curricular Activity

Monitor groups to ensure that all students participate. Encourage students to monitor their understanding of the project and to seek clarification as needed. Students should demonstrate the ability to distinguish between fact and opinion, to compare and contrast information and ideas, and to make inferences about what they hear during the discussion.

Listening and Speaking

Help students to understand that ideas about animals reflect region and culture.

Reteaching

📁 *Composition Reteaching,* p. 47

Enrichment

📁 *Composition Enrichment,* p. 47

Close

Discuss with students what makes the best evidence for a persuasive piece—fact or opinion. Encourage students to give examples of both that are strong. Help students realize that sometimes facts are more persuasive and sometimes opinions or personal experience are more effective.

Focus

Lesson Overview

Objectives

- To learn how to evaluate television programs
- To write a review of a television program

Skills

- note taking; writing to persuade

Critical Thinking

- summarizing; evaluating; identifying main ideas

Listening and Speaking

- discussing

🔔 Bellringer
Daily Language Activity

When students enter the classroom, have this assignment on the board: *Briefly describe a television show you saw recently that you particularly enjoyed.*

Grammar Link to the Bellringer

Ask students if they used any possessive nouns in their descriptions. Write some examples of these on the board and focus on the placement of the apostrophe in each.

👆 **See also** *Daily Language Practice*

Motivating Activity

Engage students in a discussion of their television viewing habits. What programs do they watch regularly? What programs do they like or dislike, and why? Students may have heard opinions about this year's newest offerings. Ask what they've heard and whether they agree. Discuss whether they watch network television, public television, cable, videotapes, or a combination of these. Explain that one way to respond to a television program is to write a review of it.

Persuasive Writing

LESSON 6.4

WRITING ABOUT LITERATURE

Writing a TV Review

Do you ever find yourself trying to convince a friend to watch a rerun of a TV show? Try writing a review and reaching a larger audience.

All week you have looked forward to the National Geographic television special about the North Pole. What's it like at the top of the world? What animals live there, and how do they survive? What would it be like there in the summer when the sun never sets?

The program not only answers your questions, but it does more. It tells you about brave explorers who faced many dangers as they mapped the frozen lands. It makes you feel as if you're taking part in a month-long dog-sled journey. The beautiful photography and the haunting music fascinate you. To share what you've learned from this show, you could write a review of the program and try to persuade people to watch it in a rerun or on videotape.

Resource Manager

Planning Resources
- Lesson Plans

👆 Transparencies
- Bellringer
- Daily Language Practice
- Fine Art 26–30
- Two-Minute Skill Drill
- Writing Process 20–22B

📂 Other Print Resources
- Composition Enrichment, p. 48
- Composition Practice, p. 48
- Composition Reteaching, p. 48
- Cooperative Learning Activities, pp. 31–36
- Listening and Speaking Activities, pp. 22, 28

- Thinking and Study Skills, pp. 17, 19
- Writing Assessment and Evaluation Rubrics

Gather Information

The best way to gather information for a TV review is to take notes while you watch the program. Jot down notes about facts or images that grab your attention.

You can use other methods, too, to help you review a TV program. If you have a videocassette recorder, tape the program and watch it again. The tape can help you strengthen your ideas about the program and add to your notes. You might watch the show with a friend. Afterward, discuss what each of you thought of the show. You can also make a chart like the one below to collect and organize information about a TV program.

Persuasive Writing

Gathering Information for a TV Review	
Name of show and network	*National Geographic Explorer,* "North to the Pole," WTBS
Subject of the show	Dog-sled expedition to the North Pole
Characters (if appropriate)	Six-member team that takes part in the expedition
Strengths	Fast-paced, exciting
Weaknesses	Not enough information on the history of such expeditions
My responses	Makes me want to travel north and learn about winter camping

Journal Writing

Make a chart like the one above, and fill it in as you watch a television program. How does the chart help you gather information about the program? What questions could you add to make the chart a better prewriting tool? How else could you improve it?

Teach

Taking Notes

Taking notes while watching a television show is difficult for many students. Remind them to jot down key words rather than writing whole sentences. They should not get so absorbed in note taking that they can't enjoy the show. They should also review their notes as soon as the show is over so they can complete them while the show is still fresh in their memory. **L1**

Making Comparisons

Students might enjoy the challenge of comparing two programs that are similar in content. Help them devise a list of criteria that they will use to assess and evaluate the programs. **L3**

Two-Minute Skill Drill

Write this description on the board. Have volunteers underline the facts that they would write down if they were taking notes on an oral presentation of the description. What abbreviations could they use to save time?

Bits and Bytes is a weekly show presented from 8 to 9 on Tuesday nights on the educational channel. It not only explains the latest software programs available, but also responds to questions viewers have about their computers. You might be interested even if you don't have a computer!

See also *Two-Minute Skill Drill Transparencies, 6.4*

Journal Writing Tip

Sharing Ideas Encourage students to share their revised charts with the rest of the class so that other students can select the chart that works best for them.

Teach

Using the Model

Discuss the order of information presented in the student model. Point out that each paragraph has a different purpose. Then ask students to identify the purpose of each paragraph. (The first paragraph identifies the program and briefly describes its content. In the second paragraph, the reviewer presents the program's strengths and weaknesses. The final paragraph sums up the reviewer's opinion of the program and gives his personal response.) **L2**

Designing a Promotional Piece

Have students work in pairs to design a promotional poster or a script for a radio or television commercial promoting a favorite television show. Students should watch the program, take notes, and then discuss their opinions. The finished piece should include a descriptive paragraph summarizing the program and quotes from student reviewers reflecting what they liked best about it. The results can be posted in the classroom or presented to the rest of the class. **L3**

Additional Resources

For persuasive **writing prompts,** see *Fine Art Transparencies* 26–30.

Daily Language Practice

Writing Process Transparencies, 20–22B

Writing Across the Curriculum

Cooperative Learning Activities, pp. 31–36

Thinking and Study Skills, pp. 17, 19

Listening and Speaking Activities, pp. 22, 28

Composition Practice, p. 48

Persuasive Writing

Grammar Tip

When you edit a review, make sure you've used tenses correctly. Most reviews discuss programs in present tense. For more information see Lesson 10.4, page 339.

TIME

For more about the drafting process, see **TIME Facing the Blank Page,** page 94.

Drafting the Review

Writing a review of a TV program is fairly straightforward. The best way to persuade people to watch a television show is to tell them what you like most about the program. Your enthusiasm can persuade your friends, teachers, parents, and anyone else who reads your review to give the show a try.

In the model below, Jack Costello's excitement about an episode of *The New Explorers* comes through in his review. How might his thumbs-up review make you want to watch the program?

Student Model

The name of the program I watched is *The New Explorers* and it is on WTTW. The subject of the program is computer art and how it is used in entertainment and medicine.

The program's strengths are that it is educational and fun to watch. I like the examples of computer graphics like *Tin Toy. Tin Toy* is an award-winning short cartoon about a toy soldier that comes to life. It is both funny and realistic. The weakness of this show is that it mentions only a few of the many people involved in making computer graphics.

Overall, I feel that the show is cool and really taught me a lot. Computer graphics can be used just about everywhere, including TV, movies, and commercials. It can also be used to help surgeons in the operating room. I think I might want to do something like this when I grow up.

Jack Costello, St. James School,
Arlington Heights, Illinois

Cooperative Learning

Working on Reviews

Have students work on their reviews in pairs. Let each partner discuss the program first and ask his or her partner questions before beginning to write. Encourage partners to go beyond general observations ("It was a great program") to more specific ones ("I enjoyed learning about what it was like for a young soldier during the Civil War"). Remind students to include examples from the program to support their views.

Write a TV Review

Imagine that the most popular segments of your favorite television program have just come out on videotape. Write a two- or three-paragraph review of the videotape that will appear on the package or on posters. The review, aimed at people who have never seen the program, should encourage people to buy the videotape.

PURPOSE To persuade someone to buy a videotape

AUDIENCE Customers of a video store

LENGTH 2–3 paragraphs

WRITING RUBRICS To write an effective review, you should

- tell what you like about the program
- give reasons that other people would enjoy it
- explain why someone would want to own a copy of the tape

Using Computers

Graphics Some computer programs allow the user to create charts. You can choose the number of columns and rows. You can even put a special border around your chart or shade certain areas. Create your own chart for reviewing TV programs. Use the chart on page 235 as a guide. Add any sections you think would be useful.

Grammar Link

Use apostrophes to form possessive nouns.

Use an apostrophe and an *–s* to form the possessive of a singular noun.

the **program's** strengths.

Where you place the apostrophe in a plural noun depends on whether or not the plural ends in *–s*:

people's   *adults'*

Write the sentences below, adding apostrophes to show possession.

1. The TV news show was about our towns plan to build a bike path.
2. The shows purpose was to include opinions from all age groups.
3. I liked the boys suggestions.

See Lesson 19.7, page 501.

Viewing and Representing

PUBLISH YOUR REVIEW Videotape your review, either alone or with a partner, or use the computer to print it out and then post it on the bulletin board. Be sure to check your spelling and punctuation if you print your review. Invite classmates to view your video or read your printed review and then evaluate your arguments in a class discussion.

Persuasive Writing

Assess

Evaluation Rubrics

Write a TV Review

Use these criteria when evaluating your students' writing.

- Does the review include a brief summary of the program's content?
- Are specific details from the program given?
- Does the review include a main idea urging readers to buy the videotape?
- Has the student listed reasons for liking the program?
- Has the student used carefully chosen descriptive words?

See also *Writing Assessment and Evaluation Rubrics.*

Using Computers

Students will enjoy the option of being able to keep the chart structure while simply changing the content to match the show. Encourage them to be creative in their chart creations.

Viewing and Representing

Make sure students understand how to videotape or print out their reviews.

Reteaching

📁 *Composition Reteaching*, p. 48

Enrichment

📁 *Composition Enrichment*, p. 48

Close

Engage students in a discussion of what they have learned about reviewing a television program. What techniques seem to have the most persuasive effect? Could these same techniques be applied to reviewing a movie?

Grammar Link

Answers

1. town's   3. boy's or boys'
2. show's

Possessive Nouns After students have checked their sentences for correct placement of apostrophes, have them rewrite the sentences, changing each possessive from singular to plural or from plural to singular. In the first sentence, for example, students might change *our town's plans* to *several towns' plans*. Have students discuss their sentence changes and changes in the placement of the apostrophe.

Teach

6+1 Trait® Writing

Ideas Ask students what important idea Swift Eagle is expressing when he says, "So I understand that you boys must have been very, very hungry to kill those little birds." *(Animals are killed only for food, never just for sport.)*

Active Reading Strategies

Summarize Ask students to summarize the two ideas Bruchac says are illustrated by the anecdote about the boys and Swift Eagle. *(People depended on the natural world for survival, and children were taught the values of their culture through example and stories.)*

Literature Model

Persuasive Writing

"Ah," he said, "I see you have been hunting. Pick up your game and come with me."

He led the boys to a place where they could make a fire and cook the birds. He made sure they said a 'thank you' to the spirits of the birds before eating them, and as they ate he told stories. It was important, he said, to be thankful to the birds for the gifts of their songs, their feathers, and their bodies as food. The last thing he said to them they never forgot—for it was one of those boys who told me this story many years later: "You know, our Creator gave the gift of life to everything that is alive. Life is a very sacred thing. But our Creator knows that we have to eat to stay alive. That is why it is permitted to hunt to feed ourselves and our people. So I understand that you boys must have been very, very hungry to kill those little birds."

I have always liked that story, for it illustrates several things. Although there was a wide range of customs, lifeways and languages—in pre-Columbian[1] times more than 400 different languages were spoken on the North American continent— many close similarities existed between virtually all of the Native American peoples. Thus ideas held by

an Apache from the Southwest fitted into the lives and traditions of Onondagas in the Northeast.

> **" . . . He told stories that pointed out the value of those birds as living beings . . . . "**

One of these ideas, expressed in Swift Eagle's words to the boys, was the continent-wide belief that mankind depended on the natural world for survival, on the one hand, and had to respect it and remain in right relationship with it, on the other. . . .

As the anecdote[2] about Swift Eagle also shows, the children were taught the values of their culture through example and stories. Instead of scolding or lecturing them, Swift Eagle showed the boys how to build a fire and cook the game they had shot, giving the songbirds the same respect he would have given a rabbit or deer.

---

1 **pre-Columbian** before Columbus's arrival in 1492
2 **anecdote** (an'ik dōt') a brief retelling of an actual event

---

6+1 Trait® Writing

Ideas

Explain to students that the ideas in a piece of writing are its theme and the details that support and develop that theme. Strong, well-developed ideas lead to a clear message that is easy for the reader to understand. Show students how the anecdote about Swift Eagle introduces and develops the idea about having a responsible relationship with nature.

Practice Ask students to write a brief explanation of the key idea contained in this sentence: "You know, our Creator gave the gift of life to everything that is alive." *(Sample response: The boys, too, are part of the natural world that the Creator has given the gift of life to. If they want their lives to be respected, they must respect the lives of everything else in the natural world.)*

Literature Model

He told stories that pointed out the value of those birds as living beings. The ritual[3] activity of making the fire, thanking the spirit of the birds, hearing the stories and then eating the game they had killed taught the boys more than a hundred stern lectures would have done, and the lesson stayed with them all their lives.

3 **ritual** (rich'ŏŏ əl) a system of special ceremonies

Teach

Critical Thinking

Interpret Ask: "What important idea is the author expressing in the last sentence of the excerpt?" *(Lessons learned from experience are more valuable and long-lasting than lessons contained in stern lectures.)*

Additional Resources

For further persuasive **writing prompts**, see *Fine Art Transparencies* 26–30

Listening and Speaking Activities, pp. 8, 24

Thinking and Study Skills, pp. 13, 19

Vocabulary and Spelling Strategies and Practice, p. 12

Active Reading Strategies

Predict

Tell students that when they make a prediction about what might happen in a piece of writing, they are making an educated guess about possible outcomes. By constantly guessing at what might happen next, readers stay engaged, because they want to see whether their predictions come true. One way to make predictions is to think about the main idea and how that might play out in the future. For example, explain to students that the boys' future lives probably will be affected by the incident with the birds.

Practice Ask students to predict how the boys' relationship to nature is likely to be different in the future. *(The boys will have a greater respect for nature in the future.)*

Linking Writing and Literature

Assess

Evaluation Rubrics

Talk About Reading

Possible answers to the questions:

1. Answers will vary, but students should note that by respecting nature they are helping to ensure the continued health of the planet on which they live.

2. Native Americans have a personal and spiritual relationship with nature. They understand that if they respect nature, nature will nurture them.

3. They learn not to abuse the bounty nature has provided. If they had been scolded or informed on, they would have learned only that they had done something wrong. They might have felt angry and resentful and not learned anything from the incident.

4. Bruchac could have written an essay in which he *tells* the reader about Native Americans and nature, but the anecdote helps him to *show* that relationship in action. The anecdote brings the theme to life for the readers. Students may discuss using anecdotes to make their own personal writing more effective.

Write About Reading

The editorial should do the following:

- clearly introduce the main idea of the editorial
- explain the concept of respect for nature
- outline the benefits of respecting nature
- close by encouraging readers to develop a positive relationship with nature

Close

Initiate a discussion about how Swift Eagle might react to some of the efforts being made today to protect the environment. To which environmental issues would he relate strongly?

246

Persuasive Writing

Literature Model

Linking Writing and Literature

Collect Your Thoughts

Think about what Joseph Bruchac is saying in "Thanking the Birds." In your journal, make some notes about the main idea of this excerpt from *Keepers of the Earth*.

Talk About Reading

Discuss "Thanking the Birds" with your classmates. Select one person to lead the discussion and another to take notes. Use the following questions to guide the discussion.

1. **Connect to Your Life** Why is it important for people to respect nature? In what ways do you respect nature in your own life?

2. **Critical Thinking: Draw Conclusions** After reading the excerpt, what conclusions can you draw about the relationship between Native Americans and nature?

3. **6+1 Trait®: Ideas** What lesson do the boys learn from Swift Eagle? What lesson might they have learned if he had simply scolded them or told their parents what they had done?

4. **Connect to Your Writing** How does Bruchac's anecdote make his theme easier for the reader to understand? When can you use anecdotes in your own writing?

Write About Reading

Editorial Write an editorial for your community newspaper that considers the following questions.

- Why it is important for everyone to develop a personal relationship with the natural world?
- How can people develop such a relationship?
- What will be the benefits for people and nature?

If appropriate, include a brief anecdote in your editorial to help readers understand your point.

Focus on Ideas Before you begin writing, spend some time thinking about the main idea of your editorial. Be sure the main idea is clear in your own mind so that you can explain it well to your readers.

For more information on ideas and the 6+1 Trait® model, see **Writing and Research Handbook,** pages 682–684.

6+1 Trait® is a registered trademark of Northwest Regional Educational Laboratory, which does not endorse this product.

Cultural Connections

Understanding Common Beliefs

The story Bruchac tells reflects the values of many Native American cultures. In fact, Bruchac says that the attitude Swift Eagle teaches the boys results from "continent-wide" beliefs held by "virtually all of the Native American peoples."

UNIT 6 Review

Reflecting on the Unit

Summarize what you learned in this unit by answering the following questions.

❶ When you write to persuade, why is it important to keep your audience in mind?

❷ What are some good ways to use opinions as supporting evidence?

❸ How can you use the revising stage to improve a piece of persuasive writing?

❹ What techniques can help you gather information to review a television program?

Adding to Your Portfolio

CHOOSE A SELECTION FOR YOUR PORTFOLIO Look over the persuasive writing you did in this unit. Select a completed piece of writing to put into your portfolio. The writing you choose should show some or all of the following:

- an attempt to get readers to believe or do something
- a clear goal statement
- reasons that support the goal statement
- evidence ordered in a way that is persuasive to the intended audience
- accurate spelling and legible cursive or manuscript writing

REFLECT ON YOUR CHOICE Attach a note to the piece you chose, explaining briefly why you chose it and what you learned from writing it.

SET GOALS How can you improve your writing? What skill will you focus on the next time you write?

Writing Across the Curriculum

MAKE A GEOGRAPHY CONNECTION Think about a weather condition or natural phenomenon that might threaten your community (a tornado, flood, electrical storm, or earthquake). Write a persuasive argument to convince people to protect themselves or their property. Put your argument in any form you wish—perhaps a newspaper article, poster, or radio announcement.

Review **247**

Review

Reflecting on the Unit
You may have students respond to the summary questions in writing or through discussion.

Writing Across the Curriculum
Remind students to state their goal or main idea and to back it up with supporting evidence.

Adding to Your Portfolio
Students should choose pieces for their portfolios that include the basic elements of persuasive writing: a strong opinion statement and supporting evidence presented in the most persuasive order. Encourage students to consider choosing those pieces that peer reviewers and others found the most persuasive.

Portfolio Evaluation
If you grade the portfolio selections, you might want to award two marks—one each for content and form. Explain your assessment criteria before students make their selections. Commend
- experimentation with creative prewriting techniques
- clear, concise writing in which the main idea, audience, and purpose are evident
- successful revisions
- work that shows a flair for language

✔ ASSESSMENT OPTIONS

📁 *Tests with Answer Key and Rubrics*
Unit 6 Choice A Test, p. 21
Unit 6 Choice B Test, p. 22
Unit 6 Composition Objective Test, pp. 23-24

💾 *Testmaker*
Unit 6 Choice A Test
Unit 6 Choice B Test
Unit 6 Composition Objective Test

You may wish to administer one of these tests as a mastery test.

📼 *Mindjogger Videoquizzes*

Troubleshooter

Viewing the Art

Puzzles can be fun or they can be frustrating, depending on how we approach them. This image depicts a jigsaw puzzle as it is being pieced together.

Interpret and Analyze Use the following questions for discussion:

- In what ways does this image capture the idea of problem solving?
- Is there anything about this image that seems odd? Explain why.
- How does the image of a jigsaw puzzle relate to the quotation from Carl Sandburg?

Discussing the Quotation

Carl Sandburg's use of repetition and rhythm in his poem "Arithmetic" creates a feeling of order and precision even as he presents the creativity of problem-solving. Students will be able to find the entire poem in *Course 1, Glencoe Literature: The Reader's Choice* beginning on page 34. Before referring students to the poem, encourage a discussion of the mood suggested by the quotation. Have students support their opinions.

Writing Prompt Ask students to write a paragraph or two explaining how the image of the puzzle extends the meaning of the quotation. Then have them connect the image and the quotation with their writing process. Ask students how writing can be like a jigsaw puzzle. Then have them compare and contrast their approach to writing with Sandburg's attitude toward arithmetic.

"Arithmetic is where the answer is right and everything is nice and you can look out of the window and see the blue sky . . ."

—Carl Sandburg, *Arithmetic*

248

Resource Manager

Planning Resources
- *Lesson Plans*
- *Block Scheduling*

Transparencies
- *Bellringer*
- *Fine Art*
- *Writing Process*
- *Two-Minute Skill Drill*

Other Print Resources
- *Grammar and Composition Handbook*
- *Grammar Workbook*
- *Sentence-Combining Practice*
- *Tests with Answer Key and Rubrics*

Video
- *MindJogger Videoquizzes*

Software
- *Presentation Plus!*
- *Testmaker*

Web Sites
- *writerschoice.glencoe.com*

UNIT 7

Troubleshooter

Use Troubleshooter to help you correct common errors that you might make in your writing. You can indicate the errors on your paper, using the handwritten codes in the left-hand column. Then the Table of Contents below will help you locate solutions to correct errors.

Objectives

- To learn how to recognize common writing errors
- To correct common usage, grammar, and style errors in writing

Key to Ability Levels

L1 Level 1 activities are within the basic ability range of students.

L2 Level 2 activities are within the ability range of average students.

L3 Level 3 activities are more challenging activities.

Using the Models

As students review their written work, have them mark errors using the abbreviations shown in the problem boxes throughout the Troubleshooter. These abbreviations can be especially useful when students share their writing during peer review.

249

Focus

Lesson Overview

Objectives

- To recognize the most common types of sentence fragments: a fragment lacking a subject, a fragment lacking a predicate, and a fragment lacking both a subject and a predicate
- To correct sentence fragments

Bellringer
Daily Language Activity

When students enter the classroom, have this assignment on the board: *Copy the following sentences. Then rewrite them correctly.*

Ellen and Sarah went to the aquarium. Saw seals. And the dolphins. Then they had lunch. At one o'clock.

Motivating Activity

Discuss with students why the sentences in the Bellringer were confusing. Explain that using sentence fragments can make writing hard to understand. This lesson will teach students how to avoid using sentence fragments in their writing.

Teach

⇄ Cross-reference: Usage

For instruction and practice of the material in Lesson 7.1, refer students to Lesson 8.2, p. 299–300.

Troubleshooter

7.1 Sentence Fragment

Problem 1

Fragment that lacks a subject

> *frag* Tess left town. (Went to Maine.)
> *frag* The horse trotted home. (Ate some hay.)
> *frag* Hasina teaches school. (Teaches English literature.)

SOLUTION Add a subject to the fragment to make a complete sentence.

Tess left town. She went to Maine.

The horse trotted home. It ate some hay.

Hasina teaches school. She teaches English literature.

Problem 2

Fragment that lacks a predicate

> *frag* The woman was singing. (The beautiful song.)
> *frag* A noise woke me up. (The dog next door again.)
> *frag* Joyce bought a skirt. (That blue linen skirt.)

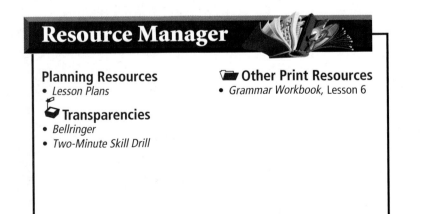

Resource Manager

Planning Resources
- *Lesson Plans*

📁 Transparencies
- *Bellringer*
- *Two-Minute Skill Drill*

📂 Other Print Resources
- *Grammar Workbook*, Lesson 6

SOLUTION Add a predicate to make the sentence complete.

The woman was singing. The song was beautiful.

A noise woke me up. The dog next door was barking again.

Joyce bought a skirt. That skirt was blue linen.

Problem 3

Fragment that lacks both a subject and a predicate

frag Miriam left work late. (With her friend.)

frag The store closed. (At two o'clock.)

SOLUTION Combine the fragment with another sentence.

Miriam left work late with her friend.

The store closed at two o'clock.

If you need more help avoiding sentence fragments, see Lesson 8.2, page 299.

Teach

Two-Minute Skill Drill

Write these sentence fragments on the board and have students rewrite them as complete sentences:

Walked three miles.
The bus driver.
At the gym.

See also *Two-Minute Skill Drill Transparencies, 7.1*

Additional Resource

Grammar Workbook, Lesson 6

Close

Have students explain in their own words the three kinds of sentence fragments. Ask them to check their current writing assignments and rewrite any sentence fragments as complete sentences.

Focus

Lesson Overview

Objectives

- To recognize and to avoid using run-on sentences
- To revise run-on sentences

🔔 Bellringer
Daily Language Activity

When students enter the classroom, have this assignment on the board: *Tell why the following sentences are difficult to read. Then write them correctly.*

I play basketball at the park, Jimmy plays baseball.
The dog barked it growled, too.
I went to the theater and I watched a movie.

Motivating Activity

Invite students to discuss why they found the sentences difficult to read. If necessary, help them to rewrite the sentences correctly. Explain that run-on sentences can be hard to read and understand. This lesson will teach students how to avoid run-on sentences in their writing.

Teach

⇄ Cross-reference: Usage

For instruction and practice of the material in Lesson 7.2, refer students to Lesson 8.6, pp. 307–308.

7.2 Run-on Sentence

Problem 1

Two main clauses separated by only a comma

run-on *I like to play volleyball, Luis prefers hockey.*

SOLUTION A Replace the comma with a period or other end mark. Begin the new sentence with a capital letter.

I like to play volleyball. Luis prefers hockey.

SOLUTION B Replace the comma between the main clauses with a semicolon.

I like to play volleyball; Luis prefers hockey.

SOLUTION C Insert a coordinating conjunction after the comma.

I like to play volleyball, but Luis prefers hockey.

Problem 2

Two main clauses with no punctuation between them

run-on *Ada writes poetry she dances, too.*

Resource Manager

Planning Resources
- *Lesson Plans*

📁 **Transparencies**
- *Bellringer*
- *Two-Minute Skill Drill*

📂 **Other Print Resources**
- *Grammar Workbook,* Lesson 7

SOLUTION A   Separate the main clauses with a period or other end mark.

Ada writes poetry. She dances, too.

SOLUTION B   Place a semicolon between the main clauses.

Ada writes poetry; she dances, too.

SOLUTION C   Insert a comma and a conjunction between the main clauses.

Ada writes poetry, and she dances, too.

Troubleshooter

Problem 3

Two main clauses with no comma before the coordinating conjunction

run-on *I climbed the mountains and I explored the forests.*

SOLUTION   Insert a comma before the coordinating conjunction.

I climbed the mountains, and I explored the forests.

If you need more help avoiding run-on sentences, see Lesson 8.6, page 307.

Teach

Two-Minute Skill Drill

Write these run-on sentences on the board and have students rewrite them correctly:

The clown juggled oranges, she sang a song.

We swim at the beach we also go fishing.

Joan did her math problems she painted her model airplane.

See also *Two-Minute Skill Drill Transparencies, 7.2*

Additional Resource

Grammar Workbook, Lesson 7

Close

Invite students to explain in their own words the three different kinds of run-on sentences presented in this Troubleshooter. Ask students to check their current writing assignment for run-on sentences and to correct them.

Focus

Lesson Overview

Objectives

- To recognize the constructions that commonly lead to lack of subject-verb agreement
- To correct the misuse of these constructions

Bellringer
Daily Language Activity

When students enter the classroom, have this assignment on the board: *Tell what is confusing about the following sentences. Then write them correctly.*

One of his answers are wrong.
Here is two slices of pizza.
Shauna and John is going to the dance.

Motivating Activity

Discuss with students why the sentences in the Bellringer are wrong. Explain that this lesson will teach students to avoid and correct subject-verb disagreement in their writing.

Teach

Cross-reference: Usage

For instruction and practice of the material in Problems 1 and 2, refer students to Lesson 15.2, pp. 441–442.

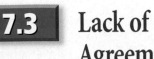

7.3 Lack of Subject-Verb Agreement

Problem 1

A subject that is separated from the verb by an intervening prepositional phrase

> *agr   One of the jars ⟨are⟩ broken.*

SOLUTION   Ignore a prepositional phrase that comes between a subject and a verb. Make sure that the verb agrees with the subject of the sentence. The subject is never the object of the preposition.

One of the jars is broken.

Problem 2

A sentence that begins with *here* or *there*

> *agr   There ⟨is⟩ private beaches all over that tropical island.*

SOLUTION   The subject is never *here* or *there*. The subject comes after the verb. The verb must agree with this subject.

There are private beaches all over that tropical island.

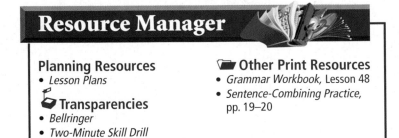

Resource Manager

Planning Resources
- *Lesson Plans*

Transparencies
- *Bellringer*
- *Two-Minute Skill Drill*

Other Print Resources
- *Grammar Workbook,* Lesson 48
- *Sentence-Combining Practice,* pp. 19–20

Problem 3

A compound subject that is joined by *and*

agr   *Music and dance ⓘⓢ taught at school.*

SOLUTION   If the parts of the compound subject refer to more than one person or thing, use a plural verb.

Music and dance are taught at school.

Problem 4

A compound subject that is joined by *or* or *nor*

agr   *Neither the bat nor the mitts ⟨belongs⟩ to me.*

agr   *Either cookies or ice cream ⟨are⟩ a good dessert.*

SOLUTION   Make the verb agree with the subject that is closer to it.

Neither the bat nor the mitts belong to me.

Either cookies or ice cream is a good dessert.

If you need more help with subject-verb agreement, see Lessons 15.1 through 15.3, pages 439–444.

Troubleshooter

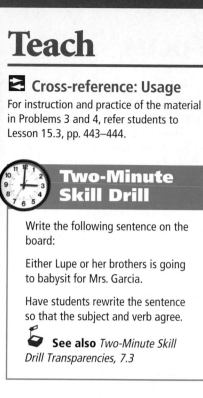

Teach

⇄ Cross-reference: Usage

For instruction and practice of the material in Problems 3 and 4, refer students to Lesson 15.3, pp. 443–444.

Two-Minute Skill Drill

Write the following sentence on the board:

Either Lupe or her brothers is going to babysit for Mrs. Garcia.

Have students rewrite the sentence so that the subject and verb agree.

See also *Two-Minute Skill Drill Transparencies, 7.3*

Additional Resources

📁 *Sentence-Combining Practice,* pp. 19–20

📓 *Grammar Workbook,* Lesson 48

Close

Have students explain in their own words the four kinds of subject-verb disagreement presented in this Troubleshooter. Ask them to check their current writing assignments for similar situations and to correct any subject-verb agreement errors.

Focus

Lesson Overview

Objective

- To learn to recognize the most common kinds of errors in verb tense or form and to avoid or correct these errors

🔔 Bellringer
Daily Language Activity

When students enter the classroom, have this assignment on the board: *Decide what is wrong with the following sentences. Then write them correctly.*

Ricky is sing in the school musical. We runned to meet Mom when she came home. Rhonda has drank her orange juice.

Motivating Activity

Discuss with students why the sentences in the Bellringer activity are wrong. Explain that this lesson will help students use the correct tense and form of verbs.

Teach

⇄ Cross-reference: Grammar

For instruction and practice of the material in Problem 1, refer students to Lesson 10.5, pp. 341–342.

Troubleshooter

 7.4 Incorrect Verb Tense or Form

Problem 1

An incorrect or missing verb ending

tense I have (learn) how to play the violin in the past year.

SOLUTION Add *-ed* to a regular verb to form the past tense and the past participle.

I have learned how to play the violin in the past year.

Problem 2

An improperly formed irregular verb

tense Jan (builded) a greenhouse in the yard.

The past and past participle forms of irregular verbs vary. Memorize these forms, or look them up.

SOLUTION Use the correct past or past participle form of an irregular verb.

Jan built a greenhouse in the yard.

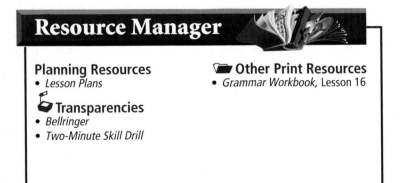

Resource Manager

Planning Resources
- *Lesson Plans*

📂 **Transparencies**
- *Bellringer*
- *Two-Minute Skill Drill*

📁 **Other Print Resources**
- *Grammar Workbook,* Lesson 16

Problem 3

Confusion between the past form and the past participle

> *tense* Carlos (has began) to play the guitar.

SOLUTION   Use the past participle form of an irregular verb, not the past form, when you use the auxiliary verb *have*.

Carlos has begun to play the guitar.

Problem 4

Improper use of the past participle

> *tense* (I seen) two plays this month.

SOLUTION   Insert the auxiliary verb *have* before the past participle of an irregular verb to form a complete verb.

I have seen two plays this month.

If you need more help with correct verb forms, see Lessons 10.3 through 10.9, pages 337–350.

Troubleshooter

Teach

Two-Minute Skill Drill

Write this sentence on the board:

Joel and Marie been looking forward to going in-line skating.

Have students rewrite the sentence so that the verb form is correct.

See also *Two-Minute Skill Drill Transparencies, 7.4*

Additional Resource

Grammar Workbook, Lesson 16

Close

Have students explain in their own words the four kinds of verb tense and form problems discussed in this Troubleshooter. Ask them to check their current writing assignments for similar situations and to correct any verb tense or form errors.

Focus

Lesson Overview

Objectives

- To recognize the constructions that give rise to incorrect pronoun use
- To use subject and object pronouns correctly

Bellringer
Daily Language Activity

When students enter the classroom, have this assignment on the board: *Tell what is confusing about the following sentence. Then write it correctly.*

Sharon and Tina went to the movies, but she didn't like it.

Motivating Activity

Discuss with students why the sentence in the Bellringer is confusing. Have volunteers write their corrected sentences on the board. If students suggest more than one solution, have them explain why each sentence is correct.

Teach

Cross-reference: Grammar

For instruction and practice of the material in Problem 1, refer students to Lesson 11.3, pp. 365–366.

Cross-reference: Grammar

For instruction and practice of the material in Problem 2, refer students to Lesson 11.1, pp. 361–362.

Troubleshooter

7.5 Incorrect Use of Pronouns

Problem 1

A pronoun that could refer to more than one antecedent

> pro   *Carla went to the concert with Ana, but (she) didn't stay long.*
>
> pro   *When the neighbors accused my brothers, (they) were angry.*

SOLUTION   Rewrite the sentence, substituting a noun for the pronoun.

Carla went to the concert with Ana, but Carla didn't stay long.

When the neighbors accused my brothers, my brothers were angry.

Problem 2

Object pronouns as subjects

> pro   *Kyoko and (me) left for summer camp.*
>
> pro   *(Her) and Satchel had an argument today.*
>
> pro   *Nita and (them) are in the school play.*

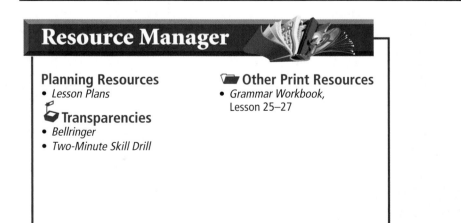

Resource Manager

Planning Resources
- *Lesson Plans*

Transparencies
- *Bellringer*
- *Two-Minute Skill Drill*

Other Print Resources
- *Grammar Workbook,* Lesson 25–27

SOLUTION   Use a subject pronoun as the subject of a sentence.

Kyoko and I left for summer camp.

She and Satchel had an argument today.

Nita and they are in the school play.

Problem 3

Subject pronouns as objects

pro   *Please help Amos and ⓘ with the groceries.*

pro   *Sonia left her books with Alan and ⓘ.*

pro   *Megan bought tickets for ⓢⓗⓔ and Ian.*

SOLUTION   Use an object pronoun as the object of a verb or a preposition.

Please help Amos and me with the groceries.

Sonia left her books with Alan and me.

Megan bought tickets for her and Ian.

If you need more help with the correct use of pronouns, see Lessons 11.1 through 11.5, pages 361–370.

Unit 7.5 Incorrect Use of Pronouns   **259**

Teach

⇄ Cross-reference: Usage

For instruction and practice of the material in Problem 3, refer students to Lesson 11.1, pp. 361–362.

Two-Minute Skill Drill

Write this sentence on the board, and have students rewrite it so that the pronouns are used correctly:

Hoang and me rode the train and Melissa waved goodbye to him and I.

✎ **See also** *Two-Minute Skill Drill Transparencies, 7.5*

Additional Resource

📙 *Grammar Workbook, Lessons 25–27*

Close

Discuss with students how recognizing the incorrect use of pronouns can help students' writing. Ask them to check their current writing assignments for incorrect pronouns and to correct any unclear pronoun references.

Focus

Lesson Overview

Objective

- To recognize the incorrect use of regular and irregular comparative and superlative adjectives
- To correct errors in the use of comparative and superlative adjectives

🔔 Bellringer
Daily Language Activity

When students enter the classroom, have this assignment on the board: *Tell what is incorrect about the following sentence. Then write it correctly.*

Helena's orange is more bigger than Alberto's.

Motivating Activity

Discuss with students the fact that comparative adjectives such as *bigger* do not use the word *more*. Have students create sentences with comparative and superlative adjectives, adding *-er* or *-est* as appropriate.

Teach

⇄ Cross-reference: Grammar

For instruction and practice of the material in Lesson 7.6, refer students to Lessons 12.3 and 12.4, pp. 383–386.

Troubleshooter

7.6 Incorrect Use of Adjectives

Problem 1

Incorrect use of *good, better, best*

adj — Selma felt (more good) after her nap.
adj — Harry is the (most good) artist in the class.
adj — Vinnie is a (more) better writer than Jenny.

SOLUTION The comparative and superlative forms of *good* are *better* and *best*. Do not use *more* or *most* before irregular forms of comparative and superlative adjectives.

Selma felt better after her nap.

Harry is the best artist in the class.

Vinnie is a better writer than Jenny.

Problem 2

Incorrect use of *bad, worse, worst*

adj — This painting is (more bad) than the one in the den.
adj — This is the (baddest) book I've ever read.
adj — That was the (most) worst speech of the day.

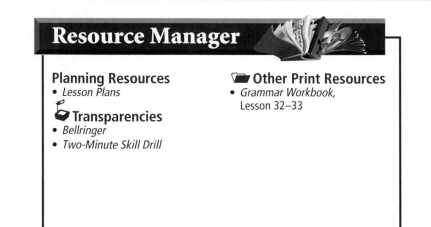

Resource Manager

Planning Resources
- *Lesson Plans*

📂 **Transparencies**
- *Bellringer*
- *Two-Minute Skill Drill*

📁 **Other Print Resources**
- *Grammar Workbook,*
  Lesson 32–33

SOLUTION The comparative and superlative forms of *bad* are *worse* and *worst*. Do not use *more* or *most* before irregular forms of comparative and superlative adjectives.

This painting is worse than the one in the den.

This is the worst book I've ever read.

That was the worst speech of the day.

Troubleshooter

Problem 3

Incorrect use of other comparative and superlative adjectives

frag Greta is (more) younger than her sister.

frag Samuel drove the (most fastest) car in the race.

SOLUTION Do not use both *-er* and *more* or *-est* and *most* at the same time.

Greta is younger than her sister.

Samuel drove the fastest car in the race.

If you need more help with the correct use of adjectives, see Lessons 12.3 and 12.4, pages 383–386.

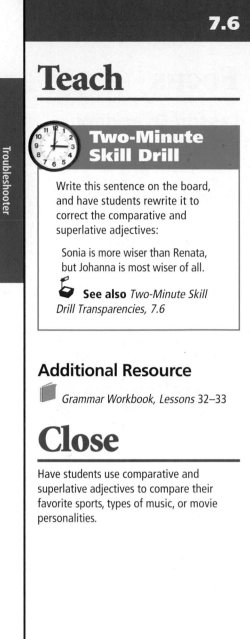

Teach

Two-Minute Skill Drill

Write this sentence on the board, and have students rewrite it to correct the comparative and superlative adjectives:

Sonia is more wiser than Renata, but Johanna is most wiser of all.

See also *Two-Minute Skill Drill Transparencies, 7.6*

Additional Resource

Grammar Workbook, Lessons 32–33

Close

Have students use comparative and superlative adjectives to compare their favorite sports, types of music, or movie personalities.

Focus

Lesson Overview

Objective

- To recognize and use commas to separate words, phrases, or clauses and to set off direct quotations

Bellringer
Daily Language Activity

When students enter the classroom, have this assignment on the board: *Tell what is missing from the following sentence, and write the sentence correctly.*

In my garden I grow cauliflower cantaloupe Brussels sprouts and eggplant.

Motivating Activity

Have a volunteer add the missing commas to the sentence on the board. Discuss with students why the sentence is not clear without the commas.

Teach

Cross-reference: Mechanics

For instruction and practice of the material in Problem 1, refer students to Lesson 19.2, pp. 491–492.

Troubleshooter

7.7 Incorrect Use of Commas

Problem 1

Missing commas in a series of three or more items

com   *Today we studied history₀science₀and mathematics.*

com   *Orson Welles wrote₀directed₀and starred in many classic films.*

SOLUTION   Use commas to separate three or more items in a series.

Today we studied history, science, and mathematics.

Orson Welles wrote, directed, and starred in many classic films.

Problem 2

Missing commas with direct quotations

com   *"This movie₀" Marcia said₀"is really exciting."*

com   *"I want to leave₀" Dorie said₀"before the storm begins."*

Resource Manager

Planning Resources
- *Lesson Plans*

Transparencies
- *Bellringer*
- *Two-Minute Skill Drill*

Other Print Resources
- *Grammar Workbook,* Lessons 72

SOLUTION The first part of an interrupted quotation ends with a comma followed by quotation marks. The interrupting words are also followed by a comma.

"This movie," Marcia said, "is really exciting."

"I want to leave," Dorie said, "before the storm begins."

If you need more help with commas, see Lessons 19.2 through 19.4, pages 491–496.

Teach

⇄ Cross-reference: Mechanics

For instruction and practice of the material in Problem 2, refer students to Lesson 19.6, pp. 499–500.

Two-Minute Skill Drill

Write this sentence on the board. Then have students rewrite it, adding commas in the correct places.

"This story" said Tory "has adventure mystery action and comedy."

✎ **See also** *Two-Minute Skill Drill Transparencies, 7.7*

Additional Resource

📖 *Grammar Workbook,* Lesson 72

Close

Spark a discussion about why using commas correctly helps make writing clear. Have students explain in their own words the rules for the correct uses of commas presented in this Troubleshooter.

Focus

Lesson Overview

Objectives

- To use possessive apostrophes correctly
- To recognize the most common instances in which possessive apostrophes are missing or misused

🔔 Bellringer
Daily Language Activity

When students enter the classroom, have this assignment on the board: *Circle and correct the punctuation errors in the following sentences:*

Billys sneakers' have red stars on them.
Ten peoples cars were towed away.
The ice skates are her's.

Motivating Activity

If necessary, help students as they correct the use of apostrophes in the Bellringer. Ask students to talk about difficulties they have had in deciding how to use apostrophes. Explain that this lesson will help them learn to use apostrophes correctly.

Troubleshooter

 Incorrect Use of Apostrophes

Problem 1

Omission of apostrophe and -*s* with singular possessive nouns

apos   *We found James calculator lying on Martas desk.*

SOLUTION   Use an apostrophe and an -*s* to form the possessive of a singular noun, even one that ends in -*s*.

We found James's calculator lying on Marta's desk.

Problem 2

Omission of apostrophe with plural possessive nouns ending in -*s*

apos   *The acrobats stunts thrilled their audience.*
apos   *The horses bridles are in the stable.*

SOLUTION   Use an apostrophe alone to form the possessive of a plural noun that ends in -*s*.

The acrobats' stunts thrilled their audience.
The horses' bridles are in the stable.

264   Unit 7 Troubleshooter

Resource Manager

Planning Resources
- *Lesson Plans*

📋 **Transparencies**
- *Bellringer*
- *Two-Minute Skill Drill*

📁 **Other Print Resources**
- *Grammar Workbook,* Lesson 80

Problem 3

Omission of apostrophe with plural possessive nouns not ending in -s

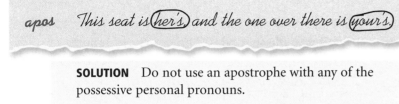

> *apos*   The childrens paints are on the table.

> **SOLUTION**   Use an apostrophe and an *-s* to form the posses-
> sive of a plural noun that does not end in *-s*.
>
> **The children's paints are on the table.**

Problem 4

Incorrect use of apostrophe with possessive personal pronouns

> *apos*   This seat is her's and the one over there is your's.

> **SOLUTION**   Do not use an apostrophe with any of the
> possessive personal pronouns.
>
> **This seat is hers, and the one over there is yours.**

If you need more help with apostrophes, see Lesson 19.7, page 501.

Teach

⇄ Cross-reference: Usage

For instruction and practice of the material
in Problems 1, 2, 3, and 4, refer students to
Lesson 19.7, pp. 501–502.

Two-Minute Skill Drill

Write these sentences on the board,
and have students correct all
apostrophe errors:

> Marias cousins visited her last
> Tuesday. They brought her two
> books' for her birthday. The
> childrens parents joined in the
> birthday party.

See also *Two-Minute Skill
Drill Transparencies, 7.8*

Additional Resource

Grammar Workbook, Lesson 80

Close

Invite students to prepare a pamphlet
explaining the proper use of the possessive
apostrophe. They can keep their pamphlet
for reference or distribute it as a guide for
other student writers.

Focus

Lesson Overview

Objective

• To recognize and correct errors in the use of capitalization when referring to nationalities, languages, and ethnic groups, and in the first word of direct quotations

🔔 Bellringer
Daily Language Activity

When students enter the classroom, have this assignment on the board: *Find the error in each of the following sentences. Then write them correctly.*

A russian diplomat wrote a letter to the newspaper.

Janelle wants to travel in Mexico, so she is studying spanish.

Dad said, "help your brother with his homework."

Teach

⇄ Cross-reference: Mechanics

For instruction and practice of the material in Problem 1, refer students to Lesson 18.4, pp. 479–480.

⇄ Cross-reference: Mechanics

For instruction and practice of the material in Problem 2, refer students to Lesson 18.1, pp. 473–474.

Troubleshooter

 Incorrect Capitalization

Problem 1

Failure to capitalize words referring to ethnic groups, nationalities, and languages

cap   A brazilian student is studying french.

SOLUTION   Capitalize proper nouns and adjectives that refer to ethnic groups, nationalities, and languages.

A Brazilian student is studying French.

Problem 2

Failure to capitalize the first word of a direct quotation

cap   Duane said, "school will begin soon."

SOLUTION   Capitalize the first word in a direct quotation.

Duane said, "School will begin soon."

 If you need more help with capitalization, see Lessons 18.1 through 18.4, pages 473–480.

Resource Manager

Planning Resources
• *Lesson Plans*

📖 Transparencies
• *Bellringer*
• *Two-Minute Skill Drill*

📁 Other Print Resources
• *Grammar Workbook,* Lessons 63–70

Proofreading Symbols

⊙	Lieut Brown	Insert a period.
∧	No one came the party.	Insert a letter or a word.
⌃;	The bell rang the students left for home.	Insert a semicolon.
≡	I enjoyed paris.	Capitalize a letter.
/	The Class ran a bake sale.	Make a capital letter lowercase.
⌒	The campers are home sick.	Close up a space.
ⓢⓟ	They visited N.Y. ⓢⓟ	Spell out.
⋏	Sue please help.	Insert a comma.
∪	He enjoyed feild day.	Transpose the position of letters or words.
#	alltogether	Insert a space.
ℐ	We went to to Boston.	Delete letters or words.
⌄⌄	She asked Who's coming?	Insert quotation marks.
/=/	mid January	Insert a hyphen.
¶	"Where?" asked Karl. "Over there," said Ray.	Begin a new paragraph.
⌄	She liked Sarah's glasses.	Insert an apostrophe.

Teach

Using Proofreading Symbols

Encourage students to use the Proofreading Symbols chart on page 267 to mark errors in capitalization, as well as other errors in usage and mechanics. Using proofreading symbols can help them correct their own work and can guide the editing process of their peer partners.

Additional Resource

Grammar Workbook, Lessons 63–70

Close

Have students imagine that they are exchange students in a foreign country. Ask them to write a paragraph or two about the country and the people they meet there. Have them include at least two lines of dialogue. Remind students to watch out for the capitalization errors addressed in this Troubleshooter.

Troubleshooter

Objectives

- To understand the types and styles of effective business letters and memos
- To write effective business letters and memos
- To become aware of the formats of application forms
- To create and fill out an application form
- To understand the characteristics of instructional writing
- To write effective instructions
- To write an effective incident report
- To understand and create an effective multimedia presentation

✔ ASSESSMENT OPTIONS

📂 *Tests with Answer Key and Rubrics*
Business and Technical Writing Pretest

💾 *Testmaker*
Business and Technical Writing Pretest

You may wish to administer the Business and Technical Writing Pretest at this point.

Key to Ability Levels

L1 Level 1 activities are within the basic ability range of students.

L2 Level 2 activities are within the ability range of average students.

L3 Level 3 activities are more challenging activities.

Business and Technical Writing

Contents

Resource Manager

Planning Resources
- *Lesson Plans*

🎞 **Transparencies**
- *Writing Process*

📂 **Other Print Resources**
- *Business and Technical Writing Activities*
- *Grammar and Composition Handbook*
- *Guide to Using the Internet and Other Electronic Resources*
- *Tests with Answer Key and Rubrics*
- *Writing Assessment and Evaluation Rubrics*

💾 **Software**
- *Presentation Plus!*
- *Revising with Style*
- *Testmaker*

💻 **Web Sites**
- *writerschoice.glencoe.com*
- *lit.glencoe.com*

Business Letters

A business letter serves a variety of purposes. Business letters are formal and are usually written to unknown people. A neat, brief, well-organized letter makes a good first impression and encourages a prompt and positive response.

The following sample business letter makes a request. The letter is written in block form. Notice how the writer follows the tips in the chart on the following page and notice also how the business letter differs from the personal letter on page 270.

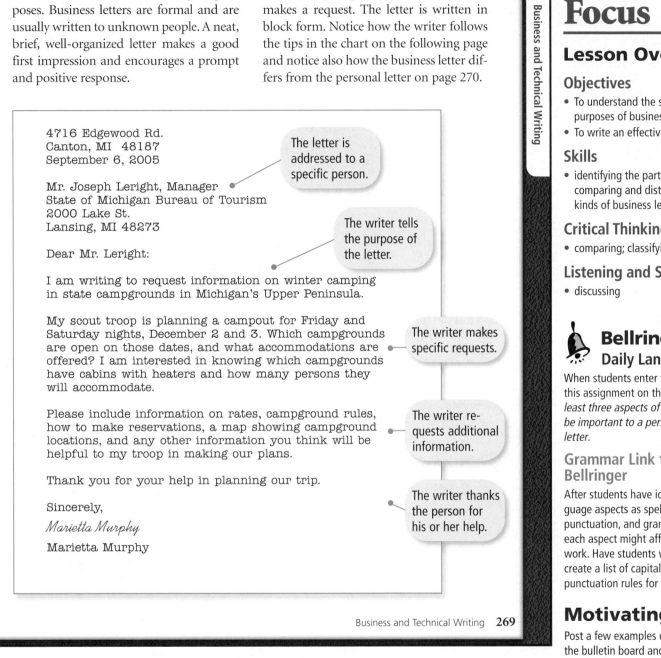

4716 Edgewood Rd.
Canton, MI 48187
September 6, 2005

Mr. Joseph Leright, Manager
State of Michigan Bureau of Tourism
2000 Lake St.
Lansing, MI 48273

Dear Mr. Leright:

I am writing to request information on winter camping in state campgrounds in Michigan's Upper Peninsula.

My scout troop is planning a campout for Friday and Saturday nights, December 2 and 3. Which campgrounds are open on those dates, and what accommodations are offered? I am interested in knowing which campgrounds have cabins with heaters and how many persons they will accommodate.

Please include information on rates, campground rules, how to make reservations, a map showing campground locations, and any other information you think will be helpful to my troop in making our plans.

Thank you for your help in planning our trip.

Sincerely,
Marietta Murphy
Marietta Murphy

> The letter is addressed to a specific person.

> The writer tells the purpose of the letter.

> The writer makes specific requests.

> The writer requests additional information.

> The writer thanks the person for his or her help.

Business and Technical Writing **269**

Focus

Lesson Overview

Objectives
- To understand the styles, types, and purposes of business letters
- To write an effective business letter

Skills
- identifying the parts of a business letter; comparing and distinguishing the various kinds of business letters

Critical Thinking
- comparing; classifying

Listening and Speaking
- discussing

🔔 Bellringer
Daily Language Activity

When students enter the classroom, have this assignment on the board: *Name at least three aspects of language that would be important to a person writing a business letter.*

Grammar Link to the Bellringer

After students have identified such language aspects as spelling, capitalization, punctuation, and grammar, discuss how each aspect might affect the letter writer's work. Have students work as a class to create a list of capitalization and punctuation rules for business letters.

Motivating Activity

Post a few examples of business letters on the bulletin board and encourage students to suggest what makes them effective or ineffective.

Enrichment and Extension

Finding Purposes for Business Writing

Suggest that students work with partners to develop lists of businesses to which they might like to write for information, for services, or just to express reactions or beliefs. For example, students might like to write a letter to the editor of the local newspaper on a subject in the news that has caught their attention. Students might plan to write a letter ordering parts for a favorite toy or piece of sports or stereo equipment. They might plan a trip and write a letter to the tourist information center for a specific location requesting brochures and information on rates. Invite volunteers to share their ideas with the class.

Teach

Comparing Styles

Have students compare the model business letter on page 269 with the friendly letter on this page. Have them note the likenesses and differences and ask if they can give reasons for the differences. **L2**

Discussing Personal Letter Style

After students have noted the differences between business and personal letters, have them work in small groups to discuss times or circumstances when the personal letter style might be used for business purposes. Have the groups share their conclusions with the class. **L1**

Business Letters

Friendly Letters

A friendly letter is a form of writing that is used to communicate with someone you know well. Notice how a friendly letter differs from a business letter.

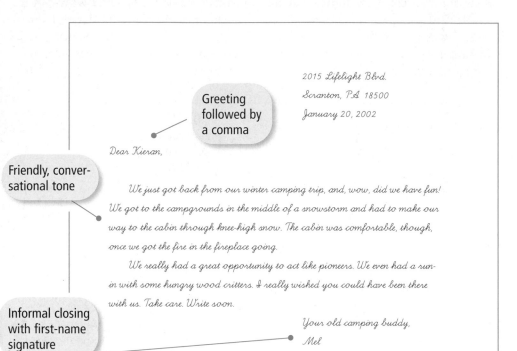

Greeting followed by a comma

Friendly, conversational tone

Informal closing with first-name signature

2015 Lifelight Blvd.
Scranton, PA 18500
January 20, 2002

Dear Kieran,

We just got back from our winter camping trip, and, wow, did we have fun! We got to the campgrounds in the middle of a snowstorm and had to make our way to the cabin through knee-high snow. The cabin was comfortable, though, once we got the fire in the fireplace going.

We really had a great opportunity to act like pioneers. We even had a run-in with some hungry wood critters. I really wished you could have been there with us. Take care. Write soon.

Your old camping buddy,
Mel

Types of Business Letters

A business letter gives information or asks for action. Knowing how to write a good business letter is a skill you will use many times throughout your life.

Use the business letter to inquire about something; order a product; make a complaint or request; express your views or apply for a job, a scholarship, or acceptance into a special program.

When you write a business letter, keep your purpose in mind. Don't include details or information not needed to achieve your purpose. Limit your letter to one page or less in length, if possible. The people you are writing to are likely to be very busy, so the shorter and neater your letter looks, the more likely it is to be read. Make the tone of your business letter formal: avoid slang and use polite language.

MEETING INDIVIDUAL NEEDS — English Language Learners

Mentoring

Pair students for whom the English language is relatively new with students who grew up with the language. Have the students for whom English is a first language act as mentors for the English language learners. Tell them that they should work with their partners, answer their questions, and help them understand the purposes, forms, and conventions of business letters.

Types of Business Letters

REQUEST LETTER	COMPLAINT LETTER	OPINION LETTER	APPLICATION LETTER
Be brief.	Be polite.	State the issue briefly.	Write to a specific person.
State your request clearly. Include all necessary information.	Identify the product or service clearly.	State your opinion in the first sentence or two.	Describe the job or program for which you're applying.
Make your request specific and reasonable.	Describe the problem accurately.	Support your opinion with reasons, facts, and examples.	List your qualifications.
Include your phone number or a self-addressed, stamped envelope.	Request a specific solution.	Summarize your main points and offer a solution, if possible.	Explain why you're the best person for the position or award.
	Keep a copy of your letter until your complaint has been resolved.		Request an application form or an interview.

Style

Business letters are usually written in one of two forms: block style or modified block style.

Block Style In block style, all lines begin at the left margin. Paragraphs are not indented but are separated by a line space. The letter on page 269 is typed in block style.

Modified Block Style In modified block style, the heading, the closing, your signature, and your typed name begin at the center of the paper. The paragraphs may be indented—five spaces on a typewriter or half an inch on a computer—or not indented. The following letter is in modified block style with paragraphs indented. There is no need to leave a line space between indented paragraphs.

Teach

Comparing Styles

To have students see the differences between the block and modified block styles of business letters, ask them to compare the models on pages 269 and 272 and identify differences. Write each difference on the board as it is named. Be sure students understand that the two styles are equally acceptable and that they can use whichever style they prefer. **L1**

Types of Business Letters

Go over the Types of Business Letters chart with students. Have the class collaborate to describe a business letter they might write for each type in the chart—for example, a letter to an expert requesting information about a topic, a letter of complaint to a restaurant that provided bad service, and so on. As each item of advice in a column is mentioned, ask student volunteers to suggest a sentence or two they might include in a letter of that type. Others in the class can offer revisions or improvements in the suggested sentence(s). **L2**

Viewing and Representing

Interpreting Graphic Organizers Ask students to explain how the chart organizes information. In this case, each column contains a group of tips for writing a particular type of business letter. Ask students to suggest other kinds of information that can be put into a similar type of chart. Invite them to find other such charts in newspapers or magazines to share with the class.

Teach

Recognizing the Parts of a Letter

As students examine each part of the letter on this page, ask volunteers to point out the same part in the block style letter on page 269. Ask students how using a consistent format like this can help the reader of the letter. (The reader will know immediately from its position what each part of the letter contains; for example, the letter writer's address will be at the top of the page.)

Business Letters

2234 Platt St.
Northville, KY 00293
January 15, 2005

Heading

Bryce Benton, Manager
Spotless Dry Cleaners
304 S. Main St.
Northville, KY 00293

Inside Address

Dear Mr. Benton:

Salutation

Now is the time to show your support for Northville Middle School and promote your business by reserving an ad in our yearbook, *The Legend.*

Last year, Northville Middle School sold more than five hundred copies of *The Legend,* and this year advance orders already exceed that number. The yearbook is read not only by students but also by their parents and other family members. When people see your ad, they will learn more about your business and will recognize that you are a supporter of our school. All profits from yearbook ads are used to support the school's football team and marching band.

Body

The enclosed reservation form lists ad sizes and prices. I've also included a self-addressed envelope for your reply. All ads and payments must be received by the yearbook committee by February 15.

Name and Signature

I look forward to hearing from you,

Juan Garcia

Juan Garcia,
Yearbook Chairman

Critical Thinking

Analyzing Persuasive Techniques

Go over the text of the letter on this page with the students and ask them what the writer's primary purpose is (to persuade). Ask them to quote specific examples of persuasive techniques the writer uses. Have them describe or give examples of other ways in which they have seen such persuasive techniques used (for example, TV or radio ads, political campaigns).

Activity

Think of a place you would like to visit, such as a zoo, museum, or factory. Write a business letter requesting the information that you need to plan your trip.

- Make a list of questions to ask.
- Use the models on pages 269 and 272 to help you plan and revise your letter.
- Use polite language and correct spelling, grammar, capitalization, and punctuation.
- For your final draft, type, use a computer, or write neatly.

PURPOSE To write a business letter

AUDIENCE Director of a recreational institution or business

LENGTH One page

WRITING RUBRICS To write an effective letter requesting information, you should

- be clear and brief
- state your request in the first paragraph
- use business-letter format
- check your letter for grammar, spelling, and mechanics.

The Parts of a Business Letter

A business letter has six parts.

Heading There are three lines in the heading:

- your street address
- your city, state, and ZIP code
- the date

Inside Address The inside address has three or more lines:

- the name of the person to whom you're writing (with or without a courtesy title such as *Ms.*, *Mr.*, or *Dr.*)
- the title of the person to whom you're writing (A short title, such as *Manager* or *Vice President,* may be placed on the same line with the person's name. A long title requires a separate line.)
- the name of the business or organization
- the street address of the business or organization
- the city, state, and ZIP code

Salutation or Greeting When you know the name of the person to whom you're writing, the salutation should include a courtesy title: *Dear Mr. Marconi* or *Dear Dr. Lewsky.* If you don't know the name of the person, you can begin with *Dear* and the person's title: *Dear Editor* or *Dear Director of Human Resources.* A colon follows the salutation of a business letter.

Body The body is the most important part of your letter. It states your message.

Closing The closing is a final word or phrase, such as *Sincerely* or *Respectfully yours.* A comma follows the closing.

Name and Signature Type your name four lines below the closing. Then sign your name in the space between the closing and your typed name. If your first name could belong to either a male or a female, include *Miss, Ms.,* or *Mr.* in parentheses before your typed name.

Business and Technical Writing **273**

Real World Connection

Addressing Business Envelopes

Encourage students to practice preparing business letters for mailing. Distribute several blank business-length envelopes to each student. Show the correct placement on the envelope of both the addressee's address and the return address. After students practice addressing the business envelopes, distribute several blank sheets of 8-$\frac{1}{2}$ × 11" paper to each student. Help students practice folding the paper in thirds to fit neatly within the business envelopes. Display copies of business letters and business envelopes so that students can study the format for addressing envelopes and folding business letters.

Business and Technical Writing

Memos

Focus

Lesson Overview

Objectives
- To understand the style, types, and purposes of memos
- To write an effective memo

Skills
- identifying the parts of a memo; comparing and distinguishing the various types of memos; using memo style

Critical Thinking
- comparing; classifying; organizing

Listening and Speaking
- discussing

Bellringer
Daily Language Activity

When students enter the classroom, have this assignment on the board: *How would you abbreviate the word memorandum?*

Grammar Link to the Bellringer

After students understand that *memo* is a shortened form of *memorandum,* point out that other abbreviations are often used in business writing. Ask them if they can name (or recognize) some such abbreviations. (For example, *Mr., Dr.,* and other titles for people; *cc* originally for "carbon copy," but still used when a copy is a photocopy; *encl* for "enclosure"; *re* for "regarding")

Motivating Activity

Post on the bulletin board several examples of memos that have recently circulated in your school. Ask students to list ways in which the memos are similar (*format, style*) or different (*topics, purposes*).

Neatness Counts

Your letter is more likely to get a serious reading if you follow closely the formal rules for business letters:

- Type your letter or create it on a computer.
- Use unlined white $8\frac{1}{2}$-by-11-inch paper.
- Leave a two-inch margin at the top of the page and margins of at least one inch at the left, right, and bottom.
- Single-space the heading. Allow one or more blank lines between the heading and the inside address, depending on the length of your letter.
- Single-space the remaining parts of the letter, leaving an extra line between the parts and between the paragraphs in the body if they are not indented.

Memos

A memo (the short form of *memorandum*) is a brief note that communicates important information. Memos use polite language and have a friendly tone.

The following model is a memo sent by the building supervisor of a school to teachers. Notice how the writer follows the tips in the chart on the following page.

TO:	All Teachers
FROM:	Joseph Macady, Building Supervisor
SUBJECT:	New Desks Are Coming
DATE:	February 28, 2005

New student and teacher desks will be placed in your classrooms over the weekend of October 2 and 3.

During the last period on Friday, March 2, please have your students remove any personal belongings left in or on their desks. I suggest that they store their things in their assigned lockers.

You will also need to empty your desk. Store the contents in the classroom closet or pile them in a corner.

Thanks for your help. When you come to school on Monday morning, your new desks will be in place.

The writer states the subject in a very few words.

The writer begins with specific information.

The writer gives instructions.

The writer thanks the readers for their help.

Types of Memos

Memos can be used to communicate on a wide variety of topics. A memo can make an announcement or request, ask or answer a question, or assign a task. In a business office, a memo can remind all employees of the date of the company picnic or ask people for suggestions on how to improve the company newsletter.

You can use a memo when you want to communicate in a brief and formal way. You might remind club members about a meeting or let teammates know about changes in the practice schedule.

One thing that all memos have in common is that they are short and to the point—ideally no longer than one page. When you write a memo, do not include any unnecessary details or information. Make the tone of your memo friendly but avoid slang. Use plain language and don't be wordy. "Please remember to sign in every morning" is better than "It's important that our records be accurate, so please try to remember to sign in each and every morning." If you are writing a memo to request something, tell your readers exactly what you want them to do. Use directions such as "Please send me the information by Monday" or "Please see me at 4 o'clock."

Types of Memos

ANNOUNCEMENT	REMINDER	REQUEST	ASSIGN A TASK
Sum up your announcement in a very few words on the subject line. Make the announcement in one or two short sentences in the first paragraph. Give details in a second paragraph or in a bulleted list. Include necessary information such as dates and phone numbers.	Begin your message with a phrase such as "Remember to . . ." or "This is to remind you . . ." Give the most important information in the first sentence or two. Give other important information in the second paragraph. Include necessary dates, times, addresses, and phone numbers.	Use the subject line to show that the memo is a request by using a phrase such as "Your help needed" or "Please help." Make your request clearly in the first sentence. Tell how the person can respond to your request. Thank the person for his or her help.	Name the assignment in the subject line. Use words such as "Your job is to . . ." or "This assignment includes . . ." in the first sentence. Briefly describe the task. Give more details if necessary. Tell when the assignment must be finished.

Teach

Using the Model
Point out that every part of a memo has a purpose. Ask students to identify the purpose of each part of the model memo on page 274.

Apply to Your School
Point out that a memo may be sent to an individual or to a group, as in the models on pages 274 and 276. Ask students to list some groups in the school that a memo might be addressed to. *(For example, sports teams, cheerleaders, clubs, a particular class)* Ask them to suggest some topics such memos might address. **L2**

Real World Connection

Evaluating Memos
Ask students to bring to class examples of memos from sources outside the school—for example, from parents' places of work, churches or other places of worship, clubs and organizations to which they or other family members belong. Display the memos in the classroom and then discuss them as a class. To what category of memos does each belong? What topics do they concern? Do they all follow the style used in the models in their book? Which are particularly effective and why?

Teach

Memos and E-mail

Point out that the form of the model memo on page 276 is similar to the form of an e-mail message. Memos and e-mail are also similar in that both are usually brief and to the point. Conciseness is a goal students should work toward when they write a memo. **L1**

Business and Technical Writing

Memos

Style

Memos are written in block style. Headings and paragraphs start at the left margin. Each heading is printed in capital letters (often in boldface type) and followed by a colon. The main words following the colons are capitalized because they form the subtitles for the memo.

Sometimes memos include bulleted or numbered lists, as in the model below. Unlike a letter, a memo does not end with a closing or signature. The last line of the message acts as a final word.

Technology Tip

If your word processing software includes a memo template, open a new document in the program. (Select **New** from the **File** menu.) You will then see a dialogue box that offers such options as letters, memos, and reports. Select the **Memo** option and open the memo template. You can then replace the filled-in copy on the template with your own message.

TO: All Scouts   (Headings)

FROM: Jason Jakola

SUBJECT: May 30 Meeting in the School Gym

DATE: May 23, 2005   (Date)

At a meeting in the school gym on May 30 at 3:00 P.M., we will be making and decorating leather vests. Vest kits will be provided.   (Message)

To decorate your vest, please bring materials such as the following.

- colored pens
- award patches
- feathers
- permanent markers
- beads
- fringe
- braid   (Bulleted list)

Glue guns will be available for attaching decorations to vests. See you at the meeting!

Technology Tip

Formatting Lists

Draw students' attention to the bulleted list in the model memo on page 276. If students use a computer for their writing, tell them that in some word processing programs they can make bulleted or numbered lists with the touch of a button. All they need to do is type their list, select all the list lines, and click on the button in the formatting toolbar for either a bulleted list or a numbered list. The bullets or consecutive numbers, as well as a hanging indentation, are added by the program almost instantly. If their software lacks this feature, they can type in the bullets or numbers and use tabs and the indent markers on the program's ruler to create a hanging indentation. If the list items are short enough, the students can use the columns feature of their software to divide the list into two columns, as the model memo does.

The Parts of a Memo

Memos have two basic parts.

The Headings Each memo heading consists of a title word in capital letters, followed by a colon and a subtitle. Most memos have at least four headings:

- the person(s) to whom the memo is addressed (Memos can be addressed to individuals or groups.)
- the sender of the memo
- the subject of the memo, a very brief description—no more than six words
- the date

The Message The message of a memo is written in one or more paragraphs. Sentences are usually short. Some memos include a bulleted or numbered list. Most memo messages end with a concluding thought, such as thanking the person if a request was made or giving an instruction on how to respond to the memo. A reminder memo might end with a friendly remark.

Neatness Counts

Write a memo on a computer or a word processor. If neither is available, use a pen to print headings in capital letters. Then fill in the heading information and the message in neat handwriting.

- Use white $8\frac{1}{2}$-by-11-inch paper.
- Leave a two-inch margin at the top of the page and margins of at least one inch at the left, right, and bottom.

- Use a line space between the heading lines, between the headings and the message, and between paragraphs.
- Single-space lines in the message.

 **Activity**

Write a Memo. Pretend that you are organizing a class picnic. Write a memo announcing the picnic. Include details about the date, the time, and the location. With a partner, read each other's memos and look for unnecessary information or wordiness. Check to make sure that information appears in order of importance. Revise the memos and post them in the classroom.

- Before writing your memo, make a list of details and rank them in order of importance.
- End your message on a friendly note.

PURPOSE To write a memo announcing an event

AUDIENCE A classmate

LENGTH Less than one page

WRITING RUBRICS To write an effective memo, you should

- use correct memo format
- convey your message clearly and briefly
- include all necessary details
- end on a friendly note
- proofread your message carefully

Assess

Evaluation Rubrics

To evaluate students' writing in the activity, use the writing rubrics given on page 277. You may also have students exchange memos for peer evaluation.

Close

Have students discuss how they might use what they learned about memos.

Applications

Focus

Lesson Overview

Objectives
- To understand the styles, types, and purposes of application forms
- To create and correctly fill out application forms

Skills
- following directions; organizing information

Critical Thinking
- comparing; classifying

Listening and Speaking
- discussing

Bellringer
Daily Language Activity

When students enter the classroom, have this assignment on the board: *Copy and fill in the following form.*

Name _____

Grade in school _____

Homeroom teacher _____

Give students a few minutes to fill out their "forms." Then collect the forms and use them to see if any students have problems in filling out a simple form.

Motivating Activity

Ask students what application forms they are familiar with. Write the names on the board as they are suggested. If necessary, add a few names of your own. Ask students to tell about forms they have filled out. What were they applying for? How complicated was the form?

Application Forms

An application is a formal request for something—a job, membership in a group, an award. The information helps the reader decide whether to accept or deny the request.

Application forms can be created for many purposes, as shown on the chart on page 279. Following the instructions on a form and filling in information neatly makes a positive impression. Below is an example of a filled-out application form.

Fifth Annual Young Writer's Workshop
November 12, 2005, at Central Middle School
1827 Windy Drive, Greenleaf, Montana 98763

To be considered as a participant in the Writer's Workshop, you must complete this application form and provide a writing sample. Applications must be received by October 12, 2005.

Participant's name: _____Kim Chan_____

Address: _____11263 Aspen Drive_____

City: ___Greenleaf_____ State: ___MT____ ZIP CODE: ___98763___

Phone: ___(206) 555-2863___

Birth date: ___June 6, 1995_____ Grade in school: ___6____

Parent name: ___Jae Chan_____

Parent's daytime phone: ___(206) 555-6827___

Please check the workshop you are most interested in attending:
- ❏ Poetry
- ☑ Writing Mystery Stories
- ❏ Writing Science Fiction Stories
- ❏ Creating Realistic Characters

Tell us why you want to participate in the Young Writer's Workshop:

I like to write and want to learn more about how to write mystery stories.

Writing Sample
Use the back of this form or attach a separate sheet of paper. The length of the sample should be 150–200 words. Please type or write neatly.
Please see attached page.

Applicant's signature: _Kim Chan_____ Date: _Sept. 10, 2005_

Mail completed application and writing sample to
Fifth Annual Young Writer's Workshop
P.O. Box 3948
Greenleaf, Montana, 98763-9876

Applicants will be notified by mail within two weeks of receipt of application.

Annotation callouts:
- This application is for a specific event.
- The application includes the rules for applying and a deadline.
- This application has space for filling in information.
- The applicant writes or prints neatly.
- The applicant indicates that he or she is attaching a separate piece of paper for this answer.
- This application requires a signature and a date.

Types of Application Form

Application forms are used in many different situations. You may be required to fill out an application form for a job; for membership in a club or other group; to attend a camp, conference, or other event; or to join a team.

When filling out an application form, read all instructions carefully and follow them exactly. Include information that will help persuade the person reading the application to consider you or grant your request.

When mailing an application form, make sure you reply to the address that appears in the instructions. Sometimes you must send a fee or other materials along with your application—for example, a writing sample, an essay, or letters of recommendation.

When you need to *create* an application form, you should include any information the applicant needs and instructions for filling out the form. If there is a date by which applicants need to reply, include it on the form. You should also include space in which the applicant can provide information.

The kinds of information you request will depend on what the application is for. If you are making an application form for admission to a backpacking group, you might ask how long the person applying has been backpacking, the length of previous backpack trips, and the person's level of physical fitness. If you are making up an application form for membership in a softball team, you might ask for the applicant's playing experience, favored position, and jersey size.

Business and Technical Writing

Types of Applications			
MEMBERSHIP OR SCHOOL APPLICATION	**EVENT APPLICATION**	**AWARD APPLICATION**	**JOB APPLICATION**
States the requirements for membership or acceptance	States the name of the event	Describes the award	Asks for personal information about the applicant
Includes instructions on how to apply	Includes information about the time and place that the event will be held	Asks for the applicant's qualifications	Asks about the applicant's qualifications and ability to do the job
Includes room for required information from the applicant	Specifies a deadline for returning the application	May ask the applicant to write an essay or answer essay questions	Sometimes includes space for listing references
Sometimes includes essay questions			May require a cover letter and a résumé
Sometimes requests a fee for applying			

Teach

Using the Model

Have students study the model application form on page 278, noticing the callouts. Then guide students through the form, directing their attention to specifics by asking questions such as the following: What is the specific event being applied for? What is the deadline for the application? If the application requires a sample or attached information, how and where does the applicant indicate this? **L2**

Studying Applications

As students read the information above the chart on page 279, ask them to find at least two important things to remember in filling out any application. Then have them note what must be included in a form that they create. After students examine the chart that lists types of applications, invite them to share experiences they have had with filling out applications. Then discuss possible scenarios for creating an application form. **L2**

Real World Connection

Planning a Creative Writing Fair

Suggest that students sponsor a creative writing fair for grades 4 to 6. Students should work in small groups to decide how the fair should be conducted and what tasks must be performed. Students will use skills previously learned to write a business letter to the administration asking permission to carry out the project. They can also write letters to the teachers of other classes, explaining how their classes will be involved. Then they should create an application form to be distributed to any interested students. All the students should be involved on various committees: a selection committee to which all applications will be submitted, a display committee to arrange writing samples in a designated area, and a publicity committee to invite the school population.

Teach

Discussing Style

Lead students in a discussion of the standard form for most applications. Basic elements include the introduction, which explains the purpose of the application; the body, which indicates the information needed and provides space for responses to be inserted; and the conclusion, which asks for the signature of the applicant and may contain information on where the application is to be sent. **L1**

Application Forms

Style

An application form begins with a heading at the top of the page. The heading can be centered or aligned with the left margin. The body of an application form is created for a specific purpose. Usually all questions begin at the left margin, but certain questions may be indented. The body of an application form may be divided into sections, as in the following model.

A colon is used after each question prompt (applicant's name: _____) and write-on lines are provided for answers.

The Northwood Observer
Application for Newspaper Carrier — Heading

To apply for the position of newspaper carrier, you must be at least twelve years old and able to deliver the *Northwood Observer* every Monday and Thursday afternoon.

Required Information — Body of application, divided into sections. Section 1

Carrier's Name: _____

Address: _____

City: _____ State: _____ ZIP CODE: _____

Telephone: _____ Age: _____ Grade: _____

Social Security Number: _____

School: _____

Use this space to tell us why you want to be a *Northwood Observer* carrier. — Answer to essay question here

_____
_____
_____

Route Preferences — Body of application, Section 2
Circle route areas for which you want to be considered.
Downtown   East Side   Kerry Town
West Side   North suburbs   Clearport

References — Body of application, Section 3
Please include as references the names and phone numbers of two adults who are not family members.

Reference 1: _____

Reference 2: _____

Applicant's signature: _____ Date: _____ — Section for signature of applicant

Parent's or Guardian's Signature: _____

Please submit your application to
Carrier Coordinator: Ms. Susan Brautmeyer — Information on where to send application
      The Northwood Observer
      29388 E. State St.
      Northwood, MN 49387-9845

The Parts of an Application Form

Most application forms include the following parts:

The Heading The heading can be the title of a contest, the name of a group or company, or simply the word *Application.*

Instructions An application form may include such instructions as

- how to fill out the form
- date by which to submit the application form
- where to send the application form

Questionnaire Section Part of the application form requests information about the applicant. Most application forms require certain basic information, such as the name, address, and phone number or e-mail address of the applicant.

Signature and Date The application form is signed and dated by the applicant.

Neatness Counts

Your application is more likely to be given favorable consideration if you follow directions exactly and fill the form in neatly. You can type your answers. Neat handwritten answers in black or blue ink are also acceptable.

When completing an application form, first write your answers on a separate sheet of paper so that you can edit them if you think changes are necessary. Then fill out the actual application form. Some companies and organizations have forms that you can fill out online while you are visiting their Web sites.

Activity

Imagine that you want to form a sports team or a hobby club. Create a membership application form for your group. Then trade application forms with a classmate and fill out the form you received, following its instructions. Collaborate with your partner to revise your applications.

- List the information you will require from applicants, such as name, address, experience, or answers to essay questions.
- Think about how to organize your application form into sections, and use clusters to list the information asked for in each section.
- Use a computer and word processing software to create and revise your application form.

PURPOSE To create and fill out an application form

AUDIENCE A classmate

LENGTH One page

WRITING RUBRICS To successfully create and fill out an application form, you should

- include instructions and request all the necessary information in your form
- organize the form into logical sections and clusters
- use computer software to create the form
- fill out all parts of the form neatly
- proofread your application and responses

Business and Technical Writing

Assess

Evaluation Rubrics

Activity

Students should carefully read the directions for creating an application form. The rubrics provided will allow them to evaluate their own work. The teacher should use the same rubrics to evaluate the students' completed work.

Close

The Real World Connection activity suggested on page 279 would provide an interesting culmination to the lesson. In place of this activity, you might have students discuss the types of applications most of them will have to complete in the next few years. Help them to summarize what they have learned about completing applications.

Instructions

Focus

Lesson Overview

Objectives

- To understand the elements of instructions
- To write a clear set of instructions

Skills

- listing; ordering

Critical Thinking

- analyzing, evaluating

Listening and Speaking

- discussing, presenting

Bellringer
Daily Language Activity

When students enter the classroom, have this assignment on the board: *List five things that you should do as soon as you enter the classroom. Be specific.*

Motivating Activity

Ask students to share their responses to the Bellringer. Explain that since beginning a lesson is so routine, there are many actions involved that they may not have thought to list: greeting friends, taking an assigned seat, arranging books and writing materials, and reading the assignment on the board. Explain that attention to small details is very important in writing instructions. This lesson will provide suggestions for writing effective instructions.

Instructions

Instructions are a set of step-by-step directions for how to do something. You can write instructions for many specific tasks. A clear and complete set of instructions will help your reader understand exactly what to do.

Here is an example of instructions on how to give a dog a bath. Notice how the writer follows some of the tips in the chart on the following page.

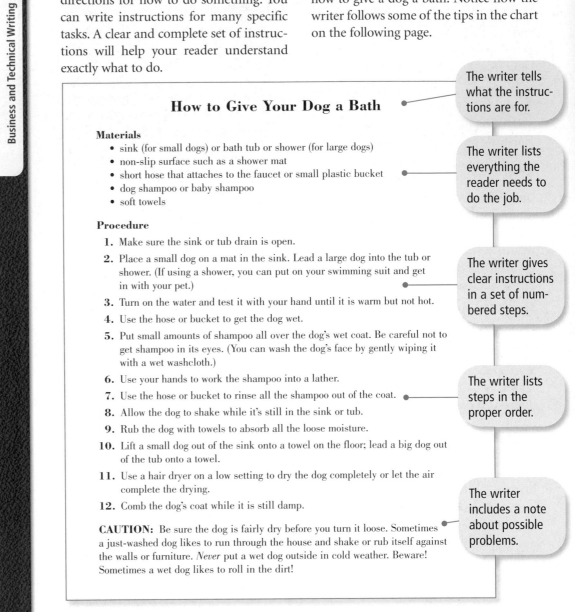

How to Give Your Dog a Bath

Materials
- sink (for small dogs) or bath tub or shower (for large dogs)
- non-slip surface such as a shower mat
- short hose that attaches to the faucet or small plastic bucket
- dog shampoo or baby shampoo
- soft towels

Procedure
1. Make sure the sink or tub drain is open.
2. Place a small dog on a mat in the sink. Lead a large dog into the tub or shower. (If using a shower, you can put on your swimming suit and get in with your pet.)
3. Turn on the water and test it with your hand until it is warm but not hot.
4. Use the hose or bucket to get the dog wet.
5. Put small amounts of shampoo all over the dog's wet coat. Be careful not to get shampoo in its eyes. (You can wash the dog's face by gently wiping it with a wet washcloth.)
6. Use your hands to work the shampoo into a lather.
7. Use the hose or bucket to rinse all the shampoo out of the coat.
8. Allow the dog to shake while it's still in the sink or tub.
9. Rub the dog with towels to absorb all the loose moisture.
10. Lift a small dog out of the sink onto a towel on the floor; lead a big dog out of the tub onto a towel.
11. Use a hair dryer on a low setting to dry the dog completely or let the air complete the drying.
12. Comb the dog's coat while it is still damp.

CAUTION: Be sure the dog is fairly dry before you turn it loose. Sometimes a just-washed dog likes to run through the house and shake or rub itself against the walls or furniture. *Never* put a wet dog outside in cold weather. Beware! Sometimes a wet dog likes to roll in the dirt!

The writer tells what the instructions are for.

The writer lists everything the reader needs to do the job.

The writer gives clear instructions in a set of numbered steps.

The writer lists steps in the proper order.

The writer includes a note about possible problems.

Types of Instructions

You can write instructions to describe a process—for example, tying a shoe, making a paper airplane, filling out an application, installing a software program, or planting a tree.

You can also use instructions to tell how to assemble something from parts, such as a bicycle, toy, model car, or doghouse.

Before you write instructions, you need to understand the process completely. Every detail must be included in your instructions, and details must appear in the correct order.

Make your instructions as simple as possible. Don't include unneeded information or details. Use plain English, and keep each step brief. Take extra care in explaining any step that might be confusing, or divide a complicated step into smaller steps. Choose words that express exactly what you mean. For example, instead of saying "Bend the pipe cleaner into a series of circles," say, "Twist the pipe cleaner into a long, slim spiral."

Style

Instructions usually begin with some form of heading or title that is centered on the page. Instructions can be written in paragraph form or in a list of numbered steps. Begin all paragraphs and numbered steps at the left margin. Leave a line space between each paragraph or between the steps of a procedure.

List each item in a materials list (if needed) on a separate line or use bullets.

If your instructions include just one illustration, it may appear before or after the numbered steps. If your instructions include a series of illustrations, you can write the steps below the illustrations as captions.

Two Types of Instructions	
INSTRUCTIONS FOR A PROCESS	**INSTRUCTIONS FOR ASSEMBLING AN ITEM**
• List the materials needed in the order in which they will be used.	• Instruct readers to put parts together in logical order.
• Number your steps in the order in which they should be completed.	• Do the assembly yourself as you write the steps so that you don't leave anything out.
• Be sure you don't leave out a step.	• Use a labeled illustration to show the different parts.
• Be brief when describing a step.	• Tell your readers everything they need to know and nothing extra.
• If instructions are complicated, use a series of illustrations to show the steps.	

Teach

Using the Model

Have students read the model on page 282, noting the precise detail in the directions. Encourage students to discuss the steps they may have omitted or combined if they had been writing in a similar set of directions. Caution students that someone familiar with a process might assume that a reader would know how to proceed, given the bare-bones directions.

It is better to err on the side of giving directions that are too explicit than to assume that a reader has knowledge that, in fact, he or she does not. **L2**

Types of Instructions

The most important characteristic of any set of instructions is clarity. Before finalizing a set of process instructions, students should try them on a friend or family member, reading each step aloud and observing whether the person has any trouble following the instructions. They should make note of any clarifications they have had to supply. When providing instructions for assembling an item, students should do the assembly themselves and include any hints that would facilitate the process. For example, if the assembly requires nails, they might suggest that the nails be stuck into a bar of soap, so that the coated nail can penetrate the wood more easily. **L2**

Enrichment and Extension

Sharing Experiences with Interpreting Instructions

Have the students recall experiences that they or members of their family have had in trying to follow printed directions. These may include hooking up a stereo or assembling a dollhouse or other toy for a younger member of the family. Encourage students to share incidents when the person following the instructions had been frustrated because of unclear directions or missing steps. They may want to each create a humorous illustration or series of illustrations that dramatize the incident.

Teach

Using the Model

Call the students' attention to the model set of instructions on page 284. Have them note the different parts of the instructions and discuss the importance of the diagram. Ask students to find details in the assembly section that make the instructions easy to follow. (They might suggest phrases like "so that they look like a plus sign" or "Wind . . . string . . . in a figure-eight pattern.") **L1**

Instructions

The Parts of a Set of Instructions

Instructions are usually divided into the following parts.

Heading or Title The heading or title tells what the instructions are for.

Materials List If materials are needed for a procedure, list them under a heading, which can be the single word *Materials*. List materials in the order in which they will be used. Describe materials exactly.

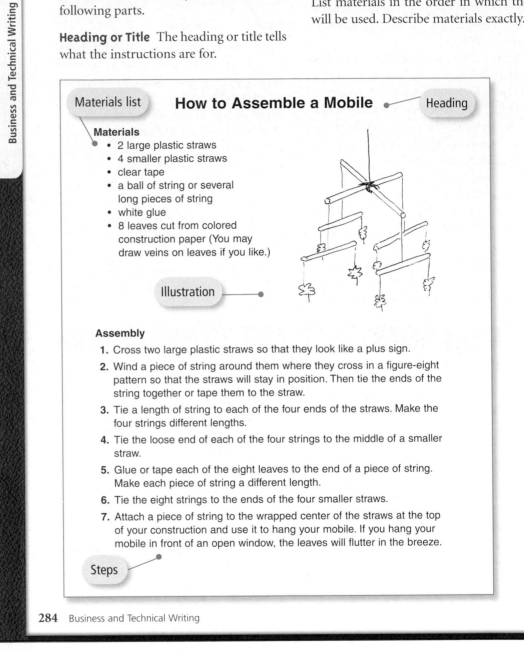

Materials list — **How to Assemble a Mobile** — **Heading**

Materials
- 2 large plastic straws
- 4 smaller plastic straws
- clear tape
- a ball of string or several long pieces of string
- white glue
- 8 leaves cut from colored construction paper (You may draw veins on leaves if you like.)

Illustration

Assembly
1. Cross two large plastic straws so that they look like a plus sign.
2. Wind a piece of string around them where they cross in a figure-eight pattern so that the straws will stay in position. Then tie the ends of the string together or tape them to the straw.
3. Tie a length of string to each of the four ends of the straws. Make the four strings different lengths.
4. Tie the loose end of each of the four strings to the middle of a smaller straw.
5. Glue or tape each of the eight leaves to the end of a piece of string. Make each piece of string a different length.
6. Tie the eight strings to the ends of the four smaller straws.
7. Attach a piece of string to the wrapped center of the straws at the top of your construction and use it to hang your mobile. If you hang your mobile in front of an open window, the leaves will flutter in the breeze.

Steps

Steps List steps in the order in which they are to be done. Numbering steps is a great way to keep your readers from getting lost.

Illustrations Some simple instructions may be clear without an illustration, but often illustrations can make your meaning clearer.

Technology Tip

Some word processing programs have an automatic numbering and bulleting feature that can organize your instructions automatically. If your software lacks this feature, you can use the indention markers on the ruler to set up lists or steps so that the lines indent uniformly after the bullets or numbers.

Activity

Write a set of instructions for how to do something or assemble something.

- Do the process or think it through carefully, noting the materials and steps needed as you go along.
- Arrange your steps in logical order.
- Use exact language to be clear.
- Draw an illustration if it will help you to be more concise.

Then trade instructions with a classmate. Follow the classmate's instructions, if possible, or imagine the process as you read. Discuss how the instructions could be made clearer.

PURPOSE To write instructions

AUDIENCE A classmate

LENGTH One page

WRITING RUBRICS To write a set of clear instructions, you should

- list any needed materials
- divide the process into clear and logical steps
- use exact language
- include an illustration if necessary
- carefully proofread your work

Assess

Evaluation Rubrics

Students should refer to the model and to the instructions in the lesson as they complete the activity. You might use the Writing Rubrics on the student page as you evaluate the students' work.

Close

Duplicate one or two sets of instructions for assembling a simple item, such as an origami bird. Distribute the materials necessary, and have each student follow the instructions. Then have the students discuss what made the instructions easy to follow or what additional information would have been helpful.

Incident Reports

Lesson Overview

Objectives

- To understand the elements of an incident report
- To create and fill out an incident report

Skills

- ordering details; describing

Critical Thinking

- evaluating

Listening and Speaking

- discussing

Bellringer
Daily Language Activity

When the students enter the classroom, have the following assignment on the board: *List three accidents or incidents that you have witnessed or heard about on the news for which you think reports would have been made. Include approximate dates or times of the occurrences.*

Motivating Activity

With the assistance of some students, prepare and stage a dramatization of an accident. Have the students discuss the details that they observe and what facts must be reported. Explain that the lesson they are now beginning will provide some concrete help in filing incident (and accident) reports.

Incident Reports

An incident report uses a specific form to record information about something that has interrupted normal activity or caused a crisis. Incident reports are written by a witness or by a person gathering information.

The following model is an incident report completed by a student bus-stop monitor. Such a report would be turned in at the principal's office.

March Middle School Incident Report

Submitter of Report

Name: _Tamika Brown_

Phone: _(622) 555-3820_

Grade and homeroom: _6th_ _Mr. Penniman's Room_

Check one:
❑ teacher ☑ student ❑ staff member ❑ other _____

> The reporter gives information on how to contact her.

Incident Information

Date of Incident: _February 12, 2005_ Time of Incident: _3:15 p.m._

Location of Incident: _Front of school — bus zone_

Type of Incident (accident, vandalism, safety violation, other):

safety violation

> The reporter answers the questions *when? where?* and *what?*

Details

(Use space below and/or additional pages if necessary.)

A red Ford pickup truck, license plate #MTS206, was parked at the curb in the bus loading zone. The buses could not pull up to the curb, so students had to walk into the street, which was icy, in order to board the bus. Some students slid on the ice, but none were injured.

> The reporter describes the incident in detail.

Date Reported: _February 13, 2005_

Signature: _Tamika Brown, Monitor_

> The reporter signs her name.

Types of Incident Report

Businesses, institutions, and schools use incident reports for recording many different kinds of situations, such as accidents, thefts, damage to property, safety violations, fights, and threats.

You may be asked to fill out a report if you witness an incident at your school. When filling out an incident report, give all the information that is asked for on the report form. Supply exact details. "On the sidewalk at the northeast corner of Brush and Fifth Avenue" is more precise than "It happened at the corner." Include the answers to the questions *who? what? where?* and *when?* Provide all you *know* about the incident but not opinions or guesses, such as why you *think* somebody did something.

You yourself could create an incident report form on which could be reported incidents in your classroom. If you make up such a form, you will want to ask for information on the person filling out the form and detailed information on the incident.

ACCIDENT	THEFT	SAFETY VIOLATION
Label blanks for listing details, including date, time, and location.	Ask for the date and time that the theft was discovered and contact information for the person who discovered it.	Make a section for information on the person reporting the incident so that he or she can be reached if needed.
Provide space for the names, addresses, and phone numbers of witnesses.	Include a fill-in section with space for listing stolen items, their descriptions, and their estimated values.	Provide a section for recording specific details, such as the date, time, and location.
Provide space or give a direction to use the back of the paper to sketch the scene.	Label a space that can be used for a description of the details of the incident.	
Give a direction to attach a photograph if available.		

Table title: Three Types of Incident Reports

Business and Technical Writing

Teach

Using the Model

Have students read the introduction and study the model incident report, noting the information described in the callouts. Ask questions such as the following:

- What might be the purpose of this report?
- What is the purpose of including detailed information about the person who submitted the report?
- What should be noted about the date the report was filed? **L2**

Read and Discuss

After students read the information on page 287, have the students discuss the differences among the three types of reports listed. Encourage students to describe experiences they may have had in filing reports or in having had to supply information for such a report. **L3**

Teach

Studying Style

Call the students' attention to the style of the incident report on page 288. Have them compare the blank report with the completed report on page 286. Direct their study with questions such as the following:

- What is the value of having a specific format for incident reports?
- Why is it helpful to have writing lines supplied throughout the report but especially in the portion of the report that calls for details? **L2**

Incident Reports

Style

Most incident reports are in block style. All of their lines begin at the left margin. A heading (title) at the top of the page may be centered. Some incident reports may have headings centered at the beginnings of sections.

The words that prompt a fill-in response are followed by a colon; for example, *Name:* _____ .

Incident Report ● — Heading

Contact Information

Name: _____ ● — Information about the person filling out the form

Address: _____

City: _____ State: _____ ZIP CODE: _____

Phone: _____

Incident Information

Date of incident: _____ Time of incident: _____ ● — Information on the incident

Location of incident: _____

Type of incident: _____

Details
(Give complete details, including quotations from people involved in the incident. Continue on the back of this form or an attached sheet if necessary.)

_____

_____

_____ ● — Space for writing in details

_____

_____

_____

Date reported: _____ ● — Date of report

Signature: _____ ● — Signature

---

288 Business and Technical Writing

The Parts of an Incident Report

Most incident reports have four basic parts.

Heading The heading or title can be simply *Incident Report* or it can include the name of the business or institution. The title can also refer to the kind of incident being reported, such as *Safety Incident Report*.

Contact Information Basic contact information includes four or more lines:
- name of person filling out report
- street address
- city, state, and ZIP code
- phone number

Incident Information Information about the incident usually includes the following:
- date
- time
- location
- type of incident

The report may also provide space for writing a more detailed description and may include an instruction to attach another sheet of paper if needed.

Signature and Date The report usually ends with the reporter's signature and the date the report was written.

Activity

Create an incident-report form on a computer. Then trade forms with a classmate. Fill out the form on any recent incident at your school. If necessary, interview witnesses to gather information. If you can't think of any recent incidents to describe, create a fictional one.

- Think about the kinds of information needed on an incident report form to be used at your school.
- Use a cluster organizer to sort the information into categories.
- Create your form on a computer.
- Exchange forms with a classmate and fill out his or her form by typing, printing, or writing neatly.

PURPOSE To create and fill out an incident report

AUDIENCE Your classmates

LENGTH 1 page

WRITING RUBRICS To create and fill out incident report, you should
- use a computer to create a form
- organize information into categories
- include all necessary information
- describe the incident clearly
- type or print your responses clearly

Teach

Using Technology

Encourage students to use a computer to create an incident report form. Remind them that, using the computer, they can produce a neat, professional-looking document that can be not only printed but also kept on file and modified as the occasion demands. **L3**

Assess

Evaluation Rubrics

Refer to the Writing Rubrics on the student's page as you evaluate the forms they have created and filled out.

Close

Have the students exchange the forms they have created. Discuss whether such forms are available to them at the school office. If not, they might decide on an appropriate form and submit it to the principal with suggestions for its use.

Multimedia Presentations

Focus

Lesson Overview

Objectives
- To understand the various elements involved in a multimedia presentation
- To create a multimedia presentation

Skills
- organizing, presenting

Critical Thinking
- analyzing, evaluating

Listening and Speaking
- discussing

🔔 Bellringer
Daily Language Activity

When students enter the classroom, have this assignment written on the board: *Briefly describe a demonstration that you've seen in a department store or grocery store. How did the demonstration appeal to sight and sound? Did the demonstration appeal to smell, touch, or taste?*

Motivating Activity

Ask several students to share the information they wrote for the Bellringer. Encourage students to speak about other presentations—live or televised—that included appeals to several senses.

Multimedia Presentations

A multimedia presentation is a report that uses several media, or means of communication. When you speak to an audience and show visuals (slides or pictures), you are giving a multimedia presentation that has both sound and graphics.

The photograph on this page shows some parts of one student's multimedia presentation. Its purpose is to persuade the audience that whale hunting should be stopped.

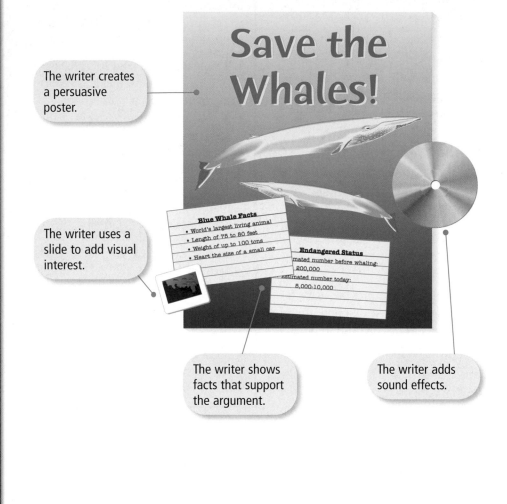

The writer creates a persuasive poster.

The writer uses a slide to add visual interest.

The writer shows facts that support the argument.

The writer adds sound effects.

Enrichment and Extension

Picturing the Process

When television commercials for food items are produced, a special food artist is employed. The task of this person is to make the food look appetizing as it is filmed. The food that you see is not as tasty as it looks! For example, dry ice is used to produce the smoke from a steaming hot cup of cocoa. Shaving cream tops dessert, since it is more durable beneath hot lights during filming than whipped cream would be. Suggest that students might research this area of art and report to the class on different techniques used by food artists.

Types of Media

You can add a combination of videos, photos, slides, music, and other media to an oral presentation. Multimedia presentations can be used to report on a wide variety of topics. They can also be used to persuade an audience to agree with an opinion or to take some kind of action. The following chart shows examples of different kinds of media.

Many multimedia presentations are persuasive, which means that their purpose is to convince others of a point of view or to prompt them to take a certain action. You can do research at the library and on the Internet to find facts, statistics, and expert opinions and use the information to support your point of view.

To persuade others to change their opinions, you must address their concerns. If you are trying to convince the school board to keep the marching band when budget cuts have to be made, you might offer a plan to raise money to pay for uniforms and instruments. If you want to convince people to write letters to support a cause, make a handout with an address to which they can write and include suggestions concerning what they might include in the letter.

Types of Media		
VISUALS	**SOUND**	**OTHER OPTIONS**
Use a video or slide show to make your subject clear.	Use a cassette recorder to help your audience hear your subject (for example, a wolf's howl or a train's whistle).	Appeal to your audience's sense of touch by passing around an object related to your topic.
Use video animation or a series of photographs, drawings, or transparencies to show a process.	Choose a CD to play in the background that will help put your audience in the right mood.	Don't neglect appeals to other senses. A food topic, for example, lends itself to appeals to smell and taste. The more senses your presentation appeals to, the more memorable it will be.
Make handouts of information you want your audience to take with them.	Add sound effects to a slide show.	
Create a poster to help convince your audience of your viewpoint.	Play a short recorded interview with an expert on your topic.	

Teach

Using the Model

Have students examine the photograph of the multimedia presentation on whale hunting. Then encourage students to share their opinions on why a multimedia presentation may be more effective than a simple report. Call attention to the various elements that appeal to the sense of sight—poster, slide, handouts. Discuss other elements that might be included in the presentation on whales. **L2**

Types of Media

The main types of media appeal to sight and sound. Within these major types, however, there are variations. For example, sounds include not only speech but musical background and other sound effects. Other options include appeals to the senses of smell, touch, and taste. Encourage students to share occasions when they witnessed presentations that appealed to these senses. **L2**

Exploring Language

Parallelism

Parallelism is the use of a series of words, phrases, or sentences that have similar grammatical form. It is often used to emphasize attributes of a commercial product. For example, the claim for a breakfast cereal might be "It's economical; it's nutritious; it's delicious!" Encourage students to share examples of parallelism that they have heard on TV or radio commercials. You might also ask that they clip and bring to class examples of parallelism that they find in print advertisements. For more on parallelism, see the **Writing and Research Handbook,** page 678.

Business and Technical Writing

Teach

Style

Multimedia presentations make use of a variety of elements, and they are ideal for persuasive purposes. After students have read the material on page 292 and studied the illustrations, have the class form groups of three or four. Direct the students to decide on one or more topics that would be suitable for a multimedia presentation. **L1**

Multimedia Presentations

Style

A multimedia presentation can be given orally or narrated on tape, with other sounds and visuals used to enrich the message. It's up to you to use the various media in the most effective way. For example, if your purpose were to convince people to support keeping the school marching band, you might introduce your topic by playing a recording of the band's most popular piece. Perhaps you might stop the music abruptly in mid-number to suggest the idea that the band may be dropped.

Technology Tip

Some computer software programs can be used to create multimedia presentations that combine text with images and sounds. These programs allow you to produce "slide shows" or a series of hypertext "cards" that can be shown on a computer monitor. Investigate the use of such software if your school has access to it. Use it to create your multimedia presentation.

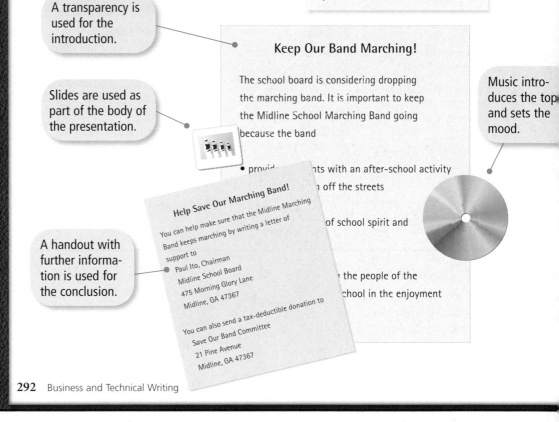

A transparency is used for the introduction.

Slides are used as part of the body of the presentation.

A handout with further information is used for the conclusion.

Music introduces the top and sets the mood.

Keep Our Band Marching!

The school board is considering dropping the marching band. It is important to keep the Midline School Marching Band going because the band

• provid... nts with an after-school activity
  ... n off the streets
  ... of school spirit and
  ... the people of the
  ... chool in the enjoyment

Help Save Our Marching Band!

You can help make sure that the Midline Marching Band keeps marching by writing a letter of support to

Paul Ito, Chairman
Midline School Board
475 Morning Glory Lane
Midline, GA 47367

You can also send a tax-deductible donation to
Save Our Band Committee
21 Pine Avenue
Midline, GA 47367

The Parts of a Multimedia Presentation

A multimedia presentation has three parts.

Introduction Begin your presentation by introducing your topic. Your introduction can also list the major points of your argument.

- Introduce yourself and your topic.
- Use a transparency or a slide to show your topic in headline form, while you introduce yourself orally.
- Use music to set the mood; then introduce yourself and your topic.

Body The body is the most important part of your presentation. In the body, you will give support for your opinion and convince your audience to agree with you.

Appeal to your listeners' sense of reason. Support your opinion with facts. For example, you could quote newspaper clippings showing that teen crime rose in a community where the school band was cut. Appeal visually to your readers' emotions. You could show a slide of happy band members in uniforms and then follow it with a slide of troubled teens on the streets. Anticipate your audience's objections and address their concerns.

Conclusion Sum up your thesis in a few sentences that are a logical conclusion of your argument.

Activity

Create a multimedia presentation to convince an audience to share your opinion on a subject or to take action. Choose the form of your presentation and the kinds of media you will use. Make your presentation to the class.

- Choose a topic you're interested in and know well or would like to learn more about.
- Research multiple resources on your topic and think of new questions for further investigation.
- Summarize and organize ideas gained from research by making outlines, maps, organizers, diagrams, graphs, or other illustrations.
- Document your sources in a bibliography.
- Include visuals and sound that will support your ideas.

PURPOSE Create a persuasive multimedia presentation

AUDIENCE Classmates and teacher

LENGTH 3–6 minutes

WRITING RUBRICS To create a successful multimedia presentation, you should

- research your topic
- present persuasive arguments to support your opinions
- include graphic organizers, other visuals, and sounds
- organize your presentation carefully
- list the sources of information you used

Business and Technical Writing (side tab)

Teach

Parts of a Multimedia Presentation

The parts of a multimedia presentation are simple: introduction, body, and conclusion. However, since a multimedia presentation has so many elements to keep track of, students may lose sight of those basics. Remind students that they must first define the purpose and audience for their presentation. Then they should select those elements that will best convey their message to that audience. Experimentation will confirm what will work to get across a persuasive message. They should strive to balance elements that appeal to sight with those that appeal to hearing and the other senses. **L2**

Assess

Evaluation Rubrics

Plan to evaluate the students' multimedia presentations during class periods. You might suggest that several students combine their efforts to create a single product. Presentations should be evaluated on the following points:

- a strong central idea
- an effective message
- the incorporation of a variety of visual and sound elements
- the careful execution of ideas

Close

Have the class decide on two or three presentations that they consider most effective. Arrange to have these presentations made to other classes.

Grammar, Usage, and Mechanics

Objectives

The units in Part 2 guide students in the development of their writing skills by helping them understand grammar, usage, and mechanics. Throughout these units, students will be asked

- to write in complete sentences, varying the kinds of sentences
- to use verb tenses appropriately and consistently
- to recognize subject-verb agreement
- to write with increasing accuracy when using pronouns and antecedents
- to use adjectives and adverbs appropriately
- to use conjunctions to connect ideas meaningfully
- to use punctuation with increasing accuracy

Viewing the Art

Katsushika Hokusai (1790 to 1849) created silkscreens, landscape paintings, wood block prints, and book illustrations inspired by the traditions, legends, and lives of the Japanese people. Among his best known work is a series of block prints entitled *Thirty-Six Views of Mount Fuji.*

Interpret and Analyze Use the following questions for discussion:

- What techniques does Hokusai use to show Fuji as a real mountain? as a powerful volcano?
- What techniques does he use to stylize the mountain—to make the mountain look less real than it might in a photograph?
- Why do you think Katsushika Hokusai made Mount Fuji the subject of more than thirty-six paintings?

"Then the volcano, which was named Mount St. Helens, began to stir."

—Patricia Lauber, *Volcano*

294

Resource Manager

Use the following resources to customize your teaching of the units in Part 2.

Planning Resources
- *Lesson Plans*
- *Block Scheduling*

Transparencies
- *Bellringer*
- *Daily Language Practice*
- *Two-Minute Skill Drill*

Other Print Resources
- *Dinah Zike's Foldables™ for Writer's Choice*
- *Grammar and Composition Handbook*

- *Grammar Enrichment*
- *Grammar Practice*
- *Grammar Reteaching*
- *Grammar Workbook*
- *Sentence-Combining Practice*
- *Spelling Power*
- *Taking Standardized Tests*
- *Tests with Answer Key and Rubrics*
- *Vocabulary Power*

Fuji in Clear
Weather by
Katsushika Hokusai.
British Museum,
London.

PART 2

Grammar, Usage, and Mechanics

295

Discussing the Quotation

In *Volcano: The Eruption and Healing of Mount St. Helens,* Patricia Lauber presents the power of nature through her detailed description of what occurred at Mount St. Helens in May of 1980. Ask students how they respond to this single short quotation. Point out Lauber's writing techniques, such as the use of a subordinate clause, commas, and specific verbs, that make this quotation clear and dramatic.

Suggest that students read or reread Lauber's book, noting her clear, straight-forward, and descriptive expository writing style. An excerpt is included in Course 1 of *Glencoe Literature: The Reader's Choice*, page 565.

Writing Prompt Have students compare the view Lauber presents of a stirring volcano with Hokusai's artistic presentation of Mount Fuji.

Video
- *MindJogger Videoquizzes*

Software
- *Interactive Grammar and Language Workbook*
- *Language Arts PASS*
- *Presentation Plus!*
- *Revising with Style*

- *Sentence Diagraming*
- *Testmaker*
- *Vocabulary Power Puzzlemaker*

Web Sites
- *TechCONNECT*
- *writerschoice.glencoe.com*

Practice and Assess

Answers: Exercise 1

1. declarative
2. interrogative
3. exclamatory
4. imperative
5. interrogative

Answers: Exercise 2

1. My favorite . . . Tinker Bell.
2. How I love fantasy stories!
3. Why did Peter . . . the window?
4. Peter lost . . . Wendy's home.
5. Please sew . . . onto my feet.
6. Come to . . . with me.
7. How excited . . . must have been!
8. The pirates . . . and the children.
9. What will . . . children?
10. Explain how . . . his friends.
11. Who walked . . . the plank?
12. The story . . . an animated movie.
13. Do you know . . . produced?
14. Believe it . . . years ago! (or .)
15. A woman . . . Broadway play.
16. How excited . . . through the air!
17. The fairy Tinker Bell helps Peter.
18. Tell me the story again.
19. Do you think adults believe in Tinker Bell?
20. What a great story this is!

Additional Resources

📁 *Grammar Practice,* p. 1
📁 *Grammar Reteaching,* p. 1
📁 *Grammar Enrichment,* p. 1

📖 *Grammar Workbook,* Lessons 1–2

Close

Have students check some of their recent writing for correct punctuation of the four kinds of sentences. Encourage students to revise their writing as needed.

Subjects, Predicates, and Sentences

| Exercise 1 | Identifying Kinds of Sentences |

Write *declarative, interrogative, exclamatory,* or *imperative* to identify each sentence.

1. Peter Pan protected a group of young orphans.
2. Did he protect them?
3. How mean Captain Hook and his pirates were!
4. Watch carefully for pirate ships on the horizon.
5. How did Peter Pan learn to fly?

| Exercise 2 | Punctuating Different Kinds of Sentences |

Write the following sentences, beginning and ending each correctly.

1. my favorite character in the story is Tinker Bell
2. how I love fantasy stories
3. why did Peter hide outside the window
4. peter lost his shadow in Wendy's home
5. please sew my shadow back onto my feet
6. come to Never-Never Land with me
7. how excited Wendy must have been
8. the pirates kidnapped Wendy and the children
9. what will the wicked pirates do to the poor children
10. explain how Peter rescued his friends
11. who walked off the end of the plank
12. the story has been a play on Broadway, a television show, and an animated movie
13. do you know when the play was first produced
14. believe it or not, it was about one hundred years ago
15. a woman played the role of Peter in the Broadway play
16. how excited audiences were to see her fly through the air
17. the fairy Tinker Bell helps Peter
18. tell me the story again
19. do you think adults believe in Tinker Bell
20. what a great story this is

MEETING INDIVIDUAL NEEDS **English Language Learners**

Forming Questions

Tell students that English forms yes-no questions in a variety of ways. One way is to insert a form of the word *do* in front of the subject: Do the pirates capture Wendy? Explain that forming yes-no questions by inserting *do* is an unusual feature of English. Most languages form yes-no questions by reordering the words or by changing the intonation. Have students practice forming questions using the correct form of *do* (*do, does,* or *did*).

8.2 Sentences and Sentence Fragments

Every sentence has two parts: a subject and a predicate.

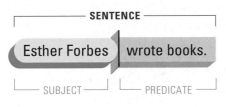

- The **subject part** of a sentence names whom or what the sentence is about.
- The **predicate part** of the sentence tells what the subject does or has. It can also describe what the subject is or is like.

A sentence must have both a subject and a predicate. It must also express a complete thought.

- A **sentence fragment** does not express a complete thought. It may be missing a subject, a predicate, or both.

You often use sentence fragments when you speak. You should avoid using them when you write, however.

Correcting Sentence Fragments		
Fragment	**Problem**	**Sentence**
Paul Revere.	The fragment lacks a predicate. *What did Paul Revere do?*	Paul Revere warned the people.
Worked for Paul Revere.	The fragment lacks a subject. *Who worked for Paul Revere?*	Johnny Tremain worked for Paul Revere.
About history.	The fragment lacks both a subject and a predicate.	Esther Forbes wrote books about history.

Focus

Lesson Overview

Objectives
- To identify subjects and predicates and to recognize complete sentences
- To identify and use strategies for correcting sentence fragments in writing
- To use subjects and predicates correctly to form complete sentences

Bellringer
Daily Language Activity

When students enter the classroom, have this assignment on the board: *Write the following phrases in the correct order to make a complete sentence:*

> walk through green forests
> Jared, Jean, and Jonah
> and colorful meadows

See also *Daily Language Practice*

Motivating Activity

Ask students how they knew which phrase would come first in the sentence. Are any of the phrases by themselves complete sentences? Why or why not? Discuss and clarify as needed.

Teach

☑ **Teaching Tip**

Point out to students that sentences follow certain patterns and that each pattern must include a subject and a predicate.

Resource Manager

Planning Resources
- *Lesson Plans*

Transparencies
- *Bellringer*
- *Daily Language Practice*

📁 **Other Print Resources**
- *Grammar and Composition Handbook*
- *Grammar Enrichment*, p. 1
- *Grammar Practice*, p. 1
- *Grammar Reteaching*, p. 2
- *Grammar Workbook*, Lesson 6

Practice and Assess

Answers: Exercise 3

1. sentence
2. fragment; missing predicate
3. sentence
4. fragment; missing predicate
5. fragment; missing subject
6. sentence
7. fragment; missing subject
8. sentence
9. fragment; missing predicate
10. sentence

Answers: Exercise 4

1. The setting is the American Revolution.
2. fragment
3. Real historical characters fill the book.
4. Americans wanted independence from England.
5. fragment
6. Johnny participated in the Boston Tea Party.
7. The Americans disliked the British tax on tea.
8. The townspeople disguised themselves.
9. fragment
10. The Sons of Liberty planned the Boston Tea Party.
11. The rebels threw the tea into the harbor waters.
12. British officials decided to close Boston Harbor.
13. fragment
14. The other colonies came to Boston's rescue.
15. Johnny's injured hand prevented him from being a soldier.

Additional Resources

📂 *Grammar Practice*, p. 1
📂 *Grammar Reteaching*, p. 2
📂 *Grammar Enrichment*, p. 1

📓 *Grammar Workbook*, Lesson 6

Exercise 3   **Identifying Sentences and Fragments**

Write *sentence* or *fragment* for each item. If an item is a fragment, explain what is missing.

1. The book *Johnny Tremain* is historical fiction.
2. A Newbery Medal winner.
3. Esther Forbes's nonfiction book on Paul Revere won a Pulitzer Prize.
4. The silversmith Paul Revere.
5. Offered Johnny a job.
6. Johnny liked his work.
7. Made things of silver.
8. Johnny burned his hand.
9. A terrible accident.
10. An operation made his hand well again.

Exercise 4   **Identifying Subjects and Predicates**

Write each sentence, underlining each subject part once and each predicate part twice. If the item is not a complete sentence, write *fragment*.

1. The setting is the American Revolution.
2. Sam Adams, John Hancock, and Paul Revere.
3. Real historical characters fill the book.
4. Americans wanted independence from England.
5. Fought for freedom of speech and other rights.
6. Johnny participated in the Boston Tea Party.
7. The Americans disliked the British tax on tea.
8. The townspeople disguised themselves.
9. As Mohawk Indians.
10. The Sons of Liberty planned the Boston Tea Party.
11. The rebels threw the tea into the harbor waters.
12. British officials decided to close Boston harbor.
13. Starved into submission.
14. The other colonies came to Boston's rescue.
15. Johnny's injured hand prevented him from being a soldier.

Subjects, Predicates, and Sentences

Close

Have students explain in their own words how they know when a sentence is complete and when it is a fragment. Encourage students to jot down in their journals for future reference any helpful hints they have learned about sentences and fragments.

Exploring Language

Discuss Fragments

Students may become confused when discussing sentence fragments because in conversational English, it is common to use fragments in response to questions. Have pairs of students practice asking each other questions and responding in complete sentences.

8.3 Subjects and Predicates

A sentence consists of a subject and a predicate, which together express a complete thought. Both a subject and a predicate may consist of more than one word.

Complete Subject	Complete Predicate
The main character	is Kit Tyler.
Kit	travels from the tropics to Connecticut.

- The **complete subject** includes all of the words in the subject of a sentence.
- The **complete predicate** includes all of the words in the predicate of a sentence.

Not all of the words in the subject or the predicate are of equal importance.

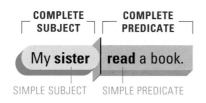

```
      COMPLETE        COMPLETE
      SUBJECT         PREDICATE

   My  sister  │ read a book.

   SIMPLE SUBJECT   SIMPLE PREDICATE
```

- The **simple subject** is the main word or group of words in the complete subject.

The simple subject is usually a noun or a pronoun. A **noun** is a word that names a person, a place, a thing, or an idea. A **pronoun** is a word that takes the place of one or more nouns.

- The **simple predicate** is the main word or group of words in the complete predicate.

The simple predicate is always a verb. A **verb** is a word that expresses an action or a state of being.

Sometimes the simple subject is also the complete subject. Similarly, the simple predicate may also be the complete predicate.

Focus

Lesson Overview

Objectives
- To identify simple and complete subjects and predicates
- To demonstrate an understanding of simple and complete subjects and predicates in written work

Bellringer
Daily Language Activity

When students enter the classroom, have this assignment on the board: *Write a complete sentence using as few words as possible.*

See also *Daily Language Practice*

Motivating Activity

Call on volunteers to write their sentences on the board. Work with students to determine the shortest complete sentence. Have students identify the subject and predicate in each short sentence they wrote. Encourage students to ask questions for clarification, as needed.

Teach

☑ Teaching Tip

A good way to teach the difference between simple and complete subjects and predicates is to write on the board a noun to use as a simple subject and a single verb to use as the predicate. Then have the students add words to create a long sentence. For example, starting with *girl reads,* students could expand this to *The little girl next door always reads my magazines in her treehouse.*

Subjects, Predicates, and Sentences

Resource Manager

Planning Resources
- *Lesson Plans*

Transparencies
- *Bellringer*
- *Daily Language Practice*

Other Print Resources
- *Grammar and Composition Handbook*
- *Grammar Enrichment,* p. 2
- *Grammar Practice,* p. 2
- *Grammar Reteaching,* p. 3
- *Grammar Workbook,* Lesson 3

Practice and Assess

Answers: Exercise 5

1. <u>My sister</u> <u><u>read</u></u> *The Witch of Blackbird Pond*.
2. <u>The book</u> <u><u>was written by Elizabeth George Speare</u></u>.
3. <u>It</u> <u><u>describes island life in the 1680s</u></u>.
4. <u>A young girl</u> <u><u>is the main character</u></u>.
5. <u>Kit</u> <u><u>lived a life of luxury</u></u>.
6. <u>She</u> <u><u>loved the island life</u></u>.
7. <u>This girl of the islands</u> <u><u>enjoyed the sun and the sea</u></u>.
8. <u>Her grandfather</u> <u><u>gave many parties</u></u>.
9. <u>Many friends</u> <u><u>attended her festive dance parties</u></u>.
10. <u>Kit's happiness</u> <u><u>ended with her grandfather's death</u></u>.
11. <u>Young Kit</u> <u><u>lost all her money</u></u>.
12. <u>Her life of luxury</u> <u><u>was over</u></u>.
13. <u>Kit</u> <u><u>had no family left in the islands</u></u>.
14. <u>Her aunt</u> <u><u>lived in the Connecticut Colony in America</u></u>.
15. <u>Kit</u> <u><u>went there to live</u></u>.
16. <u>She</u> <u><u>traveled to America by ship</u></u>.
17. <u>She</u> <u><u>was very lonely aboard ship</u></u>.
18. <u>A storm</u> <u><u>blew Kit's ship about for four days</u></u>.
19. <u>The ship</u> <u><u>approached land after many days</u></u>.
20. <u>The Connecticut Colony shore</u> <u><u>looked gray and bleak</u></u>.

Answers: Exercise 6

1. subj. *Kit*; pred. *traveled*
2. subj. *They;* pred. *were*
3. subj. *family;* pred. *worked*
4. subj. *colonists;* pred. *wore*
5. subj. *dresses;* pred. *shocked*
6. subj. *people;* pred. *discouraged*
7. subj. *customs;* pred. *made*
8. subj. *Snow;* pred. *was*
9. subj. *winters;* pred. *were*
10. subj. *Kit;* pred. *longed*

Subjects, Predicates, and Sentences

Exercise 5   **Identifying Complete Subjects and Predicates**

Write each sentence. Underline each complete subject once and each complete predicate twice.

1. My sister read *The Witch of Blackbird Pond*.
2. The book was written by Elizabeth George Speare.
3. It describes island life in the 1680s.
4. A young girl is the main character.
5. Kit lived a life of luxury.
6. She loved the island life.
7. This girl of the islands enjoyed the sun and the sea.
8. Her grandfather gave many parties.
9. Many friends attended her festive dance parties.
10. Kit's happiness ended with her grandfather's death.
11. Young Kit lost all her money.
12. Her life of luxury was over.
13. Kit had no family left in the islands.
14. Her aunt lived in the Connecticut Colony in America.
15. Kit went there to live.
16. She traveled to America by ship.
17. She was very lonely aboard ship.
18. A storm blew Kit's ship about for four days.
19. The ship approached land after many days.
20. The Connecticut Colony shore looked gray and bleak.

Exercise 6   **Identifying Simple Subjects and Simple Predicates**

Write the simple subject and simple predicate from each sentence.

1. Kit traveled far to meet her new family.
2. They were very different from Kit.
3. Kit's new family worked very hard.
4. The colonists wore plain clothing.
5. Kit's bright, colorful dresses shocked them.
6. These serious people discouraged parties.
7. Kit's strange island customs made her unpopular.
8. Snow was a surprise for Kit.
9. Kit's past winters were balmy.
10. Kit longed for her island home.

Close

Have students refer to a passage in another text to list the simple subjects and simple predicates of the sentences. Then ask students to check each other's work. Partners should discuss any needed revisions.

MEETING INDIVIDUAL NEEDS   English Language Learners

Finding Simple Subjects and Simple Predicates

Explain to students that when people learn a language, they often speak telegraphically, using just nouns and verbs to communicate. Have students make a chart with nouns or pronouns in one column and verbs in another. Have them pair words to make current, clear simple sentences. Extend the activity by having students embellish each sentence; then go back to find the subject and predicate.

8.4 Finding Subjects

Most statements begin with the subject.

Other kinds of sentences, such as questions, may begin with part or all of the predicate. The subject comes next, followed by the rest of the predicate.

To locate the subject of a question, rearrange the words to form a statement.

Predicate	Subject	Predicate
Have	all of the students	finished reading the book?
	All of the students	have finished reading the book.

Sometimes statements may have inverted word order. In these sentences, the predicate comes before the subject.

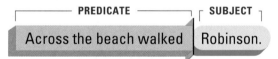

In requests and commands, the subject is usually not stated. The word *you* is understood to be the subject.

Subjects, Predicates, and Sentences

Focus

Lesson Overview

Objectives
- To identify subjects in normal and inverted sentences
- To identify and use the pronoun *you* as an understood subject in requests and commands

Bellringer
Daily Language Activity

When students enter the classroom, have this assignment on the board: *Write examples of a statement, a question, and a command.*

See also *Daily Language Practice*

Motivating Activity

Have volunteers write their sentences from the Bellringer activity on the board. Ask students to find the subject and predicate in each. Classmates should evaluate the responses and suggest changes as needed.

Teach

Critical Thinking

On the board, write the sentence *Robinson sometimes wrote in a diary while stranded on the island.* Tell students that when sentences follow normal word order, the complete subject comes before the complete predicate. Then have students move a word or phrase from the predicate to the beginning of the sentence: *Sometimes Robinson wrote . . .;* or *While stranded on the island, Robinson sometimes wrote…* Encourage students to ask questions for clarification, as needed.

Resource Manager

Planning Resources
- *Lesson Plans*

Transparencies
- *Bellringer*
- *Daily Language Practice*

Other Print Resources
- *Grammar and Composition Handbook*
- *Grammar Enrichment,* p. 3
- *Grammar Practice,* p. 3
- *Grammar Reteaching,* p. 4
- *Grammar Workbook,* Lesson 4

Practice and Assess

Answers: Exercise 7

1. <u>Robinson</u> built a house.
2. <u>The goats on the island</u> provided fresh milk.
3. <u>Robinson</u> planted corn on the island.
4. <u>The stranded man</u> carved a canoe out of a tree.
5. <u>The weather</u> was favorable.

Answers: Exercise 8

1. subj.: a parrot
2. subj.: Many years
3. subj.: the time
4. subj.: Robinson
5. subj.: (You)
6. subj.: animal skins
7. subj.: He
8. subj.: a man
9. subj.: (You)
10. subj.: the unfortunate man
11. subj.: (You)
12. subj.: Robinson
13. subj.: Defoe
14. subj.: He
15. subj.: Selkirk
16. subj.: (You)
17. subj.: Robinson Crusoe
18. subj.: England
19. subj.: Defoe
20. subj.: Many young people

Additional Resources

📁 *Grammar Practice*, p. 3
📁 *Grammar Reteaching*, p. 4
📁 *Grammar Enrichment*, p. 3

📖 *Grammar Workbook*, Lesson 4

Close

Have each student write a sentence with inverted word order, either a question or a statement. Students can then exchange papers and rewrite the sentences in normal word order. Partners should check each other's work and discuss any needed changes.

| Exercise 7 | Rewriting Questions as Statements |

Rewrite each question as a statement. Underline each complete subject.

1. Did Robinson build a house?
2. Did the goats on the island provide fresh milk?
3. Did Robinson plant corn on the island?
4. Did the stranded man carve a canoe out of a tree?
5. Was the weather favorable?

| Exercise 8 | Finding Subjects |

Write each sentence. Underline each subject. Write *(You)* before any sentence with an understood subject.

1. Did a parrot learn English from Robinson?
2. Many years passed before Robinson's rescue.
3. Did the time pass slowly without a clock?
4. Robinson explored every part of the island.
5. Read the last chapter for homework.
6. Do animal skins make good clothing?
7. He sent smoke signals from the top of a hill.
8. On the beach sat a man.
9. Tell me the ending of the story.
10. On the island waited the unfortunate man.
11. Describe how Robinson returns to London.
12. Did Robinson find his own footprint in the sand?
13. Defoe wrote the adventure almost three hundred years ago.
14. He based his story on a real person, Alexander Selkirk.
15. Selkirk survived four years on a deserted island.
16. Imagine having to survive by your wits.
17. Was Robinson Crusoe on the island twenty-four years?
18. England changed greatly in that time.
19. Defoe wrote his book for adults.
20. Many young people like the book too!

Subjects, Predicates, and Sentences

Exploring Language

Forming Questions with *Do*

English uses forms of *do* to form questions (*Did* I *see it?*) and for emphasis (I *did see it*). The *do* that makes questions is different from the *do* that indicates emphasis. When we turn a question that begins with *do* back into a statement, the *do* can disappear because there is no real need for it. For example, *Did I see it?* corresponds to two statements: *I saw it* and *I did see it.* Either is acceptable, but many writers would use the *did* version primarily where greater emphasis was required.

8.5 | Compound Subjects and Compound Predicates

Some sentences have more than one subject.

■ A **compound subject** has two or more subjects that have the same predicate. The subjects are joined by *and, or,* or *but.*

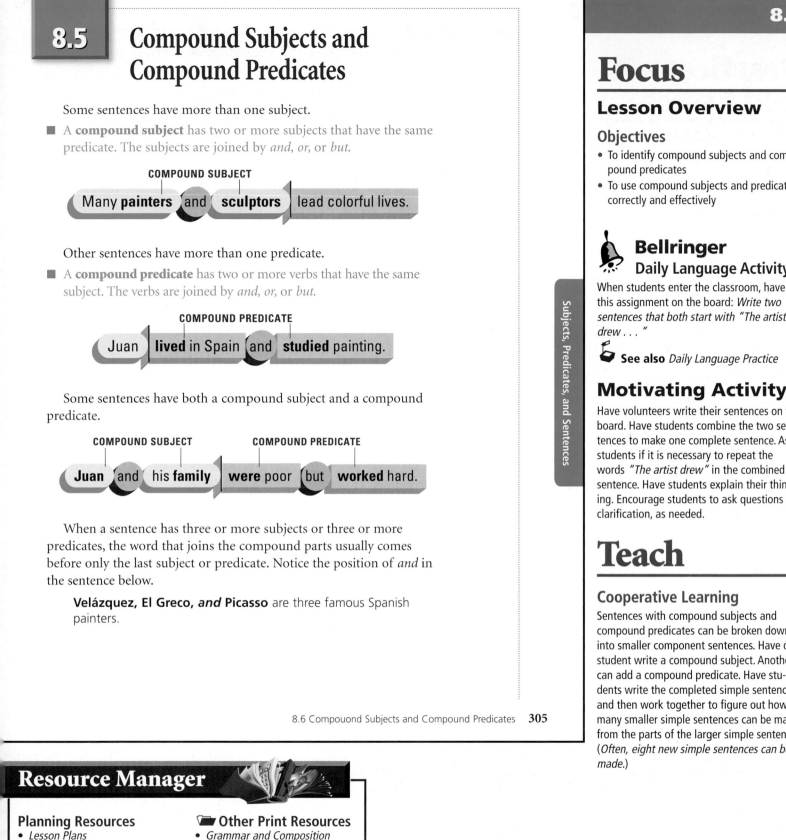

COMPOUND SUBJECT

Many **painters** and **sculptors** lead colorful lives.

Other sentences have more than one predicate.

■ A **compound predicate** has two or more verbs that have the same subject. The verbs are joined by *and, or,* or *but.*

COMPOUND PREDICATE

Juan **lived** in Spain and **studied** painting.

Some sentences have both a compound subject and a compound predicate.

COMPOUND SUBJECT   **COMPOUND PREDICATE**

Juan and his **family**   **were** poor but **worked** hard.

When a sentence has three or more subjects or three or more predicates, the word that joins the compound parts usually comes before only the last subject or predicate. Notice the position of *and* in the sentence below.

> **Velázquez, El Greco,** *and* **Picasso** are three famous Spanish painters.

Focus

Lesson Overview

Objectives
• To identify compound subjects and compound predicates
• To use compound subjects and predicates correctly and effectively

Bellringer
Daily Language Activity

When students enter the classroom, have this assignment on the board: *Write two sentences that both start with "The artist drew . . . "*

See also *Daily Language Practice*

Motivating Activity

Have volunteers write their sentences on the board. Have students combine the two sentences to make one complete sentence. Ask students if it is necessary to repeat the words *"The artist drew"* in the combined sentence. Have students explain their thinking. Encourage students to ask questions for clarification, as needed.

Teach

Cooperative Learning

Sentences with compound subjects and compound predicates can be broken down into smaller component sentences. Have one student write a compound subject. Another can add a compound predicate. Have students write the completed simple sentence and then work together to figure out how many smaller simple sentences can be made from the parts of the larger simple sentence. (*Often, eight new simple sentences can be made.*)

Subjects, Predicates, and Sentences

Practice and Assess

Answers: Exercise 9

1. comp. subj.: authors, artists
2. comp. pred.: researched, wrote
3. comp. pred.: studied, worked
4. comp. subj.: She, Juan; comp. pred.: knew, valued
5. comp. subj.: Illness, poverty
6. comp. subj.: monk, dog
7. comp. subj.: Juan, father; comp. pred.: loved, lacked
8. comp. subj.: Brushes, canvas, paint; pred.: were, cost
9. comp. pred.: left, looked
10. comp. pred.: missed, longed
11. comp. pred.: hired, paid
12. comp. pred.: did work, sleep
13. comp. pred.: left, traveled
14. comp. pred.: met, worked
15. comp. subj.: king, family
16. comp. subj.: painter, helper
17. comp. pred.: cured, won
18. comp. subj.: Juan, Velázquez; comp. pred.: traveled, studied
19. comp. pred.: have read, heard
20. comp. pred.: liked, made
21. comp. pred.: painted, showed
22. comp. subj.: portraits, portrait
23. comp. subj.: Infanta Margarita, maids, artist
24. comp. subj.: subject, composition, size
25. comp. pred.: showed, depicted

Additional Resources

📂 *Grammar Practice*, p. 4
📂 *Grammar Reteaching*, p. 5
📁 *Grammar Enrichment*, p. 4

📓 *Grammar Workbook*, Lesson 4

Close

Discuss with students why writers use compound subjects and compound predicates. (*to avoid repetitive sentences and make writing more interesting*) Have students jot down in their journal a reminder that summarizes the value of compound structures in writing.

Exercise 9   **Identifying Compound Subjects and Predicates**

For each sentence below, write the compound subject and compound predicate. Underline the compound subjects and circle the compound predicates.

1. Many authors and artists have varied interests.
2. Elizabeth Borton de Treviño researched and wrote the book *I, Juan de Pareja*.
3. She studied violin and worked at a newspaper.
4. She and Juan knew and valued hard work.
5. Illness and poverty made Juan very weak.
6. A monk and a dog nursed him back to health.
7. Young Juan and his father loved art but lacked money for art supplies.
8. Brushes, canvas, and paint were available but cost too much money for the family.
9. Juan left his hometown and looked for a job.
10. He missed his home but longed to be an artist.
11. A baker hired him but paid him very little.
12. Did Juan work in the bakery and sleep there too?
13. The boy left the bakery and traveled to Madrid.
14. Juan met an artist in Madrid and worked for him.
15. The king or his family often posed for the artist.
16. The painter and his helper worked well together.
17. Juan cured the king's sick dog and won a reward.
18. Juan and Velázquez traveled and studied together.
19. Have you read this book or heard about it?
20. King Philip IV of Spain liked Velázquez and made him the official court painter.
21. Velázquez painted people skillfully and showed the dignity and worth of each subject.
22. Sensitive portraits of ordinary people and a great portrait of Pope Innocent X are among Velázquez's well-known works.
23. The Infanta Margarita, her two maids, and the artist appear in Velázquez's famous painting *Las Meninas*.
24. The painting's subject, its composition, and its size were unique for the time.
25. Most paintings at that time showed people in formal poses and depicted important events.

Subjects, Predicates, and Sentences

MEETING INDIVIDUAL NEEDS   **English Language Learners**

Building Compounds

Students learning English may understand sentences with compound predicates more clearly if you read the component simple sentences: *Juan lived in Spain. Juan studied painting.* Ask the group to tell you how to make these two sentences into one with a compound predicate.

8.6 Simple, Compound, and Complex Sentences

A **compound sentence** is a sentence that contains two or more simple sentences. Each simple sentence in a compound sentence is called a **main clause.** A clause is a group of words containing a subject and a predicate.

COMPOUND SENTENCE

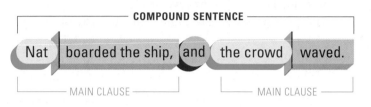

Nat | boarded the ship, (and) the crowd | waved.

MAIN CLAUSE — MAIN CLAUSE

Besides a main clause, some sentences have a **subordinate clause,** one that cannot stand alone as a sentence.

■ A **complex sentence** is a sentence that has one main clause and one or more subordinate clauses.

COMPLEX SENTENCES

The captain spoke to Nat, | who had boarded the ship.

Nat's adventures will thrill all | who read about them.

MAIN CLAUSE —— SUBORDINATE CLAUSE

When a subordinate clause is not necessary for the sentence to make sense, it is separated from the main clause by commas.

■ A **run-on sentence** is two or more sentences incorrectly written as one sentence. Notice the way run-on sentences may be corrected.

Correcting Run-on Sentences	
Run-on Sentences	**Corrected Sentences**
Nat boarded the ship the crowd waved.	Nat boarded the ship. **T**he crowd waved.
Nat boarded the ship, the crowd waved.	Nat boarded the ship**;** the crowd waved.
	Nat boarded the ship**, and** the crowd waved.

8.6 Simple, Compound, and Complex Sentences **307**

Subjects, Predicates, and Sentences

Focus

Lesson Overview

Objectives
• To identify and use simple, complex, and compound sentences
• To identify and correct run-on sentences in writing

Bellringer
Daily Language Activity

When students enter the classroom, have this assignment on the board: *Write down five different compound words.*

See also *Daily Language Practice*

Motivating Activity

Students might deepen their understanding by considering the meaning of *compound* in different contexts. A compound eye (the kind many insects have) is composed of many simple eyes. Ask students to explain what a compound word is (words, such as *hotline, ice cream,* or *cross-reference,* that are composed of two or more words). Similarly, a compound sentence is made up of two or more sentences.

Resource Manager

Planning Resources
• *Lesson Plans*

Transparencies
• *Bellringer*
• *Daily Language Practice*
• *Two-Minute Skill Drill*

Other Print Resources
• *Grammar and Composition Handbook*
• *Grammar Enrichment,* p. 5
• *Grammar Practice,* p. 5
• *Grammar Reteaching,* p. 6
• *Grammar Workbook,* Lesson 5

Practice and Assess

Answers: Exercise 10

1. simple	6. compound
2. compound	7. simple
3. simple	8. compound
4. compound	9. compound
5. simple	10. simple

Answers: Exercise 11

1. complex	6. simple
2. run-on	7. compound
3. run-on	8. complex
4. complex	9. compound
5. compound	10. compound

Two-Minute Skill Drill

Have students change the following sentences into one compound sentence:

The captain steered the ship.

The crew worked hard.

See also *Two-Minute Skill Drill Transparencies,* 8.6

Additional Resources

📁 *Grammar Practice,* p. 5
📁 *Grammar Reteaching,* p. 6
📁 *Grammar Enrichment,* p. 5

📓 *Grammar Workbook,* Lesson 5

Close

Have students look at the sentences in Exercise 10 and count the number of subjects and predicates in each one.

| **Exercise 10** | **Identifying Simple and Compound Sentences** |

Write whether each of the following sentences is *simple* or *compound.*

1. Nat and his family valued a good education.
2. His family had little money; he frequently worried about them.
3. The boy found a job and worked in a supply store for a while.
4. Nat read about sailing, or he studied mathematics.
5. Will Nat read about the stars, study navigation, and go to sea?
6. No teacher taught him, but Nat learned Spanish.
7. The boy sailed on a ship and worked as a navigator.
8. Sailors used charts of the stars, but Nat found errors in some of the measurements.
9. Nat taught the sailors mathematics, and the crew learned quickly.
10. He gathered information and wrote a book about navigation.

| **Exercise 11** | **Identifying Simple, Compound, Complex, and Run-on Sentences** |

Write whether each of the following sentences is *simple, compound, complex,* or *run-on.*

1. *The True Confessions of Charlotte Doyle* describes an adventure that takes place at sea.
2. Charlotte was brought up as a proper young lady she attended boarding school in England.
3. She returned to America her voyage to her home would not be an easy one.
4. Crew members wanted revenge on Captain Jaggery who had treated them cruelly.
5. Charlotte spoke to the captain; she told him about the planned mutiny.
6. Charlotte took responsibility and offered to help the crew.
7. The ship pitched and rolled in an awful storm, and the captain sent Charlotte aloft to fix a sail.
8. The captain who had killed his first mate accused Charlotte of the murder.
9. The crew thought Charlotte was guilty; they didn't lift a finger to save her.
10. How did Charlotte escape being hanged, and what did she do upon reaching America?

MEETING INDIVIDUAL NEEDS English Language Learners

Recognizing Compound Sentences

Students for whom English is a second language may need help in understanding the difference between a compound sentence and a run-on sentence. Write the following on the board: *Nat boarded the ship the crowd waved. Nat boarded the ship; the crowd waved. Nat boarded the ship, and the crowd waved.* Point out that each sentence expresses two complete thoughts. We use either a semicolon or a comma and a conjunction to join the thoughts. Discuss how punctuation between the thoughts makes reading a compound sentence easier.

UNIT 8 Grammar Review

SUBJECTS, PREDICATES, AND SENTENCES

In this passage from *A Tree Grows in Brooklyn*, it is 1912, and eleven-year-old Francie Nolan plans to read every book in her local library. The passage has been annotated to show some of the sentence elements and sentence structures covered in this unit.

Literature Model

from A Tree Grows in Brooklyn
by Betty Smith

Francie thought that all the books in the world were in that library and she had a plan about reading all the books in the world. She **was reading** a book a day in alphabetical order and not **skipping** the dry ones. She remembered that the first author had been Abbott. She had been reading a book a day for a long time now and she was still in the B's. Already **she** had read about bees and buffaloes, Bermuda vacations and Byzantine architecture. For all of her enthusiasm, she had to admit that some of the B's had been hard going. But Francie **was** a reader. She read everything she could find: trash, classics, time tables and the grocer's price list. **Some of the reading** had been wonderful; the Louisa Alcott books for example. She planned to read all the books over again when she had finished with the Z's.

Saturdays were different. She **treated herself by reading a book not in the alphabetical sequence. On that day she asked the librarian to recommend a book.**

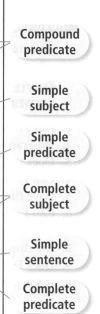

- Compound predicate
- Simple subject
- Simple predicate
- Complete subject
- Simple sentence
- Complete predicate

Teach

About the Literature

Explain that the Literature Model is a passage from Betty Smith's *A Tree Grows in Brooklyn*. After students have finished reading, use the passage to reinforce their understanding of simple subjects, complete subjects, simple predicates, and complete predicates. The exercises that follow are based on this passage and related topics.

Linking Grammar and Literature

☑ **Grammar Tip**

Some students may notice that the author fails to follow some of the rules covered in this unit: the first sentence lacks a comma before the conjunction; one sentence lacks a verb in the part following the semicolon. Emphasize that writers of fiction sometimes ignore grammar rules in order to serve some other purpose in their writing.

Critical Thinking

Ask students to think about what kind of person Francie is as you reread the passage aloud. Have students support their thoughts with details from the passage. (*She likes to read. She is interested in many different subjects. She is determined, organized, and systematic. She plans ahead. She hasn't seen libraries outside her neighborhood.*)

✔ **ASSESSMENT OPTIONS**

📁 *Tests with Answer Key and Rubrics* Unit 8 Mastery Test, pp. 35–36

💾 *Testmaker* Unit 8 Mastery Test

Resource Manager

Planning Resources
- *Lesson Plans*

📁 **Other Print Resources**
- *Grammar and Composition Handbook*
- *Grammar Workbook,* Lessons 1–7; Unit 1 Review

INTRODUCING

UNIT 9

Objectives

- To recognize and apply the rules of capitalization for common and proper nouns
- To demonstrate control over the spelling of singular and plural nouns
- To use verbs that agree in number with singular and plural collective nouns
- To punctuate and spell correctly various possessive nouns

Key to Ability Levels

L1 Level 1 activities are within the basic ability range of students.

L2 Level 2 activities are within the ability range of average students.

L3 Level 3 activities are more challenging activities.

UNIT 9 Nouns

318

Resource Manager

Planning Resources
- *Lesson Plans*
- *Block Scheduling*

📂 **Transparencies**
- *Bellringer*
- *Daily Language Practice*

📁 **Other Print Resources**
- *Grammar and Composition Handbook*

- *Grammar Enrichment*
- *Grammar Practice*
- *Grammar Reteaching*
- *Grammar Workbook*
- *Tests with Answer Key and Rubrics*

📹 **Video**
- *MindJogger Videoquizzes*

💾 **Software**
- *Interactive Grammar and Language Workbook*
- *Language Arts PASS*
- *Presentation Plus!*
- *Revising with Style*
- *Testmaker*

💻 **Web Sites**
- *writerschoice.glencoe.com*

9.1 Common and Proper Nouns

- A **noun** is a word that names a person, a place, a thing, or an idea.

Nouns	
Persons	brother, judge, athlete, teacher, mother-in-law
Places	neighborhood, county, city
Things	book, shoe, flower, pencil
Ideas	pride, skill, truth, democracy, success

There are two basic kinds of nouns: common nouns and proper nouns.

- A **common noun** names *any* person, place, thing, or idea.
- A **proper noun** names a *specific* person, place, thing, or idea.

A proper noun may consist of one or more words. You should always begin a proper noun with a capital letter. For proper nouns of more than one word, capitalize the first word and all other important words. Some examples of proper nouns are listed below.

	Common Noun	Proper Noun
People	actor	Chris O'Donnell
	singer	Mariah Carey
	athlete	Mia Hamm
Places	building	Tower of London
	city	Tucson
	river	Nile
Things	book	*Johnny Tremain*
	movie	*Peter Pan*
	song	"This Land Is Your Land"

Nouns

9.1 Common and Proper Nouns **319**

Focus

Lesson Overview

Objectives
- To identify common and proper nouns
- To demonstrate control over the rules of capitalization for proper nouns

🔔 Bellringer
Daily Language Activity

When students enter the classroom, have this assignment on the board: *List all of the nouns in the first paragraph of the passage from* Black Star, Bright Dawn *by Scott O'Dell, found on page 325.* Let students exchange papers to check each other's work.

See also *Daily Language Practice*

Teach

☑ Teaching Tip

Remind students that nouns usually follow the articles *a, an,* or *the* and that they can be either singular or plural. Tell them also that if the noun is not capitalized, it is most likely a common noun.

⇄ Cross-reference: Capitalizing

For instruction and practice in capitalizing proper nouns, refer students to Lessons 18.2–18.4, pp. 475–480.

Resource Manager

Planning Resources
- *Lesson Plans*

📀 **Transparencies**
- *Bellringer*
- *Daily Language Practice*

📁 **Other Print Resources**
- *Grammar and Composition Handbook*
- *Grammar Enrichment,* p. 6
- *Grammar Practice,* p. 6
- *Grammar Reteaching,* p. 7
- *Grammar Workbook,* Lesson 9

319

Practice and Assess

Answers: Exercise 1

1. Historians, origin, game, tennis, France
2. game, tennis, game
3. past, people, ball, hands, rackets
4. Walter Wingfield, game
5. Mr. Wingfield, form, tennis, century
6. game, lawn tennis
7. rackets, wood
8. people, aluminum, fiberglass
9. rackets, titanium
10. players, racket, games

Answers: Exercise 2

1. youngsters, people, tournaments—C
2. United States Tennis Association—P; contests, amateurs—C
3. matches, players—C; Great Britain, France, Australia—P
4. games—C; Wimbledon, England—P
5. teams, trophy—C; Davis Cup—P

Answers: Exercise 3

1. U.S. Open; Flushing Meadows, New York
2. U.S. Open; Grand Slam
3. French Open; British Open; Australian Open
4. Martina Navratilova
5. Martina; Wimbledon

Close

Have students write five common and five proper nouns. Have partners check each other's work.

Nouns

Exercise 1   Identifying Nouns

Write every noun that each sentence contains.

1. Historians trace the origin of the game of tennis to France.
2. The modern outdoor game of tennis probably evolved from an indoor game.
3. In the past, people hit the ball with their hands instead of rackets.
4. Walter Wingfield improved the game.
5. Mr. Wingfield patented his form of tennis more than a century ago.
6. Eventually the game became known as lawn tennis.
7. The first rackets were made of wood.
8. Later, people used aluminum or fiberglass.
9. Now some rackets are made of titanium.
10. Many players have a favorite racket they always use during important games.

Exercise 2   Identifying Common and Proper Nouns

Write each noun in the following sentences. Label the common nouns *C* and the proper nouns *P*.

1. Both youngsters and older people play in tournaments.
2. The United States Tennis Association sponsors contests for amateurs.
3. Matches for players also take place in Great Britain, France, and Australia.
4. The games at Wimbledon in England are very popular.
5. International teams compete for a special trophy, the Davis Cup.

Exercise 3   Using Proper Nouns

Write the proper nouns in each sentence. Use capital letters.

1. Many thousands of people attend the U.S. Open tournament in flushing meadows, new york, each year.
2. The u.s. open is one of four tournaments that are called the Grand Slam.
3. Players from all over the world also compete in the french open, the british open, and the australian open.
4. Martina navratilova was a top player for twenty years.
5. Before martina retired in 1994, she won many tournaments, in singles and doubles, but winning at Wimbledon was the most special.

MEETING INDIVIDUAL NEEDS   English Language Learners

Using Capital Letters

Some students—especially those who read or write a language such as German in which even common nouns begin with capital letters—may have difficulty with capitalization of nouns. Explain that in most cases only people's first, middle, and last names and the names of particular places are proper nouns and thus need to be capitalized.

9.2 Singular and Plural Nouns

A **singular noun** names one person, place, thing, or idea. A **plural noun** names more than one. To form the plural of most nouns, you simply add -s. Other plural nouns are formed in different ways.

Forming Plural Nouns		
Nouns Ending With	**To Form Plural**	**Examples**
-s, -ss, -zz, -ch, -sh, -x	Add **-es**.	bus buzz box bus**es** buzz**es** box**es**
-o, preceded by a vowel	Add **-s**.	cameo studio stereo cameo**s** studio**s** stereo**s**
-o, preceded by a consonant	Usually add **-es**.	hero potato echo hero**es** potato**es** echo**es**
	Sometimes add **-s**.	zero photo piano zero**s** photo**s** piano**s**
-y, preceded by a vowel	Add **-s**.	day donkey turkey day**s** donkey**s** turkey**s**
-y, preceded by a consonant	Usually change **-y** to **-i**, and add **-es**.	city dairy penny cit**ies** dair**ies** penn**ies**
-f or **-fe**	Usually change **-f** to **-v**, and add **-es**.	leaf life half lea**ves** li**ves** hal**ves**
	Sometimes add **-s**.	roof chief belief roof**s** chief**s** belief**s**

Words such as *family* and *team* are called collective nouns.

■ A **collective noun** names a group of people or things.

A collective noun can take either a singular or a plural verb, depending on how it is used. The noun is singular when all the members of the group act as a single unit. It is plural when each member of the group acts separately.

> The **team shares** the field with its opponent. [singular]
> The **team share** their jokes with each other. [plural]

Focus

Lesson Overview

Objectives
- To recognize and spell correctly various singular and plural nouns
- To identify collective nouns as singular or plural

Bellringer
Daily Language Activity

When students enter the classroom, have the following assignment on the board: *Correct any misspellings in the following sentence: Before the autumn leafs began to fall, I took photoes of donkies and fields of potatos and other things we don't see in the citys.*

See also *Daily Language Practice*

Teach

☑ Teaching Tip

The general rule is that a noun plural is formed by adding -s unless the noun stem ends in a sibilant, that is, a consonant with a hissing sound. (Some examples of sibilants are -s, -ss, -zz, -ch, -sh, or -x.) In the case of a sibilant, the plural ending is an extra syllable (-es) so that two hissing sounds do not come together. Compare, for example, *box* (which ends in a sibilant, -x) and its plural, *boxes* with *cat* (no sibilant) and its plural, *cats*.

Nouns *(side tab)*

Resource Manager

Planning Resources
- *Lesson Plans*

Transparencies
- *Bellringer*
- *Daily Language Practice*

Other Print Resources
- *Grammar and Composition Handbook*
- *Grammar Enrichment*, p. 7
- *Grammar Practice*, p. 7
- *Grammar Reteaching*, p. 8
- *Grammar Workbook*, Lessons 9–10

Practice and Assess

Answers: Exercise 4

1. stories
2. benches
3. spectators
4. heroes
5. themselves

Answers: Exercise 5

1. radishes
2. boxes
3. cherries
4. watches
5. countries
6. ants
7. bananas
8. horseshoes
9. loaves
10. valleys
11. bushes
12. buses *or* busses
13. babies
14. pianos
15. echoes
16. volcanoes
17. radios
18. selves
19. mosquitoes
20. knives

Answers: Exercise 6

1. club, S
2. team, S
3. group, P
4. committee, P
5. class, S
6. band, S
7. family, P
8. crowd, S
9. team, P
10. staff, P

Additional Resources

 Grammar Practice, p. 7
Grammar Reteaching, p. 8
Grammar Enrichment, p. 7

Grammar Workbook, Lessons 9–10

Close

Have students each write a paragraph about a favorite sport. Have them use plural and collective nouns.

Exercise 4 — Identifying Plural Noun Forms

Write the correct form of the noun in parentheses.

1. My father loves to tell funny baseball (stories, storys).
2. He said that at one game the first four (benchs, benches) in the stadium collapsed.
3. The (spectatores, spectators) crashed to the ground and were covered with mud, but no one was hurt!
4. The umpires were the (heros, heroes) at that game.
5. They interrupted the game so that the fans could clean (themselves, themselfs) off.

Exercise 5 — Forming Plural Nouns

Write the plural form of each singular noun.

1. radish
2. box
3. cherry
4. watch
5. country
6. ant
7. banana
8. horseshoe
9. loaf
10. valley
11. bush
12. bus
13. baby
14. piano
15. echo
16. volcano
17. radio
18. self
19. mosquito
20. knife

Exercise 6 — Identifying Collective Nouns

Write each collective noun and label it *S* for *singular* or *P* for *plural*. Pay close attention to the verb.

1. The volleyball club meets after school.
2. Each volleyball team has six players.
3. The group take their individual positions.
4. The committee discuss their reactions.
5. Our class watches the volleyball match.
6. The school band plays at every game.
7. Our family arrive at the stadium at different times.
8. The crowd is always friendly at the games.
9. The team share their feelings about each game at the end.
10. The coaching staff also meet after each game to discuss their strategies.

MEETING INDIVIDUAL NEEDS — English Language Learners

Nouns That Are Always Singular

Some students may have difficulty with the surprisingly large class of nouns in English that cannot be made plural. The names of some baking ingredients usually are not made plural: *flour, salt,* and *sugar.* We say or write *flour* and *salt,* for example, but not usually *flours* and *salts.*

Explain to the students that units of measure such as *cups* and *tablespoons* can be used with these nouns to show a specific quantity: **cups** of *flour* and **tablespoons** of *salt.*

9.3 Possessive Nouns

A noun that shows ownership or possession is called a **possessive noun.** Possessive nouns, like all nouns, can be singular or plural.

■ A possessive noun names who or what has something.

Notice the possessive nouns in the following sentences.

The World Cup is the amateur **skiers'** competition.
A prize is awarded for the outstanding **men's** achievement.
The **women's** division also awards a prize.

The following chart shows how to form possessives from singular and plural nouns.

Forming Possessive Nouns		
Nouns	**To Form Possessive**	**Examples**
Most singular nouns	Add an apostrophe and -*s* (*'s*).	Karen has new skis. Karen**'s** skis are new.
Singular nouns ending in -*s*	Add an apostrophe and -*s* (*'s*).	Chris got new skis last year. Chris**'s** skis are in the attic.
Plural nouns ending in -*s*	Add an apostrophe (*'*).	Many skiers wear goggles. The skiers**'** goggles are sturdy.
Plural nouns not ending in -*s*	Add an apostrophe and -*s* (*'s*).	The men have warm sweaters. The men**'s** sweaters are warm.

When you are writing, remember that possessive nouns always contain apostrophes. Plural nouns do not.

Distinguishing Between Possessive Nouns and Plural Nouns	
Singular possessive noun	Where is the **athlete's** school?
Plural possessive noun	Where is the **athletes'** school?
Plural noun	Where are the **athletes**?

Focus

Lesson Overview

Objectives
• To identify possessive nouns
• To punctuate and correctly spell possessive nouns

🔔 Bellringer
Daily Language Activity

When students enter the classroom, have this assignment on the board: *Add any needed apostrophes to the following sentence: Harrys dogs tail is always wagging.*

See also *Daily Language Practice*

Motivating Activity

Ask volunteers to explain why each apostrophe is needed in the Bellringer sentence. For example, the tail belongs to the dog, the dog belongs to the sister, and the sister is Harry's sister.

Teach

☑ Teaching Tip

Many students have great difficulty distinguishing between the plural and possessive -*s* in writing. When first beginning to use the apostrophe for possessive nouns, students often overgeneralize and use the apostrophe with plural nouns and possessive pronouns. Remind students that possessive pronouns, including *its,* are written without an apostrophe.

Nouns

Resource Manager

Planning Resources
• *Lesson Plans*

📑 **Transparencies**
• *Bellringer*
• *Daily Language Practice*

📁 **Other Print Resources**
• *Grammar and Composition Handbook*
• *Grammar Enrichment,* p. 8
• *Grammar Practice,* p. 8
• *Grammar Reteaching,* p. 9
• *Grammar Workbook,* Lesson 11

Practice and Assess

Answers: Exercise 7

1. amateurs', P
2. skier's, S
3. entrants', P
4. skiers', P
5. committee's, S

Answers: Exercise 8

1. sport's   6. skis'
2. person's   7. soldier's
3. skier's   8. Norwegian's
4. skiers'   9. men's
5. historian's   10. Koch's

Answers: Exercise 9

1. woman's, women's
2. Ms. Smith's, the Smiths'
3. child's, children's
4. senior's, seniors'
5. family's, families'

Additional Resources

📁 *Grammar Practice*, p. 8
📁 *Grammar Reteaching*, p. 9
📁 *Grammar Enrichment*, p. 8

📓 *Grammar Workbook*, Lesson 11

Close

Ask students to imagine that they are all watching a skiing exhibition. Have them each write a paragraph describing the skiing events. Remind them to include possessive nouns, both singular and plural.

324

Nouns

Exercise 7 Identifying Possessive Nouns

Write each possessive noun and label it *S* for *singular* or *P* for *plural*.

1. The *Fédération Internationale du Ski* is an amateurs' organization.
2. The World Ski Championships are a skier's goal.
3. A committee reviews all entrants' applications.
4. It considers skiers' qualifications for the races.
5. The committee's guidelines for amateur status are very strict.

Exercise 8 Using Singular and Plural Possessives

Write the possessive form of the noun in parentheses.

1. The (sport) history began thousands of years ago.
2. Each (person) skis were made of animal bone.
3. Leather straps held the (skier) boots to the skis.
4. Many (skiers) toe straps came loose.
5. One (historian) discoveries include skis from Sweden.
6. The (skis) ages ranged from 2,500 to 5,000 years.
7. In Norway a (soldier) means of travel was skiing.
8. A (Norwegian) skis were for both cross-country and downhill skiing.
9. The (men) cross-country speed record was broken by Bill Koch.
10. (Koch) average speed was 15.57 miles per hour.

Exercise 9 Forming Possessive Nouns

Copy and complete the chart, adding the possessive forms.

SINGULAR NOUN	SINGULAR POSSESSIVE	PLURAL NOUN	PLURAL POSSESSIVE
1. woman		women	
2. Ms. Smith		the Smiths	
3. child		children	
4. senior		seniors	
5. family		families	

English Language Learners

Identifying Possessive Nouns

Students whose primary language is not English may be accustomed to forming possessives in other ways. (In Spanish, possessives can be expressed by *de*, meaning *of*, plus a proper noun.) A good way for students to check whether a noun is possessive is to try using the noun in a *whose* question. For example, in the sentence *Karen's boots are new*, *Karen's* is possessive because we can ask, "*Whose* boots are new?" We then receive the possessive noun answer, "*Karen's.*" Only possessive nouns can be used in *whose* questions.

UNIT 9 Grammar Review

NOUNS

Black Star, Bright Dawn by Scott O'Dell is about a young Inuit woman named Bright Dawn who enters the Iditarod, a sled dog race. The race covers more than a thousand snow-covered miles between Anchorage and Nome, Alaska. The passage below shows some of the kinds of nouns covered in this unit.

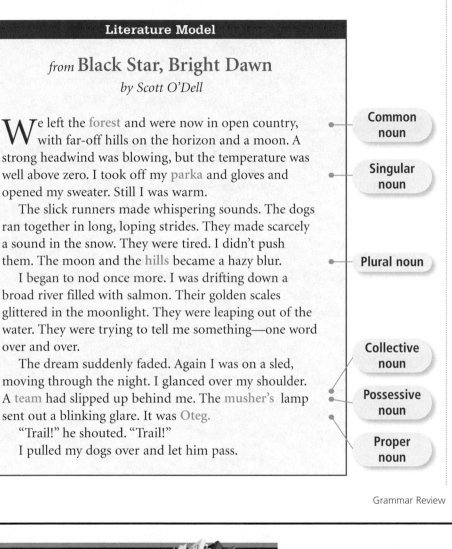

Literature Model

from Black Star, Bright Dawn
by Scott O'Dell

We left the forest and were now in open country, with far-off hills on the horizon and a moon. A strong headwind was blowing, but the temperature was well above zero. I took off my parka and gloves and opened my sweater. Still I was warm.

The slick runners made whispering sounds. The dogs ran together in long, loping strides. They made scarcely a sound in the snow. They were tired. I didn't push them. The moon and the hills became a hazy blur.

I began to nod once more. I was drifting down a broad river filled with salmon. Their golden scales glittered in the moonlight. They were leaping out of the water. They were trying to tell me something—one word over and over.

The dream suddenly faded. Again I was on a sled, moving through the night. I glanced over my shoulder. A team had slipped up behind me. The musher's lamp sent out a blinking glare. It was Oteg.

"Trail!" he shouted. "Trail!"

I pulled my dogs over and let him pass.

Common noun

Singular noun

Plural noun

Collective noun

Possessive noun

Proper noun

Grammar Review **325**

Nouns

Teach

About the Literature

Explain that the review contains a passage by Scott O'Dell, followed by exercises on related topics. Focus students' attention and have the passage read aloud. After students have listened to the passage, discuss the author's use of nouns. Ask: *How do specific nouns, such as* headwind *for wind or* parka *for coat help the reader picture the scene?*

In his book *Black Star, Bright Dawn,* writer Scott O'Dell succeeded in making the reader aware of both the ecstasy and the pain this teenager experiences as she races her dog team across a brutal land.

Linking Grammar and Literature

☑ **Teaching Tip**

Remind students that the nouns in the passage name a person, place, thing, or idea. Ask students to read each noun—both common and proper—and tell whether it names a person, a place, a thing, or an idea.

Critical Thinking

Students can compare and contrast Scott O'Dell's writing with that of another author. Suggest that they find a passage from a magazine or newspaper article. Tell them to circle all the nouns. Ask: *Are the nouns specific? Do they help create a picture in the reader's mind?* Have students explain their thinking.

> ### ✔ ASSESSMENT OPTIONS
>
> 📁 *Tests with Answer Key and Rubrics*
> Unit 9 Mastery Test, pp. 39–40
>
> 💾 *Testmaker*
> Unit 9 Mastery Test

Resource Manager

Planning Resources
• *Lesson Plans*

📁 **Other Print Resources**
• *Grammar and Composition Handbook*
• *Grammar Workbook,* Lessons 8–11; Unit 2 Review; Cumulative Review: Units 1–2

Practice and Assess

Answers: Exercise 1

1. Anchorage . . . Gulf of Alaska . . . Nome . . . Bering Sea
2. Inuit . . . Alaska's . . . wilderness
3. Bright Dawn . . . landscape
4. salmon . . . river
5. racer . . . Oteg

Answers: Exercise 2

1. Alaska
2. Nome
3. Iditarod
4. Bright Dawn
5. Black Star

Nouns

Review: Exercise 1   Using Common Nouns

Rewrite each sentence, correcting the capitalization of common and proper nouns.

SAMPLE   Bright Dawn chose her dog black star to lead her Team of dogs in the iditarod.

ANSWER   Bright Dawn chose her dog Black Star to lead her team of dogs in the Iditarod.

1. The team raced from anchorage on the gulf of alaska to nome on the bering sea.
2. The temperature rose as the inuit woman mushed across alaska's lonely, open Wilderness.
3. As bright dawn raced over the moonlit Landscape, she became sleepy.
4. Bright Dawn dreamed of golden Salmon leaping from a broad River.
5. A Racer named oteg, who had befriended the young woman, woke her.

Review: Exercise 2   Using Proper Nouns

Replace the underlined words with proper nouns. Use the information and the literature model on page 325 to help you.

SAMPLE   An author wrote *Black Star, Bright Dawn*.
ANSWER   Scott O'Dell wrote *Black Star, Bright Dawn*.

1. The state is cold for much of the year.
2. The race was between Anchorage and another city.
3. The race is one of the most dangerous races in the world.
4. The girl was in danger of freezing to death.
5. Her dog led the team.

Review: Exercise 3   Forming Plural Nouns

Write the plural form of the noun in parentheses.

SAMPLE   The real (hero) of the Iditarod are the dogs.
ANSWER   The real heroes of the Iditarod are the dogs.

1. (Husky) are the dogs most often used to pull sleds.
2. The (life) of these animals are devoted to the sport.
3. Their (reflex) are quick, and their strength is amazing.
4. They usually race over flat ground rather than hills or (valley).
5. During the Iditarod, newspapers run many (photo) of these dogs and the sleds they pull.

Review: Exercise 4   Using Collective Nouns

Write the correct form of the verb in parentheses.

SAMPLE   Bright Dawn's family (lives, live) in its home in the small village of Womengo.
ANSWER   lives

1. Her family (perform, performs) their daily activities.
2. At school Bright Dawn's class (studies, study) its English lesson.
3. A team of dogs (helps, help) its owner, Bright Dawn's father, hunt for food.
4. The team (scatters, scatter) in different directions when he drifts toward the sea on an ice floe.
5. A group of men (does, do) its best to save him.
6. Bright Dawn's family (are, is) supportive of one another.
7. Because of the difficult journey, the team (was, were) tired.
8. The team of dogs (struggle, struggles) on, listening for Bright Dawn's words of support.
9. Another group (pull, pulls) its sled in front of Bright Dawn.
10. The crowd (was, were) surprised when it saw the winner was Bright Dawn.

Nouns

Answers: Exercise 3

1. Huskies
2. lives
3. reflexes
4. valleys
5. photos

Answers: Exercise 4

1. perform
2. studies
3. helps
4. scatter
5. does
6. are
7. was
8. struggles
9. pulls
10. was

Answers: Exercise 5

1. men's
2. dog's
3. Oteg's
4. woman's
5. parents'

Answers: Exercise 6

Sentences will vary, but the correct possessive forms are given below.

1. dog's
2. women's
3. class's
4. groups'
5. man's
6. skiers'
7. snow's
8. crowd's
9. teams'
10. sleds'
11. Alaska's
12. winners'
13. sport's
14. wilderness's
15. race's
16. bear's
17. village's
18. doctors'
19. families'
20. journey's
21. newspapers'
22. river's
23. hills'
24. moonlight's
25. wolves'

Nouns

Review: Exercise 5　**Forming Possessive Nouns**

Write each possessive noun correctly.

SAMPLE　Bright Dawns father encouraged her to enter the race.
ANSWER　Bright Dawn's

1. The mens faces looked doubtful when the young woman announced she would compete.
2. Bright Dawn depended on her one lead dogs guidance.
3. Otegs advice also helped her during the race.
4. The young womans lead was erased when she stopped to help other mushers.
5. Her parents eyes teared when Bright Dawn won.

Review: Exercise 6　**Using Singular and Plural Possessive Nouns**

Write a sentence using each of the following nouns in the possessive form shown in parentheses.

SAMPLE　team (singular possessive)
ANSWER　The team's owner is Bright Dawn.

1. dog (singular possessive)
2. woman (plural possessive)
3. class (singular possessive)
4. group (plural possessive)
5. man (singular possessive)
6. skier (plural possessive)
7. snow (singular possessive)
8. crowd (singular possessive)
9. team (plural possessive)
10. sled (plural possessive)
11. Alaska (singular possessive)
12. winner (plural possessive)
13. sport (singular possessive)
14. wilderness (singular possessive)
15. race (singular possessive)
16. bear (singular possessive)
17. village (singular possessive)
18. doctor (plural possessive)
19. family (plural possessive)
20. journey (singular possessive)
21. newspaper (plural possessive)
22. river (singular possessive)
23. hill (plural possessive)
24. moonlight (singular possessive)
25. wolf (plural possessive)

Review: Exercise 7

Proofreading

The following passage is about artist Rockwell Kent, whose work appears on this page. Rewrite the passage, correcting the errors in spelling, capitalization, grammar, and usage. Add any missing punctuation marks. There are ten errors.

Rockwell Kent

[1]Rockwell Kent (1882–1971) was an important american book illustrator and landscape painter. [2]Many of his paintings depicts the open sea rugged mountains, and coastlines'. [3]Kent used these scenes to convey peoples lonelyness.

Rockwell Kent, *The Expedition*

(continued)

Nouns

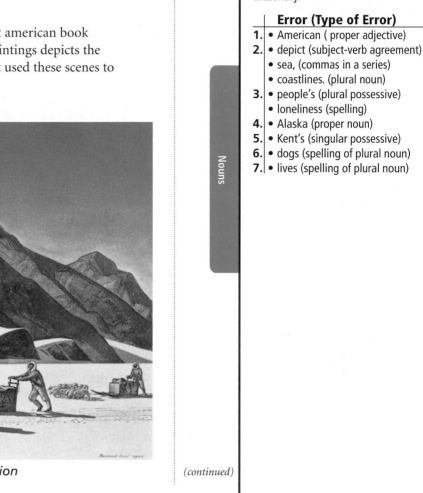

Answers: Exercise 7

Proofreading

This proofreading activity provides editing practice with (1) the current or previous units' skills, (2) the **Troubleshooter** errors, and (3) spelling errors. Students should be able to complete the exercise by referring to the units, the **Troubleshooter,** and a dictionary.

	Error (Type of Error)
1.	• American (proper adjective)
2.	• depict (subject-verb agreement)
	• sea, (commas in a series)
	• coastlines. (plural noun)
3.	• people's (plural possessive)
	• loneliness (spelling)
4.	• Alaska (proper noun)
5.	• Kent's (singular possessive)
6.	• dogs (spelling of plural noun)
7.	• lives (spelling of plural noun)

Viewing the Art

Rockwell Kent, *The Expedition*

Rockwell Kent (1892–1971) was first paid for doing fanciful letters and decorative borders at age 15. He was also a writer. He wrote this about his year in Alaska with his son: "The steel-sharp, bitter nights, the vast and heartless depths of space that they revealed, enhanced the warmth and comfort of our cabin. There we would sit, we two, the only living beings, so it seemed, in all the universe." Kent is known for his illustrations of such books as *Candide* and *Moby Dick* and for an edition of Shakespeare's works.

Answers: Exercise 8

Mixed Review

1. people—common, plural
2. Appalachian Trail—proper, singular
3. campers'—common, plural, possessive
4. camper's—common, singular, possessive
5. Berkshire Mountains—proper, plural
6. night's—common, singular, possessive
7. stores'—common, plural, possessive
8. Tents—common, plural
9. tent's—common, singular, possessive
10. class—common, singular
11. Midwest—proper, singular
12. grade—common, singular
13. buses'—common, plural, possessive
14. classes—common, plural
15. West Middle School's—proper, singular, possessive

Close

Ask students to write three sentences describing a recent sports event. Working with partners, students should list each noun and identify it as common or proper, singular or plural, and possessive if it shows ownership.

[4]The artist visited alaska in 1918 and was inspired by the vast spaces near the Arctic Circle. [5]Kents' experiences resulted in *The Expedition*. [6]The painting, which depicts figures guiding their dogs' and sleds, could be an illustration for *Black Star, Bright Dawn*. [7]It's easy to imagine the lifes of these people.

Review: Exercise 8

Mixed Review

Write all the underlined nouns. Label each one *common* or *proper*, *singular* or *plural*, and *possessive* if it shows ownership.

SAMPLE   Hikers respect natural resources.
ANSWER   Hikers – common, plural

1. <u>People</u> hike on paths and trails across America.
2. The <u>Appalachian Trail</u> goes through fourteen states.
3. The <u>campers'</u> gear must be light enough to be carried on their backs.
4. Storms are the <u>camper's</u> worst fear.
5. My family hikes in the <u>Berkshire Mountains</u> in Massachusetts.
6. Sleeping bags help provide a good <u>night's</u> sleep for a camper.
7. Many camping <u>stores'</u> supplies are limited.
8. <u>Tents</u> protect campers from rain and wind.
9. A <u>tent's</u> usefulness depends on many factors.
10. Next year my <u>class</u> is going on a trip to the Rocky Mountains.
11. We plan to travel by bus across the <u>Midwest</u>.
12. The seventh <u>grade</u> will go too.
13. The <u>buses'</u> seats will be filled with suitcases.
14. The <u>classes</u> are looking forward to the trip.
15. To raise money, we have established <u>West Middle School's</u> Dog and Car Wash.

Writing Application

Nouns in Writing

In her book *Keepers and Creatures at the National Zoo*, Peggy Thomson describes zookeeper Kathy Wallace's daily routine. In the passage below, the author describes the care of an elephant's feet. Examine the passage, paying special attention to the italicized nouns.

> *Watchers* from the *railing* can't see the foot up close. They see the *probings* with the *pick* or with the point of the *ankus*. They see *Kathy* using both *hands* on a *drawknife* to cut away a *slice* of leathery, rubbery pad and then another. (It doesn't hurt the elephant.) And they hear the *thunk* of the slice into her *bucket*.

Techniques with Nouns

When you write and revise your own work, try to use nouns in some of the ways Peggy Thomson does.

❶ Whenever possible, replace general words with precise concrete nouns.

GENERAL WORDS thing, tool

THOMSON'S VERSION pick, ankus, drawknife

❷ To identify people clearly in your writing, use proper nouns or specific common nouns.

GENERAL WORDS woman, people

THOMSON'S VERSION Kathy, watchers

❸ Whenever possible, expand single common nouns into longer word groups that create images of details.

SINGLE NOUNS noise, sound

THOMSON'S VERSION the thunk of the slice into her bucket

TIME

For more about making good word choices, see **TIME Facing the Blank Page,** pages 96–97.

Practice

Practice the techniques with nouns by revising the following passage. Use a separate sheet of paper. Pay particular attention to the underlined words.

On one <u>day,</u> <u>our teacher</u> took <u>our class</u> to a <u>zoo</u>. We took our school <u>things</u> and our <u>food</u>. The purpose of the <u>visit</u> was to study and compare the eating habits of different <u>animals</u>. A <u>person</u> from the <u>place</u> first led us to the monkey <u>place</u>. A <u>man</u> fed the <u>animals</u>. They peeled the <u>food</u> and ate as they swayed from one <u>place</u> to another. Then we went to observe the big <u>cats</u>. Lunchtime in their <u>place</u> was quite different. They were serious as they tore apart their <u>food</u>. These <u>animals</u> were not thinking about play. Later we ate our own <u>food</u>.

Nouns in Writing

Have students read the passage from *Keepers and Creatures at the National Zoo* silently. Then go back and discuss the italicized noun choices in relation to Techniques with Nouns below.

Techniques with Nouns

Discuss Peggy Thomson's use of precise, concrete nouns. Then ask students to look at sentence 4 in the proofreading practice on page 330. As an example of expanding common nouns, point out the writer's use of the expression *vast spaces near the Arctic Circle* instead of *scenery*.

Practice

The answers to this challenging and enriching activity will vary. Refer to Techniques with Nouns as you evaluate student choices.

✔ ASSESSMENT OPTIONS

📁 *Tests with Answer Key and Rubrics*
Unit 9 Mastery Test, pp. 39–40

💾 *Testmaker*
Unit 9 Mastery Test

You may wish to administer the Unit 9 Mastery Test at this point.

📼 *Mindjogger Videoquizzes*

Objectives

- To understand action verbs, linking verbs, and helping verbs
- To understand verb tenses
- To recognize regular and irregular verb formations
- To demonstrate control of the use of verbs in writing

✔ ASSESSMENT OPTIONS

📁 *Tests with Answer Key and Rubrics*
Unit 10 Pretest, pp. 41–42
Unit 10 Mastery Test, pp. 43–44

💾 *Testmaker*
Unit 10 Pretest
Unit 10 Mastery Test

You may wish to administer the Unit 10 Pretest at this point.

Key to Ability Levels

L1 Level 1 activities are within the basic ability range of students.

L2 Level 2 activities are within the ability range of average students.

L3 Level 3 activities are more challenging activities.

UNIT 10 Verbs

332

Resource Manager

📁 Planning Resources
- *Lesson Plans*
- *Block Scheduling*

🖐 Transparencies
- *Bellringer*
- *Daily Language Practice*
- *Two-Minute Skill Drill*

📁 Other Print Resources
- *Grammar and Composition Handbook*
- *Grammar Enrichment*
- *Grammar Practice*
- *Grammar Reteaching*
- *Grammar Workbook*
- *Tests with Answer Key and Rubrics*

📼 Video
- *MindJogger Videoquizzes*

💾 Software
- *Interactive Grammar and Language Workbook*
- *Language Arts PASS*
- *Presentation Plus!*
- *Testmaker*

🖥 Web Sites
- *writerschoice.glencoe.com*

10.1 Action Verbs and Direct Objects

There are two main kinds of verbs: action verbs and linking verbs. Action verbs tell what the subject does.

- An **action verb** names an action. It may contain more than one word.

Jay **has visited** Africa.

ACTION VERB

ACTION VERB

An action verb is often followed by a noun that receives the action of the verb. This noun is called the direct object. In the sentence above, the noun *Africa* is the direct object of the verb *has visited.*

- A **direct object** receives the action of a verb. It answers the question *whom?* or *what?* after an action verb.

what?

Sightseers paid the **fees.**

DIRECT OBJECT

Not all action verbs take direct objects.

- A **transitive** verb has a direct object.
- An **intransitive** verb does not have a direct object.

You must examine how an action verb is used in a sentence to determine whether it is transitive or intransitive. Some verbs can be used both ways.

> Sheila **read** a book about Africa. [transitive]
> Sheila **read** in a great hurry. [intransitive]

Verbs

Focus

Lesson Overview

Objectives
- To identify action verbs and direct objects
- To demonstrate an ability to use action verbs and direct objects in a sentence

Bellringer
Daily Language Activity

When students enter the classroom, have this assignment on the board: *Write a verb that names an action for each of the following sentences:*

1. *The hikers _____ the river to reach the other bank.*
2. *The cautious squirrels _____ the hikers as they came ashore.*

☛ **See also** *Daily Language Practice*

Motivating Activity

Discuss the verbs that students wrote in the Bellringer sentences, and ask what nouns receive the action of the verbs. Encourage students to ask questions for clarification.

Teach

☑ Teaching Tip

Explain to students that most verbs in English are action verbs. The term *action* is used in its broadest sense. In the following sentence, for example, the verb expresses mental action: *Sam forgot the meeting.* In this sentence the direct object of *forgot* is *meeting*—the noun that receives the action of the verb.

Resource Manager

Planning Resources
- *Lesson Plans*

🗐 Transparencies
- *Bellringer*
- *Daily Language Practice*

🗁 Other Print Resources
- *Grammar and Composition Handbook*
- *Grammar Enrichment,* p. 9
- *Grammar Practice,* p. 9
- *Grammar Reteaching,* p. 10
- *Grammar Workbook,* Lesson 12

Practice and Assess

Answers: Exercise 1

1. divides, <u>Africa</u>
2. create, <u>oases</u>
3. can travel
4. cross, <u>dunes</u>
5. shines
6. transport, <u>goods</u>
7. flows
8. build, <u>homes</u>
9. border, <u>Sahara</u>
10. grow
11. roam, <u>grasslands</u>
12. graze
13. tend, <u>cattle</u>
14. grow, <u>coffee</u>
15. falls
16. visit, <u>jungles</u>
17. established, <u>colonies</u>
18. crossed, <u>Mediterranean Sea</u>
19. hunted, <u>elephants</u>
20. sought, <u>gold</u>
21. won, <u>independence</u>
22. explore
23. study, <u>gorillas</u>
24. protect, <u>wildlife</u>
25. raise, <u>livestock</u>

Answers: Exercise 2

Answers will vary. A sample is given:
I <u>told</u> my (story) to the class.

Additional Resources

📁 *Grammar Practice*, p. 9
📁 *Grammar Reteaching*, p. 10
📁 *Grammar Enrichment*, p. 9

📖 *Grammar Workbook*, Lesson 12

Close

Discuss the sentences students wrote for Exercise 2. Ask students to identify the transitive and intransitive verbs in their sentences as well as any direct objects.

Exercise 1   Identifying Action Verbs and Direct Objects

For the sentences below, write each action verb. If the verb has a direct object, write it and underline it.

1. The equator divides Africa in two.
2. Streams and wells create oases in the desert.
3. Camels can travel in the desert for days without water.
4. Not even cars cross the sand dunes.
5. In the eastern Sahara, the sun shines for thousands of hours every year.
6. Boats transport goods down the Nile River.
7. In flat regions the Nile River flows slowly.
8. Many people build their homes in the Nile Valley.
9. Grasslands border the Sahara on the south.
10. Bushes and small trees grow in the grasslands.
11. Wild animals roam the grasslands of Central Africa.
12. Large herds of cattle graze on the grasslands.
13. Herders tend the cattle.
14. African farmers grow coffee.
15. Much rain falls in the tropical forests.
16. Many tourists visit the jungles.
17. Europeans established colonies in Africa.
18. Explorers crossed the Mediterranean Sea for riches.
19. Others hunted elephants for their ivory tusks.
20. Miners sought gold under the ground.
21. African ethnic groups later won their independence.
22. Anthropologists explore for evidence of early peoples.
23. Scientists study gorillas in remote forests.
24. Game parks protect wildlife.
25. Northern Africans raise livestock.

Exercise 2   Writing Action Verbs

Write five brief sentences about yourself. Use an action verb in each sentence. Underline the action verb. If the verb has a direct object, circle the direct object.

SAMPLE ANSWER   I <u>eat</u> a big (breakfast.)

Verbs

English Language Learners

MEETING INDIVIDUAL NEEDS

Transitive Verbs

To help students learning English determine whether a verb has a direct object, have them identify the simple subject and simple predicate in sentences. Have students use these parts with *what* and *whom* to form questions. If they can answer the questions, then there is a direct object and the verb is transitive. For example, *Camels travel across deserts. Camels travel what?* (can't answer) *Camels travel whom?* (can't answer) The verb is intransitive. *Many tourists visit the desert. Tourists visit what?* (the desert) This verb is transitive.

10.2 Indirect Objects

A direct object answers the question *whom?* or *what?* after an action verb. In the sentence below, the direct object is *Egypt. Egypt* answers the question *what?* after the action verb *visited.*

Rachel visited **Egypt** last year.

An action verb may also have an indirect object.

■ An **indirect object** answers the question *to whom?* or *for whom?* the action was done.

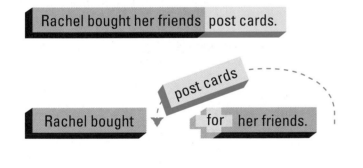

what?

Sightseers paid the **guides** fees.

to whom?

INDIRECT OBJECT

The direct object in the sentence above is *fees.* It answers the question *what?* after the action verb *paid.* The indirect object is *guides. Guides* answers the question *to whom?* after the action verb.

Indirect objects appear only in sentences that have a direct object. Two clues will help you identify indirect objects. First, the indirect object always comes before the direct object. Second, if you add the word *to* or *for* in front of the indirect object, the sentence still makes sense.

Rachel bought her friends post cards.

post cards

Rachel bought for her friends.

Verbs

Focus

Lesson Overview

Objectives
- To recognize both direct and indirect objects in sentences
- To use the objective case appropriately in writing

Bellringer
Daily Language Activity

When students enter the classroom, have this assignment on the board: *Complete each sentence, writing a word that tells to whom the action was done:*
His aunt sent _____ a birthday gift.
He wrote _____ a thank-you note.

See also *Daily Language Practice*

Motivating Activity

Discuss the Bellringer sentences. Explain that the words students have filled in are indirect objects and the words that end the sentences are direct objects. Ask students to explain the difference between the direct objects and indirect objects in these sentences.

Teach

☑ Teaching Tips

Explain that indirect objects are often used with verbs of telling, asking, and giving. Indirect objects name the receiver of the message, question, or gift.

⬦ Cross-reference: Grammar

For instruction and practice with object pronouns, refer students to Lesson 11.2, pp. 363–364.

Resource Manager

Planning Resources
- *Lesson Plans*

Transparencies
- *Bellringer*
- *Daily Language Practice*

📁 **Other Print Resources**
- *Grammar and Composition Handbook*
- *Grammar Enrichment*, p. 10
- *Grammar Practice*, p. 10
- *Grammar Reteaching*, p. 11
- *Grammar Workbook*, Lesson 13

Practice and Assess

Answers: Exercise 3

1. IO	11. IO
2. IO	12. DO
3. DO	13. IO
4. DO	14. DO
5. DO	15. DO
6. DO	16. IO
7. IO	17. IO
8. IO	18. DO
9. DO	19. DO
10. IO	20. DO

Answers: Exercise 4

1. soil, <u>farmers</u>
2. homes, <u>themselves</u>
3. bread, <u>children</u>
4. letters, <u>relatives</u>
5. food, <u>Egyptians</u>

Additional Resources

📂 *Grammar Practice,* p. 10
📂 *Grammar Reteaching,* p. 11
📂 *Grammar Enrichment,* p. 10

📖 *Grammar Workbook,* Lesson 13

Close

Students have learned to identify indirect objects by changing them into prepositional phrases. Make sure they understand this relationship by having them reverse the process, changing prepositional phrases into indirect objects in sentences such as these: *The coach told her funniest story to the team. The principal gave his usual speech for the visitors.*

Verbs

Exercise 3   **Distinguishing Between Direct and Indirect Objects**

Write whether the underlined word is a *direct object* or an *indirect object*.

1. Egypt gives <u>tourists</u> lessons in history.
2. The pyramids show <u>visitors</u> life in the past.
3. Sculptors produced <u>statues</u> for tombs and temples.
4. Artists made decorative <u>objects</u> of pottery.
5. Archaeologists study the ancient <u>tombs</u>.
6. The tombs contain valuable historic <u>scrolls</u>.
7. The guide read the <u>tourists</u> the scrolls' messages.
8. Send <u>us</u> a map of Egypt.
9. We gave my parents a <u>cruise</u> on the Nile.
10. Artists gave the <u>pharaohs</u> beautiful golden objects.
11. The ruins offer <u>historians</u> facts about a culture of long ago.
12. Ancient Egyptians built <u>pyramids</u> for their pharaohs.
13. Government leaders gave the <u>people</u> guidance.
14. Instructors taught students <u>mathematics</u>.
15. Scribes taught composition <u>skills</u> to the boys.
16. Festivals gave <u>Egyptians</u> relaxation from work.
17. Musicians offered the <u>families</u> entertainment.
18. Governors sent the pharaoh <u>taxes</u>.
19. The people gave the priests their <u>obedience</u>.
20. People sail <u>barges</u> down the Nile.

Exercise 4   **Identifying Direct and Indirect Objects**

For each sentence, write the direct object. Then write and underline each indirect object.

1. The floodwaters of the Nile gave farmers rich soil.
2. Wealthy Egyptians built themselves beautiful homes.
3. Parents fed their children bread.
4. Some Egyptians wrote relatives letters.
5. Gardens and rivers gave the Egyptians food.

MEETING INDIVIDUAL NEEDS   **English Language Learners**

Direct Objects and Indirect Objects

Students learning English may have difficulty distinguishing between direct and indirect objects. Remind them that the indirect object always comes before the direct object. Providing practice with paraphrasing indirect objects as phrases that begin with *to* or *for* will help students to recognize indirect objects confidently.

10.3 Linking Verbs and Predicate Words

■ A **linking verb** connects the subject of a sentence with a noun or an adjective in the predicate.

Africa **is** a continent.

LINKING VERB

LINKING VERB

In the sentence above, the linking verb *is* connects *Africa*, the subject, with *continent*, a noun in the predicate. *Continent* is called a *predicate noun.*

■ A **predicate noun** is a noun that follows a linking verb and tells what the subject is.

■ A **predicate adjective** is an adjective that follows a linking verb and tells what the subject is like.

Predicate Nouns and Adjectives	
Predicate Noun	Zambia is a **country.**
Predicate Adjective	Zambia is **scenic.**

In the first sentence above, the predicate noun *country* renames the subject. In the second sentence, the predicate adjective *scenic* describes the same subject. Predicate nouns and predicate adjectives follow only linking verbs.

Some linking verbs can also be used as action verbs.

The farmer **grows** tired. [linking verb]
The farmer **grows** corn. [action verb]

Common Linking Verbs			
be	seem	feel	grow
become	appear	taste	look

10.3 Linking Verbs and Predicate Words   **337**

Verbs

Focus

Lesson Overview

Objectives
• To identify linking verbs and associated predicate nouns and adjectives
• To use linking verbs appropriately in writing

Bellringer
Daily Language Activity
When students enter the classroom, have this assignment on the board: *Write two short sentences that begin with the words I am. The first sentence should tell who or what you are. The second should tell what you are like.*

See also *Daily Language Practice*

Motivating Activity
Discuss the Bellringer sentences. Explain that the first sentence should contain a predicate noun and the second sentence should contain a predicate adjective.

Teach

☑ Teaching Tip
A good way to test for a linking verb is to see whether a form of the verb *to be* can be substituted for it in a sentence. Take this sentence, for example: *The farmer* grows *tired.* If *is* is substituted for *grows*, the sentence still makes sense: *The farmer is tired.* Therefore, *grows* is a linking verb in this sentence.

Resource Manager

Planning Resources
• *Lesson Plans*

Transparencies
• *Bellringer*
• *Daily Language Practice*

📁 Other Print Resources
• *Grammar and Composition Handbook*
• *Grammar Enrichment*, pp. 9, 11
• *Grammar Workbook*, Lesson 15

Practice and Assess

Answers: Exercise 5

1. changes, action v.
2. live, action v.
3. raise, action v.
4. appear, linking v., pred. adj.
5. move, action v.
6. is, linking v., pred. adj.
7. grows, linking v., pred. adj.
8. is, linking v., pred. n.
9. respect, action v.
10. seem, linking v., pred. adj.
11. is, linking v., pred. n.
12. developed, action v.
13. became, linking v., pred. adj.
14. owned, action v.
15. was, linking v., pred. adj.
16. speak, action v.
17. is, linking v., pred. n.
18. is, linking v., pred. adj.
19. seem, linking v., pred. adj.
20. grows, action v.

Answers: Exercise 6

Answers will vary, but some suggestions are given below.

1. I feel sleepy.
2. My family is Puerto Rican.
3. I am a student.
4. My favorite food is pizza.
5. I think basketball is exciting.

Additional Resources

📁 *Grammar Practice,* pp. 9, 11

📙 *Grammar Workbook,* Lesson 15

Close

Have students each write a paragraph about favorite foods, using both action verbs and linking verbs. They should also use at least one predicate noun and one predicate adjective.

Verbs

Exercise 5 | **Identifying Action and Linking Verbs and Predicate Words**

For each sentence, write the verb. Then write whether it is an *action* verb or a *linking* verb. If it is a linking verb, write whether it is followed by a *predicate noun* or a *predicate adjective.*

1. Village life changes slowly in Zambia.
2. Many people live in grass-roofed houses.
3. Villagers raise food crops on the land.
4. Some farmers appear content with their lives.
5. Other people move to the mining towns.
6. The country is rich in copper.
7. The copper industry grows successful.
8. A common food in Zambia is corn porridge.
9. Many Zambians respect the old customs.
10. They seem happy with their traditions.
11. Zambia is a land of farmers and miners.
12. Each family group developed its own culture.
13. Traditions became important for each group.
14. No individual owned land.
15. The family group was responsible for its members.
16. Most Zambians speak a native Bantu language.
17. Sometimes communication between groups is a problem.
18. The English language is common among businesspeople.
19. Some languages seem unfamiliar to a nearby group.
20. Zambia's population grows quickly.

Exercise 6 | **Using Predicate Nouns and Adjectives**

To complete each sentence, write a predicate noun or predicate adjective as indicated in parentheses. You may need to write more than one word.

1. I feel *(predicate adjective).*
2. My family is *(predicate adjective).*
3. I am *(predicate noun).*
4. My favorite food is *(predicate noun).*
5. I think basketball is *(predicate adjective).*

MEETING INDIVIDUAL NEEDS

Special Needs

Linking Verbs

To help students understand linking verbs, focus on the verb *be.* Point out that the verb links or joins the subject with a noun, pronoun, or adjective following the verb. Give examples showing that a subject and a predicate noun name the same person, place, thing, or idea and that a predicate adjective tells about the subject.

Maria is my *cousin. She* is my *cousin. Maria* is *intelligent. She* is *intelligent.* When you feel that students understand *be* as a linking verb, give examples of other linking verbs. Show students that *be* can be substituted for other linking verbs, as in *Maria* seems *happy.*

10.4 Present, Past, and Future Tenses

A verb changes its form to show tense and to agree with its subject. The **tense** of a verb tells when an action takes place.

■ The **present tense** of a verb names an action that happens regularly. It can also express a general truth.

The present tense is usually the same as the base form of the verb. When the subject is a singular noun or *he, she,* or *it,* however, you usually form the present tense by adding **-s** to the base form. The chart below shows the present tense forms of the verb *visit.*

Present Tense Forms	
Singular	**Plural**
I **visit.**	We **visit.**
You **visit.**	You **visit.**
He, she, *or* it **visits.**	They **visit.**

Present Tense
Thousands of tourists **visit** the pyramids each year.

The present tense of the verb *be* differs from the base form *be: am, are, is.*

■ The **past tense** of a verb names an action that already happened.

Form the past tense of most verbs by adding *-ed* to the base form of the verb.

■ The **future tense** of a verb names an action that will take place in the future.

Form the future tense by adding the helping verb *will* or *shall* to the base form of the verb.

Past Tense
The people of ancient Egypt constructed the pyramids.

Future Tense
Many more tourists **will go** to Egypt next year.

Verbs

Focus

Lesson Overview

Objectives
• To understand the simple past, present, and future tenses
• To use verb tenses appropriately in writing

🔔 Bellringer
Daily Language Activity

When students enter the classroom, have this assignment on the board: *Write three sentences that tell about (1) something you do regularly, (2) something you used to do, and (3) something you will do in the future.*

See also *Daily Language Practice*

Motivating Activity

Using two or more representative sets of students' Bellringer sentences, ask students to point out the three verb forms in each set and to explain how the time of action differs in each sentence.

Teach

Cooperative Learning

Students may use the adverbs *today, yesterday,* and *tomorrow* to indicate present, past, and future tenses. When they need to identify a verb tense in a sentence, let them add the adverb they think sounds right.

Resource Manager

Planning Resources
• *Lesson Plans*

📇 **Transparencies**
• *Bellringer*
• *Daily Language Practice*

📁 **Other Print Resources**
• *Grammar and Composition Handbook*
• *Grammar Enrichment,* 12
• *Grammar Practice,* p. 11
• *Grammar Reteaching,* p. 13
• *Grammar Workbook,* Lesson 16

Practice and Assess

Answers: Exercise 7

1. learns, present
2. will travel, future
3. watched, past
4. extends, present
5. depended, past
6. provides, present
7. fertilized, past
8. flows, present
9. protected, past
10. harnesses, present
11. will increase, future
12. traps, present
13. will use, future
14. will damage, future
15. called, past
16. developed, past
17. will puzzle, future
18. help, present
19. cover, present
20. exports, present

Answers: Exercise 8

1. prospers, prospered, will prosper
2. collects, collected, will collect
3. contains, contained, will contain
4. support, supported, will support
5. extend, extended, will extend

Additional Resources

📁 *Grammar Practice,* p. 11
📁 *Grammar Reteaching,* p. 13
📁 *Grammar Enrichment,* p. 12

📙 *Grammar Workbook,* Lesson 16

Close

Ask students to imagine that they are archaeologists in Egypt. Have them write a paragraph describing what they find in the ruins and what they expect to find. Remind them to use present, past, and future tenses.

Verbs

Exercise 7   **Distinguishing Present, Past, and Future Tenses**

For each sentence write the verb. Then write whether it is in the *present, past,* or *future* tense.

1. Larry learns about archaeology in the library.
2. Someday he and his parents will travel to Egypt.
3. Larry and his friend Ann watched a film about the Sahara.
4. This vast desert extends into Egypt.
5. The survival of the ancient Egyptians depended on the Nile River.
6. The Nile still provides the country's water.
7. Silt from the Nile fertilized farmland.
8. The Nile flows into the Mediterranean Sea.
9. Silt protected land near the Mediterranean from erosion.
10. The Aswan High Dam harnesses the water of the Nile.
11. Water from the dam will increase Egypt's agricultural production.
12. The dam traps the silt from floodwaters in Lake Nasser.
13. Instead of silt, farmers will use chemical fertilizers.
14. The dam will damage the environment.
15. A Greek historian called Egypt the "gift of the Nile."
16. Like other ancient civilizations, Egypt developed on fertile land near a river.
17. Egyptian monuments will puzzle people far into the future.
18. The Nile's floods help the crops.
19. Farmlands cover less than 4 percent of the land of Egypt.
20. Today Egypt exports cotton.

Exercise 8   **Using Present, Past, and Future Tenses**

For each sentence write the present, past, and future forms of the verb in parentheses.

1. The capital, Cairo, (prosper) near the base of the Nile delta.
2. This part of the country (collect) the most rain.
3. The Western Desert (contain) few oases.
4. Oases (support) small villages and farms.
5. The sands of the Eastern Desert (extend) from the Nile River almost to the Red Sea.

340   Unit 10 Verbs

MEETING INDIVIDUAL NEEDS

English Language Learners

Verb Tenses

Students learning English may have experience forming past forms of verbs in other ways. Have students explain how past, present, and future tenses are expressed in their primary language. Encourage them to set up a chart in their journals like the one on page 339 with heads for past, present, and future verb tenses. Have students look at previous assignments, noting troublesome verbs or verb forms. Have them use a dictionary to fill in their charts. Encourage students to write context sentences to help them understand the use of each verb tense.

10.5 Main Verbs and Helping Verbs

Verbs have four principal parts. The chart below shows the principal parts of the verb *learn*.

Principal Parts of the Verb *Learn*			
Base Form	**Present Participle**	**Past Form**	**Past Participle**
learn	learning	learned	learned

The principal parts of a verb can be combined with helping verbs to form verb phrases.

■ A **helping verb** is a verb that helps the main verb tell about an action or make a statement.

■ A **verb phrase** consists of one or more helping verbs followed by a main verb.

The most common helping verbs are *be* and *have*. The helping verb *be* makes a verb phrase with the present participle of a main verb.

Be and the Present Participle			
Present		**Past**	
Singular	**Plural**	**Singular**	**Plural**
I **am** learning.	We **are** learning.	I **was** learning.	We **were** learning.
You **are** learning.	You **are** learning.	You **were** learning.	You **were** learning.
She **is** learning.	They **are** learning.	He **was** learning.	They **were** learning.

The helping verb *have* makes a verb phrase with the past participle of a main verb.

Have and the Past Participle			
Present		**Past**	
Singular	**Plural**	**Singular**	**Plural**
I **have** learned.	We **have** learned.	We **have** learned.	We **had** learned.
You **have** learned.	You **have** learned.	You **had** learned.	You **had** learned.
She **has** learned.	They **have** learned.	He **had** learned.	They **had** learned.

10.5 Main Verbs and Helping Verbs **341**

Verbs

Focus

Lesson Overview

Objectives
- To understand the principal parts of a verb
- To distinguish between main verbs and helping verbs
- To demonstrate an understanding of the use of the principal parts of verbs

Bellringer
Daily Language Activity

When students enter the classroom, have this assignment on the board: *Identify the main verb in each of the following sentences: I am going. She will go. He had gone. They should have gone.*

See also *Daily Language Practice*

Motivating Activity

Discuss the Bellringer sentences, and have students identify the verb phrase in each. Then see whether students recognize that a form of the verb *go* is the main verb in each phrase. Tell them that the main verb is always the last word in a verb phrase.

Teach

☑ **Teaching Tip**

The term *participle* can be confusing for students. First, the past and past participle forms of regular verbs are identical. Second, a participle is a verb form that may be used as a noun, an adjective, or an adverb in a sentence. To help students distinguish between these uses of participles, remind them that helping verbs are used with participles that are part of verb phrases, such as, *is learning; have learned.*

Resource Manager

Planning Resources
- *Lesson Plans*

Transparencies
- *Bellringer*
- *Daily Language Practice*

📂 **Other Print Resources**
- *Grammar and Composition Handbook*
- *Grammar Enrichment*, p. 13
- *Grammar Practice*, p. 12
- *Grammar Reteaching*, p. 13
- *Grammar Workbook*, Lessons 17–18

Practice and Assess

Answers: Exercise 9

1. <u>have</u> changed
2. <u>were</u> living
3. <u>have</u> looked
4. <u>have</u> formed
5. <u>are</u> working
6. <u>have</u> produced
7. <u>has</u> changed
8. <u>has</u> become
9. <u>had</u> called
10. <u>had</u> ruled

Answers: Exercise 10

1. had <u>acquired</u>, past participle
2. has <u>assumed</u>, past participle
3. have <u>named</u>, past participle
4. has <u>appointed</u>, past participle
5. is <u>helping</u>, present participle
6. is <u>developing</u>, present participle
7. has <u>improved</u>, past participle
8. has <u>strengthened</u>, past participle
9. are <u>training</u>, present participle
10. have <u>learned</u>, past participle
11. are <u>tending</u>, present participle
12. is <u>depending</u>, present participle
13. have <u>mailed</u>, past participle
14. are <u>growing</u>, present participle
15. are <u>living</u>, present participle
16. have <u>raised</u>, past participle
17. is <u>based</u>, past participle
18. has <u>received</u>, past participle
19. have <u>planted</u>, past participle
20. had <u>arrived</u>, past participle

Additional Resources

 *Grammar Practice*, p. 12
Grammar Reteaching, p. 14
Grammar Enrichment, p. 13

 Grammar Workbook,
Lessons 17–18

Close

Ask students to each write a paragraph describing some differences between life in Malawi and life in their own community. Have them underline any helping verbs and all past and present participles.

Verbs

Exercise 9 — Identifying Helping Verbs in Verb Phrases

Write each verb phrase. Then underline the helping verb.

1. Some African societies have changed greatly.
2. The people of Malawi were living in family groups.
3. They have looked to chiefs for leadership.
4. They have formed one nation from many different family groups.
5. Many children in Malawi are working at jobs.
6. Malawi workers have produced beautiful items for export.
7. The country's name has changed along with its society.
8. Today it has become Malawi, "land of flame."
9. Before 1964 people had called the country Nyasaland.
10. For almost thirty years, Hastings Banda had ruled the country.

Exercise 10 — Identifying Past and Present Participles

Write each verb phrase and label its main verb as a *present participle* or *past participle*.

1. Malawi had acquired independence in 1964.
2. Bakili Muluzi has now assumed leadership.
3. The people have named Mr. Muluzi president.
4. The president has appointed a cabinet.
5. The cabinet is helping the president.
6. Malawi is developing into a stable nation.
7. The government has improved agriculture.
8. Malawi's economy has strengthened.
9. Young people are training for leadership roles.
10. The people of Malawi have learned valuable skills.
11. Farmers are tending cattle, goats, and sheep.
12. Malawi is depending on other nations for access to the sea.
13. Men with jobs in cities have mailed money home.
14. Most farmers are growing enough food for themselves and their families.
15. Half of the people in Malawi are living in small villages.
16. In Malawi women historically have raised the crops.
17. The economy is based on agriculture.
18. Malawi has received money from the United States for its schools.
19. Europeans have planted tea in the highlands.
20. The Bantu people had arrived in the region of Malawi in the 1500s.

MEETING INDIVIDUAL NEEDS — **English Language Learners**

Tenses in Other Languages

Concepts of present, past, and future are reflected differently in the grammar of different languages. Chinese, for example, does not change a verb to show the time of an action, but instead adds an adverb: *I want to go* **now;** *I want to go* **tomorrow.** Some students may find it confusing that present tense in English does not usually indicate "present time." Present tense indicates "timeless" habitual actions or general truths. Explain the difference between the present and present participle forms of verbs.

10.6 Present and Past Progressive Forms

The present tense of a verb names an action that occurs regularly. To describe an action that is continuing, use the present progressive form of the verb.

■ The **present progressive form** of a verb tells about an action that is continuing right now.

    The children **are listening** to a story.

The present progressive form of a verb consists of the present participle of the main verb and the helping verb *am*, *are*, or *is*.

Present Progressive Form	
Singular	**Plural**
I **am singing.**	We **are singing.**
You **are singing.**	You **are singing.**
He, she, *or* it **is singing.**	They **are singing.**

The past tense describes an action that was started and completed in the past. To describe an action going on some time in the past, use the past progressive form.

■ The **past progressive form** of a verb names an action that continued for some time in the past.

    The women **were singing** a folk song.

The past progressive form of a verb consists of the present participle and the helping verb *was* or *were*.

Past Progressive Form	
Singular	**Plural**
I **was singing.**	We **were singing.**
You **were singing.**	You **were singing.**
He, she, *or* it **was singing.**	They **were singing.**

Verbs

10.6 Present and Past Progressive Forms **343**

Focus

Lesson Overview

Objectives
- To understand the present progressive and past progressive forms of verbs
- To demonstrate an ability to use verbs in the progressive tenses

Bellringer
Daily Language Activity

When students enter the classroom, have this assignment on the board: *Write a sentence that tells what you are doing at this moment. Write another sentence that tells what you were doing at this time yesterday.*

See also *Daily Language Practice*

Motivating Activity

Discuss students' Bellringer sentences, and point out that their first sentences use the present progressive tense, and their second sentences use the past progressive.

Teach

☑ Teaching Tip

Tell students that if the main verb in a verb phrase ends in *-ing,* then the verb is in the progressive form. The present progressive generally refers to an action taking place at the present time: *The children **are feeding** the chicks.* The past progressive refers to an action in progress at some specific moment in the past: *The chicks **were chirping** for food.*

Resource Manager

Planning Resources
- *Lesson Plans*

Transparencies
- *Bellringer*
- *Daily Language Practice*

📂 **Other Print Resources**
- *Grammar and Composition Handbook*
- *Grammar Enrichment,* p. 14
- *Grammar Practice,* p. 13
- *Grammar Reteaching,* p. 15
- *Grammar Workbook,* Lesson 19

Practice and Assess

Answers: Exercise 11

1. are learning
2. were ruling
3. were growing
4. are governing
5. are taking
6. are holding
7. are visiting
8. are finding
9. was flourishing
10. are visiting

Answers: Exercise 12

1. are seeing
2. are averaging
3. are becoming
4. are roaming
5. was constructing
6. are designing
7. is replacing
8. were cooking
9. are reducing
10. are making
11. are shopping
12. are exploring
13. is improving
14. were visiting
15. is becoming

Additional Resources

📁 *Grammar Practice*, p. 13
📁 *Grammar Reteaching*, p. 15
📁 *Grammar Enrichment*, p. 14

📘 *Grammar Workbook*, Lesson 19

Close

Ask students to write a paragraph describing a trip they took. Encourage them to use some progressive verb forms. Have them underline present progressive and past progressive forms.

Verbs

Exercise 11   Using Present and Past Progressive Forms

For each sentence, write the present progressive or past progressive form of the verb in parentheses. Be sure your sentences make sense.

1. Students today (learn) about African nations.
2. For years a few European countries (rule) some parts of Africa.
3. Many Africans (grow) eager for independence in the 1950s.
4. Today most African countries (govern) themselves.
5. Now changes (take) place in African governments.
6. Many countries now (hold) elections.
7. More Americans (visit) Africa nowadays.
8. They (find) the scenery spectacular.
9. The Mali Empire (flourish) in West Africa for about two hundred years.
10. People still (visit) Timbuktu in Mali.

Exercise 12   Using the Progressive Forms

For each sentence, write the progressive form of the verb. If the verb is in the present tense, change it to the present progressive form. If the verb is in the past tense, change it to the past progressive form.

1. Visitors see great differences across the continent.
2. Temperatures average more than 100° in the Sahara.
3. Oases become dry.
4. Nomadic herders roam across northern Africa.
5. A family constructed a house with hard mud walls.
6. Architects design modern houses or apartments.
7. Technology replaces some traditions.
8. Families cooked food over an open fire.
9. Modern stoves reduce wood use by 500 percent.
10. Textile mills in Cairo make cloth from cotton.
11. Tourists shop in Cairo.
12. Visitors explore the old parts of many cities.
13. The economy of Egypt improves.
14. In the nineteenth century, tourists visited Egypt in large numbers.
15. Each year tourism becomes more important to the economy.

344   Unit 10 Verbs

Exploring Language

Progressive Verb Forms

Many verbs, such as *know, believe, doubt,* and *love,* refer to "timeless" mental states. In English these verbs cannot be used in the present or past progressive. Note the following incorrect usage: I *am knowing* the answer. I *am believing* that you are right. I *was doubting* it. I *was loving* ice cream. Work with students to understand the correct forms: I *know* the answer. I *believe* that you are right. I *doubted* it. I *loved* ice cream.

10.7 Perfect Tenses

■ The **present perfect tense** of a verb tells about something that happened at an indefinite time in the past. It also tells about an action that happened in the past and is still happening now.

> Sheila **has collected** African jewelry for years.

In the sentence above, Sheila began to collect African jewelry at some time in the past and still collects it.

The present perfect tense of a verb consists of the helping verb *have* or *has* followed by the past participle of the main verb.

Present Perfect Tense	
Singular	**Plural**
I **have collected.**	We **have collected.**
You **have collected.**	You **have collected.**
He, she, *or* it **has collected.**	They **have collected.**

■ The **past perfect tense** of a verb names an action that happened before another action or event in the past.

> Before her last birthday, Sheila **had collected** only coins.

In the sentence above, Sheila started and finished collecting coins before another event that also occurred in the past, her last birthday.

The past perfect tense of a verb consists of the helping verb *had* and the past participle of the main verb.

Past Perfect Tense	
Singular	**Plural**
I **had** started.	We **had** started.
You **had** started.	You **had** started.
He, she, *or* it **had started.**	They **had** started.

10.7 Perfect Tenses **345**

Verbs

Focus

Lesson Overview

Objectives
- To understand present, past, and future perfect tenses
- To distinguish among simple, progressive, and perfect tenses
- To use tenses appropriately and effectively

🔔 Bellringer
Daily Language Activity

When students enter the classroom, have this assignment on the board: *Identify the two verbs in this sentence and tell which action happened first:*

Yesterday several students reported that they had finished their papers.

📓 **See also** *Daily Language Practice*

Motivating Activity

Discuss students' responses to the Bellringer assignment. Did they identify *had finished* as having happened before *reported?* Explain that *had finished* is in the past perfect tense.

Teach

☑ Teaching Tip

What is so perfect about the perfect tense? Nothing. The word *perfect* in this sense means "complete." The perfect tense indicates a completed action. The present perfect tense refers to an action begun in the past that continues up to the present moment: *The band* has completed *its performance.* The past perfect refers to an action begun in the past and completed in the past: *The band* had practiced *up to the last minute.*

Resource Manager

Planning Resources
- *Lesson Plans*

📓 Transparencies
- *Bellringer*
- *Daily Language Practice*

📁 Other Print Resources
- *Grammar and Composition Handbook*
- *Grammar Enrichment*, p. 15
- *Grammar Practice*, p. 14
- *Grammar Reteaching*, p. 16
- *Grammar Workbook*, Lesson 20

Practice and Assess

Answers: Exercise 13

1. pass, present
2. has exported, present perfect
3. invaded, past
4. ruled, past
5. had left, past perfect
6. speak, present
7. had raised, past perfect
8. have handed, present perfect
9. have learned, present perfect
10. value, present

Answers: Exercise 14

1. had created
2. had pounded
3. had constructed
4. have worked
5. have raised
6. have tended
7. has traded
8. had docked
9. had visited
10. had crowded
11. had charmed
12. have danced
13. have watched
14. had lived
15. had helped

Additional Resources

📂 *Grammar Practice*, p. 14
📂 *Grammar Reteaching*, p. 16
📂 *Grammar Enrichment*, p. 15

📕 *Grammar Workbook*, Lesson 20

Close

Have students each write a paragraph describing an event from American history. Ask them to use present perfect and past perfect tenses in at least one sentence each. When finished, students should exchange papers and work together to correct any verb tense errors.

Verbs

Exercise 13 — Review: Identifying Tenses

For each sentence, write the verb. Then write whether the verb is in the *present, past, present perfect,* or *past perfect* tense.

1. Moroccan ships pass through the Strait of Gibraltar.
2. Morocco has exported fish and minerals.
3. In the year 711, Moroccans invaded Spain.
4. For some time, they ruled most of Spain.
5. The Moroccans had left many influences in Spain.
6. Most Moroccans speak Arabic.
7. Farmers had raised dates, olives, and citrus fruit.
8. Craft workers have handed down their skills.
9. Craft workers have often learned their skills from earlier generations.
10. Tourists value Moroccan leather.

Exercise 14 — Using the Perfect Tenses

For each sentence, write the perfect tense of the verb. If the verb is in the present tense, change it to the present perfect tense. If the verb is in the past tense, change it to the past perfect tense.

1. Before modern times, Moroccan artisans created intricate silver jewelry.
2. They pounded metal into delicate shapes.
3. In the recent past, craftspeople constructed products from leather.
4. They also work on carpets for export.
5. Farmers raise barley, wheat, fruits, and vegetables.
6. Shepherds tend their flocks in green meadows.
7. Morocco trades with many other countries.
8. Long ago, ships from many countries docked in Casablanca.
9. Tourists visited the old section of the city.
10. Merchants crowded the narrow streets.
11. Marrakesh's hospitality charmed many travelers in the nineteenth century.
12. Fat bears dance in the public square.
13. Visitors watch talented jugglers and acrobats.
14. The Berbers lived in the mountains for centuries.
15. Centuries ago, the Moroccan Berbers helped the Arabs conquer Spain.

346   Unit 10 Verbs

English Language Learners

MEETING INDIVIDUAL NEEDS

Using *Have*

In American English, we usually form questions differently when *have* is a main verb than when *have* is a helping verb. Write on the board these examples of *have* as a main verb: *You* have *a friend. Do you* have *a friend?* Then write these sentences and point out to students the helping verb *have: You* have seen *my coat.* Have *you* seen *my coat?* Tell students that occasionally questions are formed in the same way whether *have* is used as a main verb or as a helping verb: Have *you a friend?* Have *you* seen *my coat?*

10.8 Irregular Verbs

Irregular verbs do not form their past forms and past participle by adding the ending -ed. The irregular verbs below are grouped according to how their past forms and past participle are formed.

Irregular Verbs			
Pattern	**Base Form**	**Past Form**	**Past Participle**
One vowel changes to form the past form and the past participle.	begin	began	begun
	drink	drank	drunk
	ring	rang	rung
	shrink	shrank or shrunk	shrunk
	sing	sang	sung
	spring	sprang or sprung	sprung
	swim	swam	swum
The past form and the past participle are the same.	bring	brought	brought
	buy	bought	bought
	catch	caught	caught
	feel	felt	felt
	get	got	got or gotten
	keep	kept	kept
	lay	laid	laid
	lead	led	led
	leave	left	left
	lend	lent	lent
	lose	lost	lost
	make	made	made
	pay	paid	paid
	say	said	said
	seek	sought	sought
	sell	sold	sold
	sit	sat	sat
	sleep	slept	slept
	swing	swung	swung
	teach	taught	taught
	think	thought	thought
	win	won	won

Verbs

Focus

Lesson Overview

Objectives
- To recognize irregular verbs
- To learn the past and past participle forms of common irregular verbs
- To use correctly the forms of regular and irregular verbs

Bellringer
Daily Language Activity

When students enter the classroom, have this assignment on the board: *Correct any errors in verb usage in the following sentence: As I set down and swang on the old swing, I sung a little song about the day I brang my toad to school and catched another one to keep it company.*

See also *Daily Language Practice*

Motivating Activity

Discuss students' corrections of the Bellringer sentence. If students have missed any of the five errors or cannot explain the errors, refer them to the chart on page 347.

Teach

☑ Teaching Tip

Ask students to look at the past and past participle forms of the irregular verbs on page 347, particularly those in the bottom part of the chart. Remind students that the past participle should follow a form of the helping verb *have*.

⇄ Cross-reference: Troubleshooter

For instruction and practice with irregular verbs, refer students to Lesson 7.4.

Resource Manager

Planning Resources
- *Lesson Plans*

Transparencies
- *Bellringer*
- *Daily Language Practice*
- *Two-Minute Skill Drill*

📂 **Other Print Resources**
- *Grammar and Composition Handbook*
- *Grammar Enrichment*, p. 16
- *Grammar Practice*, p. 15
- *Grammar Reteaching*, p. 17
- *Grammar Workbook*, Lessons 21–24

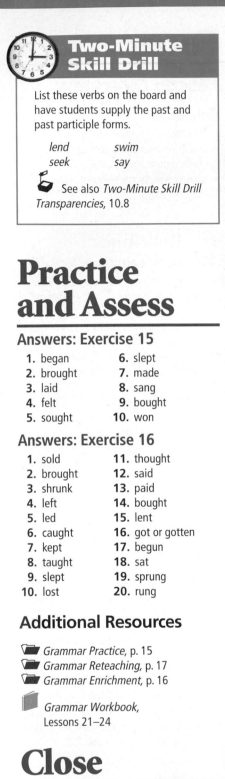

10.8

Two-Minute Skill Drill

List these verbs on the board and have students supply the past and past participle forms.

lend   swim
seek   say

👆 See also *Two-Minute Skill Drill Transparencies*, 10.8

Practice and Assess

Answers: Exercise 15

1. began   6. slept
2. brought   7. made
3. laid   8. sang
4. felt   9. bought
5. sought   10. won

Answers: Exercise 16

1. sold   11. thought
2. brought   12. said
3. shrunk   13. paid
4. left   14. bought
5. led   15. lent
6. caught   16. got or gotten
7. kept   17. begun
8. taught   18. sat
9. slept   19. sprung
10. lost   20. rung

Additional Resources

📁 *Grammar Practice*, p. 15
📁 *Grammar Reteaching*, p. 17
📁 *Grammar Enrichment*, p. 16

📓 *Grammar Workbook*, Lessons 21–24

Close

Have students write a paragraph describing some places where they have shopped. Ask them to use several irregular verbs in the past or present perfect tense. If they use irregular verbs that are not in the chart on page 347, encourage them to look up the words in the dictionary. Students should exchange papers, check each other's work, and discuss any needed corrections.

348

Verbs

Exercise 15   **Using the Past Tense of Irregular Verbs**

For each sentence, write the past tense form of the verb in parentheses.

1. African merchants (begin) work before dawn.
2. Peddlers (bring) their goods to market.
3. They (lay) out their wares in attractive displays.
4. The sun (feel) hot in the open marketplace.
5. Children (seek) the shade of date trees.
6. Infants (sleep) in spite of the chaos.
7. People (make) requests about animals for sale.
8. Some traders (sing) songs about their goods.
9. Some people (buy) gourds of all sizes.
10. A tailor (win) some new customers.

Exercise 16   **Using the Past Participle of Irregular Verbs**

For each sentence, write the past participle of the verb in parentheses.

1. Some women have (sell) bracelets and necklaces.
2. Traders had (bring) gorgeous robes and veils.
3. The material has not (shrink).
4. Herders have (leave) cattle in the stalls.
5. Herders had (lead) livestock to market.
6. The herder has (catch) the stray.
7. Some people have (keep) pots of stew warm.
8. Craft workers have (teach) their children their craft.
9. Some merchants have (sleep) in the sun.
10. The market has (lose) business to other villages.
11. The merchants had (think) competition might be good.
12. One merchant has (say) the market needs competition.
13. People have (pay) by trading.
14. How much fruit have people (buy)?
15. A mother has (lend) her child money to buy a trinket.
16. The child had (get) some candy.
17. The candy had (begin) to stick to the child's fingers.
18. Merchants have (sit) on beautiful rugs.
19. By evening a cool breeze has (spring) up.
20. Wind chimes have (ring) in the breeze.

348   Unit 10 Verbs

Exploring Language

Irregular Verbs

Show students that each verb in the first part of the chart changes *i* to *a* in the past form and *i* to *u* in the past participle. Go on to the second part of the chart, being certain that students realize that the past form and the past participle are identical.

10.9 More Irregular Verbs

Irregular Verbs			
Pattern	**Base Form**	**Past Form**	**Past Participle**
The base form and the past participle are the same.	become come run	became came ran	become come run
The past form ends in -ew, and the past participle ends in -wn.	blow draw fly grow know throw	blew drew flew grew knew threw	blown drawn flown grown known thrown
The past participle ends in -en.	bite break choose drive eat fall give ride rise see speak steal take write	bit broke chose drove ate fell gave rode rose saw spoke stole took wrote	bitten *or* bit broken chosen driven eaten fallen given ridden risen seen spoken stolen taken written
The past form and the past participle do not follow any pattern.	be (am, are, is) do go tear wear	was, were did went tore wore	been done gone torn worn
The base form, past form, and past participle are all the same.	burst cut let put	burst cut let put	burst cut let put

Verbs

Focus

Lesson Overview

Objectives

- To identify past and past participle forms of some common irregular verbs
- To use all forms of irregular verbs confidently and accurately

🔔 Bellringer
Daily Language Activity

When students enter the classroom, have this assignment on the board: *Correct any errors in verb usage in the following sentences: I seen how he run off after he had broke the window. Before he come back, he had rode his bike all over town.*

📖 **See also** *Daily Language Practice*

Motivating Activity

If students have missed any of the five errors in the Bellringer sentences or are unable to explain the errors, refer them to the chart on page 349.

Teach

☑ Teaching Tip

An effective way of learning irregular verb forms is constant exposure to the forms and occasional correction when the learner makes a mistake. Ask students to make personal dictionaries of troublesome irregular forms, including such verbs as *go, run, have,* and *see.*

🅐 Vocabulary Link

Spanish, too, has irregular verbs. The third person singular of the verb *ir*, which means "to go," is *va* in the present tense and *fue* in the past tense.

Resource Manager

Planning Resources
- *Lesson Plans*

📖 Transparencies
- *Bellringer*
- *Daily Language Practice*

📁 Other Print Resources
- *Grammar and Composition Handbook*
- *Grammar Enrichment,* p. 16
- *Grammar Practice,* p. 15
- *Grammar Reteaching,* p. 17
- *Grammar Workbook,* Lessons 21–24

Practice and Assess

Additional Resources

📁 *Grammar Practice,* p. 15
📁 *Grammar Reteaching,* p. 17
📁 *Grammar Enrichment,* p. 16

📓 *Grammar Workbook,*
Lessons 21–24

Close

Ask students to imagine that they are magazine reporters. Have them each write a paragraph describing his or her most interesting assignment. Ask them to use several irregular verbs in the past or present perfect tense. If they use irregular verbs that are not in the charts on pages 347 and 349, encourage them to look up the words in a dictionary.

Verbs

Exercise 17   Using the Past Tense of Irregular Verbs

For each sentence, write the past tense form of the verb in parentheses.

1. Crystal (do) research for her project.
2. She (go) to the library for books about Nigeria.
3. Some of her information (come) from magazines.
4. Fulani people (eat) well in the rainy season.
5. Children (ride) on cattle from camp to camp.
6. Their camps (are) temporary homes.
7. The Hausa (become) skilled potters and weavers.
8. The men (wear) long robes and loose-fitting trousers.
9. Teachers (run) schools for Nigerian children.
10. In 1954 the government (take) control of all the schools.

Exercise 18   Using the Past Participle of Irregular Verbs

For each sentence, write the past participle form of the verb in parentheses.

1. In Kenya's dry season, no rain had (fall).
2. A dry wind has (blow) over the land.
3. The families had (eat) beans and potatoes.
4. By March the farmers had (go) to the fields.
5. People have (do) the farm work by hand.
6. Pumps had (draw) water from wells.
7. Farmers had (grow) gardens close to the house.
8. By noon the sun had (rise) high in the sky.
9. Travelers have (go) to Kenya for years.
10. Tourists have (see) herders with cattle sticks.
11. The herders had (choose) each new camp carefully.
12. A fire had (drive) away mosquitoes and flies.
13. Kenyans have (grow) tea and coffee in the highlands.
14. Tourists have (fly) over Kenya's Tsavo National Park.
15. They have (ride) in trucks deep into the countryside.
16. Have you (speak) to any of them?
17. My parents had (take) many pictures on a photo safari.
18. One camera had (break).
19. They had (knew) the tour guide.
20. The tour guide has not (let) tourists off the paths.

MEETING INDIVIDUAL NEEDS   Less Proficient Readers

Mastering Irregular Verbs

Show students the charts on pages 347 and 349. Call their attention to the patterns as they read across the columns. Encourage them to use the patterns as an aid to seeing similarities and differences in the formation of the past and the past participle forms. Suggest that they can also look up a troublesome main verb in a dictionary. Tell students that a dictionary lists the past tense and the past participle of all verbs.

UNIT 10 Grammar Review

VERBS

The excerpt below is from a traditional Ashanti folktale. The Ashanti are the largest and most powerful ethnic group in the West African country of Ghana. The passage has been annotated to show some of the kinds of verbs covered in this unit.

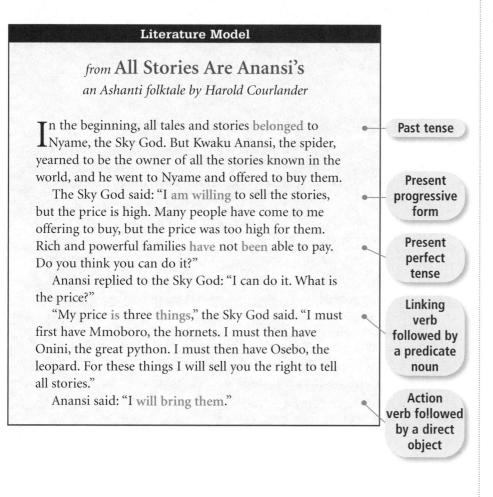

Literature Model

from All Stories Are Anansi's
an Ashanti folktale by Harold Courlander

In the beginning, all tales and stories belonged to Nyame, the Sky God. But Kwaku Anansi, the spider, yearned to be the owner of all the stories known in the world, and he went to Nyame and offered to buy them.

⟶ **Past tense**

The Sky God said: "I am willing to sell the stories, but the price is high. Many people have come to me offering to buy, but the price was too high for them. Rich and powerful families have not been able to pay. Do you think you can do it?"

⟶ **Present progressive form**

⟶ **Present perfect tense**

Anansi replied to the Sky God: "I can do it. What is the price?"

"My price is three things," the Sky God said. "I must first have Mmoboro, the hornets. I must then have Onini, the great python. I must then have Osebo, the leopard. For these things I will sell you the right to tell all stories."

⟶ **Linking verb followed by a predicate noun**

Anansi said: "I will bring them."

⟶ **Action verb followed by a direct object**

Verbs

Grammar Review **351**

Teach

About the Literature

Direct students to read the passage from "All Stories Are Anansi's," an Ashanti folktale retold by Harold Courlander. Then initiate a discussion about the characters, the setting, and the mood of the passage. Ask students to focus on the highlighted verbs in the passage. Do the shifts in verb tense and form add to or detract from the story? Would the action in the story flow as well if only past tense were used?

Linking Grammar and Literature

☑ **Teaching Tip**

Explain to students that the animal-trickster story told in the passage reflects a common theme in African folktales. The tricksters in tales from different regions of Africa include the hare, the spider, and the tortoise. Anansi, the spider-trickster, is the opponent of the Sky God. Tales about Anansi tell how he steals the Sky God's stories or tricks the Sky God into allowing disease to enter the world.

Critical Thinking

Students can use prior knowledge to discuss other folktales they know and to compare and contrast these with the passage. Ask them to name one characteristic of Anansi that they can identify from the passage. (*He is confident.*)

Listening and Speaking

Invite a volunteer to read the passage aloud. Can students follow the shifts in tense? Do they recognize that the narration is in the past tense but the dialogue is in the present?

Resource Manager

Planning Resources
- *Lesson Plans*

📁 **Other Print Resources**
- *Grammar and Composition Handbook*
- *Grammar Workbook,* Lessons 58–62; Unit 3 Review; Cumulative Review: Units 1–3

✔ **ASSESSMENT OPTIONS**

📁 *Tests with Answer Key and Rubrics*
Unit 10 Mastery Test, pp. 43–44

💾 *Testmaker*
Unit 10 Mastery Test

Practice and Assess

Answers: Exercise 1

1. boarded, <u>ship</u>
2. entered, <u>harbor</u>
3. photographed, <u>animals</u>
4. visited, <u>plateaus</u>
5. rode, <u>rapids</u>
6. walked, none
7. traveled, none
8. selected, <u>places</u>
9. traced, <u>trip</u>
10. gave, <u>tip</u>

Answers: Exercise 2

1. (adapted) <u>legends</u>
2. (collected) <u>stories</u>
3. (tells) <u>stories</u>, <u>boy</u>
4. (is)
5. (told) <u>terms</u>, <u>Brer Fox</u>
6. (used) <u>humor</u>
7. (published) <u>stories</u>
8. (visited) <u>plantation</u>
9. (told) <u>stories</u>, <u>Harris</u>
10. (influenced) <u>authors</u>

Verbs

Review: Exercise 1 — Identifying Action Verbs and Direct Objects

For the sentences below, write each action verb and direct object. Underline the direct objects. If a sentence has no direct object, write *none*.

1. We boarded the ship for Africa.
2. Our ship entered the harbor after a long wait.
3. We photographed the animals.
4. We visited several African plateaus.
5. Boaters rode the river rapids.
6. Hikers walked through the jungles.
7. Our guide traveled with us.
8. She selected the best places for overnight camps.
9. We traced our trip on a large map.
10. The tourists gave the guide a generous tip.

Review: Exercise 2 — Identifying Direct and Indirect Objects

For each sentence, write the verb plus any direct object and indirect object. Then circle the verb and underline each *direct object* once and each *indirect object* twice. (Not all sentences will have both kinds of object. One sentence has neither.)

SAMPLE   Storytellers tell children fascinating stories.
ANSWER   tell <u>stories</u>, <u>children</u>

1. Joel Chandler Harris adapted African American folk legends.
2. He collected the stories in the book *Uncle Remus, His Songs and Sayings*.
3. Uncle Remus tells a boy stories about a fox, a rabbit, and a bear.
4. Brer Rabbit is the American version of the African character Zomo.
5. Brer Rabbit told Brer Fox his terms.
6. Harris used humor in his stories.
7. The *Atlanta Constitution* published the stories.
8. As a boy, Harris visited a plantation near his home.
9. African Americans told Harris stories.
10. The stories influenced modern authors.

Review: Exercise 3 Distinguishing Linking Verbs from Action Verbs

For each sentence, write the verb and whether it is an *action verb* or a *linking verb*. If it is a linking verb, write whether it is followed by a *predicate noun* or a *predicate adjective*.

1. The Nile River is the world's longest river.
2. The Nile flows from Lake Victoria.
3. Bright blue and orange birds seem exotic.
4. Africa is a land of geographical wonders.
5. Its plateaus appear flat.
6. Wild animals graze on the plains.
7. The weather in the high plateaus and mountains is mild.
8. The mountain looks beautiful.
9. Community ceremonies are an important rural tradition.
10. Everyone gathers for celebrations of births and marriages.

Review: Exercise 4 Writing Predicate Nouns and Predicate Adjectives

Write a predicate noun or a predicate adjective as indicated to complete each sentence below. You may need to add other words. (Use the Literature Model on page 351 to help you.)

1. The Sky God was _____. (predicate noun)
2. Nyame was _____. (predicate noun)
3. Anansi was _____. (predicate adjective)
4. Anansi is a _____. (predicate noun)
5. Onini is a _____. (predicate noun)
6. Hornets are _____. (predicate noun)
7. Anansi stories are _____. (predicate noun)
8. The python is _____. (predicate adjective)
9. Osebo is _____. (predicate noun)
10. The price of the stories is _____. (predicate adjective)

Answers: Exercise 3

1. is, linking verb, predicate noun
2. flows, action verb
3. seem, linking verb, predicate adjective
4. is, linking verb, predicate noun
5. appear, linking verb, predicate adjective
6. graze, action verb
7. is, linking verb, predicate adjective
8. looks, linking verb, predicate adjective
9. are, linking verb, predicate noun
10. gathers, action verb

Answers: Exercise 4

Answers will vary. Samples follow.
1. The Sky God was the owner of stories.
2. Nyame was the Sky God.
3. Anansi was bold.
4. Anansi is a spider.
5. Onini is a python.
6. Hornets are Mmoboro.
7. Anansi stories are folktales.
8. The python is great.
9. Osebo is the leopard.
10. The price of the stories is high.

Verbs

Answers: Exercise 12

Mixed Review

1. boarded, action verb; ship, direct object
2. seemed, linking verb; large and modern, predicate adjectives
3. was, linking verb; freighter, predicate noun
4. photographed, action verb; animals, direct object
5. sent, action verb; pictures, direct object; friends, indirect object
6. had lived
7. have caused
8. are becoming
9. will protect
10. are outlawing

Close

Ask students to return to the passage and list all the verbs. Then have them label the verbs: *A* for action and *L* for linking. Have students exchange papers and check each other's work. Students should work together to correct any errors.

Remind students that action verbs make writing vivid and exciting. Encourage them to use specific action verbs in their own writing.

Verbs

saved them from extinction? ⁴That is the question Nancy Schutt addressing in her painting *Vanishing*. ⁵Many of Schutts' paintings deals with the theme of interaction among humans animals, and the natural world.

Review: Exercise 12

Mixed Review

For each sentence, write the verb and tell whether it is an *action verb* or a *linking verb*. Then write and label any *direct object*, *indirect object*, *predicate noun*, or *predicate adjective*.

SAMPLE	We left home last month for our trip.
ANSWER	left, action verb; home, direct object

1. We boarded the ship for Africa.
2. The ship seemed large and modern.
3. It was a freighter.
4. We photographed the animals.
5. We sent our friends pictures.

For each sentence, write the form of the verb indicated in parentheses.

6. Herds of elephants (past perfect tense of *live*) on many parts of the African continent.
7. People (present perfect tense of *cause*) animals' habitats to shrink.
8. The white rhinoceros and the gorilla (present progressive form of *become*) extinct.
9. Animal parks (future tense of *protect*) some endangered species.
10. Governments (present progressive form of *outlaw*) hunting in these areas.

Writing Application

Action Verbs in Writing

Jean Craighead George uses precise action verbs in this passage from *Julie of the Wolves* to make her writing lively and vivid. Examine the passage, focusing especially on the italicized verbs.

Amaroq [one of the wolves] *glanced* at his paw and slowly *turned* his head her way without *lifting* his eyes. He *licked* his shoulder. A few matted hairs *sprang* apart and *twinkled* individually. Then his eyes *sped* to each of the three adult wolves that made up his pack and finally to the five pups who were sleeping in a fuzzy mass near the den entrance. The great wolf's eyes *softened* at the sight of the little wolves, then quickly *hardened* into brittle yellow jewels as he *scanned* the flat tundra [ground].

Techniques with Action Verbs

Try to apply some of Jean Craighead George's writing techniques when you write and revise your own work.

❶ Whenever possible, replace general words with precise verbs. Compare the following:

GENERAL WORD looked

GEORGE'S VERSION glanced, scanned

❷ Expand a single verb into longer groups of words with more than one specific verb:

SINGLE VERB A few matted hairs *separated*.

GEORGE'S VERSION A few matted hairs *sprang* apart and *twinkled* individually.

TIME
For more about the importance of using interesting verbs, see **TIME Facing the Blank Page,** page 98.

Verbs

Action Verbs in Writing

Ask students to read the passage from *Julie of the Wolves* silently and then to consider the verbs, including those in italics. Suppose the author had used the verb *changed* twice in the last sentence, instead of *softened* and *hardened.* Would the sentence have been as effective?

Techniques with Action Verbs

Discuss the two techniques and ask how students would apply them to the second sentence in the practice paragraph: *Her two cubs played nearby.* How might they make the verb more specific? How might they expand it, using more than one specific verb?

Practice

The answers to this challenging and enriching activity will vary. Refer to Techniques with Action Verbs as you evaluate student choices. Some suggestions are given below.

The lioness stretched lazily in the hot sun. Her two cubs frolicked nearby. She occasionally lifted her head to look around her.

Practice Practice the Techniques with Action Verbs by revising the following passage. Use a separate sheet of paper.

The lioness lay lazily in the hot sun. Her two cubs played nearby. She occasionally moved her head to look around her. She was suddenly alert. A herd of zebra was nearby. The lioness watched her prey. Partially hidden in the tall grass, she moved close to the zebra herd. She suddenly came out of the grass. The zebras walked away, but one was small and weak. The huntress moved again and caught the zebra. She brought the dead zebra back to the cubs. They all ate their fill. Afterward they cleaned themselves, and then they rested.

Writing Application **359**

✔ ASSESSMENT OPTIONS

📁 *Tests with Answer Key and Rubrics*
Unit 10 Mastery Test, pp. 43–44

💾 *Testmaker*
Unit 10 Mastery Test

You may wish to administer the Unit 10 Mastery Test at this point.

📼 *Mindjogger Videoquizzes*

Objectives

- To identify personal, indefinite, and possessive pronouns and to recognize antecedents of pronouns
- To demonstrate control over the agreement of pronouns with antecedents
- To understand the use of various kinds of pronouns

✔ ASSESSMENT OPTIONS

📁 *Tests with Answer Key and Rubrics*
Unit 11 Pretest, pp. 45–46
Unit 11 Mastery Test, pp. 47–48

💾 *Testmaker*
Unit 11 Pretest
Unit 11 Mastery Test

You may wish to administer the Unit 11 Pretest at this point.

Key to Ability Levels

L1 Level 1 activities are within the basic ability range of students.

L2 Level 2 activities are within the ability range of average students.

L3 Level 3 activities are more challenging activities.

UNIT
11 Pronouns

360

Resource Manager

Planning Resources
- *Lesson Plans*
- *Block Scheduling*

🗂 Transparencies
- *Bellringer*
- *Daily Language Practice*
- *Two-Minute Skill Drill*

📁 Other Print Resources
- *Grammar and Composition Handbook*
- *Grammar Enrichment*
- *Grammar Practice*
- *Grammar Reteaching*
- *Grammar Workbook*
- *Tests with Answer Key and Rubrics*

📼 Video
- *MindJogger Videoquizzes*

💾 Software
- *Interactive Grammar and Language Workbook*
- *Language Arts PASS*
- *Presentation Plus!*
- *Testmaker*

🖥 Web Sites
- *writerschoice.glencoe.com*

11.1 Personal Pronouns

■ A **pronoun** is a word that takes the place of one or more nouns and the words that describe those nouns.

The most frequently used pronouns are called personal pronouns. The words *she* and *it* in the sentence below are personal pronouns.

    Dana has a favorite folktale, and **she** tells **it** often.

■ Pronouns that are used to refer to people or things are called **personal pronouns.**

Personal pronouns perform different functions in sentences. Some personal pronouns are used as the simple subject. Others are used as the direct or indirect object of a verb. In the example above, the pronoun *she* replaces the noun *Dana*, which is used as the subject. The pronoun *it* replaces the noun *folktale* and is the direct object.

■ A **subject pronoun** is a personal pronoun in the nominative case. It is used as a subject.

■ An **object pronoun** is a personal pronoun in the objective case. It is used as the direct or indirect object of a verb.

    I will read that fable. [subject pronoun]

    Jesse told **me** about the story. [object pronoun]

Personal Pronouns		
	Singular	**Plural**
Used as Subjects	I	we
	you	you
	he, she, it	they
Used as Objects	me	us
	you	you
	him, her, it	them

Pronouns

11.1 Personal Pronouns   **361**

Focus

Lesson Overview

Objectives
• To identify and use personal pronouns
• To recognize subject and object pronouns
• To demonstrate control over number and gender when using pronouns

Bellringer
Daily Language Activity

When students enter the classroom, have the following assignment on the board: *Consider what is wrong with the following sentence. Then rewrite it:*
    Jaime walked to Jaime's school, but Jaime forgot Jaime's books.

See also *Daily Language Practice*

Motivating Activity

Write the revised sentence from the Bellringer on the board. Ask students what was changed in the sentence to make it less awkward. (Pronouns replace a repeated name.) How did they decide which pronoun to use? Which sentence sounds better? Why?

Teach

Ⓐ Vocabulary Link
The prefix *pro-* in *pronoun* means "substituting for" or "taking the place of." A pronoun takes the place of a noun.

Resource Manager

Planning Resources
• *Lesson Plans*

Transparencies
• *Bellringer*
• *Daily Language Practice*

📂 **Other Print Resources**
• *Grammar and Composition Handbook*
• *Grammar Enrichment*, p. 17
• *Grammar Practice*
• *Grammar Reteaching*, p. 18
• *Grammar Workbook*, Lesson 25

Practice and Assess

Answers: Exercise 1

1. I—subject
2. It—subject; me—object
3. they—subject
4. They—subject; it—object
5. He—subject; them—object
6. They—subject; him—object
7. He—subject
8. They—subject; it—object
9. them—object
10. I—subject; you—object

Answers: Exercise 2

1. He; them
2. He; it
3. He; it
4. He; it
5. they; it
6. it
7. They; them
8. they
9. It; them
10. They

Answers: Exercise 3

1. They
2. he
3. she
4. them
5. We

Additional Resources

📁 *Grammar Reteaching,* p. 18
📁 *Grammar Enrichment,* p. 17

📖 *Grammar Workbook,* Lesson 25

Close

Discuss why writers use pronouns in place of nouns. Encourage students to ask questions for clarification. Then have students summarize in their journals an explanation as a helpful hint for writing.

Pronouns

| **Exercise 1** | **Identifying Personal Pronouns** |

Write each pronoun and label it *subject* or *object*.

1. I read "The Bundle of Sticks," a fable by Aesop.
2. It taught me the value of cooperation.
3. A man had four sons, and they always fought.
4. They started an argument in the morning and continued it all day.
5. He became impatient and scolded them.
6. They ignored him and continued to argue.
7. He decided to teach the sons a lesson.
8. They needed it.
9. The father was sure this plan would help them.
10. Now I will tell you the end of the fable.

| **Exercise 2** | **Using Pronouns in Nominative and Objective Cases** |

Write a personal pronoun to replace the underlined words.

1. The father asked the sons for a bundle of sticks.
2. The father tied the bundle up with string.
3. The father gave the bundle to the sons.
4. The father said, "Break the bundle."
5. The boys tried, but the boys were too weak to break the bundle.
6. Then the father untied the bundle.
7. The brothers easily broke the sticks one by one.
8. United, the brothers were strong.
9. The father said, "This lesson has taught my sons."
10. The sons also realized the importance of cooperation.

| **Exercise 3** | **Using Pronouns in Nominative and Objective Cases** |

For each numbered item, write the correct pronoun in parentheses.

[1]George and Maria love stories. (They, Them) especially like fables. [2]Maria wanted to go to the library with George. Could (he, him) go after school?

[3]"We can borrow some books of stories by Aesop," (she, her) said.

[4]George said, "Our friends may have checked (they, them) out already. [5](We, Us) should go to the used bookstore."

MEETING INDIVIDUAL NEEDS

English Language Learners

Practicing Pronouns

Personal pronouns are used in all languages. The form that these pronouns take frequently differs, however. For example, some languages use a single form for both subject and object pronouns. Others use the same pronoun to refer to men and women. Have students work in groups of three or more. As they pass an object around, one student announces the action. For example: *I pass the book to you. You pass it to him. He passes it to her.*

11.2 Using Pronouns Correctly

People sometimes confuse pronouns in the nominative and objective cases. They write or say *me* when they should use *I*. They use *we* when they should use *us*. Remember to use a subject pronoun as the subject. Use an object pronoun as the object of a verb.

> **She** owns a collection of fables. [subject]
>
> He told **her** an amusing fable. [indirect object]
>
> The fable entertained **us.** [direct object]

Be sure to use a subject pronoun in a compound subject and an object pronoun in a compound object.

> Richard and **I** recited the fable. [not *Richard and me*]
>
> Jennifer helped Richard and **me.** [not *Richard and I*]

In the first sentence above, *Richard and I* is the compound subject. In the second sentence, *Richard and me* is the compound object of the verb *helped.*

If you're having trouble deciding which form of the pronoun to use in a compound subject or compound object, try saying the sentence without the noun. *Me recited the fable* does not sound correct. *I recited the fable* sounds—and is—correct.

Whenever the pronoun *I* or *me* is joined with a noun or another pronoun to form a compound subject or object, *I* or *me* should come last.

> Jennifer and **I** enjoy folktales. [not *I and Jennifer*]

In formal writing and speaking, always use a subject pronoun—not an object pronoun—after a linking verb. If the sentence sounds awkward, rearrange the words.

> The winner is **she.** [not *The winner is her*]
>
> **She** is the winner.

Richard and I visited a storyteller.

She told Richard and me a fascinating story.

Pronouns

Focus

Lesson Overview

Objectives
- To identify pronouns in nominative and objective cases
- To demonstrate control over the accurate use of the subject pronoun in formal writing and speaking

Bellringer
Daily Language Activity

When students enter the classroom, have this assignment on the board: *Write this sentence, replacing the compound subject and object with just two pronouns.*
> *She and he brought it to him and her.*

See also *Daily Language Practice*

Teach

☑ Grammar Tip

To see whether a pronoun in a compound subject or object is correct, replace the compound with the correct plural pronoun: *Lia and I go. We go.*

Resource Manager

Planning Resources
- *Lesson Plans*

Transparencies
- *Bellringer*
- *Daily Language Practice*
- *Two-Minute Skill Drill*

📁 **Other Print Resources**
- *Grammar and Composition Handbook*
- *Grammar Enrichment,* p. 17
- *Grammar Practice,* p. 16
- *Grammar Reteaching,* p. 19
- *Grammar Workbook,* Lesson 26

Practice and Assess

Answers: Exercise 4

1. I
2. me
3. I
4. us
5. him
6. I
7. I
8. I
9. me
10. him

Answers: Exercise 5

1. He—subj.
2. him—obj.
3. her—obj.
4. them—obj.
5. he—subj.
6. you and I—subj.
7. He—subj.
8. she and he—subj.
9. you and me—obj.
10. them—obj.

Answers: Exercise 6

Answers will vary, but some suggestions are given below.
She and I ran after them.
They gave the box to him and me.

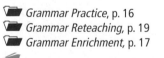

Two-Minute Skill Drill

List these pronouns on the board. Have students tell whether they are subject or object pronouns and how they know.

they	him
she	us
me	them

 See also *Two-Minute Skill Drill Transparencies,* 11.2

Additional Resources

📁 *Grammar Practice,* p. 16
📁 *Grammar Reteaching,* p. 19
📁 *Grammar Enrichment,* p. 17

📕 *Grammar Workbook,* Lesson 26

Close

Have students read a paragraph in a book, write down the pronouns, and identify them as subjects or objects. Ask students to trade papers with partners and to check each other's work. Partners should discuss any needed corrections.

364

Pronouns

Exercise 4 **Using Pronouns in Nominative and Objective Cases**

Read the following dialogue between the North Wind and the Sun. Write the correct pronoun for each item.

1. North Wind: (I, me) am the strongest power.
2. Sun: How will you show (I, me)?
3. North Wind: You and (I, me) will have a contest.
4. Sun: A traveler is approaching (we, us).
5. North Wind: I see his dog and (he, him).
6. Sun: You or (I, me) must steal his cloak from him.
7. North Wind: The winner will be you or (I, me).
8. Sun: No, (I, me) cannot lose this contest.
9. North Wind: Watch (I, me) closely as I blow the cloak from the traveler.
10. Sun: I will watch (him, he), but I know you will fail.

Exercise 5 **Using Pronoun Cases Correctly**

Write a personal pronoun to replace each underlined group of words. Label each pronoun *subject* or *object.*

1. The North Wind blew fiercely. (He, Him)
2. The traveler resisted the North Wind. (he, him)
3. The North Wind watched the Sun work. (she, her)
4. The man felt the rays of the Sun on his back. (they, them)
5. Before long the man was glad to remove the cloak. (he, him)
6. "Now North Wind and the Sun know who's more powerful," said the Sun. (you and I, you and me)
7. The North Wind could not overpower the Sun. (He, Him)
8. However, the Sun and North Wind realized that they both had powers. (she and he, her and him)
9. "This world needs both North Wind and the Sun," said the Sun. (you and me, you and I)
10. From that point on, the world respected the Sun and North Wind equally. (they, them)

Exercise 6 **Writing with Personal Pronouns**

Write five sentences. Use at least one of these pronouns in each sentence: *I, she, he, we, they, me, her, him, us, them.* Use both subject and object pronouns.

MEETING INDIVIDUAL NEEDS **Special Needs**

Testing for Compounds

Tell students that they can see whether they are using the correct pronoun in a compound subject or object by replacing the compound with a plural pronoun, such at *they* or *them.* If *they* can be used to replace the compound, then a subject pronoun should be used in the compound. (*Diana and I are reading a book.*) If *them* can replace the compound, then an object pronoun should be used. (*Darna lent the book to Diana and me.*)

11.3 Pronouns and Antecedents

■ The noun or a group of words that a pronoun refers to is called its **antecedent.**

> Albert read "Sleeping Beauty." **He** found **it** exciting.

Here, the noun *Albert* is the antecedent of the pronoun *He*. "*Sleeping Beauty*" is the antecedent of the pronoun *it*.

The pronoun must agree with its antecedent in **number** (singular or plural) and **gender.** The gender of a noun may be masculine (male), feminine (female), or neuter (referring to things).

> The king and queen were proud of the baby girl, and **they** loved **her** dearly.

In the sentence above, the pronoun *they* agrees with its antecedent, *The king and queen.* The pronoun *her* agrees with its antecedent, *the baby girl.*

The antecedent of a pronoun should be clear.

> The parents showed the baby to friends. **They** admired **her.**

In the second sentence above, does the pronoun *they* refer to *parents* or *friends*? If the antecedent is not clear, it is best to avoid using a pronoun altogether.

> **The friends** admired the baby.

Be especially careful when you use the pronoun *they.*

> They have many books of folktales at the library. [unclear]
> The library has many books of folktales. [clear]

Pronouns

Focus

Lesson Overview

Objectives

• To identify pronouns and their antecedents
• To show agreement of pronouns and antecedents

Bellringer
Daily Language Activity

When students enter the classroom, have this assignment on the board: *Write a paragraph of three sentences with at least one pronoun in each sentence.*

See also *Daily Language Practice*

Motivating Activity

Have volunteers write their paragraphs from the Bellringer activity on the board. Ask them to circle each pronoun and draw an arrow back to the antecedent. If a pronoun is unclear, have students discuss ways to correct the problem.

Teach

Cooperative Learning

Divide the class into small groups and provide each group with a pencil and paper. Then ask the groups to write their own folktale, fable, or fairy tale. Students may work together to correct errors in pronoun–antecedent agreement.

Resource Manager

Planning Resources
• *Lesson Plans*

Transparencies
• *Bellringer*
• *Daily Language Practice*

Other Print Resources
• *Grammar and Composition Handbook*
• *Grammar Enrichment,* p. 18
• *Grammar Practice,* p. 17
• *Grammar Reteaching,* p. 20
• *Grammar Workbook,* Lesson 27

Practice and Assess

Answers: Exercise 7

1. man
2. children
3. wind
4. house
5. children
6. bear
7. bear
8. request
9. daughter
10. man

Answers: Exercise 8

1. It—bear
2. them—children
3. her—daughter
4. you—girl; we—family or you—girl
5. I—girl; you—father, brothers, sisters

Answers: Exercise 9

1. They have a wolf as a main character.
2. In one story, they outsmart a wolf.
3. She meets a wolf in another story.
4. Instead of a wolf, she meets three bears.
5. Goldilocks ate it before the bears returned.

Additional Resources

📁 *Grammar Practice,* p. 17
📁 *Grammar Reteaching,* p. 20
📁 *Grammar Enrichment,* p. 18

📙 *Grammar Workbook,* Lesson 27

Close

Have students give examples of pronouns that agree in number and pronouns that agree in gender.

Pronouns

Exercise 7	Identifying Antecedents

The sentences below are about "The White Bear," a Russian folktale. Write the antecedent of each underlined pronoun.

1. A man lived in the forest. <u>He</u> was very poor.
2. He had many children. He could not feed <u>them</u>.
3. One night the wind blew hard. <u>It</u> shook the walls.
4. The house stood firm. <u>It</u> was well built.
5. The children heard a noise outside. <u>They</u> were afraid.
6. A white bear appeared. The man approached <u>it</u>.
7. The bear asked the man, "Will you give <u>me</u> your youngest daughter?"
8. This was a strange request. The man had never heard anything like <u>it</u>.
9. His daughter was dear to the man. What could he tell <u>her</u>?
10. The man listened to the bear. <u>He</u> wanted to learn what it would offer.

Exercise 8	Using Personal Pronouns

Write the correct pronoun to complete each sentence below. Then write and circle its antecedent.

1. The bear made a promise. _____ promised the family great wealth.
2. The man spoke with his children. He told _____ about the bear's request.
3. The youngest daughter became worried. The bear's request frightened _____ .
4. The girl listened to her family. They said, "If _____ go, the bear promises _____ will be rich."
5. Finally the girl told her father and her brothers and sisters, "_____ will go because I love _____ ."

Exercise 9	Writing with Personal Pronouns

Read each sentence. Rewrite the sentence, replacing the underlined antecedent with a personal pronoun.

1. <u>Many stories</u> have a wolf as a main character.
2. In one story, <u>three pigs</u> outsmart a wolf.
3. <u>Little Red Riding Hood</u> meets a wolf in another story.
4. Instead of a wolf, <u>Goldilocks</u> meets three bears.
5. Goldilocks ate <u>the porridge</u> before the bears returned.

366 Unit 11 Pronouns

MEETING INDIVIDUAL NEEDS — English Language Learners

Checking Pronoun Agreement

Point out that when the antecedent of a pronoun is another pronoun, the two pronouns should agree. Explain that a common mistake is shifting from *they* to *you* or from *I* to *you* within the same sentence; for example, *They often go to the library, where you can read folktales from all over the world* or *I like this story because you can really relate to it.* You might suggest that students try reading their own sentences aloud to make sure the pronouns agree.

11.4 Possessive Pronouns

Some personal pronouns indicate ownership or possession. These pronouns are called possessive pronouns, and they replace the possessive forms of nouns.

■ A **possessive pronoun** is a pronoun in the possessive case. It shows who or what has something.

Some possessive pronouns are used before nouns. They replace the name of the person or thing that has something.

> **Aesop's** fables are famous. **His** fables are famous.
> **A fable** is a brief tale. **Its** characters are often animals.

Other possessive pronouns stand alone in a sentence.

> This book is **yours.**
> **Aesop's Fables** is a favorite of **mine.**

The chart below shows the singular and plural forms of the two different kinds of possessive pronouns.

Possessive Pronouns		
	Singular	**Plural**
Used Before Nouns	my	our
	your	your
	her, his, its	their
Used Alone	mine	ours
	yours	yours
	hers, his, its	theirs

Possessive pronouns do not contain an apostrophe. Do not confuse the possessive pronoun *its* with the word *it's*. *It's* is a contraction, or shortened form, of the words *it is: It's a humorous tale.*

11.4 Possessive Pronouns **367**

Pronouns

Focus

Lesson Overview

Objectives
- To identify possessive pronouns
- To use possessive pronouns correctly
- To distinguish between the contraction for *it is* (*it's*) and the possessive pronoun *its*

Bellringer
Daily Language Activity

When students enter the classroom, have this assignment on the board. *Rewrite the following sentence so it is not repetitive:*
Jacob took Jacob's homework to Jacob's teacher and asked, "Is Jacob's answer correct?"

See also *Daily Language Practice*

Motivating Activity

Ask volunteers to read their revised sentences aloud. Then write the sentence on the board, inserting possessive pronouns as appropriate. Point out the repetition in the original sentence. Ask students why the corrected sentence sounds better than the original.

Teach

☑ **Grammar Tip**

To see if *its* is a contraction, students should replace *its* with *it is*. If the sentence makes sense, then students can write *it's*.

Resource Manager

Planning Resources
- *Lesson Plans*

Transparencies
- *Bellringer*
- *Daily Language Practice*

Other Print Resources
- *Grammar and Composition Handbook*
- *Grammar Enrichment,* 19
- *Grammar Practice,* p. 18
- *Grammar Reteaching,* p. 21
- *Grammar Workbook,* Lesson 28

Practice and Assess

Answers: Exercise 10

1. his—before a noun
2. its—before a noun
3. his—before a noun
4. yours—stands alone
5. mine—stands alone

Answers: Exercise 11

1. his or her
2. its
3. her
4. Their
5. its
6. their
7. yours
8. Mine
9. their
10. his

Answers: Exercise 12

Answers will vary, but some suggestions are given below.
1. The woman's idea was powerful. Her idea was powerful.
2. The friends' words were kind. Their words were kind.
3. The mule's back was sturdy. Its back was sturdy.
4. A girl's opinion was important. Her opinion was important.
5. People's thoughts were with her. Their thoughts were with her.

Additional Resources

📂 *Grammar Practice,* p. 18
📂 *Grammar Reteaching,* p. 21
📂 *Grammar Enrichment,* p. 19

📙 *Grammar Workbook,* Lesson 28

Close

Have students write four sentences using possessive pronouns before nouns and possessive pronouns that stand alone. Ask students to exchange papers and check each other's work. Students should point out any incorrectly used possessive pronouns and discuss possible revisions.

Pronouns

Exercise 10   Identifying Kinds of Possessive Pronouns

The sentences below are about a fable. List each possessive pronoun and write whether it *stands alone* or is used *before a noun.*

1. A miller, his son, and a mule walked to market.
2. "Ride on its back," a stranger suggested.
3. The boy got on, and his father walked.
4. A man they knew saw them and said, "You will spoil that son of yours."
5. The man said, "Will you follow a stranger's advice or mine?"

Exercise 11   Using Pronouns in the Possessive Case

Write a possessive pronoun to replace each underlined word or phrase.

1. The miller talked to a friend and followed <u>the friend's</u> advice.
2. The boy walked beside the mule; the man rode on <u>the mule's</u> back.
3. Next a woman gave <u>the woman's</u> opinion, and they followed that advice and rode together.
4. <u>The man and the boy's</u> weight was too great.
5. The mule collapsed, and the man and boy worried about <u>the mule's</u> health.
6. They carried the mule on <u>the man's and the boy's</u> shoulders.
7. The man's shoulders were tired. He asked the boy, "How do <u>your shoulders</u> feel?"
8. "<u>My shoulders</u> are tired as well," the boy answered.
9. The man saw that only fools think other people's opinions are better than <u>the fools'</u> own.
10. If the miller had followed <u>the miller's</u> own instincts, the mule would not have collapsed.

Exercise 12   Writing Sentences with Possessive Pronouns

Write a pair of sentences using each phrase. In one sentence of each pair, replace part of the phrase with a possessive pronoun.

SAMPLE   the boy's bike
ANSWER   The boy's bike was new. His bike was new.

1. the woman's idea
2. the friends' words
3. the mule's back
4. a girl's opinion
5. people's thoughts

368   Unit 11 Pronouns

MEETING INDIVIDUAL NEEDS

English Language Learners

Possessive Pronouns

Have students who are acquiring English work with proficient English speakers. Provide pairs with pictures from magazines and have them write a phrase describing something in the picture (the man's camera) and a related phrase using a possessive pronoun (his camera). Have them list as many of these paired phrases as they can think of.

11.5 Indefinite Pronouns

■ An **indefinite pronoun** does not refer to a particular person, place, thing, or idea.

Like possessive pronouns, indefinite pronouns can be used alone or with nouns.

> Has **any student** read this Native American folktale?
>
> Have **any** read "The Voice of the River"?

When used alone, indefinite pronouns may be singular or plural.

INDEFINITE PRONOUNS

ALWAYS SINGULAR			ALWAYS PLURAL
another	everybody	no one	both
anybody	everyone	nothing	few
anyone	everything	one	many
anything	much	somebody	others
each	neither	someone	several
either	nobody	something	

When an indefinite pronoun is used as the subject of a sentence, the indefinite pronoun may be singular or plural, depending on the noun that follows. Indefinite pronouns that change their number include *all, any, most, none,* and *some.*

> **Some** of the people **are** familiar with this folktale. [plural]
>
> **Most** of this tale **takes** place in Africa. [singular]
>
> **Most** of the characters **are** animals. [plural]

Possessive pronouns often have indefinite pronouns as their antecedents. In such cases, the pronouns must agree in number.

> **Many** are happy to share **their** folktales. [plural]
>
> **Each** must be willing to wait **his** or **her** turn. [singular]

11.5 Indefinite Pronouns **369**

Focus

Lesson Overview

Objectives
- To identify singular and plural indefinite pronouns
- To demonstrate control over the accurate use of singular and plural verbs with singular and plural indefinite pronouns

Bellringer
Daily Language Activity

When students enter the classroom, have the following assignment on the board: *Write four sentences, each beginning with one of the following words:*

Everyone	Both
Most	Somebody

See also *Daily Language Practice*

Motivating Activity

Have volunteers write their sentences from the Bellringer activity on the board. Have students underline the verb and circle the pronoun in each sentence. Tell students that the sentence starter words are indefinite pronouns and that the verb in each sentence must agree with the pronoun in number. Have students revise sentences in which the subjects and verbs do not agree.

Teach

☑ **Teaching Tip**

Many writers try to avoid the phrase *his or her* by using a plural indefinite pronoun. Compare the following sentences: *Each of the students has his or her opinion about the moral of the fairy tale. All of the students have their own opinions about the moral of the fairy tale.* As an alternative, a writer may use the indefinite article *a* or *an*: *Each student has an interesting opinion about the moral of the fairy tale.*

Pronouns

Resource Manager

Planning Resources
- *Lesson Plans*

Transparencies
- *Bellringer*
- *Daily Language Practice*
- *Two-Minute Skill Drill*

📁 Other Print Resources
- *Grammar and Composition Handbook*
- *Grammar Enrichment,* p. 20
- *Grammar Practice,* p. 19
- *Grammar Workbook,* Lesson 29

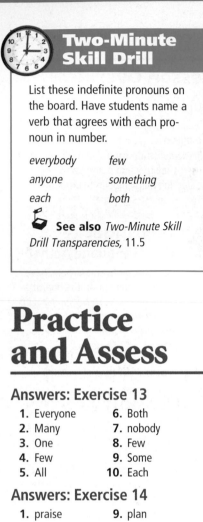

Two-Minute Skill Drill

List these indefinite pronouns on the board. Have students name a verb that agrees with each pronoun in number.

everybody	few
anyone	something
each	both

See also *Two-Minute Skill Drill Transparencies,* 11.5

Practice and Assess

Answers: Exercise 13

1. Everyone
2. Many
3. One
4. Few
5. All
6. Both
7. nobody
8. Few
9. Some
10. Each

Answers: Exercise 14

1. praise
2. their
3. is
4. escapes
5. changes
6. his or her
7. know
8. takes
9. plan
10. his
11. goes
12. see
13. flies
14. lands
15. him or her

Additional Resources

📁 *Grammar Practice,* p. 19
📁 *Grammar Enrichment,* p. 20

📖 *Grammar Workbook,* Lesson 29

Close

Ask students to write several sentences describing a conversation among three friends, using indefinite pronouns instead of the friends' names. Have students circle the indefinite pronouns. Ask students to exchange papers and discuss and explain answers.

Pronouns

Exercise 13 Using Indefinite Pronouns

For each sentence, write the correct singular or plural indefinite pronoun in parentheses.

1. (Everyone, Many) likes to read an exciting myth.
2. (Each, Many) are originally from Greece.
3. (One, Others) from Greece is about a father and a son.
4. (Anyone, Few) were able to guess the myth's ending.
5. (All, Anybody) enjoy the myth of Daedalus and Icarus.
6. (Both, One) of the mythical characters live on the island of Crete.
7. Daedalus has artistic talents; (none, nobody) can deny that.
8. (Few, Somebody) match Daedalus's skill in design.
9. (Some, Each) of these students model their work on his art.
10. (Each, Both) of the characters is interesting.

Exercise 14 Using Indefinite Pronouns

Write the word or words in parentheses that correctly complete each sentence.

1. Most of the people (praises, praise) Daedalus's ideas for the huge palace.
2. Few know (his, their) craft as well as Daedalus.
3. No one (is, are) more pleased than King Minos.
4. Although many try, no one (escapes, escape) the king's maze.
5. Everything (changes, change) when Daedalus tells the secret.
6. At last someone finds (his or her, their) way out.
7. Some of the readers (knows, know) the rest of the story: the king forbids Daedalus to leave.
8. Something (takes, take) shape in Daedalus's skilled hands—wax wings for himself and Icarus.
9. Both (plans, plan) an escape across the sea.
10. Each puts on (his, their) pair of waxy wings.
11. At first everything (goes, go) well for the pair.
12. Several (sees, see) them flying in the sky.
13. One (flies, fly) too close to the sun; the wax melts, and he plunges to his death.
14. Which one (lands, land) safely in Sicily?
15. When someone tries to do the impossible, disaster can strike (him or her, them.)

MEETING INDIVIDUAL NEEDS English Language Learners

Using Pronouns

Encourage students to copy into their journals the chart of singular and plural indefinite pronouns on page 369. Have students refer to the chart when checking a recent writing assignment for correct indefinite pronoun usage and subject–verb agreement.

Many students have difficulty determining whether *everyone* and *everybody* are singular or plural. Tell students that all indefinite pronouns that end in *-one, -body,* or *-thing* are singular. Have students jot down a reminder in their journals.

Grammar Review

PRONOUNS

In "The Wise Old Woman," a Japanese folktale, a young lord banishes everyone over seventy-one years of age from his village. A farmer disobeys the ruler and hides his mother. In the following passage, the ruler discovers that the old woman has saved the village. The passage has been annotated to show some of the pronouns covered in this unit.

Literature Model

from The Wise Old Woman

Japanese Folktale

Retold by Yoshiko Uchida

The young farmer was amazed at **his** mother's wisdom. "You are far wiser than **any** of the wise men of the village," he said, and he hurried to tell the young lord how to complete Lord Higa's third demand.

When the lord heard the answer, he was greatly impressed. "Surely a young man like you cannot be wiser than all my wise men," he said. "Tell **me** honestly, who has helped you solve all these difficult problems?"

The young farmer could not lie. "My lord," he began slowly, "for the past two years I have broken the law of the land. **I** have kept my aged mother hidden beneath the floor of my house, and it is she who solved each of your problems and saved the village from Lord Higa."

He trembled as he spoke, for he feared the lord's displeasure and rage. Surely now the soldiers would be called to throw him into the dark dungeon.

> **Possessive pronoun**

> **Indefinite pronoun**

> **Object personal pronoun**

> **Subject personal pronoun**

(continued)

Grammar Review   **371**

Pronouns

Teach

About the Literature

After students have read the passage from "The Wise Old Woman," discuss the highlighted pronouns. Encourage students to determine what noun—and its modifiers, if appropriate—could be substituted for each pronoun.

The passage reproduced in the student book appears at the end of "The Wise Old Woman," after the old woman has solved two of Lord Higa's riddles. Yoshiko Uchida often wrote about Japanese culture and the Japanese American experience.

Linking Grammar and Literature

☑ Teaching Tip

In informal speech, people tend to use pronouns carelessly, often ignoring a pronoun's antecedent. For example, many speakers use the second-person pronoun *you* to refer to a third-person antecedent: *Carlos went to the festival, where you could see a performance of* Cinderella. Explain that replacing *you* with a specific word will make the meaning of the sentence clearer: *Carlos went to the festival, where the public could see a performance of* Cinderella.

Listening and Speaking

Read the passage from "The Wise Old Woman" aloud to the class, replacing each pronoun with an appropriate noun. Then ask students to discuss how the substitutions affect the passage. Does the abundance of nouns make the writing seem repetitious and boring? Now read the passage again, but this time substitute a pronoun for each noun. Discuss the effect. Does the absence of nouns make the writing hard to understand?

Resource Manager

Planning Resources
• *Lesson Plans*

📁 Other Print Resources
• *Grammar and Composition Handbook*
• *Grammar Workbook,*
  Lessons 25–29; Unit 4 Review;
  Cumulative Review: Units 1–4

✔ ASSESSMENT OPTIONS

📁 *Tests with Answer Key and Rubrics*
Unit 11 Mastery Test, pp. 47–48

💾 *Testmaker*
Unit 11 Mastery Test

Practice and Assess

Answers: Exercise 1

1. I
2. I
3. me
4. her; she
5. I; they

Answers: Exercise 2

1. They
2. she
3. him
4. I
5. he

Subject pronoun agrees with its antecedent, *the lord*

But when he glanced fearfully at the lord, he saw that the young ruler was not angry at all. Instead, the lord was silent and thoughtful. At last **he** realized how much wisdom and knowledge old people possess.

Review: Exercise 1   **Using Personal Pronouns as Subjects and Objects**

Read the following dialogue. For each item, write the correct pronoun.

1. The Ruler: (I, Me) declare that all old people are useless.
2. Farmer: The other villagers and (I, me) do not agree with you.
3. The Ruler: What can you tell (I, me) to change my mind?
4. Farmer: It is my old mother who saved this village. You do not know (she, her), but (her, she) is wise.
5. The Ruler: Perhaps I was wrong. Let it be known to all old people. (Me, I) declare (they, them) are welcome in the land.

Review: Exercise 2   **Making Pronouns and Antecedents Agree**

Write the correct pronoun to complete the second sentence in each pair.

SAMPLE   The young farmer's mother was not troubled by Lord Higa's tasks._____ knew how to complete them.

ANSWER   She

1. The problems hadn't been solved by the wise men. _____ were bewildered.
2. The farmer told the lord that he had hidden his mother. "It is _____ who saved the village," he said.
3. The young farmer was frightened. He thought the soldiers would throw _____ into the dungeon.
4. The young lord looked thoughtful. He said, "_____ have been wrong."
5. The ruler had thought that old people were useless. At last _____ realized that they should be honored.

Review: Exercise 3 **Identifying Personal Pronouns as Subjects or Objects**

Write each pronoun and label it *subject* or *object*.

1. Aesop is famous. He wrote many fables.
2. He was a Greek writer who lived in the sixth century B.C.
3. People admire him.
4. A girl told me that Aesop's fables are fun to read.
5. I asked her to name a favorite fable.
6. She named "The Fox and the Mouse."
7. Because Aesop's stories are often about animals, children especially enjoy them.
8. Roman and medieval writers collected them.
9. We read Aesop's fables that were collected by Phaedrus.
10. You can find them in many anthologies.

Review: Exercise 4 **Using Personal Pronouns as Compound Subjects and Objects**

Write pronouns to replace the underlined words.

SAMPLE Kate and Martin read the story.
ANSWER She and he
SAMPLE Kate and Martin liked it.
ANSWER They

1. Amy and John wrote a fable.
2. They read Mr. Jackson and Ms. Diaz the tale.
3. Gina and I saw Amy and John after school.
4. Amy and John asked us to watch them act out their fable.
5. Gina and I applauded Amy and John after their great performance.
6. Amy and John thanked Gina and me.
7. They told Gina and me that they appreciated our applause.
8. Mr. Jackson and Ms. Diaz applauded too.
9. Ms. Diaz gave Amy and John a flower.
10. Mr. Jackson saluted Amy and John.

Answers: Exercise 3
1. He—subject
2. He—subject
3. him—object
4. me—object
5. I—subject; her—object
6. She—subject
7. them—object
8. them—object
9. We—subject
10. You—subject; them—object

Answers: Exercise 4
1. She; he
2. them or him and her
3. She
4. She; he
5. We
6. her
7. us
8. He; she
9. them
10. him

Pronouns

Answers: Exercise 5

1. his
2. my
3. his
4. her
5. my; your
6. their
7. its
8. his; his
9. His
10. their

Answers: Exercise 6

Answers will vary, but some suggestions are provided below.

1. Someone listens to a story.
2. All make a loud noise.
   All of this pie makes a huge serving.
3. Several talk to their friends.
4. Everybody plays the game.
5. Many enjoy the game.

Review: Exercise 5 **Using Possessive Pronouns with Nouns**

The following sentences based on passages in "The Wise Old Woman" do not appear in this textbook. Write a possessive pronoun to replace the underlined words in each sentence.

SAMPLE The villagers' leader issued a cruel decree.
ANSWER Their

1. The ruler wanted all of the ruler's people to be young and strong.
2. The lord said, "I have no use for old people in the lord's village."
3. No one guessed that the woman was hiding in the young farmer's house.
4. The ruler was amazed by the old woman's wisdom.
5. The farmer told the ruler, "It was the farmer's aged mother who solved the ruler's problems."
6. The villagers were no longer forced to abandon the villagers' parents in the mountains.
7. Lord Higa left the village alone, declaring that the village's people be allowed to live in peace.
8. The young farmer now had the farmer's worry lifted from the farmer's mind.
9. The ruler's new understanding would allow the villagers to live full lives.
10. The people would always remember how the farmer's courage had saved the people's village.

Review: Exercise 6 **Writing Sentences with Indefinite Pronouns**

Write a sentence for each item below. Use the pronoun as the subject and the correct word from each pair as the verb.

1. Someone   listens, listen
2. All   makes, make
3. Several   talks, talk
4. Everybody   plays, play
5. Many   enjoys, enjoy

Pronouns

Review: Exercise 7

Proofreading

The following passage is about African American artist Jacob Lawrence. Rewrite the passage, correcting the errors in spelling, capitalization, grammar, and usage. Add any missing punctuation. There are ten errors.

Jacob Lawrence

[1]Jacob Lawrence, who was born in 1917, growed up in Harlem. [2]This thriving artistic center influenced he. [3]Lawrence chose to become a painter in his teens and him was encouraged by artists in his community. [4]Lawrence was twenty-four years old when his' work was exhibited in a New york art gallery.

Jacob Lawrence, *Men Exist for the Sake of One Another*, 1958

(continued)

Grammar Review **375**

Pronouns

Answers: Exercise 7

Proofreading

This proofreading activity provides editing practice with (1) the current or previous units' skills, (2) the **Troubleshooter** errors, and (3) spelling errors. Students should be able to complete the exercise by referring to the units, the **Troubleshooter**, and a dictionary.

Error (Type of Error)
1. • grew (verb tense)
2. • him (object pronoun)
3. • teens, and (compound sentence)
• he (subject pronoun)
4. • his (possessive pronoun)
• York (capitalization)
5. • portray (subject-verb agreement)
6. • find (subject-verb agreement)
• appealing (spelling)
7. • no error
8. • learns (subject-verb agreement)

Viewing the Art

Jacob Lawrence, *Men Exist for the Sake of One Another*, 1958

Jacob Lawrence's paintings celebrate people and the universality of the human experience. In *Men Exist for the Sake of One Another* (1958), for example, the artist presents the universal image of children learning at an adult's knee.

Answers: Exercise 8

Mixed Review

1. Our (or My)
2. It
3. her (or him; or it)
4. they
5. her (or his; or its)
6. them
7. it
8. everyone
9. our (or my)
10. it
11. us
12. me
13. her
14. I (or he; or she)
15. We (or They)
16. My
17. Nobody
18. his (or mine)
19. It
20. her

Close

Ask students to summarize in a few sentences what is happening in Jacob Lawrence's painting *Men Exist for the Sake of One Another* on page 375. Then ask students to circle the pronouns students used in the summaries. Remind students to be sure the pronouns and antecedents agree. Have students exchange papers and check each other's work. Students should discuss any needed corrections.

Pronouns

[5]Lawrence's paintings portrays the lives and struggles of African Americans. [6]Most people finds his work apealing. [7]In the painting on the previous page, Lawrence shows a man talking to some children. [8]The painting reminds us that everyone learn from others.

Review: Exercise 8

Mixed Review

Number a sheet of paper from 1 to 20. Then choose a pronoun from the list below to fill in each blank. You will not need to use all the pronouns, but you may need to use some pronouns more than once. Use correct capitalization.

everyone	its	she
her	me	them
him	mine	they
his	my	us
I	nobody	we
it	our	yours

[1]_____ class read a fable written by Aesop. [2]_____ was the story of a very hungry fox. Some grapes tempted [3]_____. However, [4]_____ were out of [5]_____ reach. The fox knew other animals could probably reach the grapes. The fox thought of a way to reach [6]_____ too. If you want to know how this story ends, you will have to read [7]_____.

Almost [8]_____ enjoys a good folktale. Our teacher told [9]_____ class a story based on a Native American folktale. Mae and I found [10]_____ wise. The story taught [11]_____ about life in a village. It amused and surprised both her and [12]_____. Later Mae read the tale again to [13]_____ sister, Ann.

Yesterday my brother and [14]_____ went to the library. [15]_____ were both looking for a book of fables. [16]_____ brother found a book of Aesop's fables. [17]_____ is better known for fables than Aesop. The book is now a favorite of [18]_____. [19]_____ has a story has about a vixen. In it, she talks about [20]_____ cubs.

Writing Application

Pronouns in Writing

Michael Dorris uses pronouns in this passage from *Morning Girl* to make his writing clear and concise. Read the passage, paying particular attention to the pronouns that are italicized.

I knew *my* hands very well. *I* study *them* when *I* trim *my* nails with the rough edge of a broken shell, making *them* smooth and flat. *I* could spread *my* fingers and press *them* into wet sand to see the shape *they* leave. Once *I* tried to do that with *my* head, but *all I* got was a big shallow hole and dirty hair.

I knew the front of *my* body, the bottoms of *my* feet. *I* knew the color of *my* arms—tan as the inside of a yam after the air has dried *it*—and if *I* stretched *my* tongue *I* could see *its* pink tip.

Techniques with Pronouns

Use pronouns in your writing as does Michael Dorris.

❶ Always check that a pronoun agrees with its antecedent.

INCORRECT USE I knew my *hands* very well. I study *it* . . .

DORRIS'S VERSION I knew my *hands* very well. I study *them* . . .

❷ To make your writing smooth, replace repeated nouns and their modifiers with pronouns.

REPEATED WORDS I could spread *my fingers* and press my fingers into wet sand to see the shape *my fingers* leave.

DORRIS'S VERSION I could spread *my fingers* and press *them into* wet sand to see the shape they leave.

> ### TIME
> For more about usage rules, see **TIME Facing the Blank Page,** page 98.

Pronouns

Pronouns in Writing

Have students read the passage silently. Then go back and discuss the italicized pronoun choices in relation to the Techniques with Pronouns. Encourage students to ask questions for clarification as needed.

Techniques with Pronouns

Discuss the techniques described and have students examine how they are used. Students can look for examples in other books or stories and share them with a partner.

Practice

The answers to this challenging and enriching activity will vary. Refer to Techniques with Pronouns as you evaluate student choices.

Practice Practice the techniques with pronouns by revising the following passage on a separate sheet of paper.

Morning Girl spends every day with Morning Girl's brother Star Boy. Morning Girl and Star Boy go to the beach. The brother and sister walk along the shore. Star Boy finds smooth pebbles. Star Boy finds unbroken shells and gives them to Morning Girl. The boy and girl wade in the shallow water and find tiny crabs and starfish. Morning Girl and Star Boy take Morning Girl's and Star Boy's treasures home. They put their treasures in a shaded pool next to the house where they live with their parents. Morning Girl and Star Boy will watch the crabs and starfish for several hours. Then the children will return the live creatures to the sea.

Writing Application **377**

> ✔ **ASSESSMENT OPTIONS**
>
> 📁 *Tests with Answer Key and Rubrics*
> Unit 11 Mastery Test, pp. 47–48
>
> 💾 *Testmaker*
> Unit 11 Mastery Test
>
> You may wish to administer the Unit 11 Mastery Test at this point.
>
> 📼 *Mindjogger Videoquizzes*

Objectives

- To identify adjectives in sentences, and to capitalize proper adjectives
- To recognize and apply usage rules for articles, demonstrative adjectives, and demonstrative pronouns
- To use and correctly spell comparative and superlative forms of adjectives
- To use vivid adjectives correctly in writing

✔ ASSESSMENT OPTIONS

📁 *Tests with Answer Key and Rubrics*
Unit 12 Pretest, pp. 49–50
Unit 12 Mastery Test, pp. 51–52

💾 *Testmaker*
Unit 12 Pretest
Unit 12 Mastery Test

You may wish to administer the Unit 12 Pretest at this point.

Key to Ability Levels

L1 Level 1 activities are within the basic ability range of students.

L2 Level 2 activities are within the ability range of average students.

L3 Level 3 activities are more challenging activities.

UNIT
12 Adjectives

378

Resource Manager

Planning Resources
- Lesson Plans
- Block Scheduling

📑 Transparencies
- Bellringer
- Daily Language Practice

📁 Other Print Resources
- Grammar and Composition Handbook

- Grammar Enrichment
- Grammar Practice
- Grammar Reteaching
- Grammar Workbook
- Tests with Answer Key and Rubrics

📹 Video
- MindJogger Videoquizzes

💾 Software
- Interactive Grammar and Language Workbook
- Language Arts PASS
- Presentation Plus!
- Testmaker

🖥 Web Sites
- writerschoice.glencoe.com

12.1 Adjectives and Proper Adjectives

The words that we use to describe people, places, and things are called adjectives.

■ An **adjective** is a word that describes a noun or a pronoun.

Adjectives describe, or modify, nouns in three ways.

How Adjectives Describe Nouns	
What kind?	We studied **modern** history.
How many?	I read **four** volumes.
Which one?	**That** invention changed the world.

Most adjectives come before the nouns they modify. Sometimes adjectives follow linking verbs and modify the subject, as in the example below. These adjectives are called **predicate adjectives.**

These inventions are important.

Some adjectives are formed from proper nouns and begin with a capital letter. These are called **proper adjectives.**

■ **Proper adjectives** are adjectives formed from proper nouns.

Proper adjectives often have the same form as the noun. Others are formed by adding an ending to the noun form.

FORMING PROPER ADJECTIVES

PROPER NOUN	PROPER ADJECTIVE
Oranges from **Florida**	**Florida** oranges
A symphony by **Mozart**	A **Mozart** symphony
Food from **Italy**	**Italian** food

Adjectives

Focus

Lesson Overview

Objectives
- To identify adjectives and the words they modify in sentences
- To demonstrate control over the rules of capitalization for proper adjectives

Bellringer
Daily Language Activity

When students enter the classroom, have this assignment on the board: *Circle the words that describe (adjectives) in these two sentences:*

1. *The shiny green car was parked beside the Korean restaurant.*
2. *The rest of the huge parking lot was empty.*

See also *Daily Language Practice*

Teach

☑ Teaching Tip

Explain the following: 1. A predicate adjective answers the question *What kind?;* 2. The word *very* can often be inserted before a predicate adjective; 3. A predicate adjective can often be converted to a comparative or superlative.

⇄ Cross-reference: Adjectives

Refer students to Lesson 3.1, pp. 106–109 and Lesson 3.3, pp. 114–117.

Resource Manager

Planning Resources
- *Lesson Plans*

Transparencies
- *Bellringer*
- *Daily Language Practice*

📂 **Other Print Resources**
- *Grammar and Composition Handbook*
- *Grammar Enrichment,* p. 21
- *Grammar Practice,* p. 22
- *Grammar Reteaching,* p. 20
- *Grammar Workbook,* Lesson 30

Practice and Assess

Answers: Exercise 1

1. Young—Gandhi; small—school
2. busy—London
3. homesick—Gandhi, P.A.
4. inner—voice
5. courageous—He, P.A.; purposeful—He, P.A.
6. many—days
7. weak—Gandhi, P.A.; determined—he, P.A.
8. mature—Gandhi; nationalist—movement
9. nonviolent—resistance; foreign—rule
10. seven—years; that—resistance
11. long—struggle; foreign—rule
12. Two—nations; separate—nations
13. Most—Hindus; independent—India
14. Large—numbers
15. eastern—portion; new—nation

Answers: Exercise 2

1. famous—ruler; English—history
2. energetic—granddaughter
3. English—queen
4. Scottish—people; Welsh—people
5. colonial—empire
6. vast—empire; Indian—plantations
7. Asian—colonies; African—colonies
8. colonial—empire; rich—country
9. wise—Victoria; capable—Victoria
10. British—greatness
11. diamond—jubilee; immense—crowds
12. Royal—Princess Victoria; German—prince
13. next—monarch; British—monarch
14. English—history; knowledgeable—students; Victorian—era
15. Elizabethan—eras; Edwardian—eras; famous—eras

Additional Resources

📁 *Grammar Practice*, p. 22
📁 *Grammar Reteaching*, p. 20
📁 *Grammar Enrichment*, p. 21

📕 *Grammar Workbook*, Lesson 30

Adjectives

Exercise 1 · Identifying Adjectives

Write each adjective. Beside it, write the noun or pronoun it describes. If it is a predicate adjective, label it *P.A.*

1. Young Gandhi studied at a small school in India.
2. He later lived for a while in busy London.
3. Sometimes Gandhi was homesick.
4. Gandhi heard the truth of an inner voice.
5. He was courageous and purposeful.
6. Gandhi often fasted for many days.
7. After fasting, Gandhi grew weak, but he remained determined.
8. The mature Gandhi returned to India and led the nationalist movement.
9. He used nonviolent resistance as a protest against foreign rule.
10. He spent seven years in prison for that resistance.
11. The long struggle against foreign rule ended in 1947.
12. Two separate nations—India and Pakistan—were formed.
13. Most Hindus remained in independent India.
14. Large numbers of Muslims settled in Pakistan.
15. In 1971 the eastern portion of Pakistan became the new nation of Bangladesh.

Exercise 2 · Identifying Proper Adjectives

Write each adjective. Beside it, write the noun it describes. Capitalize each proper adjective.

1. Victoria was a famous ruler in english history.
2. She was the energetic granddaughter of George III.
3. Victoria was the english queen from 1837 to 1901.
4. Victoria was also the queen of the scottish and welsh people.
5. During that time, Britain built a colonial empire.
6. The vast empire included indian plantations.
7. Victoria established asian and african colonies.
8. The colonial empire made Britain a rich country.
9. Victoria was wise and capable.
10. She became the symbol of british greatness.
11.. The diamond jubilee was celebrated by immense crowds.
12. The Royal Princess Victoria married a german prince.
13. Prince Edward was crowned the next british monarch.
14. Students of english history are knowledgeable about the victorian era.
15. The elizabethan and edwardian eras are famous too.

Close

Have students look through previous writing assignments to check for capitalization of proper adjectives.

MEETING INDIVIDUAL NEEDS · English Language Learners

Learning Proper Adjectives

In some languages, proper adjectives derived from place names are identical to the proper noun. Students who speak these languages might say such things as, a Japan pear or an Italy sweater. Encourage these students to learn a group of proper adjectives in English with each of the following endings: *-ese (Chinese); -i (Israeli); -an (Nigerian); -ish (Danish).*

12.2 | Articles and Demonstratives

The words *a*, *an*, and *the* are special kinds of adjectives. They are called **articles.**

The points to a specific item or items. *A* and *an* refer to any one item of a group. Use *a* before words that begin with a consonant sound. Use *an* before words that begin with a vowel sound.

> William Shakespeare is **the** most famous English playwright.
>
> Getting a lead role in **a** Shakespeare play is **an** honor.

The words *this*, *that*, *these*, and *those* are called **demonstrative adjectives.** They are used to point out something.

> Take **this** umbrella with you.   **That** store is closed.
>
> Take **these** boots also.   **Those** clouds are lovely.

Use *this* and *that* with singular nouns. Use *these* and *those* with plural nouns. Use *this* and *these* to point out something that is close to you. Use *that* and *those* to point out something that is far from you.

Demonstratives		
	Singular	**Plural**
Near	this	these
Far	that	those

Demonstratives can be used with nouns or without them. When used alone, they are called **demonstrative pronouns.**

> **This** is mine.   **These** are for you.

Focus

Lesson Overview

Objectives
- To recognize and understand the roles of articles, demonstrative adjectives, and demonstrative pronouns
- To use articles and demonstratives correctly in sentences

Bellringer
Daily Language Activity

When students enter the classroom, have this assignment on the board: *Explain why the following sentences are confusing and write them correctly.*
> I ate a egg and an sandwich for breakfast.
> I sat at the table in a kitchen of our house.

See also *Daily Language Practice*

Teach

☑ Teaching Tip
The use of *a/an* and *the* is extraordinarily complex. A noun naming a specific item is preceded by the definite article *the*. *A/an* (the indefinite article) is used the first time that a non-specific item is mentioned. When the noun is mentioned again, it is no longer nonspecific. Since it now refers to the specific item already mentioned, *the* is used. For example, *I looked at a new car yesterday, but the car costs more than I can afford.*

Adjectives

Resource Manager

Planning Resources
- *Lesson Plans*

Transparencies
- *Bellringer*
- *Daily Language Practice*

Other Print Resources
- *Grammar and Composition Handbook*
- *Grammar Practice*, p. 21
- *Grammar Workbook*, Lesson 31

381

Teach

☑ Teaching Tip

To help students become accustomed to using *a* and *an,* have them choose a newspaper article and read through it, circling the articles *a* and *an* and indicating whether the word that follows begins with a consonant or a vowel sound. If the use of *an* as an article with words such as *hour* confuses students, remind them to listen for the beginning sound.

Practice and Assess

Answers: Exercise 3

1. an	**6.** a
2. the	**7.** the
3. The	**8.** the
4. a	**9.** a
5. a, an	**10.** The

Answers: Exercise 4

1. This	**6.** This
2. This	**7.** those
3. that	**8.** those
4. Those	**9.** This
5. This	**10.** this

Answers: Exercise 5

Answers will vary but should include the demonstratives labeled as indicated.

Additional Resources

📁 *Grammar Practice,* p. 21

📙 *Grammar Workbook,* Lesson 31

Close

Invite students to explain in their own words the rules for using articles and demonstratives.

382

Adjectives

Exercise 3 — Using Articles

For each sentence, write the correct article.

1. William Shakespeare was (an, the) English playwright.
2. Was he (a, the) greatest writer of all time?
3. (A, The) town of Stratford-on-Avon was his birthplace.
4. Shakespeare was (a, an) country boy.
5. He was (a, an) poet and (a, an) actor.
6. His plays caused (a, an) sensation in London.
7. Shakespeare had one of (a, the) largest vocabularies of any English writer.
8. Many of his plays were performed at (a, the) Globe Theatre.
9. *Romeo and Juliet* is (a, an) popular play.
10. (An, The) annual celebration of Shakespeare's birth takes place on April 23.

Exercise 4 — Using Demonstratives

For each sentence, write the correct demonstrative word.

1. (This, That) biography I'm holding is about Florence Nightingale.
2. (This, These) woman dreamed of being a nurse.
3. Her friends encouraged (that, those) dream.
4. (That, Those) sick soldiers lacked expert care.
5. (This, These) injustice created great concern.
6. (This, These) concern brought about reforms.
7. Florence Nightingale led (that, those) nurses.
8. Nightingale could organize and take care of details, and (that, those) abilities made her successful.
9. (This, These) behavior was unusual for a rich woman of her time.
10. Florence Nightingale's achievements remain famous to (this, that) day.

Exercise 5 — Writing Sentences with Demonstratives

Write a pair of sentences for each of these words: *this, that, these,* and *those.* In one sentence of each pair, use the word as a demonstrative adjective. In the other, use it as a demonstrative pronoun.

SAMPLE ANSWER These boots are too small. (demonstrative adjective)
These will fit you. (demonstrative pronoun)

Exploring Language

Provide Usage Rules for Articles

When making generalizations about a noun, use no article if the noun is plural (cats are smart). Use an article if the noun is singular (a dog is a good pet). Use *the* when the noun is unique (I saw the moon), when the noun refers to a specific one of a category (the car runs), or when the listener knows what is being said (we won the game).

12.3 Adjectives That Compare

You can use adjectives to compare two or more nouns.

■ The **comparative form** of an adjective compares two things or people.

For most adjectives of one syllable, form the comparative by adding *-er*. For most adjectives of two or more syllables, form the comparative by using *more* before the adjective.

> Is Venezuela **larger** than Peru?
>
> Is Argentina **more beautiful** than Ecuador?

■ The **superlative form** of an adjective compares more than two things or people.

For most adjectives of one syllable, form the superlative by adding *-est*. For most adjectives of two or more syllables, form the superlative by using *most* before the adjective.

> Is Brazil the **richest** country in South America?
>
> Simón Bolívar was one of South America's **most successful** generals.

Do not use *more* or *most* before adjectives that already are in the comparative or superlative form.

Comparative and Superlative Forms		
Adjective	**Comparative**	**Superlative**
small	small**er**	small**est**
dark	dark**er**	dark**est**
active	**more** active	**most** active
intelligent	**more** intelligent	**most** intelligent

Adjectives

Focus

Lesson Overview

Objectives

• To identify comparative and superlative forms of adjectives

• To use comparative and superlative adjectives correctly in sentences

Bellringer
Daily Language Activity

When students enter the classroom, have this assignment on the board: *Find and correct the errors in the following sentences.*

It was the interestingest art show I have seen. The gallery was more smaller than the other one I visited. I think Ms. Johnson's paintings were beautifuller than any of the others.

See also *Daily Language Practice*

Motivating Activity

Ask students to discuss how they were able to spot the errors in the Bellringer activity. What makes using *more, most, -er,* and *-est* correctly so difficult?

Teach

Cross-reference

Students will use comparative adjectives in expository paragraphs that compare and contrast. For instruction and practice on this writing strategy, refer students to Lesson 5.2, pp. 190–192.

Resource Manager

Planning Resources
• *Lesson Plans*

Transparencies
• *Bellringer*
• *Daily Language Practice*

Other Print Resources
• *Grammar and Composition Handbook*
• *Grammar Enrichment,* p. 23
• *Grammar Practice,* p. 23
• *Grammar Reteaching,* p. 22
• *Grammar Workbook,* Lesson 32

Teach

☑ **Teaching Tip**

Invite students to create written advertisements that compare one or more real or imaginary products. Encourage them to take the position that one product is clearly superior. Help them to include comparative and superlative adjectives in their advertisements. Students may wish to look at how comparative and superlative adjectives are used in existing advertisements.

Practice and Assess

Answers: Exercise 6

1. greatest	11. most
2. more	12. most
3. wiser	13. most
4. most	14. most
5. most	15. more
6. more	16. more
7. most	17. harder
8. most	18. most
9. more	19. most
10. most	20. more

Answers: Exercise 7

Answers will vary but should include the comparative or superlative adjective form as indicated.

Additional Resources

📁 *Grammar Practice*, p. 23
📁 *Grammar Reteaching*, p. 22
📁 *Grammar Enrichment*, p. 23

📓 *Grammar Workbook*, Lesson 32

Close

Ask students to create posters illustrating rules for using comparative and superlative forms of adjectives. Students might wish to include examples of common usage errors along with corrections and the rules that cover each example.

Exercise 6   **Using the Comparative and Superlative Forms**

Write the correct comparative or superlative form of the adjective in parentheses.

1. Simón Bolívar is one of the (great) heroes of South America.
2. He was (successful) as an older man than as a younger man.
3. The general was (wise) than before about the struggle.
4. Simón Bolívar was one of the (loyal) of patriots.
5. The general cherished the (important) dream of all.
6. He is (famous) in Europe than in the United States.
7. Maria Tallchief was one of the (noted) dancers in the world.
8. Her Canadian tour was the (challenging) of all the tours.
9. Away from home, Tallchief was (homesick) this time than ever before.
10. Maria received the (marvelous) opportunity of all.
11. The Russian composer Igor Stravinsky thought she was the (suitable) dancer for some of his ballets.
12. Tallchief is perhaps (memorable) for her role in *The Firebird*.
13. George Balanchine gave her the (prominent) roles of all.
14. George Balanchine may be the (famous) ballet choreographer of this century.
15. Some of his ballets are (inventive) than others.
16. Balanchine choreographed ballets to music that was (romantic) than Stravinsky's music.
17. Dancing requires (hard) work than some other professions.
18. Only the (dedicated) dancers become professionals.
19. Although ballets have music, scenery, and costumes, the (important) part is the dancing.
20. American ballet is often (energetic) than Russian ballet.

Exercise 7   **Writing Sentences to Show Comparison**

Write five sentences that make comparisons. After each sentence, write whether the comparison is in the *comparative* or *superlative* form.

SAMPLE ANSWER   The dancers needed longer rehearsals. (comparative)

Adjectives

Cooperative Learning

Writing Adjectives that Compare

Provide groups of students with objects or photos of objects which are similar: three cars or two books. Ask students to write comparisons of the objects. When students have finished, have them check their work for proper usage of comparative and superlative adjectives.

12.4 Special Adjectives That Compare

| Many | More | Most |

The comparative and superlative forms of some adjectives are not formed in the regular manner.

> Harriet Tubman believed in a **good** cause.
> She knew that freedom was **better** than slavery.
> The Underground Railroad was the **best** route to freedom.

In the sentences above, *better* is the comparative form of the adjective *good*. *Best* is the superlative form of *good*.

Irregular Comparative and Superlative Forms		
Adjective	**Comparative**	**Superlative**
good	**better**	**best**
bad	**worse**	**worst**
much, many	**more**	**most**
little	**less**	**least**

Do not use *more* or *most* before irregular adjectives that are already in the comparative or superlative form.

> Tubman felt **better** at the end of the day. [not *more better*]

Focus

Lesson Overview

Objectives
- To identify and correctly use irregular comparative and superlative forms of adjectives
- To demonstrate control over the spelling of irregular comparative and superlative adjectives

Bellringer
Daily Language Activity

When students enter the classroom, have this assignment on the board: *Complete the following sentences with the correct form of* good.
1. *Sara had a ____ vacation at her grandmother's farm.*
2. *Who do you think is the ____ singer of all?*
3. *Of the two plays, which do you think is ____?*

Motivating Activity

Have students discuss difficulties they had providing comparatives and superlatives for the Bellringer sentences.

See also Daily Language Practice

Teach

☑ Teaching Tip

Point out to students that the comparative and superlative forms of the adjective *good* are *better* and *best*. The comparative and superlative forms of the adverb *well* (as in *He behaved well*) are also *better* and *best*.

Adjectives

Resource Manager

Planning Resources
- *Lesson Plans*

Transparencies
- *Bellringer*
- *Daily Language Practice*

📂 Other Print Resources
- *Grammar and Composition Handbook*
- *Grammar Enrichment*, p. 24
- *Grammar Practice*, p. 24
- *Grammar Reteaching*, p. 22
- *Grammar Workbook*, Lesson 33

Practice and Assess

Answers: Exercise 8

1. comparative—good
2. superlative—good
3. comparative—good
4. comparative—many
5. comparative—little
6. superlative—good
7. comparative—much
8. superlative—bad
9. comparative—good
10. superlative—many

Answers: Exercise 9

1. more	6. more
2. better	7. best
3. best	8. more
4. best	9. worst
5. best	10. less

Additional Resources

📁 *Grammar Practice,* p. 24
📁 *Grammar Reteaching,* p. 22
📁 *Grammar Enrichment,* p. 24

📓 *Grammar Workbook,* Lesson 33

Close

Have students check the advertisements they created in Lesson 12.3 or other previous writing assignments to make sure that any irregular comparative or superlative adjectives were used correctly.

Exercise 8 **Identifying the Comparative and Superlative Forms**

Identify the form of each underlined adjective as *comparative* or *superlative.* Then write the adjective from which it was formed.

1. Martin Luther King Jr. wanted a <u>better</u> life for all Americans.
2. His <u>best</u> speeches inspired people.
3. He worked hard on his <u>better</u> speeches.
4. There were <u>more</u> people in his audience near the end of his life than there had been in the beginning.
5. King paid <u>less</u> attention to his critics than to his supporters.
6. King believed that nonviolent protest was the <u>best</u> way to achieve equality for everyone.
7. Other people believed in the use of <u>more</u> force.
8. Some of the <u>worst</u> conditions in housing were in northern cities, rather than in the South.
9. Many hoped for a <u>better</u> education for their children.
10. <u>Most</u> listeners were inspired by King's "I Have a Dream" speech.

Exercise 9 **Using the Comparative and Superlative Forms**

Write the correct comparative or superlative form of the adjectives in parentheses.

1. After her husband's death, Eleanor Roosevelt did even (much) work than before.
2. Mrs. Roosevelt's newspaper column was (good) than many other newspaper columns.
3. She gave her (good) efforts to the United Nations.
4. Perhaps she did her (good) work of all in the cause of peace.
5. Which of her speeches is the (good)?
6. She had (many) projects than the previous first ladies.
7. She may have been the (good) writer of them all.
8. When Franklin was alive, Eleanor made (many) trips than he did.
9. Being affected by polio was one of the (bad) personal problems Franklin faced.
10. Eleanor worked to help people who had (little) power and influence than she had.

MEETING INDIVIDUAL NEEDS **Less Proficient Readers**

Special Adjectives

Students who have difficulty with Exercise 9 may find it helpful to break the exercise into parts. Encourage these students to use the boxed list of Irregular Comparative and Superlative Forms on page 385. Suggest that as students write each sentence, they hold their papers next to the box, trying each form of the appropriate adjective in the blank. Having these choices in front of them may make it easier for students to select the correct form.

Grammar Review

ADJECTIVES

In the following selection, Chicago writer Studs Terkel looks at the early years of famed jazz musician Louis Armstrong. The passage has been annotated to show some of the kinds of adjectives covered in this unit.

Literature Model

from Giants of Jazz

by Studs Terkel

Kid Ory's Band was the most popular one in New Orleans. They played just about everywhere, for fancy parties as well as for rough-and-tumble get-togethers. Louis was the most sought-after jazzman. He had no days off. When the Ory group was resting, he'd be playing at some dance or funeral. Often he blew second cornet with the Papa Celestin's Tuxedo Brass Band. In later years he recalled, "I thought I was in heaven, playing with that band. They had funeral marches that would touch your heart, they were so beautiful."

One day he was approached by a red-headed band leader. It was Fate Marable, the riverboat king. Excellent jazz was being played on the excursion boats that glided up and down the Mississippi. Easily the best of these boat bands was Marable's, of the steamer *Sydney*. His repertoire was far more varied than that of any New Orleans band. His men could *read* music!

"Come on, Louis," urged Fate. "Join us and see what the rest of the country looks like." Armstrong, eager for new adventures and new learning, readily accepted.

Superlative form of popular

Demonstrative adjective

Predicate adjective

Comparative form of varied

Proper adjective

Article

Adjectives

Teach

About the Literature

Explain that the review contains a passage taken from Studs Terkel's *Giants of Jazz.*

Before he became a writer, Studs Terkel worked as an actor, a disc jockey, a radio commentator, and a television host. He is known for capturing the details of human experience, as is evidenced in this passage. He traveled extensively to interview people from all walks of life for his books, such as *Working, Giants of Jazz,* and the Pulitzer Prize-winning *The Good War: An Oral History of World War Two.*

Have students read the passage and identify the adjectives. Then ask them to discuss the ways in which these adjectives provide useful information and clarity.

Linking Grammar and Literature

Critical Thinking

Invite students to consider situations in which adjectives are necessary for accurate communication. Examples of such situations might be giving travel directions, building a birdhouse, and fixing a car.

Cooperative Learning

Invite students to work together in small groups to write a version of the passage in which all adjectives have been removed. Then ask one volunteer to read to his or her group the passage with the adjectives and another volunteer to read the passage without the adjectives. Students can then discuss the differences. Which passage was more interesting? Which provided more information? Why?

Resource Manager

Planning Resources
- *Lesson Plans*

📂 Other Print Resources
- *Grammar and Composition Handbook*
- *Grammar Workbook,* Lessons 30–33; Unit 5 Review; Cumulative Review: Units 1–5

✔ ASSESSMENT OPTIONS

📂 *Tests with Answer Key and Rubrics*
Unit 12 Mastery Test, pp. 51-52

💾 *Testmaker*
Unit 12 Mastery Test

Practice and Assess

Answers: Exercise 1

1. the
2. an
3. the
4. the, the
5. the

Answers: Exercise 2

1. rhythm—section; jazz—band
2. good—pianist; noted—composer; rag-time—music
3. special Pulitzer—award
4. popular—Gene Krupa
5. famous—drummer; new—band
6. mournful—sound; early—jazz
7. blues—singer
8. legendary—Buddy Boldon; New Orleans—musician
9. Mississippi—riverboats; new—sound
10. clarinet—player; dance—band

Adjectives

Review: Exercise 1 Using Articles

Write the correct article for each blank.

SAMPLE Jazz is truly _____ American style of music.
ANSWER an

1. While it is impossible to say when and where jazz was first played, many people call New Orleans _____ one and only "cradle of jazz."
2. Improvisation and syncopation made jazz _____ unusual form of folk music.
3. In the late nineteenth century, creative musicians combined _____ rhythms of West Africa with European harmony and American folk music.
4. Jazz historians say that before _____ turn of _____ century, this type of music was not as popular as it is today.
5. In the South, many bands played _____ new music in street parades and funeral processions.

Review: Exercise 2 Identifying Adjectives and Proper Adjectives

The following sentences are about jazz. Write each adjective. (Do not include articles.) Beside it, write the noun it describes. Capitalize any proper adjectives you find.

SAMPLE Jazz is an american style of music.
ANSWER American style

1. The rhythm section of a jazz band usually includes a piano and drums.
2. Scott Joplin was a good pianist and a noted composer of ragtime music.
3. Joplin received a special Pulitzer award in 1976.
4. The popular Gene Krupa drew attention for skill on the drums.
5. The famous drummer started a new band.
6. The mournful sound of "blues" characterized early jazz.
7. Bessie Smith was a blues singer.
8. The legendary Buddy Boldon was a new orleans musician.
9. Musicians on mississippi riverboats brought the new sound to Chicago.
10. Benny Goodman, a clarinet player, started a dance band in Chicago.

Review: Exercise 3 **Distinguishing Kinds of Adjectives**

Number your paper from 1 to 5. Identify each underlined word as a *proper adjective*, a *predicate adjective*, an *article*, or a *demonstrative adjective*.

¹<u>American</u> musicians often serve as goodwill ambassadors to other countries. ²Jazz is <u>popular</u> all over the world. ³Audiences everywhere respond enthusiastically to <u>this</u> music. ⁴<u>A</u> musician may be as well known overseas as at home. ⁵Music seems to be <u>an</u> international language.

Review: Exercise 4 **Using Demonstratives**

Write the best demonstrative—*that, this, those,* or *these*—for each sentence.

SAMPLE   A truly unique style of music is ———— music called jazz.
ANSWER   this

1. Many people living in New Orleans have said, " ———— city is the cradle of jazz."
2. When players make up some of the music they are playing, ———— players are improvising.
3. In syncopation, ———— beats that are normally unaccented are accented.
4. Improvisation and syncopation— ———— give jazz its unusual form.
5. Louis Armstrong was one of ———— early jazz musicians who became famous throughout the United States.
6. Armstrong also traveled to many foreign countries; he was very popular with fans in ———— countries.
7. In 1955 Armstrong toured Western Europe; ———— trip was a smashing success.
8. Armstrong was the first to use scat; in ———— kind of singing, meaningless syllables replace words.
9. Many other jazz singers have copied ———— style.
10. Armstrong's great trumpet playing and his famous scratchy voice are still admired ———— days.

Answers: Exercise 3
1. proper adjective
2. predicate adjective
3. demonstrative adjective
4. article
5. article

Answers: Exercise 4
1. This
2. those
3. those
4. these
5. those
6. those
7. that
8. this
9. that
10. these

Adjectives

Answers: Exercise 5

1. comparative—short
2. superlative—great
3. superlative—fine
4. comparative—good
5. superlative—good

Answers: Exercise 6

1. more persistent
2. greatest
3. best
4. more talented
5. most popular

Review: Exercise 5 **Identifying Comparative and Superlative Forms**

Write whether each underlined adjective is in the *comparative* or *superlative* form. Then write the adjective from which it is formed.

SAMPLE   Some of the <u>liveliest</u> jazz was once played on a cornet.
ANSWER   superlative, lively

1. The cornet and the trumpet are very similar brass instruments, but the cornet is the <u>shorter</u> of the two.
2. Duke Ellington had some of the <u>greatest</u> musical ideas of his time.
3. Many people think Ellington's band was the <u>finest</u> band of the swing era.
4. Was Benny Goodman a <u>better</u> clarinet player than any other clarinet player of his time?
5. Bebop was perhaps the <u>best</u> jazz style developed in the decade of the 1940s.

Review: Exercise 6 **Using Adjectives That Compare**

Write the correct comparative or superlative form of the adjective in parentheses.

SAMPLE   Louis Armstrong received his (early) formal music instruction at a children's home in New Orleans.
ANSWER   earliest

1. Being (persistent) than other teenage spectators, Armstrong borrowed clothes and went to the jazz clubs almost every evening.
2. Fate Marable's group had the (great) repertoire of any New Orleans band.
3. Was Joe "King" Oliver the (good) cornet player in Kid Ory's orchestra?
4. Many critics feel that of these two great musicians, Armstrong was the (talented).
5. Armstrong ranks high among the world's (popular) jazz musicians of all time.

Adjectives

Review: Exercise 7

Proofreading

The following passage discusses the art of Lois Mailou Jones, an African American artist, whose work appears below. Rewrite the passage, correcting the errors in spelling, capitalization, grammar, and usage. Add any missing punctuation. There are ten errors in all.

Lois Mailou Jones

¹This painting by Lois Mailou Jones combines images from a age of Egypts greatness with images from African American art drama, and music. ²The climbing figures are bathed in golden light and gold is used

Lois Mailou Jones, *The Ascent of Ethiopia*, 1932

(continued)

Answers: Exercise 7

Proofreading

This proofreading activity provides editing practice with (1) the current or previous units' skills, (2) the **Troubleshooter** errors, and (3) spelling errors. Students should be able to complete the exercise by referring to the units, the **Troubleshooter**, and a dictionary. (Note: A run-on sentence counts as one error.)

	Error (Type of Error)
1.	• an age (article before a vowel sound)
	• Egypt's (singular possessive)
	• art, (commas in a series)
2.	• light, (compound sentence)
3.	• most prominent (superlative adjective form)
4.	• studied (spelling)
	• Boston (proper adjective)
5.	• went (verb form)
	• American (proper adjective)
	• painting. She *or* painting; she (run-on sentence)

Viewing the Art

Lois Mailou Jones, *The Ascent of Ethiopia*, 1932

Lois Mailou Jones was born in 1905 in Boston and studied at the Boston Normal Art School; the School of the Museum of Fine Arts in Boston; Columbia University Teachers College in New York; Howard University in Washington, D.C.; and the Académie Julien and the École des Beaux Arts in Paris. Jones painted *The Ascent of Ethiopia* (oil on canvas, measuring 23 1/2 by 17 1/4 inches) in 1932. The painting is in the artist's own collection.

Answers: Exercise 8

Mixed Review

1. a, the
2. the, more intense
3. most important
4. a, more unusual
5. Belgian, an, English, American
6. Newport Festival, big, larger
7. more prominent
8. many, best
9. American, best
10. best

Close

Encourage students to write a descriptive passage about a place or an object of their choice, using adjectives to make their writing vivid and interesting.

Adjectives

again on the pyramids and the circle that represents music. ³The entire painting consists of shades of gold, green, blue, and violet; blue is the more prominent color of all, however.

⁴The artist was born in Boston and studied at two boston art schools. ⁵Later she gone to other american cities and to Paris to learn more about painting, she has won many awards for her work.

Review: Exercise 8

Mixed Review

For each sentence write the correct choices from the words in parentheses. When you find a proper adjective that is not capitalized, write it with the correct capitalization.

1. Boogie-woogie was (a, an) popular jazz style that used eight beats to a bar instead of (a, the) usual four beats to a bar.
2. Boogie-woogie, which developed in (a, the) 1930s, was (more intense, most intense) than other jazz styles.
3. Two of the (more important, most important) boogie-woogie artists of all were Pinetop Smith and Meade Lux Lewis.
4. Cool jazz emphasized (a, an) lagging beat and (more unusual, unusualler) orchestrations.
5. A belgian guitarist and (a, an) english pianist influenced american jazz artists.
6. The newport festival, first held in 1954, and other (big, biggest) jazz festivals introduced the new music to ever (larger, largest) audiences.
7. Since the 1950s, small combos have become (more prominent, most prominent) than before.
8. Jazz musicians continue to incorporate influences from (many, most) sources; the (better, best) among them constantly try new sounds and new combinations of instruments.
9. The american jazz musicians of the modern era that are (better, best) known include guitarist George Benson, trumpeter Wynton Marsalis, and pianist Herbie Hancock.
10. Wynton Marsalis, known for his excellent tone and flawless technique, was perhaps the (better, best) new jazz musician of the 1980s.

Writing Application

Adjectives in Writing

Yoshika Uchida uses specific words and adjectives in this passage from *The Invisible Thread* to convey her feelings about a visit to the country. Examine the passage, focusing especially on the italicized adjectives.

> They [the stars] seemed *brighter* and *closer* than they were in Berkeley. It was as though the *entire* sky had dropped closer to earth to spread out its *full* glory right there in front of me.
>
> I listened to the *slow* clop-clop of the mules as they plodded through the fields, probably wondering why they were pulling a wagonload of people in the dark, instead of hauling boxes of grapes to the shed under the *hot, dry* sun.

Techniques with Adjectives

Try to apply some of Yoshiko Uchida's writing techniques when you write and revise your own work.

❶ Whenever possible, use specific adjectives to make your descriptions more precise.

WITHOUT ADJECTIVES under the sun

UCHIDA'S VERSION under the *hot, dry* sun

❷ Use comparisons for clarity and brevity.

WITHOUT COMPARISONS [the stars] seemed bright and close

UCHIDA'S VERSION They seemed *brighter* and *closer* than they were in Berkeley.

TIME

For more about using adjectives, see **TIME Facing the Blank Page,** page 98.

Adjectives

Practice

Practice these techniques by revising the following passage, using a separate sheet of paper. Add adjectives to enhance the description. Use comparisons where appropriate.

> At dusk we were one of the groups of people enjoying a picnic on the grass. We were clustered on blankets on the hill in front of the band shell. The smells of foods floated in the air around us. The dark descended as the musicians gathered on stage and tuned their instruments. They began the concert with several jazz standards. Some people in the audience stood and began to sway to the music. Soloists took turns showing their skills. Soon everyone was standing, moving, and swaying.

Adjectives in Writing

Have students read the passage from The *Invisible Thread* silently. Then have them discuss how Yoshiko Uchida has used adjectives and specific words to make this passage interesting, informative, and enjoyable to read. Ask: *How does the writer use words to make a vivid picture in the reader's mind?*

Techniques with Adjectives

Ask students to look at another piece of writing that they have enjoyed. Then ask them to discuss how the writer of the piece used adjectives and specific words to make a vivid picture. Ask: *How was the writer's technique similar to Yoshiko Uchida's? How was it different?*

Practice

The answers to this challenging and enriching activity will vary. Refer to Techniques with Adjectives as you evaluate student choices.

✔ ASSESSMENT OPTIONS

📁 *Tests with Answer Key and Rubrics* Unit 12 Mastery Test, pp. 51–52

💾 *Testmaker* Unit 12 Mastery Test

You may wish to administer the Unit 12 Mastery Test at this point.

📼 *Mindjogger Videoquizzes*

Objectives

- To identify adverbs and the words they modify in sentences
- To recognize and use correctly comparative and superlative adverbs
- To understand the differences between adjectives and adverbs, and to use both correctly in writing
- To revise double negatives in sentences

✔ ASSESSMENT OPTIONS

📁 *Tests with Answer Key and Rubrics*
Unit 13 Pretest, pp. 53–54
Unit 13 Mastery Test, pp. 55–56

💾 *Testmaker*
Unit 13 Pretest
Unit 13 Mastery Test

You may wish to administer the Unit 13 Pretest at this point.

Key to Ability Levels

L1 Level 1 activities are within the basic ability range of students.

L2 Level 2 activities are within the ability range of average students.

L3 Level 3 activities are more challenging activities.

UNIT 13 Adverbs

394

Resource Manager

Planning Resources
- *Lesson Plans*
- *Block Scheduling*

🖍 **Transparencies**
- *Bellringer*
- *Daily Language Practice*
- *Two-Minute Skill Drill*

📁 **Other Print Resources**
- *Grammar and Composition Handbook*
- *Grammar Enrichment*
- *Grammar Practice*
- *Grammar Reteaching*
- *Grammar Workbook*
- *Tests with Answer Key and Rubrics*

📼 **Video**
- *MindJogger Videoquizzes*

💾 **Software**
- *Interactive Grammar and Language Workbook*
- *Language Arts PASS*
- *Presentation Plus!*
- *Testmaker*

13.1 Adverbs Modifying Verbs

Adjectives are words that modify, or describe, nouns and pronouns. Adverbs are another type of modifier. They modify verbs, adjectives, and other adverbs.

■ An **adverb** is a word that describes a verb, an adjective, or another adverb.

In the example below, the adverb *grandly* describes the action verb *entertained*.

Thomas Jefferson entertained **grandly** at the White House.

An adverb supplies one of three types of information.

Ways Adverbs Modify Verbs	
Adverbs Tell	**Examples**
How	grandly, royally, quickly
When	rarely, later, immediately, often, usually
Where	downstairs, below, here

When modifying an adjective or another adverb, an adverb usually comes before the word. When modifying a verb, an adverb can occupy different positions in a sentence.

Positioning of Adverbs	
Position	**Examples**
Before the Verb	Guests **often** dined in the State Dining Room.
After the Verb	Guests dined **often** in the State Dining Room.
At the Beginning	**Often** guests dined in the State Dining Room.
At the End	Guests dined in the State Dining Room **often.**

Most adverbs are formed by adding *-ly* to an adjective, as in *actively, fondly,* and *quietly.* Some adverbs are exceptions, however. These include *after, often, now,* and *later.*

13.1 Adverbs Modifying Verbs **395**

Adverbs

Focus

Lesson Overview

Objectives
- To recognize and apply the rules for using adverbs
- To identify adverbs and the words they modify in sentences

Bellringer
Daily Language Activity

When students enter the classroom, have this assignment on the board: *Circle the verbs and underline the adverbs in the following sentences:*

Alan ran quickly to the window. He had never seen anyone famous. Finally the president's motorcade arrived. Alan hoped he might see the president if he looked carefully.

See also *Daily Language Practice*

Teach

Cross-reference: Spelling Rules

When *-ly* is added to an adjective to form an adverb, the spelling of the word sometimes changes. For instruction and practice in spelling rules, refer students to Lessons 22.6–22.7, pp. 557–564.

Resource Manager

Planning Resources
- *Lesson Plans*

Transparencies
- *Bellringer*
- *Daily Language Practice*

📁 **Other Print Resources**
- *Grammar and Composition Handbook*
- *Grammar Enrichment,* p. 25
- *Grammar Practice,* p. 23
- *Grammar Reteaching,* p. 25
- *Grammar Workbook,* Lesson 34

Teach

☑ Teaching Tip

Tell students that they can use the *when, where,* or *how* test to identify adverbs that modify verbs. Words that answer these questions must be adverbs. For example, in the sentence *Guests often dined in the State Dining Room, often* is an adverb because it answers the question *when*: When did the guests dine? They dined often.

Practice and Assess

Answers: Exercise 1

1. everywhere	4. eagerly
2. finally	5. proudly
3. majestically	

Answers: Exercise 2

1. happily—lived
2. quickly—sought
3. nearly—destroyed
4. completely—rebuilt
5. further—expanded
6. indoors—built
7. thoughtfully—added
8. often—come
9. proudly—tour
10. always—sends

Answers: Exercise 3

Answers will vary, but some suggestions are given below.

1. always	4. patiently
2. often	5. quietly
3. quickly	

Additional Resources

📁 *Grammar Practice*, p. 23
📁 *Grammar Reteaching*, p. 25
📁 *Grammar Enrichment*, p. 25

📖 *Grammar Workbook*, Lesson 34

Adverbs

Exercise 1 **Identifying Adverbs**

On your paper, write the adverb to complete each sentence.

1. The federal government looked _____ for an architect. (build, eager, everywhere, official)
2. A committee _____ chose James Hoban. (decide, finally, happy, enthusiastic)
3. Hoban's White House stood _____ on a large plot of land. (proud, sit, majestically, to)
4. The Adams family _____ moved into the unfinished house. (eagerly, quick, had, grand)
5. They _____ gave visitors tours of their new home. (glad, proudly, want, famous)

Exercise 2 **Identifying Adverbs**

Write each sentence. Underline the adverb and draw an arrow to the word the adverb describes.

1. Thomas Jefferson lived happily in the White House.
2. Jefferson quickly sought the aid of another architect.
3. Fire nearly destroyed the mansion during the War of 1812.
4. Theodore Roosevelt had it rebuilt completely.
5. Franklin Roosevelt further expanded it.
6. Workers built a swimming pool indoors.
7. One president thoughtfully added a bowling alley.
8. Eager tourists often come to the White House.
9. They proudly tour their nation's capital.
10. Our school always sends the seventh graders on a trip to Washington, D.C.

Exercise 3 **Writing Adverbs to Complete Sentences**

On your paper, write an adverb that describes the verb in each sentence.

1. Our class _____ goes to the White House when visiting Washington, D.C.
2. We _____ visit the other attractions.
3. We _____ travel by bus to our nation's capital.
4. Last year the seventh graders waited _____ in line to see Congress in session.
5. The tour guide spoke _____ to us.

Close

Invite students to write five sentences that include adverbs modifying verbs. Then have students rewrite each sentence with the adverbs in as many positions as possible.

Exploring Language

Identifying Adverbs

Invite students to read through a literature passage and write down all the words that end in *-ly*. Then help students to decide if the *-ly* words are adverbs by asking if the words answer the question *when, where,* or *how.*

13.2 Adverbs Modifying Adjectives and Adverbs

Adverbs are often used to modify adjectives and other adverbs. Notice how adverbs intensify the meaning of the adjectives in the following sentences. Most often they tell **how.**

Harry Truman used **extremely** direct language.

He became a **very** popular president.

In the first sentence, the adverb *extremely* modifies the adjective *direct.* The adverb tells how direct Truman's language was. In the second sentence, the adverb *very* modifies the adjective *popular.* The adverb tells how popular Truman was.

In the sentences below, adverbs modify other adverbs.

Truman entered politics **unusually** late in life.

He moved through the political ranks **quite** quickly.

In the first sentence above, the adverb *unusually* modifies the adverb *late. Unusually* tells how late Truman entered politics. In the second sentence, the adverb *quite* describes the adverb *quickly. Quite* tells how quickly Truman moved through the ranks.

When modifying adjectives and other adverbs, adverbs almost always come directly before the word they describe. Below is a list of some adverbs that are often used to describe adjectives and other adverbs.

ADVERBS OFTEN USED TO DESCRIBE ADJECTIVES AND OTHER ADVERBS

very	really	rather	just
too	so	nearly	somewhat
almost	partly	barely	totally
quite	extremely	unusually	hardly

Adverbs

Focus

Lesson Overview

Objectives
- To recognize adverbs that describe adjectives and other adverbs
- To use adverbs to modify adjectives and other adverbs

Bellringer
Daily Language Activity

When students enter the classroom, have this assignment on the board: *Underline the adverbs in the following sentences:*
   Yesterday the weather was extremely beautiful. Today the sky is partly cloudy. Rain is falling very softly.

See also *Daily Language Practice*

Motivating Activity

Help students to decide which words are modified by each adverb in the Bellringer sentences.

Teach

Listening and Speaking

Adverbs that modify adjectives and other adverbs can never be moved away from the words they modify. Invite students to test this by writing sentences with adverbs of this type. Ask students to read the sentences aloud, move the adverbs, and read them again. Do the sentences sound right? Why not?

Resource Manager

Planning Resources
- *Lesson Plans*

Transparencies
- *Bellringer*
- *Daily Language Practice*

Other Print Resources
- *Grammar and Composition Handbook*
- *Grammar Enrichment,* p. 25
- *Grammar Practice,* p. 24
- *Grammar Reteaching,* p. 26
- *Grammar Workbook,* Lesson 35

Practice and Assess

Answers: Exercise 4

1. <u>unusually</u>—brief (adj.) **2.** <u>extremely</u>—tragic (adj.) **3.** <u>almost</u>—immediately (adv.); <u>immediately</u>—established (v.) **4.** <u>quite</u>—early (adv.); <u>early</u>—arose (v.) **5.** <u>nearly</u>—always (adv.); <u>always</u>—followed (v.) **6.** <u>Very</u>—important (adj.) **7.** <u>finally</u>—ended (v.) **8.** <u>almost</u>—immediately (adv.); <u>immediately</u>—ended (v.) **9.** <u>very</u>—often (adv.); <u>often</u>—played (v.) **10.** <u>particularly</u>—soothing (adj.) **11.** <u>regularly</u>—spent (v.) **12.** <u>Rather</u>—serious (adj.) **13.** <u>somewhat</u>—abruptly (adv.); <u>abruptly</u>—moved (v.) **14.** <u>reasonably</u>—secure (adj.) **15.** <u>nearly</u>—four (adj.) **16.** <u>next</u>—was elected (v.) **17.** <u>greatly</u>—admired (adj.) **18.** <u>quite</u>—popular (adj.) **19.** <u>most</u>—often (adv.); <u>often</u>—was referred (v.) **20.** <u>eventually</u>—was elected (v.)

Answers: Exercise 5

Answers will vary. Some suggestions are given below.
1. We hardly ever go swimming.
2. Tom brought just enough food for lunch.
3. It was unusually quiet last evening.
4. We arrived so late that we missed the boat.
5. The band's new song is very popular.
6. Matt and I are rather hungry.
7. The job is too difficult for me.
8. I can run extremely quickly.
9. He responded somewhat angrily.
10. The painting is nearly finished.

Additional Resources

📁 *Grammar Practice*, p. 24
📁 *Grammar Reteaching*, p. 26
📁 *Grammar Enrichment*, p. 25

📙 *Grammar Workbook*, Lesson 35

Adverbs

Exercise 4   **Identifying Adverbs**

Write each sentence. Underline each adverb and draw an arrow to the word the adverb modifies. Then write whether that modified word is a *verb*, an *adjective*, or an *adverb*.

1. Truman's career as vice president was unusually brief.
2. The extremely tragic death of Franklin D. Roosevelt left the presidency in Truman's hands.
3. Truman established a new procedure almost immediately.
4. He arose quite early each morning for a walk.
5. News reporters nearly always followed him.
6. Very important events took place during Truman's term.
7. World War II finally ended.
8. It ended almost immediately after Truman became president.
9. Truman very often played the piano for guests.
10. He found music particularly soothing.
11. Truman regularly spent his evenings at home.
12. Rather serious problems were discovered in the White House.
13. The Trumans moved somewhat abruptly into Blair House.
14. They felt reasonably secure in that place.
15. They lived in Blair House for nearly four years.
16. Dwight Eisenhower was elected president next.
17. Eisenhower was greatly admired as a general during World War II.
18. His wife, Mamie, was quite popular throughout the country.
19. In the newspapers, Dwight Eisenhower was most often referred to as Ike.
20. Ike's vice president, Richard Nixon, was eventually elected president.

Exercise 5   **Writing Adverbs to Modify Adjectives and Adverbs**

Choose an adverb from the box to modify each word below. On your paper, write a sentence for each pair of words you form.

nearly	hardly	just	extremely	somewhat
very	unusually	too	rather	so

1. _____ ever
2. _____ enough
3. _____ quiet
4. _____ late
5. _____ popular
6. _____ hungry
7. _____ difficult
8. _____ quickly
9. _____ angrily
10. _____ finished

Cooperative Learning

Using Adverbs
Have students work in pairs to complete Exercise 4. After each pair completes two sentences, students should check their answers with another pair of students to make sure their answers are the same.

Close

Ask students to explain in their own words how adverbs can be used to modify adjectives or other adverbs. Encourage them to illustrate their explanations with written examples.

13.3 Adverbs That Compare

■ The **comparative** form of an adverb compares two actions or things. The **superlative** form of an adverb compares more than two actions or things.

For most adverbs of only one syllable, add -*er* to make the comparative form and -*est* to make the superlative form.

Comparing One-Syllable Adverbs	
Comparative	Ronald Reagan served **longer** as president than Jimmy Carter.
Superlative	Franklin Roosevelt served **longest** of any president.

For adverbs that end in -*ly* or that have more than one syllable, use the word *more* to form the comparative and *most* to form the superlative.

Comparing Two-Syllable Adverbs	
Comparative	Our class studied Roosevelt **more thoroughly** than Reagan.
Superlative	We studied Abraham Lincoln **most thoroughly** of all.

If an adverb already is comparative or superlative, do not add *more* or *most*. Never say, for example, *more harder* or *most hardest*.

Some adverbs do not form the comparative and superlative in the regular manner. Study the irregular forms below.

IRREGULAR COMPARATIVE FORMS

ADVERB	COMPARATIVE	SUPERLATIVE
well	better	best
badly	worse	worst
little (amount)	less	least
far (distance)	farther	farthest
far (degree)	further	furthest

Adverbs

Focus

Lesson Overview

Objectives
• To use comparative and superlative adverbs correctly in sentences
• To identify various irregular comparative and superlative adverbs

🔔 Bellringer
Daily Language Activity
When students enter the classroom, have this assignment on the board: *Circle the errors in the following sentences:*
   We traveled quicklier by train than by car. We arrived more earlier than usual. Tom traveled farthest to get there than we did.

📖 **See also** *Daily Language Practice*

Motivating Activity

Invite students to discuss difficulties they have using comparative and superlative adverbs. Explain that this lesson will provide students with rules for the correct use of these adverbs.

Teach

Critical Thinking
If an adverb or adjective is comparative or superlative, do not add more *or* most. Invite students to test this statement by choosing comparative and superlative adverbs and adding *more* or *most.* Why is the addition of *more* or *most* unnecessary?

Resource Manager

Planning Resources
• *Lesson Plans*

📖 Transparencies
• *Bellringer*
• *Daily Language Practice*
• *Two-Minute Skill Drill*

📁 Other Print Resources
• *Grammar and Composition Handbook*
• *Grammar Enrichment*, p. 26
• *Grammar Practice*, p. 25
• *Grammar Workbook*, Lessons 36–37

Teach

 **Cross-reference: Comparing and Contrasting**

For practice with comparative and superlative adverbs, refer students to Lesson 5.2, pp. 190–193.

Two-Minute Skill Drill

Write the following on the board. Have students rewrite comparative and superlative adverbs that are used incorrectly.

more deeply	*more carefully*
badder	*more honestly*
most long	

✍ **See also** *Two-Minute Skill Drill Transparencies, 13.3*

Practice and Assess

Answers: Exercise 6

1. closest
2. better
3. more actively
4. hardest
5. more frequently

Answers: Exercise 7

1. most freely
2. more readily
3. farther
4. more sympathetic
5. longer
6. more busily
7. more often
8. most deeply
9. more widely
10. longer

Additional Resources

📂 *Grammar Practice,* p. 25
📂 *Grammar Enrichment,* p. 26
📕 *Grammar Workbook,* Lessons 36–37

Adverbs

Exercise 6 **Using the Comparative and Superlative Forms**

For each sentence, choose the correct form of the adverb in parentheses. Write the adverb on your paper.

1. Of all Theodore Roosevelt's nieces, Eleanor Roosevelt came (close, closest) to the presidency.
2. Many liked Mrs. Roosevelt (better, best) than they had liked any of the previous first ladies.
3. Mrs. Roosevelt worked (more actively, most actively) for human rights than for any other cause.
4. She fought (harder, hardest) of all for minorities.
5. She appeared at human-rights rallies (more frequently, most frequently) than her husband.

Exercise 7 **Writing Comparative and Superlative Forms**

Write each sentence. Use *-er, -est, more,* or *most* to make the needed form of the adverb in parentheses. Write the adverb on your paper.

1. Of all the first ladies, Eleanor Roosevelt gave (freely) of her time.
2. She traveled (readily) than any other president's wife to distant parts of the globe.
3. She journeyed (far) in her later years than in her youth.
4. She was (sympathetic) than many other people to the plight of the poor.
5. Eleanor Roosevelt lived (long) than her husband.
6. As Franklin Roosevelt became weaker, Eleanor took on some of his duties and worked (busily) than ever.
7. She (often) attended meetings in place of the president than many people realize.
8. Mrs. Roosevelt seemed to care (deeply) of all about the problems of ordinary people.
9. Eleanor Roosevelt was even (widely) recognized for her work with the United Nations than she had been for her devotion to duty as first lady.
10. Her humanitarian reputation surely will extend years (long) than her life.

Close

Invite students to create posters or pamphlets that show correct usage rules for comparative and superlative adverbs. They might consider illustrating common usage errors and how to avoid them.

Exploring Language

Comparing with Adverbs

Invite students to sort a list of adverbs, writing the adverbs that have one syllable in one column and the adverbs that have two syllables or end in *-ly* in another. Have them add *-er* or *-est* to the adverbs in the first column and *more* or *most* to the adverbs in the second column.

13.4 Telling Adjectives and Adverbs Apart

It can be hard to tell whether a word in a sentence is an adjective or an adverb. Look carefully at how the word is used.

Martha Washington was **happy** at Mount Vernon.
Martha Washington lived **happily** at Mount Vernon.

In the first sentence, *happy* is a predicate adjective. It follows the linking verb *was* and modifies the subject. In the second sentence, *happily* is an adverb. It modifies the action verb *lived*.

People sometimes confuse the words *bad, badly, good,* and *well. Bad* and *good* are both adjectives. They are used after linking verbs. *Badly* and *well* are adverbs. They are used after action verbs. *Well* can also be used after linking verbs to describe a person's health or appearance. At these times, *well* is an adjective—for example, *He looks well.*

DISTINGUISHING ADJECTIVES FROM ADVERBS

ADJECTIVE	ADVERB
The sound is **bad.**	The actor sang **badly.**
The band sounds **good.**	The band played **well.**

Three pairs of modifiers often confuse people: *real, really; sure, surely;* and *most, almost. Real* and *sure* are adjectives. *Really, surely,* and *almost* are adverbs. *Most* can be an adjective or an adverb.

DISTINGUISHING ADJECTIVES FROM ADVERBS

ADJECTIVE	ADVERB
Music is a **real** art.	Music is **really** popular.
A pianist needs **sure** hands.	Piano music is **surely** popular.
Most pianos have eighty-eight keys.	Piano strings **almost** never break.

13.4 Telling Adjectives and Adverbs Apart **401**

Adverbs

Focus

Lesson Overview

Objectives
- To distinguish between adjectives and adverbs in sentences
- To determine whether an adjective or an adverb should be used in a sentence

Bellringer
Daily Language Activity

When students enter the classroom, have this assignment on the board: *Circle the adjectives (except for the articles) and underline the adverbs in the following sentences:*

The sketches look good. Susan displays real talent. She draws really well. The subjects seem almost real.

See also *Daily Language Practice*

Motivating Activity

Invite students to discuss any strategies they have for telling whether a word in a sentence is an adjective or an adverb.

Teach

☑ Grammar Tip
Predicate adjectives describe the subject. Adverbs that modify the verb describe the action of the verb.

⇄ Cross-reference: Linking Verbs
For instruction and practice with linking verbs, refer students to Lesson 10.3, pp. 337–338.

Resource Manager

Planning Resources
- *Lesson Plans*

Transparencies
- *Bellringer*
- *Daily Language Practice*

🗁 Other Print Resources
- *Grammar and Composition Handbook*
- *Grammar Enrichment,* p. 28
- *Grammar Practice,* p. 27
- *Grammar Reteaching,* p. 28
- *Grammar Workbook,* Lesson 40

Practice and Assess

Additional Resources

🗂 *Grammar Practice,* p. 26
🗂 *Grammar Reteaching,* p. 27
🗂 *Grammar Enrichment,* p. 27

📖 *Grammar Workbook,* Lesson 38

Close

Have students read a literary passage containing adjectives and adverbs. As they read, they can make one list of the adjectives in the passage and another list of the adverbs.

Adverbs

Exercise 8 — Telling Adjectives and Adverbs Apart

On your paper, write each sentence, using the correct adjective or adverb.

1. Martha Washington lived (courageous, courageously).
2. She managed the position of first lady (good, well).
3. She supported her husband (active, actively).
4. President Washington must have felt (good, well) about his wife's support.
5. (Sure, Surely) he was appreciative.
6. Martha Washington was known as a (real, really) gracious hostess.
7. During the war, Mrs. Washington had (able, ably) organized a sewing circle.
8. The group was (quick, quickly) in mending clothes for the troops.
9. In those days, it was important to be able to sew (good, well).
10. If a woman sewed (bad, badly), she would rip her work out.
11. People (most, almost) always took notice of Mrs. Washington's common sense and charm.
12. It is also said that she was (real, really) beautiful.
13. She and her husband lived (good, well).
14. Their life together at Mount Vernon remained (cheerful, cheerfully).
15. Martha Washington had been married (previous, previously) to Daniel Parke Custis.
16. After his death, she became (popular, popularly) known as one of the richest widows in Virginia.
17. When she married George Washington, she added (substantial, substantially) to his property.
18. Martha was known as an (amiable, amiably) hostess at the many formal dinners Washington held as president.
19. She outlived her husband by a (short, shortly) time.
20. Two years after his death, Martha died (peaceful, peacefully) at Mount Vernon.

Exercise 9 — Identifying and Using Adjectives and Adverbs

On your paper, identify each word as an *adjective* or an *adverb*. Then write a sentence using the word correctly.

1. good
2. really
3. sure
4. almost
5. real
6. surely
7. well
8. badly
9. bad
10. most

Enrichment and Extension

Creating a Reference File

Students may find it helpful to keep a file of adjectives and adverbs that confuse them. The file should include sentences demonstrating the correct use of each adjective and adverb. Students can refer to the file when they need help with adjectives and adverbs.

Using *Good* and *Well*

Predicate adjectives follow linking verbs; adverbs modify action verbs. The following sentence can help students remember that *good* is an adjective used with linking verbs and *well* is an adverb used with action verbs: *The car is good because it runs well.*

13.5 Avoiding Double Negatives

The adverb *not* is a **negative word,** expressing the idea of "no" in a sentence. The word *not* often appears in its shortened form, the contraction *-n't.*

CONTRACTIONS WITH *NOT*

is not = isn't	cannot = can't	have not = haven't
was not = wasn't	could not = couldn't	had not = hadn't
were not = weren't	do not = don't	would not = wouldn't
will not = won't	did not = didn't	should not = shouldn't

Other words besides *not* may be used to express the negative. Each negative word has several opposites, or affirmative words, that show the idea of "yes." Study the following list of negative and affirmative words.

NEGATIVE AND AFFIRMATIVE WORDS

NEGATIVE	AFFIRMATIVE
never	ever, always
nobody	anybody, somebody
none	one, all, some, any
no one	everyone, someone
nothing	something, anything
nowhere	somewhere, anywhere

People sometimes mistakenly use two negative words together, as in the sentence *Lincoln hadn't never gone to college.* Avoid using a **double negative** such as this. You need only one negative word to express a negative idea.

You can correct a double negative by removing one of the negative words or by replacing it with an affirmative word, as in the following sentences.

Lincoln had **never** gone to college.
Lincoln had **not ever** gone to college.

13.5 Avoiding Double Negatives **403**

Focus

Lesson Overview

Objectives
• To recognize and avoid the use of double negatives in writing
• To revise double negatives in sentences

Bellringer
Daily Language Activity

When students enter the classroom, have this assignment on the board: *What makes the following sentences difficult to understand?*

We didn't never hear the president speak. There was not no radio where we stayed. We never read none of the speech in the paper either.

See also *Daily Language Practice*

Motivating Activity

Invite students to give suggestions for making the sentences in the Bellringer easier to read and understand.

Teach

Listening and Speaking

Prepare a group of sentences, some of which have double negatives and some of which have negative constructions used correctly. Read the sentences aloud. Encourage students to respond when they hear a double negative and to rewrite the sentence correctly.

Cross-reference: Writing Dialogue

For instruction and practice in writing dialogue, refer students to Lesson 4.3, pp. 156–159.

Resource Manager

Planning Resources
• *Lesson Plans*

Transparencies
• *Bellringer*
• *Daily Language Practice*

Other Print Resources
• *Grammar and Composition Handbook*
• *Grammar Enrichment,* p. 28
• *Grammar Practice,* p. 27
• *Grammar Reteaching,* p. 28
• *Grammar Workbook,* Lesson 40

Practice and Assess

Answers: Exercise 10

1.	ever	11.	anywhere
2.	made	12.	ever
3.	anyone	13.	anything
4.	ever	14.	anybody
5.	anyone	15.	ever
6.	ever	16.	ever
7.	anybody	17.	anywhere
8.	meant	18.	any
9.	ever	19.	any
10.	anybody	20.	any

Answers: Exercise 11

Answers will vary, but none of the sentences should contain double negatives. A sample sentence: *1. Allen couldn't ever find anyone from his group.*

Additional Resources

📁 *Grammar Practice*, p. 27
📁 *Grammar Reteaching*, p. 26
📁 *Grammar Enrichment*, p. 26

📙 *Grammar Workbook*, Lesson 40

Close

Invite students to write a paragraph or two explaining how to avoid using double negatives. It might be helpful for students to imagine they are writing their explanations for a person who knows none of the rules for using negatives in a sentence.

Adverbs

Exercise 10   **Expressing Negative Ideas**

On your paper, write each sentence so that it correctly expresses a negative idea.

1. Lincoln didn't (never, ever) have a speech writer.
2. Nothing (didn't make, made) him bitter during the war.
3. Lincoln wasn't dishonest with (no one, anyone).
4. The president didn't (never, ever) become discouraged.
5. A strong leader, Lincoln wasn't afraid of (nobody, anyone).
6. Honest Abe didn't (never, ever) try to trick the public.
7. He tried not to show favoritism to (anybody, nobody).
8. Nothing (meant, didn't mean) more to Lincoln than justice.
9. Nobody (ever, never) cared more about saving the Union than Lincoln.
10. There wasn't (nobody, anybody) more loyal to the cause of the Civil War.
11. I can't find Carl Sandburg's biography of Lincoln (nowhere, anywhere).
12. Some feared the country wouldn't (ever, never) get over the shock of Lincoln's death.
13. You can't tell me (nothing, anything) about Lincoln that I don't know.
14. I never met (nobody, anybody) who found Lincoln's life uninteresting.
15. Some people might think he didn't (never, ever) make a mistake.
16. A humble man, Lincoln wouldn't (ever, never) believe he was perfect.
17. You couldn't find a more concerned president (nowhere, anywhere).
18. The local libary hasn't got (any, no) books about Lincoln's children.
19. As a volunteer in the Black Hawk War, Lincoln didn't see (any, no) fighting.
20. There aren't (no, any) other presidents that were born in Kentucky.

Exercise 11   **Writing Sentences to Express Negative Ideas**

On your paper, write five sentences to express negative ideas. In each sentence, use the word from Column A and one of the words from Column B.

	Column A	Column B
1.	couldn't	ever, never
2.	has	anything, nothing
3.	doesn't	any, no
4.	can	anywhere, nowhere
5.	nothing	anybody, nobody

MEETING INDIVIDUAL NEEDS   **English Language Learners**

Expressing Negative Ideas

Many languages use two or more negative words to express a negative idea. As a result, students who speak these languages may have trouble avoiding double negatives in English. Encourage non-native speakers of English to read aloud sentences that express negative ideas to help them get used to the sound of the single negative word. Remind students that the contraction *-n't* also expresses "no" in a sentence. They may want to express contractions in two words so they can hear the word *not*.

UNIT 13 Grammar Review

ADVERBS

The action in Irene Hunt's *Across Five Aprils* takes place during the Civil War, which began in April 1861 and ended in April 1865. The following excerpt from the book focuses on a letter sent by a character named Shadrach Yale to a younger boy named Jethro. The passage has been annotated to show some of the adverb uses covered in this unit.

Literature Model

from Across Five Aprils
by Irene Hunt

Shadrach wrote that he and Jenny had seen the President and General Grant as they drove through the Washington streets together.

". . . The President's face is deeply lined, and his cheeks are gaunt. I have seen so many soldiers whose cheeks have had that sunken look, even though they were young faces. . . . The President looks at least twenty years older than the pictures you and I used to study together in the early days of the war. But his face was full of light as the crowds cheered; I think he knew they were cheering Grant and that pleased him, for I'd guess that he, too, wanted to cheer the little man who sat beside him.

Grant does *not* have the appearance of a great general; he looks awkward, ill at ease, and carelessly dressed. But we have had enough of charm and polish; this commander who doesn't even walk like a military man is the one who will, I believe, restore the Union."

> Adverb modifying the verb *drove*

> Adverb modifying the adjective *lined*

> Adverb modifying the adjective *many*

> Negative adverb modifying the verb *does have*

Adverbs

Grammar Review **405**

Teach
About the Literature

Explain that the review features a passage from Irene Hunt's historical novel about the Civil War, *Across Five Aprils*. This passage details one character's reaction to General Grant and his position as commander of the Union Army. *Across Five Aprils* is Irene Hunt's first book.

After students have read the passage, initiate a discussion of the characters, the setting, and the mood of the passage. Then ask students to focus on the highlighted adverbs. Invite them to decide which words are essential to the meaning of the passage and which are not. The exercises that follow are based on this passage and related topics.

Linking Grammar and Literature

☑ **Teaching Tip**

To help students distinguish between adjectives and adverbs, remind them that adverbs can modify only verbs, adjectives, or other adverbs.

Cooperative Learning

Invite students to work together to choose a literature passage that exemplifies an effective use of adverbs. Suggest that students start by looking for examples of adverb use in several books they enjoy. Students can then give short presentations explaining how the effective use of adverbs contributes to the strength of the passage.

Listening and Speaking

Listening for adverbs can help students reinforce what they have learned. Encourage students to listen for adverbs in their daily speech. How often, for example, do they use adverbs such as *very*, *always*, or *really?* When they compare things, how often do they use adverbs?

Resource Manager

Planning Resources
• *Lesson Plans*

📂 **Other Print Resources**
• *Grammar and Composition Handbook*
• *Grammar Workbook,* Lessons 34–40; Unit 6 Review; Cumulative Review: Units 1–6

✔ **ASSESSMENT OPTIONS**

📂 *Tests with Answer Key and Rubrics*
Unit 13 Mastery Test, pp. 55–56

💾 *Testmaker*
Unit 13 Mastery Test

Practice and Assess

Answers: Exercise 1

Answer will vary, but some suggestions are given below.

1. always
2. Occasionally
3. once
4. here
5. quite

Answers: Exercise 2

1. Soon—when
2. proudly—how
3. rapidly—how
4. there—where
5. often—when
6. Sometimes—when
7. privately—how
8. outside—where
9. together—how
10. firmly—how

Review: Exercise 1 **Writing Adverbs to Modify Verbs**

On your paper, write an adverb to complete each sentence correctly.

SAMPLE Students _____ read *Across Five Aprils* in sixth grade.
ANSWER sometimes

1. Librarians _____ order new copies of *Across Five Aprils* because of the book's popularity.
2. _____ our teacher assigns a group book report to the class.
3. My friends and I _____ volunteered to write about *Across Five Aprils*.
4. I thought I left my copy of *Across Five Aprils* _____.
5. Irene Hunt was _____ honored when she received the Newbery Award for her book.

Review: Exercise 2 **Identifying Adverbs That Modify Verbs**

On your paper, identify the adverb in each sentence and write whether it tells *how*, *when*, or *where*.

SAMPLE I read the book quickly.
ANSWER quickly—how

1. Soon Shadrach would write to his friend Jethro.
2. He proudly described his experience.
3. War can age a president rapidly.
4. Shadrach saw President Lincoln there.
5. Grant was often criticized.
6. Sometimes Grant felt uncomfortable around people.
7. Lincoln privately admired Grant.
8. Lincoln sat outside with Grant.
9. They drove together through Washington, D.C.
10. Shadrach firmly believed in Grant's ability as a leader.

Review: Exercise 3 **Identifying Adverbs and the Words They Modify**

On your paper, write each sentence. Underline each adverb. Then write the word that the adverb describes and write whether the word is a *verb, adjective,* or *adverb.* (Some sentences have more than one adverb.)

SAMPLE President Lincoln and General Grant rode through the streets together.

ANSWER President Lincoln and General Grant rode through the streets together. (rode—verb)

1. Jethro read the letter, and he placed it carefully in a big envelope.
2. Shadrach wrote thoughtfully; he described events in Washington.
3. The large crowd cheered loudly for the popular General Grant.
4. Lincoln was very pleased that the crowd reacted enthusiastically.
5. Union troops fought extremely well under General Grant.
6. Eventually Grant would be elected president.
7. He triumphed quite easily over his Democratic opponent.
8. Grant carefully organized his presidency as he had organized the army.
9. Grant was unanimously renominated by his party to run for a second term as president.
10. Scandals were quite widespread during his second term.

Review: Exercise 4 **Writing Adverbs in Sentences**

On your paper write each sentence, replacing the blank with an adverb that describes the underlined word.

SAMPLE Being a large-boned man, Lincoln was _____ suited for hard work.

ANSWER Being a large-boned man, Lincoln was **quite** suited for hard work.

1. As a boy, Lincoln was a _____ gifted speaker.
2. He worked _____ hard as a clerk in a store.
3. In 1832 Lincoln _____ bought a grocery store with a partner.
4. _____ the grocery store failed.
5. Even though his partner died, Lincoln _____ paid off the debts from the store.

Answers: Exercise 3

1. carefully—placed (verb)
2. thoughtfully—wrote (verb)
3. loudly—cheered (verb)
4. very—pleased (adjective); enthusiastically—reacted (verb)
5. extremely—well (adverb); well—fought (verb)
6. Eventually—would be elected (verb)
7. quite—easily (adverb); easily—triumphed (verb)
8. carefully—organized (verb)
9. unanimously—was renominated (verb)
10. quite—widespread (adjective)

Answers: Exercise 4

Answers will vary, but some suggestions are given below.

1. very
2. extremely
3. finally
4. Eventually
5. determinedly

Adverbs

Answers: Exercise 5

1. more loudly
2. worse
3. farther
4. better
5. less
6. longer
7. more carelessly
8. more deeply
9. most
10. longer

Answers: Exercise 6

1. most frequently
2. more grandly
3. more carefully
4. least
5. longest

Adverbs

Review: Exercise 5   Using the Comparative and Superlative Forms

On your paper, rewrite each sentence, using the correct comparative or superlative form in parentheses.

SAMPLE   The troops fought (harder, more harder) under General Grant.
ANSWER   The troops fought harder under General Grant.

1. The crowd applauded (more loudly, loudlier) than they had for any other Union general.
2. The North fared (worse, worst) than the South until Grant took command.
3. Grant drove his armies (farther, farthest) into the South than they had gone before.
4. Grant commanded (better, best) than the other Union generals.
5. Crops in the North suffered (less, lesser) from the war than crops in the South did.
6. The divisions caused by the war lasted far (longer, more longer) than anyone expected.
7. Grant was (more careless, more carelessly) dressed than Shadrach had expected.
8. President Lincoln's face was (more deeper, more deeply) lined than it had been in the days before the war.
9. Of all his generals, Lincoln admired Grant (more, most).
10. The Civil War lasted years (longer, longest) than people had thought it would.

Review: Exercise 6   Using Comparative and Superlative Adverbs

On your paper, write each sentence, using the comparative or superlative adverb form of the word in parentheses.

1. Which is the (frequently) visited building in the city?
2. Who entertained (grandly), Dolley Madison or Elizabeth Monroe?
3. Of the two, who guarded her privacy (carefully)?
4. Of all the presidents, who enjoyed the White House the (little)?
5. Who lived there (long) of all?

Review: Exercise 7 **Telling Adjectives and Adverbs Apart**

On your paper, write the correct word from parentheses. Then write whether the word is an *adverb* or *adjective*.

1. Dolley Madison gave (lavish, lavishly) parties.
2. She entertained (good, well).
3. She (proud, proudly) wore rich silks.
4. She was (great, greatly) admired.
5. Her parties were (most, almost) always a success.
6. From 1801 to 1817, Dolley was an (elegant, elegantly) Washington hostess.
7. While the White House was being rebuilt, she lived with President Madison in a (private, privately) mansion.
8. Wherever she lived, Dolley entertained (extravagant, extravagantly).
9. She (real, really) enjoyed her role as hostess.
10. After her husband's death, Dolley (surprising, surprisingly) returned to live in Washington.

Review: Exercise 8 **Using Adverbs and Adjectives Correctly**

On your paper, write the following paragraph. Choose an adjective or adverb from the list below to go in each blank. Write *adjective* or *adverb* to identify each word you add.

difficult	good	least	best
very	less	better	easily
easy	quite	great	eventually

Elizabeth Blackwell had a(n) ¹_____ desire for a medical education. Her goal was not a(n) ²_____ one. She faced a(n) ³_____ struggle to become a doctor. Blackwell began by writing letters to doctors all over the country. ⁴_____ few answered her. Most people thought it was ⁵_____ foolish for a woman to think of becoming a doctor, but Blackwell was not ⁶_____ discouraged. She wrote to the ⁷_____ medical schools in the country, hoping they would admit her. She then wrote to schools that were ⁸_____ famous than the others. She was accepted by one school in Geneva, New York, and ⁹_____ became the first American woman to receive a medical degree. Elizabeth Blackwell's example remains a ¹⁰_____ model for young women today.

Answers: Exercise 7
1. lavish—adjective
2. well—adverb
3. proudly—adverb
4. greatly—adverb
5. almost—adverb
6. elegant—adjective
7. private—adjective
8. extravagantly—adverb
9. really—adverb
10. surprisingly—adverb

Answers: Exercise 8
Answers will vary, but some suggestions are given below.
1. a great—adjective
2. an easy—adjective
3. a difficult—adjective
4. Very—adverb
5. quite—adverb
6. easily—adverb
7. best—adjective
8. less—adverb
9. eventually—adverb
10. good—adjective

Answers: Exercise 9

1. ever
2. anyone
3. anything
4. ever
5. any
6. anywhere
7. anybody
8. any
9. anything
10. anyone

Answers: Exercise 10

Answers will vary, but some suggestions are given below.

1. weren't ever
2. never met anyone
3. hadn't gone anywhere
4. had known nothing
5. had never seen anything
6. Nobody . . . had ever seen
7. could never
8. hadn't ever
9. Never before had
10. no one should

Adverbs

Review: Exercise 9 **Avoiding Double Negatives**

On your paper, complete each sentence so that it correctly expresses a negative idea.

1. No one (ever, never) forgets our twenty-sixth president.
2. I can't find (anyone, no one) else in history like Theodore Roosevelt.
3. I didn't know (nothing, anything) about him until recently.
4. I wasn't (ever, never) expecting to be so impressed.
5. I didn't expect to find (any, no) books about Teddy Roosevelt at the library.
6. I couldn't have learned more about him (anywhere, nowhere) else.
7. You might think there isn't (nobody, anybody) else as interested in him as I am.
8. There wasn't (no, any) other president who worked harder.
9. It seemed he didn't do (anything, nothing) else.
10. There isn't (anyone, no one) I admire more.

Review: Exercise 10 **Expressing Negative Ideas**

On your paper, rewrite each sentence to express a negative idea correctly. (There is more than one correct way to write most sentences.)

SAMPLE   The Browns didn't never expect to visit Washington, D.C.
ANSWER   The Browns didn't ever expect to visit Washington, D.C.

1. The Browns weren't never planning to go to the capital.
2. Margie Brown had never met no one who had been there.
3. They hadn't gone nowhere near Washington before last summer.
4. Little Billy hadn't known nothing about the surprise trip.
5. The family hadn't never seen nothing as impressive as the White House.
6. Nobody in their family had never seen the Cherry Blossom Festival.
7. They couldn't never have imagined the beauty of the mall in springtime.
8. They hadn't never before visited the Senate Office Building.
9. Never before hadn't they imagined the thrill of the Air and Space Museum.
10. They concluded that no one shouldn't turn down an opportunity to visit the nation's capital.

Review: Exercise 11

Proofreading

The following passage is about American artist Roger Brown, whose painting *Lost America* appears below. Rewrite the passage, correcting the errors in spelling, capitalization, grammar, and usage. Add any missing punctuation. There are ten errors.

Roger Brown

[1]Born in 1941, Roger Brown a painter who lives in Chicago. [2]His works, such as *Lost America*, have sure made him influential in the art world. [3]Brown has develop a highly individualized style over the past

Roger Brown, *Lost America*, 1989

(continued)

Adverbs

Answers: Exercise 11

Proofreading

This proofreading activity provides editing practice with (1) the current or previous units' skills, (2) the **Troubleshooter** errors, and (3) spelling errors. Students should be able to complete the exercise by referring to these units, the **Troubleshooter**, and a dictionary.

	Error (Type of Error)
1.	• Brown is a (sentence fragment)
2.	• surely (adverb form)
3.	• developed (verb form)
4.	• clearly (adverb form)
5.	• immediately (adverb form)
6.	• It's nothing as, *or* It's not anything as (double negative)
7.	• against (spelling)
8.	• soldiers (plural noun)
9.	• entirely (adverb form)
10.	• really (adverb form)

Viewing the Art

Roger Brown, *Lost America*, 1989

In *Lost America,* Abraham Lincoln contemplates his responsibilities as president of the United States at a time when the country indeed seemed lost. Ask students to identify some of the images in Roger Brown's painting that symbolize the Civil War and its effect on Lincoln. (The threatening clouds symbolize the storm of dissent in the nation. The rows of vegetation suggest lines of soldiers at the ready. Lincoln's face is purple, as if the war had physically bruised him.)

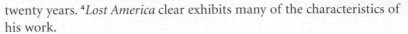

Answers: Exercise 12

Mixed Review

1. certainly
2. actually
3. willingly
4. seriously
5. specially
6. really
7. ever
8. partly
9. almost
10. surely

Close

Ask students to write a paragraph comparing two United States presidents. Encourage students to use adjectives and adverbs correctly and to make vivid comparisons.

Adverbs

twenty years. ⁴*Lost America* clear exhibits many of the characteristics of his work.

⁵The painting is immediate recognizable as a portrait of Abraham Lincoln. ⁶It's not nothing as simple as that. ⁷Lincoln is silouetted agenst a sky full of threatening clouds lined up in tightly packed rows. ⁸At the bottom of the painting is vegetation that resembles the kind of fence that soldiers' erect in battle.

⁹Except for the dark purple of his face, the figure of Lincoln is entire in black and white. ¹⁰Lincoln appears real gloomy and thoughtful; perhaps, as the title *Lost America* suggests, he is thinking about the war and the possible division of the United States into two separate countries."

Review: Exercise 12

Mixed Review

Rewrite each sentence, replacing the underlined word with an adverb that makes sense. Underline your adverb.

SAMPLE   An eccentric *usual* behaves in an unexpected way.
ANSWER   An eccentric *usually* behaves in an unexpected way.

1. Claiming to be emperor of the United States would <u>certain</u> be considered eccentric behavior.
2. In the middle of the nineteenth century, Joshua Norton <u>actual</u> claimed to be Norton I, Emperor of the United States.
3. The people of San Francisco <u>willing</u> accepted his claim.
4. Emperor Norton took his job quite <u>serious</u>.
5. The best clothing store in the entire city made clothing <u>special</u> for him.
6. Their "emperor" was <u>real</u> loved by the people of San Francisco.
7. The people of San Francisco haven't <u>never</u> forgotten Norton.
8. Perhaps Norton's ideas were inspired <u>part</u> by Napoleon.
9. Napoleon conquered <u>most</u> all of Europe.
10. Norton <u>sure</u> would have heard about Napoleon.

Writing Application

Adverbs in Writing

In this excerpt from Betsy Byars's novel *Coast to Coast*, 13-year-old Birch tries to convince her grandfather to take her up in his 1940 airplane. As you read, pay special attention to the underlined words.

"I <u>really</u> want to go!" As she said it, she realized it was true. She needed to get <u>away</u> from this world, and this was the way to do it. "What are we waiting for?"

"I don't guess it would hurt to fly to the beach and back."

"Then get <u>in</u>! Let's go!"

"Don't get in <u>too</u> big a hurry." Her grandfather smiled. It was his first real smile of the afternoon.

Birch followed him around the plane. "What are you doing?"

"Well, <u>right now</u>, I'm doing a preflight inspection. I check the tires, the control surfaces, move them for freedom and cable looseness."

Examine the passage, focusing on the underlined words.

Techniques with Adverbs

> **TIME**
>
> For more about usage rules, see **TIME Facing the Blank Page,** page 98.

Try to apply some of Betsy Byars's writing techniques when you write and revise your own work.

❶ To make your writing more vivid, add adverbs to tell exactly when the action is occurring. Compare the following:

GENERAL WORDS Well, I'm doing a preflight inspection.

BYARS'S VERSION Well, *right now* I'm doing a preflight inspection.

❷ Use adverbs to reinforce the mood and tone of your writing.

UNSPECIFIED TONE I want to go.

BYARS'S VERSION I *really* want to go.

Adverbs

Adverbs in Writing

Ask students to read silently this passage from Betsy Byars's novel *Coast to Coast.* Discuss with them how the author has used adverbs to make her writing more vivid and to enhance the mood and tone of the passage.

Techniques with Adverbs

Discuss with students the techniques for using adverbs that are outlined here. Then have students look at the proofreading passage on pages 411–412. Ask: *How has the writer used adverbs to make the piece more vivid or to enhance its mood and tone?*

Practice

The answers to this challenging and enriching activity will vary. Refer to Techniques with Adverbs as you evaluate student choices.

Practice Practice these techniques by revising the following passage on a separate sheet of paper. Remember that adverbs can modify verbs, adjectives, and other adverbs.

Many people read Betsy Byars's books. She is one of the popular young adult authors of our time. In her book *Coast to Coast,* Ms. Byars's love of flying comes across to her readers. Thirteen-year-old Birch does not want her grandfather to sell his plane. She is sure the plane can keep him young at heart. Birch talks her grandfather into letting her get into the plane. He shows her how to operate it. He gets into the plane with her. Will Birch and her grandfather fly the old airplane? You'll have to read this exciting book to find out.

Writing Application **413**

Objectives

- To recognize and understand the function of prepositions and prepositional phrases
- To identify and use the correct pronoun form after a preposition
- To recognize and use prepositional phrases as adjectives and as adverbs
- To understand conjunctions and the specific uses of both coordinating and correlative conjunctions
- To recognize and use interjections in a meaningful way

✔ ASSESSMENT OPTIONS

📁 *Tests with Answer Key and Rubrics*
Unit 14 Pretest, pp. 57–58
Unit 14 Mastery Test, pp. 59–60

💾 *Testmaker*
Unit 14 Pretest
Unit 14 Mastery Test

You may wish to administer the Unit 14 Pretest at this point.

Key to Ability Levels

L1 Level 1 activities are within the basic ability range of students.

L2 Level 2 activities are within the ability range of average students.

L3 Level 3 activities are more challenging activities.

UNIT
14

Prepositions, Conjunctions, and Interjections

Resource Manager

Planning Resources
- *Lesson Plans*
- *Block Scheduling*

📂 **Transparencies**
- *Bellringer*
- *Daily Language Practice*
- *Two-Minute Skill Drill*

💻 **Web Sites**
writerschoice.glencoe.com

📁 **Other Print Resources**
- *Grammar and Composition Handbook*
- *Grammar Enrichment*
- *Grammar Practice*
- *Grammar Reteaching*
- *Grammar Workbook*
- *Sentence-Combining Practice*
- *Tests with Answer Key and Rubrics*

📺 **Video**
- *MindJogger Videoquizzes*

💾 **Software**
- *Interactive Grammar Workbook*
- *Language Arts PASS*
- *Presentation Plus!*
- *Revising with Style*
- *Testmaker*

14.1 Prepositions

■ A **preposition** is a word that relates a noun or a pronoun to some other word in a sentence.

The dictionary **on** the desk was open.

An almanac was **under** the dictionary.

Meet me **at** three o'clock tomorrow.

COMMONLY USED PREPOSITIONS

aboard	as	despite	near	since
about	at	down	of	through
above	before	during	off	to
across	behind	except	on	toward
after	below	for	onto	under
against	beneath	from	opposite	until
along	beside	in	out	up
amid	between	inside	outside	upon
among	beyond	into	over	with
around	by	like	past	without

A preposition can consist of more than one word.

I borrowed the almanac **along with** some other reference books.

PREPOSITIONS OF MORE THAN ONE WORD

according to	along with	because of	in spite of	on top of
across from	aside from	in front of	instead of	out of

Read each sentence below. Any word that fits in the blank is a preposition.

Use the almanac that is _____ the table.

I took the atlas _____ your room.

Prepositions, Conjunctions, and Interjections

Focus

Lesson Overview

Objectives
- To recognize common prepositions and prepositions of more than one word
- To demonstrate the ability to use prepositions accurately

Bellringer
Daily Language Activity

When students enter the classroom, have this assignment on the board: *Write a few sentences that explain how to find the closest public library.*

See also *Daily Language Practice*

Motivating Activity

Explain that prepositions are words such as *down, to, under,* or *near* that show the relationship between a noun or pronoun and another word. Have each student exchange the Bellringer sentences with a partner and underline the prepositions. Encourage volunteers to share their sentences on the board.

Teach

☑ Teaching Tip

English usage allows the terminal preposition, as in *This is the new library I told you about.* Attempts to avoid the terminal preposition often result in strained, wooden sentences: *This is the new library about which I told you.* Perhaps the most famous sentence used to defend the terminal preposition is that attributed to Winston Churchill: *This is the kind of nonsense up with which I will not put.*

Resource Manager

Planning Resources
- *Lesson Plans*

Transparencies
- *Bellringer*
- *Daily Language Practice*

📂 Other Print Resources
- *Grammar and Composition Handbook*
- *Grammar Enrichment,* p. 29
- *Grammar Practice,* p. 28
- *Grammar Reteaching,* p. 29
- *Grammar Workbook,* Lesson 41

Practice and Assess

Answers: Exercise 1

1. around
2. on
3. in front of
4. of, on, of
5. during
6. of
7. of, in
8. in, in
9. during
10. for, of

Answers: Exercise 2

1. of, upon, of, below
2. (Along with)
3. into
4. (in front of,) of
5. of, into, of
6. in, (because of,) of, in
7. (Aside from,) of, in, of, before
8. among, in, of
9. (According to,) (along with,) for
10. On, of

Additional Resources

📂 *Grammar Practice*, p. 28
📂 *Grammar Reteaching*, p. 29
📂 *Grammar Enrichment*, p. 29

📕 *Grammar Workbook*, Lesson 41

Close

Ask students to write directions for getting from their classroom to the school library. Then have them circle all the prepositions they used.

Exercise 1 **Identifying Prepositions**

Write each preposition from the following sentences.

1. Many famous libraries around the world are tourist attractions.
2. The New York Public Library on Fifth Avenue serves the New York metropolitan community.
3. Two marble lions in front of the library greet visitors.
4. The library houses a large number of books on a vast range of topics.
5. The library also holds several exhibitions during the year.
6. Its branches hold millions of volumes.
7. The New York Public Library is one of the largest library systems in the world.
8. The first public library in America was built in the year 1833.
9. Many important library developments occurred during the nineteenth century.
10. Melvil Dewey established a system for the classification of books.

Exercise 2 **Identifying Prepositions of More Than One Word**

Write the preposition or prepositions from each sentence. Circle each preposition of more than one word.

1. The classification number of a library book is found upon the spine of the book, usually below the title.
2. Along with the Dewey Decimal Classification system, Melvil Dewey also established the American Library Association and the *Library Journal*.
3. The Dewey system organizes books into ten main categories.
4. The research library in front of the administration building uses a different system of classifying books.
5. The Library of Congress classification system categorizes books into twenty-one major areas of knowledge.
6. This system was developed in the early twentieth century because of the large number of books in this library.
7. Aside from being one of the largest research libraries in the world, the Library of Congress has the largest collection of books printed before 1501.
8. Among the books in its collection is a perfect copy of the Gutenberg Bible.
9. According to the guide, the library provides reference assistance along with research for the United States Congress.
10. On the back of a book's title page, you will find cataloging data.

English Language Learners

Choosing Prepositions

Because many prepositions are part of idiomatic phrases, students who are acquiring English may have difficulty identifying which preposition to use. To give them practice in using prepositions correctly, write on slips of paper a few simple sentences that contain prepositions.

(Examples: *The student stands behind the desk. She sits in front of the blackboard.*) Then ask student volunteers to act out the sentences. Have other students guess what each sentence is; then write the sentence on the board, underlining the preposition.

14.2 Prepositional Phrases

■ A prepositional phrase is a group of words that begins with a preposition and ends with a noun or pronoun, which is called the object of the preposition.

> Dr. Chin has an almanac **from the nineteenth century.**
> The almanac has a special meaning **for him.**

A preposition can have a compound object.

> Almanacs contain lists **of facts and figures.**
> Grace showed one **to her sisters and her classmates.**

A sentence can have more than one prepositional phrase.

> We left our notes **under the almanac on the shelf.**

A prepositional phrase can appear anywhere in a sentence—at the beginning, in the middle, or at the end.

> **At the library** students examined the almanac.
> Students **at the library** examined the almanac.
> Students examined the almanac **at the library.**

Sometimes you can use a prepositional phrase to combine sentences.

> Gary wrote a newspaper article.
> He wrote about old almanacs.
> Gary wrote a newspaper article **about old almanacs.**

In the second sentence above, the prepositional phrase *about old almanacs* tells more about the newspaper article. You can combine the sentences by adding the phrase to the first sentence.

14.2 Prepositional Phrases **417**

Focus

Lesson Overview

Objectives
- To identify prepositional phrases
- To use prepositional phrases in sentence combining

🔔 Bellringer
Daily Language Activity

When students enter the classroom, have this assignment on the board: *Write a sentence or two that tells where and when you might read a book.*

✎ **See also** *Daily Language Practice*

Motivating Activity

Tell students that prepositional phrases are often the words that tell where and when something takes place. (Example: *We met in front of the library at noon. In front of the library* tells where and *at noon* tells when.) Have students exchange Bellringer sentences and circle the prepositional phrases that tell where and when.

Teach

☑ Teaching Tip

Write one of the sentences from the lesson on the board and draw an arrow from the preposition to its object. Then write several sentences on the board and ask volunteers to supply the arrows.

Resource Manager

Planning Resources
- *Lesson Plans*

📂 Transparencies
- *Bellringer*
- *Daily Language Practice*

📂 Other Print Resources
- *Grammar and Composition Handbook*
- *Grammar Enrichment,* p. 29
- *Grammar Practice,* p. 28
- *Grammar Reteaching,* p. 29
- *Grammar Workbook,* Lesson 42

417

Practice and Assess

Answers: Exercise 3

1. in <u>almanacs</u>
2. through a certain <u>year</u>; on <u>population</u>
3. with special <u>information</u>
4. from the American colonial <u>period</u>
5. in <u>1733</u>
6. with <u>facts</u> and <u>lists</u>; of various <u>sorts</u>
7. of reference <u>books</u>; in the <u>library</u>
8. from <u>nine</u> o'clock; in the <u>morning</u>; to <u>nine</u> o'clock; at <u>night</u>
9. in the reference <u>section</u>; of most school and public <u>libraries</u>
10. about <u>foods</u>; from various <u>countries</u>
11. of a <u>dictionary</u>; of <u>words</u>
12. for the <u>study</u>; of many <u>kinds</u>; of <u>information</u>
13. about the <u>location</u>; of all the <u>countries</u>; in the <u>world</u>
14. In most <u>libraries</u>; out of the <u>building</u>
15. of phonograph <u>records</u>, <u>CDs</u>, and <u>videotapes</u>
16. in various <u>neighborhoods</u>
17. by <u>taxes</u> and <u>contributions</u>
18. Because of the rising <u>cost</u>; of <u>material</u> and <u>equipment</u>; under <u>pressure</u>
19. of the public <u>libraries</u>; in the <u>United States</u>
20. of reference <u>materials</u>, current <u>magazines</u>, and technical <u>reports</u>

Additional Resources

📂 *Grammar Practice,* p. 28
📂 *Grammar Reteaching,* p. 30
📂 *Grammar Enrichment,* p. 29

📖 *Grammar Workbook,* Lesson 42

Close

Ask students how to identify the object of a preposition. (Find a preposition, look at the whole prepositional phrase, and then find the noun or pronoun that ends the phrase.)

(side tab) Prepositions, Conjunctions, and Interjections

Exercise 3 **Identifying Prepositions and Their Objects**

Write each prepositional phrase. Underline each object of the preposition. Some sentences have more than one prepositional phrase.

1. Calendars are often included in almanacs.
2. Many almanacs predict the weather through a certain year and give information on population.
3. Some newspapers and organizations publish almanacs with special information.
4. *Poor Richard's Almanac* is a well-known almanac from the American colonial period.
5. Benjamin Franklin published the book in 1733.
6. It is filled with facts and lists of various sorts.
7. Many other kinds of reference books are found in the library.
8. The library is open from nine o'clock in the morning to nine o'clock at night.
9. Encyclopedias are located in the reference section of most school and public libraries.
10. International cookbooks contain information about foods from various countries.
11. The pages of a dictionary list many different kinds of words.
12. Almanacs are useful for the study of many kinds of information.
13. An atlas can help you learn about the location of all the countries in the world.
14. In most libraries the reference material cannot be taken out of the building.
15. Many libraries today have collections of phonograph records, CDs, and videotapes.
16. Many large cities have branch libraries in various neighborhoods.
17. School libraries and public libraries are funded by taxes and contributions.
18. Because of the rising cost of material and equipment, library budgets have been under pressure.
19. One-third of the public libraries in the United States are branch libraries.
20. A library should have a good collection of reference materials, current magazines, and technical reports.

MEETING INDIVIDUAL NEEDS **English Language Learners**

Identifying Prepositions

Students learning English as a second language may have difficulty identifying prepositions. Explain that the prefix *pre-* means "before." A *pre*position, then, usually comes *before* a noun or a pronoun; it doesn't stand by itself.

14.3 Pronouns After Prepositions

When a pronoun is the object of a preposition, remember to use an object pronoun and not a subject pronoun.

> Yoshi handed the dictionary to Akilah.
> Yoshi handed the dictionary to **her.**

In the example above, the object pronoun *her* replaces *Akilah* as the object of the preposition *to.*

Sometimes a preposition will have a compound object consisting of a noun and pronoun. Remember to use an object pronoun in a compound object.

> I borrowed the almanac from Jorge and Lisa.
> I borrowed the almanac from Jorge and **her.**

An object pronoun is used in the sentence above. *Jorge and her* is the compound object of the preposition *from.*

If you are unsure about whether to use a subject pronoun or an object pronoun, try saying the sentence aloud with only the pronoun following the preposition.

The pronouns *who* and *whom* are often confused. *Who* is a subject pronoun, and *whom* is an object pronoun. Note how the pronouns are used in the following sentences.

> **Who** told you about it?
> To **whom** did you lend the almanac?

Focus

Lesson Overview

Objectives
- To identify the object of a preposition when the object is a pronoun
- To distinguish between the nominative and objective forms of pronouns
- To use the object pronoun when it occurs in a prepositional phrase

Bellringer
Daily Language Activity

When students enter the classroom, have this assignment on the board: *Tell what is wrong with this sentence and write it correctly:*
Lisa's dog ran to Lisa, jumped on Lisa, and stole a cookie from Lisa.

See also *Daily Language Practice*

Motivating Activity

Remind students that using pronouns helps writers to avoid repeating nouns over and over. Check that students have substituted pronouns for the noun *Lisa* in the Bellringer. Have them underline the prepositional phrases and circle the pronouns.

Teach

☑ Teaching Tip

Sometimes the compound object of a preposition consists of two pronouns. A sentence such as the following may confuse students: *Yuri gave the thesaurus to you and me.* When students want to use a compound object with two pronouns, suggest they say the sentence aloud with only one pronoun at a time following the preposition.

Prepositions, Conjunctions, and Interjections

Resource Manager

Planning Resources
- *Lesson Plans*

Transparencies
- *Bellringer*
- *Daily Language Practice*
- *Two-Minute Skill Drill*

📁 **Other Print Resources**
- *Grammar and Composition Handbook*
- *Grammar Enrichment,* p. 30
- *Grammar Practice,* p. 29
- *Grammar Reteaching,* p. 31
- *Grammar Workbook,* Lesson 43

Practice and Assess

Answers: Exercise 4

1. whom
2. him
3. them
4. her
5. him
6. her
7. them
8. him
9. him
10. them

Answers: Exercise 5

1. her
2. him
3. them
4. him
5. her
6. him
7. her
8. her
9. her
10. them

Answers: Exercise 6

Answers will vary, but some suggestions are given below.
1. She visited with me.
2. I went to dinner with her.
3. I borrowed the book from them.
4. I gave a magazine to them.
5. I wrote about him.

Additional Resources

Grammar Practice, p. 29
Grammar Reteaching, p. 31
Grammar Enrichment, p. 30

Grammar Workbook, Lesson 43

Close

Have students write sentences with object pronouns after prepositions.

Prepositions, Conjunctions, and Interjections

Exercise 4   **Choosing Pronouns After Prepositions**

For each sentence, write the correct pronoun.

1. Jorge and Lisa told you about (who, whom)?
2. Vanessa spoke to Lisa and (he, him) at the game.
3. What did Vanessa show to (them, they)?
4. Mr. Valdes bumped into Vanessa and (she, her) in the corridor.
5. Lisa had still not given her homework assignment to (him, he).
6. He walked with Lisa and (her, she) to the door.
7. Who knows what he said to (they, them)?
8. After class they had lunch with Jorge and (he, him).
9. Lisa is going to the library with (he, him).
10. She picked a topic that would interest both of (they, them).

Exercise 5   **Using Pronouns After Prepositions**

In each item, a proper noun is underlined. Replace the proper noun with the correct object pronoun.

1. Mr. Valdes handed an almanac to <u>Alice</u>.
2. Alice learned about Ukraine from <u>Mr. Valdes</u>.
3. Ukraine had been one of <u>the Soviet republics</u>.
4. Alice wanted information for <u>Uncle Oscar</u>.
5. Uncle Oscar often speaks of <u>Greta</u>, his sister.
6. Greta lives with <u>Victor</u>, her husband.
7. Alice mailed a package to <u>Greta</u>.
8. Faraway places are exciting to <u>Alice</u>.
9. Alice wants to learn much more about <u>Greta</u>.
10. She plans a visit to <u>Greta</u> and <u>Victor</u> next year.

Exercise 6   **Writing Sentences with Prepositions and Object Pronouns**

Write a sentence for each item. Use the pronouns listed as objects of a preposition. Underline the preposition and its object pronoun.

SAMPLE   them

ANSWER   We wrote a letter <u>to them</u>.

1. me
2. her
3. her and him
4. them
5. him

Enrichment and Extension

Using *Who* or *Whom*

Help students decide whether to use the subject pronoun *who* or the object pronoun *whom* in a question. Suggest they rewrite the question as a statement and substitute *he* or *she* or *him* or *her* for *who* or *whom*.

14.4 Prepositional Phrases as Adjectives and Adverbs

Prepositional phrases function as adjectives and adverbs in sentences.

■ A prepositional phrase functioning as an **adjective** describes a noun or a pronoun.

These phrases can describe subjects, direct and indirect objects, predicate nouns, or objects in other prepositional phrases. An adjective phrase usually comes directly after the noun or pronoun it describes.

Africa is a continent **with many natural resources.**

One **of the articles** describes Africa vividly.

The wildlife **of Africa** is varied and abundant.

■ A prepositional phrase functioning as an **adverb** describes a verb, an adjective, or another adverb.

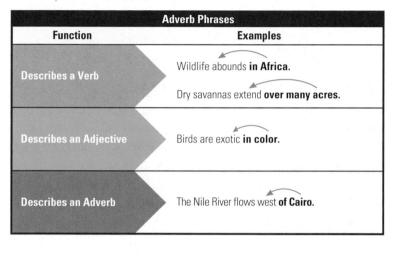

Adverb Phrases	
Function	**Examples**
Describes a Verb	Wildlife abounds **in Africa.**
	Dry savannas extend **over many acres.**
Describes an Adjective	Birds are exotic **in color.**
Describes an Adverb	The Nile River flows west **of Cairo.**

Focus

Lesson Overview

Objectives
- To identify prepositional phrases used as adjectives and adverbs
- To use adverb and adjective phrases effectively and correctly to modify nouns, pronouns, adjectives, and adverbs

Bellringer
Daily Language Activity

When students enter the classroom, have this assignment on the board: *Write five sentences with at least one prepositional phrase in each.*

See also *Daily Language Practice*

Motivating Activity

Have students exchange papers and underline the prepositional phrase or phrases in each sentence. Later, after students have read about how prepositional phrases function as adjectives and adverbs, have them draw a line from each phrase to the word being described.

Teach

☑ **Teaching Tip**

An adverb phrase that modifies a verb can usually be moved to another position in the sentence. An adjective phrase, however, cannot be separated from the noun it modifies.

Resource Manager

Planning Resources
- *Lesson Plans*

Transparencies
- *Bellringer*
- *Daily Language Practice*

☞ Other Print Resources
- *Grammar and Composition Handbook*
- *Grammar Enrichment*, p. 31
- *Grammar Practice*, p. 30
- *Grammar Workbook*, Lesson 44

Practice and Assess

Answers: Exercise 7

1. on the equator—adv.
2. near the rain forests—adv.
3. on the northeast—adv.
4. of Cairo—adj.
5. in the Sahara—adv.
6. about new African nations—adj.
7. of Somalia—adj.; of hardship—adj.
8. between Mali and Ghana—adv.
9. of the Atlantic Ocean—adj.; of the Ivory Coast—adj.
10. from years—adv.; of conflict—adj.
11. of this kind—adj.; of information—adj.; in an atlas—adv.
12. to Cheryl—adv.; for her birthday—adv.
13. beside the globe—adv.
14. about geography—adv.
15. on maps—adv.; in tables—adv.
16. of an atlas—adj.
17. to the riches—adj.; of an atlas—adj.
18. in an atlas—adj.; for research—adv.
19. about their countries—adj.
20. by cartographers—adv.

Answers: Exercise 8

Answers will vary. A sample sentence:
1. An atlas gives information about countries. (*about countries* modifies *information*)

Additional Resources

📂 *Grammar Practice,* p. 30
📂 *Grammar Enrichment,* p. 31

📖 *Grammar Workbook,* Lesson 44

Close

Have students describe the difference between an adjective phrase and an adverb phrase.

Exercise 7   **Identifying Adjective and Adverb Phrases**

Write each prepositional phrase and whether it is used as an *adjective* or an *adverb*.

1. The Congo Basin lies on the equator.
2. The grass grows quickly near the rain forests.
3. The Red Sea borders Africa on the northeast.
4. What is the climate of Cairo?
5. There is little vegetation in the Sahara.
6. I read a brief article about new African nations.
7. The people of Somalia are suffering a great deal of hardship.
8. Burkina Faso is a small country that lies between Mali and Ghana.
9. The waters of the Atlantic Ocean wash the shores of the Ivory Coast.
10. Southern African nations have recently emerged from years of conflict.
11. Much of this kind of information can be found in an atlas.
12. Bill gave an atlas to Cheryl for her birthday.
13. Cheryl left it beside the globe.
14. An atlas tells about geography.
15. Facts and figures are shown on maps and in tables.
16. An index is an important part of an atlas.
17. It is the guide to the riches of an atlas.
18. Information in an atlas is useful for research.
19. Several governments publish national atlases about their countries.
20. Early atlases had maps that were hand-drawn by cartographers.

Exercise 8   **Writing Adjective and Adverb Phrases**

On your paper, expand each sentence below by adding at least one adjective or adverb phrase to the sentence. Draw a line from each phrase to the word it describes.

1. An atlas gives information.
2. The birds are colorful.
3. The zebras gather.
4. The monkeys are calling.
5. The lion dozes.
6. The climate is humid.
7. The desert seems endless.
8. The plants bloom.
9. A traveler needs water.
10. The sunset glows.

Prepositions, Conjunctions, and Interjections

MEETING INDIVIDUAL NEEDS

English Language Learners

Identifying Adjective and Adverb Phrases

Students might benefit from going step by step through the process of determining whether prepositional phrases are adjective or adverb phrases. Provide students with a passage containing prepositional phrases. Have students go through the sentences and circle all of the prepositional phrases. Then help the students to determine whether the phrases modify nouns or pronouns (adjective phrases), or verbs, adjectives, or adverbs (adverb phrases).

14.5 | Telling Prepositions and Adverbs Apart

Sometimes it is difficult to tell whether a word is a preposition or an adverb. Both types of words can answer the questions *where?* and *when?* In addition, some words can be used as either prepositions or adverbs.

**WORDS THAT CAN BE
USED AS PREPOSITIONS
OR ADVERBS**

about	below	out
above	down	outside
around	in	over
before	inside	through
behind	near	up

If you're having trouble deciding whether a word is used as a preposition or as an adverb, look at the other words in the sentence. If the word is followed closely by a noun, the word is probably a preposition, and the noun is the object of the preposition.

We ate our lunch **outside** the **library**.

In the sentence above, the word *outside* is followed closely by the noun *library. Outside* is a preposition, and *library* is the object of the preposition.

If the word is not followed closely by a noun, then the word is probably an adverb.

We ate our lunch **outside**.

In this sentence, the word *outside* answers the question *where?* but is not followed by a noun. In this sentence, *outside* is an adverb.

We ate our lunch **outside.**

We ate our lunch **outside** the **library.**

Prepositions, Conjunctions, and Interjections

14.5 Telling Prepositions and Adverbs Apart **423**

Focus

Lesson Overview

Objectives
- To identify words used as both prepositions and adverbs
- To demonstrate an understanding of the function of a word used as an adverb or as a preposition

🔔 Bellringer
Daily Language Activity

When students enter the classroom, have this assignment on the board: *Create four sentences using the following words:*

above	*inside*
over	*before*

See also *Daily Language Practice*

Motivating Activity

Have students look over the sentences they wrote in the Bellringer activity. For each sentence, write the word or words that answer the question *where?* or *when?* For example: *The clock is above the door. Where is the clock?* (above the door)

Teach

☑ Teaching Tip

To help students decide whether a word is used as a preposition or as an adverb, suggest they check to see whether the word is contained within a prepositional phrase. A prepositional phrase begins with a preposition and usually ends with a noun or pronoun—the object of the preposition. A word used as an adverb does not have an object and is not contained within a prepositional phrase.

Resource Manager

Planning Resources
- *Lesson Plans*

📖 Transparencies
- *Bellringer*
- *Daily Language Practice*

📁 Other Print Resources
- *Grammar and Composition Handbook*
- *Grammar Practice,* p. 31
- *Grammar Workbook,* Lesson 45

Practice and Assess

Answers: Exercise 9

1. adverb	14. preposition
2. preposition	15. adverb
3. preposition	16. preposition
4. adverb	17. preposition;
5. preposition	adverb
6. preposition	18. preposition
7. adverb	19. preposition
8. adverb	20. preposition
9. preposition	21. preposition
10. preposition	22. adverb
11. preposition	23. adverb
12. preposition; adverb	24. preposition
13. adverb; adverb	25. adverb

Answers: Exercise 10

Answers will vary, but some suggestions are given below.
1. The shelf is above my head. 2. The book is in the bag. 3. Cookbooks are around the corner. 4. Travel books are near the window. 5. To see the sign, look up. 6. The student walked out the door. 7. Read through the introduction. 8. I read that book before. 9. Study time is over. 10. The librarian put the book down.

Additional Resources

📁 *Grammar Practice*, p. 31

📓 *Grammar Workbook*, Lesson 45

Close

Ask students to use the words from the list on page 423 to write sentences. Have them exchange papers and tell whether each word was used as a preposition or as an adverb.

Exercise 9 · Distinguishing Between Adverbs and Prepositions

Write whether each underlined word is used as a *preposition* or as an *adverb*.

1. Who left this book of quotations <u>behind</u>?
2. Gene found the book <u>behind</u> the lockers.
3. We searched <u>through</u> the biographical dictionary.
4. I had read the same article <u>before</u>.
5. I will report on the article <u>before</u> Friday.
6. Please look <u>inside</u> the almanac.
7. Jeff will bring the encyclopedia <u>inside</u>.
8. Kim pointed to the important notes <u>below</u>.
9. My note cards lie <u>below</u> the top shelf.
10. Did you read the article <u>about</u> Gandhi?
11. It was <u>about</u> his early life.
12. <u>Outside</u> class I shall have a chance to read the article <u>carefully</u>.
13. I can think my impressions <u>over</u> while taking a walk <u>outside</u>.
14. I enjoy a walk <u>in</u> the park.
15. Kim carried the atlas <u>around</u>.
16. She walked hastily <u>around</u> the library.
17. Lee carried his article <u>up</u> the stairs but came <u>down</u> without it.
18. Bob's dictionary was found <u>near</u> his desk.
19. Kim reads <u>down</u> the pages of the almanac.
20. Her conversation goes <u>over</u> my head.
21. A map of the United States hangs <u>near</u> the front door.
22. A portrait of the president hangs <u>above</u>.
23. Mr. Cleese brought <u>in</u> an overdue video about India.
24. Did I leave my card <u>in</u> that book?
25. The librarians searched <u>around</u> for my card.

Exercise 10 · Using Words as Prepositions or Adverbs

Write each word below in a sentence. If you use the word as a preposition, underline the prepositional phrase.

1. above	6. out
2. in	7. through
3. around	8. before
4. near	9. over
5. up	10. down

Viewing and Representing

Interpreting Visuals

Use the pictures on page 423 to help students find the preposition in the sentence *We ate our lunch outside the library.* Ask: Which word answers the question *outside what?* (the library). Point out that this noun is represented in the larger picture. In the sentence *We ate our lunch outside,* there is no answer to the question *outside what?* In this sentence, *outside* is an adverb. Suggest students work with partners to practice with their own pairs of sentences. Ask the students to label prepositions and adverbs.

14.6 Conjunctions

■ A **conjunction** is a word that joins words or groups of words in a sentence.

The most common conjunctions are *and, but,* and *or.* They are called **coordinating conjunctions.** *And* and *or* are used to form compound subjects. *And, but,* and *or* are used to form compound predicates and compound sentences.

Using Conjunctions to Form Compounds	
Compound Subject	Mexico **and** Canada are both on a map of North America.
Compound Predicate	Students can check the map **or** use the globe.
Compound Sentence	I would lend you my atlas, **but** Felicia already borrowed it.

A comma should be placed before the conjunction in a compound sentence. Do not, however, place a comma between the two parts of a compound subject or a compound predicate.

Although the conjunctions are used in a similar fashion, they are not interchangeable. Each has a different meaning.

Coordinating Conjunctions		
Conjunction	**Meaning**	**Example**
And	Introduces an additional idea	The map **and** the globe are in the classroom.
But	Introduces a contrasting idea	The map is old, **but** the globe is new.
Or	Introduces a choice or second possibility	Students check the map **or** use the globe.

Pairs of conjunctions such as *either, or; neither, nor;* and *both, and* are called **correlative conjunctions.** They join the same kinds of words as do the conjunctions *and, but,* and *or.*

Either Lucy **or** I will use the atlas.

Focus

Lesson Overview

Objectives
- To identify coordinating conjunctions and their function in forming compound sentences and compound elements within sentences
- To identify correlative conjunctions and to distinguish between these and coordinating conjunctions
- To use both correlative and coordinating conjunctions appropriately and effectively in writing

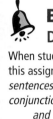 **Bellringer**
Daily Language Activity

When students enter the classroom, have this assignment on the board: *Write four sentences using each of the following conjunctions:*
and   but
or   either, or

See also *Daily Language Practice*

Motivating Activity

Invite volunteers to write their sentences from the Bellringer activity on the board. Work with students to figure out whether their sentences have compound subjects or compound predicates or whether they are compound sentences.

Teach

☑ **Teaching Tip**

Conjunctions join words or groups of words that have equal grammatical weight in a sentence: subjects, predicates, phrases, and independent clauses. Point out that correlative conjunctions make the relationship between words or groups of words a little clearer than do coordinating conjunctions.

Prepositions, Conjunctions, and Interjections

Resource Manager

Planning Resources
- *Lesson Plans*

Transparencies
- *Bellringer*
- *Daily Language Practice*

📁 **Other Print Resources**
- *Grammar and Composition Handbook*
- *Grammar Enrichment,* p. 32
- *Grammar Practice,* p. 32
- *Grammar Reteaching,* p. 32
- *Grammar Workbook,* Lesson 46

425

Practice and Assess

Answers: Exercise 11

1. and—compound subject
2. and —compound predicate
3. and—compound predicate
4. but—compound sentence
5. or—compound predicate
6. and—compound subject
7. or—compound sentence
8. Either, or—compound subject
9. but—compound predicate
10. but—compound sentence

Answers: Exercise 12

1. and	6. but
2. and	7. Both, and
3. or	8. and
4. or	9. but *or* and
5. or	10. Neither, nor

Additional Resources

📁 *Grammar Practice,* p. 32
📁 *Grammar Reteaching,* p. 32
📁 *Grammar Enrichment,* p. 32

📕 *Grammar Workbook,* Lesson 46

Close

Ask students to explain, in their own words, the differences between the coordinating conjunctions *and, or,* and *but.* Then have them tell what a correlative conjunction is.

Exercise 11 Identifying Conjunctions and Compounds

Write each conjunction. Then write whether it forms a *compound subject, compound predicate,* or *compound sentence.*

1. Ramón and Sal are using the class atlas.
2. They are studying rivers and comparing figures.
3. The Mississippi River flows southward and increases in width along the way.
4. The Amazon is long, but it is not the longest river.
5. Who has studied or visited mountains in Europe?
6. The Chaco and the Serengeti are vast plains.
7. Sal has been to Argentina, or he is planning to go there.
8. Either the Himalayas or the Urals are the world's highest mountains.
9. Bolivia contains some of the highest mountains in South America but also has some very hot, humid lowlands.
10. Denver is called the mile-high city, but Leadville is at an even higher altitude.

Exercise 12 Using Conjunctions

Write the conjunctions that best fit in the sentences.

1. Judy wrote a report _____ drew a map of the Himalayas.
2. Tibet _____ Nepal lie north of India.
3. Is the Upper Nile in north _____ south Egypt?
4. Australia _____ New Zealand is easy to reach from North America.
5. Is Mount Everest in Asia, _____ is it in Europe?
6. I have a map of India, _____ I do not have one of Japan.
7. _____ Tokyo _____ Hiroshima are in Japan.
8. Her ambition was to climb the highest mountain on each continent, _____ she planned to start with Mt. McKinley in Alaska.
9. Mt. Everest is the highest at 29,028 feet, _____ two other Himalayan peaks are more than 28,000 feet high.
10. _____ Mt. Fuji in Japan _____ Mt. Etna in Italy is nearly as high.

Exploring Language

Joining with Conjunctions

Tell students that conjunctions are like a glue that joins similar things. Write sentences with conjunctions on the board. Discuss why the pairs go together. Ask students to make up their own sentences and identify the compound parts in each.

Correlative Conjunctions

Tell students that when the correlative conjunction *not only ... but also* joins clauses, the verb in the first clause precedes the subject. For example: *Not only have I studied Japan's history, but I have also studied its language.* Ask students to create sentences using this conjunction.

14.7 Interjections

© Watterson. 1987 Universal Press S.

■ An **interjection** is a word or group of words that expresses strong feeling.

COMMON INTERJECTIONS

aha	great	oh	phew
alas	ha	oh, no	well
eek	hey	oops	wow
goodness	hooray	ouch	yes

An interjection that expresses a very strong feeling may stand alone, either before or after a sentence. Such interjections are followed by an exclamation mark.

Oh, no! I wrote *horse* instead of *hoarse*.

When an interjection expresses a milder feeling, it appears as part of the sentence. In that case, it is separated from the rest of the sentence by a comma.

Oh, I thought I knew the definition of that word.

Use interjections sparingly. Overuse ruins the effect.

Prepositions, Conjunctions, and Interjections

Focus

Lesson Overview

Objectives
- To recognize interjections as a means of expressing strong feeling
- To understand that an interjection may stand alone or be part of a longer sentence
- To use interjections appropriately

🔔 Bellringer
Daily Language Activity

When students enter the classroom, have this assignment on the board: *Write three sentences, each of which expresses strong feelings about something.*

See also *Daily Language Practice*

Motivating Activity

Invite volunteers to share their sentences with the class. Then ask students to look at the list of common interjections on page 427. Have them add one of the interjections to their sentences. Discuss how the tone of the sentence may have changed when the interjection was added.

Teach

☑ Teaching Tip

Students often confuse interjections with imperative sentences. Interjections are sentence fragments when they stand alone. An imperative sentence only appears to be a fragment; its subject is always understood to be *you,* and it always contains a verb.

Resource Manager

Planning Resources
- *Lesson Plans*

Transparencies
- *Bellringer*
- *Daily Language Practice*

📁 **Other Print Resources**
- *Grammar and Composition Handbook*
- *Grammar Enrichment*, p. 32
- *Grammar Practice*, p. 32
- *Grammar Reteaching*, p. 33
- *Grammar Workbook*, Lesson 47

Practice and Assess

Answers: Exercise 13

1. Phew,	13. Well!
2. Hooray!	14. Ha!
3. Great!	15. Oh,
4. Oh, no!	16. Oops,
5. Oops,	17. Great!
6. Hey!	18. Aha!
7. Aha!	19. Phew!
8. Well,	20. Ouch!
9. Ouch!	21. Hey,
10. Yes!	22. Oh, no!
11. Awesome!	23. Hey,
12. Oh, no!	24. Well,
	25. Wow!

Answers: Exercise 14

Answers will vary. Make sure that an interjection expressing strong feeling is followed by an exclamation mark. An interjection expressing milder feeling should be separated from the rest of the sentence by a comma.

Additional Resources

 *Grammar Practice*, p. 32

Grammar Reteaching, p. 35

Grammar Enrichment, p. 32

Grammar Workbook, Lesson 47

Close

Have volunteers say aloud a sentence with an interjection. The rest of the students can write the sentence they hear. Check that punctuation of the interjection is appropriate.

Prepositions, Conjunctions, and Interjections

Exercise 13   Identifying Interjections

Write each interjection. Include any punctuation mark that goes with it.

1. Phew, this dictionary is heavy.
2. Jack will carry it for me. Hooray!
3. Great! I made no mistakes on my spelling test.
4. Oh, no! I forgot the double *b* in *hobble*.
5. Oops, I think I forgot to sign my name.
6. Hey! Studying the English language is fun!
7. Simon has the answer to our problem. Aha!
8. Well, I would like to know more about Old English.
9. Ouch! Spelling rules can be complicated.
10. I am going to the state spelling bee. Yes!
11. Mr. Robinson just showed me the unabridged dictionary. Awesome!
12. Oh, no! Do I need that to prepare for the spelling bee?
13. So this is Middle English. Well!
14. Ha! I recognize a few words.
15. Oh, I didn't hear you, Mr. Lyons.
16. Oops, I lost my English book.
17. Mr. Lyons found it on the floor. Great!
18. Aha! I dropped it in the reference room.
19. Mr. Lyons, you saved the day. Phew!
20. Ouch! It's time to get back to that dictionary.
21. Hey, spellers! Watch out for me.
22. Oh, no! I think I spelled *accommodate* with one *m* and two *d*'s.
23. Hey, do you know how to spell *embarrass*?
24. Well, if *alto* is from an Italian word meaning "high," why does it refer to low female singing voices?
25. I had no idea so many common expressions were originally written by Shakespeare. Wow!

Exercise 14   Writing Sentences with Interjections

Write ten sentences, using a different interjection in each. Take care to punctuate each sentence correctly.

MEETING INDIVIDUAL NEEDS   English Language Learners

Recognizing Interjections

Students whose second language is English may not readily recognize the situations in which some interjections are used. Pair these students with native English speakers and have the partners go over the sentences in Exercise 13. The more fluent student should explain why the interjection in each sentence is appropriate, and both students should suggest other interjections that could be substituted. If a student doesn't understand a particular interjection, encourage the partner to explain it—perhaps by acting it out.

UNIT 14

Grammar Review

PREPOSITIONS, CONJUNCTIONS, AND INTERJECTIONS

Eudora Welty is an American short story author and novelist who writes about small-town life in the South. In her book *One Writer's Beginnings*, published in 1984, she describes the influence of her family and surroundings on her writing. The following passage has been annotated to show some uses of prepositions and conjunctions.

Literature Model

from One Writer's Beginnings
by Eudora Welty

Mrs. Calloway made her own rules **about** books. You could not take back a book to the Library on the same day you'd taken it out; it made no difference to **her** that you'd read every word in it **and** needed another to start. You could take out two books at a time and two only; this applied as long as you were a child and also for the rest of your **life**, to my mother as severely as to me. So two by two, I read library books as fast as I could go, rushing them home in the basket **of my bicycle**. From the minute I reached our house, I started to read. Every book I seized on, from *Bunny Brown and His Sister Sue at Camp Rest-a-While* to *Twenty Thousand Leagues Under the Sea*, stood for the devouring wish to read being instantly granted. I knew this was bliss, knew it **at the time**. Taste isn't nearly so important; it comes in its own time. I wanted to read *immediately*. The only fear was that of books coming to an end.

- Preposition
- Pronoun as object of the preposition
- Conjunction connecting compound predicate
- Noun as object of the preposition
- Prepositional phrase (adjective phrase)
- Prepositional phrase (adverb phrase)

Grammar Review **429**

Teach

About the Literature

After students have read the passage by Eudora Welty, initiate a discussion of the characters and the mood of the excerpt. Then ask students to focus on the high-lighted words in the passage. Have them identify the prepositional phrases that are not highlighted and determine whether each functions as an adjective or adverb.

The passage from *One Writer's Beginnings* tells about Eudora Welty's early love of books. The book is composed of a series of lectures the author delivered at Harvard University in 1983.

Linking Grammar and Literature

☑ **Teaching Tip**

Ask students to make up sentences based on their reaction to the passage from *One Writer's Beginnings*. Tell students they may explain their own relationship to books, imagine a dialogue between themselves and the young Eudora Welty, or respond in some other way to the passage. Each sentence should contain a preposition, a conjunction, or an interjection. After the students have completed the assignment, invite them to share their sentences with the rest of the class.

Listening and Speaking

Interjections are often used in writing dialogue. Invite students to imagine a short dialogue between Eudora Welty and Mrs. Calloway, the librarian. Have them use interjections as appropriate. Suggest students work in pairs and share their dialogues with a partner. Can students hear and identify the interjection?

Resource Manager

Planning Resources
- *Lesson Plans*

📂 **Other Print Resources**
- *Grammar and Composition Handbook*
- *Grammar Workbook,* Lessons 41–47; Unit 14 Review; Cumulative Review: Units 1–13

✔ **ASSESSMENT OPTIONS**

📂 *Tests with Answer Key and Rubrics*
Unit 14 Mastery Test, pp. 59–60

💾 *Testmaker*
Unit 14 Mastery Test

Answers: Exercise 1

1. of
2. by; to
3. for
4. for
5. by; about

Answers: Exercise 2

Answers will vary, but some suggestions are provided below.

1. with
2. of
3. for
4. through; around
5. in
6. Within
7. at; along
8. on; behind
9. near
10. between

Review: Exercise 1 Identifying Prepositions

Write each preposition in the sentences below.

SAMPLE Eudora Welty writes about the beginning of her love for books.
ANSWER about, of, for

1. Mrs. Calloway was an important part of Welty's early reading life.
2. The rules made by Mrs. Calloway seemed ridiculous to a young reader.
3. The library's rules were the same for all.
4. The important thing for Eudora Welty was having books available.
5. Welty read books by any author about any topic.

Review: Exercise 2 Using Prepositions

Write an appropriate preposition to replace each blank. Try to use a different preposition in each sentence.

SAMPLE Libraries _____ very large communities often have several branches.
ANSWER in

1. People _____ library cards can take home any of the books on the shelves.
2. All _____ the branches are available to anyone with a library card in the city.
3. There are library rules _____ children and adults.
4. A librarian is usually available to help you find your way _____ the library.
5. Short story collections are _____ the fiction section.
6. _____ this library is a wonderful section of young-adult fiction.
7. The section is _____ the back wall.
8. You can find it _____ the librarian's desk.
9. The librarian's desk is _____ the reference section.
10. The reference section is _____ the rare-book room and the fiction section.

Review: Exercise 3 Identifying Prepositional Phrases
and Their Objects

Write the prepositional phrases from each sentence. Underline the object of
each preposition.

SAMPLE Scholars often go to specialized libraries for information.
ANSWER to specialized <u>libraries</u> for <u>information</u>

1. Researchers needing information about fine arts or early printed books may
   go to the Morgan Library in New York City.
2. Near the Capitol in Washington, D.C., is the Folger Shakespeare Library.
3. Opposite the Folger, across the street, sits the huge Library of Congress.
4. The Beinecke Rare Book and Manuscript Library at Yale University is housed
   inside a six-story glass enclosure on campus.
5. Because of the excellent collections within these libraries, scholars can study
   any subject along with you and me.

Review: Exercise 4 Choosing Object Pronouns

Write the correct pronoun for each sentence.

1. Books were Mrs. Calloway's subject, and she made rules about (they, them).
2. To (who, whom) did Mrs. Calloway's rules apply?
3. The rules applied equally to the two of (they, them), Eudora and her mother.
4. Eudora read so many books that she seemed to race through (they, them).
5. According to (she, her), she started to read as soon as she returned from the
   library.
6. Although Eudora may not have liked Mrs. Calloway, despite (she, her), the
   girl certainly enjoyed reading.
7. Although Eudora does not mention her father in this passage, her love of
   books may have been influenced by (he, him).
8. I, too, have always loved having books around (I, me).
9. My family and I always keep stacks of unread books near (we, us).
10. Without (they, them) we feel lost.

Answers: Exercise 3
1. about fine <u>arts</u> or early printed <u>books</u>;
   to the <u>Morgan Library</u>; in <u>New York City</u>
2. Near the <u>Capitol</u>; in <u>Washington, D.C.</u>
3. Opposite the <u>Folger</u>; across the <u>street</u>;
   of <u>Congress</u>
4. at <u>Yale University</u>; inside a six-story
   glass <u>enclosure</u>; on <u>campus</u>
5. Because of the excellent <u>collections</u>;
   within these <u>libraries</u>; along with <u>you</u>
   and <u>me</u>

Answers: Exercise 4
1. them
2. whom
3. them
4. them
5. her
6. her
7. him
8. me
9. us
10. them

Answers: Exercise 5

1. preposition—life
2. adverb
3. preposition—stories, novels
4. preposition—drawer
5. adverb

Answers: Exercise 6

1. of Welty's early reading life—part—adjective
2. for an ardent reader—tiresome—adverb
3. except her mother—everyone—adjective; of Mrs. Calloway—afraid—adverb
4. for silence—asked—adverb
5. to adults and children—applied—adverb
6. to the library—rode—adverb
7. Because of her love—obeyed—adverb; of books—love—adjective
8. by any author—books—adjective
9. of *One Writer's Beginnings*—parts—adjective; from Welty—gift—adjective; to her readers—gift—adjective; to her
10. in the bookcase—had—adverb; in the living room—bookcase—adjective

Prepositions, Conjunctions, and Interjections

Review: Exercise 5   Telling Prepositions from Adverbs

The following sentences are about Eudora Welty's life. Identify each underlined word as a *preposition* or an *adverb*. If the word is a preposition, write its object or objects.

1. *One Writer's Beginnings* is Eudora Welty's book <u>about</u> her own life.
2. The book discusses how the effects of her early years in the South come <u>through</u> in her stories.
3. Eudora Welty is an important Southern writer known <u>for</u> both her short stories and her novels.
4. <u>In</u> a library drawer, Welty's father kept musical instruments of all kinds.
5. Welty often looked <u>inside</u> to see the wonderful instruments.

Review: Exercise 6   Identifying Adjective and Adverb Phrases

Write each sentence. Underline each prepositional phrase and draw an arrow to the word it describes. Write whether the phrase functions as an *adjective* or an *adverb*.

SAMPLE   Eudora Welty writes about her love of books.

ANSWER   Eudora Welty writes <u>about her love</u> <u>of books</u>.
                           adverb phrase   adjective phrase

1. Mrs. Calloway was an important part of Welty's early reading life.
2. Mrs. Calloway's rules were tiresome for an ardent reader.
3. Welty said everyone except her mother was afraid of Mrs. Calloway.
4. Mrs. Calloway asked everyone for silence.
5. The library's rules applied to adults and children.
6. Eudora rode her bike to the library.
7. Because of her love of books, she obeyed Mrs. Calloway's rules.
8. Eudora read books by any author.
9. A critic said parts of *One Writer's Beginnings* are a gift from Welty to her readers.
10. The Weltys had five encyclopedias in the bookcase in the living room.

Review: Exercise 7 Using Conjunctions to Combine Sentences

Combine each pair of sentences below by using the conjunction in parentheses to form a compound sentence, compound subject, or compound object. Write whether your sentence is a *compound sentence* or a sentence with a *compound subject* or a *compound predicate*.

SAMPLE Public libraries provide useful services. Budget problems are forcing some public libraries to cut back the services they provide. (but)

ANSWER Public libraries provide useful services, but budget problems are forcing some public libraries to cut back the services they provide. compound sentence

1. What do you think of your local library? How do you use your library? (and)
2. Consider the function of the library. Also think about the ways in which it serves the community. (and)
3. Our library is in a municipal building. The same building houses the town government. (and)
4. Some libraries provide a place for community meetings. Other libraries are just for reading and research. (or)
5. Small towns have limited funds for a library. Small towns may join with other nearby communities to form a regional library. (but)
6. Large cities have more than one library. Each of those libraries may house a specialized collection, such as business or health and medicine. (and)
7. No library can contain all the books its users need. Interlibrary loans allow readers to borrow books from other libraries. (but)
8. At the library, people can exchange community information and post notices. People can pick up tax forms and other printed material. (either, or)
9. A library exhibit can highlight special events and seasonal activities. The exhibit can suggest reading related to the topic. (or)
10. Libraries often have special collections of books for children. Libraries may provide story hours, films, and workshops for children. (and)

Answers: Exercise 7

Answers will vary, but some suggestions are given below.

1. What do you think of your local library, and how do you use it? —compound sentence
2. Consider the function of the library and also think about the ways in which it serves the community. —compound sentence
3. Our library and the town government are in a municipal building. —compound subject
4. Some libraries provide a place for community meetings or exist just for reading and research. —compound predicate
5. Small towns have limited funds for a library but may join with other nearby communities to form a regional library. —compound predicate
6. Large cities have more than one library, and each may house a specialized collection, such as business or health and medicine. —compound sentence
7. No library can contain all the books its users need, but inter-library loans allow readers to borrow books from other libraries. —compound sentence
8. At the library, people can either exchange community information and post notices, or they can pick up tax forms and other printed material. —compound sentence
9. A library exhibit can highlight special events and seasonal activities, or it can suggest reading related to the topic. —compound sentence
10. Libraries often have special collections of books for children, and libraries may provide story hours, films, and workshops for children. —compound sentence

Answers: Exercise 8

Answers will vary. Students' sentences should employ what they have learned in this unit.

Review: Exercise 8 **Writing Sentences**

Write fifteen sentences, following the directions given below.

SAMPLE Write a sentence that begins with an interjection and contains a compound predicate.

ANSWER Oh, I fell and skinned my knee!

1. Write a sentence with a compound subject.
2. Write a compound sentence joined by the conjunction *and*.
3. Write a sentence that begins with an interjection followed by a comma.
4. Write a sentence with a compound predicate.
5. Write a sentence that uses the correlative conjunction *either, or*.
6. Write a sentence that is preceded by an interjection followed by an exclamation mark.
7. Write a compound sentence joined by the conjunction *but*.
8. Write a sentence that includes a prepositional phrase with a compound object.
9. Write a sentence that uses the conjunctions *both* and *and*.
10. Write a compound sentence that is joined by the conjunction *or* and contains an interjection.
11. Write a sentence that begins with a prepositional phrase in which the object is a pronoun.
12. Write a sentence that ends with a prepositional phrase in which the object is made up of two pronouns.
13. Write a sentence in which one part of the compound object of a preposition is a pronoun.
14. Write a compound sentence that contains a preposition of more than one word.
15. Write a sentence that contains two prepositional phrases, one used as an adjective and one as an adverb.

Proofreading

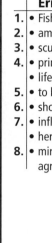

The following passage is about Janet Fish, whose painting *Toby and Claire Reading* appears on this page. Rewrite the passage, correcting the errors in spelling, capitalization, grammar, and usage. Add any missing punctuation. There are ten errors.

Janet Fish

¹'Janet Fish' early interest in art is similar to Eudora Welty's love of books ²Her ambiton from early childhood was to be a sculptor. ³Fish's mother was a sculptor and her grandfather was a painter. ⁴Fish studied sculpture, printmaking and abstract painting in college, but painting was to become her lifes work. ⁵The effects of light on various surfaces are especially interesting to she. ⁶The painting *Toby and Claire Reading* show the importance of light and color for her. ⁷Although Fish's paintings are realistic, her art is strongly influence by she training in abstract painting. ⁸The painting *Toby and Claire Reading* mirror Eudora Welty's early love of books.

Janet Fish, *Toby and Claire Reading*, 1984

Prepositions, Conjunctions, and Interjections

Answers: Exercise 9

Proofreading

This proofreading activity provides editing practice with (1) the current or previous units' skills, (2) the **Troubleshooter** errors, and (3) spelling errors. Students should be able to complete the exercise by referring to the units, the **Troubleshooter,** and a dictionary.

	Error (Type of Error)
1.	• Fish's (singular possessive)
2.	• ambition (spelling)
3.	• sculptor, (run-on sentence)
4.	• printmaking, (comma in a series)
	• life's (singular possessive)
5.	• to her (object pronoun)
6.	• shows (subject-verb agreement)
7.	• influenced (verb form)
	• her training (possessive pronoun)
8.	• mirrors (subject-verb agreement)

Viewing the Art

Janet Fish, *Toby and Claire Reading*, 1984

In *Toby and Claire Reading,* Janet Fish presents the effect of full summer sunlight on an outdoor scene. The light emphasizes some of the painting's details and blurs others. As a result, the painting has an almost photo-graphic realism. The observer peers into the picture to try to read the comics and the titles of the books on the grass. This 1984 oil-on-canvas painting measures 50 by 100 inches and is held by the Robert Miller Gallery.

Answers: Exercise 10

Mixed Review

Answers will vary, but some suggestions are given below.

1. on—adverb
2. from the fibers—made
3. Because of
4. Ptolemy I and II made …
5. Wow!
6. … tablets, but scholars …
7. them
8. … Bible and preserved …
9. Both paper and movable type …
10. Before

Close

Ask students how they like to spend a carefree summer's day. Do they like to read voraciously, like Eudora Welty? Or do they like to lie in the sun and do nothing? After the discussion, ask students to write sentences based on their responses. Each sentence should contain one or more of the following: a prepositional phrase *(We meet our friends at the pool.)*, a conjunction *(We blow bubbles, and our dog chases them.)*, or an interjection *(Gee! I wish it were summer right now!)*.

Prepositions, Conjunctions, and Interjections

Review: Exercise 10

Mixed Review

Rewrite each item, following the directions in parentheses.

SAMPLE The Maya wrote their history _____ stone monuments. (Add a preposition.)

ANSWER on

1. Information was written _____ clay tablets in Mesopotamia and on papyrus in Egypt. (Add a preposition. Write whether the prepositional phrase is used as an *adjective* or an *adverb*.)
2. Papyrus was a writing material made _____ the fibers of water reeds. (Add a preposition. Draw an arrow from the prepositional phrase to the word it describes.)
3. _____ the fragile nature of papyrus, many ancient writings have not survived. (Begin with a preposition of more than one word.)
4. Ptolemy I made the Alexandrian Library the greatest in the ancient world. Ptolemy II made the Alexandrian Library the greatest in the ancient world. (Use a conjunction to form one sentence with a compound subject.)
5. It is amazing that not a trace of such a great library has ever been found. (Add an interjection.)
6. In 1859 British archaeologists found thousands of clay tablets. Scholars have not been able to understand the writing on them. (Use a conjunction to form a compound sentence.)
7. To _____, the cuneiform script on the tablets has been an unbreakable code. (Add an object pronoun to replace the words *the archaeologists*.)
8. Monks in monasteries copied religious works such as the Bible. They preserved the works of ancient scholars. (Use a conjunction to write one sentence with a compound predicate.)
9. Paper made books easier to produce. Movable type made books easier to produce. (Use a pair of correlative conjunctions to write one sentence with a compound subject.)
10. _____ the invention of the printing press, it took many hours of hand-copying to produce a Bible. (Add a preposition.)

Writing Application

Prepositions and Conjunctions in Writing

Freeman Hubbard uses prepositions and conjunctions in this passage from *The Great Days of the Circus* to help him convey the excitement of the circus's arrival. Examine the passage, focusing especially on the italicized words.

The street was alive *with noise* as the first four lovely ladies on horseback, trumpets lifted to their lips, came into sight. They were always lithe and lovely, *and* the plumes they wore danced as their horses pranced. Then came the band, *in red uniforms with gold braid,* riding *on a gilded band wagon* that was sometimes drawn by as many as forty horses. The band never stopped playing: the big bass drum thumped steadily, the trumpets *shrilled and blared,* the cymbals flashed *in the sun.* Behind the band came great floats.

Techniques with Prepositions and Conjunctions

Try to apply some of Hubbard's writing techniques when you write and revise your own work.

❶ Use prepositional phrases as adjectives and adverbs to add specific details to your writing.

WITHOUT PREPOSITIONAL PHRASES Then came the band.

HUBBARD'S VERSION Then came the band, in red uniforms with gold braid, riding on a gilded band wagon.

❷ To vary your writing, use conjunctions to form compound subjects, predicates, and sentences.

WITHOUT CONJUNCTIONS The trumpets shrilled. The trumpets blared.

HUBBARD'S VERSION The trumpets shrilled and blared.

> **TIME**
> For more about the importance of using language effectively, see **TIME Facing the Blank Page,** page 98.

Prepositions, Conjunctions, and Interjections

Prepositions and Conjunctions in Writing

Have students read the passage silently to themselves. Then discuss the italicized words with the class. Discuss these choices in relation to the Techniques with Prepositions and Conjunctions section.

Techniques with Prepositions and Conjunctions

Discuss the examples of the use of prepositional phrases and conjunctions. Encourage students to find additional examples in books or stories. Students can examine a current writing project of their own to find places to apply the techniques.

Practice

The answers to this challenging and enriching activity will vary. Refer to Techniques with Prepositions and Conjunctions as you evaluate student choices.

Practice Practice these techniques by revising the following passage on your own paper. Use prepositional phrases to add details and conjunctions to vary your sentences.

Marty and Josh had some free time. They decided to go to the library. It was a favorite place. The reading corner was surrounded by shelves. There were chairs and a couch. Marty chose a best-seller. Josh picked out a magazine. They settled down for a good read. They had an hour before Josh's mother was to pick them up. The room was quiet. The light was soft. No one disturbed them. It was so restful that both boys forgot the time.

Writing Application **437**

✔ ASSESSMENT OPTIONS

📁 *Tests with Answer Key and Rubrics*
Unit 14 Mastery Test, pp. 59–60

💾 *Testmaker*
Unit 14 Mastery Test

You may wish to administer the Unit 14 Mastery Test at this point.

📼 *Mindjogger Videoquizzes*

Objectives

- To recognize and use correctly singular and plural subjects and verbs
- To locate the subject in sentences with interrupting phrases and sentences that begin with *here* or *there*
- To use verbs that agree with compound subjects
- To identify and revise errors in subject-verb agreement

✔ ASSESSMENT OPTIONS

📂 *Tests with Answer Key and Rubrics*
Unit 15 Pretest, pp. 61–62
Unit 15 Mastery Test, pp. 63–64

💾 *Testmaker*
Unit 15 Pretest
Unit 15 Mastery Test

You may wish to administer the Unit 15 Pretest at this point.

Key to Ability Levels

L1 Level 1 activities are within the basic ability range of students.

L2 Level 2 activities are within the ability range of average students.

L3 Level 3 activities are more challenging activities.

UNIT
15

Subject-Verb Agreement

438

Resource Manager

Planning Resources
- *Lesson Plans*
- *Block Scheduling*

📇 Transparencies
- *Bellringer*
- *Daily Language Practice*

📂 Other Print Resources
- *Grammar and Composition Handbook*

- *Grammar Enrichment*
- *Grammar Practice*
- *Grammar Reteaching*
- *Grammar Workbook*
- *Tests with Answer Key and Rubrics*

📼 Video
- *MindJogger Videoquizzes*

💾 Software
- *Interactive Grammar and Language Workbook*
- *Language Arts PASS*
- *Presentation Plus!*
- *Testmaker*

🖥 Web Sites
- *writerschoice.glencoe.com*

15.1 Making Subjects and Verbs Agree

A subject and its verb are the basic parts of a sentence. The subject and its verb must *agree in number*. A singular noun subject takes a singular form of the verb. A plural noun subject takes a plural form of the verb. In the present tense, the singular form of the verb usually ends in *-s* or *-es*.

Read the sentences in the chart below. You can see that the subjects and verbs agree in number.

Subject Noun and Verb Agreement	
Singular	**Plural**
A **mountain rises** sharply to the sky.	**Mountains rise** sharply to the sky.
A **naturalist teaches** us about nature.	**Naturalists teach** us about nature.

Verbs and subject pronouns must also agree in number. In the present tense, the *-s* ending is used with the subject pronouns *it*, *he*, and *she*.

Subject Pronoun and Verb Agreement	
Singular	**Plural**
He, she, or it **travels.**	We **travel.**
You **travel.**	You **travel.**
I **travel.**	They **travel.**

The irregular verbs *be, do,* and *have* can be main verbs or helping verbs. They must agree with the subject, whether they are main verbs or helping verbs.

> I **am** fine. He **is** ready. [main verb]
> They **are** questioning a ranger. [helping verb]
>
> She **does** well. [main verb]
> She **does** work hard. They **do** sing. [helping verb]
>
> He **has** a boat. [main verb]
> He **has** visited Utah. They **have** eaten. [helping verb]

15.1 Making Subjects and Verbs Agree **439**

Focus

Lesson Overview

Objectives
- To identify singular and plural subjects and verbs
- To use verbs that agree in number with their subjects

Bellringer
Daily Language Activity

When students enter the classroom, have this assignment on the board: *Choose the correct verbs in the following sentences:*
Many tourists (visits, visit) Acadia National Park each year. Acadia (features, feature) a rocky coastline.

See also *Daily Language Practice*

Teach

☑ Teaching Tip
The following helping verbs do not change to show subject-verb agreement: *can, may, must, will,* and *shall.* Ask students to explain why the word *cans* in the following sentence is or is not an exception to this rule: *Every summer she cans tomatoes.*

⇄ Cross-reference: Grammar
For instruction and practice in using singular and plural subject pronouns, refer students to Lesson 11.1, pp. 361–362.

Subject-Verb Agreement

Resource Manager

Planning Resources
- *Lesson Plans*

Transparencies
- *Bellringer*
- *Daily Language Practice*

📂 Other Print Resources
- *Grammar and Composition Handbook*
- *Grammar Enrichment,* p. 33
- *Grammar Practice,* p. 33
- *Grammar Reteaching,* p. 34
- *Grammar Workbook,* Lesson 48

Practice and Assess

Answers: Exercise 1

1. lies	**14.** do
2. are	**15.** approach
3. features	**16.** do
4. is	**17.** carries
5. travel	**18.** has
6. photograph	**19.** contain
7. is	**20.** has
8. wind	**21.** line
9. flows	**22.** lie
10. lead	**23.** includes
11. enjoy	**24.** fill
12. does	**25.** protects
13. has	

Answers: Exercise 2

Answers will vary, but some suggestions are given below.

My 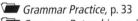brothers love to go camping. (plural)
Ana often comes with us. (singular)

Additional Resources

📁 *Grammar Practice,* p. 33
📁 *Grammar Reteaching,* p. 34
📁 *Grammar Enrichment,* p. 33

📖 *Grammar Workbook,* Lesson 48

Close

Discuss the sentences students wrote for Exercise 2.

Exercise 1 **Using Subject and Verb Agreement**

For each sentence, write the correct form of the verb in parentheses.

1. Acadia National Park (lies, lie) along Maine's coast.
2. Several islands (is, are) in the park.
3. Acadia (features, feature) a rocky coastline.
4. Mount Desert Island (is, are) very beautiful.
5. Many people (travels, travel) to Acadia every year.
6. They (photographs, photograph) the wildlife.
7. Mammoth Cave (is, are) in Kentucky.
8. The passageways (winds, wind) for nearly two hundred miles.
9. An underground river (flows, flow) through the caves.
10. Tour guides (leads, lead) people through the chambers.
11. Many visitors (enjoys, enjoy) the sense of adventure.
12. For example, my mother (does, do).
13. Yellowstone National Park (has, have) some of the few surviving grizzly bears.
14. Campers (does, do) enjoy the wilderness.
15. Large bears sometimes (approaches, approach).
16. Park visitors (does, do) require protection.
17. A camper (carries, carry) bedding and supplies.
18. Yellowstone (has, have) a beautiful waterfall.
19. Our national parks (contains, contain) natural wonders.
20. Wind Cave (has, have) unusual crystals.
21. Tiny white crystals (lines, line) the cave walls and ceiling.
22. Ancient animal fossils (lies, lie) in the Agate Fossil Beds.
23. The park (includes, include) the remains of two-horned rhinoceroses.
24. Unusual rock formations (fills, fill) Death Valley.
25. The National Park Service (protects, protect) Death Valley and other national monuments.

Exercise 2 **Writing Sentences with Subject and Verb Agreement**

Write ten original sentences. Use singular subjects in some sentences and plural subjects in others. Be sure each verb agrees with its subject. In each sentence, underline the subject once and the verb twice. Write whether the subject is *singular* or *plural.*

SAMPLE ANSWER: My friends are packing for a camping trip. (plural)

(side tab) Subject-Verb Agreement

MEETING INDIVIDUAL NEEDS

English Language Learners

Learning About Agreement

Students whose first language is non-European often have great difficulty with subject-verb agreement in English. They cannot see what meaning subject-verb agreement adds to the sentence (as opposed, for example, to a past tense ending, which changes the time of the action, or a plural ending on a noun, which changes its number). You might point out to these students that English speakers often have a similar problem with adjective-noun gender agreement in other languages.

15.2 Problems with Locating the Subject

You know how to make a subject and a verb agree when the verb directly follows the subject. However, sometimes a prepositional phrase comes between the subject and the verb. When that happens, make sure that the verb agrees with the subject of the sentence and not with the object of the preposition.

> A **park** in the islands **contains** a volcano.
> The **parks** of Hawaii **contain** volcanoes.

In the first sentence, *in the islands* is a prepositional phrase. The singular verb *contains* agrees with the subject of the sentence, *park*, not with the plural noun *islands*, which is the object of the preposition.

In the second sentence, *of Hawaii* is a prepositional phrase. The plural verb *contain* agrees with the plural subject *parks*, not with the singular noun *Hawaii*, which is the object of the preposition.

Some sentences begin with *here* or *there*. *Here* or *there* is never the subject of a sentence. Look for the subject after the verb in this type of sentence.

> There **is** a **park** on Maui.
> Here in the park **are** tropical **forests**.

To make it easier to find the subject, try rearranging these sentences and placing the subject and verb in their usual positions. This rearrangement makes clear how the subject and the verb agree in number.

> A **park is** there on Maui.
> Tropical **forests are** here in the park.

Focus

Lesson Overview

Objectives
- To locate the subject in sentences with interrupting phrases and sentences that begin with *here* or *there*
- To demonstrate control over subject-verb agreement in complicated sentences

Bellringer
Daily Language Activity

When students enter the classroom, have this assignment on the board: *Write these sentences. Then underline the subject and circle the verb in each.*

> Here is a wilderness.
> There are people in the city who are lonelier than I.
>
> Jean Craighead George,
> *My Side of the Mountain*

See also *Daily Language Practice*

Motivating Activity

Ask students to rearrange each sentence from the Bellringer activity, placing the subject and verb in their more typical positions, with the subject first.

Teach

 Grammar Tip

By deleting a prepositional phrase that comes between the subject and the verb, students can more easily check for subject-verb agreement.

Resource Manager

Planning Resources
- *Lesson Plans*

Transparencies
- *Bellringer*
- *Daily Language Practice*

📂 Other Print Resources
- *Grammar and Composition Handbook*
- *Grammar Enrichment*, p. 34
- *Grammar Practice*, p. 34
- *Grammar Reteaching*, p. 35
- *Grammar Workbook*, Lesson 50

Practice and Assess

Answers: Exercise 3

1. has	**6.** delights
2. rise	**7.** arrives
3. see	**8.** have
4. is	**9.** need
5. are	**10.** are

Answers: Exercise 4

1. Protection—subj.; is—verb
2. system—subj.; includes—verb
3. islands—subj.; contain—verb; correct
4. student—subj.; prepares—verb
5. Studies—subj.; occur—verb
6. Protectors—subj.; work—verb
7. opportunities—subj.; are—verb; correct
8. list—subj.; is—verb; correct
9. system—subj.; has protected—verb
10. park—subj.; is—verb; correct
11. National Park Service—subj.; oversees—verb; correct
12. activities—subj.; are—verb; correct
13. guides—subj.; describe—verb
14. Visitors—subj; hike—verb; correct
15. adventures—subj.; are—verb

Answers: Exercise 5

Answers will vary, but some suggestions are given below.
1. Here is my <u>house</u>.
2. Here are my <u>sisters</u>.
3. There are two <u>cats</u> in the yard.
4. There is a <u>bowl</u> of apples.
5. Here are my <u>books</u>.

Additional Resources

📁 *Grammar Practice*, p. 34
📁 *Grammar Reteaching*, p. 35
📁 *Grammar Enrichment*, p. 35

📕 *Grammar Workbook*, Lesson 50

Close

Give students complicated sentences, and have them identify phrases that interrupt the subject and verb.

Subject-Verb Agreement

Exercise 3 **Choosing the Correct Verb Form**

For each sentence, write the correct form of the verb in parentheses.

1. The island of Oahu (has, have) a mild climate.
2. Islands of volcanic origin (rises, rise) in the Pacific.
3. Travelers to Haleakala (sees, see) a huge crater.
4. A hike along the cliffs (is, are) exciting.
5. There (is, are) lush green trees everywhere.
6. Our trip to the islands (delights, delight) us.
7. A busload of tourists (arrives, arrive) in the park.
8. Parts of Kauai (has, have) served as movie locations.
9. The rain forests of Hawaii (needs, need) protection.
10. There (is, are) many visitors to the Hawaii Volcanoes National Park.

Exercise 4 **Making Subjects and Verbs Agree**

Write each sentence. Underline the simple subject once and its verb twice. If they agree, write *correct*. If they do not agree, correct the verb.

1. Protection of rare plants are vital.
2. Our system of parks include forests.
3. The islands of Hawaii contain two national parks.
4. A student of volcanoes prepare an exhibit.
5. Studies of plant life occurs in the parks.
6. Protectors of the environment works there.
7. There are many opportunities for research.
8. Here is a list of the national parks.
9. Our system of national parks have protected natural wonders.
10. The oldest park in the system is Yellowstone.
11. The National Park Service oversees our parks and monuments.
12. There are many activities throughout the park system.
13. Tour guides from the service describes points of interest to guests.
14. Visitors to the Appalachian National Scenic Trail hike from Maine to Georgia.
15. There is rafting adventures at the Delaware Scenic River Park.

Exercise 5 **Using Subject-Verb Agreement in Sentences**

Write five original sentences. Begin each sentence with *Here is, Here are, There is,* or *There are*. Underline the subject of each sentence.

MEETING INDIVIDUAL NEEDS

English Language Learners

Recognizing Prepositions

Students acquiring English may have difficulty recognizing prepositional phrases, which may make it difficult to locate the subject of a sentence. Write the following list of prepositions on the board: *of, for, to, in, by, with.* Explain that these words often begin a prepositional phrase and that a prepositional phrase sometimes comes between a subject and a verb. Remind students that the noun in a prepositional phrase is never the subject of a sentence.

15.3 Agreement with Compound Subjects

A subject and its verb must agree in number. A singular noun subject takes a singular form of the verb. A plural noun subject takes a plural form of the verb. In the present tense, the singular form of the verb usually ends in -s or -es.

A hawk soars.

SINGULAR SUBJECT

Two hawks soar.

PLURAL SUBJECT

A **compound subject** contains two or more subjects that have the same verb. You can tell whether the compound subject takes a singular or a plural verb form by looking at the way the subjects are joined. When two or more subjects are joined by *and* or by *both . . . and*, the verb is plural.

Both a grizzly bear **and** a bobcat **live** near here.

This sentence refers to more than one thing, so the form of the verb is plural. When two or more subjects are joined by *or*, *nor*, or *either . . . or* or *neither . . . nor*, the verb must agree in number with the subject that is closest to it.

An eagle **or** a hawk **soars** in the sky.
Either the loon **or** its chicks **swim** nearby.
Neither the bears **nor** the bobcat **crosses** our path.

In the first sentence, the verb *soars* agrees in number with *hawk*, which is the subject closer to the verb. The verb is singular in form because *hawk* is a singular subject. In the second sentence, the verb *swim* agrees with *chicks*, which is the closer subject. The verb is plural in form because *chicks* is a plural subject. In the third sentence, the verb *crosses* agrees with *bobcat*, which is the closer subject. The verb is singular in form because *bobcat* is a singular subject.

Subject-Verb Agreement

15.3 Agreement with Compound Subjects **443**

Focus

Lesson Overview

Objectives
- To identify compound subjects joined by *and, both . . . and, or, nor, either . . . or* and *neither . . . nor*
- To use verbs that agree in number with different kinds of compound subjects

Bellringer
Daily Language Activity

When students enter the classroom, have this assignment on the board: *Write these sentences and underline the compound subject in each:*

1. *Tony and the dogs are out for a walk.*
2. *Neither Harry nor the twins eat cereal.*
3. *Dirt and rocks cover the road.*

See also *Daily Language Practice*

Motivating Activity

Write the following sentence on the board: *Neither my parents nor my brother cook dinner.* Ask students whether they can figure out what is wrong with it.

Teach

☑ **Teaching Tip**

Many students see the parts of a compound subject as separate units. In a sentence such as *The salt and pepper are gone,* students may want to use a singular verb. Remind students that compound subjects connected by *and* are treated as plural.

Resource Manager

Planning Resources
- *Lesson Plans*

Transparencies
- *Bellringer*
- *Daily Language Practice*

Other Print Resources
- *Grammar and Composition Handbook*
- *Grammar Enrichment*, p. 35
- *Grammar Practice*, p. 35
- *Grammar Reteaching*, p. 36
- *Grammar Workbook*, Lesson 51

Practice and Assess

Answers: Exercise 6

1. wade	**6.** thrive
2. outrun	**7.** leads
3. is	**8.** disturb
4. hunt	**9.** are
5. have	**10.** report

Answers: Exercise 7

1. Either the <u>factories</u> or the <u>swamp</u> <u>is</u> in danger.
2. Both <u>bears</u> and <u>frogs</u> <u>hibernate</u> in winter.
3. Neither <u>alligators</u> nor <u>crocodiles</u> <u>like</u> the cold.
4. The <u>blue</u> <u>heron</u> and the <u>egret</u> <u>live</u> in the Everglades.
5. Our national <u>seashores</u> and <u>parks</u> <u>are</u> a great resource.
6. The <u>grizzly</u> <u>bear</u> and the <u>polar</u> <u>bear</u> <u>are</u> carnivorous.
7. Both <u>Florida</u> and <u>Hawaii</u> <u>have</u> underwater parks.
8. There <u>are</u> breeding <u>sea</u> <u>lions</u> and nesting <u>birds</u> at Channel Islands National Park in California.
9. A rare <u>orchid</u> or brilliantly colored <u>birds</u> <u>attract</u> many photographers.
10. <u>Wolves</u> and a large moose <u>herd</u> <u>roam</u> the Isle Royale National Park.

Answers: Exercise 8

Answers will vary, but some suggestions are given below.
1. Mary and Eva live here.
2. Cats or a dog sleeps in this bed.
3. Both you and I love ice cream.
4. Either Jodi or Leo is singing.
5. Neither a new bike nor a million dollars tempt me.

Close

Have students write a short paragraph about their families, using at least three compound subjects.

444

Subject-Verb Agreement

Exercise 6 | **Identifying the Correct Verb Form**

For each sentence, write the correct form of the verb in parentheses.

1. A deer and a heron (wades, wade) in the lake.
2. Both a coyote and an antelope (outruns, outrun) a bear.
3. Neither hunting nor mining (is, are) allowed in protected areas.
4. An alligator and an egret (hunts, hunt) for food in the swamp.
5. Both Bryce Canyon Park and Yellowstone Park (has, have) wonderful hiking trails.
6. Birds and insect life (thrives, thrive) in the swamp.
7. Either experienced campers or the ranger (leads, lead) the evening talks.
8. Neither heat nor mosquitoes (disturbs, disturb) us.
9. Dams and pollution (is, are) destroying the swamp.
10. Newspapers and television (reports, report) on this problem.

Exercise 7 | **Making Verbs Agree with Compound Sentences**

Write each sentence, correcting the verb if necessary. Underline the subject once and its verb twice. Remember to underline the complete compound subjects.

1. Either the factories or the swamp are in danger.
2. Both bears and frogs hibernate in winter.
3. Neither alligators nor crocodiles likes the cold.
4. The blue heron and the egret lives in the Everglades.
5. Our national seashores and parks are a great resource.
6. The grizzly bear and the polar bear is carnivorous.
7. Both Florida and Hawaii have underwater parks.
8. There is breeding sea lions and nesting birds at Channel Islands National Park in California.
9. A rare orchid or brilliantly colored birds attracts many photographers.
10. Wolves and a large moose herd roams the Isle Royale National Park.

Exercise 8 | **Using Compound Subjects in Sentences**

Write five original sentences with compound subjects. Join the subjects in each sentence by using the word or words indicated.

1. and	3. both . . . and	5. neither . . . nor
2. or	4. either . . . or	

MEETING INDIVIDUAL NEEDS

English Language Learners

Understanding Compounds

Students acquiring English may need extra practice in determining whether a subject takes a singular or plural verb. First, explain that a compound subject has more than one subject in it. Review with students the rules for using verbs with compound subjects and give a few examples. Then show students a variety of pictures, each showing more than one person or thing. Have students work in pairs to write sentences about the pictures that contain compound subjects.

Grammar Review

SUBJECT-VERB AGREEMENT

John Muir by Eden Force is a biography of the naturalist and explorer whose efforts influenced Congress to pass the Yosemite National Park Bill in 1890. The bill established both Yosemite and Sequoia National Parks. Both of these parks are justly famous for their variety of breathtaking natural wonders. In the following excerpt from the book, the writer describes the beautiful scenery of Yosemite Valley, which Muir explored for six years. The passage has been annotated to show some examples of subject-verb agreement covered in this unit.

Literature Model

from John Muir
by Eden Force

Yosemite Valley includes some of the world's most awe-inspiring natural wonders. El Capitan, a block of stone more than 600 times Muir's height, faces Bridalveil Fall. Bridalveil tumbles 620 feet from high rocks into the valley. Farther up the Merced River is Yosemite Falls, rushing down in two sections to Yosemite Valley. North of the river is North Dome, a dome-shaped peak about as high as El Capitan. It towers above the landscape. South of North Dome and east of Tenaga Creek stands a strange peak even taller than North Dome. It is Half Dome. As the name suggests, Half Dome looks like a dome that a giant has sliced down the middle from top to bottom. Only one half of the rock dome remains.

Agreement between a singular noun subject and a singular verb

Agreement between a singular pronoun subject and a singular verb

Agreement between a singular subject and verb that have a prepositional phrase between them

Subject-Verb Agreement

Teach

About the Literature

Explain that the review contains a passage from Eden Force's biography of John Muir followed by exercises on related topics. The passage describes some of the natural wonders of Yosemite Valley. Thanks in large part to Muir's efforts, the valley appears today much as it did when the conservationist first explored the area in 1868. Encourage students to read through the Literature Model for information and enjoyment, reminding them that regular reading is the best way to develop a feeling for standard usage. After students read the passage, discuss examples it contains of subject-verb agreement.

Linking Grammar and Literature

☑ **Teaching Tip**

Have students reread the passage and look for any phrases that separate subjects and verbs.

Listening and Speaking

Have students take turns reading aloud sentences from the passage. After each sentence, the students who are listening can write down the subject and the verb and note whether each is singular or plural.

Resource Manager

Planning Resources
- *Lesson Plans*

📂 **Other Print Resources**
- *Grammar and Composition Handbook*
- *Grammar Workbook,* Lessons 48–51; Unit 8 Review; Cumulative Review: Units 1–8

✔ **ASSESSMENT OPTIONS**

📂 *Tests with Answer Key and Rubrics*
Unit 15 Mastery Test, pp. 63–64

💾 *Testmaker*
Unit 15 Mastery Test

Practice and Assess

Answers: Exercise 1

1. stops
2. rises
3. resembles
4. are
5. attract
6. hike
7. is
8. are
9. create
10. has

Answers: Exercise 2

1. correct, singular
2. grace, plural
3. measures, singular
4. correct, singular
5. correct, plural
6. correct, singular
7. features, singular
8. correct, plural
9. grows, singular
10. grow, plural

Subject-Verb Agreement

Review: Exercise 1 **Making Subjects and Verbs Agree**

Write the correct form of the verb in parentheses.

SAMPLE Merced River (forms, form) a white ribbon through the valley.
ANSWER forms

1. Sometimes a family of bears (stops, stop) to swim and play in the river.
2. El Capitan (rises, rise) high above Yosemite Valley.
3. In shape it (resembles, resemble) a boot.
4. Yosemite's natural wonders (is, are) awe-inspiring.
5. They (attracts, attract) thousands of visitors.
6. The visitors (hike, hikes) seven hundred miles of trails.
7. The most spectacular scenery (is, are) in Yosemite Valley.
8. The peaks of California's Sierra Nevada (is, are) millions of years old.
9. Deep gorges (creates, create) beautiful views.
10. The National Park Service (has, have) begun a public transportation system to reduce traffic in the park.

Review: Exercise 2 **Making Subjects and Verbs Agree**

Write each sentence, correcting the verb if necessary. Write whether the subject is *singular* or *plural*.

1. Yosemite National Park lies in the mountains two hundred miles east of San Francisco.
2. Giant sequoias graces three groves in the park.
3. The Grizzly Giant Tree measure thirty-four feet in diameter, more than most roads.
4. This huge tree stands in the famous Mariposa Grove.
5. The sequoias are some of the oldest living things on earth.
6. The wood of the sequoias resists fire.
7. Sequoia National Park feature some giant trees with the names of Civil War generals.
8. Redwoods are related to giant sequoias.
9. The redwood grow even taller than the giant sequoia.
10. These enormous trees grows from tiny seeds.

Review: Exercise 3   Identifying Subjects and Making Verbs Agree

Write the correct form of the verb in parentheses.

SAMPLE   There (is, are) books written by John Muir.
ANSWER   are

1. The Sierra Club, with branches throughout the United States, (owes, owe) its existence to Muir.
2. Muir's campaign for preserving forests (continues, continue) to inspire environmentalists.
3. In California there (is, are) a redwood forest called Muir Woods.
4. The forest near San Francisco (honors, honor) the achievements of John Muir.
5. A glacier in Alaska also (bears, bear) his name.
6. *The Yosemite* by John Muir (is, are) a classic.
7. Copies (is, are) available at my local library.
8. Muir, in his journals, (describes, describe) the natural wonders of Yosemite.
9. The governor of California (declares, declare) each April 21 "John Muir Day."
10. Admirers of Muir and his causes (celebrates, celebrate) at the John Muir National Historic Site.

Review: Exercise 4   Locating Subjects and Making Verbs Agree

Locate and write the subject of each sentence. If the verb in the sentence is correct, write *correct*. If the verb is not correct, rewrite the sentence, correcting the verb.

1. There is the Merced River in Yosemite Valley.
2. There are rough terrain in some Yosemite wilderness areas.
3. There is lovely landscapes in the valley.
4. Here in Yosemite Valley are effects of volcanoes and glaciers.
5. There is a book about Muir's glacial theory.

Answers: Exercise 3

1. Sierra Club owes
2. campaign continues
3. forest is
4. forest honors
5. glacier bears
6. *The Yosemite* is
7. Copies are
8. Muir describes
9. governor declares
10. Admirers celebrate

Answers: Exercise 4

1. Merced River, correct
2. terrain, is
3. landscapes, are
4. effects, correct
5. book, correct

Subject-Verb Agreement

Answers: Exercise 5

1. provide
2. is
3. pour
4. discourage
5. steal
6. walk
7. wait
8. lies
9. sing
10. crown

Answers: Exercise 6

1. forms
2. boast
3. are
4. are
5. pose

Subject-Verb Agreement

Review: Exercise 5 **Making Verbs Agree with Compound Subjects**

For each sentence, write the correct form of the verb in parentheses.

1. Both Glacier Point and Taft Point (provides, provide) a great view.
2. Neither Half Dome nor El Capitan (is, are) the highest point in the valley.
3. Both Vernal Falls and Nevada Falls (pours, pour) over giant rocks formed by glaciers.
4. Neither cold weather nor drenching rains (discourages, discourage) backpackers.
5. Bears or other animals sometimes (steals, steal) the backpackers' food.
6. A student and a backpacker (walks, walk) toward the glacier.
7. A van and a camper (waits, wait) at the entrance to the park.
8. Snow or ice (lies, lie) in many of the ravines of the Sierra Nevada.
9. Both a robin and a yellow warbler (sings, sing) near the campsite.
10. Either a dome or spires (crowns, crown) the granite mountains forming the valley.

Review: Exercise 6 **Writing the Correct Verb Form for Compound Subjects**

For each sentence, write the correct present-tense form of the verb in parentheses. Make sure your verb agrees with the subject of the sentence.

SAMPLE   Parks and other areas (be) part of the National Park System.
ANSWER   are

1. A noteworthy landscape or a historic site (form) the basis of most national parks.
2. Both Indiana and Wisconsin (boast) national lakeshores.
3. The Blue Ridge and the Natchez Trace (be) national parkways.
4. National battlefields and a national scenic trail (be) part of the National Park System.
5. Air and water pollution and overcrowding (pose) threats to the most popular parks.

Review: Exercise 7 Choosing Verbs

Write the subject of each sentence and the correct present tense of the verb in parentheses.

1. Geysers (attract) visitors to Yellowstone National Park.
2. We (photograph) the geysers and hot springs at the park.
3. Yellowstone, in the northwest corner of Wyoming, (be) the oldest national park in the United States.
4. Pools of hot mud (bubble) in the Lower Geyser Basin section of the park.
5. Steam (change) the hard surrounding rock into soft clay.
6. Yellowstone Lake, with geysers and hot springs along its shores, (be) the largest high-altitude lake in North America.
7. Evergreen forests of fir, spruce, and pine (cover) much of the park.
8. The feeding of bears within the park's boundaries (defy) park regulations.
9. Park regulations about fishing in the lakes and rivers (be) also strict.
10. The variety of landscapes in the region (surprise) new visitors to the park.
11. Memorials to past events (exist) in every state.
12. Some of these memorials (become) national historical parks.
13. The junction of two rivers (form) one such park.
14. The Potomac River (meet) the Shenandoah River at Harpers Ferry, West Virginia.
15. The park by the rivers (be) Harpers Ferry National Historical Park.
16. Students of the Civil War (visit) this park.
17. They (learn) about John Brown's attack on the arsenal at Harpers Ferry in 1859.
18. A museum at the park (record) how John Brown worked for the end of slavery.
19. John Brown's actions at his trial for treason (become) an inspiration to some writers.
20. John Brown (be) the subject of an epic poem by Stephen Vincent Benét.

Subject-Verb Agreement

Answers: Exercise 7

1. Geysers attract
2. We photograph
3. Yellowstone is
4. Pools bubble
5. Steam changes
6. Yellowstone Lake is
7. forests cover
8. feeding defies
9. regulations are
10. variety surprises
11. Memorials exist
12. Some become
13. junction forms
14. Potomac River meets
15. park is
16. Students visit
17. They learn
18. museum records
19. actions become
20. John Brown is

Answers: Exercise 8

1. designate
2. form
3. honor
4. are
5. are
6. is
7. range
8. occupy
9. include
10. are
11. are
12. have
13. exist
14. contains
15. are
16. connects
17. extends
18. create
19. form
20. has

Review: Exercise 8 **Making Verbs Agree**

For each sentence, write the correct present-tense form of the verb in parentheses.

1. Acts of Congress (designate) areas as part of the National Park System.
2. Unique natural landscapes or historic sites (form) the basis of the majority of national parks.
3. The Edgar Allan Poe National Historic Site and the Georgia O'Keeffe National Historic Site (honor) famous Americans.
4. Prehistoric dwellings (be) preserved at a number of different sites.
5. Some people (be) surprised to learn that the White House is part of the National Park System.
6. The largest of the national parks (be) the Wrangell-St. Elias system in Alaska.
7. National parks (range) in area from 8 million acres to about 6 thousand acres.
8. The John F. Kennedy birthplace and some other national historic sites (occupy) less than an acre.
9. National battlefield parks and national battlefield sites (include) Civil War and Revolutionary War sites.
10. There (be) other areas primarily for recreational use.
11. There (be) national parklands along rivers in eleven states.
12. The Alganak Wild River Park and New River Gorge Park (have) exciting stretches of white water.
13. There (exist) national recreation areas in states across the country from New York to California.
14. Alaska or Texas (contain) most of the national preserves.
15. Blue Ridge and Natchez Trace (be) the only national parkways.
16. The John D. Rockefeller Jr. Memorial Parkway (connect) two beautiful national parks, Yellowstone and Grand Teton.
17. The Appalachian National Scenic Trail (extend) for two thousand miles from Maine to Georgia.
18. The Glen Canyon Dam and the Hoover Dam (create) the largest national recreation areas.
19. Sand dunes in both Colorado and Indiana (form) part of the National Park System.
20. Arizona (have) many national monuments and two national parks.

Review: Exercise 9

Proofreading

The following passage is about artist Thomas Moran, whose work appears below. Rewrite the passage, correcting the errors in spelling, capitalization, grammar, and usage. Add any missing punctuation. There are eleven errors.

Thomas Moran

¹When he were an art student, Thomas Moran (1837–1926) admirred European landscape painters. ²However, Moran wanted to "paint as an american." ³His paintings, such as *Cliffs of the Upper Colorado River, Wyoming Territory,* captures the beauty of the American West.

Thomas Moran, *Cliffs of the Upper Colorado River, Wyoming Territory,* **1882**

Answers: Exercise 9

Proofreading

This proofreading activity provides editing practice with (1) the current or previous units' skills, (2) the **Troubleshooter** errors, and (3) spelling errors. Students should be able to complete the exercise by referring to the units, the **Troubleshooter**, and a dictionary.

	Error (Type of Error)
1.	• was (subject-verb agreement)
	• admired (spelling)
2.	• American (proper noun)
3.	• capture (subject-verb agrement)
4.	• shows (subject-verb agreement)
5.	• separate (spelling)
	• appear (subject-verb agreement)
6.	• bathes (subject-verb agreement)
7.	• tan, (commas in a series)
8.	• pause (subject-verb agreement)
	• nature's (singular possessive)

(continued)

Viewing the Art

Thomas Moran, *Cliffs of the Upper Colorado River, Wyoming Territory,* **1882**
In his life, Moran returned often to the American West. He conveyed the scenery of the western landscape through paintings like this 16-by-24-inch oil-on-canvas.

Subject-Verb Agreement

Answers: Exercise 10

Mixed Review

1. record, compound
2. characterize, compound
3. include, plural
4. shows, singular
5. record, plural
6. correct, singluar
7. correct, singular
8. overtake, compound
9. have, compound
10. is remembered, singluar
11. correct, compound
12. spring, plural
13. correct, plural
14. correct, singular
15. correct, plural

Close

Suggest that students write a paragraph describing an ideal park. Have them check their writing for subject-verb agreement.

⁴The painting on page 451 show a scene in the West. ⁵Two seperate rocks appears in the distance. ⁶The sun bathe the rocks in light and shadow. ⁷Tones of rust, brown, tan orange, and sand are used by the artist. ⁸The riders and horses pauses near the river to view natures majesty.

Review: Exercise 10

Mixed Review

Rewrite each sentence, correcting the verb if necessary. Write whether the subject is *singular*, *plural*, or *compound*.

1. The sculptures and paintings of Frederic Remington records the changing West of the nineteenth century.
2. Action and drama characterizes the best of Remington's art.
3. Other recorders of the land and life of the Old West includes Albert Bierstadt, Charles M. Russell, and George Catlin.
4. Russell's experience as a cowboy and trapper show in his detailed artwork.
5. George Catlin's paintings records the life of Native Americans along the Missouri River and the Western Plains.
6. Catlin's portrait of a Blackfeet chief hangs in The Smithsonian Institution.
7. Albert Bierstadt is one of the great American Romantic landscape painters.
8. Drama and grandeur sometimes overtakes realism in his huge canvases.
9. Both Bierstadt and Thomas Moran has large paintings on display in the U.S. Capitol.
10. George Caleb Bingham are remembered for his scenes of frontier life.
11. The Metropolitan Museum of Art and the National Gallery house his colorful work.
12. Events from the Wild West springs to life through these works.
13. What forms of art depict today's events?
14. A great twentieth-century photographer of the American West is Ansel Adams.
15. The granite domes of Yosemite are the subjects of many of Adams's photos.

Writing Application

Subject-Verb Agreement in Writing

Peggy Thomson uses singular, plural, and compound subjects in this passage from "Bathing Elephants." Examine the passage, noting how subjects and verbs agree in number.

Bath and foot-care time now flows into demonstration time directed by the keeper team of Kathy and Morna out in the yard. Here people clap to see the elephants maneuver on command, present a foot, balance on tiny stools, and move huge logs with their trunks. By the time Ambika and Shanthi take their bows, the keepers are beginning to wilt. There's an element of tension in the playful-looking baths they give and in the training shows—in just dealing with animals who could so easily pulverize them if they chose to.

Techniques with Subjects and Their Verbs

Try to use singular, plural, and compound subjects when you write and revise your own work. Be sure your subjects and their verbs agree in number. Look at these examples from "Bathing Elephants."

❶ With a singular subject, be sure you use the singular form of the verb. With a plural subject, be sure you use the plural form of the verb.

THOMSON'S EXAMPLES Bath and foot-care <u>time</u> now <u>flows</u>; <u>people</u> <u>clap</u>; <u>keepers</u> <u>are</u>

❷ With a compound subject using *and*, be sure to use the plural form of the verb.

THOMSON'S EXAMPLES <u>Kathy and Morna speak</u>; <u>Ambika and Shanthi take</u>

TIME

For more about the importance of using verbs correctly, see **TIME Facing the Blank Page,** page 98.

Subject-Verb Agreement

Practice Revise the following passage. Be sure all the subjects and their verbs agree in number.

¹My family and I am going on a car trip through Colorado and Wyoming this summer. ²We plan stops at a number of different national parks and historic sites. ³The first stop on our journey are Yellowstone, the oldest park in the national park system. ⁴We have reservations at Old Faithful Inn. ⁵The beautiful open lobby of the inn rise more than ninety feet.

Writing Application **453**

Subject-Verb Agreement in Writing

Ask students to read the passage from "Bathing Elephants." Ask them to point out examples of singular subjects, plural subjects, compound subjects, and subjects in sentences that begin with *here* or *there.* Have students name the verb for each of these subjects. Encourage them to discuss anything in the passage that they find confusing, such as why a particular subject takes a singular or plural verb.

Techniques with Subjects and Their Verbs

Remind students that using a variety of types of subjects helps make writing clearer and more interesting. Discuss the examples from "Bathing Elephants," and then have students look back to page 452 at the last paragraph from the proofreading passage. Have students find the subject and verb in each sentence and determine whether the subject is singular, plural, or compound.

Practice

The answers to this challenging and enriching activity will vary according to how much rewriting students do. Refer to Techniques with Subjects and Their Verbs as you evaluate students' choices. They should at least correct the verbs in sentences 1, 3, and 5, which should be *are, is,* and *rises,* respectively.

✔ ASSESSMENT OPTIONS

📁 *Tests with Answer Key and Rubrics* Unit 15 Mastery Test, pp. 63–64

💾 *Testmaker* Unit 15 Mastery Test

You may wish to administer the Unit 15 Mastery Test at this point.

📼 *Mindjogger Videoquizzes*

INTRODUCING

UNIT 16

Objectives

- To recognize and use correctly various groups of troublesome words
- To demonstrate control over the spelling of troublesome words

Key to Ability Levels

L1 Level 1 activities are within the basic ability range of students.

L2 Level 2 activities are within the ability range of average students.

L3 Level 3 activities are more challenging activities.

UNIT 16

Glossary of Special Usage Problems

454

Resource Manager

Planning Resources
- *Lesson Plans*
- *Block Scheduling*

Transparencies
- *Bellringer*
- *Daily Language Practice*

Other Print Resources
- *Grammar and Composition Handbook*

- *Grammar Enrichment*
- *Grammar Practice*
- *Grammar Reteaching*
- *Grammar Workbook*
- *Tests with Answer Key and Rubrics*

Video
- *MindJogger Videoquizzes*

Software
- *Interactive Grammar and Language Workbook*
- *Language Arts PASS*
- *Presentation Plus!*
- *Testmaker*

Web Sites
- *writerschoice.glencoe.com*

16.1 Using Troublesome Words I

Like all languages, English contains a number of confusing words. The following glossary will help you understand some of the more troublesome ones.

Word	Meaning	Example
accept **except**	"to receive" "other than"	Ships **accept** most cargo. Ships move at a rapid speed **except** in storms.
all ready **already**	"completely prepared" "before" or "by this time"	The flight crew is **all ready.** The plane had **already** left when I arrived at the airport.
all together **altogether**	"in a group" "completely"	The wagons traveled **all together** for protection. Wagons are **altogether** too slow.
a lot	"very much" *A lot* is two words. Its meaning is vague; avoid using it.	Sailors travel **a lot.** [vague] Sailors travel frequently. [more precise]
beside **besides**	"next to" "in addition to"	Railroad tracks often run **beside** roads. **Besides** trains we ride buses.
between **among**	Use *between* when referring to two people or things. Use *among* when talking about groups of three or more.	Ships sail **between** ports. Trains are **among** the best ways to travel.
choose **chose**	"to select" "selected"	Many people **choose** a window seat when they fly. I **chose** an aisle seat the last time I flew to New York.
in **into**	"inside" indicates movement from outside to a point within	Freight is stored **in** cargo bays. The pilot guided the ship **into** port.
its **it's**	the possessive form of *it* the contraction of *it is*	The ship is moving to **its** pier. **It's** hard to dock a ship.

16.1 Using Troublesome Words I   **455**

Focus

Lesson Overview

Objectives

- To recognize various groups of troublesome words
- To use troublesome words correctly in sentences

Bellringer
Daily Language Activity

When students enter the classroom, have this assignment on the board: *Find two words in the following sentence that sound similar. Except for this part, I accept the plan. Now write two more sentences using these two words correctly.*

👉 **See also** *Daily Language Practice*

Motivating Activity

Invite volunteers to share their sentences from the Bellringer activity. Ask students to suggest other word pairs that they confuse. Explain that often the only way to remember which word or expression to use is to master both the meaning and spelling.

Teach

☑ **Teaching Tip**

The possessive pronoun *its (The cat chased its tail)* and the contraction *it's (It's the fastest train)* are often confused. Have students replace *it's* or *its* with *it is* in a particular sentence. If the sentence makes sense, then the contraction is correct. If it does not make sense, then the possessive form (*its*) should be used.

Resource Manager

Planning Resources
- *Lesson Plans*

Transparencies
- *Bellringer*
- *Daily Language Practice*

📁 Other Print Resources
- *Grammar and Composition Handbook*
- *Grammar Enrichment*, p. 36
- *Grammar Practice*, p. 36
- *Grammar Reteaching*, p. 37
- *Grammar Workbook*, Lessons 58–60

Practice and Assess

Answers: Exercise 1

1. all together
2. accept
3. except
4. choose
5. It's
6. beside
7. all ready
8. already
9. into
10. choose
11. its
12. among
13. besides
14. among
15. into

Answers: Exercise 2

1. beside
2. into
3. altogether
4. all ready
5. already
6. choose
7. accept
8. between
9. Besides
10. except

Additional Resources

📁 *Grammar Practice*, p. 36
📁 *Grammar Reteaching*, p. 37
📁 *Grammar Enrichment*, p. 36

📕 *Grammar Workbook*, Lessons 58–60

Close

Have students write two lines of dialogue, each line containing one word from the troublesome word pairs in the lesson. Invite students to write their dialogue on the board, omitting the troublesome words. Have volunteers complete the sentences. Write the following example on the board: *"Let's swim to the other side of the pond _____," he said to the group. (all together) Alex responded, "The water is _____ too cold for me!" (altogether)*

456

Exercise 1 Choosing the Correct Word

Write each sentence, choosing the correct word or words in parentheses.

1. We are traveling (altogether, all together).
2. The conductor will (accept, except) our tickets.
3. Every railroad car (accept, except) ours is going all the way to Chicago.
4. Did we (choose, chose) the wrong one?
5. (Its, It's) difficult to choose without checking the schedule.
6. The train that is (beside, besides) ours at the station is headed for Omaha.
7. The conductor says we are (all ready, already) to leave.
8. Before you know it, the train has (all ready, already) left the station.
9. We settle (in, into) our seats and look out the window.
10. My friend let me (choose, chose) the seat closest to the window.
11. The train is moving along (its, it's) track at a steady speed.
12. We talk (between, among) ourselves about the passing scenery.
13. There are many people on this train (besides, beside) my family.
14. Freight trains are (between, among) the busiest carriers.
15. Elevators load grain (in, into) railroad hoppers.

Exercise 2 Using the Correct Word

Write each sentence, using the correct word or words from the lesson as defined in parentheses.

1. Truckers stop _____ highways to rest. (next to)
2. Truckers can drive _____ the city. (from outside to a point within)
3. Heavy trucks can cause _____ too much damage to highways. (completely)
4. Our moving van is _____. (completely prepared)
5. The circus trucks have _____ left. (by this time)
6. Of all the trucks on this lot, which one would you _____ to drive? (select)
7. Does this parkway _____ trucks? (receive)
8. This highway runs _____ Baltimore, Maryland, and Washington, D.C. (referring to two places)
9. _____ truck traffic, the highway gets much commuter traffic. (in addition to)
10. The highway is crowded _____ on weekends. (other than)

Enrichment and Extension

Using Troublesome Words

Help students understand troublesome word pairs by describing situations in the classroom. Andy sits *between* Ramon and Claudia. Andy sits *among* many students. Celia put her notebook *into* her desk. Celia's notebook is *in* her desk. Invite students to present examples to the class.

Using Descriptive Words

Challenge students to think of alternatives for the vague phrase *a lot*. Encourage them to use their substitutions in sentences. Provide examples: There was *a lot* of food at the picnic. There was an *abundance* of food at the picnic.

16.2 Using Troublesome Words II

Like all languages, English contains a number of confusing words. The following glossary will help you understand some of the more troublesome ones.

Word	Meaning	Example
lay	"to put" or "to place"	Sailors **lay** the ropes in coils.
lie	"to recline" or "to be positioned"	Passengers **lie** in bunks.
learn	"to receive knowledge"	Crews **learn** rescue tactics.
teach	"to give knowledge"	Some pilots **teach** flying.
leave	"to go away"	Most buses **leave** on time.
let	"to allow"	**Let** the children board.
loose	"not firmly attached"	**Loose** cargo is dangerous.
lose	"to misplace" or "to fail to win"	You could **lose** your luggage.
raise	"to cause to move upward"	The sailors **raise** the anchors before the ships depart.
rise	"to move upward"	The anchors **rise** slowly.
set	"to place" or "to put"	Cranes **set** cargo in the hold.
sit	"to place oneself in a seated position"	I will **sit** by you.
than	*Than* introduces the second part of a comparison.	Ships are larger **than** boats.
then	"at that time" or "soon after"	Raise the anchor and **then** sail.
their	*Their* is the possessive form of *they.*	We like **their** fast trains.
they're	*They're* is the contraction of *they are.*	**They're** designed for speed.
to	"in the direction of"	Trains carry coal **to** ports.
too	"in addition to" or "excessively"	Coal is **too** bulky for planes.
two	the number after one	The supertanker is as long as **two** football fields.
who's	*Who's* is the contraction of *who is.*	I have a friend **who's** a pilot.
whose	*Whose* is the possessive form of *who.*	**Whose** flight leaves first?

Glossary of Special Usage Problems

Resource Manager

Planning Resources
• *Lesson Plans*

Transparencies
• *Bellringer*
• *Daily Language Practice*

Other Print Resources
• *Grammar and Composition Handbook*
• *Grammar Enrichment,* p. 36
• *Grammar Practice,* p. 36
• *Grammar Reteaching,* p. 37
• *Grammar Workbook,* Lessons 60–62

Focus

Lesson Overview

Objectives
• To demonstrate control over the spelling and meaning of various troublesome words
• To use troublesome words correctly in sentences

Bellringer
Daily Language Activity

When students enter the classroom, have this assignment on the board: *What does the following quote mean? Write your explanation.*

> Sometimes you can *learn* things people don't even know they're *teaching.*
>
> —Bette Greene, *Summer of My German Soldier*

See also *Daily Language Practice*

Motivating Activity

Invite volunteers to share their explanations of the quote. Explain the distinction between the words *teach* and *learn.* Students might distinguish between the two words by remembering this sentence: If you want to be sure you learned something, try teaching it to someone else.

Teach

☑ Grammar Tip

Help students distinguish between the pairs *lay* and *lie, raise* and *rise,* and *set* and *sit* by explaining that the first verb in each pair involves causing something to happen. For example, *to lay something down* is "to cause it to lie."

Practice and Assess

Answers: Exercise 3

1. Whose
2. teach
3. too
4. set
5. than
6. lie
7. lose
8. rise
9. raises
10. then
11. sit
12. they're
13. who's
14. They're
15. Whose
16. Raise
17. than
18. loose
19. Their
20. leave

Answers: Exercise 4

1. Sit
2. leave
3. Let
4. rise
5. raise

Additional Resources

📁 *Grammar Practice*, p. 36
📁 *Grammar Reteaching*, p. 37
📁 *Grammar Enrichment*, p. 36

📓 *Grammar Workbook*, Lessons 60–62

Close

Ask students to write questions using *who's* and *whose*. Examples:

Whose lunch is this?
Who's going tomorrow?

Glossary of Special Usage Problems

Exercise 3   **Choosing the Correct Word**

Write each sentence, choosing the correct word in parentheses.

1. (Who's, Whose) instructions will the pilot follow?
2. The pilot will (learn, teach) you to use radar.
3. The pilot will help you with math (to, too).
4. The best pilots (set, sit) their planes down gently.
5. Planes are faster (than, then) trains.
6. Once in flight, passengers may (lay, lie) back in their seats.
7. Planes almost never (loose, lose) their way.
8. After taking off, planes (raise, rise) to a suitable flying height.
9. During this time, the plane's pilot (raises, rises) the landing gear.
10. The plane reaches its cruising altitude; (than, then) the crew can relax more.
11. They may (set, sit) and chat.
12. They may study the navigational charts that (their, they're) using.
13. They understand (who's, whose) responsible for what duties.
14. (Their, They're) well trained, and all crew members know their jobs.
15. (Who's, Whose) job is it to fly the plane?
16. (Raise, Rise) your hand if you know the answer.
17. I sometimes wonder whether flying the plane is more difficult (than, then) tending the passengers.
18. Flight attendants see that all (loose, lose) luggage is safely secured.
19. (Their, They're) primary responsibility is the safety and comfort of the passengers.
20. They (leave, let) the flying to the pilot and copilot.

Exercise 4   **Using the Correct Word**

Write each sentence, using the correct word or words from the lesson as defined in parentheses.

1. _____ near the bow so that we can see the harbor. (place yourself in a seated position)
2. Ships will not _____ port until high tide. (go away)
3. _____ me help you down the gangplank. (allow)
4. The crew saw the playful whale _____ from the water. (move upward)
5. Vessels _____ flags as signals. (cause to move upward)

MEETING INDIVIDUAL NEEDS   **English Language Learners**

Some students do not hear the difference between such word pairs as *accept, except; choose, chose; loose, lose;* and *set, sit.* Pair them with English speakers who can help them practice. Ask students to exaggerate the pronunciation to help their partners detect subtle differences in the words.

To help students distinguish the meaning of these troublesome word pairs, have volunteers act them out. For example, after a student puts a book on a desk, another student describes the action: *Anna is setting the book on the desk.* Have volunteers write the words on the board.

UNIT 16
Grammar Review

GLOSSARY OF SPECIAL USAGE PROBLEMS

In *Exploring the* Titanic, Robert D. Ballard writes about his explorations of the largest ship of its time, the *Titanic,* which sank after hitting an iceberg in the North Atlantic Ocean on April 15, 1912. More than 1,500 passengers and crew died; fewer than half that number survived.

Literature Model

from Exploring the *Titanic*
by Robert D. Ballard

It looked as though the metal hull was slowly melting away. What seemed like frozen rivers of rust covered the ship's side and spread out over the ocean bottom. It was almost as if the blood of the great ship **lay** in pools on the ocean floor.

As *Alvin* rose in slow motion up the ghostly side of the ship, I could see our lights reflecting off the still-unbroken glass of the *Titanic*'s portholes. They made me think of cats' eyes gleaming in the dark. In places the rust formations over the portholes looked like eyelashes with tears, as though the *Titanic* were crying. I could also see **a lot** of reddish-brown stalactites of rust over the wreck, like long icicles. I decided to call them "rusticles." This rust turned out to be very fragile. If touched by our sub, it disappeared like a cloud of smoke.

As we **rose** further and began to move across the mighty forward deck, I was amazed at the sheer size of everything: giant bollards and shiny bronze capstans that were used for winding ropes and cables; the huge links of the anchor chains. When you were there on the spot, the ship was truly titanic.

> Past tense of the verb *lie,* meaning "to be positioned"

> *A lot* spelled as two words

> Past tense of the verb *rise,* meaning "to move upward"

Glossary of Special Usage Problems

Grammar Review **459**

Teach

About the Literature

Explain that the review features a passage from Robert D. Ballard's *Exploring the* Titanic. The passage recounts Ballard's impressions of the *Titanic* as he and his crew observed the ship from their submarine and their efforts to explore the *Titanic* and the watery world that surrounds the sunken ship. The exercises that follow are based on this passage and related topics.

After students have read the passage, initiate a discussion about the author's description of the *Titanic*. Then ask students to focus on the highlighted words in the passage. Would the meaning of the passage be as clear if the writer had used these words incorrectly?

Linking Grammar and Literature

☑ Grammar Tip

Students may be confused by the use of the past tense of *lie* in the passage. Explain the distinction between *lay,* the past tense of *lie,* and present tense *lay,* meaning to put or place (something). Remind students that the verbs *lie* and *rise,* used in the past tense in the passage, never take an object.

☑ Teaching Tip

Students might point out that they were advised to avoid the use of the vague expression *a lot.* You might explain that because Robert Ballard's passage is so descriptive and visual, the use of *a lot* in this instance is acceptable. Invite students to think of alternative words that the author could have used.

Resource Manager

Planning Resources
• *Lesson Plans*

📂 Other Print Resources
• *Grammar and Composition Handbook*
• *Grammar Workbook,* Lessons 58–62; Unit 10 Review; Cumulative Review: Units 1–10

✔ ASSESSMENT OPTIONS

📂 *Tests with Answer Key and Rubrics*
Unit 16 Mastery Test, pp. 67–68

💾 *Testmaker*
Unit 16 Mastery Test

Practice and Assess

Answers: Exercise 1

1. to
2. into
3. among
4. already
5. than

Answers: Exercise 2

1. lies
2. beside
3. learn
4. except
5. altogether

Review: Exercise 1 **Making Usage Choices**

Write each sentence, choosing the correct word or words in parentheses.

> SAMPLE The *Titanic* hit an iceberg (in, into) the North Atlantic.
> ANSWER The *Titanic* hit an iceberg in the North Atlantic.

1. The *Titanic* was on its way (to, too, two) New York when it hit an iceberg.
2. Passengers hurriedly crowded (in, into) the lifeboats.
3. Crew members sat (between, among) the passengers in the crowded boats.
4. The *Titanic* had (all ready, already) sunk by the time other ships got to the area.
5. More passengers died (than, then) survived.

Review: Exercise 2 **Making Usage Choices**

Write each sentence, choosing the correct word or words in parentheses.

> SAMPLE The explorers could see the *Titanic*'s (to, too, two) anchors.
> ANSWER The explorers could see the *Titanic*'s two anchors.

1. The *Titanic* (lays, lies) on the ocean floor nearly two and a half miles below the surface.
2. The sub *Alvin* rose slowly (beside, besides) the ship.
3. By exploring the wreck up close, Ballard was able to (learn, teach) what he wanted to know about the *Titanic*.
4. The entire ship was visible (accept, except) for the bow.
5. The *Titanic*'s bow was (all together, altogether) buried in the mud.

Review: Exercise 3

Proofreading

The following passage is about American artist Richard Shaw, whose work appears on this page. Rewrite the passage, correcting the errors in spelling, capitalization, grammar, and usage. Add any missing punctuation. There are ten errors.

Richard Shaw

¹Richard Shaw was born in 1941 he was risen in Hollywood, California. ²His father worked as a cartoonist for Walt Disney Studio and his mother was an artist two. ³They're friends were all artists, cartoonists, and writers. ⁴Shaw remembers spending much time as a child drawing train wrecks, battles and maritime disasters.

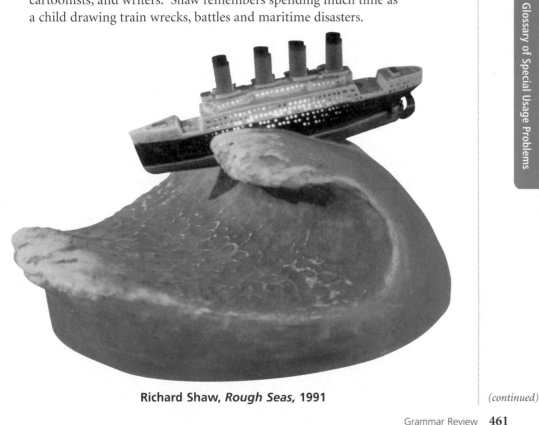

Richard Shaw, *Rough Seas*, 1991

(continued)

Answers: Exercise 3

Proofreading

This proofreading activity provides editing practice with (1) the current or previous units' skills, (2) the **Troubleshooter** errors, and (3) spelling errors. Students should be able to complete the exercise by referring to the units, the **Troubleshooter,** and a dictionary. (Note: A run-on sentence counts as one error.)

	Error (Type of Error)
1.	• 1941. He *or* 1941; he *or* 1941, and he (run-on sentence)
	• raised (troublesome word)
2.	• Studio, (compound sentence)
	• too (troublesome word)
3.	• Their (troublesome word)
4.	• battles, (commas in a series)

Viewing the Art

Richard Shaw, *Rough Seas*, 1991

Richard Shaw (1941–) began painting and making movies in high school. Shaw later studied at the San Francisco Art Institute, where he became interested in ceramic sculpture. He received his B.F.A. from the school in 1965 and has taught there since 1966. Although he lives and works primarily in California, Shaw's influence on younger ceramic artists extends throughout the country.

Rough Seas is made of porcelain, measures 8 1/2 by 12 inches, and is in the Franklin/Adams Gallery in New York.

Answers: Exercise 3

(continued from previous page)

Error (Type of Error)
5. • Besides (troublesome word)
6. • sea (spelling)
7. • sits (troublesome word)
8. • its (troublesome word)

Answers: Exercise 4

Mixed Review

1. altogether
2. loose
3. lies
4. rise
5. among
6. lies
7. too
8. than
9. they're
10. beside
11. choose
12. It's
13. between
14. sit
15. Let

Close

Have students write a paragraph from the point of view of one of the passengers or crew members from the *Titanic*. They should include in their paragraph some of the troublesome words discussed in this unit.

⁵Beside his interest in painting, Shaw also became interested in filmmaking and ceramic sculpture. ⁶In the work on the previous page, he uses ceramic to show the immense power of the see. ⁷The ocean liner sets precariously on the top of a huge wave. ⁸The *Titanic*, of course, met it's fate in the form of an iceberg, not a wave.

Review: Exercise 4

Mixed Review

The following sentences provide information about icebergs. For each sentence, write the correct word in parentheses.

1. An iceberg is a large drifting piece of ice that has broken off (altogether, all together) from a freshwater glacier.
2. It is really a (loose, lose) piece of ice floating in the sea.
3. In the Northern Hemisphere, the main source of icebergs (lays, lies) along the southwestern coast of Greenland.
4. In the south, the glacial flow from Antarctica releases large icebergs, some of which (raise, rise) hundreds of feet into the air.
5. Moving (among, between) a large number of icebergs is dangerous for ships, since only a small portion of each iceberg is visible above the water.
6. Most of the iceberg (lays, lies) under the water.
7. The biggest of the icebergs are (to, too) large to be easily recognized as icebergs.
8. They are much larger (than, then) the largest supertankers.
9. Sometimes (their, they're) over sixty miles long.
10. If you were on a big ship (beside, besides) one of these giant icebergs, you might think you were next to an island.
11. Would you (choose, chose) to live in such an icy place?
12. (Its, It's) hard to imagine, but some animals do!
13. Emperor penguins swim (between, among) ice and land.
14. Seals (set, sit) on the frigid surfaces.
15. (Leave, Let) me bask on a sunny, sand-filled beach!

Glossary of Special Usage Problems

Writing Application

Usage of Glossary Words in Writing

In this passage from *The Jacket*, Gary Soto uses several of the words you have studied to describe the boy's reactions to his new jacket. As you read, concentrate on the italized words.

"I threw my books on the bed and approached the jacket slowly, as if it were a stranger *whose* hand I had to shake. I touched the vinyl sleeve, the collar, and pecked at the mustard-colored lining.

From the kitchen Mother yelled that my jacket was *in* the closet. I closed the door *to* her voice and pulled at the rack of clothes *in* the closet, hoping the jacket on the bedpost wasn't for me but my mean brother."

Techniques with Correct Usage

Gary Soto was careful to use the correct word of a pair that could easily be confused. When you draft and revise your writing, try to be as careful.

TIME

For more about usage rules, see **TIME Facing the Blank Page,** page 98.

❶ Remember the difference between the use of *who's* and *whose.*

INCORRECT . . . as if it were a stranger *who's* hand I had to shake.

CORRECT . . . as if it were a stranger *whose* hand I had to shake.

❷ Learn the difference between *in* and *into.*

INCORRECT My jacket was *into* the closet.

CORRECT My jacket was *in* the closet.

❸ Don't confuse *to, too,* and *two.*

INCORRECT I closed the door *too* her voice . . .

CORRECT I closed the door *to* her voice . . .

Glossary of Special Usage Problems

Usage of Glossary Words in Writing

Have students read the passage silently, paying particular attention to the italicized words. Discuss the italicized words in relation to the Techniques with Correct Usage.

Techniques with Correct Usage

Discuss the techniques used to determine correct usage. Then have students refer to the first paragraph of the passage on page 459. Ask why Robert Ballard said *lay in pools* and not *lay into pools.* Then have students refer to the first paragraph on page 463 and explain the use of *whose* in the first sentence.

Practice

Answers:
1. in
2. to
3. in
4. into
5. two
6. too
7. Whose
8. into
9. Who's
10. into

Practice Practice these techniques by rewriting the following paragraph, making the correct choice from each word pair.

What was (in, into) the back of the closet? I tiptoed nervously (to, too) the closet door. Gingerly, I opened the door and reached (in, into). Slowly, I edged my hand further (in, into) the closet. My hand slid between (too, two) coats that seemed almost (to, too) silky to the touch. (Who's, Whose) could they be? A sudden screech sent me crashing sideways (in, into) the door. "(Who's, Whose) that?" I managed to whisper. The answer launched itself (in, into) me, knocking me backwards. My dog!

Writing Application **463**

Objectives

- To recognize sentence parts
- To identify and use simple subjects and predicates, direct and indirect objects, and parts of speech
- To practice representing these parts in sentence diagrams

✓ ASSESSMENT OPTIONS

📂 *Tests with Answer Key and Rubrics*
Unit 17 Pretest, pp. 69–70
Unit 17 Mastery Test, pp. 71–72

💾 *Testmaker*
Unit 17 Pretest
Unit 17 Mastery Test

You may wish to administer the Unit 17 Pretest at this point.

Key to Ability Levels

L1 Level 1 activities are within the basic ability range of students.

L2 Level 2 activities are within the ability range of average students.

L3 Level 3 activities are more challenging activities.

UNIT 17 Diagraming Sentences

464

Resource Manager

Planning Resources
- *Lesson Plans*
- *Block Scheduling*

🗇 **Transparencies**
- *Bellringer*

📂 **Other Print Resources**
- *Grammar and Composition Handbook*

- *Grammar Enrichment*
- *Grammar Practice*
- *Grammar Reteaching*
- *Grammar Workbook*
- *Tests with Answer Key and Rubrics*

📺 **Video**
- *MindJogger Videoquizzes*

💾 **Software**
- *Interactive Grammar and Language Workbook*
- *Language Arts PASS*
- *Presentation Plus!*
- *Testmaker*

🖥 **Web Sites**
- *writerschoice.glencoe.com*

17.1 Diagraming Simple Subjects and Simple Predicates

Every sentence contains a subject and a predicate. To diagram a sentence, first draw a horizontal line. Then draw a vertical line that crosses the horizontal line.

To the left of the vertical line, write the simple subject. To the right of the vertical line, write the simple predicate. Use capital letters as they appear in the sentence, but do not use punctuation.

Waves crash.

| Waves | crash |

Be sure to write only the simple subject and the simple predicate in this part of the diagram. Remember that the simple predicate can include a helping verb.

The **breakers are pounding** the rocks.

| breakers | are pounding |

Exercise 1 **Diagraming Simple Subjects and Simple Predicates**

Diagram the simple subject and simple predicate of each sentence.

1. Families arrive.
2. They began the day early.
3. Some people are swimming.
4. A child has found a shell.
5. Gwen has built a sand castle.

Focus

Lesson Overview

Objectives
- To identify simple subjects and simple predicates
- To recognize their function as parts of a sentence

Bellringer
Daily Language Activity

When students enter the classroom, have the assignment on the board: *Write three sentences and label the subject and predicate in each one.*

Practice and Assess

Answers: Exercise 1

1. Families | arrive

2. They | began

3. people | are swimming

4. child | has found

5. Gwen | has built

Close

Ask students to contribute ideas for a paragraph about summer experiences. Write the sentences on the board and have students diagram the simple subject and predicate in each sentence.

Diagraming Sentences

Resource Manager

Planning Resources
- *Lesson Plans*

Transparencies
- *Bellringer*

Other Print Resources
- *Grammar and Composition Handbook*
- *Grammar Workbook,* Lesson 52

Focus

Lesson Overview

Objectives
• To identify the four kinds of sentences
• To diagram declarative, imperative, interrogative, and exclamatory sentences

 **Bellringer**
Daily Language Activity

When students enter the classroom, have this assignment on the board: *Write one declarative, one imperative, one interrogative, and one exclamatory sentence.*

Ask volunteers to read aloud their sentences and to explain the difference between each type.

Practice and Assess

Answers: Exercise 2

1. you | Have seen

2. Oceans | cover

3. planet | Does look

4. (you) | Think

5. continents | seem

6. ocean | is

7. (you) | Look

8. Pacific Ocean | Does extend

9. Indian Ocean | Is

10. (you) | Find

Close

Have students diagram the simple subjects and predicates of the sentences they wrote for the Bellringer activity.

466

Diagraming Sentences

17.2 **Diagraming the Four Kinds of Sentences**

The simple subject and the simple predicate of the four kinds of sentences are diagramed below. Note that the location of the simple subject and the simple predicate in a sentence diagram is always the same, regardless of word order in the sentence.

DECLARATIVE

Fishers depend upon the sea.

Fishers | depend

INTERROGATIVE

Do you live near the ocean?

you | Do live

IMPERATIVE

Read this book about the sea.

(you) | Read

EXCLAMATORY

How majestic the **oceans are!**

oceans | are

In an interrogative sentence, the simple subject often comes between the two parts of a verb phrase. In an imperative sentence, the word *you* is understood to be the simple subject.

Exercise 2 **Diagraming Simple Subjects and Simple Predicates**

Diagram the simple subject and simple predicate of each sentence.

1. Have you seen an ocean?
2. Oceans cover about seventy percent of the earth's surface.
3. Does our planet look like one large ocean?
4. Think about that.
5. How small the continents seem!
6. The largest ocean on earth is the Pacific Ocean.
7. Look at the map in this atlas.
8. Does the Pacific Ocean extend to Japan?
9. Is the Indian Ocean the smallest one?
10. Find it on the globe.

Resource Manager

Planning Resources
• *Lesson Plans*

Transparencies
• *Bellringer*

Other Print Resources
• *Grammar and Composition Handbook*
• *Grammar Workbook,* Lesson 53

17.3 Diagraming Direct and Indirect Objects

The predicate of a sentence often contains an action verb and a direct object. In a sentence diagram, place the direct object to the right of the action verb. Draw a vertical line to separate the action verb from the direct object. This vertical line, however, does *not* cross the horizontal line.

The sea contains many **creatures.**

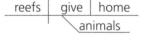

| sea | contains | creatures |

In some sentences, an indirect object comes between the action verb and the direct object. In a diagram, place the indirect object on a line below and to the right of the verb. Draw a slanted line to connect the indirect object to the verb.

Coral reefs give some **animals** a home.

| reefs | give | home |
         \animals

Exercise 3   Diagraming Sentences

Diagram the simple subject, simple predicate, and direct object of each sentence. If the sentence contains an indirect object, diagram it too.

1. Sea plants get minerals from the water.
2. Seaweeds include the long, thin kelp.
3. Scientists have found animal life at impressive depths.
4. Many sea animals show us their picturesque behavior.
5. Some anemones make homes in crab shells.
6. They attach their bodies to the shells of hermit crabs.
7. Hermit crabs use the shells of sea snails for homes.
8. They must protect their soft abdomens.
9. The crabs twist their bodies into the snail shells.
10. The Atlantic hermit crab makes itself a home in a whelk shell.

Diagraming Sentences (sidebar)

Focus

Lesson Overview

Objectives
• To identify action verbs and direct objects
• To identify indirect objects
• To recognize the functions of objects as parts of a sentence and to represent these functions in a sentence diagram

Bellringer
Daily Language Activity

When students enter the classroom, have the following assignment on the board: *Write three sentences that contain both direct objects and indirect objects. Circle the direct object and underline the indirect object in each.*

Practice and Assess

Answers: Exercise 3

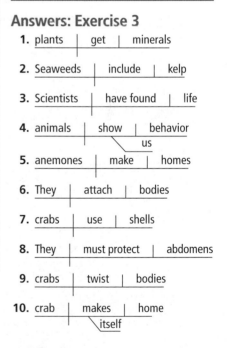

1. | plants | get | minerals |

2. | Seaweeds | include | kelp |

3. | Scientists | have found | life |

4. | animals | show | behavior |
            \us

5. | anemones | make | homes |

6. | They | attach | bodies |

7. | crabs | use | shells |

8. | They | must protect | abdomens |

9. | crabs | twist | bodies |

10. | crab | makes | home |
          \itself

Close

Have students diagram the simple subject, predicate, direct object, and indirect object of each sentence they wrote in the Bellringer activity.

17.4

Focus

Objectives

- To identify adjectives and adverbs
- To recognize their functions as parts of a sentence and to represent these functions in a sentence diagram

Practice and Assess

Answers: Exercise 4

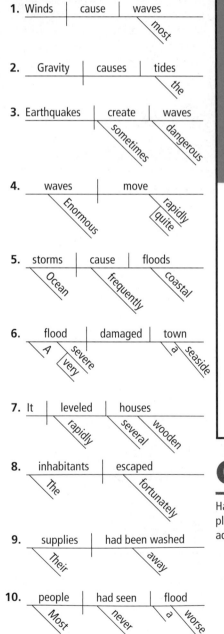

1. Winds | cause | waves / most

2. Gravity | causes | tides / the

3. Earthquakes | create | waves / sometimes / dangerous

4. waves | move / Enormous / rapidly / quite

5. storms | cause | floods / Ocean / frequently / coastal

6. flood | damaged | town / A / severe / very / a / seaside

7. It | leveled | houses / rapidly / several / wooden

8. inhabitants | escaped / The / fortunately

9. supplies | had been washed / Their / away

10. people | had seen | flood / Most / never / a / worse

Diagraming Adjectives and Adverbs

An adjective modifies a noun or pronoun. In a diagram, write the adjective on a slanted line beneath the noun or pronoun it modifies. Diagram possessive nouns and pronouns and the articles *a*, *an*, and *the* just as you would diagram other kinds of adjectives.

Our new boat encountered **a stormy** sea.

An adverb can modify a verb, an adjective, or another adverb. Note how adverbs are diagramed.

We have **almost never** seen **such** violent weather.

Exercise 4 **Diagraming Sentences**

Diagram each sentence.

1. Winds cause most waves.
2. Gravity causes the tides.
3. Earthquakes sometimes create dangerous waves.
4. Enormous waves move quite rapidly.
5. Ocean storms frequently cause coastal floods.
6. A very severe flood damaged a seaside town.
7. It rapidly leveled several wooden houses.
8. The inhabitants fortunately escaped.
9. Their supplies had been washed away.
10. Most people had never seen a worse flood.

Close

Have students write and diagram four simple sentences that have an adjective or an adverb.

Diagraming Sentences

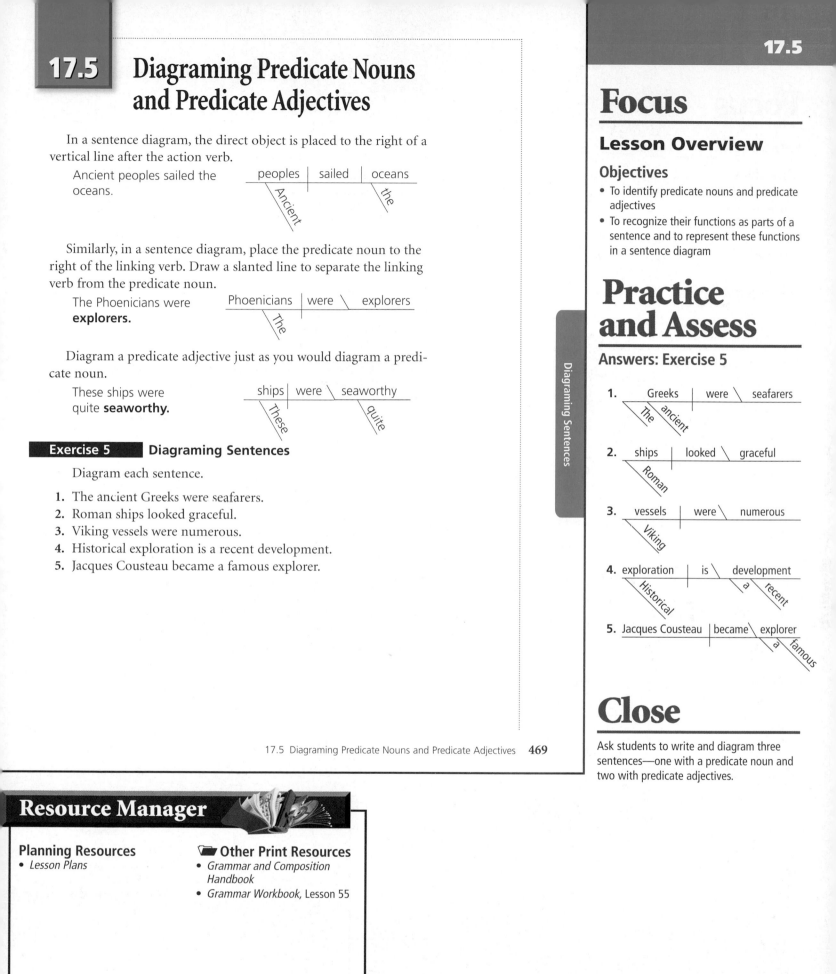

17.5 Diagraming Predicate Nouns and Predicate Adjectives

In a sentence diagram, the direct object is placed to the right of a vertical line after the action verb.

Ancient peoples sailed the oceans.

Similarly, in a sentence diagram, place the predicate noun to the right of the linking verb. Draw a slanted line to separate the linking verb from the predicate noun.

The Phoenicians were **explorers.**

Diagram a predicate adjective just as you would diagram a predicate noun.

These ships were quite **seaworthy.**

Exercise 5   Diagraming Sentences

Diagram each sentence.

1. The ancient Greeks were seafarers.
2. Roman ships looked graceful.
3. Viking vessels were numerous.
4. Historical exploration is a recent development.
5. Jacques Cousteau became a famous explorer.

Diagraming Sentences

Focus

Lesson Overview

Objectives
* To identify predicate nouns and predicate adjectives
* To recognize their functions as parts of a sentence and to represent these functions in a sentence diagram

Practice and Assess

Answers: Exercise 5

1. Greeks | were \ seafarers
   The / ancient

2. ships | looked \ graceful
   Roman

3. vessels | were \ numerous
   Viking

4. exploration | is \ development
   Historical / a \ recent

5. Jacques Cousteau | became \ explorer
   a \ famous

Close

Ask students to write and diagram three sentences—one with a predicate noun and two with predicate adjectives.

Resource Manager

Planning Resources
* *Lesson Plans*

📂 **Other Print Resources**
* *Grammar and Composition Handbook*
* *Grammar Workbook,* Lesson 55

Focus

Lesson Overview

Objectives

- To identify prepositional phrases
- To recognize and use prepositional phrases as both adjectives and adverbs
- To represent both functions in a sentence diagram

Practice and Assess

Answers: Exercise 6

1. floor | has | features — The, of ocean the, remarkable

2. mountains | exist — Many, beneath surface the

3. mountains | include | volcanoes — These, below waves the, active

4. islands | are \ mountains — Many, Pacific, really, on floor the ocean

5. trenches | cut — Deep, into floor the South Pacific

17.6 Diagraming Prepositional Phrases

To diagram a sentence with a prepositional phrase used as an adjective, follow the model below.

The waves **along the rocky shore** crashed loudly.

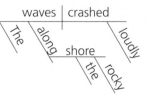

The prepositional phrase, *along the rocky shore*, is connected to the word that it modifies, the noun *waves*.

The following example shows the same prepositional phrase used as an adverb.

Enormous waves crashed **along the rocky shore**.

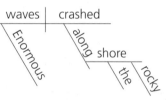

The prepositional phrase, *along the rocky shore*, is connected to the word that it modifies, the verb *crashed*.

Exercise 6   Diagraming Sentences

Diagram each sentence.

1. The floor of the ocean has remarkable features.
2. Many mountains exist beneath the surface.
3. These mountains below the waves include active volcanoes.
4. Many Pacific islands are really mountains on the ocean floor.
5. Deep trenches cut into the South Pacific floor.

Close

Have students write and diagram three simple sentences, each having a prepositional phrase.

Resource Manager

Planning Resources
- *Lesson Plans*

📁 Other Print Resources
- *Grammar and Composition Handbook*
- *Grammar Workbook,* Lesson 56

17.7 Diagraming Compound Sentence Parts

Conjunctions such as *and, but,* and *or* are used to join words, phrases, and sentences, creating compound constructions. When you diagram compound parts of a sentence, place the second part of the compound below the first.

COMPOUND SUBJECT
The sea and its products benefit people.

COMPOUND PREDICATE
Sea creatures **eat and sleep.**

COMPOUND SENTENCE
Some sea creatures are plentiful, but others are scarce.

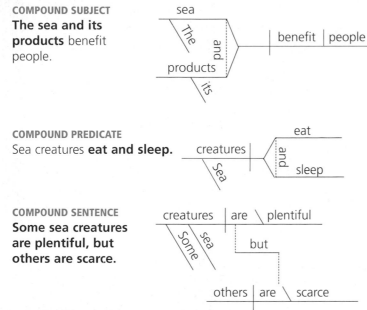

Exercise 7 Diagraming Sentences

Diagram each sentence.

1. Fish and shellfish are plentiful ocean products.
2. The undersea world lives and grows.
3. Herring and cod are good food.
4. The ocean is unpredictable, but it lures many travelers.
5. The water wears many faces, and it shows different moods.

Focus

Lesson Overview

Objectives
• To identify parts of a compound sentence
• To represent elements of a compound sentence in a diagram

Practice and Assess

Answers: Exercise 7

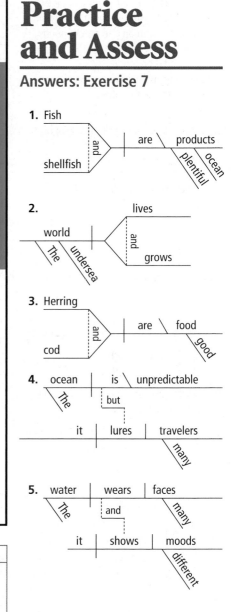

Objectives

- To recognize and apply the rules of capitalization for sentences, quotations, and salutations in letters
- To demonstrate control over the conventions of capitalization for the names of places and the names and titles of people
- To identify common and proper nouns and adjectives, and to capitalize proper nouns and proper adjectives
- To identify and revise errors in the conventions of capitalization

✔ ASSESSMENT OPTIONS

📁 *Tests with Answer Key and Rubrics*
Unit 18 Pretest, pp. 73–74
Unit 18 Mastery Test, pp. 75–76

💾 *Testmaker*
Unit 18 Pretest
Unit 18 Mastery Test

You may wish to administer the Unit 18 Pretest at this point.

Key to Ability Levels

L1 Level 1 activities are within the basic ability range of students.

L2 Level 2 activities are within the ability range of average students.

L3 Level 3 activities are more challenging activities.

UNIT
18 Capitalization

472

Resource Manager

Planning Resources
- *Lesson Plans*
- *Block Scheduling*

📖 Transparencies
- *Bellringer*
- *Daily Language Practice*

💻 Web Sites
- *writerschoice.glencoe.com*

📁 Other Print Resources
- *Grammar and Composition Handbook*
- *Grammar Enrichment*
- *Grammar Practice*
- *Grammar Reteaching*
- *Grammar Workbook*
- *Tests with Answer Key and Rubrics*

📹 Video
- *MindJogger Videoquizzes*

💾 Software
- *Interactive Grammar Workbook*
- *Language Arts PASS*
- *Presentation Plus!*
- *Testmaker*

18.1 Capitalizing Sentences, Quotations, and Salutations

A capital letter appears at the beginning of a sentence. A capital letter also marks the beginning of a direct quotation and the salutation and closing of a letter.

RULE 1: 'Capitalize the first word of every sentence.

The country of Canada extends across North America.

RULE 2: Capitalize the first word of a direct quotation that is a complete sentence. A direct quotation gives a speaker's exact words.

Duane said, "**A**bout twenty-nine million people live in Canada."

"**M**any Canadians live near the southern border," Regina said.

RULE 3: When a quoted sentence is interrupted by explanatory words, such as *she said*, do not begin the second part of the sentence with a capital letter.

"Most Canadians," said Minh, "**l**ive in cities or towns."

"Canada's largest city," Lois added, "**i**s Toronto."

When the second part of a quotation is a new sentence, put a period after the interrupting expression and begin the second part of the quotation with a capital letter.

"I've been to Toronto," said Paul. "**M**y mother was born there."

RULE 4: Do not capitalize an indirect quotation. An indirect quotation does not repeat a person's exact words and does not appear in quotation marks. It is often introduced by the word *that*.

Paul said **that h**is mother was born in Toronto.

RULE 5: Capitalize the first word in the salutation and closing of a letter. Capitalize the title and name of the person addressed.

Dear **M**rs. **M**oulin,   **Y**ours truly,

To whom it may concern,   **S**incerely yours,

Capitalization

Focus

Lesson Overview

Objectives

- To recognize and apply the rules of capitalization for sentences and salutations
- To understand and apply capitalization rules for direct and indirect quotations

🔔 Bellringer
Daily Language Activity

When students enter the classroom, have this assignment on the board: *Capitalize and punctuate the following sentence correctly.*

    That's my point," she said "that's it exactly."

📖 **See also** *Daily Language Practice*

Motivating Activity

Explain that the second part of the quotation—"that's it exactly"—is a separate sentence that must be preceded by a period and must begin with a capital letter.

Teach

☑ Teaching Tip

Many students have difficulty distinguishing between direct and indirect quotations. Suggest that students look for the word *that*, which is often (though not always) inserted after the verb in indirect quotations.
Indirect: *Lois said that Canada's largest city was Toronto.* Direct: *Lois said, "Canada's largest city is Toronto."*

Resource Manager

Planning Resources
- *Lesson Plans*

📖 **Transparencies**
- *Bellringer*
- *Daily Language Practice*

📁 **Other Print Resources**
- *Grammar and Composition Handbook*
- *Grammar Workbook, Lessons 63–64*

Practice and Assess

Answers: Exercise 1

1. We were …
2. Renée said, "Last …"
3. "You were …"
4. correct
5. correct
6. "Does that …"
7. correct
8. correct
9. "Anyway, …"
10. correct

Answers: Exercise 2

Dear Jack,

My family and I are having a great vacation here in the New Hampshire mountains. Dad says that **w**e may come back again next year. The snow is perfect, and we love the town where we are staying.

Believe it or not, your cousin is also here on vacation. She told me today that you were not feeling well. "**P**erhaps a letter," I said, "**w**ill cheer him up." So I sat down after lunch and wrote you this letter. I hope **y**ou are feeling better. Next week I will be returning home. **T**hen I can visit you in person.

> **Y**our good **f**riend,
> Pete

Additional Resources

Grammar Workbook,
Lessons 63–64

Close

Ask students to imagine they are taking a trip to Canada. Have them write a letter describing the trip using one direct and one indirect quotation.

Capitalization

Exercise 1   **Capitalizing Sentences, Quotations, and Salutations**

Write each sentence. Use capital letters where needed. If a sentence contains no errors, write *correct.*

1. we were talking about our summer vacations.
2. Renée said, "last summer I visited Canada."
3. "you were lucky," said Paul, "because you went in the summer."
4. "Canada has cold winters," Jim remarked.
5. Paul said that summer winds from the Gulf of Mexico often bring hot weather to Canada.
6. "does that mean that on some days it's as hot in Canada as it is in Mexico?" asked Jim.
7. Jim said that in the Northwest Territories the summers are very short.
8. "I'm not surprised," said Renée, "for the Northwest Territories reach up to the North Pole."
9. "anyway," she said, "we visited only Quebec."
10. Paul said that he'd go to Quebec next year.

Exercise 2   **Using Capitalization in a Letter**

Rewrite the letter, using correct capitalization. The letter contains ten errors.

January 2, 2000

dear Jack,

my family and I are having a great vacation here in the New Hampshire mountains. Dad says that We may come back again next year. The snow is perfect, and we love the town where we are staying.

believe it or not, your cousin is also here on vacation. She told me today that you were not feeling well. "perhaps a letter," I said, "Will cheer him up." So I sat down after lunch and wrote you this letter. I hope You are feeling better. Next week I will be returning home. then I can visit you in person.

your good Friend,
Pete

MEETING INDIVIDUAL NEEDS   **Less Proficient Readers**

Capitalizing Quotations

Some students may have difficulty determining when to begin a direct quotation with a capital letter. Remind them that the rule is the same as for any other sentence: If a group of words is a complete sentence, it should begin with a capital letter. Encourage pairs of students to work together on Exercise 1 so that they have the benefit of each other's reasoning.

18.2 Capitalizing Names and Titles of People

A common noun is the general name of a person, place, or thing. A common noun is not capitalized. A proper noun names a particular person, place, or thing and is capitalized.

RULE 1: Capitalize the names of people and the initials that stand for their names.

Louis **H**. **L**afontaine   **S**. **D**. **T**hompson   **J**ohn **C**abot

RULE 2: Capitalize a title or an abbreviation of a title when it comes before a person's name or when it is used in direct address.

General James Wolfe   **D**r. Michelle Turner   **M**s. Chavez
In 1610 **C**aptain Hudson searched for a passage to Asia.
Later people asked him, "Did you find it, **C**aptain?"

Do not capitalize a title that follows or stands for a person's name.

Henry Hudson was captain of a ship.

RULE 3: Capitalize the names and abbreviations of academic degrees that follow a person's name. Capitalize *Jr.* and *Sr.*

Tina Ibarra, **P**h.**D**.   Linda Tsang, **M**.**D**.   David Melo, **J**r.

RULE 4: Capitalize words that show family relationships when used as titles or as substitutes for a person's name.

Last year **F**ather and **A**unt Beth retraced Cartier's journey.

Do not capitalize words that show family relationships when they follow a possessive noun or pronoun.

Jody's **u**ncle took photographs of the voyage.

RULE 5: Always capitalize the pronoun *I*.

Champlain is the explorer **I** admire most.

Capitalization

18.2

Focus

Lesson Overview

Objectives
- To understand the difference between common and proper nouns that refer to people
- To recognize and apply the rules of capitalization for the names and titles of people

Bellringer
Daily Language Activity

When students enter the classroom, have this assignment on the board: *Capitalize the following names correctly:*

billy the kid	*donald duck*
jabba the hut	*peggy o'neal*
mr. mcdonald	*catherine the great*

See also *Daily Language Practice*

Teach

☑ Teaching Tip

Explain to students that when we refer to a person by his or her title only (usually after an article or a possessive noun or pronoun), the title is a common noun and is not capitalized. When we use a title to address someone directly, the title is a proper noun and, therefore, capitalized. Compare *This is the commander* (common noun) and *Good evening, Commander* (proper noun, direct address).

Resource Manager

Planning Resources
- *Lesson Plans*

🔖 Transparencies
- *Bellringer*
- *Daily Language Practice*

📁 Other Print Resources
- *Grammar and Composition Handbook*
- *Grammar Enrichment*, p. 38
- *Grammar Practice*, p. 38
- *Grammar Reteaching*, p. 39
- *Grammar Workbook*, Lessons 65–66

Practice and Assess

Answers: Exercise 3

1. Ms. Lucy Jojola
2. Dr. Claude C. Islas
3. Captain Richards
4. Aunt Anna
5. Richard Bennett Jr.
6. Daniel Roget, Ph.D.
7. Uncle Louis
8. Jeanette Canales, M.D.
9. Judge Jean Luc
10. W. R. Mackenzie
11. President Jefferson
12. Sir James Smith
13. Mr. Robert Townsend Sr.
14. Queen Victoria
15. Madame Marie Curie
16. Lord Roy Nesbett
17. Warren G. Malloy Jr.
18. Professor Talmon
19. Mr. and Mrs. Ortiz
20. General Davidson

Answers: Exercise 4

1. King Henry VII
2. John Cabot
3. Verrazano
4. King Francis I; I; Jacques Cartier
5. Champlain
6. Joliet; Marquette
7. La Salle
8. Sir Alexander Mackenzie
9. Dad; Bill
10. Mr. Zebulon Pike

Additional Resources

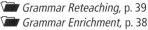 *Grammar Practice*, p. 38
Grammar Reteaching, p. 39
Grammar Enrichment, p. 38

 Grammar Workbook, Lessons 65–66

Close

Have students write a journal entry with names and titles about yesterday's events.

Exercise 3 Capitalizing Names and Titles

Write each item. Use capital letters where needed.

1. ms. lucy jojola
2. dr. claude c. islas
3. captain richards
4. aunt anna
5. richard bennett jr.
6. daniel roget, ph.d.
7. uncle louis
8. jeanette canales, m.d.
9. judge jean luc
10. w. r. mackenzie
11. president jefferson
12. sir james smith
13. mr. robert townsend sr.
14. queen victoria
15. madame marie curie
16. lord roy nesbett
17. warren g. malloy jr.
18. professor talmon
19. mr. and mrs. ortiz
20. general davidson

Exercise 4 Using Capital Letters in Names and Titles

Write each sentence. Use capital letters where needed for names and titles.

1. In 1497 king henry VII of England hired a navigator.
2. This navigator, john cabot, landed in what is now Canada.
3. The Italian navigator verrazano probably reached Canada in 1524.
4. In 1534 king francis I of France, i believe, sent jacques cartier to the New World.
5. In 1608 another French explorer, champlain, founded Quebec.
6. In 1673 joliet and marquette sailed down the Mississippi River.
7. Nine years later, the explorer la salle claimed for France all the land drained by the Mississippi River.
8. In 1789 sir alexander mackenzie followed a river to the Arctic Ocean.
9. Last year dad and Uncle bill traveled down this river.
10. Pike's Peak was first sighted by mr. zebulon Pike in 1806.

The **d**octor will see you now.

This is **D**r. Gonzales.

Less Proficient Readers

Capitalizing Words That Show Family Relationships

Some students may need practice in determining when to capitalize words that show family relationships. Have students write two sentences using the word *aunt*. Then have them work with a partner to determine in which sentences *aunt* should be capitalized. Remind students that when such a word is modified by a possessive word or article, the word is usually a common noun and should not be capitalized.

18.3 Capitalizing Names of Places

The names of specific places are proper nouns and are capitalized. Do not, however, capitalize articles and prepositions that are part of geographical names.

RULE 1: Capitalize the names of cities, counties, states, countries, and continents.

Toronto	Mexico	Europe
New Hampshire	Cook County	Hong Kong

RULE 2: Capitalize the names of bodies of water and other geographical features.

Atlantic Ocean	Hudson Bay	Cape Cod
Mojave Desert	the Great Lakes	Monument Valley

RULE 3: Capitalize the names of sections of the country.

the Southwest	New England	Midwest

RULE 4: Capitalize compass points when they refer to a specific section of the country.

the East Coast	the South	the Northeast

Do not capitalize compass points when they are used to indicate direction.

Mexico is south of San Diego.

Do not capitalize adjectives formed from words showing direction.

northerly wind	eastern Texas

RULE 5: Capitalize the names of streets and highways.

Hyde Street	Hollywood Freeway

RULE 6: Capitalize the names of specific buildings, bridges, and monuments.

Washington Monument	Empire State Building

Focus

Lesson Overview

Objectives
- To identify common and proper nouns that refer to places
- To capitalize proper nouns that name places

Bellringer
Daily Language Activity

When students enter the classroom, have this assignment on the board: *Add capital letters as needed in the following phrases:*

1. *along the Hudson river*
2. *the river known as the Rio Grande*
3. *born in the south*
4. *south of the border*

See also *Daily Language Practice*

Teach

☑ **Teaching Tip**

Explain to students that the popular names of regions are usually capitalized: Back Bay (Boston); the Channel (English Channel); Bay Area (San Francisco); the Badlands (South Dakota). The word *state* is capitalized if it follows the name of the state (Washington State), but it is not capitalized if it precedes the name of the state (the state of Washington).

Capitalization (side tab)

Resource Manager

Planning Resources
- *Lesson Plans*

Transparencies
- *Bellringer*
- *Daily Language Practice*

📂 **Other Print Resources**
- *Grammar and Composition Handbook*
- *Grammar Enrichment*, p. 39
- *Grammar Practice*, p. 39
- *Grammar Reteaching*, p. 40
- *Grammar Workbook*, Lessons 67–68

Practice and Assess

Answers: Exercise 5

1. New Mexico
2. Acapulco
3. Asia
4. Peru
5. Brooklyn Bridge
6. Yucatán Peninsula
7. the Pacific Northwest
8. Amarillo Avenue
9. northern Texas
10. San Diego Freeway
11. Interstate 80
12. Chrysler Building
13. the Southeast
14. Indian Ocean
15. Alaska
16. Portola Valley
17. southern Oregon
18. Washington Monument
19. Rocky Mountains
20. the United States

Answers: Exercise 6

1. Mexico, United States of America
2. Latin America
3. Mexico City
4. North America, South America
5. Mexico, Plateau of Mexico
6. Gulf of California, Baja California
7. Sierra Madre, Rockies
8. North America, Mount McKinley
9. Mount McKinley, Alaska
10. Hawaii, Pacific Ocean, Puerto Rico, Atlantic, Caribbean Sea

Answers: Exercise 7

Answers will vary, but a sample is given below.

I live in the state of Michigan. It has two peninsulas, the Upper Peninsula and the Lower Peninsula. Four of the Great Lakes— Huron, Erie, Michigan, and Superior— almost surround my state. It borders the states of Ohio, Indiana, and Wisconsin, and also Canada on its eastern side. The capital of Michigan is Lansing, and the largest city is Detroit.

Additional Resources

 *Grammar Practice,* p. 39
Grammar Reteaching, p. 40
Grammar Enrichment, p. 39

Grammar Workbook, Lessons 67–68

Exercise 5 — Capitalizing Place Names

Write each word or group of words. Use capital letters where needed.

1. new mexico
2. acapulco
3. asia
4. peru
5. brooklyn bridge
6. yucatán peninsula
7. the pacific northwest
8. amarillo avenue
9. northern texas
10. san diego freeway
11. interstate 80
12. chrysler building
13. the southeast
14. indian ocean
15. alaska
16. portola valley
17. southern oregon
18. washington monument
19. rocky mountains
20. the united states

Exercise 6 — Using Capital Letters for Place Names

Write each sentence. Use capital letters where needed for geographical names.

1. The country of mexico is south of the united states of america.
2. Mexico is the most northern country in latin america.
3. Its capital and largest city is mexico city.
4. This city of 19 million people has the largest population of any city in north america and south america.
5. The largest cities in mexico exist in the region known as the plateau of mexico.
6. The large peninsula located west of the gulf of california is known as baja california.
7. The sierra madre is part of the rockies.
8. The highest mountain in north america is mount mckinley.
9. Mount mckinley is in central alaska.
10. hawaii is surrounded by the pacific ocean, and puerto rico has the atlantic to the north and the caribbean sea to the south.

Exercise 7 — Writing Place Names in a Paragraph

Write at least five sentences telling about the state you live in. Include the names of cities, rivers, and other specific places. Name the states that border your state.

Capitalization

478   Unit 18 Capitalization

Close

Have students plan a trip to Mexico. Ask them to use a map to write a paragraph about the trip, including place names and direction words.

18.4 Capitalizing Other Proper Nouns and Adjectives

Many nouns besides the names of people and places are proper nouns and, therefore, are always capitalized. The adjectives that are formed from proper nouns are called proper adjectives and are also always capitalized.

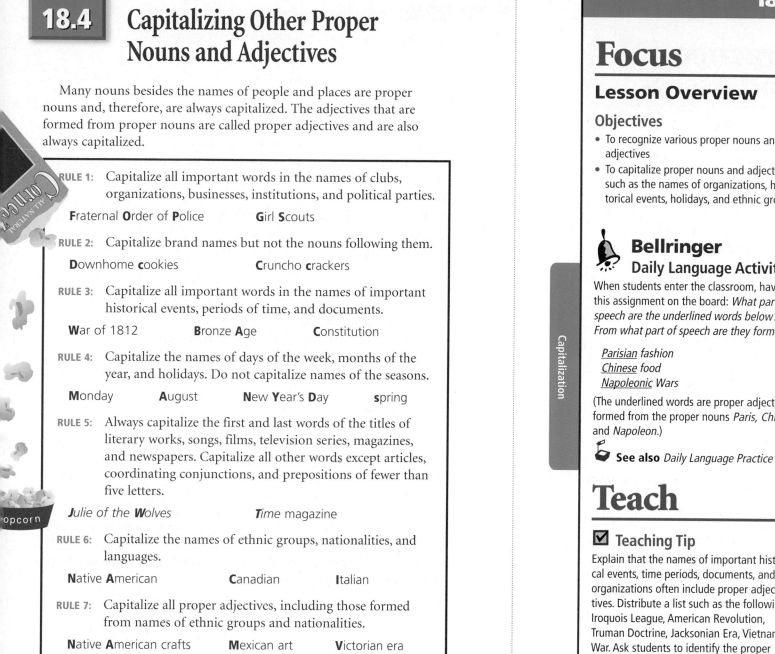

RULE 1: Capitalize all important words in the names of clubs, organizations, businesses, institutions, and political parties.

Fraternal Order of Police   Girl Scouts

RULE 2: Capitalize brand names but not the nouns following them.

Downhome cookies   Cruncho crackers

RULE 3: Capitalize all important words in the names of important historical events, periods of time, and documents.

War of 1812   Bronze Age   Constitution

RULE 4: Capitalize the names of days of the week, months of the year, and holidays. Do not capitalize names of the seasons.

Monday   August   New Year's Day   spring

RULE 5: Always capitalize the first and last words of the titles of literary works, songs, films, television series, magazines, and newspapers. Capitalize all other words except articles, coordinating conjunctions, and prepositions of fewer than five letters.

Julie of the Wolves   Time magazine

RULE 6: Capitalize the names of ethnic groups, nationalities, and languages.

Native American   Canadian   Italian

RULE 7: Capitalize all proper adjectives, including those formed from names of ethnic groups and nationalities.

Native American crafts   Mexican art   Victorian era

Focus

Lesson Overview

Objectives

- To recognize various proper nouns and adjectives
- To capitalize proper nouns and adjectives, such as the names of organizations, historical events, holidays, and ethnic groups

Bellringer
Daily Language Activity

When students enter the classroom, have this assignment on the board: *What part of speech are the underlined words below? From what part of speech are they formed?*

Parisian fashion
Chinese food
Napoleonic Wars

(The underlined words are proper adjectives formed from the proper nouns *Paris, China,* and *Napoleon.*)

See also *Daily Language Practice*

Teach

☑ Teaching Tip

Explain that the names of important historical events, time periods, documents, and organizations often include proper adjectives. Distribute a list such as the following: Iroquois League, American Revolution, Truman Doctrine, Jacksonian Era, Vietnam War. Ask students to identify the proper adjectives in the list and name the proper noun from which each was formed.

Capitalization

Resource Manager

Planning Resources
- *Lesson Plans*

Transparencies
- *Bellringer*
- *Daily Language Practice*

📂 Other Print Resources
- *Grammar and Composition Handbook*
- *Grammar Enrichment,* p. 40
- *Grammar Practice,* p. 40
- *Grammar Reteaching,* p. 41
- *Grammar Workbook,* Lessons 69–70

Practice and Assess

Answers: Exercise 8

1. Madison School
2. December
3. World War I
4. Native American poetry
5. "Casey at the Bat"
6. *Oliver Twist*
7. Input Corporation
8. Mello yogurt
9. French
10. Japanese
11. "We Are the World"
12. *Chicago Tribune*
13. International Workers Union
14. "My Life and Difficult Times"
15. African American stories
16. Valentine's Day
17. Girl Scouts of the United States of America
18. *Popular Mechanics* magazine
19. Spanish dances
20. Declaration of Independence

Answers: Exercise 9

1. Latin American
2. Mexican
3. America, Maya, Toltec
4. Aztec
5. Mexican Revolution
6. "Wind and Water and Stone," Mexican
7. Independence Day, September
8. Mexico
9. Mexico, North America
10. United States, Mexican, Spanish

Additional Resources

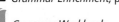
Grammar Practice, p. 40
Grammar Reteaching, p. 41
Grammar Enrichment, p. 940

Grammar Workbook,
Lessons 69–70

Close

Ask students to imagine they are starting their own country. Have them write a description of some new holidays using proper nouns and adjectives.

480

Capitalization

Exercise 8 **Capitalizing Proper Nouns and Adjectives**

Write the following items. Use capital letters where needed.

1. madison school
2. december
3. world war I
4. native american poetry
5. "casey at the bat"
6. *oliver twist*
7. input corporation
8. mello yogurt
9. french
10. japanese
11. "we are the world"
12. *chicago tribune*
13. international workers union
14. "my life and difficult times"
15. african american stories
16. valentine's day
17. girl scouts of the united states of america
18. *popular mechanics* magazine
19. spanish dances
20. declaration of independence

Exercise 9 **Using Capital Letters for Proper Nouns and Adjectives**

Write each sentence. Use capital letters where needed for proper nouns and adjectives.

1. Mexico is a latin american country rich in art and tradition.
2. For centuries the arts have played a very important part in mexican life.
3. Long before Columbus discovered america, the maya and toltec peoples built beautiful temples.
4. The aztec people composed music and poetry.
5. The mexican revolution of 1910 changed the course of Mexico's art and literature.
6. Have you read the poem "wind and water and stone," by the famous mexican writer Octavio Paz?
7. In Mexico independence day is in september.
8. Holidays in mexico are colorfully celebrated.
9. We learned that mexico is the most southern part of the continent of north america.
10. The names of many cities in the southwestern united states originated from mexican and spanish words.

English Language Learners

MEETING INDIVIDUAL NEEDS

Adjectives Made from Proper Nouns

Students who are acquiring English may have difficulty identifying the adjectives made from proper nouns in Exercise 9. Pair these students with more proficient students who can act as coaches and help them identify the proper adjectives in Exercise 9.

UNIT 18 Grammar Review

CAPITALIZATION

A Secret for Two, by Quentin Reynolds, tells the story of a visually impaired milk deliverer, Pierre Dupin, and Joseph, the horse that drew his wagon. The passage has been annotated to show some of the rules of capitalization covered in this unit.

Literature Model

from A Secret for Two

by Quentin Reynolds

Montreal is a very large city, but, like all large cities, it has some very small streets. Streets, for instance, like **P**rince **E**dward **S**treet, which is only four blocks long, ending in a cul-de-sac. No one knew Prince Edward Street as well as did **P**ierre **D**upin, for Pierre had delivered milk to the families on the street for thirty years now.

During the past fifteen years the horse which drew the milk wagon used by Pierre was a large white horse named Joseph. In **M**ontreal, especially in that part of Montreal which is very **F**rench, the animals, like children, are often given the names of saints. When the big, white horse first came to the **P**rovincale **M**ilk **C**ompany, he didn't have a name. They told Pierre that he could use the white horse henceforth. Pierre stroked the softness of the horse's neck; he stroked the sheen of its splendid belly, and he looked into the eyes of the horse.

"**T**hat is a kind horse, a gentle and a faithful horse," Pierre said. . . .

- Name of a street
- Name of a person
- First word of a sentence
- Name of a city
- Proper adjective
- Name of a company
- First word of a direct quotation

Capitalization

Grammar Review **481**

Teach

About the Literature

Focus students' attention and have a volunteer read aloud the passage from Quentin Reynolds's *A Secret for Two*. Ask students which words are or are not essential to the meaning of the passage, paying particular attention to the large number of capital letters in the passage. Go over the highlighted words with them. Ask students to identify other examples of capitalization in the text. The exercises that follow are based on this passage and related topics.

Critical Thinking

Point out that capitalization can indicate the use of specific information. After listening to the passage, invite students to determine which sentences contain facts (verifiable information) and which represent opinions.

Linking Grammar and Literature

Cooperative Learning

Bring to class several newspapers and magazines. Have teams of three or four students find examples that demonstrate each rule of capitalization in this unit. Teams can then work together to create a chart of their findings.

Critical Thinking

Encourage students to consider the reasons for the rules they have learned about capitalization. Remind them that capital letters make it easier to understand the meaning of what we read. Call on students to explain how the capital letter in each of the highlighted words on page 481 helps them understand the sentences more quickly.

Resource Manager

Planning Resources
- *Lesson Plans*

Other Print Resources
- *Grammar and Composition Handbook*
- *Grammar Workbook,* Lessons 63–70; Unit 11 Review; Cumulative Review: Units 1–11

✔ ASSESSMENT OPTIONS

📂 *Tests with Answer Key and Rubrics* Unit 18 Mastery Test, pp. 75–76

💾 *Testmaker* Unit 18 Mastery Test

Practice and Assess

Answers: Exercise 1

1. For …
2. After …
3. The …
4. … "What … friend …"
5. correct
6. All …
7. Pierre said, "Fifteen … "
8. "This …"
9. … his …
10. … that … "

Answers: Exercise 2

Dear Sara,

Today we read a story about a milk deliverer. My teacher said, "Class, I know you will like this story. It is one of my favorites." I can see why my teacher says he likes the story so much.

Last summer you said to me, "Someday I hope I can have my own horse." You might like to read this story. It's called "A Secret for Two." Tell me what you think of it.

Your friend,
Chris

Review: Exercise 1 Capitalizing Sentences and Quotations

Rewrite each sentence, correcting any errors in capitalization. If a sentence has no errors, write *correct*.

SAMPLE   Pierre Dupin said, "no one loves Joseph as much as I do."
ANSWER   Pierre Dupin said, "No one loves Joseph as much as I do."

1. for most of his adult life, Pierre Dupin delivered milk to the families on Prince Edward Street.
2. after fifteen years of delivering milk, Pierre got his horse, Joseph.
3. the horse would lead his master to each house on the street.
4. Pierre thought, "what would I do without my loyal Friend, Joseph?"
5. Pierre and Joseph spent many years together in Montreal, Canada.
6. all the families on the street recognized Pierre and Joseph.
7. Pierre said, "fifteen years ago my supervisor gave me a horse to pull my milk wagon."
8. "Look into his eyes," said the supervisor. "this horse will be your faithful friend."
9. Pierre thought His new horse was kind and gentle.
10. "I think," said Pierre, "That I will name him Joseph."

Review: Exercise 2 Using Capitalization in a Letter

Rewrite the following letter, using correct capitalization. The letter contains ten errors.

March 19, 2001

dear Sara,

Today we read a story about a milk deliverer. My teacher said, "class, I know you will like this story. it is one of my favorites." I can see why my teacher says He likes the story so much.

last summer you said to me, "someday I hope I can have my own horse." you might like to read this story. It's called "A Secret for Two." tell me What you think of it.

your friend,
Chris

Review: Exercise 3 Capitalizing Names and Titles of People

Rewrite the following names and titles, using correct capitalization. If an item contains no errors, write *correct*.

1. mr. robert chang
2. uncle john
3. the club's president
4. professor r. d. diego
5. my aunt and uncle
6. queen elizabeth
7. margaret lee, m.d.
8. lieutenant juarez
9. the captain of the ship
10. ms. evert
11. governor whitman
12. dr. chris cross
13. president lincoln
14. emily cox, ph.d.
15. e. b. white
16. mrs. doubtfire
17. sir edmund hillary
18. aunt maria and i
19. ken griffey jr.
20. lady jane grey

Review: Exercise 4 Capitalizing Titles and Names of People and Places

Write each sentence. Use capital letters where needed.

SAMPLE   Our art teacher, ms. whitney, showed us paintings from mexico.
ANSWER   Our art teacher, Ms. Whitney, showed us paintings from Mexico.

1. The brilliant Mexican artist diego rivera painted murals.
2. Born in 1886, rivera became famous for his murals of mexico.
3. Last summer aunt sharice saw the murals in the national palace in mexico city.
4. My aunt then visited the yucatán peninsula.
5. That peninsula is surrounded by the gulf of mexico and the caribbean sea.
6. Her tour guide was juan perez, ph.d.
7. One evening dr. perez discussed general santa anna.
8. In 1833 the general became president of mexico.
9. Santa anna led the fight against the American colonists who wanted to take texas from mexico.
10. He was captured in a famous battle fought on the banks of the san jacinto river in 1836.

Capitalization

Answers: Exercise 3
1. Mr. Robert Chang
2. Uncle John
3. correct
4. Professor R. D. Diego
5. correct
6. Queen Elizabeth
7. Margaret Lee, M.D.
8. Lieutenant Juarez
9. correct
10. Ms. Evert
11. Governor Whitman
12. Dr. Chris Cross
13. President Lincoln
14. Emily Cox, Ph.D.
15. E. B. White
16. Mrs. Doubtfire
17. Sir Edmund Hillary
18. Aunt Maria and I
19. Ken Griffey Jr.
20. Lady Jane Grey

Answers: Exercise 4
1. Diego Rivera
2. Rivera; Mexico
3. Aunt Sharice; National Palace; Mexico City
4. Yucatán Peninsula
5. Gulf of Mexico; Caribbean Sea
6. Juan Perez, Ph.D.
7. Dr. Perez; General Santa Anna
8. Mexico
9. Anna; Texas; Mexico
10. San Jacinto River

Answers: Exercise 5

1. Provincale Milk Company
2. Pierre; Prince Edward Street
3. supervisor
4. Pierre
5. I

Answers: Exercise 6

1. southern
2. France; European; Montreal
3. French and Indian War
4. French
5. French-speaking
6. French; English
7. Lawrence River; northeast; Quebec
8. New England; Canadian; east
9. southern; York; Vermont
10. national; Canada; Ottawa

Capitalization

Review: Exercise 5 **Capitalizing Proper Nouns**

Rewrite each sentence, correcting any errors in capitalization.

SAMPLE   Within a year joseph knew the milk route as well as Pierre.
ANSWER   Within a year Joseph knew the milk route as well as Pierre.

1. Pierre began his work for the provincale milk company every morning at five o'clock.
2. Without any direction from pierre, Joseph stopped at each house on prince edward street.
3. Jacques, the Supervisor of the company, thought that Pierre should retire after thirty years of work.
4. Jacques didn't know that pierre was visually impaired.
5. Only Joseph, i believe, knew Pierre couldn't see.

Review: Exercise 6 **Capitalizing Proper Nouns and Proper Adjectives**

Rewrite each sentence, correcting any errors in capitalization.

SAMPLE   Montreal is in the canadian province of quebec.
ANSWER   Montreal is in the Canadian province of Quebec.

1. The city is located in Southern Quebec, the province's most fertile region.
2. In 1535 Jacques Cartier of france became the first european explorer to reach present-day montreal.
3. The British captured the city in 1760 during the french and indian war.
4. Today french is the official language of Montreal.
5. Montreal is the largest french-speaking city in the world after Paris.
6. In addition to french, english is spoken in Montreal.
7. The St. lawrence river runs Northeast through quebec, a province of Canada.
8. Two states in new england and two canadian provinces border Quebec on the East.
9. Quebec shares its Southern border with New york and vermont.
10. The National capital of canada is ottawa.

Capitalization

Review: Exercise 7

Proofreading

The following passage is about the artist John Kane, whose work appears below. Rewrite the passage, correcting the errors in spelling, capitalization, grammar, and usage. Add any missing punctuation. There are ten errors.

John Kane

¹Born in scotland, John Kane (1860–1934) immigrated to Pennsylvania with his family when he was nineteen. ²Kane began sketching as a youth, but he couldn't afford to go to Art school.

John Kane, *Across the Strip*, 1929

(continued)

Grammar Review   **485**

Answers: Exercise 7

Proofreading

This proofreading activity provides editing practice with (1) the current or previous units' skills, (2) the **Troubleshooter** errors, and (3) spelling errors. Students should be able to complete the exercise by referring to the units, the **Troubleshooter,** and a dictionary.

	Error (Type of Error)
1.	• Scotland (capitalization of place names)
2.	• art (capitalization; common noun)
3.	• artist (capitalization; common noun) • recognition (spelling)
4.	• Kane's (singluar possessive)
5.	• rise (verb form)
6.	• Two (capitalization of titles)
7.	• Like (capitalization of first word in a sentence) • are (subject-verb agreement) • city's (capitalization; common noun)

Viewing the Art

John Kane, *Across the Strip*, 1929

John Kane's painting *Across the Strip* depicts details of urban life in Pittsburgh along with its steel mills, structures, and natural features. At one time, Kane painted railroad cars for a living. During his lunch hours, he painted his landscapes on the sides of the railroad cars; when he returned to work, he painted them out. Kane's work was first exhibited in 1927 at Carnegie International Exhibition in Pittsburgh. At the age of 67, he became a celebrity. *Across the Strip,* an oil-on-canvas painting, measures 32 1/4 inches by 34 1/2 inches. It is now in the Phillips Collection in Washington, D.C.

Answers: Exercise 8

Mixed Review

April 21, 19—

Dear Lenny,

Since you were absent last week, I thought I would tell you what we did in our history class. We are learning about pyramids. Ms. Nelson said that great civilizations thrived in Mexico a thousand years ago.

Barry asked, "Is it true that some Native Americans built pyramids?"

Anna answered, "At the town of Teotihuacán, people built pyramids dedicated to the sun."

Our teacher added, "In the religious centers of southern Mexico, the Mayan people built pyramids with temples on top. In addition," she continued, "there are other ancient pyramids."

Ms. Nelson then told us about the pyramids in Egypt. The Great Pyramid stands near the Nile River. It is believed to have been built about 2700 B.C. when Pharaoh Khufu reigned. Some pyramids were actually the tombs of Egyptian pharaohs.

Maybe we will still be studying pyramids when you return next week. All of us at West Middle School miss you.

Your pal,
Stan

Close

Ask students to write a paragraph describing the city or town they live in. Remind them to check their capitalization of place names and proper adjectives.

486

Capitalization

³The self-taught Artist finally achieved reckognition at the age of sixty-seven with the exhibition of one of his paintings in Pittsburgh.

⁴Many of Kanes' paintings present detailed images of everyday life in Pittsburgh, where the artist spent much of his life. ⁵In *Across the Strip*, for example, mills and warehouses risen up behind apartment buildings, where clothes are hung out to dry. ⁶A man in a horse-drawn wagon delivers bread on a route similar to that in "A Secret for two." ⁷like Pierre and Joseph, the man and horse is a familiar part of their City's daily life.

Review: Exercise 8

Mixed Review

Rewrite the following letter, capitalizing all necessary words. You will need to capitalize twenty-five letters.

april 21, 2001

dear lenny,

Since you were absent last week, I thought I would tell you what we did in our history class. we are learning about pyramids. ms. nelson said that great civilizations thrived in Mexico a thousand years ago.

Barry asked, "is it true that some native americans built pyramids?"

Anna answered, "at the town of teotihuacán, people built pyramids dedicated to the sun."

Our teacher added, "in the religious centers of southern Mexico, the mayan people built pyramids with temples on top. In addition," she continued, "there are other ancient pyramids."

Ms. Nelson then told us about the pyramids in egypt. The Great Pyramid stands near the nile river. It is believed to have been built about 2700 B.C. when pharaoh khufu reigned. some pyramids were actually the tombs of egyptian pharaohs.

Maybe we will still be studying pyramids when you return next week. All of us at west middle school miss you.

your pal,
stan

Writing Application

Capitalization in Writing

Study the italicized examples of capitalization in this excerpt from Joseph Bruchac's essay "Thanking the Birds." Think about why each is capitalized.

> *One* day 30 years ago, *Swift Eagle,* an *Apache* man, visited some friends on the *Onondaga Indian Reservation* in central *New York. While* he was out walking, he heard sounds of boys playing in the bushes.
>
> *"There's* another one. Shoot it!" said one of the boys.
>
> *When* he pushed through the brush to see what was happening, he found that they had been shooting small birds with a BB gun.

Techniques with Capitalization

Try to apply the rules of capitalization in your own writing, just as Joseph Bruchac has done in his.

❶ Capitalize adjectives that are formed from proper nouns.

INCORRECT VERSION an apache man
BRUCHAC'S VERSION an Apache man

❷ Capitalize the names of specific geographical places.

INCORRECT VERSION the onondaga indian reservation
BRUCHAC'S VERSION the Onondaga Indian Reservation

❸ Do not capitalize adjectives formed from words showing direction or location.

INCORRECT VERSION
Central New York
BRUCHAC'S VERSION
central New York

TIME
For more about proofreading for capitalization errors, see **TIME Facing the Blank Page,** page 98.

Capitalization *(side tab)*

Practice Practice using correct capitalization by revising the following passage on a separate sheet of paper.

today the official languages of canada are english and French. however, most of the people of quebec are French-speaking canadians. Although it was the french explorer champlain who founded quebec, the english captured Quebec City during the french and indian war. They acquired quebec by the Treaty of Paris in 1763. Over the next few decades thousands of british colonists came to canada from the british Isles and the american colonies.

Writing Application **487**

Capitalization in Writing

Encourage students to read the passage in their books silently. Then discuss the italicized words in relation to the Techniques with Capitalization.

Techniques with Capitalization

Discuss the techniques described and ask students to apply them to the letter in Exercise 8 on page 486. They will find examples of proper adjectives (Egyptian pharaohs), place names (Egypt), and direction or location words (southern Mexico).

Practice

The answers to this challenging activity may vary if students have made revisions in addition to correcting errors. Corrections are as follows:

Today . . . Canada . . . English . . . However . . . Quebec . . . Canadians . . . French . . . Champlain . . . Quebec . . . English . . . French and Indian War . . . Quebec . . . British . . . Canada . . . British . . . American

Objectives

- To identify the conventions of punctuation in written works
- To understand the use of end marks, commas, quotation marks, apostrophes, and hyphens and to use them appropriately
- To understand the use of abbreviations and written numbers and to use them appropriately

✔ ASSESSMENT OPTIONS

📁 *Tests with Answer Key and Rubrics*
Unit 19 Pretest, pp. 77–78
Unit 19 Mastery Test, pp. 79–80

💾 *Testmaker*
Unit 19 Pretest
Unit 19 Mastery Test

You may wish to administer the Unit 19 Pretest at this point.

Key to Ability Levels

L1 Level 1 activities are within the basic ability range of students.

L2 Level 2 activities are within the ability range of average students.

L3 Level 3 activities are more challenging activities.

UNIT 19 Punctuation

488

Resource Manager

Planning Resources
- *Lesson Plans*
- *Block Scheduling*

🖥 **Transparencies**
- *Bellringer*
- *Daily Language Practice*
- *Two-Minute Skill Drill*

📁 **Other Print Resources**
- *Grammar and Composition Handbook*

- *Grammar Enrichment*
- *Grammar Practice*
- *Grammar Reteaching*
- *Grammar Workbook*
- *Tests with Answer Key and Rubrics*

📼 **Video**
- *MindJogger Videoquizzes*

💾 **Software**
- *Interactive Grammar and Language Workbook*
- *Language Arts PASS*
- *Presentation Plus!*
- *Testmaker*

🖥 **Web Sites**
- *writerschoice.glencoe.com*

19.1 Using the Period and Other End Marks

Different end marks are used with the different types of sentences. The period is used for declarative and imperative sentences. The question mark is used for interrogative sentences. And the exclamation point is used for exclamatory sentences.

| RULE 1: | Use a period at the end of a declarative sentence. A declarative sentence makes a statement. |

The Wright brothers built the first successful airplane.

They built this pioneering machine at a cost of about $1,000.

| RULE 2: | Use a period at the end of an imperative sentence. An imperative sentence gives a command or makes a request. |

Open your book to the chapter on airplanes. [command]

Please read about the first successful flight. [request]

| RULE 3: | Use a question mark at the end of an interrogative sentence. An interrogative sentence asks a question. |

When did jet planes first begin flying?

Do most jet planes have space for more than a hundred passengers?

| RULE 4: | Use an exclamation point at the end of an exclamatory sentence. An exclamatory sentence expresses strong feeling. |

What a wonderful invention the jet engine was!

How fast jet planes fly!

| RULE 5: | Use an exclamation point at the end of an interjection. An interjection is a word or group of words that expresses strong emotion. |

Wow!   Whew!

My goodness!   Ouch!

Focus

Lesson Overview

Objectives

- To identify periods and other end marks
- To demonstrate control of the use of end marks

Bellringer
Daily Language Activity

When students enter the classroom, have this assignment on the board: *Can you end the following sentence with three different punctuation marks? How does the meaning of the sentence change?*
   You have a gift for me

➤ **See also** *Daily Language Practice*

Motivating Activity

Invite volunteers to read aloud their sentences from the Bellringer activity and to tell which punctuation marks they used.

Teach

☑ Teaching Tip

To reinforce how end marks can change the meaning of a sentence, write this sentence on the board: *She enjoyed that movie.* Ask students to identify the sentence type (declarative), and then have them change it into an interrogative sentence (*Did she enjoy that movie?*) and an exclamatory sentence (*She really enjoyed that movie!*).

Punctuation

Resource Manager

Planning Resources
- *Lesson Plans*

Transparencies
- *Bellringer*
- *Daily Language Practice*

📂 Other Print Resources
- *Grammar and Composition Handbook*
- *Grammar Enrichment*, p. 41
- *Grammar Practice*, p. 41
- *Grammar Reteaching*, p. 42
- *Grammar Workbook*, Lesson 71

Practice and Assess

Answers: Exercise 1

1. . (declarative)
2. ! (exclamatory)
3. ? (interrogative)
4. . (declarative)
5. ! (exclamatory)
6. . (imperative)
7. . (declarative)
8. . (declarative)
9. ! (exclamatory)
10. . (declarative)
11. ? (interrogative)
12. . (declarative)
13. ! (exclamatory)
14. ? (interrogative)
15. ? (interrogative)
16. . (declarative)
17. ? (interrogative)
18. . (declarative)
19. . (imperative)
20. . (declarative)
21. . (declarative)
22. . (declarative)
23. ! (exclamatory)
24. . (declarative)
25. . (imperative)

Additional Resources

📁 *Grammar Practice,* p. 41
📁 *Grammar Reteaching,* p. 42
📁 *Grammar Enrichment,* p. 41

📖 *Grammar Workbook,* Lesson 71

Close

Ask students to imagine how the Wright brothers would react to today's modern flying technology. Have the students write five sentences about the brothers' reactions. The interjection and the four types of sentences presented in the lesson should be represented in the five sentences.

Punctuation

Exercise 1 Using End Marks

Write the correct end mark for each sentence. Then write whether the sentence is *declarative*, *imperative*, *interrogative*, or *exclamatory*.

1. Leonardo da Vinci drew a design of an airplane more than four hundred years ago
2. How imaginative da Vinci was
3. Did the Wright brothers make the first successful airplane flight
4. On December 17, 1903, Orville Wright made the first successful piloted flight in a power-driven airplane
5. What an important day in history it was
6. Please tell me the name of Orville's brother
7. On that day Wilbur Wright also made a successful flight
8. The Wright brothers did not believe airplanes would ever be able to fly at night
9. How wrong they were
10. The Wright brothers were from Dayton, Ohio
11. Why did the brothers begin flying
12. The Wright brothers read about the death of a glider pilot named Otto Lilienthal
13. How that man's work affected them
14. Why did they make their flights in Kitty Hawk, North Carolina
15. Did the Weather Bureau in Washington advise them
16. In 1900 they tested their own glider
17. Did that early glider have good lifting power
18. They received a patent on a glider they made in 1902
19. Describe that machine
20. Later the two brothers built a motor-powered airplane
21. They took experimental flights for several years
22. In 1905 they made 105 flights, totaling only forty-five minutes in the air
23. Imagine that
24. Newspapers began giving longer reports on their flights after that time
25. Don't forget the Wright brothers' important role in history

---

MEETING INDIVIDUAL NEEDS

English Language Learners

Using Question Marks

Deciding when to use the question mark in standard English may be confusing for some nonnative speakers. For example, the question mark is not used with an indirect question: *He asked me whether I was going out.* With a polite request or courtesy question in business letters, the question mark is also usually left out: *Will you* *please send six boxes of computer paper.* Remind Spanish-speaking students, who are accustomed to putting the question mark at both the beginning and end of the sentence, that the mark is used only at the end of a question in English.

19.2 | Using Commas I

Commas can make sentences easier to understand because the commas signal a pause or separation between sentence parts.

RULE 1: Use commas to separate three or more items in a series.

Mary McLeod Bethune served as a teacher, adviser, and administrator.

Bethune lived, studied, and worked in the South.

RULE 2: Use a comma to show a pause after an introductory word.

Yes, she became the first African American woman to head an agency in the United States government.

No, her family had very little money.

RULE 3: Use a comma after two or more prepositional phrases at the beginning of a sentence.

For a number of years, she served as director of the National Youth Administration's Division of Negro Affairs. [two prepositional phrases—*For a number* and *of years*]

You need not use a comma after a single prepositional phrase, but it is not incorrect to do so.

For years she served as President Roosevelt's special adviser on minority affairs. [one prepositional phrase—*For years*]

RULE 4: Use commas to set off words that interrupt the flow of thought in a sentence.

Bethune, as you might imagine, spent her life improving educational opportunities for African Americans.

Mary McLeod Bethune, of course, served as president of the famous Bethune-Cookman College.

RULE 5: Use commas to set off names used in direct address.

Clarisse, did you know that Ms. Bethune opened a school for girls?

Pardon me, Ms. Moeti, when did she open this school?

Read about Bethune-Cookman College in Florida, Derek.

Punctuation

Focus

Lesson Overview

Objectives
- To identify comma use between words in a series, before an introductory word, after prepositional phrases when appropriate, and to set off names or other words that interrupt the flow of a sentence
- To demonstrate the ability to use commas correctly within a sentence

🔔 Bellringer
Daily Language Activity

When students enter the classroom, have this assignment on the board: *Explain the difference between these two sentences:*
  I will divide the pizza into equal pieces for Bobbie, Jo, Lou, Ann, and me.
  I will divide the pizza into equal pieces for Bobbie, Jo, Lou Ann, and me.

✎ **See also** *Daily Language Practice*

Motivating Activity

Invite volunteers to describe the difference between the two sentences in the Bellringer activity. Students should understand that commas can make a difference in the meaning of a sentence.

Teach

☑ Teaching Tip

Ask students to write sentences modeled after the example sentences in the text. Assign the example sentences to individual students. Have the students write the sentences on the board along with an original sentence following the form of the model.

Resource Manager

Planning Resources
- *Lesson Plans*

✎ Transparencies
- *Bellringer*
- *Daily Language Practice*

📂 Other Print Resources
- *Grammar and Composition Handbook*
- *Grammar Enrichment,* p. 43
- *Grammar Practice,* pp. 42–43
- *Grammar Reteaching,* p. 43
- *Grammar Workbook,* Lesson 72

Practice and Assess

Answers: Exercise 2

1. . . . Bethune, we have learned, was . . .
2. . . . a mission school, a seminary, and the . . .
3. . . . the twentieth century, she . . .
4. . . . Coolidge, Hoover, Roosevelt, and . . .
5. From 1935 to 1944, she . . .
6. Mr. Fenster, is . . .
7. Yes, she was, and . . .
8. . . . and, I think, an . . .
9. From 1913 to the present, the . . .
10. correct

Answers: Exercise 3

1. Yes, Mrs. Roosevelt . . . (Rule 2)
2. . . . women, or so I've read, worked . . . (Rule 4)
3. . . . young, poor, and . . . (Rule 1)
4. . . . in 1921, Eleanor . . . (Rule 3)
5. . . . famous, Mr. Branwell, for . . . (Rule 5)

Additional Resources

 *Grammar Practice,* p. 42–43

Grammar Reteaching, p. 43

Grammar Enrichment, p. 43

Grammar Workbook, Lesson 72

Close

Have students choose a famous person or a period in history they have studied. Invite them to think of sentences about this person or historical period. Their sentences should include examples of the comma rules presented in this lesson. Write the students' sentences on the board as they are presented.

Exercise 2 **Using Commas**

Write the following sentences, adding commas where needed. Write *correct* if a sentence needs no commas.

1. Mary McLeod Bethune we have learned was the daughter of enslaved persons.
2. Bethune attended a mission school a seminary and the Moody Bible Institute.
3. In the early part of the twentieth century she opened a girls' school.
4. Bethune served in various capacities for presidents Coolidge Hoover Roosevelt and Truman.
5. From 1935 to 1944 she served as President Franklin Roosevelt's special adviser on minority affairs.
6. Mr. Fenster is it true Bethune was the first African American woman to head a federal agency?
7. Yes she was and she also was awarded the Spingarn Medal.
8. Joel E. Spingarn was a leader of the National Association for the Advancement of Colored People and I think an American literary critic.
9. From 1913 to the present the Spingarn Medal has been awarded to African Americans for outstanding achievement.
10. In 1958 the Spingarn Medal was given to the eight young people who were the first African Americans to attend Little Rock Central High School.

Exercise 3 **Identifying Comma Rules**

Write the following sentences, adding commas where needed. Write whether the commas are needed because of Rule 1, 2, 3, 4, or 5 on page 491.

SAMPLE   Ms. Lamm is it true that Bethune became a friend of Eleanor Roosevelt?

ANSWER   Ms. Lamm, is it true that Bethune became a friend of Eleanor Roosevelt? (Rule 5)

1. Yes Mrs. Roosevelt was a great admirer of Bethune.
2. Both women or so I've read worked hard during World War II.
3. Bethune and Roosevelt worked with people who were young poor and illiterate.
4. After her husband's illness in 1921 Eleanor became active on his behalf.
5. Both Bethune and Roosevelt are famous Mr. Branwell for their noble work.

MEETING INDIVIDUAL NEEDS **English Language Learners**

Using Commas in a Series

Students may be accustomed to using commas differently when writing a language other than English. Spanish, for example, does not use a final comma before the conjunction in a series. Explain that in formal English the comma is used before *and* or *or* in a series to prevent confusion. Pair English language learners with students who are more proficient in English. Ask students to write a few simple sentences using a series of three or more items. For example, *I like apples, oranges, and bananas.* Students can then exchange papers and check each other's use of commas.

19.3 Using Commas II

You need to use commas correctly in compound sentences, after salutations and closings in letters, and to prevent misreading.

RULE 6: Use a comma before *and, or,* or *but* when it joins simple sentences into a compound sentence.

Phillis Wheatley began to write poetry at the age of fourteen, and she became the first important African American poet.

She was born in Africa, but she was enslaved and taken to Boston.

Phillis Wheatley's poems discuss the question of religion, or they treat the issue of slavery.

RULE 7: Use a comma after the salutation of a friendly letter and after the closing of both a friendly letter and a business letter.

Dear Dad,   Your friend,   Yours truly,

RULE 8: Use a comma to prevent misreading.

Instead of one, two friends visited Phillis.

Dear General Washington,

Dear George,

Dear Mr. President,

19.3 Using Commas II **493**

Punctuation

Focus

Lesson Overview

Objectives
- To recognize the function of commas as aids to clarity in writing
- To demonstrate control of the uses of commas in compound sentences, after salutations and closings in letters, and for general clarity in writing

Bellringer
Daily Language Activity

When students enter the classroom, have this assignment on the board: *Add any necessary commas to the following sentence: Phillis Wheatley was a slave and she was also a poet.*

See also *Daily Language Practice*

Motivating Activity

Discuss the sentence in the Bellringer. Did students insert a comma before the conjunction *and* ? Ask them to write two compound sentences of their own and remind them of the proper use of the comma.

Teach

☑ Teaching Tip

Sentence combining is an excellent means for teaching the difference between joining two simple sentences with a comma and a coordinating conjunction and joining a compound predicate with a coordinating conjunction but no comma.

Resource Manager

Planning Resources
- *Lesson Plans*

Transparencies
- *Bellringer*
- *Daily Language Practice*

📂 **Other Print Resources**
- *Grammar and Composition Handbook*
- *Grammar Enrichment,* pp. 44–45
- *Grammar Practice,* p. 44
- *Grammar Reteaching,* p. 44
- *Grammar Workbook,* Lesson 73

Practice and Assess

Answers: Exercise 4

1. . . . ship, and . . .
2. . . . family, and . . .
3. . . . talents, and . . .
4. . . . geography, history, and . . .
5. . . . poets, and . . .
6. . . . teenager, and . . .
7. correct
8. . . . was, I believe, . . .
9. . . . Schofield, . . .
10. . . . London, but . . .

Answers: Exercise 5

1. Dear Phillis,
2. . . . today, and . . .
3. . . . local newspaper, or maybe . . .
4. . . . London, but I . . .
5. . . . one, two people . . .
6. . . . Westminster Abbey, and . . .
7. . . . damage, thank goodness, during . . .
8. . . . rebuilt, and . . .
9. Of course, we . . .
10. . . . friend, *Hannah*

Additional Resources

📁 *Grammar Practice*, p. 44
📁 *Grammar Reteaching*, p. 44
📁 *Grammar Enrichment*, p. 44–45

📖 *Grammar Workbook*, Lesson 73

Close

Ask students to write a letter to Phillis Wheatley or some other important person in history. Tell them to make their letters realistic and to use the correct punctuation for letter writing. They should also include compound sentences and sentences that require commas for clarity.

Punctuation

Exercise 4 ▪ Using Commas

Write the following sentences, adding commas where needed. Write *correct* if a sentence needs no commas.

1. Phillis Wheatley was taken to Boston on a slave ship and there she was sold at a slave auction.
2. She was sold to a wealthy family and this family gave her their name and their religion.
3. The Wheatleys recognized Phillis's great talents and they taught her to read and write.
4. They encouraged her to study geography history and Latin.
5. Phillis read the great English poets and she studied the famous Latin writers.
6. She began writing poetry when she was a teenager and many of her poems were published.
7. A book of her poems was published in London in 1773.
8. The title of the book was I believe *Poems on Various Subjects, Religious and Moral.*
9. Ms. Schofield have you read any of her poems?
10. Wheatley traveled to London but she returned to Boston.

Exercise 5 ▪ Using Commas

Write each numbered item or sentence. Add a comma or commas where needed.

¹Dear Phillis

²I read your poem today and I thought it showed great promise. ³You should send it to the local newspaper or maybe a magazine would publish it. ⁴You'll be able to travel to London but I know you'll want to return to Boston. ⁵Instead of one two people will go to London with you. ⁶I suggest that you see Westminster Abbey and Mr. Garns thinks you should visit the Tower of London while you are there. ⁷These buildings escaped damage thank goodness during London's Great Fire of 1666. ⁸Mr. Garns says that most of the city has been rebuilt and the new buildings are of brick and stone. ⁹Of course we all hope that you have a wonderful trip.

¹⁰Your friend
Hannah

494   Unit 19 Punctuation

MEETING INDIVIDUAL NEEDS

English Language Learners

Using Commas in Compound Sentences

Students may be confused about the comma in compound sentences. Point out that because a compound sentence consists of two simple sentences joined by a coordinating conjunction, a comma must be placed before the conjunction. Compare the sentence *I went to the store* and *bought some dessert* (no comma) with *I went to the store, and I bought some dessert* (comma). In the first sentence, *and* joins a compound predicate; the sentence is simple. In the second sentence, *and* joins simple sentences, making a compound sentence.

19.4 Using Commas III

Several rules for using commas, including those for punctuating dates, addresses, and titles, are a matter of standard usage.

RULE 9: Use commas before and after the year when it is used with both the month and the day. Do not use a comma if only the month and the year or the month and the day are given.

The flight began on June 18, 1983, and lasted six days.

The flight ended in June 1983 and lasted six days.

RULE 10: Use commas before and after the name of a state or a country when it is used with the name of a city. Do not use a comma after the state postal abbreviation followed by a ZIP code.

People came from as far away as Albany, New York, and Guatemala City, Guatemala, to watch the launch.

The address on the envelope was 42 Campus Drive, Stanford, CA 94305.

RULE 11: Use a comma or pair of commas to set off an abbreviated title or degree following a person's name.

The first American woman to participate in a space mission was Sally Ride, Ph.D.

Norman E. Thagard, M.D., accompanied Sally Ride on that memorable mission.

RULE 12: Use a comma or pair of commas to set off *too* when *too* means "also."

Kathy Sullivan, too, is a famous astronaut.

RULE 13: Use a comma or pair of commas to set off a direct quotation.

Claude said, "Sally Ride received her doctor's degree from Stanford University in 1978."

"I think," said Lotoya, "that Kathy Sullivan became the first woman spacewalker in history."

Punctuation

19.4 Using Commas III **495**

Focus

Lesson Overview

Objectives
- To recognize the function of commas when punctuating dates, addresses, and other special purposes
- To demonstrate control of the uses of commas to punctuate dates, addresses, and titles

Bellringer
Daily Language Activity

When students enter the classroom, have this assignment on the board: *Write a sentence that contains your date of birth and the place (city, state, and country) where you were born. Be sure to use commas correctly.*

See also *Daily Language Practice*

Motivating Activity

Discuss the Bellringer activity with students. Ask volunteers to write their sentences on the board. Does the rest of the class agree with the placement of the commas?

Teach

☑ **Teaching Tip**

Numbers other than dates usually have a comma after the digit representing the thousands: *More than 1,500 people came to hear Nelson Mandela's speech.* However, do not use a comma in page or date numbers (except for dates of five figures or more) or after a decimal point: *3500 B.C.; p. 2345; 0.76854; and 35,000 B.C.*

Resource Manager

Planning Resources
- *Lesson Plans*

Transparencies
- *Bellringer*
- *Daily Language Practice*

Other Print Resources
- *Grammar and Composition Handbook*
- *Grammar Enrichment,* pp. 46–47
- *Grammar Practice,* pp. 46–47
- *Grammar Reteaching,* p. 45
- *Grammar Workbook,* Lesson 74

Practice and Assess

Answers: Exercise 6

1. . . . Houston, Texas, arrived . . .
2. . . . postmarked March 19, 1995.
3. It focused attention on Sally Ride, Ph.D.
4. space mission, the . . . *or* . . . space mission, the other astronauts with Ride were Hauck, Fabian, and Crippen.
5. . . . conducted experiments, and they tested . . .
6. correct
7. correct
8. Yes, I think Sally Ride . . .
9. Before her mission in 1983, Sally Ride . . .
10. "It's true," Lee said . . . letter, "that Sally Ride . . ."

Answers: Exercise 7

1. 16 Wallace Avenue
2. Richmond, VA 23203
3. October 4, 2000
4. Dear Monica,
5. On April 6, 2000, my class . . .
6. Alice Perri, M.A., was . . .
7. "With . . . each part," she said, "we . . ."
8. . . . got a part, too.
9. . . . on May 1, 2000, and on May 8, 2000.
10. Your friend, *Deling*

Additional Resources

📁 *Grammar Practice,* p. 46–47
📁 *Grammar Reteaching,* p. 45
📁 *Grammar Enrichment,* p. 46–47

📓 *Grammar Workbook,* Lesson 74

Close

Review the use of commas in this lesson. Then ask students to write a letter to a real or an imaginary person. Students should be attentive both to the way their letters are written and to the placement of commas.

Exercise 6   Using Commas

Write the following sentences, adding commas where needed. Write *correct* if a sentence needs no commas.

1. A letter from a friend in Houston Texas arrived in the mail yesterday.
2. The letter was postmarked March 19 1995.
3. It focused attention on Sally Ride Ph.D.
4. On the June 1983 space mission the other astronauts with Ride were Hauck Fabian and Crippen.
5. Ride and Fabian conducted experiments and they tested the shuttle's remote manipulator arm.
6. They launched a communications satellite for the Indonesian government and one for the Canadian government too.
7. Sally Ride became an astronaut candidate the same year she got her Ph.D. in physics.
8. Yes I think Sally Ride should inspire young women to learn everything they can about math and science.
9. Before her mission in 1983 Sally Ride married a fellow astronaut.
10. "It's true" Lee said in the letter "that Sally Ride is a pioneer and is very brave."

Exercise 7   Using Commas

Write each numbered item or sentence in the following letter. Add a comma or commas where needed.

¹16 Wallace Avenue
²Richmond VA 23203
³October 4 2000

⁴Dear Monica,

⁵On April 6 2000 my class held auditions for a play. ⁶Alice Perri M.A. was our director. ⁷"With two students for each part" she said "we can perform the play twice." ⁸I won a major role, and my friend Sonia got a part too. ⁹We performed the play on May 1 2000 and on May 8 2000.

¹⁰Your friend
Deling

MEETING INDIVIDUAL NEEDS — English Language Learners

Understanding Commas

Students acquiring English may find comma use confusing. You might help them by explaining that in many cases commas separate words or phrases that are not essential to the meaning of the sentence. To show this, write the following sentence on the board: *I, too, am going on the trip.* Tell students you could take the commas, along with the word *too,* out of the sentence and leave the basic meaning of the sentence intact.

19.5 Using Semicolons and Colons

The semicolon and the colon are punctuation marks that separate parts of a sentence that might otherwise be confused.

RULE 1: Use a semicolon to join parts of a compound sentence when a conjunction such as *and, but,* or *or* is not used. Remember that a compound sentence has two or more simple sentences that are joined by a conjunction.

Albert Einstein made many discoveries in science; his theory of relativity changed scientific thought.

Einstein was born in Germany in 1879; he moved to the United States in 1933.

Einstein liked classical music; he played the violin.

RULE 2: Use a colon to introduce a list of items that ends a sentence. Use a phrase such as *these, the following,* or *as follows* before the list.

A list of the greatest scientists in history usually begins with **these** names: Newton and Einstein.

Einstein's relativity theory advanced new ideas about **the following:** time, space, mass, and motion.

Einstein wrote his famous equation **as follows:** $E = mc^2$.

Do not use a colon immediately after a verb or a preposition. Either leave out the colon, or reword the sentence.

Einstein **studied** mathematics, physics, and English.

During his lifetime he lived **in** Germany, Switzerland, and the United States.

RULE 3: Use a colon to separate the hour from the minute when you write the time of day.

Einstein's train left Princeton at 10:15 A.M. and arrived at New York City at 12:33 P.M.

RULE 4: Use a colon after the salutation of a business letter.

Dear Sir or Madam: Dear Mrs. Santiago:

(side tab) Punctuation

Focus

Lesson Overview

Objectives
- To recognize conventions for the use of semicolons and colons
- To demonstrate control of the use of semicolons in compound sentences and the use of colons in lists, the time of day, and salutations for business letters

Bellringer
Daily Language Activity

When students enter the classroom, have this assignment on the board: *Correct these sentences by adding words or punctuation:*
The play will begin promptly at seven everyone must be ready. We still need the following props an alarm clock, a camera, and a trumpet.

 See also *Daily Language Practice*

Motivating Activity

Ask volunteers to tell how they corrected the sentences in the Bellringer activity. Students may suggest making the first item into two sentences, adding the coordinating conjunction *and* or *so,* or using a semicolon. The second sentence requires a colon.

Teach

☑ **Teaching Tip**

Explain to students that a semicolon is part period, part comma, and that it indicates that the reader should pause a little longer, when reading it aloud, than for a comma but not as long as for a period.

Resource Manager

Planning Resources
- *Lesson Plans*

 Transparencies
- *Bellringer*
- *Daily Language Practice*

 Other Print Resources
- *Grammar and Composition Handbook*
- *Grammar Enrichment,* p. 48
- *Grammar Practice,* p. 48
- *Grammar Reteaching,* pp. 46–47
- *Grammar Workbook,* Lesson 77

Practice and Assess

Answers: Exercise 8

1. …thinker; he…
2. correct
3. …light; no object…
4. …Office; this job…
5. …as follows: we…
6. …these inventions: motion…
7. …day; he wrote…
8. 6:45 A.M.
9. … Israel; he…
10. …New Jersey; he…

Answers: Exercise 9

1. Dear Ms. Ntinga:
2. correct
3. I have Glee Club practice at 1:30 P.M. and…
4. …about Einstein's life; I hope you…
5. I bought these books: *The Theory of* …

Additional Resources

📁 *Grammar Practice,* p. 48
📁 *Grammar Reteaching,* p. 46–47
📁 *Grammar Enrichment,* p. 48

📖 *Grammar Workbook,* Lesson 77

Close

Have students look for examples of semi-colons and colons in textbooks or magazine articles to present in class. As each example is presented, ask students to explain why the semicolon or colon was used.

Punctuation

Exercise 8 **Using Semicolons and Colons**

Write each sentence. Add any needed semicolons or colons. Write *correct* if the sentence needs no semicolon or colon added.

1. Albert Einstein was an original thinker he changed our view of the universe.
2. His relativity theory contained new ideas about time, space, mass, motion, and gravitation.
3. Einstein speculated about speeds faster than light no object has yet moved that fast.
4. Einstein worked for seven years at the Swiss Patent Office this job gave him the free time to carry out his scientific investigations.
5. Einstein summarized his relativity theory as follows we can never talk about space without talking about time.
6. Einstein's quantum theory led to the development of these inventions motion pictures with sound, television, and sophisticated security devices.
7. Einstein also thought about the problems of his day he wrote a letter to Franklin Roosevelt about developing the atomic bomb.
8. An atomic bomb was dropped on Hiroshima, Japan, at 645 A.M. on August 6, 1945.
9. In the 1950s Einstein was offered the presidency of the state of Israel he insisted he was not right for this position.
10. Einstein lived the last part of his life in Princeton, New Jersey he considered himself a citizen of the world.

Exercise 9 **Using Semicolons and Colons**

Write each numbered item in the business letter below. Add semicolons or colons where needed.

¹Dear Ms. Ntinga

²I am sorry that I missed your talk on Albert Einstein. ³I have Glee Club practice at 130 P.M. and could not be at the talk. ⁴I am planning to write about Einstein's life I hope you can suggest some good books. ⁵I bought these books *The Theory of Relativity* and *Einstein, Profile of the Man.*

Sincerely,

Jerome

MEETING INDIVIDUAL NEEDS **English Language Learners**

Using Colons to Introduce a List

To help students understand the use of a colon in introducing a list, pair students acquiring English with those who are proficient in the language. Write sentences such as the following on the board: *We bought cereal, milk, and bread. The boys prepared a meal of chicken, salad, and rice. We will study art, science, and history.* Have the paired students work together to change each sentence so that it requires the use of a colon. Encourage students to think of some sentences of their own to demonstrate colon use.

19.6 Using Quotation Marks and Italics

RULE 1: Use quotation marks before and after a direct quotation.

"Sojourner Truth was born enslaved," said Graciela.

RULE 2: Use quotation marks around each part of an interrupted quotation.

"She was," explained Kazuko, "a great fighter against slavery."

RULE 3: Use a comma or commas to separate a phrase such as *he said* from the quotation itself. Place the comma outside opening quotation marks but inside closing quotation marks.

Victoria said, "Sojourner Truth became free in 1828."

"She finally received her freedom under a New York law," Manny added.

RULE 4: Place a period inside closing quotation marks.

Ms. Yu said, "Sojourner Truth preached concern for the welfare of others."

RULE 5: Place a question mark or an exclamation mark inside the quotation marks when it is part of the quotation.

Chi asked, "Did she find jobs for enslaved persons who escaped?"

RULE 6: Place a question mark or an exclamation mark outside the quotation marks when it is part of the entire sentence but not part of the quotation.

Did Ms. Yu say, "Sojourner Truth visited President Lincoln"?

RULE 7: Use quotation marks for the title of a short story, essay, poem, song, magazine or newspaper article, or book chapter.

"The Open Boat" [short story]   "Shenandoah" [song]

RULE 8: Use italics (underlining) to identify the title of a book, play, film, television series, magazine, or newspaper.

The Grapes of Wrath [book]   *National Geographic* [magazine]

19.6 Using Quotation Marks and Italics **499**

Focus

Lesson Overview

Objectives

- To recognize conventions for the use of quotation marks and italics
- To demonstrate control of quotation marks with direct quotations and with the titles of short works
- To demonstrate control of the use of italics in print and the use of underlining to indicate italics when identifying titles of long works

Bellringer
Daily Language Activity

When students enter the classroom, have this assignment on the board: *Describe the difference between these two sentences: Ana asked Ty what he was doing after school. Ana asked, "Ty, what are you doing after school?"*

See also *Daily Language Practice*

Teach

☑ Teaching Tip

To help students understand question marks in quotations, explain that if the quoted sentence itself is a question, the question mark goes inside the quotation marks. (*"Am I late?"*) If the quoted sentence is a statement within a question, the question mark goes outside the quotation marks. (*Who said, "You are late"?*) Ask students to include a famous quotation in a question using correct punctuation. (*Who said, "We have nothing to fear but fear itself"?*)

Resource Manager

Planning Resources
- *Lesson Plans*

Transparencies
- *Bellringer*
- *Daily Language Practice*

📁 **Other Print Resources**
- *Grammar and Composition Handbook*
- *Grammar Enrichment,* p. 49
- *Grammar Practice,* p. 49
- *Grammar Reteaching,* p. 48–49
- *Grammar Workbook,* Lessons 78–79

Practice and Assess

Answers: Exercise 10

1. "The Necklace"
2. "By the Sea"
3. *Newsweek*
4. *A Midsummer Night's Dream*
5. "Women in Sports"
6. *Back to the Future*
7. *Ivanhoe*
8. "Treasures of Lascaux Cave"
9. *Home Improvement*
10. "Self-Reliance"
11. *Hoop Dreams*
12. "Amazing Grace"
13. *New York Times*
14. "Casey at the Bat"
15. "The Morning"

Answers: Exercise 11

1. "Sojourner . . . Baumfree," said Winona.
2. "Sojourner . . . name," said Winona, "when . . . preach."
3. "Don't . . . truth?" asked Maya.
4. "That . . . day," said Mr. Scruggs.
5. "Abolitionists . . . slavery," said Ms. Yu.
6. . . . asked, "What is a sojourner?"
7. . . . replied, "A sojourner is a traveler."
8. . . . say, "Sojourner . . . Washington"?
9. . . . exclaimed, "What . . . was!"
10. "Go to the library," Ms. Yu said, "and . . . Truth."

Additional Resources

📁 *Grammar Practice*, p. 49
📁 *Grammar Reteaching*, p. 48–49
📁 *Grammar Enrichment*, p. 49

📖 *Grammar Workbook*, Lessons 78–79

Close

Have students work in pairs. One partner writes an indirect quotation. (*Carl said that he would be late.*) The other partner changes it into a direct quotation. (*Carl said, "I will be late."*) This partner then returns the paper to the original partner, who checks for proper use of quotation marks.

Punctuation

Exercise 10 — Using Quotation Marks and Italics

Write each of the following titles. Add the necessary quotation marks or underlining for italics.

1. The Necklace (short story)
2. By the Sea (poem)
3. Newsweek (magazine)
4. A Midsummer Night's Dream (play)
5. Women in Sports (newspaper article)
6. Back to the Future (film)
7. Ivanhoe (book)
8. Treasures of Lascaux Cave (magazine article)
9. Home Improvement (television series)
10. Self-Reliance (essay)
11. Hoop Dreams (film)
12. Amazing Grace (song)
13. New York Times (newspaper)
14. Casey at the Bat (poem)
15. The Morning (book chapter)

Exercise 11 — Using Quotation Marks with Other Punctuation

Write each sentence. Add quotation marks and other punctuation marks where needed.

1. Sojourner Truth's real name was Isabella Baumfree said Winona
2. Sojourner Truth changed her name said Winona when she decided to preach.
3. Don't you think her talks and lectures have the ring of truth asked Maya
4. That helped make her one of the best-known American abolitionists of her day said Mr. Scruggs.
5. Abolitionists worked to end slavery said Ms. Yu.
6. Bertha asked What is a sojourner
7. Ms. Yu replied A sojourner is a traveler
8. Did Ms. Yu say Sojourner Truth worked to improve the lives of African Americans living in Washington
9. Bertha exclaimed What a brave woman she was
10. Go to the library Ms. Yu said and find a book about Sojourner Truth

---

MEETING INDIVIDUAL NEEDS

English Language Learners

Using Quotation Marks

Students acquiring English may have difficulty determining which words to enclose in quotation marks in a sentence containing dialogue. Have students work in pairs to write dialogue for a cartoon, writing the words from the cartoon bubble first, enclosing them in quotation marks, and then adding the words indicating the speaker.

19.7 Using Apostrophes and Hyphens

An apostrophe shows possession and points out the missing letters in a contraction. A hyphen divides a word between syllables and joins the parts of compound words.

RULE 1:	Use an apostrophe and an *-s* (*'s*) to form the possessive of a singular noun.
	girl + **'s** = girl**'s** Charles + **'s** = Charles**'s**
RULE 2:	Use an apostrophe and an *-s* (*'s*) to form the possessive of a plural noun that does not end in *-s*.
	women + **'s** = women**'s** mice + **'s** = mice**'s**
RULE 3:	Use an apostrophe alone to form the possessive of a plural noun that ends in *-s*.
	girls + **'s** = girls**'** cities + **'s** = citie**s'**
	Do not use an apostrophe in a possessive pronoun.
	These skates are **hers.** **Theirs** are in the car.
RULE 4:	Use an apostrophe to replace letters that have been omitted in a contraction. A contraction is a word that is made by combining two words into one and leaving out one or more letters.
	it is = it**'s** you + are = you**'re**
RULE 5:	Use a hyphen to show the division of a word at the end of a line. Always divide a word between its syllables.
	With her husband, Pierre, Marie Sklodowska Curie dis-covered radium and polonium.
RULE 6:	Use a hyphen in compound numbers.
	sixty-five pianos forty-two experiments
RULE 7:	Use a hyphen or hyphens in certain compound nouns. Consult a dictionary to be sure.
	great-uncle brother-in-law
	attorney-at-law editor in chief

19.7 Using Apostrophes and Hyphens   **501**

Punctuation

Focus

Lesson Overview

Objectives
• To identify hyphens and to recognize the use of apostrophes in possessives and contractions
• To use apostrophes correctly in singular and plural possessives and to use hyphens when appropriate

Bellringer
Daily Language Activity

When students enter the classroom, have this assignment on the board: *Choose the correct word in the following sentence:*
We learned today that (its, it's) Marie Curie who discovered radium.

See also *Daily Language Practice*

Motivating Activity

Discuss the correct answer in the Bellringer activity. Ask students how they decided which form to use. Then have them write two sentences, one using *it's* and the other using *its*.

Teach

Cross-reference: Hyphens
Tell students that dictionaries usually use hyphens, bullets, or spaces to separate the syllables in each entry word. For instruction and practice with dictionary entries, refer students to Lesson 21.6.

Resource Manager

Planning Resources
• *Lesson Plans*

Transparencies
• *Bellringer*
• *Daily Language Practice*

📁 **Other Print Resources**
• *Grammar and Composition Handbook*
• *Grammar Enrichment*, p. 50
• *Grammar Practice*, p. 50
• *Grammar Reteaching*, p. 50
• *Grammar Workbook*, Lessons 80–81

Practice and Assess

Answers: Exercise 12

1. men's	11. Mrs. Jacobs's
2. child's	12. wolves'
3. Lois's	13. day's
4. Rossi's	14. Ford's
5. oxen's	15. sheep's
6. horses'	16. Mr. Sanchez's
7. countries'	17. reefs'
8. babies'	18. girls'
9. pig's	19. his
10. house's	20. teams'

Answers: Exercise 13

1. correct	9. Curie's, son-in-law
2. correct	
3. correct	10. daughter's
4. Curies'	11. Curie's
5. didn't	12. It's
6. twenty-five	13. correct
7. correct	14. Curie's, fifty-two
8. Curie's	15. Mayer's

Additional Resources

📁 *Grammar Practice*, p. 50
📁 *Grammar Reteaching*, p. 50
📁 *Grammar Enrichment*, p. 50

📕 *Grammar Workbook*, Lessons 80–81

Close

Discuss Exercise 13 with students, especially any parts of the exercise that they found difficult.

Punctuation

Exercise 12 · Using the Possessive Form

Write the possessive form of each word or group of words that follows. Remember to use an apostrophe and an *s* (*'s*) or an apostrophe alone (*'*).

1. men	6. horses	11. Mrs. Jacobs	16. Mr. Sanchez
2. child	7. countries	12. wolves	17. reefs
3. Lois	8. babies	13. day	18. girls
4. Ms. Marie Rossi	9. pig	14. President Ford	19. his
5. oxen	10. house	15. sheep	20. teams

Exercise 13 Using Apostrophes and Hyphens

Write each sentence. Add apostrophes and hyphens where needed. Write *correct* if a sentence needs no changes.

1. Marie and Pierre Curie discovered radium in 1898.
2. The daughter of teachers, Marie studied chemistry and physics in Paris.
3. In 1895 Pierre Curie became her husband.
4. The Curies interest in the discovery of radioactivity led to their discovery of radium.
5. The Curies, however, didnt discover radium until two years later.
6. From more than twenty five tons of uranium ore, they isolated radium and polonium.
7. For their work with radium and polonium, the Curies were awarded the Nobel Prize for physics in 1903.
8. Marie Curies work with the chemical properties of radium and polonium won her a second Nobel Prize in 1911.
9. Madame Curies daughter Irene and son in law Frederic Joliot also won a Nobel Prize for chemistry.
10. In 1934 Marie Curie died of leukemia, the same disease that took her daughters life twenty years later.
11. Eve Curies biography of her famous mother has been published in more than twenty languages.
12. Its amazing to think of how much the Curies accomplished.
13. In 1963 Maria Goeppert Mayer became the second woman ever to win a Nobel Prize in physics.
14. Her award followed Marie Curies second Nobel Prize by fifty two years.
15. Goeppert Mayers husband, Joseph E. Mayer, was a chemist.

MEETING INDIVIDUAL NEEDS

English Language Learners

Using Possessive Apostrophes

The possessive apostrophe may puzzle students whose first language is not English, because many languages do not have a possessive form of the noun. Instead, they use a phrase with the preposition *of* to show possession.

For example, the English language allows the use of *the building's designer* (possessive noun) or *the designer of the building* (possessive phrase). Some students learning English may find the possessive phrase easier to use.

19.8 Using Abbreviations

| RULE 1: | Abbreviate the titles *Mr., Mrs., Ms.,* and *Dr.* before a person's name. Also abbreviate the professional or academic degrees that follow a person's name, as well as the titles *Jr.* and *Sr.* |

Mr. Ed Hall **Jr.**   Henry Wong, **M.D.**   **Dr.** Ann Chu

Juan Diaz, **Ph.D.**   **Ms.** Ava Danko, **M.F.A.**

| RULE 2: | Use all capital letters and no periods for abbreviations that are pronounced letter by letter or as words. Exceptions are *U.S.* and *Washington, D.C.,* which do use periods. |

NASA National Aeronautics and Space Administration

MVP most valuable player

| RULE 3: | Use the abbreviations A.M. (*ante meridiem,* "before noon") and P.M. (*post meridiem,* "after noon") for exact times. For dates use B.C. (before Christ) and, sometimes, A.D. (*anno Domini,* "in the year of the Lord," after Christ). |

6:15 **A.M.**   5:30 **P.M.**   20 **B.C.**   **A.D.** 476

| RULE 4: | Abbreviate calendar items only in charts and lists. |

Mon.   Wed.   Thurs.   Jan.   Apr.   Aug.   Nov.

| RULE 5: | In scientific writing, abbreviate units of measure. Use periods with abbreviations of English units but not of metric units. |

inch(es) **in.**   foot (feet) **ft.**   gram(s) **g**   liter(s) **l**

| RULE 6: | On envelopes abbreviate the words that refer to streets in street names. Spell them out everywhere else. |

Street **St.**   Avenue **Ave.**   Road **Rd.**   Court **Ct.**

We live at the corner of Polaris **Avenue** and Maple **Court.**

| RULE 7: | On envelopes use state postal service abbreviations for the names of states. Everywhere else, spell out state names. |

Indiana **IN**   Arizona **AZ**   Alabama **AL**   Delaware **DE**

Maryland **MD**   Georgia **GA**   Florida **FL**   California **CA**

Focus

Lesson Overview

Objectives

- To recognize common abbreviations
- To demonstrate control of the use of abbreviations, including those for personal titles, academic degrees, and addresses

Bellringer
Daily Language Activity

When students enter the classroom, have this assignment on the board: *Rewrite the following sentences, spelling out the abbreviations:*

Geo. Washington was the first pres. of our country. Gen. Washington's army crossed the DE River and defeated the British in NJ.

See also *Daily Language Practice*

Teach

☑ Teaching Tip

Explain to students that names of organizations—government agencies (CIA), networks (CBS), professional organizations (AMA), trade unions (AFL-CIO)—usually do not have periods with their abbreviations.

☑ Grammar Tip

Tell students that in most formal writing *United States* is spelled out. However, the abbreviation U.S. may be used in informal writing as an adjective: *U.S. government.*

Punctuation

Resource Manager

Planning Resources
- *Lesson Plans*

Transparencies
- *Bellringer*
- *Daily Language Practice*
- *Two-Minute Skill Drill*

📁 **Other Print Resources**
- *Grammar and Composition Handbook*
- *Grammar Enrichment,* p. 51
- *Grammar Practice,* p. 51
- *Grammar Reteaching,* p. 51
- *Grammar Workbook,* Lessons 82–83

Teach

Two-Minute Skill Drill

List these words on the board. Have students supply the correct abbreviations.

Illinois	ounces
Captain	Saint
Mount	Associated Press

☞ **See also** *Two-Minute Skill Drill Transparencies, 19.8*

Practice and Assess

Answers: Exercise 14

1. Mr.	11. Fri.
2. B.C.	12. in.
3. Mar.	13. FL (with ZIP code)
4. Jr.	14. Mr.
5. Ct.	15. Sept.
6. Sun.	16. CA (with ZIP code)
7. A.D.	17. IRS
8. St.	18. ft.
9. l.	19. Rd.
10. FBI	20. Jan.

Answers: Exercise 15

1. Rep.	6. Jr.
2. Dr.	7. Dr.
3. NOW	8. B.C., A.D.
4. Sen.	9. IN
5. A.M., P.M.	10. Mr.

Additional Resources

🗀 *Grammar Practice,* p. 51
🗀 *Grammar Reteaching,* p. 51
🗀 *Grammar Enrichment,* p. 51

📖 *Grammar Workbook,* Lessons 82–83

Close

Have students write a brief essay about a famous person. They should use at least two abbreviations.

504

Punctuation

Exercise 14 — Using Abbreviations

Write the correct abbreviation for each underlined item.

1. <u>Mister</u> Dean Paxton
2. 4000 <u>before Christ</u>
3. <u>March</u> 2, 1988
4. Hugh Hunt <u>Junior</u>
5. 43 Palm <u>Court</u>
6. <u>Sunday</u>
7. <u>anno Domini</u> 63
8. 456 Laguna <u>Street</u>
9. 8 <u>liters</u>
10. <u>Federal Bureau of Investigation</u>
11. <u>Friday</u>
12. 16 <u>inches</u>
13. Tampa, <u>Florida</u>
14. <u>Mister</u> Harold Wong
15. <u>September</u>
16. San Francisco, <u>California</u>
17. <u>Internal Revenue Service</u>
18. 6 <u>feet</u>
19. 109 Van Dyke <u>Road</u>
20. <u>January</u>

Exercise 15 — Using Abbreviations

Write the correct abbreviation for each underlined item in the following sentences.

1. <u>Representative</u> Mari Ramos plans to speak about Elizabeth Blackwell.
2. <u>Doctor</u> Blackwell received her medical degree in 1849 from a college in Geneva, New York.
3. My <u>National Organization for Women</u> chapter will honor another Blackwell; Antoinette Brown Blackwell was the first ordained woman minister.
4. The first woman elected to the United States Senate was <u>Senator</u> Margaret Chase Smith from Maine.
5. The museum director presented a seminar on ancient Rome from 11:45 <u>in the morning</u> until 1:30 <u>in the afternoon</u>.
6. Juan Bosch <u>Junior</u> is known for giving interesting and lively seminars on various topics.
7. The museum is located at 1680 Sequoia <u>Drive</u>.
8. We learned that the first Roman emperor, Augustus, ruled from 27 <u>before Christ</u> to <u>anno Domini</u> 14.
9. Write to the Organization of American Historians at 112 North Bryan Street, Bloomington, <u>Indiana</u> 47401.
10. If you call, ask for <u>Mister</u> Bosch.

Enrichment and Extension

Using B.C. and A.D.

Have students look in a history book to see how the abbreviations B.C. and A.D. are used. Do they appear before or after the date? The answer may surprise students: B.C. appears after the date (30 B.C.), and A.D. appears before the date (A.D. 30).

19.9 Writing Numbers

In charts and tables, you always write numbers as figures. However, in ordinary sentences, you sometimes spell out numbers and sometimes write them as numerals.

RULE 1:	Spell out numbers that you can write in one or two words.

Jackie Robinson helped the Dodgers win **six** pennants.

RULE 2:	Use numerals for numbers of more than two words.

The field at Dodger Stadium is **330** feet down the left-field line.

RULE 3:	Spell out any number that begins a sentence or reword the sentence so that it does not begin with a number.

Fifty-five thousand fans turned out on opening day.

RULE 4:	Write a very large number in numerals followed by the word *million* or *billion*.

In 1991 major league baseball attracted more than **56 million** fans.

RULE 5:	If related numbers appear in the same sentence, use all numerals even though you might spell out one of the numbers if it appeared alone.

In 1953 the Dodgers won **105** games and lost **49.**

RULE 6:	Spell out ordinal numbers (such as *first, second,* and *third*).

Jackie Robinson was the **first** African American to play in the majors.

RULE 7:	Use words to express the time of day unless you are writing the exact time with the abbreviation A.M. or P.M.

Today's baseball game began at **two o'clock.**

Work ended at **5:15 P.M.**

RULE 8:	Use numerals to express dates, house and street numbers, apartment and room numbers, telephone numbers, page numbers, amounts of money of more than two words, and percentages. Write out the word *percent.*

May **16, 1865**   **241** Bryant St.   Apartment **3**G   **50 percent**

Punctuation

Focus

Lesson Overview

Objectives
- To recognize the conventions for the use of numerals and spelled-out numbers
- To use numerals and spelled-out words in writing

Bellringer
Daily Language Activity

When students enter the classroom, have this assignment on the board: *Study the passage below. Explain why each number is either spelled out or expressed as a numeral.*

> When I was seventeen, Dad let me enlist as a mess boy in the U.S. Coast Guard . . . By 1949 the Coast Guard had made me its first "journalist"; finally, . . . I retired at the age of thirty-seven, determined to make a full-time career of writing . . .
>
> —Alex Haley, *My Furthest-Back Person—"The African"*

See also *Daily Language Practice*

Teach

A Vocabulary Link

Call students' attention to Rule 6. Explain that the word *ordinal* comes from the Latin *ordo,* meaning "order." Ordinal numbers— *third, fourth,* and so on—indicate order, or position in a series.

Resource Manager

Planning Resources
- *Lesson Plans*

Transparencies
- *Bellringer*
- *Daily Language Practice*

Other Print Resources
- *Grammar and Composition Handbook*
- *Grammar Enrichment,* p. 52
- *Grammar Practice,* p. 52
- *Grammar Reteaching,* p. 52
- *Grammar Workbook,* Lessons 84–85

Teach

☑ **Teaching Tip**

Summarize for students as follows: Spell out one- and two-digit numbers (*zero* to *ninety-nine*). Spell out large numbers ending in *hundred, thousand, million,* or *billion* if they can be written in two words—for example, *eight hundred, twelve billion.* Express other numbers ending in *million* or *billion* as a combination of numerals and words—*53 million, 100 billion.* Spell out fractions (*two-thirds*), except in scientific usage.

Practice and Assess

Answers: Exercise 16

1.	correct	11.	first; $11,200
2.	12:30 P.M.	12.	one million
3.	30 percent	13.	twenty
4.	1947	14.	1948; 1971
5.	First	15.	755
6.	second	16.	Second
7.	correct	17.	correct
8.	three; seventh	18.	four; four
9.	tenth	19.	240
10.	54	20.	Twenty-three

Additional Resources

📁 *Grammar Practice,* p. 52
📁 *Grammar Reteaching,* p. 52
📁 *Grammar Enrichment,* p. 52

📖 *Grammar Workbook,* Lessons 84–85

Close

Invite students to choose their favorite athlete and to discuss their choice in a paragraph. Ask them to use at least three numbers correctly.

Punctuation

Exercise 16   **Writing Numbers**

Use the correct form for writing numbers in the following sentences. Write *correct* if the sentence needs no changes.

1. In the 1930s, many baseball games began at three o'clock in the afternoon.
2. Some World Series games began at twelve thirty P.M.
3. A good batter hits safely thirty percent of the time.
4. Jackie Robinson entered major league baseball in nineteen hundred forty-seven.
5. Robinson was born at the end of the 1st World War.
6. Later he gained fame as an all-star 2nd baseman for the Brooklyn Dodgers.
7. Robinson helped the Dodgers win the World Series for the first time in 1955.
8. In that World Series, each team won 3 times before the Dodgers won an exciting 7th game.
9. Robinson retired from baseball after his 10th season.
10. In his career, Robinson hit 273 doubles, 137 home runs, and fifty-four triples.
11. In Robinson's 1st season in the majors, the average salary was eleven thousand two hundred dollars.
12. In 1992 the average salary for major leaguers was more than 1,000,000 dollars.
13. Satchel Paige was a star pitcher in the Negro baseball leagues for more than 20 years.
14. Paige entered the major leagues in nineteen hundred forty-eight and was elected to the National Baseball Hall of Fame in nineteen hundred seventy-one.
15. Hank Aaron broke Babe Ruth's home-run record and hit a total of seven hundred fifty-five home runs in his career.
16. During the 2nd World War, many people attended women's-league baseball games.
17. A film about the women's leagues, titled *A League of Their Own,* was made in 1992.
18. Willie Mays led the National League in stolen bases 4 times and in home runs 4 times.
19. In 1961 the New York Yankees hit a record two hundred forty home runs.
20. 23 teams played in the National League between 1876 and 1900.

Real World Connection

Spelling Out Numbers

Give students some practice in spelling out numbers by reading aloud several sentences that include numbers in numerical form. Have students pair up to decide together which numbers to spell out and which to use figures for. Partners can explain to each other which rule they think applies to each case. Then pairs can exchange papers and check each other's answers.

UNIT 19 Grammar Review

PUNCTUATION

Harriet Tubman: The Moses of Her People by Langston Hughes tells about the African American woman who escaped from slavery and then helped free hundreds of other enslaved people. The following excerpt from the biographical sketch describes Tubman's activities during the Civil War. The passage is annotated to show some of the rules of punctuation covered in this unit.

Literature Model

from Harriet Tubman:
The Moses of Her People
by Langston Hughes

Harriet Tubman's war activities were amazing. She served under General Stevens at Beaufort, South Carolina. She was sent to Florida to nurse those ill of dysentery, small pox, and yellow fever. She was with Colonel Robert Gould Shaw at Fort Wagner. She organized a group of nine Negro scouts and river pilots and, with Colonel Montgomery, led a Union raiding contingent of three gunboats and about 150 Negro troops up the Combahee River. As reported by the Boston *Commonwealth,* for July 10, 1863, they "under the guidance of a black woman, dashed into the enemy's country, struck a bold and effective blow, destroying millions of dollars worth of commissary stores, cotton and lordly dwellings, and striking terror into the heart of rebeldom, brought off near 800 slaves and thousands of dollars worth of property."

> **Apostrophe to show possession**

> **Comma before a state name when used with a city name**

> **Comma to separate items in a series**

> **Italics for the title of a newspaper**

> **Period inside closing quotation marks**

Punctuation

Grammar Review   **507**

Grammar Review

Teach

About the Literature

Explain that the review contains a passage from Langston Hughes's essay about Harriet Tubman, followed by exercises on related topics. Discuss the setting and mood of the passage as well as the character of Harriet Tubman. Then ask students to read the annotations and to observe how following the rules of punctuation helps make the passage clear and coherent.

Linking Grammar and Literature

☑ **TeachingTip**

Dialogue is often used to develop character in literature. Discuss what part punctuation marks play in written dialogue. (Quotation marks set off the words of each speaker.) How does the reader know that a new person is speaking? (Quotation marks close the first speaker's words, a new paragraph is started, and new quotation marks signal the words of the second speaker.)

Critical Thinking

Ask students to think about why the essay has the subtitle *"The Moses of Her People."* What did Harriet Tubman have in common with Moses? Some students may know that Moses led his people—the Jews—out of bondage in Egypt and into the Promised Land of Canaan.

Resource Manager

Planning Resources
• *Lesson Plans*

📂 Other Print Resources
• *Grammar and Composition Handbook*
• *Grammar Workbook,* Lessons 71–85; Unit 12 Review; Cumulative Review: Units 1–12

✔ ASSESSMENT OPTIONS

📂 *Tests with Answer Key and Rubrics*
Unit 19 Mastery Test, pp. 79–80

💾 *Testmaker*
Unit 19 Mastery Test

Practice and Assess

Answers: Exercise 1

1. period, declarative
2. question mark, interrogative
3. exclamation point, exclamatory
4. period, imperative
5. period, declarative

Answers: Exercise 2

1. … Montgomery, and …
2. … woman,
3. … houses, provisions, and cotton.
4. … July 10, 1863.
5. Yes, Tubman …
6. … her, you may be surprised to learn, when …
7. … Auburn, New York, and … to live there too.
8. Ms. Buchman, do …
9. … in the war, Tubman …
10. … in Auburn, New York, and …

Review: Exercise 1 **Using End Marks**

Write the correct end mark for each sentence, and then write whether the sentence is *declarative*, *imperative*, *interrogative*, or *exclamatory*.

1. Harriet Tubman was born enslaved in Maryland
2. Why did she serve in the Union Army
3. What an amazing woman she was
4. Read about her heroic actions in Hughes's book
5. Tubman worked in the fields before escaping to freedom in 1849

Review: Exercise 2 **Using Commas**

Rewrite each sentence, inserting commas as needed.

SAMPLE   During the Civil War Harriet Tubman served as a nurse a scout and a spy.

ANSWER   During the Civil War, Harriet Tubman served as a nurse, a scout, and a spy.

1. Tubman served with Colonel Montgomery and she helped him lead a raid on enemy territory.
2. With the help of an African American woman the troops made a successful raid.
3. During the raid Tubman helped destroy houses provisions and cotton.
4. The *Commonwealth* reported her heroic actions on July 10 1863.
5. Yes Tubman was seen as an extraordinary woman even while she was alive.
6. Harriet's husband discouraged her you may be surprised to learn when she wanted to escape to freedom.
7. Harriet settled in Auburn New York and she brought her parents to live there too.
8. Ms. Buchman do you know how many enslaved persons she helped escape?
9. During one military campaign in the war Tubman helped free more than 750 enslaved people.
10. After the war, Tubman helped African Americans by establishing a home for the elderly and needy in Auburn New York and by raising money for schools.

Review: Exercise 3 — Using Semicolons and Colons

Rewrite each sentence, inserting semicolons and colons as needed. Write *correct* if the sentence needs no semicolons or colons.

1. Alexander Graham Bell invented the telephone he received the patent for his invention in 1876.
2. I admire Henry Fonda's performance in the following film *The Story of Alexander Graham Bell.*
3. Thomas Edison was a great inventor some of his inventions include the phonograph, the electric lightbulb, the carbon telephone transmitter, and a duplicating machine.
4. I'll pick you up at 315 P.M. to visit Edison's research laboratory in West Orange.
5. Tourists can see Bell's home in Nova Scotia and tour Edison's home in Florida.

Review: Exercise 4 — Using Quotation Marks and Italics

Rewrite each sentence, inserting quotation marks and underlining for italics as needed.

1. Rachel Carson was an artist, a poet, a scientist, an author, and a reformer, replied Ms. Erlich.
2. The journalist Eric Sevareid compared her to Harriet Beecher Stowe, Mr. Santiago added.
3. Sevareid said that Carson's book Silent Spring sparked a war against pesticides just as Stowe's book Uncle Tom's Cabin helped start the Civil War.
4. A New York Times article called Silent Spring Is Now Noisy Summer stirred great interest across the country, and other newspapers picked up the story.
5. In response to the excitement, Rachel Carson said, As you listen to the present controversy about pesticides, I recommend that you ask yourself who speaks and why.

Answers: Exercise 3

1. … telephone; he …
2. … film: *The Story* …
3. … inventor; some …
4. … 3:15 P.M. …
5. correct

Answers: Exercise 4

1. "Rachel Carson was an artist, a poet, a scientist, an author, and a reformer," replied Ms. Erlich.
2. "The journalist Eric Sevareid compared her to Harriet Beecher Stowe," Mr. Santiago added.
3. Sevareid said that Carson's book <u>Silent Spring</u> sparked a war against pesticides just as Stowe's book <u>Uncle</u> <u>Tom's</u> <u>Cabin</u> helped start the Civil War.
4. A <u>New</u> <u>York</u> <u>Times</u> article called *"Silent Spring* Is Now Noisy Summer" stirred great interest across the country, and other newspapers picked up the story.
5. In response to the excitement, Rachel Carson said, "As you listen to the present controversy about pesticides, I recommend that you ask yourself who speaks and why."

Punctuation

Answers: Exercise 5

1. … Booker T. Washington's …
2. … twenty-five …
3. correct
4. It's … Washington's …
5. … African Americans' …

Answers: Exercise 6

1. … three hundred …
2. Six … Alabama.
3. … 1901.
4. … fifty-six …
5. On September 18, … Georgia
6. … twenty …
7. … first …
8. … 54 percent …
9. … first …
10. … March 31 …

Punctuation

Review: Exercise 5　Using Apostrophes and Hyphens

Rewrite each sentence, inserting apostrophes and hyphens as needed. Write *correct* if a sentence needs no apostrophes or hyphens.

1. Probably Booker T. Washingtons greatest contribution was founding the Tuskegee Institute, a vocational school for African Americans.
2. Washington opened the school when he was twenty five years old.
3. Washington advised President Theodore Roosevelt and President William H. Taft on their racial policies.
4. Its not surprising that W. E. B. Du Bois disagreed with some of Washingtons views on civil rights.
5. Theirs was a disagreement about different ways to achieve a similar end: the improvement of African Americans lives.

Review: Exercise 6　Using Abbreviations and Numbers

Rewrite each sentence, correcting the errors in abbreviations and numbers.

1. In 1872, when he was sixteen, Washington traveled 300 miles to enter an industrial school for African Americans—Hampton Institute.
2. 6 years after he graduated from Hampton, Washington founded Tuskegee Institute in Tuskegee, AL.
3. Washington told about his rise from slavery to national prominence in *Up from Slavery,* published in nineteen hundred one.
4. The autobiography was reprinted 56 years after Washington died.
5. On September eighteenth, 1895, Washington made a speech before a large crowd at the Cotton Exposition in Atlanta, GA.
6. He spoke for less than 20 minutes, explaining his theory that African Americans could accept segregation in exchange for economic advancement.
7. The speech was widely quoted and was the 1st event to make Washington a national figure and adviser to presidents.
8. Today fifty-four percent of the students at Tuskegee are female.
9. The school 1st looks for students with outstanding records.
10. Applications received by March thirty-one are given priority.

Review: Exercise 7 — Using End Marks, Commas, Semicolons, and Colons

Rewrite each sentence, inserting end marks, commas, semicolons, and colons as needed.

SAMPLE By overplanting cotton year after year southern plantation owners ruined their land George Washington Carver helped bring the land back to life

ANSWER By overplanting cotton year after year, southern plantation owners ruined their land; George Washington Carver helped bring the land back to life.

1. Carver's radical ideas included rotating these crops peanuts soybeans and sweet potatoes
2. Carver's innovations helped restore the land they also helped diversify the South's economy
3. Did you know that he discovered more than three hundred uses for the peanut
4. These uses included the following a milk substitute printer's ink and face powder
5. Yes he discovered more than one hundred uses for the sweet potato too
6. Carver was born enslaved in 1861 on a farm near Diamond Missouri
7. Carver faced many obstacles to getting an education but he finally graduated from Iowa State Agricultural College in 1894
8. In 1896 with his master's degree behind him Carver joined the faculty at Tuskegee Institute in Alabama
9. Carver put his laboratory onto a mule-driven wagon and his traveling exhibit helped farmers in Alabama and other states
10. Carolyn do you plan to visit the George Washington Carver National Monument after you graduate on June 6 2001

Review: Exercise 8 — Using Correct Punctuation in a Letter

To request information about what Tuskegee Institute is like today, write a sample business letter to Suite 101, Old Administration Building, Tuskegee, AL 36088. Punctuate your letter with end marks, commas, semicolons, and colons as needed. For a model letter, turn to pages 496 and 498.

Grammar Review **511**

Answers: Exercise 7

1. . . . these crops: peanuts, soybeans, and sweet potatoes.
2. . . . the land; they also helped diversify the South's economy.
3. . . . uses for the peanut?
4. . . . the following: a milk substitute, printer's ink, and face powder.
5. Yes, he discovered more than one hundred uses for the sweet potato too.
6. Carver was born enslaved in 1861 on a farm near Diamond, Missouri.
7. . . . education, but he finally graduated from Iowa State Agricultural College in 1894.
8. In 1896, with his master's degree behind him, Carver joined the faculty at Tuskegee Institute in Alabama.
9. . . . mule-driven wagon, and his traveling exhibit helped farmers in Alabama and other states.
10. Carolyn, do you . . . after you graduate on June 6, 2001?

Answers: Exercise 8

Answers will vary, but a sample letter is given below.

[student's street address]
[student's city and state]
[date]

Tuskegee Institute
Suite 101
Old Administration Building
Tuskegee, AL 36088
November 11, 2004

Dear Sir or Madam:

I am thinking of applying for admission to Tuskegee on September 1, 2005.

Is Tuskegee still a leading university in agricultural research? Soil erosion is one of my special interests; crop rotation is another. I would like to request information about your classes in these subjects, and I would like information about campus life too.

Yours truly,
[name]

Answers: Exercise 9

1. Du Bois's other books include <u>Black Reconstruction in America</u> and <u>The Autobiography of W. E. B. Du Bois</u>.
2. "I heard he was the first African American to receive a doctorate from Harvard University," said Jarell.
3. "Du Bois was dissatisfied with the progress of race relations, and he moved to Ghana in Africa as a result," said the history professor.
4. Du Bois helped found the National Association for the Advancement of Colored People in 1909, and he was editor of its magazine, <u>The Crisis</u>.
5. For information on current activities, Amanda suggested that we write to the NAACP's national headquarters at this address: 4805 Mt. Hope Drive, Baltimore, MD 21215.

Answers: Exercise 10

1. … twenty-three …
2. … Supreme Court's …
3. … four …
4. … first …
5. … Maryland …

Review: Exercise 9 **Using Commas, Quotation Marks, Italics, and Apostrophes**

Rewrite each sentence, inserting commas, quotation marks, italics (underlining), and apostrophes as needed.

SAMPLE Mr. Garns answered Du Bois wrote about his disagreements with Booker T. Washington in his book The Souls of Black Folk.

ANSWER Mr. Garns answered, "Du Bois wrote about his disagreements with Booker T. Washington in his book *The Souls of Black Folk.*"

1. Du Boiss other books include Black Reconstruction in America and The Autobiography of W. E. B. Du Bois.
2. I heard he was the first African American to receive a doctorate from Harvard University said Jarell.
3. Du Bois was dissatisfied with the progress of race relations and he moved to Ghana in Africa as a result said the history professor.
4. Du Bois helped found the National Association for the Advancement of Colored People in 1909 and he was editor of its magazine The Crisis.
5. For information on current activities Amanda suggested that we write to the NAACPs national headquarters at this address: 4805 Mt. Hope Drive Baltimore MD 21215

Review: Exercise 10 **Using Apostrophes, Hyphens, Abbreviations, and Numbers**

Rewrite each sentence, inserting apostrophes and hyphens as needed and correcting errors in abbreviations and numbers.

1. Thurgood Marshall was chief counsel for the NAACP for twenty three years.
2. As counsel he presented the argument that resulted in the Supreme Courts 1954 decision to end segregation in public schools.
3. For 4 years, he was a United States Appeals Court judge.
4. In 1967 he became the 1st African American to sit on the Supreme Court of the United States.
5. Marshall was born in Baltimore, MD, in 1908.

Review: Exercise 11

Proofreading

The following passage is about African American artist Aaron Douglas, whose work appears below. Rewrite the passage, correcting the errors in spelling, capitalization, grammar, and usage. Add any missing punctuation. There are 10 errors.

Aaron Douglas

[1]Aaron Douglas (1899–1979) is 1 of the best-known artists of the Harlem Renaissance movement of the 1920s. [2]Many African american

Aaron Douglas, *Aspiration*, 1936

(continued)

Answers: Exercise 11

Proofreading

This proofreading activity provides editing practice with (1) the current or previous units' skills, (2) **Troubleshooter** errors, and (3) spelling errors. Students should be able to complete the exercise by referring to the units, the **Troubleshooter**, and a dictionary.

	Error (Type of Error)
1.	• one (numbers)
2.	• American (proper adjective)
	• artists (plural noun)
3.	• Douglas's (singular possessive)
	• expressed (spelling)
4.	• sculpture. (end punctuation)
5.	• represent (spelling)
6.	• past, (comma after two introductory prepositional phrases)
	• look (subject-verb agreement)
7.	• following: (colon before a list)

Viewing the Art

Aaron Douglas, *Aspiration*, 1936

This painting symbolizes African Americans' struggle for full freedom. Ask students to discuss the image in the painting and how it represents this struggle. (The figures have their backs to the past and are looking toward the future, represented by the city in the background; note the globe, the book, and the builder's tools.)

The 60-by-60-inch oil painting is part of the Evans-Tibbs/Thurlough Tibbs Collection in Washington, D.C.

Practice and Assess

Answers: Exercise 5

Answers will vary, but some suggestions are given below.

1. Elephants in the wild normally bathe themselves in rivers.
2. Elephant baths at the zoo are fun for the keepers and the elephants.
3. Elephants in the wild live in herds, or social groups.
4. Hay protects the elephants from sunburn.
5. Before the baths, the veterinarians check the elephants' backs.
6. The keeper sprays water on the elephants' foreheads and feet.
7. The elephants' backs are soaked with green oil soap and carefully scrubbed with brushes.
8. Scrapes on the elephants' backs are treated with soothing salve.
9. In the last part of the bath, the elephants' feet are examined for pebbles and other irritants.
10. The keeper has the special ankus stick nearby at all times as a sign to the elephants of authority.

Answers: Exercise 6

Answers will vary, but some suggestions are given below.

One of the Washington Zoo's most colorful elephants is named Shanthi. Shanthi was rescued and raised with 21 other elephants in an elephant orphanage. At the age of one, she was sent from Sri Lanka to Washington as a gift to the children of the United States. Her keeper, Sam, came to the United States with Shanthi and slept near his young charge on a cot in the Elephant House.

Before going back to Sri Lanka, Sam gave the zoo a tape recording of his special commands for Shanthi. According to Sam, if the zookeepers used the commands, they would have no trouble with Shanthi. In spite of Sam's assurances, however, the young elephant turned out to be quite a handful. She probably misbehaves to get special attention from her keepers.

Sentence Combining

4. a. Hay protects the elephants.
   b. It protects them **from sunburn.**
5. a. The veterinarians check the elephants' backs.
   b. They check the elephants' backs before the baths.
6. a. The keeper sprays water.
   b. She sprays water on the elephants' foreheads and feet.
7. a. The elephants' backs are soaked and carefully scrubbed.
   b. They are soaked with green oil soap.
   c. They are scrubbed with brushes.
8. a. Scrapes are treated.
   b. The scrapes are on the elephants' backs.
   c. The scrapes are treated with soothing salve.
9. a. The elephants' feet are examined.
   b. Their feet are examined in the last part of the bath.
   c. Their feet are examined for pebbles and other irritants.
10. a. The keeper has the special ankus stick nearby at all times.
    b. The keeper has the ankus as a sign of authority.
    c. The ankus is a sign of authority to the elephants.

| Exercise 6 | Combining Sentences with Prepositional Phrases |

Rewrite the following paragraphs, combining sentences with prepositional phrases. Make any other changes in wording that you feel are necessary.

One of the Washington Zoo's most colorful elephants is named Shanthi. Shanthi was rescued and raised in an elephant orphanage. She was raised with twenty-one other elephants. At the age of one, she was sent from Sri Lanka. She was sent to Washington. She was a gift. The gift was to the children of the United States. Her keeper, Sam, came with Shanthi. He came to the United States. Sam slept near his young charge. He slept in the Elephant House. He slept on a cot.

Before going back to Sri Lanka, Sam gave a tape recording to the zoo. The recording was of his special commands. If the zoo-keepers used the commands, they would have no trouble with Shanthi. This was according to Sam. However, the young elephant turned out to be quite a handful. This is in spite of Sam's assurances. She probably misbehaves to get special attention. She wants attention from her keepers.

MEETING INDIVIDUAL NEEDS

Less Proficient Readers

Prepositional Phrases

Students may mistake an infinitive phrase for a prepositional phrase beginning with *to.* Remind them that a prepositional phrase consists of a preposition followed by a noun or pronoun. List some common prepositions, and then let students take turns adding prepositional phrases first to the verb and then to the subject of an incomplete sentence such as the following: *The street leads ___.* (Answers will vary. Sample: *The street leads to the school. The street on the left leads to the school.*)

Exercise 7

Mixed Review

The sentences below are based on a passage from *Coast to Coast* by Betsy Byars, which you can find on pages 82–86. Combine the sentences from each numbered item into one new sentence. Combine sentences and compound elements by using a coordinating conjunction; add new information as prepositional phrases.

1. a. Birch wanted to take a ride in the plane.
   b. She knew this was her last chance.
2. a. Her grandfather seemed to have lost his desire for fun.
   b. Perhaps he did not want to take any chances.
3. a. Her grandfather glanced at the sky.
   b. Her grandfather decided to fly.
4. a. Birch grinned with delight.
   b. Her grandfather smiled for the first time that afternoon.
5. a. It was a beautiful day for a flight.
   b. Birch knew it.
   c. Her grandfather knew it.
6. a. Birch wanted to go right away.
   b. Her grandfather needed to perform a preflight inspection.
7. a. Her grandfather found no problems with the tires.
   b. Her grandfather found no problems with the gas.
   c. Her grandfather found no problems with the oil.
8. a. The old plane sat on the pavement.
   b. The pavement was in front of the hangar.
9. a. Pop steered the plane off the ramp.
   b. He steered it down the taxiway.
   c. He steered the plane onto the runway.
10. a. The wind rushed through the open window.
    b. The wind blew on Birch's face.

Practice and Assess

Answers: Exercise 7

Mixed Review

Answers will vary, but some suggestions are given below.

1. Birch wanted to take a ride in the plane and knew this was her last chance.
2. Her grandfather seemed to have lost his desire for fun, or perhaps he did not want to take any chances.
3. Her grandfather glanced at the sky and decided to fly.
4. Birch grinned with delight, and her grandfather smiled for the first time that afternoon.
5. It was a beautiful day for a flight, and Birch and her grandfather knew it.
6. Birch wanted to go right away, but her grandfather needed to perform a preflight inspection.
7. Her grandfather found no problems with the tires, the gas, or the oil.
8. The old plane sat on the pavement in front of the hangar.
9. Pop steered the plane off the ramp, down the taxiway, and onto the runway.
10. The wind rushed through the open window and blew on Birch's face.

Additional Resources

📁 *Sentence-Combining Practice*, pp. 9–10

📕 *Grammar Workbook*, Lesson 42

Close

Divide the class into small groups for a partners activity. Direct the partners in each group to exchange a piece of writing, possibly from a previous assignment or their writing portfolios. Ask partners to underline any sentences they think could be combined to make the writing more concise and to help it flow better.

✔ ASSESSMENT OPTIONS

📁 *Tests with Answer Key and Rubrics*
Unit 20 Mastery Test, pp. 83–84

💾 *Testmaker*
Unit 20 Mastery Test

You may wish to administer the Unit 20 Mastery Test at this point.

📼 *Mindjogger Videoquizzes*

PART 3

Resources and Skills

Objectives

The units in Part 3 guide students as they develop their skills in studying, note taking, using information resources, taking tests, and communicating—in written, oral, and electronic formats. Throughout these units, students will be asked

- to use the library and reference sources effectively and with increasing familiarity
- to understand ways in which words become part of a language and to become familiar with common spelling rules
- to develop an organized method of study
- to explore and practice taking standardized tests
- to learn through formal and informal speaking and listening experiences
- to understand and analyze mass media
- to become increasingly skilled at using electronic resources

Viewing the Art

Emile Bernard, a French painter of the late nineteenth and early twentieth centuries, was noted for his friendships with van Gogh, Gauguin, and Cézanne. In 1886 Bernard developed a style termed *cloisonnism*— using bold forms separated by dark contours. The style reminded viewers of the stained glass windows and metalwork of the Middle Ages. He is considered a major contributor to the understanding of modern art.

Interpret and Analyze Use the following questions for discussion:

- What mood would you attribute to this painting?
- What techniques does the painter use to create that mood? For example, consider the colors and the ways in which the people in the picture seem to be moving.
- Might a modern painter create a picture like this one? Why or why not?

"The scientists were saying ... that the sun, the global problem, would begin to get better. Perhaps for her grandchildren's children ... Perhaps they would feel the delicious warmth of the sun."

—Alma Luz Villanueva, "The Sand Castle"

524

Resource Manager

Use the following resources to customize your teaching of the units in Part 3.

Planning Resources
- *Lesson Plans*
- *Block Scheduling*

Transparencies
- *Bellringer*
- *Daily Language Practice*
- *Two-Minute Skill Drill*

Other Print Resources
- *Dinah Zike's Foldables™ for Writer's Choice*
- *Guide to Using the Internet and Other Electronic Resources*
- *inTime*

- *ITBS® Preparation and Practice Workbook*
- *Listening and Speaking Activities*
- *SAT-9 Preparation and Practice*
- *Spelling Power*
- *Taking Standardized Tests*
- *TerraNova Preparation and Practice*
- *Tests with Answer Key and Rubrics*
- *Thinking and Study Skills*

Resources and Skills

Breton Women with Umbrellas, by Emile Bernard. 1892

525

Discussing the Quotation

In "The Sand Castle," Alma Luz Villanueva describes the sun as "the global problem" and presents a picture of life without its "delicious warmth." Discuss the reasons people may have for enjoying the sunshine, as they are doing in the painting; for being cautious in the sun, as many are today; and for living without it, as the quotation implies.

Encourage students to read "The Sand Castle" in Course 1 of *Glencoe Literature: The Reader's Choice*, page 787, and to share their own imaginings about the kind of world presented there.

Writing Prompt Encourage students to use one or two reference sources to learn more about the relationship of the sun and the earth and to write a story, a poem, or an essay in which they use some of the facts they learned.

- *Viewing and Representing Activities*
- *Vocabulary and Spelling Strategies*
- *Vocabulary Power*

📼 **Video**
- *MindJogger Videoquizzes*

💾 **Software**
- *Presentation Plus!*
- *Testmaker*

- *Vocabulary Power Puzzlemaker*

🖥 **Web Sites**
- *TechCONNECT*
- *writerschoice.glencoe.com*

Objectives

- To develop understanding of the resources available in the library
- To recognize additional reference resources
- To use reference and library resources effectively

✔ ASSESSMENT OPTIONS

📁 *Tests with Answer Key and Rubrics*
Unit 21 Pretest, pp. 85–86

💾 *Testmaker*
Unit 21 Pretest

You may wish to administer the Unit 21 Pretest at this point.

Key to Ability Levels

L1 Level 1 activities are within the basic ability range of students.

L2 Level 2 activities are within the ability range of average students.

L3 Level 3 activities are more challenging activities.

UNIT **21**

Library and Reference Resources

526

Resource Manager

Planning Resources
- *Lesson Plans*
- *Block Scheduling*

📑 **Transparencies**
- *Bellringer*
- *Daily Language Practice*

📁 **Other Print Resources**
- *Guide to Using the Internet and Other Electronic Resources*
- *Tests with Answer Key and Rubrics*
- *Thinking and Study Skills*
- *Vocabulary and Spelling Strategies and Practice*

📹 **Video**
- *MindJogger Videoquizzes*

💾 **Software**
- *Presentation Plus!*
- *Testmaker*

💻 **Web Sites**
- *writerschoice.glencoe.com*

21.1 Using a Library

The first free public library in the United States was opened in 1833. Libraries have changed since then.

Today's libraries contain books of all sorts. They also offer magazines, newspapers, audio recordings, videos, and many other resources. In fact, some libraries are now called media centers or resource centers. You can find information about anything from skateboards to Shakespeare, from Persian poetry to pickles.

No two libraries are exactly alike, but all libraries group similar things together. Stories and novels (fiction) are separate from information books (nonfiction). Magazines and audio-visual materials have their own sections. Turn the page to explore the different parts of a library.

Focus

Lesson Overview

Objectives
- To become familiar with the library
- To recognize the librarian as a valuable source of information
- To consult the librarian as needed

Skills
- locating library resources

Critical Thinking
- classifying

Listening and Speaking
- discussing

🔔 Bellringer
Daily Language Activity

When students enter the classroom, have this assignment on the board: *List four library reference sources you might want to use.*

👆 **See also** *Daily Language Practice*

Motivating Activity

Ask students to draw a map of their school library. Have students identify where they would expect to find the four resources they named in the Bellringer.

Library and Reference Resources

Resource Manager

Planning Resources
- *Lesson Plans*

👆 **Transparencies**
- *Bellringer*
- *Daily Language Practice*

📂 **Other Print Resources**
- *Thinking and Study Skills,* pp. 23–29
- *Vocabulary and Spelling Strategies and Practice,* pp. 23–24

Teach

Asking for Help

Tell students that the librarian is the best resource that a library has. When they are in doubt, they can always ask for help. Ask volunteers to list some of the materials they might need help finding. Then have them discuss what the librarian might do for them. **L2**

Library and Reference Resources

Librarian A librarian can help you use the library wisely by directing you to different resources, showing you how to use them, and giving you advice when needed.

Young Adult and Children's Section Find books written for young readers in a separate area of the library. Sometimes reference materials for students, along with periodicals and audiovisual materials, are also shelved here.

Stacks The stacks are the bookshelves that hold most of the library's books. Stacks for fiction books are usually in a different area than those for nonfiction.

Circulation At the circulation desk you can use your library card to check out materials you want to take home.

No two libraries are alike, but most of them share the same characteristics and have similar resources.

MEETING INDIVIDUAL NEEDS Gifted and Talented

Mapping

Encourage partners to map out the placement of resources in the school or community library. Suggest that the students take notes and sketch the various areas of the library as they tour it. They might use the map on pages 528–529 as a guide or checklist for the types of materials they should locate, if available, and include on their maps. After note taking and sketching, encourage partners to work together to create a map of the library. Invite volunteers to share their maps and descriptions of different areas of the library with the class.

Reference The reference area holds dictionaries, encyclopedias, atlases, and other reference works. Computer database systems in the reference area allow you to search for facts or articles from periodicals and newspapers.

Audiovisual Materials Audiocassettes, compact discs (CDs), videotapes, and computer software are in the audiovisual section. Some libraries have listening and viewing areas to allow you to review materials before checking them out.

Newspapers and Periodicals Find current issues of newspapers and periodicals in the general reading area. Periodicals are arranged alphabetically and by date. Older issues of periodicals may be available. Use the computer catalog to locate them or ask a librarian to help you.

Computer Card Catalog or Card Catalog A card catalog contains a card or listing for each book in the library. Each card or listing describes the book and tells its location in the library.

Practice and Assess

Answers: Exercise 1
1. Newspapers and Periodicals
2. Reference
3. Stacks (general fiction) or Young Adult and Children's Section
4. Audio-Visual Materials
5. Reference

Additional Resources

📁 *Vocabulary and Spelling Strategies and Practice,* pp. 23–24
📁 *Thinking and Study Skills,* pp. 23–29

Close

Ask students to describe the library resources that they have found the most helpful. You can also have them share any research tips or strategies they know about.

Exercise 1

In which section of the library would you find each of the following items? Share your results with the class.

1. The monthly magazine *National Geographic*
2. *Atlas of the American Revolution*
3. The novel *My Side of the Mountain*
4. A video of the movie *Old Yeller*
5. *Encyclopedia of Black America*

Library and Reference Resources

MEETING INDIVIDUAL NEEDS

English Language Learners

Discussing Periodicals

Students whose first language is not English may not be familiar with common periodicals. Discuss the periodicals carried by your school or local library. You may wish to have some samples of the most useful and interesting periodicals available in class, such as *National Geographic, National Geographic World, National Wildlife, Time,* and *Newsweek.*

Focus

Lesson Overview

Objectives
- To become familiar with the Dewey Decimal System
- To locate materials in a local or school library, using that library's system

Skills
- using the Dewey Decimal System

Critical Thinking
- classifying

Listening and Speaking
- discussing

Bellringer
Daily Language Activity

When students enter the classroom, have this assignment on the board: *Write the titles of at least three books you have read.*

See also *Daily Language Practice*

Motivating Activity

Discuss the titles students have listed in the Bellringer activity. Have volunteers write on the board two or three of the titles they chose. Then ask them to list the classification of these books.

Library and Reference Resources

21.2 How Books Are Organized

A large library may have hundreds of thousands of books. How can you find what you want among all those books? In 1876 librarian Melvil Dewey set up a system for organizing books. His system, the Dewey decimal system, is still used in libraries today.

In this system, all nonfiction books are given numbers. Dewey divided the numbers into groups by topic. Books about science, for example, make up the 500s group. A book about magnets would be placed in the science group. One about the English language would go into the language group—the 400s. The chart shows how the Dewey groups are broken into smaller subgroups. As you search for a book, begin by asking yourself what group it might be classified in.

Dewey Decimal System		
Numbers	**Major Groups**	**Examples of Subgroups**
000–099	General works	Encyclopedias, library science
100–199	Philosophy	Dreams, the senses
200–299	Religion	World religions, mythology
300–399	Social sciences	Law, education, money
400–499	Language	Grammar, foreign languages
500–599	Science	Animals, math, astronomy
600–699	Technology	Tools, medicine, farming
700–799	The arts	Music, painting, sports
800–899	Literature	Poetry, plays
900–999	Geography, history	Travel, biography, U.S. history

Each nonfiction book has a call number on its spine. In most libraries, this is a Dewey decimal number. It's a short code telling the subject of the book. Each digit in the number narrows down the topic. For example, look at the call number for a book called *The Great American Baseball Scrapbook*.

Resource Manager

Planning Resources
- *Lesson Plans*

Transparencies
- *Bellringer*
- *Daily Language Practice*

Other Print Resources
- *Thinking and Study Skills,* pp. 23–29
- *Vocabulary and Spelling Strategies and Practice,* pp. 23–24

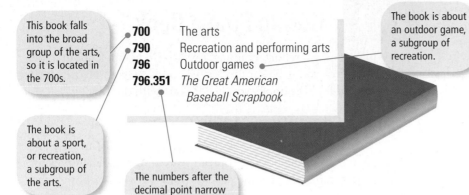

This book falls into the broad group of the arts, so it is located in the 700s.

The book is about a sport, or recreation, a subgroup of the arts.

700 The arts
790 Recreation and performing arts
796 Outdoor games
796.351 *The Great American Baseball Scrapbook*

The book is about an outdoor game, a subgroup of recreation.

The numbers after the decimal point narrow down the topic even further. This book is about baseball.

As a student, you don't need to memorize the Dewey code. It's a good idea, however, to learn the main groups in the Dewey decimal system. Knowing them will make it easier to find the books you need.

Books are shelved by Dewey decimal number and then alphabetically by the author's last name. You might find six books about whales, each book with the number 599.5 on its spine. Within this group a book by Dorothy Hinshaw Patent would appear before a book by John F. Waters.

Fiction works usually don't have Dewey decimal numbers. They are shelved in alphabetical order by the author's last name. The call number may have *F* or *FIC*, for *fiction*, on the first line. The second line has the first three letters of the author's last name. Different books by the same author are shelved alphabetically by title.

Exercise 2

In what Dewey group would you expect each of the following books to be shelved? Give the main group name and the number in hundreds.

1. A book about the solar system
2. A book with the title *A History of the Ancient World*
3. A book about Greek gods and goddesses
4. A book about the origins of jazz
5. A book of poems by Shel Silverstein

21.2 How Books Are Organized **531**

Teach

Promoting Discussion

Ask students whether they have at home collections of books, CD-ROMs, video games, or any other articles that could be classified. When might it be necessary to classify such a collection? Ask them to discuss methods, such as categorizing and sequencing information, that might be used at home to organize the various kinds of collections. **L2**

Practice and Assess

Answers: Exercise 2

1. Science, 500s
2. History and geography, 900s
3. Religion (mythology), 200s
4. Arts, 700s
5. Literature, 800s

Additional Resources

📂 *Vocabulary and Spelling Strategies and Practice,* pp. 23–24
📂 *Thinking and Study Skills,* pp. 23–29

Close

Have students read the titles of the books they listed in the Bellringer and tell how the books would be classified in a library that uses the Dewey Decimal System.

Less Proficient Readers

Practicing Alphabetical Order

Students who are new to English may need practice with alphabetical order. Bring in a number of works of fiction, including some books written by the same author. Ask students to arrange the books in alphabetical order by the author's name and where necessary by the book's title.

Explain that book titles beginning with the word *a* or *the* are alphabetized by using the second word in the title. Students can discuss why libraries follow this practice. You may prefer to do this activity using three-by-five index cards instead of actual books.

Focus

Lesson Overview

Objectives
- To become familiar with computer and/or card catalogs
- To use the catalog information effectively and easily

Skills
- using a card catalog

Critical Thinking
- categorizing; classifying

Listening and Speaking
- discussing; explaining a process

Bellringer
Daily Language Activity

When students enter the classroom, have this assignment on the board: *Write down the titles and authors of a work of fiction and a work of nonfiction that you know. For the nonfiction book, write a word or phrase telling the book's subject.*

See also *Daily Language Practice*

Teach

Making Cards

Bring into class several library books, including nonfiction works on various topics. Divide the class into small groups, and give each group three books and three three-by-five index cards. Ask each group to create cards that would show computer catalog entries for the group's books. **L2**

Library and Reference Resources

21.3 | How to Find a Book

While writing a report, you may need to find a book about a particular topic or you may want to locate a book by your favorite writer. How do you find the books you need? Start with the catalog.

Using a Computer Catalog

The computer catalog lists all the books, periodicals, and audiovisual materials in the library. You can search for these materials by title, author, subject, or keyword. A *keyword* is a word or phrase that describes your topic. If you type an author's name, you can view a list of all the books written by that author. By typing a subject, you can view all the books about that particular topic. The computer catalog tells you the title, author, and call number of each book, and whether it is available to check out.

For example, suppose you are looking for books by the writer Milton Meltzer. Your computer search might proceed as follows:

1. **Enter A for Author-Name. A prompt will then ask you for the author's name. Key in Meltzer, Milton.**
2. **The computer will show a list of all the books in the library by this author. Each item will have a call number. These are two of the books you will see by Milton Meltzer.**

```
1.Title:      All Times, All Peoples: A
              World History of Slavery
  Author:     Meltzer, Milton
  Published:  1980
  Media:      Book
  Call No:    326 M528a

2.Title:      American Politics: How It
              Really Works
  Author:     Meltzer, Milton
  Published:  1989
  Media:      Book
  Call No:    320.473 M528a
```

3. **You can also type the call number of the book that interests you. Information about the book will appear, including the book's location and availability.**

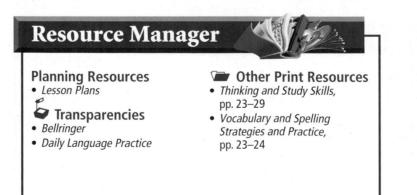

Resource Manager

Planning Resources
- *Lesson Plans*

Transparencies
- *Bellringer*
- *Daily Language Practice*

Other Print Resources
- *Thinking and Study Skills,* pp. 23–29
- *Vocabulary and Spelling Strategies and Practice,* pp. 23–24

Information on Cards

Some libraries use an older method of organizing books called a card catalog. A card catalog is a cabinet of long narrow drawers that holds cards arranged alphabetically. Each card contains the description of a book and has that book's call number in the upper left-hand corner. Fiction books have an author card and a title card. Nonfiction books have a subject card as well. Because each book has two or three cards, it can be found by searching under its title, its author, or sometimes its subject.

Finding a Book

After you look up an author's name, a book title, or any subject in the catalog, carefully copy down the call number of the book you want. Then go to the shelves to see if the book is available.

Nonfiction books are arranged in numerical order by call number. You can look at the signs at the end of each row of shelves to see which call numbers are in that row.

Exercise 3

At your school or neighborhood library, use the catalog to find a book about each of the following topics. List the author, title, and call number of each book.

1. Endangered animals
2. How to build kites
3. South Africa
4. A book by Jean Craighead George
5. The ocean
6. The American Civil War
7. Musical instruments
8. Women in sports

21.3

Practice and Assess

Answers: Exercise 3

Each response should include an author's name, a title, and a call number. Most titles and call numbers will reflect the following Dewey Decimal System categories:
1. 500s (Science)
2. 700s (The Arts—Recreation)
3. 900s (Geography and History)
4. Fiction (F or FIC) or 600 (Cook books)
5. 500s (Science)
6. 900s (Geography and History)
7. 700s (The Arts—Music)
8. 700s (The Arts—Recreation) or 900s (Biography)

Additional Resources

📂 *Vocabulary and Spelling Strategies and Practice*, pp. 23–24
📂 *Thinking and Study Skills*, pp. 23–29

Close

Each student can find the call numbers for the books they listed in the Bellringer activity. They can either give the appropriate number range from the list on page 530 or look up the precise call number when they carry out Exercise 3.

Library and Reference Resources

Technology Tip

Using Computers

If your school library or local neighborhood library has a computer catalog, encourage students to investigate its use. You may wish to have experienced students help those who are less familiar with library computers. You may also want to have students explore databases that may be available at the library. Have students identify which print resources are available to them and tell how they might use their resources.

Focus

Lesson Overview

Objectives
- To identify useful reference sources
- To use reference sources appropriately

Skills
- using an encyclopedia; using an atlas

Critical Thinking
- evaluating reference sources

Listening and Speaking
- oral reporting

Bellringer
Daily Language Activity

When students enter the classroom, have this assignment on the board: *List five reference books you would expect to see in a library.*

See also *Daily Language Practice*

Teach

Researching Information

Tell students that references can be very helpful, but they must know what topics to look up in order to use these resources effectively. Ask students to name the subjects of papers they have written or are in the process of writing. Discuss entries they could look up in an encyclopedia or other print or CD-ROM reference sources. Suggest that students look up information on the Civil War under the subject categories Civil War, United States Wars, Abraham Lincoln, and Gettysburg. Then ask them to compare the kind of information they find. Point out that they should think about related topics that would give them additional information. **L2**

21.4 Using References

If you are curious about a topic and want to know more about it, or if you need information for a report, look first in a reference work. Reference books (or on-line reference sources) make it easy to locate information about a person, a place, or almost any other topic. Encyclopedias and atlases are two examples of useful reference works.

Encyclopedias

You can find information on many different topics in an encyclopedia. Major encyclopedias contain a number of volumes. *The World Book Encyclopedia*, for example, is divided into twenty-two volumes.

Guide words at the top of each two-page spread show the first and last entries on that spread.

Articles may contain a list of books you can turn to for more information on the topic.

Encyclopedia entries appear in alphabetical order.

The article or an entry word may refer you to another entry in the encyclopedia.

Library and Reference Resources

TIME

For more about the importance of using accurate information in your writing, see **TIME Facing the Blank Page,** page 97.

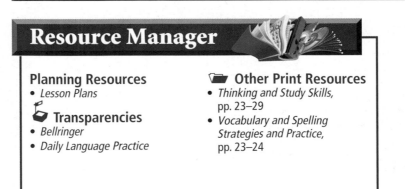

Resource Manager

Planning Resources
- *Lesson Plans*

Transparencies
- *Bellringer*
- *Daily Language Practice*

Other Print Resources
- *Thinking and Study Skills,* pp. 23–29
- *Vocabulary and Spelling Strategies and Practice,* pp. 23–24

An encyclopedia is a good place to check dates and specific facts, such as when Texas became a state or whether a fungus is a plant. You can also use an encyclopedia to get basic information on a topic quickly.

Atlases

An atlas is a collection of maps. A general atlas contains maps of all parts of the world. It may also have special maps that give information about climate or population. You might use a general atlas when you are writing a report about a particular country.

Other atlases deal with one part of the world, such as Asia, Republic of the Congo, or Oklahoma. Still others cover special topics—for example, an atlas of wildlife. Historical atlases contain maps that show changes over time. Some historical atlases cover lengthy periods of time. Others cover shorter periods, perhaps only a few years. Similarly, they may deal with world history or the history of a single country or region.

Exercise 4

Tell which reference work—an encyclopedia or an atlas—would best answer each question below. Then choose one of the questions to answer. Give the answer and the title of the reference work you used to find it.

1. What countries border the country of Iraq?
2. Which planet has the most moons?
3. How many bones are in a human hand?
4. What sea is between Saudi Arabia and India?
5. How large is the Sahara?

Library and Reference Resources

Answers: Exercise 4

Answers should include the name of the encyclopedia or atlas that furnished the information.

1. atlas; Turkey, Iran, Saudi Arabia, Jordan, Syria, Kuwait
2. encyclopedia; Saturn
3. encyclopedia; 27
4. atlas; Arabian Sea
5. encyclopedia or atlas; /3,320,000 sq.mi.

Additional Resources

📂 *Vocabulary and Spelling Strategies and Practice,* pp. 23–24
📂 *Thinking and Study Skills,* pp. 23–29

Close

Ask students to describe their experiences using encyclopedias and atlases. Did they find some sources to be more helpful than others? With what types of reference materials did they have difficulty?

Listening and Speaking

Checking References

Ask volunteers to make a list of the atlases and encyclopedias available in their school library. Then ask each student to examine one of these references and report on it to the class. Tell students to respond to questions such as the following: What kinds of information does this reference contain? Does it seem to be up-to-date? How complete is the information provided on a specific topic? Is the information clear and easy to understand? For what kinds of assignments would this reference be useful?

Focus

Lesson Overview

Objectives
- To identify types of dictionaries and their uses
- To identify and use a thesaurus

Skills
- using a dictionary; using a thesaurus

Critical Thinking
- comparing; categorizing

Listening and Speaking
- discussing

Bellringer
Daily Language Activity

When students enter the classroom, have this assignment on the board: *Name five things you can find in a dictionary.*

See also *Daily Language Practice*

Motivating Activity

Bring to class several different types of dictionaries (corresponding to those in the text) for students to examine. Have them compare the dictionaries and tell what is different about them. After students have read the first page of the lesson, have them decide in which category each dictionary belongs.

Library and Reference Resources

21.5 Using a Dictionary

The Dictionary

People often speak of dictionaries as though they were all alike. In fact, people often say that they've looked up a word in *the* dictionary. After all, every dictionary is an alphabetically arranged collection of words and their definitions. However, dictionaries come in different sizes and have different uses. They are meant for different users. The chart below shows some of the ways in which dictionaries differ.

Types of Dictionaries		
Type	**Description**	**Examples**
Unabridged Dictionaries 250,000 or more entries	Detailed word histories and definitions Found mostly in libraries	*Random House Unabridged Dictionary* *Webster's Third New International Dictionary*
Desk or College Dictionaries 130,000–250,000 entries	Detailed enough to answer most questions on definitions and word histories Used in schools, homes, and businesses	*Webster's New World Dictionary* *The American Heritage Dictionary*
School Dictionaries 90,000 or fewer entries	Often in separate versions for primary, elementary, and high school students Definitions suitable for students' grade levels	*Macmillan Dictionary for Students* *Webster's School Dictionary*

Resource Manager

Planning Resources
- *Lesson Plans*

Transparencies
- *Bellringer*
- *Daily Language Practice*

Other Print Resources
- *Thinking and Study Skills,* pp. 23–29
- *Vocabulary and Spelling Strategies and Practice,* pp. 23–24

The sample dictionary page shows how the entries on a page are arranged. An entry includes the word, its definitions, and other information about the word. The bold type used for each entry term helps you see what words are defined on each page. The entries are in alphabetical order.

Teach

Using the Pronunciation Key

Review the pronunciation key at the bottom of a student dictionary page. Write the phonetic pronunciations for several words on the board, and ask students to identify the words. Then ask students to take turns looking up words and writing only the phonetic spellings on the board. Ask other students to identify the words from those spellings. **L2**

Comparing Dictionaries

Emphasize to students that dictionaries differ in ways other than just the numbers of word entries they provide. Even very similar dictionaries—such as various college dictionaries—differ in the order, type, and completeness of information. After students have compared the entries for two or three words in several dictionaries, ask them which dictionary provides the most complete definitions. Which provides word histories that are easy to understand? Which would they prefer to use? Why? **L3**

Guide words at the top of each page show the first and last entries on the page. These guide words help you locate an entry.

Illustrations help you understand some definitions. How does the picture of a privet help you understand that word's definition?

A pronunciation key appears at the bottom of each page or each pair of facing pages. The pronunciation key gives examples of each pronunciation symbol by using familiar words such as at, āpe, and cär.

Library and Reference Resources

21.5 Using a Dictionary **537**

Enrichment and Extension

History

The first dictionaries translated words from one language into another. Early English dictionaries translated French and Latin into English. In the seventeenth century, the first completely English dictionaries appeared, but these provided definitions only for difficult words. Authors then wrote more complete dictionaries for scholars only. In 1721, for example, a 60,000-word dictionary was published that assumed readers knew the meaning of common words. The word *horse,* for example, was defined as "a beast well known."

Practice and Assess

Answers: Exercise 5

1. Guide words will depend on the dictionary used.
2. plane, planetarium, plaid
3. grain
4. Examples:
   a. tremble, quake, quiver, vibrate, shiver, shudder, wobble
   b. affluent, wealthy, opulent, well-to-do

Additional Resources

📁 *Vocabulary and Spelling Strategies and Practice*, pp. 23–24
📁 *Thinking and Study Skills*, pp. 23–29

Close

Have students discuss how dictionaries and thesauruses can help writers improve their writing. Encourage students to share their past experiences in using dictionaries or thesauruses.

Library and Reference Resources

The Thesaurus

A thesaurus is a dictionary of synonyms, or words with similar meanings. A thesaurus is a helpful tool when you're revising your writing. In fact, if you use word processing software, you may even have a thesaurus as part of your software package. You can use a thesaurus to find a more exact or more colorful word to replace a vague or overused word.

In a dictionary-style thesaurus, entries are arranged alphabetically, as in a dictionary. Several synonyms may be listed for a single definition. A cross-reference to another entry or entries may follow the definition.

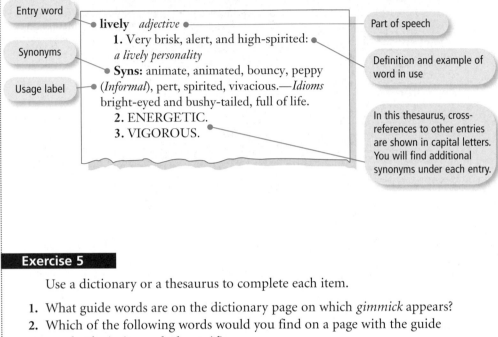

Entry word

Synonyms

Usage label

lively *adjective*
  1. Very brisk, alert, and high-spirited: *a lively personality*
  Syns: animate, animated, bouncy, peppy (*Informal*), pert, spirited, vivacious.—*Idioms* bright-eyed and bushy-tailed, full of life.
  2. ENERGETIC.
  3. VIGOROUS.

Part of speech

Definition and example of word in use

In this thesaurus, cross-references to other entries are shown in capital letters. You will find additional synonyms under each entry.

Exercise 5

Use a dictionary or a thesaurus to complete each item.

1. What guide words are on the dictionary page on which *gimmick* appears?
2. Which of the following words would you find on a page with the guide words *plagiarism* and *planetoid*?

   plane   plantation   placid
   plank   planetarium   plaid
3. Does the word *skein* rhyme with *green, shine,* or *grain*?
4. List three synonyms for the following:
   a. the verb *shake*
   b. the adjective *rich*

Enrichment and Extension

Using Vivid and Precise Words

Write the following on the board:

It's a <u>bad</u> night, and a <u>cold rain</u> is falling. Father <u>watches</u> the bumpy dirt road. We <u>worry</u> that the <u>old</u> car will become stuck. It's <u>extremely</u> muddy. Finally, we arrive at a <u>little</u> cabin. Inside, a <u>nice</u> fire <u>burns</u> in the fireplace.

Have students use thesauruses to replace the underlined words with more vivid and precise words. Discuss how the choice of synonyms affects the paragraph's meaning.

21.6 Understanding a Dictionary Entry

Which is the right spelling: *life style, life-style,* or *lifestyle*? How do you divide *environment* into syllables? Is *domestic* a noun, an adjective, or both? These are just a few of the types of questions you can answer with a dictionary.

The Entry Word and Definition

The entry word begins the entry. If the word has more than one syllable, the entry word shows how it is divided, or hyphenated. Notice how *ba•sin* is divided by the dot. A dictionary will show you that some entries are two words, as in *high school*. Other words are hyphenated, as in *runner-up*. Still others are spelled as one word: *lifeboat*.

Most of the time, you probably look up a word to find a definition. Words usually have more than one definition. Some words, in fact, have many definitions. Your dictionary probably includes more than a dozen different meanings for the word *set*. School dictionaries generally list the most common definition first, as in the entry below.

> **ba•sin** (bāʹsin) *n.* **1.a.** container that is usually round with a wide, flat bottom and sloping sides; shallow bowl, esp. for holding liquids. **b.** bathroom sink. **2.** contents or capacity of a basin. **3.** the entire region drained by a river and its tributaries. **4.** depression in the earth usually holding water, like a pond, but sometimes dry.

Entry word

Numbered definitions

Other Information in Entries

How do you say *reign*? Where does the word *caribou* come from? Are there any good synonyms for *slow*? What is the plural of *calf* ? Dictionary entries can also answer questions like these. Look at the entry on the next page to locate some of the important parts of a dictionary entry.

Library and Reference Resources

21.6 Understanding a Dictionary Entry **539**

Focus

Lesson Overview

Objectives
• To recognize elements in dictionary entries
• To use various types of dictionaries appropriately

Skills
• reading a dictionary entry; using word origins

Critical Thinking
• analyzing dictionary entries; identifying types of information

Listening and Speaking
• discussing; pronouncing difficult words

Bellringer
Daily Language Activity

When students enter the classroom, have this assignment on the board: *List five words that you are not sure how to pronounce.*

See also *Daily Language Practice*

Teach

Exploring Dictionary Entry Words

As students look at the sample dictionary entry, ask them to describe the types of information given—entry word divided into syllables, pronunciation, part(s) of speech, definitions, and so on. Encourage students to discuss when each of these kinds of information might be useful. Have students look up the words that they would like to know how to pronounce and share their lists with the class. **L2**

Practice and Assess

Answers: Exercise 6

1. quad • ran • gle
2. Spanish (or Latin by way of Spanish)
3. Examples: voyage, trip, tour, jaunt, expedition
4. noun
5. oxen, loaves, brothers-in-law

Additional Resources

📁 *Vocabulary and Spelling Strategies and Practice*, pp. 23–24

📁 *Thinking and Study Skills*, pp. 23–29

✔ ASSESSMENT OPTIONS

📁 *Tests with Answer Key and Rubrics* Unit 21 Mastery Test, pp. 87–88

💾 *Testmaker* Unit 21 Mastery Test

You may wish to administer the Unit 21 Mastery Test at this point.

📼 *Mindjogger Videoquizzes*

Close

Point out to students that different dictionaries may give information in somewhat different ways and that the pronunciation keys may differ. Tell students to look up two or three of the same words in different dictionaries to see how the entries compare. Have students discuss the differences they find.

Pronunciation The pronunciation follows the entry word. Refer to the key at the bottom of the page if you are not sure what the pronunciation symbols mean. Notice that the second syllable of *fragile* can be pronounced two ways.

Part of Speech An abbreviation shows how the word is used as a part of speech. In this entry, *adj.* stands for *adjective* and *adv.* for *adverb.*

Word Origin Many entries include information about the word's origin, or a history of the word.

frag•ile (fraj´əl,-ī́l) *adj.* easily broken, damaged, or destroyed; delicate. [Latin *fragilis.* Doublet of FRAIL.] —**frag•ile•ly**, *adv.* —**fra•gil•i•ty** (frə jil´ə tē), n. Syn. **Fragile, frail, brittle** mean tending to break easily. **Fragile** suggests that the substance of which a thing is made may result in its breaking if it is not handled with care: *The movers carefully packed the fragile china into cartons.* **Frail** implies that a thing is of weak construction and that it will tend to collapse under strain: *The frail wooden bridge cracked and swayed in the heavy winds.* **Brittle** suggests hardness of such rigidity that the thing may easily break if pressure is applied unwisely: *The bones of an aged person are often quite brittle.*

Synonyms Some entries list synonyms, words with similar meanings. Explanations and examples are often included to help you understand the different meanings. For more information on synonyms, turn to page 552.

Library and Reference Resources

Exercise 6

Use a school dictionary to answer the following questions.

1. How is the word *quadrangle* divided into syllables?
2. What is the origin of the word *patio*?
3. What synonyms are given for *journey*?
4. Is *bramble* a noun or a verb?
5. What is the plural of *ox*? Of *loaf*? Of *brother-in-law*?

MEETING INDIVIDUAL NEEDS   English Language Learners

Exploring Dictionaries

Students not proficient in English may have difficulty interpreting the symbols and abbreviations used in dictionary entries. Explain the table of symbols and the list of abbreviations in the front matter of the dictionary. Give particular attention to pronunciation symbols. Use

commonwords to demonstrate each sound aloud, and ask students to repeat the words after you. Then read through several dictionary entries that demonstrate the various symbols and abbreviations.

UNIT
22 Vocabulary and Spelling

541

Objectives

- To understand the influence of other languages and cultures on the spelling of English words
- To use context clues to decipher the meaning of unfamiliar words
- To break a word into its parts, such as the root, the prefix, and the suffix
- To identify synonyms and antonyms of various words, and to distinguish between pairs of homographs
- To recognize and apply spelling rules for compound words, plural nouns, and other commonly misspelled words

✔ ASSESSMENT OPTIONS

📂 *Tests with Answer Key and Rubrics*
Unit 22 Pretest, pp. 89–90

💾 *Testmaker*
Unit 22 Pretest

You may wish to administer the Unit 22 Pretest at this point.

Key to Ability Levels

L1 Level 1 activities are within the basic ability range of students.

L2 Level 2 activities are within the ability range of average students.

L3 Level 3 activities are more challenging activities.

Resource Manager

Planning Resources
- *Lesson Plans*
- *Block Scheduling*

🗂 Transparencies
- *Bellringer*
- *Daily Language Practice*

📂 Other Print Resources
- *Tests with Answer Key and Rubrics*
- *Thinking and Study Skills*
- *Spelling Power*
- *Vocabulary and Spelling Strategies and Practice*
- *Vocabulary Power*

📹 Video
- *MindJogger Videoquizzes*

💾 Software
- *Presentation Plus!*
- *Testmaker*
- *Vocabulary Power Puzzlemaker*

🖥 Web Sites
- *writerschoice.glencoe.com*

Focus

Lesson Overview

Objectives
- To identify English words that were borrowed from other languages
- To understand the influence of other languages and cultures on the spelling of English words

Skills
- using a dictionary; reading a map

Critical Thinking
- classifying; analyzing

Listening and Speaking
- oral reporting

Bellringer
Daily Language Activity

When students enter the classroom, have this assignment on the board: *List five foods with names that come from languages other than English.*

See also *Daily Language Practice*

Motivating Activity

Point out to students that they really know and recognize many words from other languages, whether they regularly speak another language or not. Have students share the words they listed in the Bellringer activity. Encourage students to speculate on the origins of each word.

Vocabulary and Spelling

22.1 Borrowed Words

The English language contains more than 600,000 words, more than any other language. Many of these words have been borrowed from other languages.

Many of the foods you eat originally came from other lands. The names of those foods came from other languages. Think about pizza (Italian), hamburger (German), chili (Spanish), taco (Mexican Spanish), and gumbo (West African). You can probably add more examples of your own. Every time you ask for these foods, you use a borrowed word.

English has also borrowed words for clothing, sports, cars, and hundreds of other items in daily use. Parts of words have also been borrowed. Our word *television*, for example, comes from the Greek *tele*, "far off," and the Latin *visio*, "to see."

Often a word passes from one language to another before becoming a part of English. Our word *theater*, for example, was first used in ancient Greece, where the idea of theater itself began. The word was borrowed by the Romans, who spoke Latin. French speakers later borrowed it from Latin. English speakers then borrowed it from the French.

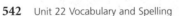

Resource Manager

Planning Resources
- *Lesson Plans*

Transparencies
- *Bellringer*
- *Daily Language Practice*

Other Print Resources
- *Vocabulary and Spelling Strategies and Practice,* pp. 13–16, 21–34, 41–52

The map below shows just a few examples of borrowed words. You have probably used many of them without knowing that they came from another language.

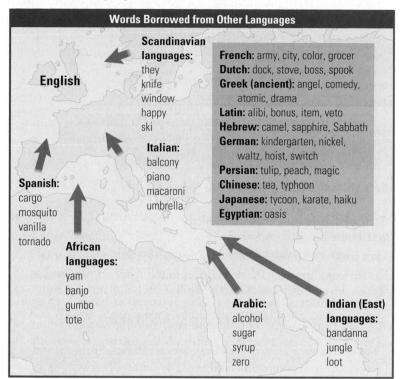

Words Borrowed from Other Languages

English

Scandinavian languages:
they
knife
window
happy
ski

Italian:
balcony
piano
macaroni
umbrella

Spanish:
cargo
mosquito
vanilla
tornado

African languages:
yam
banjo
gumbo
tote

Arabic:
alcohol
sugar
syrup
zero

Indian (East) languages:
bandanna
jungle
loot

French: army, city, color, grocer
Dutch: dock, stove, boss, spook
Greek (ancient): angel, comedy, atomic, drama
Latin: alibi, bonus, item, veto
Hebrew: camel, sapphire, Sabbath
German: kindergarten, nickel, waltz, hoist, switch
Persian: tulip, peach, magic
Chinese: tea, typhoon
Japanese: tycoon, karate, haiku
Egyptian: oasis

Exercise 1

Working in a group, choose one foreign language. See how many words you can find that came into English from that language. Use what group members already know, interviews, and library resources. Present your list to the class.

Teach

Finding Word Origins

Discuss how technology and contact with speakers of other languages have added new vocabulary to English. Have students name words of foreign origin used in sports, films, games, dances, and music. Have students use dictionaries to find word origins. **L2**

Practice and Assess

Evaluation Rubrics

Exercise 1

Answers will vary. Students should list as many borrowed words as possible. Encourage students to research languages that are not listed on the student page.

Additional Resources

📁 *Vocabulary and Spelling Strategies and Practice*, pp. 13–16, 21–34, 41–52

Close

English has borrowed a large number of loan words from the French language. Ask students to locate France and England on a detailed map. How might the proximity of these countries have contributed to French influence on the English language?

Vocabulary and Spelling

MEETING INDIVIDUAL NEEDS ▸ **English Language Learners**

Recognizing Borrowed Words

Highlight the advantage of bilingualism by asking students whose first language is not English to supply additional English words borrowed from their first language. Students might create another map on which they write words their first languages have contributed to English.

543

Focus

Lesson Overview

Objectives
- To identify different types of context clues in sentences
- To use context clues to decipher the meaning of unfamiliar words

Skills
- using context clues

Critical Thinking
- synthesizing

Listening and Speaking
- discussing

Bellringer
Daily Language Activity

When students enter the classroom, have this assignment on the board: *List three different ways you can find out the meaning of a word you don't know.*

See also *Daily Language Practice*

Motivating Activity

Let students discuss their strategies from the Bellringer activity. Then have students look in a nonfiction book or textbook from another subject and point out words they don't know. Have students discuss ways of determining the meanings of these words.

Vocabulary and Spelling

22.2 | Clues to Word Meanings

One way to learn the meaning of a new word is to use a dictionary. However, you won't always have a dictionary handy. Try to figure out the meaning of the word yourself. Look for clues in the words and sentences around it. These surrounding words and sentences are called the context.

Specific Context Clues

DEFINITION   The meaning, or definition, of an unfamiliar word is sometimes given in the sentence that includes the word. Definitions are usually introduced with clue words.

> The plant has begun to germinate, which means that it is starting to sprout.

The clue words *which means* tell you that the definition of the word *germinate* is "to start to sprout."

EXAMPLE   Familiar examples can help a reader understand an unfamiliar word. See how the writer uses examples in the sentence below.

> Felines, such as lions, domestic cats, and leopards, are natural hunters.

The words *such as* introduce examples of felines. From the examples you can guess that *felines* refers to the cat family.

Interpreting Clue Words		
Type of Context Clue	**Clue Words**	**Example**
Definition: The meaning of the unfamiliar word is given in the sentence.	that is in other words which means	Jerry *inscribed* his name; that is, he wrote his name in the book.
Example: The meaning of the unfamiliar word is explained by familiar examples.	like such as for example including	Some people are afraid of *arachnids,* such as spiders and ticks.

544   Unit 22 Vocabulary and Spelling

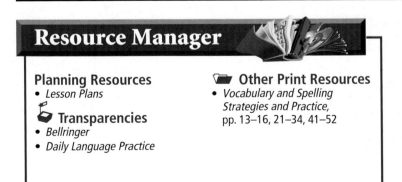

Resource Manager

Planning Resources
- *Lesson Plans*

Transparencies
- *Bellringer*
- *Daily Language Practice*

📂 **Other Print Resources**
- *Vocabulary and Spelling Strategies and Practice,* pp. 13–16, 21–34, 41–52

General Context

Sometimes there are no special clue words to help you understand a new word. However, you can still use the general context. That is, you can use the details in the words or sentences around the new word. Look at the following sentences:

> Andrea carefully mixed several pigments with an oil base to produce just the right colors. Then she began her painting.

The sentences tell you that pigments have something to do with painting. They also tell you that pigments can be mixed to produce various colors. From those clues, you can figure out that pigments are a kind of dye or color used to make paint.

Exercise 2

Use context clues to figure out the meaning of the underlined word in each sentence. Write the meaning of the word. Then tell what type of context clue you used to figure out each meaning. The types of context clues will be definition, example, or general context.

1. Brian used a <u>template</u>, or pattern, for cutting the wood he used to build a birdhouse.
2. <u>Vipers</u>, such as rattlesnakes, cobras, and copperheads, can be very dangerous, even deadly.
3. Birds, mammals, and even plants can be <u>insectivores</u>. For example, flycatchers and anteaters are insectivores. So is the Venus's flytrap, a plant that traps flies and then digests them.
4. The scene by the lake was <u>tranquil</u>. There was only a slight breeze, and the surface of the lake was as smooth as glass. Even the birds and insects seemed hushed.
5. Margot is studying <u>calligraphy</u>, which is the art of fine handwriting.

Vocabulary and Spelling

Teach

Identifying Context Clues

On the chalkboard, write this sentence: *Grant was so hungry that he grabbed the roll and sooled it, hardly chewing before he swallowed.* Ask students to use context words to guess the meaning of the nonsense word *sooled*. (*Roll, chewing,* and *swallowed* indicate that *sooled* could mean ate, gulped, or wolfed down.) **L2**

Practice and Assess

Answers: Exercise 2
1. a pattern; definition
2. dangerous (or poisonous) snakes; example
3. insect eaters; example (general context is also acceptable)
4. peaceful; general context
5. the art of fine handwriting; definition

Additional Resources

📁 *Vocabulary and Spelling Strategies and Practice,* pp. 13–16, 21–34, 41–52

Close

Discuss additional strategies that students can use to determine the meanings of unfamiliar words. (Use a dictionary or ask someone what the unknown word means.)

Exploring Language

Science

Point out that writing in the field of science may include words that are not familiar to readers. Have students quickly look through articles or books about science. Encourage them to identify any unfamiliar words. Ask volunteers to use context clues to figure out the meanings of the words. Did students use definitions, examples, or general context clues?

Focus

Lesson Overview

Objectives

- To identify English words that were borrowed from French
- To understand the influence of French on the spelling of English words

Skills

- using borrowed words

Critical Thinking

- defining; clarifying

Listening and Speaking

- discussing

Teach

Discussion

Have students read Wordworks, p. 546, and discuss the following questions: *What language was spoken in England before the Norman Conquest? How did Old English change?*

Finding Word Origins

Supply students with a dictionary that includes word origins. Have students find out as much as they can about the history of the borrowed words on this page. They can find out which language or languages the word came from, how the word was spelled, and the original meaning of the word. **L2**

Practice and Assess

Answer: Challenge

The examples given on this page indicate that many speakers of English think of French as a superior, or at least more beautiful, language.

Answers: Parlez-vous français?

1. salon
2. matinee
3. petite
4. R.S.V.P.
5. document

Wordworks

Oui! French Is Spoken Here

Which do you think would smell better, a perfume called Eau de Cochon or one called Happiness? If you guessed Eau de Cochon, you're not alone. Many Americans associate French names with something fancier or more fashionable. Actually, Eau de Cochon means "aroma of pig."

Admiration of the French language began more than 900 years ago. In A.D. 1066 French-speaking Normans conquered England. The people living there spoke a language we now call Old English. The Normans became England's rulers. They controlled the government, the land, the laws, the military, and most of the wealth. Everybody who was anybody spoke French! And people who wanted to be somebody soon began using French words. While English peasants ate the meat of *cows* and *pigs* (words from Old English), ladies and gentlemen of the court dined on *beef* and *pork* (words from French).

> **Challenge**
>
> Based on your reading of this page, under what circumstances do you think one language might borrow words from another?

Shall we visit the *boutique*?

Do you mean the "small shop"?

Vocabulary and Spelling

ACTIVITY

Parlez-vous français?

Write the word or phrase that completes each sentence.

document	*matinee*	*petite*
salon	*R.S.V.P.*	

1. I had my hair cut at the beauty _____.
2. The _____ begins at 2:00 P.M.
3. Angela is very _____.
4. _____ by next Tuesday.
5. The _____ is on my desk.

546   Unit 22

Close

Begin a discussion about how languages change. Ask students why a language might need a new word. Point out that *cyberspace* and *blading* are recent additions to English. Ask students to think of some other words that are new to English. The fields of music, science, and computers frequently require the addition of new words.

546

22.3 Using Word Parts

You often can figure out the meaning of an unfamiliar word by dividing it into parts. The main part of the word is called the **root,** and it carries the word's basic meaning. A root is often a simple word in itself. For example, *read* is a word. When a prefix or a suffix is added to it, *read* becomes a root.

Prefixes and suffixes can be attached to a root to change its meaning. A **prefix** is added to the beginning of a root. A **suffix** is added to the end. A word can have both a prefix and a suffix.

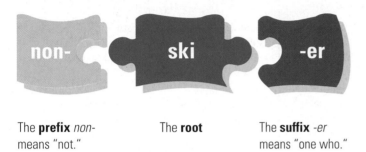

The **prefix** *non-* means "not."

The **root**

The **suffix** *-er* means "one who."

You know what *ski* means. Look at the meanings of the prefix *non-* and the suffix *-er.* You can easily see that a nonskier is "one who does not ski."

The prefix *non-* and the suffix *-er* can be attached to other roots as well. In each case they will produce the meaning "one who does not [do whatever the word root says]." For example, a *nonobserver* is someone who does not observe. A *nonvoter* is a person who does not vote. Try to think of some other root words that would fit between *non-* and *-er.*

Words usually have only one prefix, but may have several suffixes. For example, you can start with *nation,* add *-al* to get *national,* and add *-ity* to get *nationality.* You can see how learning about prefixes and suffixes can help increase your vocabulary. Knowing the meanings of these word parts can also help you understand unfamiliar words.

Vocabulary and Spelling

Focus

Lesson Overview

Objectives
- To identify the parts of a word, such as the root, the prefix, and the suffix
- To analyze the parts of a word to determine a word's meaning

Skills
- using prefixes and suffixes; changing the spelling of words when adding suffixes

Critical Thinking
- defining and clarifying

Listening and Speaking
- discussing; creating riddles

Bellringer
Daily Language Activity

When students enter the classroom, have this assignment on the board: *List five words that have a prefix or a suffix.*

See also *Daily Language Practice*

Motivating Activity

Have students choose a paragraph in a book or article. Let them read the paragraph and then scan it for any words with prefixes or suffixes. Begin a list on the chalkboard of words the students find.

Resource Manager

Planning Resources
- *Lesson Plans*

📠 **Transparencies**
- *Bellringer*
- *Daily Language Practice*

📁 **Other Print Resources**
- *Vocabulary and Spelling Strategies and Practice,* pp. 13–16, 21–34, 41–52

Teach

Adding Prefixes

On the chalkboard, write the word *prefix.* Remind students that a prefix is a word part added to a root to form a new word. A prefix changes or adds to the meaning of the original word. Ask students how the word *prefix* tells them where the added part can be found. If necessary, point out that *pre-* means "before." A prefix comes before the root. Ask students to name other words that begin with *pre-.* Familiar words include *preview, prepare,* and *preschool.* **L2**

Using Word Parts

Before students attempt to read the charts of prefixes and suffixes, help them manipulate word parts. Make flash cards, writing the prefix *un-* on one card and the suffix *-ness* on another. On additional cards write the root words *kind, fit,* and *sound.* Use cards to demonstrate pairing a prefix with a root word to form a new word. Repeat the process with the suffix cards and the suffix chart on p. 549. **L1**

Vocabulary and Spelling

Prefixes

pre-

The following chart shows some prefixes and their meanings. Notice that some prefixes have more than one meaning. Sometimes two or more prefixes have the same or a similar meaning.

Prefixes		
Prefixes	**Words**	**Meanings**
in- means "not"	inactive incomplete indirect	not active not complete not direct
non- means "without" or "not"	nonfat nonstop nonreturnable	without fat without stopping not able to be returned
dis- means "opposite of" or "not"	disadvantage disagree disarm	an unfavorable condition to not agree to take away arms (weapons)
un- means "opposite of" or "to reverse"	unable unclean untie unset	not able not clean to loosen not yet firm or set
pre- means "before"	prejudge prepay preview	to judge in advance to pay in advance to view in advance
re- means "again" or "back"	rewrite repay reappear	to write again to pay back to appear again

Suffixes

A suffix added to a word can change the word's part of speech as well as its meaning. For example, adding the suffix *-er* to *read* (a verb) makes *reader* (a noun). Adding *-less* to *rain* (a noun) makes *rainless* (an adjective).

548   Unit 22 Vocabulary and Spelling

MEETING INDIVIDUAL NEEDS

English Language Learners

Using Prefixes

Students learning English may have difficulty with prefixes that have similar meanings, such as *in-, non-, dis-, un-,* and *de-.* Suggest that they be alert to the use of these and other prefixes as they read and listen to others speak. You might read the following sentences and ask volunteers to repeat the words that begin with prefixes.

- Lupe was unsure of how to get to the library.
- The magician made the rabbit disappear.
- Sam feels insecure in his new job.

The following chart shows some common suffixes and their meanings. As the examples show, sometimes a suffix has more than one meaning. In addition, two or more suffixes may have the same meaning. For example, the suffixes -er, -or, and -ist can all mean "one who."

See if you can identify the part of speech of each example word with and without its suffix. You can review parts of speech in Part 2 of this book.

Suffixes		
Suffixes	**Words**	**Meanings**
-er means "one who," "that which," or "more"	runner baker toaster weaker	one who runs one who bakes that which makes toast more weak
-or means "one who"	actor conductor demonstrator	one who acts one who conducts one who demonstrates
-ist means "one who"	typist violinist scientist	one who types one who plays the violin one who works at science
-less means "without"	hairless spineless merciless	without hair without a spine without mercy
-able means "can be" or "having the quality of"	believable washable valuable	can be believed can be washed having value
-ible means "can be" or "having the quality of"	deductible digestible sensible	can be deducted can be digested having sense
-ness means "quality of" or "state of being"	darkness mildness kindness	being dark quality of being mild state of being kind

Teach

Adding Suffixes

To illustrate how adding a suffix can change a word to a different part of speech, have students work within sentence frames. Write on the chalkboard: *The girl will run fifty yards in the race tomorrow.* Ask a volunteer to add the suffix *-er* to *run.* Can the new word be used in the same place in the sentence? (no) Which word in the sentence can *runner* replace? (girl) **L2**

Cross-reference: Vocabulary and Spelling

For more information on spelling rules that apply when adding prefixes or suffixes to words, refer students to Lesson 22.6, pp. 557–560.

Additional Resources

Vocabulary and Spelling Strategies and Practice, pp. 13–16, 21–34, 41–52

Vocabulary and Spelling

Enrichment and Extension

Adding Prefixes and Suffixes

Tell students that with some words, you can add both a prefix and a suffix. Write the following words on the board: *fix, comfort, join, agree, pay, correct.* Challenge students to come up with a prefix and a suffix for each. *(unfixable, uncomfortable, nonjoiner, disagreeable, prepayable, incorrectness)*

Practice and Assess

Answers: Exercise 3

(Students' column-four words will vary.)

1. pre-teen	preview
2. non-drive -er	nonjoiner
3. un-forgive -able	unbelievable
4. non-profit	nonskid
5. de-forest	defrost
6. collect-ible	digestible
7. dis-approve	discomfort
8. in-complete -ness	indecisiveness

Answers: Exercise 4

1. waiter, server
2. pianist, piano player
3. teacher, instructor, professor
4. actor, player
5. biker, cyclist, rider

Close

Have students practice writing words with prefixes and suffixes in sentences. Each student can choose a word with a prefix, a suffix, or both and use it in a sentence. A partner can say the word aloud and identify the root word and the prefix or suffix.

Adding a suffix sometimes changes the spelling of a word. As the chart shows, when adding *-er* to *run,* you also must add another *n* to make *runner.* To learn more about spelling changes when adding suffixes, see pages 557-560.

Exercise 3

Divide the following words. Write their parts in three columns headed *prefix, word root,* and *suffix.* (Note that not all the words have both a prefix and a suffix.) In a fourth column, write another word that uses the same prefix or the same suffix (or both if you can). Check your words in a dictionary to make sure the prefixes and suffixes are correctly used.

1. preteen
2. nondriver
3. unforgivable
4. nonprofit
5. deforest
6. collectible
7. disapprove
8. incompleteness

Exercise 4

To name each person described below, use a word that ends in the suffix *-er, -or,* or *-ist.* You should be able to list more than one word for some of the descriptions. Remember that sometimes the addition of a suffix changes the spelling of the root word. Check your answers in a dictionary to be sure you have the correct spelling and suffix.

1. A person who serves food in a restaurant
2. A person who plays a keyboard instrument
3. A person who instructs others
4. A person who appears in plays
5. A person who rides a bicycle

Cooperative Learning

Creating Riddles

Have students use words from the prefixes and suffixes lists on pages 548 and 549 to create riddles for each other like the following:

- What is a story that can be believed? (a believable story)
- Who is a person who bakes cakes? (a cake baker)

Tell students to look at the meaning of the prefix or suffix and use it as a clue in their riddles. For example, *-er* means "one who," so the clue might say "a person who."

Wordworks

Sounds Like . . .

"How much wood would a woodchuck chuck if a woodchuck could chuck wood?" But if a woodchuck can't chuck wood, how did it get the name *woodchuck*?

When people hear an unfamiliar word, they often try to understand the word by relating it to words they know. The process of inventing an origin for a word is called folk etymology (et´ ə mol´ ə jē).

As to *woodchuck*—English speakers new to North America heard the Cree word for the animal, which is *otchek*. They changed its unfamiliar sounds to the familiar sounds of *wood* and *chuck*. People would later guess that a woodchuck had something to do with wood simply because of its name.

Sometimes people change the pronunciation of a word because the word not only sounds like one they know but also seems to be related. During the Middle Ages, the French word for "young woman," *femelle*, was borrowed into English. Because *femelle* sounded like *male* and seemed related to *male*, *femelle* eventually was pronounced and spelled *female*.

> **Challenge**
>
> Look up the origin of the word *shamefaced* in a college dictionary. How did this word get its spelling and pronunciation?

ACTIVITY

In Other Words

Figure out the English words related to the following word origins.

1. from the Natick word *musquash* (a North American rodent)
2. from the Middle English word *berfrey* (tower)
3. from the Old English words *brȳd* (bride) and *guma* (man)

Vocabulary and Spelling

551

Cooperative Learning

Misunderstood Words

Children learning the Pledge of Allegiance often substitute a known word for an unfamiliar one. One small child began: "Congratulations to the flag . . . ," and another ended with the words: "liver tea and justice for all." Ask students to recall and list some words they have misunderstood and pronounced incorrectly. They might then work with a partner to share their lists and brainstorm additional words. Then have pairs of students share their recollections with the class.

Focus

Lesson Overview

Objectives
- To understand the usefulness of word origins in developing vocabulary
- To use resources to determine the origins of words

Skills
- finding word origins

Critical Thinking
- synthesizing

Listening and Speaking
- discussing; listening to word sounds

Teach

Discussion

Have students read Wordworks, p. 551, and discuss the following questions: *How might someone create the meaning of an unfamiliar word? Why might speakers change the pronunciation of a borrowed word?*

Practice and Assess

Answer: Challenge

Shamefaced comes from Old English *sceamfaest,* which combines *sceamu* (shame) + *faest* (firm). *Shamefaced* suggests a face held firm by shame.

Answers: In Other Words

1. muskrat
2. belfry
3. bridegroom

Close

Have students make a list of words with unusual sounds and look up their words' origins.

Focus

Lesson Overview

Objectives

- To identify synonyms and antonyms of words
- To use synonyms and antonyms to expand vocabulary

Skills

- recognizing and using synonyms and antonyms

Critical Thinking

- comparing and contrasting

Listening and Speaking

- informal speaking

🔔 Bellringer
Daily Language Activity

When students enter the classroom, have this assignment on the board: *Make two lists. In the first list, put words that mean the same as* cold. *In the second list, put words that mean the opposite of* cold.

📖 **See also** *Daily Language Practice*

Teach

☑Teaching Tip

Call on a volunteer to make up a sentence using the word *walk.* Invite other students to brainstorm synonyms for *walk,* such as *stroll, amble, stride, march, plod, pace,* or *tramp.* Ask students to act out and define each synonym. Discuss how a careful selection of synonyms can make writing more vivid. **L2**

Vocabulary and Spelling

22.4   Synonyms and Antonyms

Suppose that you were describing a rainy day. Imagine how dull your writing would be if you could use only the word *rain.* Fortunately, the English language has many words with meanings similar to *rain.* In describing the rain, you might use the word *downpour.* You could also choose *flood, cloudburst, shower, sprinkle,* or *drizzle.*

English also contains many pairs of words that have opposite meanings. On a rainy day the streets are *wet.* On a sunny day the streets are *dry.*

Synonyms

Words that have similar meanings are called **synonyms.** Knowing synonyms can improve your vocabulary and your writing. It can also help you understand the meanings of unfamiliar words. For example, you may not know what the word *obstinate* means. However, suppose that you knew that its synonyms included *hardheaded* and *stubborn.* Then you'd probably have a pretty good idea of what *obstinate* means.

Synonyms can help you be more precise in your speaking and writing. Synonyms have similar meanings, but they hardly ever have exactly the same meaning. The words *cloudburst* and *downpour* both refer to heavy rain. *Drizzle* and *shower* bring to mind a different, more gentle rain. There's a big difference between a *sprinkle* and a *deluge,* even though both words can mean "rain." When you write about rain—or about anything at all—synonyms help you say exactly what you mean.

You'll find synonyms listed in some dictionary entries. Another place to look for them is in a dictionary of synonyms. Such a dictionary is called a thesaurus. See page 538 for more information on how to use a thesaurus.

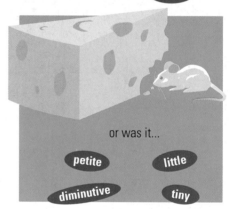

The mouse was **small**

or was it...

petite   **little**

diminutive   **tiny**

Resource Manager

Planning Resources
- *Lesson Plans*

📖 Transparencies
- *Bellringer*
- *Daily Language Practice*

📁 Other Print Resources
- *Vocabulary and Spelling Strategies and Practice,* pp. 13–16, 21–34, 41–52

Antonyms

Antonyms are words that have opposite or nearly opposite meanings. Knowing antonyms can help you build your vocabulary and help you understand the meanings of other words. Perhaps you don't know the meaning of the word *taciturn*. Knowing that an antonym of the word is *talkative,* you could guess that *taciturn* describes someone who is silent, or untalkative.

You probably know such common antonyms as *hot—cold, love—hate,* and *short—tall.* One common way to form antonyms is to add a prefix meaning "not" or "the opposite of" to a word. (Page 548 has a list of some prefixes with those meanings.) For example, you can make an antonym of *believable* by adding the prefix *un-.*

Exercise 5

In each pair of synonyms below, the first word may be unknown to you. The second word, however, is probably familiar. Use your knowledge of each familiar word to figure out the meaning of its synonym. Then write a sentence using the first word in each pair.

1. benevolent, good
2. apparition, ghost
3. malevolent, evil
4. fatigued, tired
5. nourish, feed

Exercise 6

Write an antonym for each word below by adding the proper prefix to it. Review the list of such prefixes on page 548 if you need to. Check each word in a dictionary to make sure you used the correct prefix.

1. appear
2. sense
3. true
4. equal
5. direct

Vocabulary and Spelling

Practice and Assess

Evaluation Rubrics

Exercise 5

Answers will vary. Sentences should demonstrate an understanding of the word's meaning. Examples:
1. Her kindness to the poor showed her to be a benevolent person.
2. He claimed to have seen an apparition of the dead man.
3. His malevolent grin frightened everyone who saw him.
4. The vigorous workout left us fatigued.
5. We must nourish the hungry children.

Answers: Exercise 6

1. disappear
2. nonsense
3. untrue
4. unequal
5. indirect

Additional Resources

Vocabulary and Spelling Strategies and Practice, pp. 13–16, 21–34, 41–52

Close

Ask students to each write a paragraph explaining what synonyms and antonyms are and how synonyms help a writer.

Technology Tip

Using the Thesaurus

Many word-processing programs include a thesaurus. Ask students who have used such programs for their writing to compare their program thesaurus to a thesaurus in book form. Is one of the two faster? Easier to use? Do both have a sufficient number of synonyms? Does either provide antonyms?

Focus

Lesson Overview

Objectives

- To understand the different meanings and word origins of homographs
- To use homographs to expand vocabulary

Skills

- recognizing homographs; using a dictionary

Critical Thinking

- analyzing

Listening and Speaking

- discussing

Teach

Discussion

Have students read Wordworks, p. 554, and discuss the following questions: How might a word have a twin? How might words that are spelled alike have different origins?

Homographs

Have students brainstorm homographs. List these on the chalkboard. Invite students to make up sentences or sentence pairs using both meanings of selected homographs. You may wish to suggest some common homographs such as *wound, tire, wind,* and *bear.* **L2**

Practice and Assess

Answers: Challenge

Bale, meaning "sorrow" or "woe," comes from Middle English derived from Old English. This word is rarely used today. In the more common word *baleful,* the word part *bale-* means "foreboding evil." A *baleful* stare is an ominous look. *Bale,* meaning "a large bundle of goods," comes from Middle English derived from Old French.

Answers: Reading Double

1. palm   3. can
2. close   4. slip

Wordworks

Word Twins

Some English words, called *homographs,* look identical. Homographs are sometimes pronounced differently, but they always have identical spellings. However, homographs have different origins.

Meal (ground grain) and *meal* (eating time) are homographs. Since both refer to food, you might think they have the same origin. Actually, the two words are not related.

The meal used in bread comes from the Old English word *melu,* meaning "to grind." During the Middle Ages (from about A.D. 476 to about A.D. 1450), the word *melu* developed into *meele. Meele* was used as a noun referring to ground grain. By the eighteenth century, the spelling had changed to *meal.*

The meal that refers to an eating time, such as breakfast or lunch, comes from the Old English word *mael,* meaning "appointed time." By the Middle Ages, *mael* had developed into *meel.* In modern English, this word began to be spelled as *meal* and referred to the regular eating times in a day.

Challenge

Using a college dictionary, trace the origins of the homographs *bale* (sorrow) and *bale* (a large bundle of goods). List each form and its meaning.

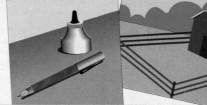

Vocabulary and Spelling

ACTIVITY

Reading Double

Write the homographs for each pair of definitions below and for the pair of illustrations at right.

1. inner surface of the hand; a tropical tree
2. to shut; nearby
3. able to; a metal container
4. to move or slide out of place; a small piece of paper

Close

Have students write pairs of definitions or draw pictures of homographs similar to those shown in "Reading Double." Students can exchange their definitions and guess the homograph.

22.5 Words That Sound Alike

How are a pair and a pear alike? How about a rein and a rain and a reign? The answer, of course, is that these groups of words sound alike. You probably noticed that the words have different meanings and different spellings.

Understanding Homonyms

Words that sound alike but have different meanings are called homonyms. Some homonyms not only sound alike but are spelled alike as well. Such words usually don't cause too many problems. Whether you *ring* a bell or wear a *ring* on your finger, it's still spelled *ring*. You can *file* your nails or *file* some papers. You can even *file* for a job or *file* down the hall with your friends. The spelling of the word *file* remains the same even though its meaning changes.

Homonyms that sound alike but are spelled differently can be tricky. These are the ones you need to be careful with. You don't want to write *new* instead of *knew* in a written report. Imagine writing *threw* on a spelling test when you meant to write *through*. The chart on this page has some more examples of such homonyms. Maybe you can think of other examples.

Homonyms
break to crack, split, or smash
brake to stop a movement
piece a part of something
peace the opposite of war
holey having holes
holy sacred
wholly completely

knight

Using Homonyms

Have you ever been confused about whether to use *their* or *there* in a sentence? Does the difference between *your* and *you're* confuse you sometimes? Because homonyms sound alike, people occasionally don't remember which spelling to use. The chart on the following page shows some common homonyms.

night

Vocabulary and Spelling

22.5 Words That Sound Alike **555**

Focus

Lesson Overview

Objectives
- To identify and understand the difference between various homonyms
- To use words with homonyms correctly in sentences

Skills
- using homonyms

Critical Thinking
- defining and clarifying

Listening and Speaking
- telling riddles based on sound words

Bellringer
Daily Language Activity

When students enter the classroom, have this assignment on the board: *Name five words that have more than one meaning.*

See also *Daily Language Practice*

Motivating Activity

Have students share the words they named in the Bellringer activity. Then have students use those words in context sentences that illustrate each meaning.

Resource Manager

Planning Resources
- *Lesson Plans*

Transparencies
- *Bellringer*
- *Daily Language Practice*

📁 **Other Print Resources**
- *Vocabulary and Spelling Strategies and Practice,* pp. 13–16, 21–34, 41–52

Teach

Understanding Homonyms

To help students with the concept of words that sound alike but are spelled differently, use both auditory and visual clues. Ask students to close their eyes and listen as you read pairs of homonyms. Next, reread the words and their meanings as students find the words in the chart and copy them onto paper or on the chalkboard. Then ask students to circle or highlight the letters that are different in each pair or draw a cartoon to show the meaning of the words. **L1**

Practice and Assess

Answers: Exercise 7

1. they're
2. you're
3. Who's
4. principal
5. it's
6. too

Additional Resources

Vocabulary and Spelling Strategies and Practice, pp. 13–16, 21–34, 41–52

Close

Discuss words that sound alike but are spelled differently. Ask students how they know which homonym to use in a sentence.

Vocabulary and Spelling

Common Homonyms

Words	Meanings
their	belonging to them
there	in that place
they're	contraction for *they are*
its	belonging to it
it's	contraction for *it is* or *it has*
to	in the direction of
too	also
two	the number
your	belonging to you
you're	contraction for *you are*
hear	listen
here	this place
principal	the head of a school; most important
principle	a rule, law, or truth
who's	contraction for *who is* or *who has*
whose	the possessive form of *who*

Exercise 7

Write the correct homonym to fit each sentence.

1. The children are concentrating on what (their, there, they're) doing.
2. Be sure to let me know when (your, you're) going to arrive.
3. (Who's, Whose) responsible for this mess?
4. Coffee is one of the (principle, principal) exports of Colombia.
5. I think (it's, its) going to rain today.
6. Mandy heard the noise; John said that he heard it (to, too, two).

556   Unit 22 Vocabulary and Spelling

Listening and Speaking

Riddles and Jokes

Discuss riddles and jokes based on words that have the same sound but different meanings. For example:
• Why are socks and seeds alike? They both come in pairs (pears).
• How did the queen flood her country? She had a long reign (rain).
• Why did the students bring emery boards to school? (They wanted to be ready to file down the hall.)
Ask students whether they know of any other riddles or jokes based on homonyms, or challenge students to make up their own.

22.6 Spelling Rules I

Improving your spelling can improve your writing. You can improve your spelling skills by noticing common spelling patterns in words with similar sounds and by learning some basic spelling rules.

Suffixes and the Silent *e*

Words that end in a silent *e* can be a spelling problem. They're especially troublesome when you have to add a suffix to them. The rules in the following chart will help you.

Adding Suffixes to Words that End With Silent *e*	
Rules	**Examples**
When adding a suffix that begins with a consonant to a word that ends with a silent *e*, keep the *e*.	pure + -ly = purely grace + -ful = graceful **Common exceptions** awe + -ful = awful argue + -ment = argument
When adding -*ly* to a word that ends with an *l* plus a silent *e*, always drop the *e*.	terrible + -ly = terribly whole + -ly = wholly
When adding a suffix that begins with a vowel or *y* to a word that ends with a silent *e*, usually drop the *e*.	write + -ing = writing shine + -y = shiny **Common exceptions** dye + -ing = dyeing mile + -age = mileage
When adding a suffix that begins with *a* or *o* to a word that ends with *ce* or *ge*, keep the *e* so the word will still have the soft *c* or *g* sound.	change + -able = changeable courage + -ous = courageous
When adding a suffix that begins with a vowel to a word that ends in *ee* or *oe*, keep the *e*.	agree + -able = agreeable hoe + -ing = hoeing

Vocabulary and Spelling

Focus

Lesson Overview

Objectives
- To identify spelling rules for adding suffixes and forming compound words
- To spell correctly words with suffixes, compound words, and other commonly misspelled words

Skills
- identifying misspelled words; spelling words with suffixes correctly

Critical Thinking
- recognizing patterns

Listening and Speaking
- discussing

🔔 Bellringer
Daily Language Activity

When students enter the classroom, have this assignment on the board: *List five words that you have trouble spelling correctly.*

📋 **See also** *Daily Language Practice*

Motivating Activity

On the chalkboard, have students group their lists of words according to the source of the spelling problem. For example, list *ie* and *ei* words in one group, and in another group, list words formed by adding a suffix to a root word.

Resource Manager

Planning Resources
- *Lesson Plans*

📋 **Transparencies**
- *Bellringer*
- *Daily Language Practice*

📁 **Other Print Resources**
- *Vocabulary and Spelling Strategies and Practice,* pp. 13–16, 21–34, 41–52

Teach

Adding Suffixes

List vowels on the chalkboard to help students visualize the final -y rule for words ending in *vowel-plus-y*. Tell them to list all the vowels, then cross out *i* and *y*. Dictate four words, each ending in one of the remaining four vowels plus *y* (for example, *stay, obey, toy, buy*). Students can write the words as you dictate them, then write the same words and add suffixes. **L2**

Vocabulary and Spelling

Suffixes and the Final *y*

Adding suffixes to words that end in *y* can cause spelling problems. The chart below shows the rules for changing the *y* to *i* when adding suffixes.

Adding Suffixes to Words That End In *y*	
When a word ends in a consonant + *y*, change the *y* to *i*.	cry + -ed = cried deny + -es = denies
When the suffix begins with an *i*, do not change the *y* to *i*.	cry + -ing = crying deny + -ing = denying
When a word ends in a vowel + *y*, keep the *y*.	joy + -ful = joyful also stay + -ing = staying

Spelling *ie* and *ei*

Some writers get confused when spelling words containing *ie* or *ei*. One way to help with these letter combinations is to memorize a simple rhyming rule.

Rhyming Rule	Examples
Put *i* before *e*	believe, chief, grieve
except after *c*	receive, deceit, receipt
and when sounded like *a*, as in *neighbor* and *weigh*.	eight, weight, veil, freight

Fortunately, there are very few exceptions to the *ie* and *ei* rule. The box below lists the only exceptions you need to remember.

Exceptions to the *ie* and *ei* Rule
species, seize, leisure, weird, either, neither, height

MEETING INDIVIDUAL NEEDS — English Language Learners

Distinguishing Sounds

Some students cannot distinguish certain English speech sounds. Students may not hear the sound differences in such words as *hit/heat, let/late, cat/cot/cut*. They can benefit from practice with minimal pairs of words. Have them practice with sentences such as *Pick up the cap; pick up the cup.* Have a volunteer repeat the sentence several times, varying use of *cap* and *cup*. Then have the student pronounce a list of words while a student who is more proficient in English writes down what he or she hears. Compare the lists.

Doubling the Final Consonant

When a word ends in a consonant, you may need to double the final consonant when adding a suffix.

DOUBLE THE FINAL CONSONANT WHEN a word ends in a single consonant following one vowel AND

- the word is one syllable

  sit + -ing = sitting   run + -er = runner

- the word has an accent on the last syllable and the accent stays there after the suffix is added

  prefer + -ed = preferred   reset + -ing = resetting

DO *NOT* DOUBLE THE FINAL CONSONANT WHEN

- the suffix begins with a consonant

  forget + -ful = forgetful   pain + -less = painless

- the accent is not on the last syllable

  develop + -ing = developing   offer + -ed = offered

- the accent moves when the suffix is added

  prefer + -ence = preference   refer + -ence = reference

- two vowels come before the final consonant

  train + -ing = training   moan + -ed = moaned

- the word ends in two consonants

  remind + -er = reminder   bang + -ed = banged

SPECIAL CASE: When a word ends in *ll* and the suffix *-ly* is added, drop one *l*.

  dull + -ly = dully   full + -ly = fully

Using Syllable Boundaries

Some students like to use the syllables or beats in a word to help them with pronunciation as they read or with spelling as they write. Each **syllable** in a word should have one, and only one, vowel sound. Try clapping out the word *wel-come.* You should get two beats. It is easy to find each syllable in two syllable words that contain two consonants in the middle of two vowels (VCCV). Divide the word between the two consonants. How would you separate the following words into syllables?

    basket   lantern   dollar   mustard   funny

Teach

Understanding Syllables and Accents

Spelling rules for doubling the final consonant involve recognizing the syllables and stress of a word. If students have trouble hearing syllables in a word, or if they cannot always recognize a stressed or accented syllable, suggest that they clap out the rhythm of each word, using soft and loud claps to distinguish the accented and unaccented syllables. Begin by clapping out rhythms yourself; then ask students to clap with you. **L1**

⇄ Cross-reference: Vocabulary and Spelling

For more information on spelling rules, refer students to Lessons 22.7 and 22.8 on pp. 561–567.

Vocabulary and Spelling

Exploring Language

History

Geoffrey Chaucer, who died about 1400, wrote in Middle English. Speakers of Middle English were the first to stop pronouncing the final *e* that is silent in many modern English words. Other vowel sounds and some consonant sounds also differed from those in modern English words. Many words that come from Old or Middle English conform to the same spelling pattern, such as *eight, weight,* and *freight.* Words from a different language, such as Latin, conform to different patterns, for example, *fate, date,* and *plate.*

Practice and Assess

Additional Resources

📁 *Vocabulary and Spelling Strategies and Practice*, pp. 13–16, 21–34, 41–52

Close

Have students write a list of ways in which learning spelling rules help them to improve their writing. Have them discuss their ideas.

An **open syllable** is one where a vowel is not followed by a consonant. Sometimes open syllables can be words themselves, such as *a* or *I*. Usually, open syllables are parts of a word, such as in *pro-vide* or *fla-vor*. A **closed syllable** contains consonants on either side of the vowel, such as in the words *champ* and *blast*.

Here are some guidelines to help you divide words into syllables.

- Prefixes form separate syllables, such as in the words *un-hap-py* or *re-pay*.

- Suffixes also form separate syllables, because they, too, contain a vowel. Consider the words *kind-ness* or *help-ful*.

- Endings that form plurals may or may not create a new syllable. If you add *-s* to make a plural, such as in the word *plants*, you won't add a syllable, but if you add *-es*, as in *wishes*, you will add a syllable.

- Compound words divide into syllables according to their word boundaries, such as in *black-bird* or *out-side*.

- A final *-le* picks up the preceding consonant to form a syllable, such as in *ta-ble*, *sam-ple*, or *un-cle*.

Exercise 8

Carefully examine each set of words below. Find the one word that is misspelled in each set and write the word correctly.

1. blackness, roundness, sterness
2. recieve, achieve, veil
3. dullly, purely, rarely
4. stating, shineing, mileage
5. commited, stopped, regretting

Exercise 9

Correctly complete each of the following word + suffix problems.

1. big + -er =
2. supply + -ing =
3. explain + -able =
4. label + -ed =
5. expel + -ing =
6. choose + -ing =
7. occur + -ed =
8. hoe + -ing =
9. differ + -ence =
10. use + -able =

Vocabulary and Spelling

Enrichment and Extension

Changes in English

Play a recording of a reading from one of Chaucer's *Canterbury Tales* to demonstrate for students how different Chaucer's English was from the English students know today. Ask students to identify words or phrases they can understand. You might write several Middle English words on the board with their modern English equivalents. Ask students to describe how spelling has changed from Middle English to modern English.

22.7 Spelling Rules II

A handful of spelling rules can help you spell thousands of words. For example, the few rules that follow deal with the spelling of plurals. These rules will help you spell the plurals of nearly every English noun.

Forming Plurals

Most nouns in English form plurals by adding an -s or -es. However, there are other ways to form plurals. The charts that follow show some general and special rules for plurals.

General Rules for Plurals		
If the Noun Ends in	**The Rule is**	**Example**
s, ch, sh, x, or z	add -es	loss → losses watch → watches bush → bushes box → boxes fizz → fizzes
a consonant + y	change y to i and add -es	berry → berries body → bodies baby → babies
a vowel + y	add -s	key → keys day → days boy → boys
a vowel + o	add -s	stereo → stereos studio → studios rodeo → rodeos
a consonant + o	usually add -s	piano → pianos photo → photos solo → solos
	Common exceptions but sometimes add -es	potato → potatoes hero → heroes echo → echoes

Vocabulary and Spelling

Focus

Lesson Overview

Objectives
- To understand spelling rules for plural nouns
- To spell the plural forms of words correctly

Skills
- forming plural nouns; using a dictionary

Critical Thinking
- visualizing

Listening and Speaking
- discussing; spelling aloud

Bellringer
Daily Language Activity
When students enter the classroom, have this assignment on the board: *List five plural nouns.*

See also *Daily Language Practice*

Motivating Activity

On the chalkboard, work with students to sort into groups the plural nouns that they listed. Have them group or cluster words according to the way the plurals are formed. For example, *lice, mice, men,* and *feet* would be in one group; *cats, boys,* and *skates* in another; and *dishes, matches,* and *foxes* in a third group.

Resource Manager

Planning Resources
- *Lesson Plans*

Transparencies
- *Bellringer*
- *Daily Language Practice*

Other Print Resources
- *Vocabulary and Spelling Strategies and Practice,* pp. 13–16, 21–34, 41–52

Teach

Forming Plurals

Encourage students to list additional examples of each spelling rule in the chart. Discuss exceptions as well. Students might take turns naming objects in the room and challenging classmates to spell the plurals. **L2**

Tracing Difficult Words

Some students may need to engage a number of senses as an aid for memorizing individual words. Have students use kinesthetic tracing methods. You may wish to pair students. One student should read a word aloud for the other student to write. The reader should then show the word to the listener. Finally, the listener should write the correct spelling of the word, and then spell it aloud while tracing the outline of each letter. **L1**

Vocabulary and Spelling

General Rules for Plurals		
If the Noun Ends in	**The Rule is**	**Example**
f or *ff*	add *-s*	reef → reefs cuff → cuffs
	Common exceptions change *f* to *v* and add *-es*	leaf → leaves loaf → loaves
lf	change *f* to *v* and add *-es*	half → halves wolf → wolves
fe	change *f* to *v* and add *-s*	life → lives knife → knives

Special Rules for Plurals	
Special Case	**Examples**
To form the plurals of most proper names, add *-s*. But add *-es* if the name ends in *s, ch, sh, x,* or *z*.	Krey → Kreys Jones → Joneses Hatch → Hatches Bush → Bushes Marx → Marxes Sanchez → Sanchezes
To form the plural of one-word compound nouns, follow the general rules for plurals.	textbook → textbooks icebox → iceboxes penknife → penknives blackberry → blackberries
To form the plural of hyphenated compound nouns or compound nouns of more than one word, make the most important word plural.	brother-in-law → brothers-in-law ice cream → ice creams chief of staff → chiefs of staff
Some nouns have irregular plural forms and do not follow any rules.	woman → women ox → oxen foot → feet
Some nouns have the same singular and plural forms.	series → series deer → deer sheep → sheep

562 Unit 22 Vocabulary and Spelling

English Language Learners

Writing Plural Nouns

Because different languages form plurals in different ways, students may have difficulty understanding the concept of plural nouns and developing the habit of changing singular nouns to a plural form. To provide additional practice for students who need it, you may team them with peers who can make up and dictate sentences. Go over the rules for formation of plurals. Ask students to find examples of each rule in available reading materials.

Becoming a Better Speller

By following a few simple steps, you can learn to spell new words. Pay attention to unfamiliar words or hard-to-spell words in your reading. Notice and remember spelling patterns in words. As you write, note words that you have trouble spelling. Then use the steps below to learn to spell those difficult words.

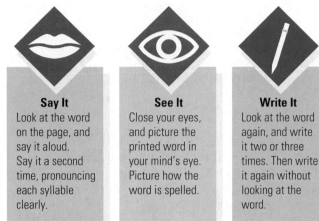

Say It
Look at the word on the page, and say it aloud. Say it a second time, pronouncing each syllable clearly.

See It
Close your eyes, and picture the printed word in your mind's eye. Picture how the word is spelled.

Write It
Look at the word again, and write it two or three times. Then write it again without looking at the word.

Check It
Check what you have written. Did you spell it correctly? If not, go through each step again until you can spell the word correctly.

Get into the habit of using your dictionary to find the correct spelling of a word. How do you find it in a dictionary if you can't spell it? Jot down letters and letter combinations that could stand for the sound you hear at the beginning of the word. Try each of these possible spellings as you look for the word in the dictionary. Then *Say It, See It, Write It, Check It,* and learn to spell the word.

Exercise 10

Write the plural form of each of the following words.

1. fox	**4.** echo	**7.** bench	**10.** mosquito
2. fly	**5.** radio	**8.** trouble	**11.** strawberry
3. elf	**6.** dairy	**9.** Juarez	**12.** zebra

Practice and Assess

Answers: Exercise 10
1. foxes
2. flies
3. elves
4. echoes
5. radios
6. dairies
7. benches
8. troubles
9. Juarezes
10. mosquitoes
11. strawberries
12. zebras

Additional Resources

Vocabulary and Spelling Strategies and Practice, pp. 13–16, 21–34, 41–52

Close

Have students discuss strategies for spelling plural nouns. Ask students these questions: *What works best for remembering tricky spellings? What strategies would you like to try in the future?*

Vocabulary and Spelling

Exploring Language

History

In Old English, inflections (word endings), rather than syntax (word order), were used to designate changes in grammatical form. However, by the end of the Middle English period, most of the inflections of Old English had disappeared. Among the inflections remaining today are the final *-es* or *-s* for plural nouns and the past tense suffix, *-ed.*

Focus

Lesson Overview

Objectives

- To analyze the system used to create a code
- To create a code and analyze the codes of others

Skills

- understanding code systems

Critical Thinking

- patterning

Listening and Speaking

- discussing

Teach

Discussion

Have students read Wordworks, p. 564, and discuss the following questions: *Why might someone send a message in a code? How can you create a code?*

Creating a Code

Have students work in teams to create original codes and exchange their coded messages with other teams. **L2**

Practice and Assess

Evaluation Rubrics

Challenge

Answers will vary. Students may discover that language is simply a set of symbols that combine to create words that express ideas.

Answer: Crack the Code

The message says: "Attack Caesar at dawn." The code is based on the numerical order of the letters in the alphabet.

Wordworks

Secret Codes

Suppose that you want to send a secret note to a friend but need to make sure no one else can read it. Do what the ancient Greeks did—code it!

People have sent coded messages, or cryptograms, for thousands of years. Messengers first used codes during wartime to carry secret messages across enemy lines.

One common code system substitutes letters. Julius Caesar, a Roman general, used such a system. In his system, you replace each letter in the message with a letter three spaces to the right in the regular alphabet. For example, the message FIGHT would be written as ILJKW in code. Anyone who knows the code can easily figure out the message. To decode the message, you replace each letter with a letter three spaces to the left in the alphabet.

Another code system reverses the order of letters. Suppose that you want to code the message SUE WILL NOT GO WITH JACK. First, divide the letters of the message into groups of five: SUEWI LLNOT GOWIT HJACK. Then reverse the letters in each group: IWEUS TONLL TIWOG KCAJH. This message would be pretty hard to figure out—unless you knew the code.

Challenge

Working with a friend, experiment with coded messages. Use a system discussed here, or create your own. What fact about language can you learn from your experiments?

1 - 20 - 20 - 1 - 3 - 11

3 - 1 - 5 - 19 - 1 - 18

1 - 20 - 4 - 1 - 23 - 14

ACTIVITY

Crack the Code

Suppose that you are one of Caesar's messengers. You have just intercepted this coded message from one of Caesar's enemies. All you know is that the numbers in the code stand for letters in the alphabet. Can you crack the code?

Vocabulary and Spelling

564 Unit 22

Close

Have students discuss how creating codes and figuring out codes can help them learn about language.

Real World Connection

History

During World War II, the U.S. Marine Corps used a "code" for sending messages by telephone or radio that the Germans and Japanese never succeeded in cracking. This baffling "code" was simply a spoken Native American language—most often Navajo. Reportedly, only a handful of non-Navajos, none of them German or Japanese, could speak the Navajo language. By the end of the war, the Marine Corps included 420 Navajo "codetalkers."

22.8 Problem Words

Like most people, you probably have trouble spelling certain words. Some words are harder to spell than others. Some words don't follow basic spelling rules, but there are some ways you can learn to spell even the most difficult words.

Make a personal word list. List the words that you find especially difficult or that you often misspell. Keep your list up-to-date, adding new words as you come across them. Study them by using the steps shown on page 563. When you're sure you can spell a word, you can remove it from your list.

Difficult Words

The following is a list of words that people often misspell. Are any of your problem words on this list? What other words would you add to the list?

Often Misspelled Words			
absence	definite	leisure	recommend
accidentally	descend	library	restaurant
adviser	disease	license	rhythm
all right	embarrass	misspell	schedule
answer	environment	molasses	sense
athlete	February	muscle	separate
attendant	foreign	necessary	similar
ballet	forty	neighborhood	sincerely
beautiful	funeral	niece	succeed
beginning	genius	ninety	technology
believe	government	occasion	theory
business	grammar	original	traffic
cafeteria	guarantee	parallel	truly
canceled	height	permanent	usually
canoe	humorous	physical	vacuum
cemetery	immediate	probably	variety
choir	jewelry	receipt	various
colonel	laboratory	recognize	Wednesday

Focus

Lesson Overview

Objectives
- To identify commonly misspelled words
- To use easily confused words correctly in sentences

Skills
- creating a personal word list

Critical Thinking
- defining and clarifying

Listening and Speaking
- tape recording sentences

Bellringer
Daily Language Activity

When students enter the classroom, have this assignment on the board: *List three pairs of words that are easily confused because they sound alike but have different meanings and spellings.*

See also *Daily Language Practice*

Motivating Activity

Form groups and have each group choose a pair of homonyms from their Bellringer lists to use in sentences. Each group member should write one sentence using the wrong homonym. Then students can exchange papers, make corrections, and share their corrected sentences with one another.

Vocabulary and Spelling

Resource Manager

Planning Resources
- *Lesson Plans*

Transparencies
- *Bellringer*
- *Daily Language Practice*

Other Print Resources
- *Vocabulary and Spelling Strategies and Practice,* pp. 13–16, 21–34, 41–52

Teach

Exploring Misspelled Words

After students look at the list of often-misspelled words, discuss possible reasons that these words are often misspelled. Ask students to read a word from the list aloud, such as *absence,* and listen to the way it sounds. The pronunciation doesn't make the second vowel sound clear, since it is in an unaccented syllable. Memorizing the spellings of some problem words is important, since sounds can sometimes be deceiving. **L2**

Using Homonyms Creatively

Students may search telephone directories and periodicals for advertisements that show an intentional misuse (or creative use) of homonyms. For example, a secretarial service was called The Write Type. Other business names, logos, or slogans may use homonyms correctly but in clever ways. The editing program RIGHTWriter is one example. After researching and discussing examples, students might invent their own names for products or businesses, using homonyms in creative ways. **L3**

Easily Confused Words

Did you ever get confused over the spelling of *through* and *threw?* How about *hour* and *our?* Would you describe a smell as a *sent,* a *cent,* or a *scent?*

Some words are often confused because they sound alike but have different spellings and meanings. You can review many of these troublesome words on pages 455–458. Following are a few more. You may want to add some of these words to your personal word list.

Words That Are Often Confused	
to	toward, in the direction of; as far as Go **to** the corner, and then turn **to** the left.
too	also; as well as; more than enough Mario was **too** tired to dance. His sister was tired **too.**
two	the number 2 The **two** of us were the last pair to arrive.
principle	a basic rule, truth, or law The **principle** of free speech is important in a democracy.
principal	first in rank; the head of a school The **principal** announced that school would close early.
desert (dez′ ərt)	a dry, barren region They hoped to cross the **desert** before their water ran out.
desert (di zurt′)	to abandon; to leave without permission The soldier was warned not to **desert** his post.
dessert (di zurt′)	a sweet course served at the end of a meal I'll have the chocolate cake for **dessert.**
passed	to have moved on or ahead; completed satisfactorily Donna **passed** the test with only one error.
past	time gone by; existed earlier Jake learned from his **past** mistakes.
weather	the daily conditions of temperature, moisture, wind, etc. The northern wind brought a sudden change in the **weather.**
whether	conjunction used in indirect questions Everyone wondered **whether** the plane would leave on time.

Exploring Language

History

Some troublesome spelling words are explained by the way the English language has developed. Originally, spelling reflected changes in pronunciation. When printing became common in the late fifteenth century, spelling became more standardized because people saw words in print. The use of dictionaries, starting in the eighteenth century, standardized spellings even more, but pronunciation continued to change. For example, the word *knight* is spelled as it is because the letters *k, g,* and *h* in the word were pronounced by people in Chaucer's time.

Another way to learn problem words is to use memory devices, or tricks for remembering. For example, do you have trouble remembering the difference between *principal* and *principle?* You might memorize: *Your principal is a pal. A principle is a rule.* Do you confuse *to, too,* and *two?* Perhaps you could remember: *Two horses are one too many for me to tend.* Sometimes these memory devices are little rhymes, such as the following:

> *Poor little Emma,*
> *Caught in a dilemma.*

Think of other sentences or rhymes that will help you remember how to spell troublesome words. Do you know any?

Exercise 11

On a separate sheet of paper, write the word in the parentheses that correctly completes each sentence.

1. There were only (to, too, two) of us at breakfast this morning.
2. Camels can travel in the (desert, dessert) better than most other animals.
3. We all wondered (weather, whether) the test would be as hard as the last one was.
4. My parents think I spend (to, too, two) much money on CDs.
5. The helicopter (passed, past) overhead, frightening the animals.
6. My favorite teacher will be the new (principle, principal) next year.
7. I ate so much that I hardly had room for (desert, dessert).
8. Isn't this rainy (weather, whether) ever going to end?
9. I like studying history. The (past, passed) has always interested me.
10. The (principle, principal) purpose of our club is to raise money to help feed the homeless.

Vocabulary and Spelling

Practice and Assess

Answers: Exercise 11

1. two
2. desert
3. whether
4. too
5. passed
6. principal
7. dessert
8. weather
9. past
10. principal

✔ ASSESSMENT OPTIONS

📁 *Tests with Answer Key and Rubrics*
Unit 22 Mastery Test, pp. 91–92

💾 *Testmaker*
Unit 22 Mastery Test

You may wish to administer the Unit 22 Mastery Test at this point.

📼 *Mindjogger Videoquizzes*

Additional Resources

📁 *Vocabulary and Spelling Strategies and Practice,* pp. 13–26, 21–34, 41–52

Close

Students may work with partners to write sentences that help them identify and clarify homonyms and other words that can cause spelling problems.

Technology Tip

Recording Homonyms

Tape-record students reading sentences containing homonyms. As you play the tape recording back, have students write the correct homonym. Ask them whether they think certain homonyms are more difficult to distinguish than others.

Objectives

- To use the table of contents, index, and glossary of a book to gather information and direct research
- To set study goals and schedule time to complete assigned work
- To use an effective study method to gather information
- To organize information using note cards, outlines, and graphic aids

✔ ASSESSMENT OPTIONS

📁 *Tests with Answer Key and Rubrics*
Unit 23 Pretest, pp. 93–94

💾 *Testmaker*
Unit 23 Pretest

You may wish to administer the Unit 23 Pretest at this point.

Key to Ability Levels

L1 Level 1 activities are within the basic ability range of students.

L2 Level 2 activities are within the ability range of average students.

L3 Level 3 activities are more challenging activities.

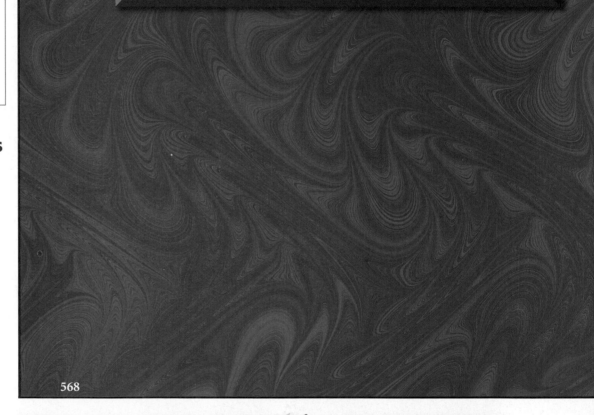

UNIT
23 Study Skills

568

Resource Manager

Planning Resources
- *Lesson Plans*
- *Block Scheduling*

✋ **Transparencies**
- *Bellringer*
- *Daily Language Practice*

📁 **Other Print Resources**
- *Listening and Speaking Activities*
- *Tests with Answer Key and Rubrics*
- *Thinking and Study Skills*

📺 **Video**
- *MindJogger Videoquizzes*

💾 **Software**
- *Presentation Plus!*
- *Testmaker*

🖥 **Web Sites**
- *writerschoice.glencoe.com*

23.1 Exploring a Book

Imagine that you are researching a report for science class. In the library you find a book that may help you. Can you find out if the book has what you need without reading all of it?

The pictures on this page show some helpful parts of a book. Learning to use these parts will make it easier for you to find the information you need. The chart on page 570 answers some questions you might ask about a book.

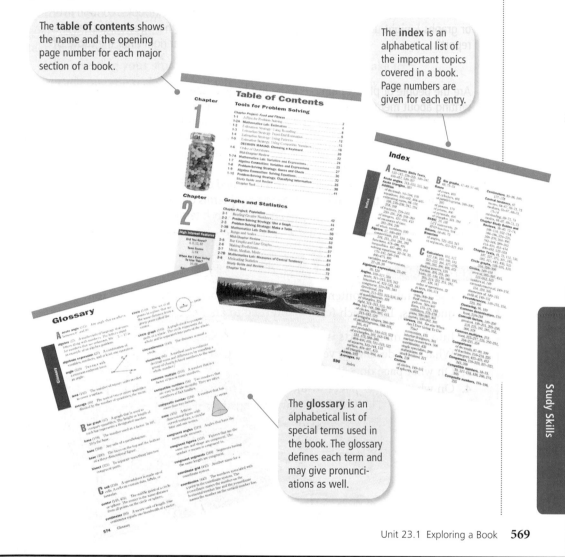

The **table of contents** shows the name and the opening page number for each major section of a book.

The **index** is an alphabetical list of the important topics covered in a book. Page numbers are given for each entry.

The **glossary** is an alphabetical list of special terms used in the book. The glossary defines each term and may give pronunciations as well.

Resource Manager

Planning Resources
- *Lesson Plans*

Transparencies
- *Bellringer*
- *Daily Language Practice*

Other Print Resources
- *Thinking and Study Skills,* pp. 30–32, 35–40

Focus

Lesson Overview

Objectives
- To recognize the table of contents, index, and glossary of a book
- To use these parts of a book to gather information and frame questions to direct research

Skills
- reading a table of contents; using a glossary; using an index

Critical Thinking
- analyzing; classifying; evaluating

Listening and Speaking
- discussing

Bellringer
Daily Language Activity

When students enter the classroom, have this assignment on the board: *List at least five ways you can find out about a book's contents.*

See also *Daily Language Practice*

Motivating Activity

Ask students to imagine they are writing a report on a specific topic such as volcanic islands. They have a large stack of books and five minutes to decide what books they need. How would students find out a book's content? What parts of the book would students check?

Teach

Providing Support

Ask students to turn to the index. Have students put a ruler under the topic *Library*. Have students slide the ruler down, noting subtopics. How are they different? **L1**

Study Skills

Teach

Understanding Time

Point out to students that the time it takes to do a specific task varies from person to person. Students should be aware of their strengths when planning. If someone thinks up ideas for a paper in nothing flat, but has trouble putting the ideas into words, he or she should schedule less time for prewriting and more for drafting. **L2**

Practice and Assess

Evaluation Rubrics

Exercise 2

Answers will vary, but completed calendars should reflect a reasonable allocation of study time for each goal and demonstrate an understanding of how to plan each day's work realistically.

Additional Resources

 Thinking and Study Skills, pp. 30–32, 35–40

Close

Ask students how they currently keep track of school assignments, tutoring dates, special class activities, and other events and tasks.

Study Skills

Using a Calendar

One important tool for making a study plan is a calendar. As you set your goals, write each one on the calendar. For longer tasks, first write the final due date. Then work backward from there, filling in each task. For example, say that a report is due on the fifteenth. Mark the fourteenth on your calendar for proofreading the final report. Then set aside the twelfth and the thirteenth to revise your first draft and write the final draft. Continue working backward in this manner through all the needed tasks.

As you schedule your study time, try to keep all your class assignments balanced. Suppose that an English report is due on Friday—the same day you have a social studies test. You'll need to set aside study time for both goals. Also, keep in mind other important activities. You don't want to schedule writing a report on the day you have a track meet.

Exercise 2

Draw a thirty-day calendar with the first day falling on a Wednesday. Then set study goals, and schedule the following assignments:

- You must read four chapters (about eighty pages) of your social studies text by the end of the month. You must also review an earlier unit (eighty pages) for a test on Friday the tenth.
- A written report for English is due the seventeenth.
- In science a unit test covering five chapters will be given Friday the twenty-fourth.
- You need to review for a short quiz your math teacher gives every Monday.
- You are on the basketball team and have practice every Thursday from 3:30 to 5:00.

Cultural Connections

Using Calendars

The calendar now used in the United States and in many other countries is called the Gregorian calendar. It has been in use since 1582. In the past, calendars changed as people learned more about the relation of the earth to the sun and moon. The calendar was changed in 1582 because over the centuries the dates had begun to fall behind the seasons! Other calendars still in use are the Chinese, Jewish, and Muslim calendars. Differences among the various calendars include the names of the months, the number of the year, and how leap year is handled.

23.3 | Using a Study Method

When you study, your most important job is to understand and remember information and ideas. You might say that, in order to study well, you need to monitor how well you are thinking. If you don't understand something you've read, stop. Go back and reread the passage more slowly, focusing on finding main ideas and on understanding important vocabulary. Jot down questions and comments. Whatever study strategy or method you use, be sure you find one that works for you—one that helps you learn and remember information.

Look at the diagram below. Can you guess why this study strategy is called SQ3R?

Survey	**Question**	**Read**	**Record**	**Review**
Survey the material by skimming it. Read the headings and any highlighted key terms or ideas. Examine the illustrations, and read their captions.	After surveying the material, ask questions about it. Important questions to ask usually begin with *who, what, when, where, why,* and *how.*	Read the material slowly and carefully. Decide the main idea of each section. As you read, take notes about important points.	After finishing the reading, write the answers to your questions without looking in the book.	Check your written answers against the text to see if they are correct. Continue to study the material until you can answer all the questions correctly.

You can use the SQ3R method with any subject. Once you've learned the method and use it regularly, it will become a habit. Effective studying will save you time. In addition, it will help you become better prepared in all your classes.

Survey

To survey means to look something over to get a general view of it. You can do that by looking for the main ideas of the material. Read all the headings that divide the material into smaller sections. These headings may help you find the main ideas. They also will show you

Study Skills

Focus

Lesson Overview

Objectives
- To identify the steps of an effective study method
- To use a study method to gather information from a text

Skills
- skimming text; generating questions; taking notes; reviewing

Critical Thinking
- recalling; identifying the main idea

Listening and Speaking
- note taking; informal speaking

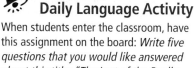

Bellringer
Daily Language Activity

When students enter the classroom, have this assignment on the board: *Write five questions that you would like answered about this title: "The Last of the Really Great Oompaloompas."*

See also *Daily Language Practice*

Motivating Activity

Ask students what they think the abbreviation *SQ3R* stands for. Explain that it is not pronounced as a word but is a memory device for a study method. Write the words *Survey, Question, Read, Record,* and *Review* on the board. Ask a volunteer to come to the board and draw a box around the first letter of each word. Repeat that *SQ3R* stands for these five words.

Resource Manager

Planning Resources
- *Lesson Plans*

Transparencies
- *Bellringer*
- *Daily Language Practice*

Other Print Resources
- *Thinking and Study Skills,* pp. 30–32, 35–40

Focus

Lesson Overview

Objectives

- To use note cards to record information for research
- To organize information for research using an outline

Skills

- taking notes; creating an outline

Critical Thinking

- observing and organizing; summarizing

Listening and Speaking

- discussing

🔔 Bellringer
Daily Language Activity

When students enter the classroom, have this assignment on the board: *List five questions that you would research to write a report on Aesop's fables.*

📖 **See also** *Daily Language Practice*

Motivating Activity

Create an overhead transparency or a handout by drawing a box about the size of a 3-by-5-inch or 4-by-6-inch note card. Ask students how they might organize notes about the animals in Aesop's fables. (The name of the fable and the animal might appear at the top of the card; the animal's traits and other details can appear below.) Have each student create a sample card.

576

Study Skills

23.4 Notes and Outlines

While working on a report, you'll find many facts and ideas. Most people can't count on memory alone to keep track of everything they read. You need to make notes of the facts and ideas you might use in your report.

Taking Notes

Use a separate note card for each piece of information. The cards will allow you to organize your notes easily. Write the name of your source on the card. (Use the sample note card below as a model.) Then, in your own words, summarize the information from your research.

Write only the details and ideas that relate to your topic. Use a quotation if a sentence or phrase is especially interesting. You may also need to use the words of an authority to strengthen your report. When you do quote something from a source, copy it word for word. Enclose it in quotation marks. The quotation marks will make it clear that you have used another person's thoughts.

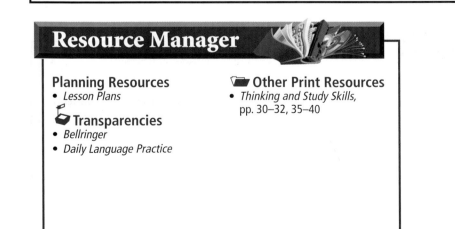

History of Surfing Surf ridi[ng]
pastime of the ancient Polyn[esians on]
the islands in the Pacific Oc[ean . . .]
land to Tahiti and who are[. . .]
brought the sport to Haw[aii . . .]
explorer James Cook wit[h . . .]
he discovered the Sand[wich Islands]
in 1778. He wrote in th[e . . .]
surf broke in Kealakek[ua . . .]
board "place themsel[ves . . .]
largest surge by whic[h . . .]
amazing rapidity towar[d the shore."]

Encyclopedia Americana Vol. 26, p. 54.
Capt. James T. Cook saw surfers in Hawaii in 1778. Wrote that they "place themselves on the summit of the largest surge by which they are driven along with amazing rapidity toward the shore."

Resource Manager

Planning Resources
- *Lesson Plans*

📖 Transparencies
- *Bellringer*
- *Daily Language Practice*

📁 Other Print Resources
- *Thinking and Study Skills,* pp. 30–32, 35–40

Tips on Taking Notes

1. Use a new 3 x 5 card for each important piece of information.

2. At the top of each card, identify the source of the information (the reference you used).

3. Summarize information in your own words.

4. Use direct quotations only when the words are especially useful or come from an important source.

Outlining

After completing your research, you're ready to organize the information in an outline. Look through your note cards and write down the main ideas you want to cover. Then decide on the right order for presenting them. For example, suppose that you're writing about the history of ballooning. You'll probably use time order—from earliest event to latest event. For other kinds of topics, think about how you can best group your ideas.

Write your outline. Begin by listing main ideas. Then fill in the supporting details. Look at the outline below.

TIME

For more about the value of using outlines, see **TIME Facing the Blank Page,** page 93.

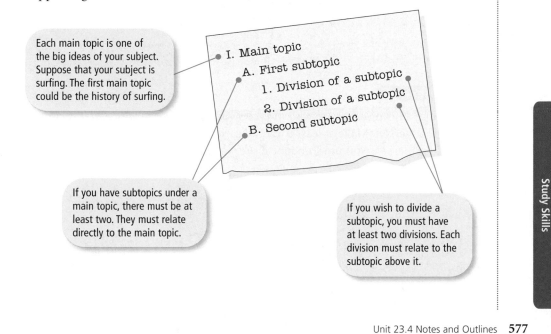

Each main topic is one of the big ideas of your subject. Suppose that your subject is surfing. The first main topic could be the history of surfing.

I. Main topic
  A. First subtopic
    1. Division of a subtopic
    2. Division of a subtopic
  B. Second subtopic

If you have subtopics under a main topic, there must be at least two. They must relate directly to the main topic.

If you wish to divide a subtopic, you must have at least two divisions. Each division must relate to the subtopic above it.

Study Skills

Teach

Organizing Note Cards

Show students how to manipulate note cards before writing an outline. Tell them to place the main topic note card at the top of their desk, and then to group together the subtopic cards. They should arrange the group of subtopic cards below their main topic card. They should then do the same with the divisions cards, placing them below the subtopics. When they have arranged the cards in descending order, they can create an outline. **L1**

Organizing an Outline

Ask students to think of events they have heard or read about in the news in recent months. They might make an outline showing each event (main topic), the date and people, country, or group involved (subtopics), and details (divisions of subtopics). Students may think of other original ways to organize the information. **L3**

Cross-reference: Note-taking

For more information on note-taking, refer students to Lesson 3.2, pp. 110–113.

Technology Tip

Writing Note Cards

If students have access to computer software with an outline option, they can write their note cards using the computer. When they organize their outline, they may want to use the search function to locate information on a particular topic.

Practice and Assess

Evaluation Rubrics

Exercise 4
Answers will vary, but check that students have followed the Tips on Taking Notes on page 577. Emphasize the need to use quotation marks around any material that is copied directly from a source.

Additional Resources

📁 *Thinking and Study Skills,* pp. 30–32, 35–40

Close

Some students may feel that making up note cards is an unnecessary step in their research. Ask students to discuss the pros and cons of using note cards. (Pro: Note cards allow them to organize and outline information, encourage them to keep notes brief, and keep them focused on the main topic and important details. Con: Note cards take time to write; it might be difficult to fit all information on one card; cards can get separated, lost, or out of order.)

Study Skills

Put your note cards in order according to your outline. You may not need all the information you've found. Don't try to include ideas that don't fit your outline. An example of a completed outline follows. Notice that you don't have to use complete sentences in an outline.

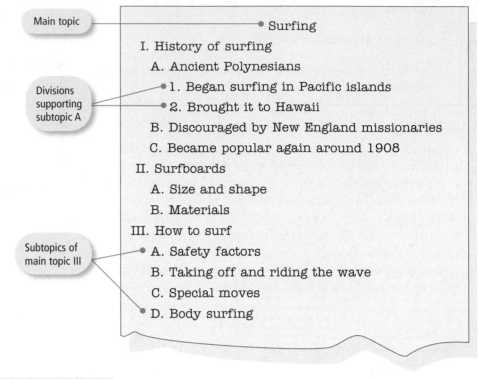

Main topic → Surfing

I. History of surfing
   A. Ancient Polynesians

Divisions supporting subtopic A →
   1. Began surfing in Pacific islands
   2. Brought it to Hawaii
   B. Discouraged by New England missionaries
   C. Became popular again around 1908
II. Surfboards
   A. Size and shape
   B. Materials
III. How to surf

Subtopics of main topic III →
   A. Safety factors
   B. Taking off and riding the wave
   C. Special moves
   D. Body surfing

Exercise 4

Choose a historical figure who interests you. Read an encyclopedia article about that person. Make at least five note cards from the article. Be sure to use quotation marks if you use someone else's words.

Enrichment and Extension

Using Topics and Outlines
Give students topics, such as surfing in the 1950s, analyzing waves, movies about surfing, and wooden surfboards. Ask them to decide how each topic would fit into the outline shown on this page. Ask students to suggest other possible topics for their classmates to fit into the outline.

23.5 Using Graphic Aids

Sometimes you need to present complicated information. You'll find that words don't always provide the best way to do it. Certain kinds of information call for graphic aids, such as tables, graphs, time lines, and maps.

Tables

Tables show pieces of information in a way that makes sense of them. Tables use columns and rows to organize information, which often includes groups of numbers. Look at the table below. Notice how easily you can tell which groups of animals include the most endangered species.

The title identifies the table's topic.

The left column names the groups of animals that are endangered.

Numbers of Endangered Species in the United States and the Rest of the World		
Group	U.S.	Rest of World
Mammals	61	251
Birds	75	178
Reptiles	14	65
Amphibians	9	8
Fishes	69	11
Insects	28	4

Source: Fish and Wildlife Service, U.S. Department of Interior, 1999

Columns 2 and 3 divide the world into two areas. One column shows figures for the United States. The other gives figures for the rest of the world.

Each row gives the numbers of endangered species for one group.

You can read this table from left to right or from top to bottom. Suppose that you want to know how many species of birds in the United States are endangered. To find out, you don't have to read the whole table. First find the row that shows birds. Then move your eye across the row to the column for the United States. The table also makes it easy to compare numbers for the United States with those for the rest of the world. The numbers for each group of animals are side by side in columns 2 and 3.

Study Skills

Focus

Lesson Overview

Objectives
- To interpret information that is represented visually
- To select, organize, and produce a graphic aid to present information

Skills
- interpreting tables; reading bar graphs and line graphs; reading time lines; using maps

Critical Thinking
- synthesizing; categorizing; relating images to concepts; summarizing; comparing

Listening and Speaking
- questioning; informal speaking

🔔 Bellringer
Daily Language Activity

When students enter the classroom, have this assignment on the board: *On a sheet of paper, give directions on how to get to your house from school.*

See also *Daily Language Practice*

Motivating Activity

Ask students if they wrote the directions to their house in words or if they made a map. Point out that sometimes it is simpler and more effective to explain things graphically instead of verbally. Have students identify kinds of information that are best presented using graphic aids.

Resource Manager

Planning Resources
- *Lesson Plans*

Transparencies
- *Bellringer*
- *Daily Language Practice*

📁 **Other Print Resources**
- *Thinking and Study Skills,* pp. 30–32, 35–40

Teach

Formulating Questions

Divide the class into groups with two sets of partners. Have one pair in each group formulate at least three questions based on the television viewing graph. (For example, How many hours a week do children ages six to eleven watch television?) The second pair should formulate questions about the United States population graph. The pairs will then try to answer each other's questions. The groups should conclude by discussing their questions and answers. **L2**

Graphing Knowledge

To make the use of graphs more accessible, help students create their own graphs. On the board draw the bottom axis and label it "Students." Draw the side axis and label it "Height." Mark height in six-inch segments, explaining what you are marking. Ask for volunteers to tell how tall they are, or if possible, measure them in the classroom. Have volunteers write their names on the bottom axis and draw lines up from their names to the level of the number representing their heights. When all volunteers are finished, discuss what they have recorded on the graph (for example, Yoko is taller than Reggie; Ken and Elizabeth are the same height). **L1**

Study Skills

Graphs

Graphs always deal with numbers of some kind. They can show the same kinds of information that tables show. However, graphs organize information differently.

BAR GRAPHS Numbers in a bar graph appear as bars. The bar graph below shows the number of hours young people spend watching television. Notice how easily you can see the highest bar and find the group that watches the most television. You also can easily compare the viewing times of all the groups.

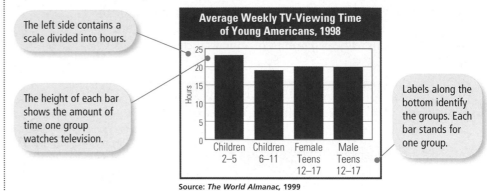

The left side contains a scale divided into hours.

The height of each bar shows the amount of time one group watches television.

Labels along the bottom identify the groups. Each bar stands for one group.

Source: *The World Almanac*, 1999

To find the number a bar represents, use the scale along the left side. You can see that three of the groups watch close to twenty hours of television per week. Which group watches more than twenty hours per week?

LINE GRAPHS A line graph shows changes in numbers or amounts over a period of time. For example, a line graph can show the rise and fall of daily temperatures. A line graph can also show any other numbers that change over time. Read the title of the line graph below. What does it show?

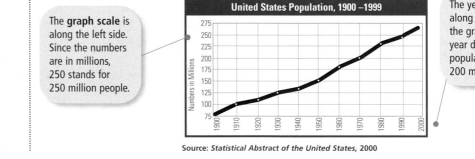

The **graph scale** is along the left side. Since the numbers are in millions, 250 stands for 250 million people.

The years are shown along the bottom of the graph. In what year did the U.S. population go over 200 million?

Source: *Statistical Abstract of the United States*, 2000

English Language Learners

Using a Time Line

Students from other cultural backgrounds who have recently moved to the United States may not be familiar with the events shown on the time line. You might have them make a time line of events related to their country of origin. Invite volunteers to share their time lines.

Time Lines

A time line shows events that happened over a period of time. Time is shown along a line or sometimes a bar. The amount of time shown on a time line can be anything from seconds to eons. A time line allows you to see easily the order in which the events occurred. You can also see how much time passed between certain events. On the time line below, for example, which two events occurred closest in time?

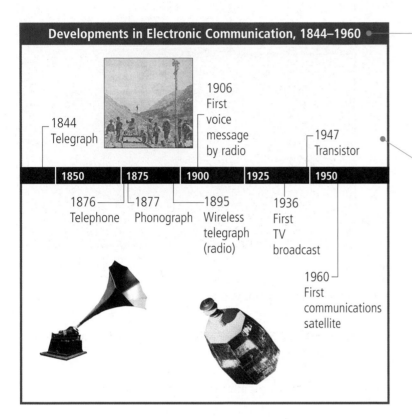

Developments in Electronic Communication, 1844–1960

1844 Telegraph

1906 First voice message by radio

1947 Transistor

1850 1875 1900 1925 1950

1876 Telephone

1877 Phonograph

1895 Wireless telegraph (radio)

1936 First TV broadcast

1960 First communications satellite

> The title shows the subject of the time line. It also may include the dates covered.

> Space between events shows the amount of time that passed between them. Which two events came closest together?

Maps

Maps show some part of the earth's surface. The area shown can be as small as a playground or as large as the entire world.

Teach

Exploring Careers

Ask students to describe jobs in which a person might rely on tables and graphs. How would people in those professions use them? (A meteorologist might use a graph to record changes in temperature or rainfall; a truck driver might use a chart to record times and locations of deliveries; a nurse might use a chart to record a patient's temperature, pulse, and other vital signs.) Encourage students to choose a profession and create a "mock-up" of a table, chart, or graph that would be used in a work setting. **L3**

Additional Resources

📁 *Thinking and Study Skills,*
pp. 30–32, 35–40

Study Skills

Viewing and Representing

Making a Time Line

Producing Visual Images After students have looked at the time line on this page, tell them to make their own time lines that focus on a topic of interest to them. An individual's time line might show the history of a favorite sports team, the development of a musical ability, a scouting career, volunteer work, a hobby, or another area of interest.

Practice and Assess

Evaluation Rubrics

Exercise 5

The graphic aids will vary but should demonstrate a mastery of the concepts and skills introduced in the lesson.

Close

Ask students to find examples of tables, graphs, time lines, and maps in their social studies textbooks. Discuss the various types of information shown. Ask students what other ways they might visually show dates and events (lists, charts).

✔ ASSESSMENT OPTIONS

📁 *Tests with Answer Key and Rubrics*
Unit 23 Mastery Test, pp. 95–96

💾 *Testmaker*
Unit 23 Mastery Test

You may wish to administer the Unit 23 Mastery Test at this point.

📼 *MindJogger Videoquizzes*

Study Skills

Maps are drawn to scale. That is, a certain distance on the map stands for a certain distance on the earth. Maps usually contain a line or bar scale that you can use to measure distances. Use the scale on the map to see if you can tell the distance between New York City and Chicago.

The United States

A **legend** explains the symbols and sometimes the colors used on a map. What does a dot indicate on this map? What does a star indicate?

The top line of this **scale** shows miles. The bottom line shows kilometers.

★ National capital
● Cities with more than 1 million

Exercise 5

Make a graphic aid of your own. Some possibilities include the following:

- a map of your room, your schoolyard, or your neighborhood
- a bar graph that compares the heights or weights of four or five classmates
- a line graph showing the batting averages of your favorite baseball player over several years
- a time line of your life or the life of a historical figure you admire

🌐 Cultural Connections

History of Maps

The oldest known map was made about 2300 B.C. It is a small clay tablet from Babylonia that appears to show a man's estate in a valley. The Egyptians made maps as early as 1300 B.C. One of the few remaining ancient Egyptian maps shows the route from the Nile Valley to the gold mines of Nubia. The Greeks made maps in the early 300s B.C. and were among the first to realize that the earth is spherical. The Romans used maps for taxing land and to assist in military campaigns.

UNIT
24 Taking Tests

Objectives

- To improve study skills for tests
- To recognize different types of test items and use strategies for each type
- To prepare for standardized test items such as analogies

✔ ASSESSMENT OPTIONS

📁 *Tests with Answer Key and Rubrics*
Unit 24 Pretest, pp. 97–98

💾 *Testmaker*
Unit 24 Pretest

You may wish to administer the Unit 24 Pretest at this point.

Key to Ability Levels

L1 Level 1 activities are within the basic ability range of students.

L2 Level 2 activities are within the ability range of average students.

L3 Level 3 activities are more challenging activities.

583

Resource Manager

Planning Resources
- *Lesson Plans*
- *Block Scheduling*

🖇 **Transparencies**
- *Bellringer*
- *Daily Language Practice*

📁 **Other Print Resources**
- *ITBS® Preparation and Practice Workbook*
- *SAT-9 Preparation and Practice*

- *Taking Standardized Tests*
- *TerraNova Preparation and Practice*
- *Tests with Answer Key and Rubrics*
- *Thinking and Study Skills*

📼 **Video**
- *MindJogger Videoquizzes*

💾 **Software**
- *Presentation Plus!*
- *Testmaker*

🖥 **Web Sites**
- *writerschoice.glencoe.com*

Focus

Lesson Overview

Objectives
- To prepare effectively for tests
- To learn and use time-saving strategies for tests

Skills
- preparing for a test; planning your time

Critical Thinking
- evaluating

Listening and Speaking
- discussing

Bellringer
Daily Language Activity
When students enter the classroom, have this assignment on the board: *List five hints for doing well on a test.*

See also *Daily Language Practice*

Teach

Getting Ready for a Test
Ask students to think about a test that they have coming up, in any subject. Have them write the strategies from the list on page 584 that they think will help them prepare for it. Now ask students to be as specific as possible: When will they have time to study? Can they arrange to study with classmates? What types of materials will they need to look at? Have them write a few questions that they think might be on the test. **L2**

584

Taking Tests

24.1 Tips for Test Taking

"There will be a test on Friday." Do those words throw you into a panic or are you usually well prepared? Either way, you can improve your test-taking skills. This lesson will help you learn a few strategies for taking tests.

Preparing for a Test

Preparing for a test can get you off to a good start. Here are some simple but effective strategies:
- Allow plenty of time to study. Don't wait until the day before the test. Several short review sessions are better than one long one.
- Gather information about the test. When will it be given? How long will it take? Exactly what material will it cover? What types of test items will be used (multiple choice, true or false, essay)?
- Review material from your textbook, class notes, homework, quizzes, and handouts.
- Make up some sample test questions, and answer them.
- Study with a partner or a small group. Quiz one another on topics you think the test will cover.

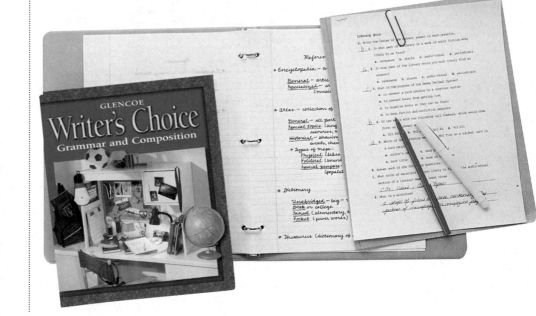

Resource Manager

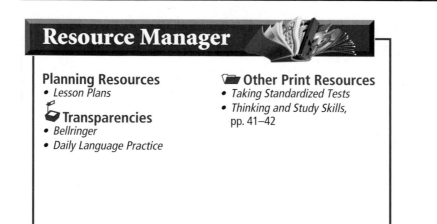

Planning Resources
- Lesson Plans

Transparencies
- Bellringer
- Daily Language Practice

Other Print Resources
- Taking Standardized Tests
- Thinking and Study Skills, pp. 41–42

Planning Your Time

You normally have a limited amount of time to take a test. Using your time wisely will help you do your best work. Before you begin, plan a general amount of time for each section of the test.

Tips for Using Time Well
• Read all test directions carefully. Understanding the directions will keep you from making mistakes.
• Answer the easier items first. By skipping the hard items, you give yourself time to answer all the easy ones.
• In whatever time is left, return to the items you skipped. Answer them as best you can. If you won't be penalized for doing so, guess.
• Save some time to check your answers before you turn in your test.

Exercise 1

The following statements give advice on taking a test. Which statements give *bad* advice? Write their numbers. Then rewrite each statement so that it gives *good* advice.

1. Do all your studying for the test the night before you take the test.
2. Always study alone for a test.
3. Review your homework and quizzes.
4. Try to learn what the test will cover.
5. Try to study without using your textbook.
6. Always avoid answering any of the difficult test questions.
7. Read the test directions carefully.
8. Answer every test question in order.
9. Never guess at an answer.
10. Check your answers carefully before turning in your test.

Practice and Assess

Evaluation Rubrics

Exercise 1

Statements 1, 2, 5, 6, 8, and 9 are bad advice. Examples of rewritten sentences follow. Accept other valid revisions.

1. Don't put off studying until the night before you take a test.
2. Study alone, with a friend, or with a small group.
5. Use your textbook to review for a test.
6. Save the difficult questions for last.
8. Answer the easy questions first.
9. Guess at answers only if guessing is not penalized.

Additional Resources

📁 *Taking Standardized Tests*
📁 *Thinking and Study Skills,* pp. 41–42

Close

Ask students to tell which tips for preparing for a test and planning their time they already knew and have used. Also ask students to discuss which new tips they think will be most helpful to incorporate into their test-taking strategies. See if they have other test-taking tips they would like to share with classmates.

Taking Tests

Viewing and Representing

Producing a Visual

Ask a small group of volunteers to make a chart on "How to Prepare for a Test" or on "How to Plan Your Time on a Test." Remind students that these strategies can be used for tests in any of their classes. You might suggest that the students use color and illustrations to highlight key ideas. When the poster is complete, display it in the classroom so that students can refer to it.

Focus

Lesson Overview

Objectives
- To identify different types of test items
- To recognize and apply strategies for each type of test item

Skills
- applying appropriate strategies for solving true-false; multiple choice; and matching items

Critical Thinking
- evaluating

Listening and Speaking
- discussing

Bellringer
Daily Language Activity

When students enter the classroom, have this assignment on the board: *Write down as many different kinds of test questions as you can think of.*

See also *Daily Language Practice*

Motivating Activity

Survey student responses to the Bellringer activity. Have students give examples of each type of item and name situations in which those items are likely to occur.

The best way to prepare for a test, of course, is to learn the material that will be tested. You can also help yourself by mastering the different types of test items.

True-False Items

A true-false item gives only two choices, true or false. An answer is true only if the *entire* statement is true. If any part of the statement is false, you must mark it *false*. Look at the statement below.

> The earth circles the sun once each day.

The earth does circle the sun. However, it does so once each *year*, not each *day*. The statement is false.

Multiple-Choice Items

In a multiple-choice item you must answer a question or complete a sentence. You do so by picking the *best* response out of the three or four given.

> What is included in our solar system?
> a. the earth and the sun
> b. all the sun's planets
> c. asteroids and moons
> d. all of the above

Item *a* seems true, but be sure to read all the choices before answering.

Reading all responses is especially important when one choice is "all of the above" or "none of the above." The answer is *d.*

Matching Items

In the matching test format, you have two groups or lists of items. You must match each item from the first group with an item in the second group. Complete the easy matches first. That will leave fewer items to choose from when you get to the difficult ones.

Taking Tests

Resource Manager

Planning Resources
- *Lesson Plans*

Transparencies
- *Bellringer*
- *Daily Language Practice*

Other Print Resources
- *Taking Standardized Tests*
- *Thinking and Study Skills,* pp. 41–42

> Complete the items you are sure of first. Doing so will increase your chance of choosing correctly from the remaining items.

Match each river with its continent.
1. Rhine River
2. Nile River
3. Mississippi River
4. Amazon River

a. North America
b. South America
c. Africa
d. Asia
e. Europe

> Notice that column 2 has more items than column 1. One item in column 2 will not be used.

Exercise 2

Read the passage below. Then use your test-taking skills to answer the questions.

Kilauea is one of the most active volcanoes in the Hawaiian Islands. Since 1983 it has erupted dozens of times. When Kilauea erupts, it rarely explodes. Instead, fast-running lava pours out from cracks and vents. Sometimes it shoots up in fountains hundreds of feet high. Usually the lava runs down the sides of the mountain and cools. These layers of lava have formed Mt. Kilauea's long, gentle slopes. When the lava reaches the ocean, it quickly cools into rugged black rock.

1. Kilauea is an explosive volcano. True or false?
2. The lava from Kilauea
   a. forms mile-high fountains.
   b. has created the mountain's gentle slopes.
   c. is driven back by the ocean.
   d. none of the above
3. Match the terms in column 1 with the descriptions in column 2.
   1. Kilauea   a. a sudden release of lava
   2. eruption   b. a volcano
   3. lava   c. melted rock

Taking Tests

24.2 Test Items **587**

Teach

Scanning Questions

Point out to students that when they take reading comprehension tests, it often helps to look at the questions before reading the selection. That way students will know what they should look for as they read. Tell them to practice this strategy as they work on Exercise 2. **L2**

Practice and Assess

Answers: Exercise 2
1. false
2. b
3. 1. b; 2. a; 3. c

Additional Resources

📁 *Taking Standardized Tests*
📁 *Thinking and Study Skills,*
   pp. 41–42

Close

Ask students which types of test items they find easy and which they find difficult. Encourage them to discuss why this might be. Do they have better strategies for a certain type of test item? Have students make up test questions on a topic that interests them (for example, cars or music). They can exchange tests with a partner for extra practice on any problem areas.

Listening and Speaking

Telling Tales

Write on the chalkboard the titles of some familiar folk or fairy tales, such as "The Ugly Duckling," "Beauty and the Beast," and "The Three Little Pigs." Call on one or more volunteers to retell briefly one of the tales. Then have students help you write several true-false, multiple choice, and matching test items related to the tale. Write these items on the board, and then call on students to give the answers. Ask them to discuss the strategies they used to arrive at each answer.

Focus

Lesson Overview

Objectives

- To prepare effectively for standardized tests
- To recognize and apply strategies for solving analogies

Skills

- taking standardized tests, doing well on analogy items

Critical Thinking

- analyzing

Listening and Speaking

- discussing

🔔 Bellringer
Daily Language Activity

When students enter the classroom, have this assignment on the board: *Write down three kinds of problems that were on a standardized test you have taken.*

📖 **See also** *Daily Language Practice*

Teach

Creating Test Items

Direct students to create several test items like those in Exercise 3 (analogy, grammar usage, and mechanics). Pairs of students will meet to exchange and complete each other's items. If some items are particularly difficult to solve, have volunteers solve them on the board. **L2**

⇄ Cross-reference: Vocabulary

For more information on the use of synonyms and antonyms, refer students to Lesson 22.4, pp. 552–554.

Taking Tests

24.3 Standardized Tests

In addition to classroom tests, you will sometimes take standardized tests. Students all over the country take these tests.

Taking Standardized Tests

Some standardized tests measure your abilities or how well you think. Others measure your knowledge in such subjects as English, math, and science. The following tips can help you do well on standardized tests.

Tips for Taking Standardized Tests
1. Sleep well the night before the test. Eat well in the morning. Try to arrive early for the test. Relax.
2. Listen carefully as directions are given before the test. Ask questions if you don't understand the directions.
3. Complete all the easy items first. Leave hard items until the end.
4. Compare the numbers for test items with the numbers on your answer sheet. Be sure your answers are in the right place.
5. If you can, find out whether points are subtracted for wrong answers. If they are not, you should guess at questions you aren't sure of.

Analogies

Analogy items test how well you can compare the meanings of words. For example, *stop* and *go* have opposite meanings.

Resource Manager

Planning Resources
- *Lesson Plans*

📁 **Other Print Resources**
- *Taking Standardized Tests*
- *Thinking and Study Skills,* pp. 41–42

A typical analogy item shows one relationship and asks you to complete another. They are often written as follows.

First figure out the relationship in the first pair of words. Eyes are used for seeing.

```
eyes: seeing:: ears:_____
a. smelling    b. hearing    c. touching
```

Then complete the second pair with the same kind of relationship. You use eyes to see and ears to hear. The correct answer is *b*.

The single colon (:) stands for "are to" or "is to." The double colon (::) stands for "as." So you would read the top line as "eyes are to seeing as ears are to ___."

COMMON TYPES OF ANALOGIES		
Antonyms	One word means the opposite of the other	light : dark
Synonyms	Two words have the same general meaning	tired : sleepy
Use	The thing named by one word uses or is used by the other.	rider : horse
Cause and effect	One item causes or results from the other.	cold : shiver

Teach

Working Through Analogies
On the board write the following analogy: *canoe : water :: ski : snow.*
Discuss the relationship of each pair of words. Encourage students to name other ways in which words may be related: as synonyms or antonyms or by use (users and tools, for example). Then have students write their own analogies. Invite them to share their analogies with the class.

Taking Tests

MEETING INDIVIDUAL NEEDS

English Language Learners

Following Tips and Asking Questions
Students who lack confidence in their English skills may be especially intimidated by standardized tests. Language is likely to be an added burden for these students. Emphasize the importance of following the tips listed in the chart on page 588. Explain that it is particularly important to ask questions if they do not understand all the directions given before the test. Students could also work as partners to practice analogy test items.

Practice and Assess

Answers: Exercise 3

1. b
2. b
3. c
4. d

Additional Resources

📁 *Taking Standardized Tests*
📁 *Thinking and Study Skills,*
   pp. 41–42

Close

Ask students to discuss how classroom tests and standardized tests are similar and how they are different. Which type of test do most students prefer to take? Why? Ask students to discuss which of the tips on page 588 they usually follow when taking standardized tests. Encourage them to explore how these tips could work for them.

Grammar, Usage, and Mechanics

Standardized tests often will ask you to identify errors in grammar, usage, and mechanics. These errors might include incorrect capitalization, punctuation, or spellings, as well as errors in the use of pronouns, verb tenses, and subject-verb agreement.

Most sentence correction test items will ask you to identify an error in underlined text. Study the item below. Identify the underlined section that contains an error. If the sentence is correct as is, choose d to indicate no error.

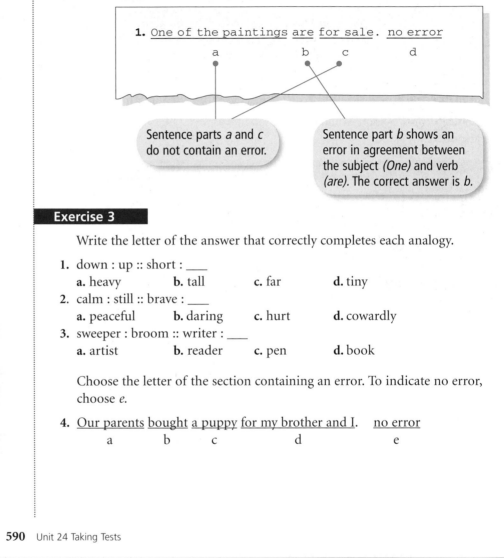

1. One of the paintings are for sale. no error
   a   b   c   d

Sentence parts *a* and *c* do not contain an error.

Sentence part *b* shows an error in agreement between the subject *(One)* and verb *(are)*. The correct answer is *b*.

Exercise 3

Write the letter of the answer that correctly completes each analogy.

1. down : up :: short : ____
   a. heavy   **b.** tall   **c.** far   **d.** tiny
2. calm : still :: brave : ____
   a. peaceful   **b.** daring   **c.** hurt   **d.** cowardly
3. sweeper : broom :: writer : ____
   a. artist   **b.** reader   **c.** pen   **d.** book

Choose the letter of the section containing an error. To indicate no error, choose *e*.

4. Our parents bought a puppy for my brother and I.   no error
      a   b   c   d   e

Standardized Test Practice

INTRODUCTION

The following pages of exercises have been designed to familiarize you with the standardized writing tests that you may take during the school year. These exercises are very similar to the actual tests in how they look and what they ask you to do. Completing these exercises will not only provide you with practice, but also will make you aware of areas you might need to work on.

These writing exercises—just like the actual standardized writing tests—are divided into three sections.

SENTENCE STRUCTURE   In this section, pages 592 to 599, you will be given a short passage in which some of the sentences are underlined. Each underlined sentence is numbered. After you finish reading the passage, you will be asked questions about the underlined sections. The underlined sections will be either incomplete sentences, run-on sentences, correctly written sentences that should be combined, or correctly written sentences that do not need to be rewritten. You will need to select which is best from the four choices provided.

USAGE   In this section, pages 600 to 607, you will also be asked to read a short passage. However, in these exercises, a word or words in the passage will be omitted and a numbered blank space will be in their place. After reading the passage, you will need to determine which of the four provided words or groups of words best belongs in each numbered space.

MECHANICS   Finally, in the third section, pages 608 to 615, the short passages will have parts that are underlined. You will need to determine if, in the underlined sections, there is a spelling error, capitalization error, punctuation error, or no error at all.

Writing well is a skill that you will use the rest of your life. You will be able to write more accurate letters to your friends and family, better papers in school, and more interesting stories. You will be able to express yourself and your ideas more clearly and in a way that is interesting and engaging. These exercises should help to improve your writing and to make you comfortable with the format and types of questions you will see on standardized writing tests.

Standardized Test Practice

One way you may wish to use this section of *Writer's Choice* is to have students complete an exercise or a series of exercises in an environment that resembles a testing environment. Students should be encouraged to work slowly and carefully. After students have completed the assigned exercises, you may want to go over the answers with students. You can explain the correct answers and review the grammar skills being tested.

Not covered in these test practices is the section in many standardized test situations that requires students to write a composition based on a provided topic. In this section, students are tested on their ability to write clear, concise, and persuasive compositions. You may want to assign topics to your students and have them write one- or two-page compositions so that they get practice for this section. When assigning a topic, choose subjects that require the student to have an opinion and to write convincingly as to why their opinion is valid. When advising students on how to prepare for the composition section, tell students that the following abilities may earn not only a higher grade on the test, but may also result in good writing skills: use specific examples to illustrate your point; organize your argument in a logical manner; carefully choose words that effectively and descriptively state your thoughts and opinion; be consistent in style and purpose throughout the composition. These are some of the ways that students can create interesting, persuasive, and clearly-written compositions.

Students are often anxious about taking standardized tests. Part of a teacher's responsibility is to provide support and instruction and to assure students that thorough preparation will enable them to meet the challenges of the test.

Taking Tests

Resource Manager

Planning Resources
• *Lesson Plans*

Other Print Resources
• *Taking Standardized Tests*
• *Thinking and Study Skills,* pp. 41–42

Standardized Test Practice

Tested Objective

- To recognize appropriate English usage and sentence structure within the context of a written passage

Answers and Analyses

1. B The original sentence is a run-on because it is made up of two sentences that are combined without punctuation. The correct answer choice removes the second, repeated, subject *(it)* and verb *(was)* and adds a comma.

2. H Make sure students understand that the underlined sentences contain one sentence fragment, or dependent clause beginning with *In wording similar,* and an independent clause. The correct answer choice combines the sentences with a comma.

3. A The two sentences are both grammatically correct, but are better when combined. The second sentence adds information to the object of the first sentence. The correct answer choice removes the subject *The 19th Amendment,* which is already mentioned in the first sentence, and replaces it with the relative pronoun *which.*

Test-Taking Tip

Make sure students know that a complete sentence has a subject and verb and states one complete thought.

Test-Taking Tip

Point out to students that with questions in which both sentences are correct, there is never a *Correct as is* option. Why is this? Because the sentences are grammatically correct but can be improved.

Read each passage. Some sections are underlined. The underlined sections may be one of the following:

- Incomplete sentences
- Run-on sentences
- Correctly written sentences that should be combined
- Correctly written sentences that do not need to be rewritten

Choose the best way to write each underlined section and mark the letter for your answer on your paper. If the underlined section needs no change, mark the choice "Correct as is."

> Elizabeth Cady Stanton was one of the first Americans to push for women's voting rights, or suffrage. <u>One of her earliest contributions was to help organize the Seneca Falls Convention it was the first women's rights assembly in the U.S.</u> (1) There, in 1848, she unveiled her Declaration of Sentiments. <u>In wording similar to that of the Declaration of Independence. This document called for full voting rights for women.</u> (2)
>
> The Seneca Falls convention and the Declaration of Sentiments established women's rights as a movement in the U.S. <u>They were the first major steps towards the 19th Amendment to the Constitution. The 19th Amendment finally gave women the right to vote in 1920.</u> (3)

1 A One of her earliest contributions was to help organize. The Seneca Falls Convention was the first women's rights assembly in the U.S.

B One of her earliest contributions was to help organize the Seneca Falls Convention, the first women's rights assembly in the U.S.

C One of her earliest contributions she helped organize the Seneca Falls Convention, the first women's rights assembly in the U.S.

D Correct as is

2 F In wording similar to that of the Declaration of Independence, calling for full voting rights for women.

G In wording it was similar to that of the Declaration of Independence, it called for full voting rights for women.

H In wording similar to that of the Declaration of Independence, this document called for full voting rights for women.

J Correct as is

3 A They were the first major steps towards the 19th Amendment to the Constitution, which finally gave women the right to vote in 1920.

B They were the first major steps towards the 19th Amendment to the Constitution, or the 19th Amendment finally gave women the right to vote in 1920.

C They were the first major steps towards the 19th Amendment to the Constitution, and the right to vote in 1920 finally gave women.

D They were the first major steps towards the 19th Amendment to the Constitution because finally giving women the right to vote in 1920.

Gardeners struggle to keep insects away from their gardens. Some plants, however, need insects to survive. A jungle plant called a Dischidia, for instance, needs ants. The ants live inside its large, hollow leaves. Ants drag dead insects and other materials back to their nest to eat. What the ants are unable to finish, the Dischidia soaks up into its leaves. Scientists call this kind of relationship symbiosis because both sides get something from the situation. The ants get a place to build a safe, dry nest, and the Dischidia plant gets a constant source of nutrients. Scientists believe the Dischidia does this. Because there are so few natural nutrients in the soil where it grows.

(1) (2) (3)

1 A A jungle plant called a Dischidia, for instance, needs the ants that live inside its large, hollow leaves.

  B A jungle plant called a Dischidia, for instance needs, and the ants live inside its large, hollow leaves.

  C A jungle plant called a Dischidia, for instance, that needs the ants that live inside its large, hollow leaves.

  D A jungle plant called a Dischidia, for instance, that needs and lives inside its large, hollow leaves, the ants.

2 F Scientists call this kind of relationship symbiosis. Because both sides get something from the situation.

  G Scientists call this kind of relationship symbiosis, they get something from the situation.

  H Scientists calling this kind of relationship symbiosis and both sides getting something from the situation.

  J Correct as is

3 A Scientists believe the Dischidia does this, this is because there are so few natural nutrients in the soil where it grows.

  B Scientists, believing the Dischidia does this, and so few natural nutrients in the soil where it grows.

  C Scientists believe the Dischidia does this because there are so few natural nutrients in the soil where it grows.

  D Correct as is

Answers and Analyses

1. A The underlined sentences are grammatically correct but would read more smoothly if combined. Notice how the object of the first sentence (*the ants*) is the subject of the second sentence. It sounds repetitive. The correct answer removes the second *the ants* and replaces it with the relative pronoun *that*.

2. J Students should recognize that the underlined sentence is correct as is. The sentence consists of two independent clauses combined by the linking conjunction *because*.

3. C The underlined sentences should be combined. As in question 2, there are two independent clauses that should be combined with the conjunction *because*. They should not be separated by a period.

Test-Taking Tip

Students should have a solid understanding of the function of a clause. A clause contains a subject and a verb. Clauses are either dependent or independent. An independent clause has a subject and a verb and can stand on its own. A dependent (or subordinate) clause cannot stand on its own. It is dependent on the rest of the sentence to complete its meaning.

Tested Objective

- To recognize appropriate English usage and sentence structure within the context of a written passage

Answers and Analyses

1. A Explain to students that the underlined portion contains a run-on sentence. Two complete sentences are combined without punctuation. The correct answer combines the sentences with the coordinating conjunction *but*.

2. G Students should be able to recognize that the underlined section contains a dependent or subordinate clause (beginning with *As the sun*) and an independent clause. The dependent clause does not make sense on its own. The correct answer simply combines the clauses with a comma.

3. A The underlined section contains two grammatically correct sentences. However, they are short, choppy, and redundant. To create one flowing sentence, the correct answer removes the redundant pronoun *it* (which refers to *clockwise*) and adds the conjunction *and*.

Test-Taking Tip

Make sure that students can identify a dependent clause. A dependent clause, which requires more information to complete its meaning, can be joined to independent clauses to create complete sentences. Relative pronouns *(that, which, who)* or linking conjunctions *(after, although, as, because, before, if, since, unless, until, when, while)* serve to connect the clauses. A dependent clause by itself is a sentence fragment.

Standardized Test Practice

Read each passage. Some sections are underlined. The underlined sections may be one of the following:

- Incomplete sentences
- Run-on sentences
- Correctly written sentences that should be combined
- Correctly written sentences that do not need to be rewritten

Choose the best way to write each underlined section and mark the letter for your answer on your paper. If the underlined section needs no change, mark the choice "Correct as is."

It might seem strange that all clock hands revolve in the same direction there is actually a very good reason. (1) It started with ancient clocks called sundials. Sundials use the angle of the shadow made by a central pole to tell the time. As the sun moves from east to west. The shadow crosses numbers that represent the time. (2)

Throughout the day, the shadow moves from left to right across the face of the sundial, crossing the 12 in the middle at noon. The first mechanical clocks imitated this. Their hour hands swept from left to right across the top of the face. This direction became known as clockwise. It is still used today. (3)

---

1 A It might seem strange that all clock hands revolve in the same direction, but there is actually a very good reason.

B It might seem strange that all clock hands revolve in the same direction. There being actually a very good reason.

C It might seem strange that all clock hands. It revolves in the same direction, but there is actually a very good reason.

D Correct as is

2 F As the sun moves from east to west, the shadow crosses numbers. That represent the time.

G As the sun moves from east to west, the shadow crosses numbers that represent the time.

H As the sun moving from east to west, the shadow it crosses numbers that represent the time.

J Correct as is

3 A This direction became known as clockwise and is still used today.

B This direction became known as clockwise, that is still used today.

C This direction became known and is still clockwise today.

D This direction became known and used as clockwise today.

Tracy was thinking of tying knots. She was thinking it as she fell asleep. The next day would be the first
(1)
day of sailing camp. Tracy got up early and left for the harbor. At eight o'clock, she got off the bus at the
(2)
pier the sailboats were kept there. She smelled the salty wind and saw boats of all sizes moored to the docks.
It looked like it had on other mornings since Tracy had started sailing six years ago. Only one thing was
(3)
different —when she got to her classroom, she did not sit at the back. She went right up to the front, she sat
(4)
facing the class. This year Tracy was an assistant instructor!

1 A Tracy was thinking of tying knots, and thinking it as she fell asleep.
B Tracy was thinking of tying knots when it was asleep.
C Tracy was thinking of tying knots as she fell asleep.
D Tracy was thinking of tying knots but she was falling asleep.

2 F At eight o'clock, she got off the bus at the pier. The sailboats kept there.
G At eight o'clock, she got off the bus at the pier. Where the sailboats were kept.
H At eight o'clock, she got off the bus at the pier, where the sailboats were kept.
J Correct as is

3 A It looked like it had on other mornings. Since Tracy had started sailing six years ago.
B It looked like it on other mornings since Tracy had started sailing six years ago.
C It looked like it had. On other mornings since Tracy had started sailing six years ago.
D Correct as is

4 F She went right up to the front. And sat facing the class.
G Going right up to the front. She sat facing the class.
H She went right up to the front and sat facing the class.
J Correct as is

STOP

Answers and Analyses

1. C Students should be able to recognize that the underlined portion contains two grammatically correct but redundant sentences. The second sentence begins with the same structure as the first, except it uses a pronoun *(She)*. The repeated subject and verb *(She was thinking)* can be removed to create one complete, flowing sentence.

2. H This is a run-on sentence. Two sentences run into each other in a clumsy, difficult to read sentence. The correct answer adds the linking conjunction *where* and removes the pronoun *there.*

3. D The sentence is correct as is. Two clauses are connected with the linking conjunction *since.*

4. H Students should be aware that this is a run-on sentence. Two complete sentences with the same subject are combined with only a comma. The correct answer removes the repeated subject *(she)* and replaces it with the conjunction *and.*

Test-Taking Tip

Remind students that sentences can be linked with conjunctions. The coordinating conjunction connects equal parts of sentences. Encourage students to make a list of coordinating conjunctions: *and, but, for, nor, so, yet.*

Test-Taking Tip

Tell students that this is a common page layout for writing tests. They should become familiar with it, so they will be more comfortable during the real test.

Tested Objective

- To recognize appropriate English usage and sentence structure within the context of a written passage

Answers and Analyses

1. **C** The original sentence is a run-on. The correct answer replaces the second verb with the preposition *from*, making the second part into a prepositional phrase.

2. **G** Students should recognize that the two sentences are grammatically correct. The correct answer choice combines the two into a better flowing sentence with the conjunction *and*.

3. **A** The original contains a sentence fragment beginning with *Of brightly colored*. The correct answer simply removes the period to make the fragment into a prepositional phrase. Students should be made aware that this is a common error type.

Test-Taking Tip

Suggest that students identify the parts of each sentence in the original text. If they are unable to find a subject or verb, it might be a fragment.

Test-Taking Tip

Make sure that students can identify a run-on sentence. A run-on sentence is two complete sentences put together without punctuation or with only a comma. Encourage students to read some sample run-on sentences out loud. Is it hard to read the entire sentence without a pause?

Standardized Test Practice

Read each passage. Some sections are underlined. The underlined sections may be one of the following:

- Incomplete sentences
- Run-on sentences
- Correctly written sentences that should be combined
- Correctly written sentences that do not need to be rewritten

Choose the best way to write each underlined section and mark the letter for your answer on your paper. If the underlined section needs no change, mark the choice "Correct as is."

<u>Mrs. Chen, the sixth-grade science teacher, smiled brightly at her students she was beside the large gray machine.</u> (1) She had brought the class on a field trip to the university microscopy laboratory.

A university technician was wearing a white lab coat. <u>She switched on the machine. She turned to the class.</u> (2) "This is called a Nomarski interference microscope," she said. "It uses polarized light to make objects more distinct. Today we are going to look at a drop of ordinary pond water."

The first student looked through the microscope eyepiece and let out a gasp. <u>The water had been transformed into a land. Of brightly colored amoeba twisting slowly across the plane of view.</u> (3) The other students waited for their turn to look.

---

1 A Mrs. Chen, the sixth-grade science teacher. She smiled brightly at her students from beside the large gray machine.
 B Mrs. Chen, the sixth-grade science teacher, smiled brightly at her students. Beside the large gray machine.
 C Mrs. Chen, the sixth-grade science teacher, smiled brightly at her students from beside the large gray machine.
 D Correct as is

2 F She switched the class on the machine.
 G She switched on the machine and turned to the class.
 H She switched on the machine because she turned to the class.
 J She switched on the machine, and she turned, and it was to the class.

3 A The water had been transformed into a land of brightly colored amoeba twisting slowly across the plane of view.
 B The water transformed into a land of brightly colored amoeba twisting slowly across the plane of view.
 C The water had been transformed into a land, brightly colored amoeba twisted slowly across the plane of view.
 D Correct as is

Standardized Test Practice

Do you know what an elephant really uses its trunk for? Just about everything. <u>You have probably seen</u>
<u>elephants using their trunks at the zoo. To pick up peanuts or straw for food.</u> In the wild, these powerful
(1)
appendages help elephants strip branches and leaves from trees to eat and dig minerals out of the earth. <u>An</u>
<u>elephant can swim underwater for up to six hours straight.</u> <u>It breathes by keeping the end of its trunk out of</u>
(2)
<u>the water like a snorkel.</u>

Elephants also have very poor eyesight and use their trunks to recognize each other and communicate.
<u>When young elephants wrestle by entwining their trunks, it strengthens the trunks, they learn how to</u>
(3)
<u>recognize others in their herd.</u>

1 **A** You have probably seen elephants using
their trunks at the zoo to pick up peanuts.
Or straw for food.

B You have probably seen elephants using
their trunks at the zoo, they use them to
pick up peanuts or straw for food.

C You have probably seen elephants using
their trunks at the zoo to pick up peanuts
or straw for food.

D Correct as is

2 **F** An elephant can swim underwater for up
to six hours straight, or it breathes by
keeping the end of its trunk out of the
water like a snorkel.

G An elephant can swim underwater for up
to six hours straight, by keeping the end of
its trunk out of the water like a snorkel.

H An elephant can swim underwater for up
to six hours straight, keeping the end of its
trunk out of the water like a snorkel.

J An elephant can swim underwater for up
to six hours straight because it is like a
snorkel with its trunk out of the water.

3 **A** When young elephants wrestle by entwining their trunks, it strengthens the trunks,
and they learn how to recognize others in
their herd.

B When young elephants, entwining their
trunks it strengthens the trunks. They
learn how to recognize others in their herd.

C When young elephants wrestle by entwining their trunks it strengthens the trunks.
And they learn how to recognize others in
their herd.

D Correct as is

Answers and Analyses

1. C Explain to students that the underlined portion contains a sentence
fragment beginning with *To pick up*.
This fragment does not make sense
on its own because there is no subject. The correct answer removes the
period to make the fragment into a
prepositional phrase.

2. H The two sentences are grammatically
correct, but notice that the two sentences both begin with the same subject *(An elephant and it, which refers
to the elephant)*. When combined, the
sentence reads more smoothly. The
correct answer removes the subject,
verb, and preposition *by* from the
second sentence and adds a comma.

3. A Students should be able to recognize
that this is a run-on sentence. Two
complete sentences are combined
with only a comma. The correct
answer adds the conjunction *and* after
the comma, correctly combining the
two independent clauses.

Test-Taking Tip

If students are not sure how the original
sentence should be changed, they
should look for errors in the answer
choices and eliminate ones they know
are wrong.

Test-Taking Tip

Suggest to students that when they read
the answer choices, they make sure that
the meaning of the original sentence or
sentences is retained.

Tested Objective

- To recognize appropriate English usage and sentence structure within the context of a written passage

Answers and Analyses

1. **B** The original sentence is a run-on because it is composed of two sentences combined with only a comma. The correct answer choice removes the second, repeated subject and verb.

2. **H** Students should recognize that the underlined section contains a sentence fragment beginning with *When she was.* This is a dependent clause that cannot stand on its own. The correct answer replaces the period with a comma.

Test-Taking Tip

Encourage students to come up with ways to correct run-on sentences by either making them into two complete sentences, or by removing some words to shorten the sentence.

Standardized Test Practice

Read each passage. Some sections are underlined. The underlined sections may be one of the following:

- Incomplete sentences
- Run-on sentences
- Correctly written sentences that should be combined
- Correctly written sentences that do not need to be rewritten

Choose the best way to write each underlined section and mark the letter for your answer on your paper. If the underlined section needs no change, mark the choice "Correct as is."

<u>In 1884, Sarah Winchester began building one of the strangest homes in the world, it is in San Jose,</u>
<u>California.</u> The enormous mansion, which took thirty years to complete, later became known as the
(1)

"Winchester Mystery House." When Sarah bought the house, it was a modest six-room dwelling. <u>When she</u>
<u>was finally done with it. The house contained 160 rooms and stood five stories.</u>
(2)

    The mansion has stairways that lead nowhere, rooms within rooms, and skylights in the floor. It is difficult to understand what could have driven Sarah to build such a bizarre home. In fact, no one really knows.

---

1 A In 1884. Sarah Winchester began building one of the strangest homes in the world in San Jose, California.

  B In 1884, Sarah Winchester began building one of the strangest homes in the world in San Jose, California.

  C In 1884, Sarah Winchester began building one of the strangest homes in the world. In San Jose, California.

  D Correct as is

2 F When she was finally done with it, the house contained 160 rooms, it stood five stories.

  G When she was finally done with it, the house contained 160 rooms. And it stood five stories.

  H When she was finally done with it, the house contained 160 rooms and stood five stories.

  J Correct as is

Standardized Test Practice

Sam was visiting his Aunt Theresa in San Francisco for Thanksgiving. When they were on the Bay Area
(1)
Rapid Transit Train travelling to a museum, Sam noticed something odd.

"Aunt Theresa," Sam said with astonishment, "there was nobody driving that train!"

Aunt Theresa smiled and explained that the trains were electronically controlled. When they were first
(2)
built in 1972, there were frequent equipment malfunctions. There were also frequent control malfunctions.

However, for the past twenty years, they had run quite well, carrying more than 200,000 passengers per day.

The train stopped it dropped Sam and his aunt at the museum.
(3)
"Instead of going to the museum, let's ride the train again!" exclaimed Sam. Aunt Theresa laughed and

they boarded the train again.

1 A Sam, visiting his Aunt Theresa in San
Francisco for Thanksgiving.
  B Sam was visiting his Aunt Theresa. He was
in San Francisco for Thanksgiving.
  C Sam was visiting his Aunt Theresa in San
Francisco, it was also for Thanksgiving.
  D Correct as is

2 F When they were control malfunctions
first built in 1972, there were frequent
equipment.
  G When they, which were frequent equipment and control malfunctions, were first
built in 1972.
  H When they were first built in 1972, there
were frequent equipment malfunctions,
and there were also frequent control
malfunctions.

  J When they were first built which was in
1972, frequent equipment and control
malfunctions.

3 A The train stopped and dropped Sam and
his aunt at the museum.
  B The train stopping. The train dropped Sam
and his aunt at the museum.
  C The train stopped. And dropped Sam and
his aunt at the museum.
  D Correct as is

Answers and Analyses

1. D The sentence is correct as is. The
prepositional phrase *for Thanksgiving
weekend* is appropriate and correct.
The sentences in choice B are grammatically correct, but result in choppy
sentences in which the subject is
named twice.

2. H The two sentences are correct. The
answer choice combines them.

3. A The original sentence is a run-on. The
conjunction *and* correctly combines
the clauses.

Test-Taking Tip

Students should become accustomed to
recurring error types. For example, correct sentences that need to be combined
often describe two actions performed by
the same subject.

Tested Objective

• To recognize appropriate English usage within the context of a written passage

Answers and Analyses

1. D Students should recognize that the sentence is missing the second half of the verb *were (to be)*. The students were clearly what? The only verb in the answer choice is *excited.*

2. F The second-person verb form must follow the subject "you" and the auxiliary verb "are." Only answer F provides it. "Leaving" also works better than either "left" or "have left."

3. C The sentence is missing a verb in the present perfect tense. This tense indicates that the action started in the past and is continuing into the present.

4. J Students should understand that the missing word is the comparative adjective of *hard—harder.* Although the word is acting as an adverb (modifying *to try*), and adverbs usually end in -ly, *hardly* is incorrect in this case, as it is a word with another meaning. It means "with difficulty; scarcely; almost not at all."

Test-Taking Tip

Encourage your students to review superlative and comparative adjectives. Superlatives describe the most or best of something. The superlative is created with the word *most* + the adjective. The comparative adjective compares two things. For one-syllable words such as *fast,* a comparative adjective is formed by adding -er to the adjective *(faster).*

Standardized Test Practice

Read each passage and choose the word or group of words that belongs in each space. Mark the letter for your answer on your paper.

> The students crowded around Jorry's locker. They were clearly ____(1)____ about the trip to the amusement park that Saturday. Suddenly, Jorry saw Will walking out the door. "Will, are you ____(2)____ without making plans for Saturday?"
>
> "I can't come," Will replied. "I need to use the extra day to paint my parents' garage. It ____(3)____ for weeks."
>
> Later that afternoon, Will was watching TV at home when he heard a noise from out in the backyard. He looked out the window and saw his friends. They had brought ladders, paint, and brushes, and were busy scraping the old paint from the garage.
>
> "If we all help, the garage will be painted by the weekend," called Jorry when she saw Will. "You'll have to try ____(4)____ than that to get away from us!"

1 A excitement
  B excite
  C exciting
  D excited

2 F leaving
  G have left
  H left
  J had been leaving

3 A had been planned
  B will be planned
  C has been planned
  D is being planned

4 F more hard
  G hardly
  H most hardly
  J harder

Most people ____(1)____ of finding a pirate's treasure. Barry Clifford actually found one. Using a map from the year 1717, Mr. Clifford spent fifteen years searching the coast off Massachusetts for the sunken remains of a ship called the *Whydah*. Mr. Clifford has found more than 100,000 items from the ship already, but says he ____(2)____ find everything. The sea has spread the treasures far and wide.

Some preservationists feel that the *Whydah* should be ____(3)____ property. They ____(4)____ historic artifacts such as the sunken ship should be kept in museums. However, Massachusetts law says that the ship and everything Mr. Clifford finds belong to him.

1 **A** has dreamed
   B have dreamed
   C is dreaming
   D were dreaming

2 **F** will barely never
   G will not never
   H will hardly never
   J will probably never

3 **A** publicly
   B publicize
   C publics
   D public

4 **F** think
   G thought
   H had thought
   J was thinking

Answers and Analyses

1. **B** Students should recognize that since the subject of the sentence, *most people,* is plural, the verb must also be plural. Of the two plural answer choices, *have dreamed* is correct because the action continues (people still dream of treasures) and because the period in which they do the dreaming is not time-specific.

2. **J** Students should be able to recognize the double negative and understand why it is not correct in the English language.

3. **D** Students should recognize that the answer is an adjective. It is a word that modifies the noun *property. Public* is the only answer choice that is an adjective.

4. **F** The sentence requires a verb in the present tense. It must agree with the subject *they.* The clue for identifying what tense the verb should be in is the tense of the surrounding verbs. In the previous sentence, the verb is in the present tense *(feel).*

Test-Taking Tip

Encourage students to review subject-verb agreement. In a sentence, the form of the verb needs to agree with the subject. This means that if the sentence has a singular subject *(I, the man)* it should also have a singular verb *(I ran, the man climbed the stairs).* If the subject is plural, the verb must also be plural.

STOP

Tested Objective

- To recognize appropriate English usage within the context of a written passage

Answers and Analyses

1. D The sentence requires a verb in the present tense. The subject of the verb is the pronoun *it,* which is singular. The tense of the surrounding verbs is present *(sells, is).* The passage describes a food, caviar, that exists and is eaten today (present tense). The correct answer is the singular present tense of the verb *to come (comes).*

2. H Students should recognize that the sentence requires a verb in the present tense. The subject of the verb is *caviar,* which is singular. The tense of the second verb in the sentence is present *(comes).* The correct answer is the singular present tense of the verb *to sell (sells).*

3. A This question looks for an adjective to modify the noun *amount.* Note that the superlative, answer choice D, is inappropriate because no comparison is made. The correct answer is the adjective *precise.*

4. G The sentence requires a verb in the present tense. The subject is *he,* which is singular. The second verb in the sentence is in the present tense *(are).* The correct answer is the verb *to know* in the singular present tense *(knows).*

Test-Taking Tip

Students should be able to identify when to use the different forms of verbs. Regular verbs are conjugated (or changed into their different forms) by adding suffixes (for example, *-ed* for the past tense). Irregular verbs do not follow the same rules. Encourage your students to make a list of irregular verbs *(to be, to dive, to hang).*

Standardized Test Practice

Read each passage and choose the word or group of words that belongs in each space. Mark the letter for your answer on your paper.

Have you ever eaten caviar? Not many people have. Caviar is a very expensive preparation of fish eggs and salt. It only ___(1)___ from certain kinds of fish, in certain regions of the world. The finest caviar sells for more than $1,000 per pound.

A less expensive caviar, which ___(2)___ for $630 per pound, comes from a fish called a chalbash. The chalbash can easily grow to be five feet long, and weigh more than thirty-five pounds. A master caviar artisan adds a ___(3)___ amount of salt to the chalbash's eggs, then rubs them with his fingers, tasting them from time to time, until he ___(4)___ they are ready. It is a very difficult thing to learn, and that may be one reason why caviar is so expensive.

1 **A** had come
  B came
  C have come
  D comes

2 **F** selling
  G have sold
  H sells
  J sold

3 **A** precise
  B precisely
  C more precisely
  D most precise

4 **F** knew
  G knows
  H has known
  J know

Latorry's class was playing volleyball in physical education. The ball came down towards Latorry, but it was too far away for him to reach. Without thinking, he __(1)__ out his foot and kicked it. The ball sailed over the net and bounced inside the lines.

When Latorry __(2)__ off the court, Mr. Russel, the PE instructor, came over to him. "That was a nice move, Latorry," he said.

"But Mr. Russel, __(3)__ was illegal," Latorry said. "The other team got the point."

"That's true, Latorry, but maybe you'll invent a new game," Mr. Russel replied. "Once a young English soccer player named William Webb Ellis picked up the ball and ran. The move was against soccer's rules, but people enjoyed playing that way. Without William Webb Ellis we __(4)__ of the sport of rugby."

1 A sticked
  B has stuck
  C sticks
  D stuck

2 F will rotate
  G rotated
  H rotating
  J rotates

3 A I
  B we
  C it
  D you

4 F would never have heard
  G wouldn't never have heard
  H wouldn't barely have heard
  J would never hardly hear

STOP

Answers and Analyses

1. **D** This question requires a verb that agrees with the subject *he*. The second verb in the sentence is in the past tense *(kicked)*. Students should recognize that the correct answer is the past tense of the verb *to stick (stuck)*.

2. **G** The sentence requires a verb that agrees with the subject, *Latorry*. What did Latorry do? He *rotated*. Students should see that the second verb in the sentence is in the past tense *(came)*, so the answer choice should be as well.

3. **C** Explain to students that the sentence requires a pronoun. The antecedent of the pronoun, or the noun the pronoun is replacing, is *the move*, which is singular. *The move* is an inanimate object and therefore is replaced by the pronoun *it*.

4. **F** This question asks students to correctly negate the phrase *would have heard*. Students should be aware that *never, barely,* and *hardly* are all negative words, and therefore cannot be combined either with each other or with the negative of *would (would not or wouldn't)*.

Test-Taking Tip

Remind students that a double negative is comprised of two negative words used together to make a single idea negative. In English, only one negative word is needed to negate an idea. Make sure that students can identify negative words such as *never, hardly, scarcely, not,* etc.

Tested Objective

- To recognize appropriate English usage within the context of a written passage

Answers and Analyses

1. C The sentence requires a verb to agree with the subject *lightning*. *Lightning* is singular because it describes a single *group* of light flashes. The first verb in the sentence *(believe)* is in the present tense, so this verb should be as well. Students should also understand the need for the present tense by the context of the sentence. The singular present form of *to flash* is *flashes*.

2. J This question asks students to correctly identify the superlative adjective. Explain to students that the superlative is formed by adding the word *most* to the adjective. The correct answer is *most frequent*.

3. A The sentence requires a verb in the present tense. The verb must agree with the subject *(this type)* and with the tense of the second verb in the sentence *(develops)*. In this case, the passive construction is used: *is caused*.

4. H Students are asked to choose the correct pronoun to agree with the antecedent *cloud,* which is a singular noun with neutral gender. The correct answer is *it*.

Test-Taking Tip

Assure students that on writing tests, the names of the tenses of verbs or the parts of speech will not be tested. What will be tested, and what students should review, is how words function in a sentence and why.

Standardized Test Practice

Read each passage and choose the word or group of words that belongs in each space. Mark the letter for your answer on your paper.

> At any time, there may be 2,000 thunderstorms in activity on earth. Scientists believe that lightning ___(1)___ an average of 100 times per second. Some lightning flashes occur inside a cloud, but the ___(2)___ type of lightning flashes from a cloud down to the ground. This type ___(3)___ when the bottom of the cloud develops a negative charge. As the negatively charged cloud moves over the ground, a positive charge builds below ___(4)___. The positive and negative charges get stronger until they balance themselves in what we call lightning.

1 A was flashing
   B had flashed
   C flashes
   D flashed

2 F frequent
   G more frequently
   H frequentest
   J most frequent

3 A is caused
   B has caused
   C was causing
   D have caused

4 F me
   G you
   H it
   J they

When bicycles were first invented,
___(1)___ did not have pedals. Pedals
___(2)___ in 1839 by the Scottish blacksmith, Kirkpatrick Macmillan.

The first pedals ___(3)___ to the rear
wheel of the bicycle. The wheel turned
once with each rotation of the pedals.
Speed depended upon how big the front
wheel was. The pennyfarthing bicycles of
the time had front wheels that were five
feet high. The back wheels were ___(4)___
than the wheels of modern bicycles.

1 A they
  B our
  C your
  D their

2 F was inventing
  G invented
  H had invented
  J were invented

3 A has been attached
  B were attached
  C is attached
  D are attached

4 F much smaller
  G more smaller
  H smallest
  J small

Answers and Analyses

1. A Students are asked to use the correct pronoun. Students should recognize that the pronoun refers to the antecedent *bicycles,* which is plural. The subject pronoun *they* is correct.

2. J This question asks students to form the past tense, passive voice of the verb *to invent.* The subject is *Pedals,* which is plural. The verb in the first sentence is in the past tense passive voice (*were invented*). This verb should agree with the tense of the first verb. The correct answer is *were invented.*

3. B Explain to students that the sentence requires a verb. The tense of the verb in the preceding sentence is past (*were invented*). The subject of the verb is plural (*pedals*). The plural past form of *to attach* is *were attached.*

4. F This question tests the students' ability to use the comparative adjective. Students should be aware that a comparison is being made of the back wheels of pennyfarthings and the wheels of today's bicycles. The comparative adjective *much smaller* is correct.

Test-Taking Tip

Point out to students that on writing tests, made-up words, or words that don't really exist, are often provided as answer choices. They can be easily eliminated.

STOP

Tested Objective

- To proofread for spelling, punctuation, and capitalization errors within the context of a written passage

Answers and Analyses

1. **C** The error is an error in punctuation. *After all* is a parenthetical phrase, and needs to be set off by two commas.

2. **G** Students should recognize that *music* is not a proper noun and therefore should not be capitalized.

3. **C** Point out to students that the error is one of punctuation because direct quotations should be enclosed in quotation marks on both sides.

4. **F** Students should recognize that the error is one of spelling because *beating* is misspelled.

5. **D** No comma is needed between two actions. All the words are spelled correctly.

6. **G** Since Carter Brothers Band is the name of a band and therefore a proper name, all the first letters in the band's name should be capitalized.

Test-Taking Tip

Watch out for vowel combinations such as *ie* and *ea* in words—they will often be misspelled on writing tests.

Test-Taking Tip

Encourage students to pay attention to how words change when they are made plural. Words that end in -*y*, for instance, often change to -*ies* when made plural. Ask students to think of examples of words that change their spelling when made plural.

Standardized Test Practice

Read each passage and decide which type of error, if any, appears in each underlined section. Mark the letter for your answer on your paper.

Carlos looked suspiciously at his little brother, Ry. <u>Ry was only seven, after all and Carlos wasn't sure a</u>
(1)
seven-year-old would be able to sustain an interest in <u>playing Music long enough to get it right. Carlos</u>
(2)
carefully explained that all Ry had to do was beat on the drum. He showed him the rhythm he needed.

"As long as you keep it <u>steady, everything will be fine, said Carlos encouragingly.</u>
(3)

Ry <u>started beeting on the drum. "Is that okay?"</u> he asked.
(4)

Carlos <u>answered by picking up his clarinet and playing</u> the melody he had invented that morning. The
(5)
notes mixed in with the drum's beat and became a song.

"It's music!" cried Ry, and missed a beat.

"It sure was," said Carlos. "We'll call ourselves <u>the Carter brothers Band. Let's</u> take it again from the top!"
(6)

1 **A** Spelling error
    B Capitalization error
    C Punctuation error
    D No error

2 **F** Spelling error
    G Capitalization error
    H Punctuation error
    J No error

3 **A** Spelling error
    B Capitalization error
    C Punctuation error
    D No error

4 **F** Spelling error
    G Capitalization error
    H Punctuation error
    J No error

5 **A** Spelling error
    B Capitalization error
    C Punctuation error
    D No error

6 **F** Spelling error
    G Capitalization error
    H Punctuation error
    J No error

One day in 1992 <u>Iwan Stössel, a swiss geology student, was</u> walking along the coast of Ireland. He came
<u>(1)</u>
across a <u>strange set of imppressions in a stone that</u> looked like footprints. There were 150 of these fossilized
<u>(2)</u>
<u>footprints, each about the size of a dogs foot.</u> Paleontologists believe that the tracks were left 365 <u>million</u>
<u>(3)</u>
<u>years ago by a tetrapod one of the first creatures ever to walk</u> rather than swim. <u>The tetrapod waded</u>
<u>(4)</u>   <u>(5)</u>
<u>through shallow water, Scientists believe, at</u> a time when Ireland was south of the equator. Just how its
ancestors' fins became legs, and <u>how it moved from the shallos up onto dry land, is still a mystery.</u>
<u>(6)</u>

1 A Spelling error
   B Capitalization error
   C Punctuation error
   D No error

2 F Spelling error
   G Capitalization error
   H Punctuation error
   J No error

3 A Spelling error
   B Capitalization error
   C Punctuation error
   D No error

4 F Spelling error
   G Capitalization error
   H Punctuation error
   J No error

5 A Spelling error
   B Capitalization error
   C Punctuation error
   D No error

6 F Spelling error
   G Capitalization error
   H Punctuation error
   J No error

Answers and Analyses

1. B Explain to students that the error is one of capitalization. Names of countries and the adjective used to describe people or things from that country should be capitalized. *Swiss* should be capitalized.

2. F There is a spelling error. *Impressions* is spelled incorrectly.

3. C Students should recognize that the error is a punctuation error because an apostrophe is required after *dog* to show possession. Whose foot is it? *A dog's.*

4. H Explain to students that since *one of the first creatures to walk* is a modifying phrase, it should be set off with commas.

5. B *Scientists* is a general noun, not a proper noun, so should not take a capital letter.

6. F The error is a spelling error. *Shallows* is misspelled.

Test-Taking Tip

Remind students of the rules regarding apostrophes—'*s* is used to indicate possession.

Tested Objective

- To proofread for spelling, punctuation, and capitalization errors within the context of a written passage

Answers and Analyses

1. A Students should recognize that there is a spelling error. *Carefully* requires two *l*'s.

2. G Remind students that days of the week are capitalized *(Saturday)*.

3. C Explain to students that the underlined portion contains a punctuation error. The introductory, dependent clause ending with *time* should be set off with a comma.

4. G Since *red* is not a proper noun, it should not be capitalized.

5. D There is no error in the underlined portion.

6. H The underlined portion contains a punctuation error that students should recognize. To show possession, the noun requires *-'s*. The pieces belong to Jodie's mother. They are her *mother's pieces.*

Test-Taking Tip

It might be useful to review the rules for using quotation marks with students. Quotation marks should be placed around direct quotations. Quotation marks always come in pairs. Make sure your students find an opening and closing quotation mark when someone is speaking in the text.

A comma appears within the quotation marks to separate the quote from explanatory words that follow (for example, "I like chocolate cake," said Francis). Commas do not appear if the quotation ends with an exclamation point or a question mark (for example, "Would you like to be my partner?" she asked).

Standardized Test Practice

Read each passage and decide which type of error, if any, appears in each underlined section. Mark the letter for your answer on your paper.

Jodie looked carefuly across the checkerboard at her opponent. She was playing with her mother. Jodie and her mother played checkers every saturday. Sometimes Jodie won and sometimes her mother won. Hoping that she would win this time Jodie concentrated very hard. She had worked out a strategy and she was feeling confident.

Today, Jodie had the Red pieces and her mother had the black. Her mother hopped over two of Jodie's pieces.

"I might just win this time," Jodie's mother said.

"Don't be so sure!" Jodie said and jumped over four of her mothers pieces. She had won the game!

"I'll get you next time!" laughed Jodie's mother. As was their tradition, they went into the kitchen and had some milk and cookies after their game.

1
 A Spelling error
 B Capitalization error
 C Punctuation error
 D No error

2
 F Spelling error
 G Capitalization error
 H Punctuation error
 J No error

3
 A Spelling error
 B Capitalization error
 C Punctuation error
 D No error

4
 F Spelling error
 G Capitalization error
 H Punctuation error
 J No error

5
 A Spelling error
 B Capitalization error
 C Punctuation error
 D No error

6
 F Spelling error
 G Capitalization error
 H Punctuation error
 J No error

Test-Taking Tip

Point out to students that on writing tests, they should not assume that just because an underlined portion consists of punctuation, it does not mean the punctuation is incorrect.

Standardized Test Practice

In the last half of 1998, a number of scientists mounted <u>donkeys in Dana Jordan. They</u> set out into the

(1)

desert with hand-mined copper ore. They wanted to reduce the ore to metal the way people in that region

did <u>6,500 years ago. Tom levy, an archeologist</u> from California, was one of the leaders of the group.

(2)

After a ten-day <u>trek accross the desert, the team</u> arrived at the site of the ancient village of Shiqmim,

(3)

whose ruins lie in modern day Israel. They used <u>the towns original firepits to try</u> to heat the copper ore and

(4)

reduce it to metal. When they had <u>kept the ore at temperatures of nearly 2000 degrees for a</u> whole hour,

(5)

they were left with only a few pea-sized lumps of copper. They <u>left with a new apreciation of what hard</u>

(6)

<u>work the ancient</u> metalworkers had been faced with!

1 **A** Spelling error
   B Capitalization error
   C Punctuation error
   D No error

2 **F** Spelling error
   G Capitalization error
   H Punctuation error
   J No error

3 **A** Spelling error
   B Capitalization error
   C Punctuation error
   D No error

4 **F** Spelling error
   G Capitalization error
   H Punctuation error
   J No error

5 **A** Spelling error
   B Capitalization error
   C Punctuation error
   D No error

6 **F** Spelling error
   G Capitalization error
   H Punctuation error
   J No error

Answers and Analyses

1. **C** The error is one of punctuation because a comma is required after the state and before the country *(Dana, Jordan)*. Students should be aware that this is a very common error type.

2. **G** Students should be aware that because *Tom Levy* is a proper name, it should be capitalized.

3. **A** The error is a spelling error. *Across* is the correct spelling.

4. **H** This question requires students to recognize and correctly punctuate a possessive. Whose original firepits? The *town's*.

5. **D** There is no error in the underlined section.

6. **F** There is a spelling error. The correct spelling is *appreciation*.

Test-Taking Tip

Students should take extra care with double consonants in words. It is a frequent error type on writing tests.

STOP

Tested Objective

• To proofread for spelling, punctuation, and capitalization errors within the context of a written passage

Answers and Analyses

1. B There is an error in capitalization: *Science Club.*

2. F Students should recognize that there is a spelling error. The word *interesting* is misspelled.

3. C There is a punctuation error. There should be a comma after *studies.*

4. G Students should recognize that the error is in capitalization. *P.M.*

5. B Capitalization: *Dr.* is abbreviated and capitalized when used as a title.

Test-Taking Tip

Point out to students that this is a functional passage, or one that serves a purpose (that of contacting Ms. Burke). A letter is a document that students will need to write in daily life. Other types of functional passages are flyers from restaurants or stores.

Standardized Test Practice

Read each passage and decide which type of error, if any, appears in each underlined section. Mark the letter for your answer on your paper.

Ms. Julie Burke

Koch Laboratories

1800 Abrams Parkway

Dallas, TX 75214

Dear Ms. Burke:

I am the president of the science Club at Roosevelt High School. I read an article recently about your
(1)
company in the newspaper. The tests that you are conducting sound very intresting to me. Would you be
(2)
willing to speak to our club about the work that you do? It would be very informative to hear about your
(3)
studies your background, and your thoughts about the profession.

The Science Club meets every Tuesday at 4 p.m., but we would be willing to work around your schedule
(4)
if necessary. You can contact our faculty advisor, dr. Harold Ripley, at the school's main office. Thank you in
(5)
advance for your time. I hope we will have the opportunity to meet soon.

Sincerely,

Zachary Dunham

---

1 A Spelling error
  B Capitalization error
  C Punctuation error
  D No error

2 F Spelling error
  G Capitalization error
  H Punctuation error
  J No error

3 A Spelling error
  B Capitalization error
  C Punctuation error
  D No error

4 F Spelling error
  G Capitalization error
  H Punctuation error
  J No error

5 A Spelling error
  B Capitalization error
  C Punctuation error
  D No error

Standardized Test Practice

Crocodiles first emerged in the pre-historical record 200 million years <u>ago. More than eighty million</u>
(1)
<u>years later there</u> were crocodiles forty feet long that may have preyed on dinosaurs. <u>Today, crocodiles vary in</u>
(2)
<u>size. Dwarf crocodiles</u> are as short as five feet long, while saltwater <u>crocodiles from southeastern asia, can</u>
(3)
<u>grow</u> up to twenty feet in length, and weigh one ton or more.

The female crocodile <u>burries her eggs in a bed of vegetation near</u> the water. Heat from <u>the Sun and the</u>
(4)(5)
<u>rotting plants</u> incubate the eggs, which hatch about three months later. When the <u>baby crocodiles hatch they</u>
(6)
<u>are still buried.</u> They must call to their mother to dig them out. She then brings them down to the water.

1 A Spelling error
B Capitalization error
C Punctuation error
D No error

2 F Spelling error
G Capitalization error
H Punctuation error
J No error

3 A Spelling error
B Capitalization error
C Punctuation error
D No error

4 F Spelling error
G Capitalization error
H Punctuation error
J No error

5 A Spelling error
B Capitalization error
C Punctuation error
D No error

6 F Spelling error
G Capitalization error
H Punctuation error
J No error

STOP

Answers and Analyses

1. C Students should recognize that there is a punctuation error. There should be a comma setting off the phrase *more than eighty million years later* from the independent, main clause beginning with *there were*.

2. J There is no error in the underlined section.

3. B Explain to students that the error is in capitalization. *Asia,* as the name of a region, should be capitalized. See the Test-Taking Tip below.

4. F The underlined portion contains a spelling error. *Buries* is spelled incorrectly.

5. B Explain to students that *sun* does not need to be capitalized. Point out to students that the names of planets are capitalized.

6. H The underlined portion contains a punctuation error. The subordinate clause that ends with *hatch* should be set off from the main clause by a comma.

Test-Taking Tip

Remind students that compass headings—*north, south, east, west,* etc.—are capitalized only when they indicate specific regions. The rule is: capitalize locations, but not directions.

Test-Taking Tip

Students should pay close attention to words that are capitalized that are not at the beginning of a sentence. They could be capitalized incorrectly.

Tested Objective

- To proofread for spelling, punctuation, and capitalization errors within the context of a written passage

Answers and Analyses

1. **A** Students should be able to recognize that there is a spelling error. *Practice* is misspelled.

2. **G** The underlined portion contains a capitalization error. Names of cities, such as *Chicago,* should be capitalized. The word is also a part of the name of a newspaper *(Chicago Legal News)* which requires that it be capitalized.

3. **C** Point out to students that the error is in punctuation. *Women* requires an -'s to indicate possession. Whose rights are they? They are *women's rights.*

4. **F** The underlined portion contains a spelling error. *Application* is misspelled.

5. **C** Two main clauses joined by a coordinating conjunction *(and)* should be separated by a comma before *and.*

Test-Taking Tip

Remind students of the basic rules for commas. Commas are used to separate two independent clauses connected by conjunctions (*and, but, or,* etc.); to separate items in a list or a series of words; to separate an introductory phrase or clause from the independent clause; to set off words or phrases that interrupt the sentence; to separate a full sentence quotation from surrounding comments.

Standardized Test Practice

Read each passage and decide which type of error, if any, appears in each underlined section. Mark the letter for your answer on your paper.

The bar is a legal term for the body of <u>lawyers who have been qualified to practise at trials.</u> Myra Colby
(1)
Bradwell was one of the first American women to be admitted to the bar. <u>Bradwell was the editor of the</u>
(2)
<u>chicago Legal News, and was</u> very influential through <u>editorials she wrote on womens rights.</u> She herself was
(3)
the object of substantial discrimination. <u>Her first aplication to the Illinois bar, in 1869, was rejected because</u>
(4)
<u>she was a woman, even though Illinois law prohibited the</u> barring of persons from any occupation on the
basis of gender. It took eleven years for <u>the Illinois bar to admit her and finally in 1892 she was admitted to</u>
(5)
<u>practice</u> before the U.S. Supreme Court.

1 **A** Spelling error
  B Capitalization error
  C Punctuation error
  D No error

2 **F** Spelling error
  G Capitalization error
  H Punctuation error
  J No error

3 **A** Spelling error
  B Capitalization error
  C Punctuation error
  D No error

4 **F** Spelling error
  G Capitalization error
  H Punctuation error
  J No error

5 **A** Spelling error
  B Capitalization error
  C Punctuation error
  D No error

Earthquakes are more <u>common occurences than you might expect. During</u> the 1980s, 15,436 earth-
(1)
quakes with a magnitude of five or greater on the Richter scale were recorded. The vast majority of earthquakes are very <u>small and cause little damage but the largest</u> can be among the most destructive of natural
(2)
catastrophes.

The largest earthquakes occur at subduction <u>zones, where one part of the earths crust</u> is forced beneath
(3)
another. <u>For example, in 1960, an earthquake in chile had a</u> magnitude of 8.5. <u>Another earthquake in kobe,</u>
(4) (5)
<u>Japan in 1995 was also very destructive.</u>

However, smaller earthquakes can be just as intense. Poor construction and certain soil types can make
even a <u>medium-sized earthquake highly destructive.</u>
(6)

1 **A** Spelling error
  B Capitalization error
  C Punctuation error
  D No error

2 **F** Spelling error
  G Capitalization error
  H Punctuation error
  J No error

3 **A** Spelling error
  B Capitalization error
  C Punctuation error
  D No error

4 **F** Spelling error
  G Capitalization error
  H Punctuation error
  J No error

5 **A** Spelling error
  B Capitalization error
  C Punctuation error
  D No error

6 **F** Spelling error
  G Capitalization error
  H Punctuation error
  J No error

Answers and Analyses

1. A The underlined portion consists of a spelling error. The correct spelling is *occurrences*.

2. H The error is in punctuation. The two independent clauses are separated by the conjunction *but* and should also be separated by a comma.

3. C *Earth's crust* requires an apostrophe because it indicates possession. Students should understand that this means *the crust of the earth*.

4. G Names of countries should be capitalized. *Chile* is a country in South America.

5. B Explain to students that names of states or towns should be capitalized. *Kobe, Japan*.

6. J The underlined portion contains no errors.

Test-Taking Tip

On some writing tests, there are only three different types of errors to look for: spelling, punctuation, or capitalization. Encourage students to first read the text with only spelling errors in mind. If no error is found, reread the text with only capitalization errors in mind. Finally, if still no errors are found, reread the text one last time for punctuation errors. If your students narrow their focus, these questions may become easier for them.

Objectives

- To take notes and summarize spoken ideas
- To learn how to listen and speak effectively when communicating on the phone, giving directions, and participating in informal discussion
- To demonstrate effective communication skills when storytelling or presenting an oral report

Key to Ability Levels

L1 Level 1 activities are within the basic ability range of students.

L2 Level 2 activities are within the ability range of average students.

L3 Level 3 activities are more challenging activities.

✔ ASSESSMENT OPTIONS

📁 *Tests with Answer Key and Rubrics*
Unit 25 Pretest, pp. 101–102

💾 *Testmaker*
Unit 25 Pretest

You may wish to administer the Unit 25 Pretest at this point.

UNIT 25

Listening and Speaking

616

Resource Manager

Planning Resources
- *Lesson Plans*
- *Block Scheduling*

📷 Transparencies
- *Bellringer*
- *Daily Language Practice*

📁 Other Print Resources
- *Listening and Speaking Activities*
- *Tests with Answer Key and Rubrics*
- *Thinking and Study Skills*

📼 Video
- *MindJogger Videoquizzes*

💾 Software
- *Presentation Plus!*
- *Testmaker*

🖥 Web Sites
- *writerschoice.glencoe.com*

25.1 Listening

Imagine yourself taking a trip and using a map for directions. How would you know where to go if a part of your map were missing? Traveling without a complete set of directions can be difficult. The same is true in listening. You must listen for *all* the important "road signs." Miss one, and you may not understand what you hear.

Following Instructions

Understanding exactly what your teacher expects of you begins with listening to instructions. The following suggestions can help you improve your listening skills.

Listening to Instructions in Class

1. First try to eliminate any distractions that may make it difficult to listen.
2. Make sure you understand what you are listening for. Are you receiving instructions for homework or for a test? What you listen for depends upon the type of instructions being given.
3. Think about what you are hearing, and keep your eyes on the speaker. This will help you stay focused on the important points.
4. Listen for word clues the speaker is using. Examples of word clues are expressions such as *above all, the most important,* and *the three basic parts.* These clues can help you identify important points you should remember.
5. Take notes on what you hear. Write down only the most important parts of the instructions.
6. If you don't understand something, ask questions. Then, if you're still unsure about the instructions, repeat them aloud to your teacher to receive correction on any key points you've missed.

Listening and Speaking

Resource Manager

Planning Resources
• *Lesson Plans*

Transparencies
• *Bellringer*
• *Daily Language Practice*

Other Print Resources
• *Listening and Speaking Activities,* pp. 6–11, 17–18
• *Thinking and Study Skills,* pp. 33–34

Focus

Lesson Overview

Objectives
• To eliminate barriers to listening effectively to instructions
• To take notes and summarize spoken ideas

Skills
• listening to instructions; taking notes

Critical Thinking
• evaluating; determining important information

Listening and Speaking
• listening to instructions; discussing

Bellringer
Daily Language Activity

When students enter the classroom, have this assignment on the board: *List five situations when it would be important for you to listen carefully to instructions or information. What might your purpose be for listening in each of these situations?*

See also *Daily Language Practice*

Teach

Listening to Instructions

Draw a simple design on a piece of paper. Have one student study the design and then give instructions to the class on how to draw it. Suggest that other students take notes on the instructions, and then try to duplicate the original design, using the instructions given. Then have them compare their drawings to the original design. Ask students why there are differences in their drawings. Were the instructions clear and complete? **L2**

Teach

Evaluating a Persuasive Speech

If possible, bring a video of a persuasive speech to class. You might videotape the speech of a politician campaigning for office. Have students listen carefully to the speech and take notes to summarize the spoken ideas. After listening to the speech, have students evaluate the content, credibility, and delivery of the message, using their notes. Are students persuaded by the speaker? Why or why not? Finally, help students recognize and understand barriers to effective listening, such as internal and external distractions, personal bias, and conflicting demands. **L2**

Thinking About Persuasive Content

Remind students to evaluate the information they hear, especially in persuasive speeches. Review that a fact is something that can be proved. A reference source or an expert in the field can verify that the information is correct. Opinions are based on feelings and experiences, but they cannot be proved to be true. In a persuasive speech, the speaker will present his or her ideas and opinions in a way that will encourage the listener to accept them as true. It is up to the listener to sort out the facts and opinions and to decide whether the message being presented is valid. **L2**

Listening and Speaking

Taking Notes

Taking notes as you listen is a good way to sort out main ideas and supporting details. The process of taking notes also helps you remember what you've heard. You may already have your own way of taking notes. Here are a few useful note-taking tips you may want to keep in mind:

- **Have a purpose for listening.** Are you trying to gain information or solve a problem? Asking these questions will give you a focus when you are taking notes.
- **Key ideas** are the ones you want to remember. Listen for them.
- **Don't be in a hurry** to start writing. It can take time to complete an idea. Make sure the speaker has completed a key idea before you write it down.
- **Keep listening** as you take notes. Stay alert so that you don't miss important information as you write.
- **Keep your notes brief.** Don't try to take down everything the speaker says. You don't need to write complete sentences. A few words are usually enough to help you remember a key idea. Remember, your notes are for you.
- **Use graphic aids** to organize information clearly. Charts, pictures, tables, or even arrows and lines can help you understand and remember how points are related. You can review the information about graphic aids on pages 579–582.
- **Review your notes.** Read over your notes a few hours after you have written them. Reviewing what you have written will help you remember the information.

Listening to Persuasive Speech

Have you ever listened to a politician speak or to an editorial on the news? Do you listen to radio or television commercials? If you said *yes*, you have heard persuasive speech. All of these speakers have one thing in common—they are trying to convince you of something. They may want to get your vote, to sell you a certain product, or to change your mind about an issue that is important to them.

MEETING INDIVIDUAL NEEDS — English Language Learners

Summarizing

Students who are just learning English may have difficulty understanding and summarizing verbal information. You might suggest that as they listen to people speak they notice nonverbal as well as verbal cues. Demonstrate examples of nonverbal communication. Show how stress and intonation can change meaning. Ask them to share verbal and nonverbal cues used in their native cultures in order to focus their thoughts. Then, ask students to suggest their own examples of nonverbal cues in American culture.

Listening to Commercials

Nowhere is persuasive speech more obvious than in commercials. Commercials provide information, but they also try to sell you products. Advertisers use many different techniques to convince you to buy their products. They know you often decide what to buy based on your feelings rather than on the facts.

- **Endorsement.** In an endorsement, a famous person or an expert, such as a doctor, tells you that he or she uses a certain product. For example, a famous basketball player may be shown wearing a certain brand of shoes. The advertiser hopes that if you see someone you know or respect with a product, you will be more likely to buy it. Or, you may think that if you buy that product, it will make you as successful or even as good-looking as the person who is endorsing the product.
- **Exaggeration.** Some advertisers use exaggeration to persuade you to buy their products. Commercials are sprinkled with words and slogans such as "new and improved," "the greatest," "perfect," and so on. If a spot remover product promises "amazing" results, what exactly does that mean? What is amazing to one person may not be to another. Exaggerations in advertising are often just statements of opinion that are not based on facts.

25.1 Listening **619**

Listening and Speaking

25.1

Teach

Making a Commercial

Have students break into small groups and write their own commercials using some of the persuasive techniques presented on student pages 619–620. Ask volunteers to present their commercials to the class. Have classmates identify the persuasive techniques used in the commercials. Ask students to evaluate whether the techniques would be effective in making viewers want to buy the product advertised in each commercial presented to them. Why or why not? **L2**

Responding to Commercials

Focus students' attention and ask a volunteer to read aloud the Garfield comic strip. Invite students to share their own responses to various commercials they recall, identifying the commercial techniques they noticed. You may wish to have students represent their analyses and responses to various commercials in comic strips of their own. Students might use the Garfield comic strip, in which a viewer responds to what he sees on the television, as a format or model for their own comic strips. **L2**

Evaluating Persuasive Messages in Different Media

Have students locate advertisements on the Internet. If possible, students might print their advertisements and present them to the class. Initiate a discussion on how persuasive techniques used on the Internet differ from those used in TV commercials. Ask students to assess how the choice of media contributes to the message.

Practice and Assess

Evaluation Rubrics

Exercise 1

Answers will vary. Responses should reflect an understanding of the listening and note-taking skills introduced in the lesson. Each student should take brief notes in order to understand the program's major ideas and supporting evidence. Ask them to use an effective rate, volume, pitch, and tone to help the audience "see" the program described.

Exercise 2

To complete this exercise, encourage students to refer to the techniques used in commercials that are listed on pages 619–620. Students should choose a chart or other graphic aid that clearly communicates techniques and examples from commercial messages. When students present their graphic aids, encourage them to speak clearly in order to communicate their ideas.

Additional Resources

📁 *Listening and Speaking Activities,*
   pp. 6–11, 17–18
📁 *Thinking and Study Skills,*
   pp. 33–34

Close

Explain to students that part of being a good listener is letting the speaker know that you are really listening by making eye contact, nodding your head, and asking good questions.

620

- **Hidden Fears.** Some commercials appeal to your fears. They suggest that by using a certain product you will be protected from something unpleasant or even dangerous. For instance, some soap manufacturers try to convince buyers that their special "germ-killing formula" will protect you from all kinds of illness. Other advertisers might suggest that if you don't use their perfume or their mouthwash, other people won't want to be around you.
- **Bandwagon.** Some advertisers encourage buyers to "jump on the bandwagon" and buy their product because it is the most popular of its kind. A blue jean commercial might claim that everyone at school will be wearing a certain brand of blue jean this year. Advertisers who use the bandwagon technique often try to convince consumers that if they don't buy the most popular brand, then they will not be popular themselves.

Exercise 1

Working with a small group, pick several programs to watch on television. Choose different types of programs, such as news, comedy, drama, science, and sports. Each group member should watch one program and take notes on it. Afterward, share with the group your notes on the program you watched. Try to help the group members "see" the program you describe for them.

Exercise 2

Listen carefully to several radio or television commercials. If possible, tape record them. Then choose one that uses one or more of the techniques listed above. Create a chart to list a sample of how each technique is used in the commercial you chose. Then use your chart as a graphic aid to prepare and present a short oral report on your findings.

Listening and Speaking

Critical Thinking

Target Audiences

Evaluating Messages Discuss the target audiences of specific commercials with students. For example, you might mention a perfume commercial or one for a shaving cream. Explain that every commercial "aims" at a specific group of people. Point out to students that the actors in commercials are often selected to represent the target audience for the product. Sometimes such actors present an ideal view of the person who might buy the product. Invite students to identify and discuss commercials that specifically target them. They might list the range of products which seem specifically targeted toward their age group.

25.2 Informal Speaking

Did you know that you're already an expert in at least one type of public speaking—informal speaking? Most of your talking with other people is informal. There are many ways to speak informally. Examples include talking with friends, speaking in small groups in class, and communicating on the telephone.

Using the Telephone

When you call someone on the telephone, always identify yourself right away. Don't make the person on the other end try to guess who you are. You might say, "Is Gabriel there? This is Maria calling."

Here are some more tips for using the telephone:

- Speak clearly. Make sure the person on the other end can understand you easily. If a listener keeps asking you to repeat what you're saying, you may be mumbling.
- If the person you called is not there, try to leave a message. First ask if you can do so. Then give the person who answered time to get a pencil and paper.
- Speaking clearly becomes especially important if you must leave a recorded message. Remember, the recording can't ask you to repeat something.
- Deliver your message clearly. Give your name and your phone number. Then tell what information you'd like to leave for the person you've called. Try to make your message short and to the point.
- Be polite. Good telephone communication depends on how willing the other person is to listen to you. Good manners can help keep the other person interested.

Listening and Speaking

25.2 Informal Speaking **621**

Focus

Lesson Overview

Objectives
- To learn how to give and receive telephone messages
- To give clear directions and participate effectively in an informal discussion

Skills
- using the telephone; giving directions; taking part in informal discussions

Critical Thinking
- clarifying; evaluating

Listening and Speaking
- leaving and taking messages; giving directions; discussing

Bellringer
Daily Language Activity

When students enter the classroom, have this assignment on the board: *Write down what types of oral traditions you participate in within your family or culture. Why are these traditions important?* Then have students share their thoughts with the class.

See also *Daily Language Practice*

Motivating Activity

Ask students to imagine they are new to the school. Invite volunteers to give directions to the main office, library, gym, and cafeteria. Ask other students to evaluate the directions. Were the directions clear and complete?

Resource Manager

Planning Resources
- *Lesson Plans*

Transparencies
- *Bellringer*
- *Daily Language Practice*

Other Print Resources
- *Listening and Speaking Activities,* pp. 6–11, 17–18
- *Thinking and Study Skills,* pp. 33–34

Teach

Participating in Discussions

Encourage the students to get involved in discussion. Stress that in an informal discussion everyone's opinion is valid; there may be differences of opinion, but everyone's ideas should be listened to. Still, students should support their ideas with evidence or examples. Ask volunteers to suggest do's and don'ts of participating in a discussion, such as "Do be an active listener," "Do ask questions," "Don't interrupt." **L2**

Keeping Direction Steps in Order

Students may need suggestions for ordering steps when giving directions. Suggest that they actually go through the steps needed to complete a process, such as entering a computer program, setting up a telephone answering machine, or programming a VCR. Have students complete the first step, and then write what they did on a piece of paper. Repeat this process for all the following steps. **L1**

Listening and Speaking

Giving Directions

When someone asks you for directions, it's important to give detailed and exact information. You want to be sure that the person listening understands exactly what you're saying. The examples in the following chart will help you understand how to give clear directions.

Giving Directions		
Unclear	**Clear**	**Remember to**
Go a few blocks, then turn, and go two more blocks.	Go straight ahead for three blocks. Then turn left, and go on for two more blocks.	**Be precise.**
Mix the eggs and milk and the flour.	First mix the eggs and milk. Next sift the flour, and then combine it with the eggs and milk.	**Use proper ordering.**
Graham stopped by. He wants you to meet him later.	Graham stopped by at noon. He wants you to meet him in the library at about seven tonight.	**Give complete information.**
That's how you do it. Now you try it.	Before you try it yourself, do you have any questions about what I've said?	**Make sure you've been understood.**

Taking Part in an Informal Discussion

A small-group meeting in class is one example of an informal discussion. Other examples include planning a party with friends or discussing vacation plans with your family. Informal discussions should be relaxed. You usually don't have to prepare for what you'll say. You should, however, be ready to talk about the topic the group wishes to discuss.

Group members should express their own opinions and argue in favor of them. Members should feel free to disagree with one another, but in a polite way. The chart on the following page presents some useful tips on taking part in an informal discussion.

Real World Connection

History

The telephone was invented in 1876 by Alexander Graham Bell. The first commercial telephone exchange opened in New Haven, Connecticut, on January 28, 1878. According to the *Guinness Book of Records,* the United States has the greatest number of telephones—more than 130 million. The United States also holds the record for the greatest number of calls made in a year—over 400 billion. Invite students to learn more about Alexander Graham Bell and his motivation for inventing the telephone. Ask volunteers to share their findings with the class.

Tips For Informal Discussions

1. Be sure you've listened carefully to what other people have said. To respond well, you should have considered your classmates' points and perspectives.
2. Decide what ideas you want to get across when you speak. You need not have the wording completely planned ahead of time.
3. Help the discussion move forward. Make sure each comment adds something important to the topic.
4. Take turns listening and speaking without interrupting other speakers.
5. Speak in a normal tone of voice. Feel free to use gestures to stress a point you want to make strongly. The idea in informal speaking is to express yourself as naturally as you can.
6. Accept and evaluate criticism of your ideas.

Exercise 3

Working in pairs, take turns pretending to speak to each other on the telephone. Each caller should leave a short, clear message after asking for someone who is not available. The person receiving the call should write an accurate, complete message. Calls might be made to the dentist, to a friend, to a grandparent or other relative, or to a teacher or instructor.

Exercise 4

Work with a small group. Use a topic from the list below or one of your own choosing and hold a ten-minute discussion on it.
- Using cellular phones in public places
- Eliminating the long summer vacation in schools
- Watching television versus reading a book

Practice and Assess

Evaluation Rubrics

Exercise 3

Answers will vary. The caller should
- identify him- or herself immediately
- speak clearly and politely
- ask if he or she can leave a message
- give a brief, clear message that includes his or her name and phone number

The listener should
- speak clearly and politely
- record the message clearly and accurately
- repeat the caller's name and phone number to verify their accuracy

Exercise 4

Answers will vary. In group discussions, each student should
- listen carefully in order to avoid repeating points already made
- make comments that move the discussion forward
- speak naturally and expressively
- communicate using appropriate delivery (volume, rate, enunciation, and gestures)
- listen politely to other members without interrupting
- accept criticism of his or her ideas

Additional Resources

📁 *Listening and Speaking Activities,* pp. 6–11, 17–18
📁 *Thinking and Study Skills,* pp. 33–34

Listening and Speaking

MEETING INDIVIDUAL NEEDS

English Language Learners

Following Directions

Many students acquiring English can be helped when giving or listening to directions if they pay attention to some basic elements: verbs (*draw, write*), transition words (*next, then*), directional words (*above, left*), and non-verbal communication. Have students discuss these tips and then practice giving and following simple directions. (For example, students might describe how to get to the principal's office or how to draw a cube.) Ask students to take notes when they are listening and provide non-verbal clues when they are speaking.

Focus

Lesson Overview

Objectives
- To present an effective oral report
- To choose a story and present it to the class

Skills
- preparing and presenting oral reports

Critical Thinking
- determining main points

Listening and Speaking
- oral reporting

🔔 Bellringer
Daily Language Activity

When students enter the classroom, have this assignment on the board: *Your friend is nervous about having to present an oral report tomorrow. List five pieces of advice you would give so that your friend will be better prepared and less nervous.*

✍ **See also** *Daily Language Practice*

Teach

Preparing to Speak

During prewriting, work with students to narrow their topics. Before students revise reports, remind them that speakers usually use shorter sentences than writers do, and that they should include transition words to show how they organized their material. These techniques help listeners follow the main idea of an oral report. **L2**

25.3 How to Give an Oral Report

Speaking in front of an audience can be exciting. You can make sure your talk goes smoothly by taking care as you prepare it. Good planning also will help your audience gain the most from what you say.

TIME
For more about using the writing process, see **TIME Facing the Blank Page,** page 90.

Preparing an Oral Report

The following five-step plan can help you prepare and deliver an oral report. You'll find the plan familiar. It's very much like the one you use to do a written report.

1. **Prewriting** Decide on your topic. Make sure it's narrow enough to cover in a short oral report. Do research, take notes, and outline as you would for a written report.

2. **Drafting** Write out your report just as you'd like to deliver it orally. Let your thoughts flow, but keep to your outline. Make sure all the details help support your main ideas.

3. **Revising** Review what you've written. Do your ideas flow from one to another? Is there a better way to organize your material? Is it the right length? Does it need revision for style? Rework your draft as needed. Keep reworking it until you're satisfied it's right.

Listening and Speaking

624   Unit 25 Listening and Speaking

Resource Manager

Planning Resources
- *Lesson Plans*

✍ Transparencies
- *Bellringer*
- *Daily Language Practice*

📁 Other Print Resources
- *Listening and Speaking Activities,* pp. 6–11, 17–18
- *Thinking and Study Skills,* pp. 33–34

4. **Practicing** Practice giving your report in front of a mirror. Try not to read from your written copy. Use it only as notes for your talk. You might ask a friend or relative to listen to you and offer suggestions. You can also tape-record your talk.

5. **Presenting** Relax! If you've prepared well, you can trust that your oral report will go smoothly.

Presenting an Oral Report

Actually, it's not unusual to feel a bit nervous when speaking before an audience. Even well-known actors feel nervous, no matter how often they've performed. Here are some suggestions for giving an oral report.

Tips For Effective Speaking
1. Speak slowly, clearly, and in a normal tone of voice. Raise your voice a bit or use gestures to stress important points.
2. Pause a few seconds after making an important point. This lets your audience think about what you've said.
3. Use words that will help your audience picture what you're talking about. Visual aids such as pictures, graphs, charts, and maps can also help make your information clear to the audience.
4. Stay in contact with your audience. Make sure your eyes move from person to person in the group you're addressing.

Storytelling

For thousands of years, people from many different cultures used storytelling as a way to pass on their history, to teach the young, to explain why things happen in nature, and to entertain. Today, in the United States, storytelling has become an art and is mostly used to entertain and delight audiences of all ages. Good storytellers rely on their voices and words to create pictures in the minds of their listeners. use the plan on the following page to help you sharpen your story-telling skills and prepare a storytelling performance that your audience won't soon forget.

Listening and Speaking

Discussion Prompt
Discuss the Tips for Effective Speaking with the class. How are the criteria for presenting an oral report different from the criteria for having informal discussions? What are imporant tips for speaking, overall? Can students think of any additional tips for presenting a report?

Enrichment and Extension

Effective Speaking
Model both effective and ineffective speaking for the class. For ineffective speaking, you might speak too quickly, use unclear words, or lose contact with your audience. Have students evaluate both of your speeches using the Tips for Effective Speaking on the student page.

25.3

Teach

Finding a Story
Some students might choose to tell published stories that have always been treasured within their families. Encourage them to ask family members and friends to suggest ideas for stories to retell. **L1**

Sharing Cultures
Some students may wish to share special stories that are orally told and retold in their families or among people who share the same culture. Encourage students to share with the class any special knowledge they have of the importance of a story within a culture. After students listen to several story presentations, invite them to compare how stories, especially those from various cultures, are alike and different. **L2**

Planning Story Delivery
Have students plan where in the story they will pause, or speak loudly or softly. They might place sticky notes, with appropriate hints on telling the story, at those particular points in the book. **L2**

Listening and Speaking

1. **Finding the right story to tell.** Check at your library for books of folktales. You will want to visit the young people's section as well as the adult section. You might wish to choose a story that is from your own culture, or a culture that is similar to yours. The story should be short and interesting. It should capture the audience's attention with a surprise twist, a remarkable moment, or a satisfying ending.

2. **Familiarize yourself with the story.** Read the story several times. First read it for pleasure. Then read the story over and over again to become familiar with the style and structure of the story. Are there any unusual words and phrases, or ones that are repeated? What happens in the beginning and at the end?

   Think about what the story's characters are like. How does each one speak? What is the setting? What does it look like? What is it about the story that you would like to share with your listener? its humor? its sense of wonder?

3. **Practice telling the story.** Be yourself as you practice retelling your story in your own words. First tell it to your family, friends, or stand in front of a mirror. The following tips will help you as you practice.

   a. Don't memorize. Just remember the main details of the plot and go from there. Your story will probably be a little different every time you tell it, and that's fine. The more you let your own words and imagination flow, the more interesting the story will be.

   b. Make sure that you pace the story correctly. Each story has its own pace. Some stories, like "The Gingerbread Man," have a brisk pace, while others have a slow and steady pace. Some stories are made up of both slow and fast parts. Study your story to determine how you should pace it. Limit your first story to a length of five to ten minutes.

   c. Take time to come up with vivid descriptions of sounds, colors, smells, and other details in the story. If you forget what you want to say for a moment, use these descriptions to fill in the space. No one will know, because it's your story.

   d. Use your voice to make your storytelling interesting. Use a pleasant, low-pitched voice, and speak loudly enough so that all of your listeners can easily hear. Try to give each character a

Real World Connection

Visit the Library
Schedule a field trip to a local library. Ask the librarian to address how to locate various types of stories in the library. For example, students may want to browse in the folktale section or consider retelling a narrative poem, such as "Casey at the Bat," by Ernest Lawrence Thayer, from the poetry section. Have pairs of students work together to "find the right story to tell" in the library.

distinct voice. You don't need to give a shy character a high, squeaky voice and a pushy character a low, growling voice; you may simply have one character speak more softly. Whichever voice you choose for your characters, make sure it suits the character and that you use the same voice for each one throughout.

e. Don't be afraid to pause to allow an idea to sink in or to create a feeling of suspense. Stress important words by saying them more loudly, or even by whispering them. Sometimes a whisper captures your audience's attention more than a shout.

f. Look directly at your audience, moving your eyes from face to face. Your gestures and facial expressions should be natural—don't try to act out every action in the story. Remember that you are telling a story, not putting on a play.

4. **Limit distractions as much as possible.** Make sure that your audience is comfortable and ready to give you their full attention.

Exercise 5

Work with a small group. Each member should select a topic and write a two- to three-minute oral report about it. Be sure to narrow your topic before you begin. Practice giving your talk before your group. Allow group members to suggest improvements. Group members may give their oral reports later before the entire class.

Exercise 6

Work with a partner. Each of you should select a story and prepare to tell it to a group of people. Your story should be no longer than ten minutes and no less than five. Practice telling your story to your partner first. Have your partner time your story, evaluate your presentation, and make suggestions for improvement. Then tell each of your stories to the class.

Practice and Assess

Evaluation Rubrics

Exercise 5
Answers will vary. Oral reports should be evaluated according to the Tips for Effective Speaking on p. 625.

Exercise 6
Answers will vary. Story presentations should be evaluated according to how well students have used the storytelling techniques on pp. 626–627. As a further challenge, teachers could arrange for their students to deliver their oral presentations to an unfamiliar audience, such as another class.

Additional Resources
Listening and Speaking Activities, pp. 6–11, 17–18
Thinking and Study Skills, pp. 33–34

Close

Have students explain in writing what they would do to prepare a short oral report on a topic such as "How to Listen to Instructions" or "How to Use the Telephone." You may want to have volunteers use their plans to each give a short impromptu report.

✔ ASSESSMENT OPTIONS
Tests with Answer Key and Rubrics Unit 25 Mastery Test, pp. 103–104

Testmaker Unit 25 Mastery Test

You may wish to administer the Unit 25 Mastery Test at this point.

MindJogger Videoquizzes

English Language Learners

Practicing for a Report
Encourage students who are acquiring English to each practice his or her oral report with a more fluent partner. Students should continue to practice until they feel comfortable with their delivery.

Videotaping for Review
Depending on the needs of your class, you may want to videotape students as they present their oral reports. Students can review the tapes within their groups and use them to interpret, analyze, and evaluate the reports. They may also want to compare their own perceptions of the reports with those of others. **L3**

INTRODUCING

UNIT 26

Objectives

- To interpret and evaluate various kinds of visual messages
- To compare and contrast different types of media
- To evaluate how different media forms influence and inform
- To produce communications using technology or appropriate media

✔ ASSESSMENT OPTIONS

📂 *Tests with Answer Key and Rubrics*
Unit 26 Pretest, pp. 105–106

💾 *Testmaker*
Unit 26 Pretest

You may wish to administer the Unit 26 Pretest at this point.

Key to Ability Levels

L1 Level 1 activities are within the basic ability range of students.

L2 Level 2 activities are within the ability range of average students.

L3 Level 3 activities are more challenging activities.

UNIT 26 Viewing and Representing

628

Resource Manager

Planning Resources
- *Lesson Plans*
- *Block Scheduling*

📂 Other Print Resources
- *Tests with Answer Key and Rubrics*
- *Viewing and Representing Activities*

📺 Video
- *MindJogger Videoquizzes*

💾 Software
- *Presentation Plus!*
- *Testmaker*

🖥 Web Sites
- *writerschoice.glencoe.com*

26.1 Interpreting Visual Messages

Statistics show that nearly one out of every five nine-year-olds watches six or more hours of television every day. By the time many of those nine-year-olds graduate from high school, they will have spent more time experiencing television and other forms of **mass media** than they will have spent going to school!

The term *mass media* means "a form of communication that is widely available to many people." Examples include newspapers, magazines, television, radio, movies, videos, and the Internet. Television and other forms of mass media have a great influence on your life. The influences can be both positive and negative.

You can enjoy the benefits of the media and still protect yourself from its problems. The best way to do this is to learn how to interpret, analyze, and evaluate the many messages that are sent to you—by the press, over the airwaves, and through the Web. This unit will help.

Understanding Visual Design

You know that written and spoken words contain verbal messages. Pictures, however, carry *visual messages.* You have learned to read verbal messages carefully and to evaluate them. You can do the same thing when you "read" visual messages. Like written messages, some visual messages are valuable and truthful, but others are not.

Photographs, paintings, cartoons, and drawings are all created very carefully to send messages to you, the viewer. So are advertisements, television programs, videos, movies, Internet graphics, and video games. Understanding how pictures send messages will help you to "read" each message and then decide whether the message is valuable.

Photographers and artists carefully plan the design of their pictures. They think about how they want to arrange the people and objects so that you, the viewer, will "read" their message and then respond in a certain way. The arrangement of features in a picture is called **composition.** The chart on the following page lists some basic elements of a picture's composition. It also describes how the artist or photographer can work with these elements to send visual messages.

Viewing and Representing

Lesson Overview

Objectives

- To understand the design of visual messages
- To interpret how meanings are expressed through design, composition, and various techniques

Skills

- identifying and analyzing visual elements; understanding visual design and composition

Critical Thinking

- interpreting; drawing conclusions; classifying; speculating

Listening and Speaking

- discussing; asking and answering questions; informal speaking

Bellringer
Daily Language Activity

When students enter the classroom, have this assignment on the board: *Sketch an image that communicates how you feel today.*

Motivating Activity

Ask volunteers to "read" their sketches to the class. Discuss the meaning of *mass media* ("a form of communication that is widely available to many people"). Call on volunteers to name types of mass media that contain pictures, citing specific examples.

26.1 Interpreting Visual Messages   **629**

Resource Manager

Planning Resources
- *Lesson Plans*

📁 Other Print Resources
- *Viewing and Representing Activities*

Teach

Understanding the Chart

Have small groups each select one element from the Elements of Picture Design and Composition chart on page 630. Students should work together to find examples in magazines, newspapers, and posters that illustrate the use of that element to suggest meaning. Encourage groups to present their examples to the class. **L3**

Elements of Picture Design and Composition

What to Look For	Possible Effect
Lines	
Heavy, thick lines	Suggest boldness or power
Thin or broken lines	Suggest weakness or lightness
Straight lines	Point in a direction, or lead the eye, to something else
Curved lines	Suggest motion
Vertical lines	Suggest power
Horizontal lines	Suggest peace or stillness
Diagonal lines	Suggest tension, action, energy
Colors	
Cool colors (blue, green, gray)	Can suggest either calmness or coldness
Warm colors (orange, yellow, red)	Often suggest energy and pep
Bright colors	Often suggest joy, action, or excitement
Subdued or pastel colors	Suggest innocence or softness
Position of subjects	
Center of picture	Suggests strength, dominance; draws attention to the subject
Top of picture	Suggests power, importance
Bottom of picture	Suggests weakness, lack of power
Space	
Large space around subject	Draws attention to subject; can suggest loneliness, vastness
Small amount of space around subject	Makes subject seem very powerful

Enrichment and Extension

Analyzing Artwork

Applying Information Suggest to students that they use the chart on page 630 to analyze art pieces they have completed for art class. They might list ways in which they could improve their art, based on the information in the chart. Invite volunteers to present their artwork and analyses to the class.

Study this drawing that illustrator Lynn Munsinger created for the children's book *Listen Buddy*, by Helen Lester. The bear is in the center of the picture. As the chart shows, the bear's central position makes him dominate the picture. The reader's eyes are drawn to him first. Also, the curved lines in the bear's body suggest motion. The diagonal line created by his position suggests tension, action, and energy. How do the colors of the bear's clothing and his facial expression work together with these design elements?

Exercise 1

Use the Elements of Picture Design and Composition chart and the interpretation of the bear to interpret what visual message the artist aims to send through the rabbit. Explain how lines and position, as well as colors and facial expression, work together to send that message. Include reasons that the artist might have chosen to use thick, heavy lines to outline the bear and thin or broken lines to outline the rabbit.

26.1 Interpreting Visual Messages **631**

Teach

Using the Chart

Help students use the chart on page 630 to interpret elements of picture design and composition in Munsinger's illustration. Point out the dominant position of the bear; the curved form of his body; and the heavy, thick lines used to outline his body and to emphasize his hair, teeth, and claws. Lead them to understand that the blues suggest coldness, and the bright colors suggest excitement. Have students suggest ways in which the bear's facial expression and body language contribute to the overall visual message. **L2**

Practice and Assess

Evaluation Rubrics

Exercise 1

Have partners or small groups apply the information in the chart to interpret the visual messages Munsinger meant to send through her portrayal of the rabbit. Allow time for students to discuss their ideas. Then, as a class, compare and contrast the use of lines and body language used in presenting the bear and the rabbit. Students might mention that the diagonal lines of the rabbit, along with its expression, suggest tension. The overshadowing of the rabbit by the bear suggests the rabbit's lack of power.

Viewing and Representing

Cultural Connections

Expressing Culture Through Art

Have students locate images that in some way express important ideas about their cultures or backgrounds. Ask volunteers to present their images to the class, explaining how their images communicate or represent information about their cultures. If students have difficulty finding images to share with the class, urge them to consult the art teacher or school librarian.

Practice and Assess

Evaluaton Rubrics

Exercise 2

Complete Exercise 2 in a whole-class discussion. Call on volunteers to interpret the messages that the cartoonist meant to send through his use of lines, position, and space. Point out, if necessary, that the "bruin" is huge and fierce-looking to suggest power. Lead them to contrast this rough, strong physical presence with the verbal message. Then work with students to compare the cartoon bear with the bear in the Munsinger illustration. Lead them to understand that the Munsinger bear is a truly fierce bear, whereas the Szep bear is not as fierce as his physical presence suggests.

Many artists and photographers work in black and white rather than in color. Some choose to do so because the absence of color lets them emphasize dark, light, and shadows. Others, like many newspaper cartoonists, must work in black and white because their medium, the newspaper, is in black and white.

Paul Szep, the *Boston Globe* political cartoonist, drew this cartoon. The local NHL hockey team, the Boston Bruins (*bruins* means "bears"), had just lost an important game, and many people felt that the team had played poorly.

THE MIGHTY BRUINS KNOCKED OUT OF STANLEY CUP

MEE YOW!

Exercise 2

Think about the cartoonist's use of lines, position, and space in this cartoon. Then note the facial expression and the words that the character is speaking. Summarize in your own words the message that the cartoonist wanted to send to viewers of this cartoon. Then compare the bear in this cartoon with the bear in the first drawing you examined. How are they alike and different? What different visual messages did each artist aim to send to the viewer?

Viewing and Representing

*inter*NET CONNECTION

Cartoons on the Web

Encourage students to use Web sites such as that of the International Museum of Cartoon Art (http://cartoon.org) to find information and sample art by other cartoonists, including Charles Schulz ("Peanuts"), Scott Adams ("Dilbert"), and Brant Parker and Johnny Hart ("The Wizard of Id").

Understanding Film Techniques

Think of a time you have seen a movie based on a book you have read. How did the two versions compare? Did seeing the film or reading the book help you better understand characters, themes, or twists in the plot? Or did seeing one version after the other change your first opinion of the entire story?

Creators of movies and videos use the same elements of picture design and composition that artists and photographers use. In addition to those elements, they use many different camera and lighting techniques to tell stories and send visual messages. This chart shows some of these techniques and the effects they can have.

Film and Video Techniques for Sending Visual Messages	
Technique	**Possible Effects**
Camera angle	
High (looking down on subjects)	Often makes subject seem smaller, less important, or more at risk
Low (looking up at subject)	Emphasizes subject's importance
Straight on (eye level)	Puts viewer on equal level with subject; can make viewer identify with subject
Camera shots	
Close-up (picture of subject's face)	Emphasizes character's facial expressions; leads viewer to identify with him or her
Long shot (wide view, showing character within larger setting)	Shows relationship between character and setting
Lighting	
High, bright lighting	Creates cheerful tone
Low, shadowy lighting	Creates gloomy or scary tone
Lighting from above	Makes subject seem to glow with power or strength
Lighting from below	Often creates tension or fear
Background music	
Loud, strong music	Creates tone of action or power
Soft melodies	Create tone of sadness or sweetness
Music that builds from slow to fast or from soft to loud	Often creates suspense or fear

Viewing and Representing

26.1 Interpreting Visual Messages **633**

Teach

Comparing Media
Have students compare and contrast information from the Film and Video Techniques for Sending Visual Messages chart (p. 633) with the information in the Elements of Picture Design and Composition chart (p. 630). In what ways is a picture different from a film? How are they similar? Ask students to assess how an artist's choice of media contributes to his or her message. **L3**

Enrichment and Extension

Planning a Film
Have students work in small groups to plan short films. They might plan to film a favorite story or a new version of a favorite movie or TV program. Students should describe the camera angles, camera shots, lighting, and background music for at least three scenes. Some students may wish to sketch their scenes. Have students present their film plans to the class. Students can then display their work in the classroom.

Teach

Using the Chart

Work with students to use the chart on page 633 to interpret the movie still from *E.T. The Extra Terrestrial.* Allow time for students to offer suggestions about the types of background music they would choose for this scene. Stress that each suggestion is "correct"; part of the creative process of visual design and composition involves experimenting with different techniques until the desired effect is achieved. **L2**

Practice and Assess

Evaluation Rubrics

Exercise 3

Have students work independently to write answers to Exercise 3. Have them use both the Elements of Picture Design and Composition on page 630 and the Film and Video Techniques for Sending Visual Messages chart on page 633.

Use these criteria when evaluating the written assignment:

- Do the answers include details concerning the director's use of lines, color, lighting, camera angle, and camera shot?
- Do the answers indicate a reasonable interpretation of the director's intended visual message?
- Does the choice of background music support the interpretation they have presented?

Close

Call on volunteers to identify specific visual techniques used by artists, cartoonists, and film directors. Which techniques do they feel are particularly effective in getting across verbal messages? Why is it helpful for readers and viewers to be aware of these techniques?

Examine the elements of visual design and film techniques used in this still from the movie *E.T. The Extra Terrestrial.* The movie director wants us to identify with E.T. and Elliott. Therefore, the camera angle is straight on, and viewers are at eye level with both characters. Note also that this shot is a close-up. Our attention is drawn to the facial expressions of both characters. How do you think each character feels? What clues help you to read that verbal message?

Note also in this movie still that E.T. and Elliott are lit from above, in high, bright lights. Such lighting gives the characters a positive glow and gives the still a cheerful tone.

If you were on the creative staff of this movie, what type of background music would you choose for this scene?

Exercise 3

Study this movie still from *The Empire Strikes Back.* It shows the giant camel-like "Imperial Walkers" shooting laser weapons at the rebel heroes of the film. What visual message does this scene send you? Explain how the movie director used lines, color, lighting, camera angle, and camera shot to create that message. Then describe the type of background music you imagine in this scene. Explain your choice.

Viewing and Representing

MEETING INDIVIDUAL NEEDS — Gifted and Talented

Critical Thinking

Evaluating Media After discussing the movie still from *E.T. The Extra Terrestrial,* challenge students by asking such questions as *How might the visual message be different if the director had chosen a high camera angle?* *Or a low camera angle? How does the visual design of E.T. contribute to the viewer's understanding of his gentle personality? How might the visual design be altered to represent a visual message about a frightening alien?*

26.2 Analyzing Media Messages

Drawings, cartoons, photographs, movies, and television programs often seem realistic. However, every medium is made with one goal—to send the viewer a message that carries a particular point of view and to use such techniques as color, line, and camera angles to persuade the viewer to accept that point of view.

In a documentary film about endangered animals, for example, the director makes decisions about pictures and information to include, what camera angles will prove most effective, and what information should *not* be included. Every time you view an example of mass communications, analyze it carefully. Begin by using these steps.

KEY QUESTIONS

To analyze a media message, ask yourself these Key Questions:
- What message is this visual medium trying to send to readers or viewers? (The visual might be a photo, drawing, cartoon, television program, movie, video, or commercial.)
- What techniques were used to try to persuade readers or viewers to agree with that message?
- What do I already know about this subject?
- How can I use what I already know to judge whether this message is
  - fair or unfair?
  - based on reality or fantasy?
  - based on facts or opinions?
- What additional sources might I use to find other viewpoints that I can trust on this subject?
  - parent, teacher, or other trustworthy adult
  - reliable books or other reference sources

On the basis of your answers and of viewpoints you can trust, make a decision about the message. Make sure you can support that decision.
  - I agree with the visual message because . . . .
  - I disagree with the visual message because . . . .

Viewing and Representing

Focus

Lesson Overview

Objectives
- To compare and contrast different forms of media
- To learn how to analyze and evaluate media messages

Skills
- evaluating the purposes and effects of varying media, contrasting techniques used in various forms of mass media

Critical Thinking
- interpreting; analyzing; evaluating; drawing conclusions; classifying; speculating

Listening and Speaking
- discussing; asking and answering questions; informal speaking; interpreting, analyzing, and evaluating

Bellringer
Daily Language Activity
When students come into the classroom, have this assignment on the board: *List the techniques you remember that are often used in presenting your favorite TV program.*

Motivating Activity
Ask volunteers to share their lists from the Bellringer activity with the class. Discuss the meaning or effect that different techniques help create.

Resource Manager

Planning Resources
- *Lesson Plans*

Other Print Resources
- *Viewing and Representing Activities*

Teach

Practice Using the Key Questions

Use a photograph or other "realistic" visual image with a clear point of view to lead the students through the Key Questions. Then have them refer back to the Szep cartoon on page 632 as they read and discuss the "practice" use of the Key Questions shown on page 636. **L1**

Practice and Assess

Evaluation Rubrics

Exercise 4

Make sure students address all the Key Questions in their presentations. Remind students that they should use an effective rate, volume, pitch, and tone for the audience in their presentations.

Viewing and Representing

You can practice using the Key Questions by examining again the Paul Szep cartoon on page 632.

- **What the message is:** During the big game, the Boston Bruins hockey players acted more like gentle little cats than fierce bears.
- **What techniques were used:** All cartoonists use humor and exaggeration to get their messages across. In this cartoon, Paul Szep made the bear look very big and tough. Also, he added the bandage and the missing tooth to suggest that the bear had been injured during the game. However, he then showed the bear meowing like a little cat instead of growling like a big, tough bear.
- **What you know:** You might have watched the game. You might have followed the team during the season and have observed that the players are usually good.
- **How you can use what you know:** If you watched the game, you can form your own opinion about how well the team played. You can also look back on the season and decide that although the team may not have played a great game this time, it's unfair to picture the players as weak or gentle. Maybe they just had a bad day!
- **Other sources you might use to find other viewpoints that you can trust:** You might seek viewpoints from hockey fans in your family or at school. You might also read *factual* newspaper or magazine articles about the game and weigh these new points of view against your own feelings and the visual message in the cartoon.

   Decision time! You could then make a well thought-out decision, based on your analysis, about agreeing or disagreeing with the cartoon's visual message. Your decision would be valuable because *it would be backed up by careful analysis.*

Exercise 4

Working with a partner, find a cartoon in a current newspaper or newsmagazine. With your partner, use the Key Questions on page 635 to help you analyze the visual message of the cartoon. Present your findings to the class.

MEETING INDIVIDUAL NEEDS — Gifted and Talented

Analyzing Visual Media

Recognizing Stereotypes Point out that stereotyping falls under the fairness category in the Key Questions on page 635. Have students find videos or other visual media that contain gender, race, or other stereotypes. Ask them to analyze the stereotypes and to offer alternative representations.

Analyzing Movies, Music Videos, Television Shows, and Video Games

You can use the Key Questions to help you identify and judge a variety of types of mass-media messages. In this section, use the Key Questions to help you analyze the messages that the producers of movies, music videos, television shows, and video games send viewers.

Most people have fictional characters, movies, television shows, and games that they particularly like. Sometimes, however, the actors and performers in these forms of media, or the forms of media themselves, seem more "real" than they actually are. Actors in movies and television shows play fictional characters. Characters in video games are fictional characters living only in fantasy settings. What visual messages do such characters and settings send viewers, and are these messages valuable and fair? Use the Key Questions on page 635 to help you decide.

Exercise 5

Watch carefully as your teacher plays a scene or two from a popular movie or television show. Then work together as a class to use the Key Questions on page 635 to help you analyze and evaluate the visual messages you received.

Exercise 6

Choose a favorite movie, television show, music video, or video game. Use the Key Questions to analyze and evaluate its visual messages. Write a brief report on your findings and conclusions.

Practice and Assess

Evaluation Rubrics

Exercise 5

Play thought-provoking scenes from one or more movies and television programs that the students regularly watch. Then work together with them to apply the Key Questions and draw conclusions about the messages conveyed.

Exercise 6

Have students complete Exercise 6 independently. Make sure students address all the Key Questions in their reports. Challenge students to offer suggestions that would make the message each student chose more effective.

Viewing and Representing

Enrichment and Extension

Comparing Original Texts with Film Adaptations

Deconstructing Media Select a videotape or the film version of a book that students have read and enjoyed, such as *The Black Stallion, Treasure Island,* or *Old Yeller.* Depending on the time available, play the entire video or one or more pivotal scenes. Discuss how the original print version and the film adaptation differ.

Teach

Analyzing Advertising Materials

Write the terms *fact, opinion,* and *persuasive language* on the board. Remind students that advertisements are carefully crafted and may blend facts and opinions to persuade the viewer or reader to buy a product. Display several advertisements for products that are of interest to the students. Help them evaluate the techniques used to make the products appealing. **L2**

Critical Thinking

Explain the concept of "target audiences" to students. Point out that each commercial "aims" at a target audience, or a specific group of people that the maker of the product wants to persuade to buy this product. Ask students to identify commercials that target them. Which persuasive techniques do commercials often use to persuade them? **L2**

Viewing and Representing

Analyzing Advertisements and Commercials

You can also use the Key Questions to help you identify and judge the value of the media messages appearing in newspaper and magazine advertisements and on television commercials.

More than any other form of media, advertisements and commercials have one main goal: *to persuade the viewer to buy the product being advertised.* Along with the Elements of Picture Design and Composition listed on page 630, and the Film and Video Techniques for Sending Visual Messages listed on page 633, advertisers often use one or more of the following advertising techniques to accomplish that goal.

Leading Advertising Techniques

Technique	Description	Example
Bandwagon: "Jump on the bandwagon and join in the fun!"	showing images or using words implying that popular, attractive, well-liked people use this product	an advertisement for jeans, showing attractive people having fun
Testimonial: "Be like your favorite celebrity!"	showing a popular star, athlete, or musical performer using the product	an advertisement for running shoes, showing a leading basketball player
Partial truth: "Use this for incredible results!"	using oils, dyes, and other substances to make the results of using the product look "too good to be true"	an advertisement for shampoo, in which a model's hair shows a terrific, but unrealistic, silkiness and shine
Card stacking: "Leading experts are convinced that you should use this product."	using actors that pretend they are experts to present the advertiser's message	an advertisement for a toothbrush; an actor portrays a dentist
Name calling or appeal to guilt: "You mean you don't know how nutritious this product is?"	manipulating data to convince viewers that another product would be foolish or wasteful	an advertisement for breakfast cereal, suggesting to parents that it is the most healthful

MEETING INDIVIDUAL NEEDS — English Language Learners

Understanding Advertising Techniques

Sharing Cultures Students acquiring English may have a different perspective on some of the advertising techniques described on the student page. Encourage students to describe commercials presented in their first language or culture. Help students analyze what appeals were used to make viewers want to buy the product. Are these appeals different than those used in U.S. TV commercials? As a class, identify the advertising techniques in various commercials.

How can viewers "cut through" the nonsense and hard-sell tactics of advertisements and commercials to make informed, wise decisions about which products to buy? The Key Questions can help! Examine the following model of an advertisement.

Food for Champions

When CHAMPION tennis player **Marie Ziegler's** pups tell her it's time for a treat, they scramble for **PUPPY FOOD**!

Her tennis game isn't the only thing that Marie has perfected! She has learned that leading veterinarians and animal nutrition experts agree that **PUPPY FOOD** is the best food for healthy young dogs. It delivers all the essential nutrients, including calcium and protein, that her puppies need for strong bones and muscles!

Terrific tennis player, terrific dogs! Shouldn't you feed your puppies **PUPPY FOOD** too?

Puppy Approved! ✓

PUPPY FOOD

Exercise 7

Use the Key Questions on page 635 to help you analyze and evaluate this advertisement. Discuss your findings with classmates.

Exercise 8

Watch carefully as your teacher plays a video clip of one or more television commercials. Then work as a class to use the Key Questions to identify, analyze, and evaluate the messages that the commercials convey.

26.2 Analyzing Media Messages   **639**

Teach

Critical Thinking

To extend discussion of the Puppy Food ad, ask students: *Which group of consumers might be attracted by this ad? How might the advertisers change the ad so that it appeals to a different audience? What might the effect be of showing a veterinarian rather than a professional athlete if you were a consumer who might buy this product?* **L2**

Practice and Assess

Evaluation Rubrics

Exercise 7

Check that students address all of the Key Questions in a written report format. You might assign Exercise 7 as a homework project. Have volunteers present their written reports as oral presentations to the class, followed by discussion.

Exercise 8

Select at least one commercial that targets your students' age group. Assist students in using the Key Questions to analyze the commercial you selected.

Close

Challenge students to analyze two videotaped news broadcast segments on the same subject, using the Key Questions on page 635. Have students compare their findings and draw conclusions about which news source they found more trustworthy and why.

Viewing and Representing

Real World Connection

Becoming a Smart Consumer

Using Media Display sample copies of consumer magazines such as *Consumer Reports* and *Consumer's Digest.* Point out that these magazines report on products that are tested and evaluated in their independent laboratories. The magazines often do not accept advertising, which may allow them to remain more objective about the products they review. Display sample articles for students to review.

Focus

Lesson Overview

Objectives
- To produce media messages using available technology
- To assess how each medium contributes to its message

Skills
- selecting, organizing, and producing visuals to complement and extend textual meanings

Critical Thinking
- establishing goals; considering audience and purpose; organizing; drawing conclusions; classifying

Listening and Speaking
- discussing; asking and answering questions; informal speaking; interpreting, analyzing, and evaluating

🔔 Bellringer
Daily Language Activity

When students come into the classroom, have this assignment on the board: *Think of a message that you can communicate visually. Write three sentences about how you would communicate the message.*

Motivating Activity

Ask volunteers to share their answers to the Bellringer activity. Ask them how they could express these messages as cartoons and advertisements.

Viewing and Representing

26.3 Producing Media Messages

There is another great way in which you can increase your knowledge about the techniques that mass media producers use to send visual messages. Practice those techniques yourself by creating your own media messages! This section will help you to create two forms of media messages: cartoons and advertisements.

Creating a Cartoon

The artist often uses one or more of the following elements of humor in cartoons.

ELEMENTS OF HUMOR OFTEN USED BY CARTOONISTS

- **Exaggeration:** Making something bigger or greater than it really is
  Examples: Paul Szep gave his bear an enormous face and a fiercer-than-normal expression. Similarly, a cartoon about the problem of having too much homework might show a student buried under a mile-high stack of books and papers.
- **Surprise:** Providing an outcome that is completely unexpected or unusual
  Examples: Paul Szep's fierce-looking bear "meows" in the gentle voice of a cat. Similarly, a cartoon about the importance of avoiding accidents might show someone smiling confidently while stepping carefully over a banana peel—straight into an open manhole.
- **Puns:** Making a play on words
  Examples: A "fly swatter" might be portrayed as a fly dressed up as a baseball batter "swatting" (hitting) a baseball. Similarly, a "baseball batter" might be portrayed as a bowl of pancake batter into which someone is stirring several baseballs.
- **Satire:** Poking fun at a person, event, or situation
  Examples: Each day, political cartoonists publish satirical cartoons in newspapers to poke fun at politicians, news events, or situations that they find amusing. This type of cartoon often carries the strongest visual message, because its purpose is not only to create humor but to carry a message of criticism about a person, event, or situation.

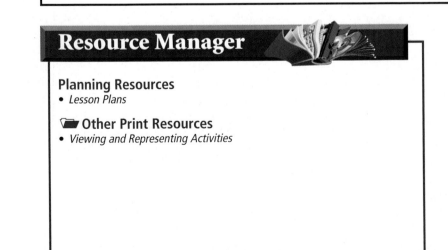

Resource Manager

Planning Resources
- *Lesson Plans*

📂 **Other Print Resources**
- *Viewing and Representing Activities*

TIPS FOR CREATING A CARTOON

1. **Begin by brainstorming.** Think about situations that you find funny or that you would like to poke fun at. It might be a rule that you think is unnecessary, a part of human behavior that you think is silly, a famous person that you'd enjoy poking fun at, or a personal experience that made you laugh. Jot down several ideas and then pick one to develop into a cartoon.

2. **Identify your purpose and message.** What underlying message do you want your cartoon to send to your readers? Is your purpose merely to make your readers laugh at your humor, or do you also want them to agree with your point of view? On notebook paper, write a sentence that states your purpose. Then write another sentence that states your message. Keep both in mind as you draw.

3. **Make sketches.** On scrap paper, draw several versions of the cartoon. Refer to the Elements of Picture Design and Composition chart on page 630 for ideas about use of lines, colors, and positions of your subjects. Experiment with different elements and techniques, always keeping in mind the techniques that will be most effective in getting your message across.

4. **Decide whether to use words.** Will your message be clear from your picture alone, or do you need a caption to make your message precisely clear? Experiment with using and omitting a caption. In addition, consider whether any characters in your cartoon should speak. If you feel that their words will help to make your message clear, write the words in speech balloons.

5. **Make your final copy.** When you are satisfied with your sketches and your decision about whether to include words in your cartoon, make a final copy.

6. **Publish your cartoon.** Share your cartoon with viewers—friends, classmates, and family members who share your sense of humor or who might particularly understand and enjoy the message you want to send. Ask for comments and suggestions. Find out whether your viewers "read" and agreed with your message.

Exercise 9

Use the tips to create a cartoon that uses one or more elements of humor to send a media message.

Teach

Guiding the Project

Display several cartoons and point out effective uses of elements of humor in them. Encourage students to keep these elements in mind as they plan and create their own cartoons. Encourage students to follow the steps of the Writing Process (Prewriting, Drafting, Revising, Editing/Proofreading, and Publishing/Presenting) to plan, create, and present their cartoons. Refer them to the Elements of Picture Design and Composition chart on page 630 for ideas on effective techniques used by visual artists. **L2**

Practice and Assess

Evaluation Rubrics

Exercise 9

Use these criteria when evaluating students' cartoons. The cartoons should:

- reflect comprehension and application of elements from the Elements of Picture Design and Composition chart on page 630
- reflect comprehension and application of Elements of Humor Often Used by Cartoonists on page 640
- show application of the Tips for creating a cartoon listed on page 641

Viewing and Representing

MEETING INDIVIDUAL NEEDS Less Proficient Readers

Getting Started

Creating Cartoons If students have difficulty getting started, invite all students to each bring in a cartoon strip. Each student should write a one-sentence summary of what happens in the strip or what the character's problem is without using characters' names. (For example, "The dog needs water in his dish.") Gather all the summaries. Students who are "stuck" for a cartoon idea can draw a summary from the collection and frame a cartoon around the summary.

Teach

Introducing the Project

Review with students that the purpose of each advertising message is to persuade the viewer or reader to buy a particular product. Discuss how advertisers blend facts and opinions to create media containing both verbal and visual persuasive messages. Emphasize that advertisers also spend time planning before they create advertisements. They identify their audience and keep that audience in mind as they create their ads. Provide several examples of print ads as examples and as models for students to refer to as they plan and create their own ads. **L2**

Guiding the Project

Encourage students to use the basic steps of the Writing Process (Prewriting, Drafting, Revising, Editing/Proofreading, and Publishing/Presenting) as they plan, create, and present their ads. Encourage them to refer back to the Elements of Picture Design and Composition chart on page 630 for ideas regarding effective techniques used by visual artists in general, as well as the Leading Advertising Techniques chart on page 638 for ideas on crafting effective advertisements. **L2**

TIME

For more about brainstorming and generating ideas for writing, see **TIME Facing the Blank Page,** page 92.

Viewing and Representing

Creating an Advertisement

What product would you like to convince viewers to buy? It might be a realistic product, such as jeans, running shoes, or in-line skates. Or, you might dream up a fantastic product, such as a robot that does a student's homework, a hat that allows the wearer to fly, or a dog food that enables a dog to sing rap songs.

You can write an ad with a strong, persuasive message for any product you choose. The following tips will help.

TIPS FOR CREATING AN ADVERTISEMENT

1. **Begin by looking at published advertisements.** Look at several different types of advertisements in newspapers and magazines. What techniques did the advertisers use? Which of these techniques do you think are most effective at getting the message across? Clip out samples to look at as you think about your topic.

2. **Brainstorm.** Jot down the names of several realistic products that you particularly enjoy using. Your own enthusiasm for the product will help you to write a convincing ad. Then make a second list of "fantastic" products that might be fun to advertise, such as the examples listed in the first paragraph of this section. Review your lists carefully. Select one product for your ad.

3. **Mold your message.** As you begin to draft the words and visual images you'll use in your ad, keep in mind that you have one and only one purpose: to convince the viewer to buy your product. Think carefully about how you can most effectively get your message across. Refer to the Leading Advertising Techniques chart on page 638 for ideas. Jot down phrases and sentences that you think work well.

4. **Make layout sketches.** On scrap paper, draw several layout sketches for your ad, showing what visual images you will use, where they will appear in the ad, and how you might use lines, colors, and space to enhance your message. Refer to the Elements of Picture Design and Composition chart on page 630 for ideas. Then, once you have decided on the placement of your images, add the words. Looking once again at the published ads you gathered earlier may give you additional ideas about the placement of visual images and words.

Enrichment and Extension

Planning an Advertising Campaign

Some students may enjoy extending their advertising projects into ad campaigns. Point out that many products are advertised through radio and television commercials, as well as through print media. Challenge students to rework the ideas in their print advertisements to make television and radio commercials. If possible, have students audio- or videotape the commercials and share them with the class.

5. **Make your final copy.** Once you are satisfied with your layout sketches, make a final copy of your ad, using color and lines in a way that seems most effective.

6. **Publish your advertisement.** Think carefully about where to display your ad. An ad for in-line skates would probably not appear in a magazine geared toward senior citizens. Nor would an ad for baby clothes appear in a magazine geared toward people your age. Where in the school would the people most interested in your product be most likely to see and respond to your ad? Place a response box next to your ad, asking people for comments. Find out whether your viewers "read" and accepted your message.

Exercise 10

Use the tips to create an advertisement that uses elements of picture design and composition, as well as leading advertising techniques. Convince your viewers to buy your product!

Practice and Assess

Evaluation Rubrics

Exercise 10

Use these criteria when evaluating the advertisements. Advertisements should:
- reflect understanding of elements from the Elements of Picture Design and Composition chart on page 630
- reflect understanding of Leading Advertising Techniques, shown on page 639
- include carefully crafted verbal and visual images that are persuasive
- show application of the Tips for creating an Advertisement listed on page 642

Close

Point out to students that they have learned how to interpret, analyze, and evaluate visual messages and have experimented with making their own visual messages. Ask: *How might the process of creating advertising help you as a consumer?*

✔ ASSESSMENT OPTIONS

📂 *Tests with Answer Key and Rubrics*
Unit 26 Mastery Test, pp. 107–108

💾 *Testmaker*
Unit 26 Mastery Test

You may wish to administer the Unit 26 Mastery Test at this point.

📺 *MindJogger Videoquizzes*

Viewing and Representing

Real World Connection

Recognizing Facts and Opinions

Have students practice recognizing facts and opinions. With partners, have students leaf through magazines and select advertisements of special interest. Have students find examples of facts and opinions, marking each with a different color highlighting marker. Remind students that facts can be proven to be true. Opinions express a person's beliefs and cannot be proven. (Students might review Lesson 6.3 on page 230 for more information about facts and opinions.) Have students share their examples with the class.

Objectives

- To become familiar with the Internet and to learn how to access Web sites
- To evaluate the accuracy of information presented on a Web site
- To learn how to send and edit e-mail messages
- To identify and use other electronic resources, such as CD-ROMs and DVDs

✔ ASSESSMENT OPTIONS

📂 *Tests with Answer Key and Rubrics*
Unit 27 Pretest, pp. 109–110

💾 *Testmaker*
Unit 27 Pretest

You may wish to administer the Unit 27 Pretest at this point.

Key to Ability Levels

L1 Level 1 activities are within the basic ability range of students.

L2 Level 2 activities are within the ability range of average students.

L3 Level 3 activities are more challenging activities.

UNIT 27 Electronic Resources

644

Resource Manager

Planning Resources
- *Lesson Plans*
- *Block Scheduling*

📂 **Other Print Resources**
- *Guide to Using the Internet and Other Electronic Resources*
- *Tests with Answer Key and Rubrics*

📼 **Video**
- *MindJogger Videoquizzes*

💾 **Software**
- *Presentation Plus!*
- *Testmaker*

🖥 **Web Sites**
- *writerschoice.glencoe.com*

27.1 The Internet

The Internet is like a giant storehouse of information that you can tap into by using a computer. It uses telephone lines, cable lines, and satellites to link your computer to computers all over the world. As recently as the 1980s, few people even knew about the Internet. Today, the computer terms *cyberspace, information superhighway,* and *surfing the Web* have become part of our vocabulary.

History

The Internet was developed in 1969 to connect computers at four different universities. This early version of the Internet, called ARPANET, was all words, or text, and very unorganized. It was used for research, educational, and government purposes. Most of the users were computer experts, scientists, and engineers. Commands had to be given in computer language. As the demand for information grew, so did the Internet. By the early 1990s, the Internet had become popular with home computer users.

Today, what most people generally refer to as the Internet is actually only a part of the Internet called the **World Wide Web.** Using the World Wide Web is one of the best ways to explore the Internet. It is designed to make it easy to connect to millions of different Web sites. Web sites may include video, graphics, animation, and sound as well as text.

The Internet has changed the way we live, think, and communicate. In the years since the Internet was developed, the number of users has skyrocketed. Today, the Internet reaches over 200 million people worldwide. Eighty million of these people live in the United States. Americans spend an average of 8.8 hours a week online viewing news, information, travel, weather, music, shopping, and technology Web sites. In the next five years, more than 500 million people will be surfing the Web.

Focus

Lesson Overview

Objectives
- To become familiar with the Internet
- To listen to and organize ideas in order to gain information
- To evaluate the influence of a medium
- To assess how language contributes to a message

Skills
- using the Internet

Critical Thinking
- recalling; comparing and contrasting; predicting

Listening and Speaking
- discussing

🔔 Bellringer
Daily Language Activity

When students enter the classroom, have this assignment on the board: *When was the last time you used the Internet or the World Wide Web? What did you use it for?*

Motivating Activity

Ask students to contribute to a chart or graph on the board to record the information elicited in the Bellringer. Which are the most common reasons for using the Internet? The least?

Electronic Resources

Resource Manager

Planning Resources
- *Lesson Plans*

📁 **Other Print Resources**
- *Guide to Using the Internet and Other Electronic Resources*

Teach

Getting Online

Divide the class into small groups and allow each group to spend one class period learning how to access the Internet. Ask each group to create a list of the steps they took to get online and have them share those steps with the class. **L2**

Practice and Assess

Evaluation Rubrics

Exercise 1

Students' glossaries should include common terms, such as *modem, Web site,* and *e-mail,* as well as definitions for these terms. It can include all boldfaced terms throughout the unit. If more than one group has defined the same word, discuss the different definitions and, as a class, reach a consensus on the most appropriate definition for the classroom "Internet Dictionary."

Close

Ask students to describe ways in which the World Wide Web might be helpful in completing school assignments. Have them discuss why they think the Web has become so popular.

Electronic Resources

Affordable computers, easy-to-use software, and speedy Internet connections have boosted the Internet's popularity. With the click of a mouse button, a person using the Internet can search through millions of documents without leaving home. Students can use the Internet for help with their homework, families can use it to plan vacations, and doctors can use it for medical research.

Exercise 1

Work with a small group to make a glossary that lists and defines words related to using the Internet. Combine your group's glossary with the glossaries of other groups to create a classroom "Internet Dictionary." The **boldfaced** terms in this unit will give you a good start.

Cultural Connections

Planning for Internet Use

Have students work in small groups to make lists of three or four questions about a topic discussed in a social studies, science, or English class that they think could be answered on an Internet site. Encourage students for whom English is a second language to investigate Web sites in their first languages as they try to answer the questions and share information with other students.

27.2 Getting on the Internet

The three basic things you need to access the Internet are a computer, a modem, and an Internet service provider. A **modem** is a device that allows a computer to communicate and share information with other computers over telephone or cable lines. Most computers now come with a modem built in. An **Internet service provider,** or ISP, provides a service (for a fee) that allows your computer to dial into the Internet. You can also get onto the Internet by using an online service, such as America Online or Microsoft Network. These services let you access the Internet as well as their own private services. For example, America Online users can use private chat rooms and message boards. **Message boards** are places where you can read or write messages about subjects that interest you.

To display the contents of a Web site, your computer must have a browser. A **browser** is a software program that displays Web pages as text, graphics, pictures, and video on your computer. The best-known browsers are Netscape Navigator and Microsoft Internet Explorer. Once you have a browser, you'll be able to navigate, or get around, the Web. You don't have to own a computer to get on the Internet. Many public libraries now have Internet terminals that their patrons can use, and most schools have some that their students can use.

Net Addresses

The World Wide Web is made up of millions of Web sites. A **Web site** is a page, or collections of pages, created by a person, a company, or an organization such as a university. A **Webmaster** is the person who is in charge of building and maintaining a Web site. Some Web sites consist only of text, while others include photos, artwork, sound, and video.

To get to a particular Web site, you need to know its address. Every Web site on the Internet has a unique address or URL. **URL** stands for Uniform Resource Locator. No two Web sites can have the same URL.

Each part of its URL provides information about a site.

Electronic Resources

Focus

Lesson Overview

Objectives
• To learn how to use Web site addresses to access Web sites
• To compare and contrast the significance of various media images

Skills
• accessing and using the World Wide Web

Critical Thinking
• observing; synthesizing

Listening and Speaking
• discussing; explaining a process

Bellringer
Daily Language Activity

When students enter the classroom, have this assignment on the board: *List four subjects that you might want to investigate on the Internet.*

Motivating Activity

Ask volunteers to share their answers to the Bellringer activity. Have students identify where they would expect to find the four subjects they named in the Bellringer.

Resource Manager

Planning Resources
• *Lesson Plans*

📂 Other Print Resources
• *Guide to Using the Internet and Other Electronic Resources*

Teach

URL Components

Give pairs of students a list of five URLs. Have students break down each part of the URL and name each component. **L1**

Identifying Clues

Write the following URL on the chalkboard: http://www.spaceflight.nasa.gov/mars/missions/. Ask students to predict what they will find when they type in the address. Have them identify the clues that help them make their prediction. Students should infer that NASA owns the site and that the specific page is about NASA's missions to Mars. **L2**

Following is the address for the Web site that lists the six pillars of character supported by the AYSO (American Youth Soccer Organization).

http://www.soccer.org/abc/c_pillar.htm#sixpillars

1. The http:// at the beginning of an address stands for **hypertext transfer protocol.** These are the rules by which your computer gets information from any other computer hooked to the Web. All computers on the Web use this protocol and this four-letter prefix.

2. The *www* in an address refers to the World Wide Web, the part of the Internet in which this site is located.

3. The second part of a Web site address, called the **domain name,** tells your Web browser about the computer (or server) that stores the Web files. The domain name is usually the name (sometimes shortened) of the company or organization that maintains the site.

4. A suffix usually follows the domain head, separated from it by a period, or "dot." The suffix tells what type of organization the domain belongs to. The most common suffixes are *.com* (a business), *.gov* (a government agency), and *.edu* (an educational organization, such as a school).

5. The **path** identifies the route followed to get to a particular part or page of a site.

6. The **file name** follows the path; it leads you to the specific file that you're looking for on a Web site.

Write down the addresses of some of your favorite Web sites and see if you can identify the parts of the addresses. Remember that some URLs do not have paths or file names. When that's the case, the URL will take you to the site's **home page,** or opening page.

Enrichment and Extension

Sketching a Web Site

Have students break into groups and sketch designs of their own Web sites. Students should create an address and illustrate a home page with different path options. Ask volunteers to present their plans for Web sites to the class. Students can then suggest improvements that would make these Web sites easier to use.

As an Internet user, you may want to keep track of some Web sites that you visit. You can keep a record of them by using your browser's **Bookmark** or **Favorites** option. This option lets you keep a list of the addresses of your favorite sites so that you do not have to type an address each time you want to view a Web site. Instead, simply go to the Bookmark or Favorites menu of your browser and click on the site's name.

File Edit View Go Favorites Window Help
Apple presents Excite
Back Forward Stop Refresh Home Favorites History Search AutoFill Larger Smaller Print Mail Preferenc
Address: http://apple.excite.com/

Hyperlinks

You may notice as you begin to investigate various Web sites that some words or phrases are underlined or are in a color that is different from the rest of the text. These words or phrases are called hyperlinks. **Hyperlinks** are text or graphics that, when clicked on, take you to a new page or a related Web site. Sometimes it may be difficult to find the hyperlinks on a Web page. If you are not sure whether the text or graphics contain a hyperlink, drag the cursor arrow over the possible hyperlink. If the arrow changes to a pointing finger, you've found a hyperlink.

Searching the Internet

When writing a report, doing research, or using the Internet for pleasure, you may want to find specific information. How do you find the Web sites you are looking for? The fastest way is start with a search engine. A **search engine** helps you look for information on the Web by searching for keywords. A keyword is a word or phrase that describes your topic.

If you haven't narrowed your search to a specific topic, you can start with a subject directory. A **subject directory** lists general topics, such as arts and humanities, science, education, entertainment, sports, and health. After you select a broad topic, the directory will offer a list of possible subtopics from which to choose. Each subtopic may lead to topics that are even more specific. Various search engines and subject directories, such as those in the chart on the following page, are available for your use on the Internet.

Teach

Using a Dictionary
Encourage students to find or suggest the etymology of the word *hyperlink*. Ask them to search for other words containing one of the word parts and to discuss ways in which these words are and are not related.

Electronic Resources

interNET CONNECTION

Using Keywords

Ask students to generate and list keywords for the following searches. Students can then try out these keywords and evaluate their search results.

1. Search for a recipe for chocolate cake. (*recipes, desserts, chocolate*)

2. Search for a map of your city or state. (*maps, name of city or state*)

Practice and Assess

Evaluation Rubrics

Exercise 2

Students' answers will vary depending on the search engines they use to find the different Web sites. *The New York Times,* Will Smith, the Toledo Mudhens, and Princeton University all have official Web sites. Students may find unofficial Web sites that mention these subjects as well. There is no official Web site for hammerhead sharks but many unofficial Web sites. Check the Web sites that students have provided to verify their results.

Exercise 3

Have students exchange their lists of hyperlinks and check each other's answers. Those who have exchanged papers can discuss what they found at each Web site.

Close

Have students discuss how search engines can help them find the information they might need for reports, research papers, or presentations.

Electronic Resources

Some Popular Search Tools		
Search Tool	**Type**	**URL**
Alta Vista	search engine	http://www.altavista.com
Excite	search engine	http://www.excite.com
Galaxy	subject directory	http://www.galaxy.com
Yahoo!	subject directory	http://www.yahoo.com

Exercise 2

Use a search engine to find Web sites about the following subjects. Write down the URL of one Web site for each subject. Briefly describe each of the Web sites and compare your findings with those of other students.

1. *New York Times*
2. Will Smith
3. The Toledo Mudhens
4. Princeton University
5. Hammerhead sharks

Exercise 3

Find a Web site that has hyperlinks to other Web sites. Select one of the links and follow it to the next Web site. (If you find a site with no links, try another site.) Find the links on that Web site and choose one to follow. Continue doing this until you have been to five different Web sites. Write down in order the URL and the name of each Web site that you visit. Share information about the sites with your class.

Real World Connection

Tips for Using the Computer

Let students know techniques they can use when using the computer over longer periods of time. Students can exercise their hands by alternately spreading their fingers out and then bringing each hand together as in a fist. They can stretch their necks by moving their heads as close to each shoulder as possible and then looking back over each shoulder. Encourage students to hold their wrists above the keyboard as they type. Resting their wrists on the desk or keyboard will actually make their hands tire more quickly.

27.3 Evaluating Internet Sources

As you search the Internet and discover new Web sites, remember that anyone can create a Web site. As a result, you cannot always be sure that the Web site information is correct. It is your responsibility to determine what information is useful to you, whether that information is accurate, and how current the information is.

You'll want to make sure the sources you use in a presentation or research paper are reliable. How can you be sure? One way is to find out who owns the Web site or who created it. For instance, if you are looking for the batting average of a baseball player, www.majorleaguebaseball.com, the official site of major league baseball, should be accurate. A reputable sports news organization, such as ESPN, should also be useful. However, if the site was created by a baseball fan, you may want to find a second source to back up the information.

How to Evaluate the Usefulness of a Web Site

When evaluating a Web site, ask these questions:

1. What person, organization, or company created the Web site? Generally, you can expect a government or university site to be more accurate than an individual's site.
2. Does the site provide information on where the information was gathered or for what purpose?
3. Is there a way to check the information by contacting the person or organization that created the site?
4. Was the site recommended by a reliable person or reference book?

Exercise 4

Choose a famous person from the past and find a Web site that provides information about that person. Write down the URL and five to ten facts that you find about the person on the Web site. Check the accuracy of the facts in another source, such as an encyclopedia. Then report on the accuracy of the Web site.

27.3 Evaluating Internet Sources **651**

Focus

Lesson Overview

Objectives
- To learn how to determine the accuracy of Internet information
- To assess how presentation contributes to a message

Skills
- using the Internet; verifying and recording information

Critical Thinking
- analyzing and evaluating reference sources; identifying fact and opinion

Listening and Speaking
- discussing

🔔 Bellringer
Daily Language Activity

When students enter the classroom, have this assignment on the board: *Answer this question on a sheet of paper: How do you know if information on the Internet is accurate?*

Motivating Activity

List five facts on the board. Ask students how they would verify each of the facts.

Practice and Assess

Evaluation Rubrics

Exercise 4

Students should provide their written list of facts, URLs, and the other sources they used to verify the facts they found on the Web sites.

Resource Manager

Planning Resources
- *Lesson Plans*

📂 **Other Print Resources**
- *Guide to Using the Internet and Other Electronic Resources*

Teach

Making a Troubleshooting Search

Have students use the keywords "troubleshooting+Web" to research other troubleshooting issues and solutions. Students can take notes and present their discoveries to the class. You might ask volunteers to organize students' notes on a troubleshooting chart to display in the classroom. **L2**

Determining Reliable Web Sites

Have students explain what elements make a Web site reliable. Ask students to search the Internet and to provide at least two examples of Web sites that they believe are reliable. Have them give reasons for selecting these Web sites. **L2**

Electronic Resources

Troubleshooting Guide

As you work on the Web, you may need help in dealing with possible problems.

Here are some error messages that you might see as you spend time on the Web. They are followed by their possible causes and some suggestions for eliminating the errors.

Message: Unable to connect to server. The server may be down. Try connecting again later.

Possible Causes: The server is having technical problems. The site is being updated or is not communicating properly with your browser.

Suggestion: It usually helps if you try again in a few minutes; however, it could be a few days before the server is working properly.

Message: Unable to locate the server: www.server.com. The server does not have a DNS (Domain Name System) entry. Check the server name in the URL and try again.

Possible Causes: You have typed in the URL incorrectly, or the site no longer exists.

Suggestion: Be sure you have entered the URL correctly—check for proper capitalization and punctuation. If you have entered it correctly, try using a search engine to find the site. Keep in mind, though, the possibility that the site may have been abandoned.

Message: File Not Found: The requested URL was not found on this server.

Possible Causes: You have reached the server, but that particular file no longer exists or you have entered the path or file name incorrectly.

Suggestion: Check the URL again. If you have entered it correctly, try searching for the page from the server's home page.

Enrichment and Extension

Using Print Resources

Have students locate instruction manuals and troubleshooting guides for Internet searches at their local library. Students can present these materials to the class to facilitate their Internet searches.

Message: Network connection refused by the server. There was no response.

Possible Causes: You have reached the server, but it is too busy (too many other people are trying to access it) or temporarily shut down.

Suggestion: Try to access the site later.

Message: Connection timed out.

Possible Causes: Your browser attempted to contact the host, but the host took too long to reply.

Suggestion: Try to access the site later.

Message: Access denied. You do not have permission to open this item.

Possible Causes: The URL has moved, the Webmaster no longer allows public access to the site, or you have been denied access to the site.

Suggestion: Contact the Webmaster to verify the URL or try the site again in a few days. Sometimes there is nothing you can do if access has been denied. Many colleges, for example, allow access to parts of their sites only to faculty and registered students.

Teach

Troubleshooting for Software

Have students search troubleshooting Web sites for specific computer software, such as a well-known word processing program. Students should use the key word *troubleshooting* plus the name of the software to search for possible Web sites. Ask volunteers to present their search results to the class. **L2**

Sorting Fact and Opinion

Select a Web site that contains both facts and opinions (for example, any site where something is reviewed). Have students read through the Web site. Then work with them to find statements of fact and of opinion. List the statements on the board under the heading *Fact* or *Opinion*. **L1**

Close

Engage students in a discussion of what they have learned about evaluating Web sites. Could these same evaluation techniques be applied to books, magazines, or newspapers?

Electronic Resources

MEETING INDIVIDUAL NEEDS | English Language Learners

Recognizing Opinions

Some students whose first language is not English might have difficulty distinguishing between facts and opinions. Share the following phrases with students. Explain to them that these phrases usually indicate that an opinion is being expressed.

I think . . .	*I don't like . . .*
I believe . . .	*. . . is beautiful*
I really like . . .	

Focus

Lesson Overview

Objectives
- To learn how to use e-mail
- To use technology to support publishing efforts
- To edit e-mail drafts

Skills
- using the Internet and exploring its features

Critical Thinking
- categorizing; analyzing; identifying types of information

Listening and Speaking
- discussing; explaining ideas

Bellringer
Daily Language Activity

When students enter the classroom, have this assignment on the board: *Write your ideas about what the "e" in e-mail stands for.*

Motivating Activity

Point out that e-mail ("electronic mail") has become a popular form of communication. Ask students how e-mail is used for informal communication (among friends and relatives) as well as formal communication (at and between businesses).

Teach

Adding to the Internet Dictionary

Have students add terms to the Internet dictionary that they made at the beginning of the unit using terms from this lesson. Each word in the dictionary should include a definition, an example, and, whenever possible, an illustration. **L1**

Electronic Resources

27.4 Using E-Mail

Electronic mail, or **e-mail,** is a popular feature of the Internet. Millions of Americans send or receive e-mail every day. With the click of a button, e-mail lets you send messages to anyone in the world. You can also add computer files of text or graphics as **attachments** to an e-mail message. You can send pictures of yourself to an e-mail pen pal, send a sound clip of your favorite song to a friend, or send a report you have written to one of your teachers.

To send e-mail, you need an e-mail address. Like Web site addresses, e-mail addresses are unique. No two people can have the same e-mail address. Your Internet service provider should provide you with an e-mail address. You can also use a service, such as Yahoo!, to provide you with an e-mail account.

A typical e-mail address has four parts. The first part is the **user name.** This is the name you have chosen for yourself or that is assigned to you by your Internet service provider. The second part is the @ symbol, which stands for "at." This symbol separates the user name from the rest of the e-mail address. The third part is the **domain name,** which is the name of your ISP's server or the service that hosts your e-mail account. The last part of an e-mail address is the suffix. The **suffix** indicates the type of organization that provides your e-mail service.

Just as you can send an e-mail message to any address in the world, anyone in the world can send an e-mail message to you. Sometimes you will receive junk e-mail, or **spam.** It is similar to the junk mail you receive at home. Advertisements are the main form of spam, and sometimes this kind of e-mail can be offensive. If you receive e-mail from someone whose e-mail address you do not recognize, show it to an adult. Do not write back unless the adult gives you permission. Some people send links to Web sites through e-mail. If you receive a message with a link to a Web site, show it to an adult before clicking on the link. When you send e-mail, be sure to extend courtesy to those you are addressing.

654 Unit 27 Electronic Resources

Resource Manager

Planning Resources
- *Lesson Plans*

Other Print Resources
- *Guide to Using the Internet and Other Electronic Resources*

E-Mail Etiquette

When sending e-mail, you should follow the Internet rules etiquette, which are usually referred to as **Netiquette.** Here are some of the important Netiquette rules.

- Use the subject line wisely. Be as brief as you can, but let the person to whom you are sending e-mail know what your message is about.
- Keep messages short and to the point.
- Use appropriate capitalization. Using all capital letters is considered SHOUTING.
- Avoid sending unfriendly e-mail. Sending an unfriendly e-mail message is called "flaming."
- Always check your spelling before sending an e-mail message. Your e-mail software may have a spelling-check function you can use.
- Always include your e-mail address at the bottom of any message you send.
- Be careful when using humor or sarcasm. It can be difficult to indicate emotion in print. Use "smileys" if you want to show emotion. Smileys are also called *emoticons*, a term made up of the words *emotion* and *icons*. They are little faces made by the characters on a keyboard. Tilt your head to the left to see them.

      :-)   (a smile)   ;-)   (a wink)

      :-((frown)   :-D   (laughing)

- Remember that good behavior on the Internet is no different from good behavior in face-to-face situations. Treat others as you would like them to treat you.

Exercise 5

If at some time you want to set up your own e-mail account, with your parents' approval, you can do so by accessing one of the free e-mail providers on the Web. Your teacher can explain how to establish your account. You will need to create a name for your e-mail address and to share addresses with friends, classmates, and relatives with whom you want to correspond.

Discuss in a small group the reasons you might have for wanting e-mail access. Discuss the rules of etiquette listed above and be sure you understand the meaning of each rule and the reason for its inclusion on this list.

Electronic Resources

Teach

Using Global Communication

Obtain the e-mail addresses of colleagues and other reliable adults who are willing to correspond with your students and who live in a variety of geographic areas. Have students work together to write e-mail messages asking questions about the climate and geography of the places where the recipients live. Write the messages on the board and proofread them as a class before sending them. As students receive responses, print the responses and post them on a map. **L3**

Practice and Assess

Evaluation Rubrics

Exercise 5

Students should discuss establishing their own e-mail addresses and list purposes for their doing so. They should participate in the creation of a directory of e-mail addresses.

Close

Have students discuss how they can use e-mail for fun and for getting information.

*inter*NET CONNECTION

Choosing an E-Mail Provider

Point out to students that there are many free e-mail providers. Some of these providers have their own programs for accessing e-mail. Encourage students to try out a few different e-mail providers to see which program they like best.

Focus

Lesson Overview

Objectives

- To identify electronic resources other than the Internet that provide useful information
- To evaluate sources of information
- To frame questions to direct research

Skills

- understanding the value of electronic resources; using a CD-ROM

Critical Thinking

- evaluating reference resources

Listening and Speaking

- discussing

🔔 Bellringer
Daily Language Activity

When students enter the classroom, have this assignment on the board: *List resources, other than the Internet and books, that you can use to find information.*

Motivating Activity

Have students discuss their answers to the Bellringer activity. Ask students for examples of the types of things that can be found on CD-ROMs. Ask volunteers who have educational CD-ROMs at home to bring them in to share with the class.

Electronic Resources

27.5 Other Electronic Resources

In your search for information, you may use sources of electronic information other than the Internet. CD-ROMs, DVDs, and diskettes all store information electronically.

CD-ROMs

A **CD-ROM,** or Compact Disc–Read-Only Memory, looks like an audio compact disc, but it stores more than just audio information. **Read-only memory** is computer memory on which data has been prerecorded. Once data has been written onto a CD-ROM, it cannot be removed or changed. It can only be read. A CD-ROM can store text, graphics, and video files. Because a CD-ROM can store large amounts of information, many dictionaries, encyclopedias, and other reference works are stored on CD-ROMs. In fact, one CD-ROM can store as much information as hundreds of floppy diskettes. You can use CD-ROMs to read text and look at pictures. You can also use them to view video and audio files.

To use a CD-ROM, your computer must have a CD-ROM drive. A CD-ROM drive is standard on most new computers. Some CD-ROM drives are "read only"—that is, they can only use the information put on the disc. Other drives are able to record information on the disc just as you might record music on an audiocassette. Once recorded, that information cannot be changed. The newest CD-ROM drives, however, can record over and over on the same disc, just as you can do with a tape.

DVDs

A **DVD,** or Digital Video Disc, can store up to six times the data of a CD-ROM on the same surface area. Similar in size and shape to a CD-ROM, a DVD can hold enough information for a full-length movie. A DVD player can be used like a VCR to watch movies. Like a CD-ROM, a DVD requires a special drive on a computer. Although a DVD drive can play CD-ROMs, a CD-ROM drive cannot play DVDs.

Resource Manager

Planning Resources
- *Lesson Plans*

📁 **Other Print Resources**
- *Guide to Using the Internet and Other Electronic Resources*

Removable Storage

Diskettes, also called floppy disks, are commonly used to store text documents. The average computer still uses diskettes to store information, although most software is now distributed on CD-ROMs rather than diskettes. Some newer computers no longer contain diskette drives. Instead, they have a Zip drive, which uses a small disc that can store about seventy times as much information as a diskette. Other types of removable discs can hold even more information. The greater capacity of such discs has become necessary, now that users deal with large graphic files. A file for a single large color photo, for example, simply won't fit on a diskette.

Digital magnetic tape for a computer is similar to tape for an audiocassette player. The tape stores information on a magnetically coated strip of plastic. The tape can store large amounts of information, but it is not as convenient to use as a CD-ROM or a removable disc. It is more difficult to access information from a magnetic tape. If you need to view information that is at the end of a tape, you must sort through all of the information on the tape until you find it. CD-ROMs and removable discs let you choose the information you wish to view with the click of a button. Magnetic tape is used mainly for backing up information or storing large quantities of information that do not have to be accessed quickly.

Exercise 6

At your local library, check out a CD-ROM on any subject that interests you. Before viewing it, make a list of five questions that you have about the subject. Then look for the answers to your questions as you view the CD-ROM. Draw a diagram that shows each step you have to take to find each answer.

Practice and Assess

Evaluation Rubrics

Exercise 6
Students' diagrams should demonstrate the steps taken to find each answer to their five questions.

Close

Ask students to look up two or three subjects in different resources to see how presentation and type of information differ. Have students discuss the differences they find. Suggest that they use books, film, and Internet sources to compare information, reviews, and styles of presentation.

✔ ASSESSMENT OPTIONS

📁 *Tests with Answer Key and Rubrics*
Unit 27 Mastery Test, pp. 111–112

💾 *Testmaker*
Unit 27 Mastery Test

You may wish to administer the Unit 27 Mastery Test at this point.

📼 *Mindjogger Videoquizzes*

Electronic Resources

Cooperative Learning

Planning a CD-ROM
Have students break into small groups and plan a list of information that they would include on a CD-ROM on a topic of interest to them. Each group should work together to sketch at least three "pages," including both text and illustrations, that might be included on their CD-ROM. Have students present their lists and pages to the class.

WRITING AND LANGUAGE
GLOSSARY

This glossary will help you quickly find definitions used in writing and grammar.

A

Adjective. A word that modifies, or describes, a noun or a pronoun. An adjective may tell *what kind, which one, how many,* or *how much.*
> The **comparative degree** of an adjective compares two people, places, things, or ideas. (*worse, sadder*)
> The **superlative degree** of an adjective compares more than two people, places, things, or ideas. (*worst, saddest*)
> A **possessive adjective** is a possessive pronoun used before a noun.
> A **predicate adjective** always follows a linking verb. It modifies the subject of the sentence.
> A **proper adjective** is formed from a proper noun. It always begins with a capital letter.
> A **demonstrative adjective** is the word *this, that, these,* or *those* used before a noun.

Adverb. A word that modifies a verb, an adjective, or another adverb. Adverbs may tell *how, when, where, in what manner,* and *how often.* Some adverbs have different forms to indicate **comparative** and **superlative degrees.** (*loud, louder, loudest; sweetly, more sweetly, most sweetly*)

Allusion. A reference in a piece of writing to a well-known character, place, or situation from a work of literature, music, or art or from history.

Analysis. The act of breaking down a subject into its separate parts to determine its meaning.

Anecdote. A short story or incident usually presented as part of a longer narrative.

Antecedent. *See* Pronoun.

Appositive. A noun placed next to another noun to identify it or add information about it. (My basketball coach, *Ms. Lopes,* called for a time out.)

Argument. A statement, reason, or fact for or against a point; a piece of writing intended to persuade.

Article. The adjectives *a, an,* and *the. A* and *an* are **indefinite articles.** They refer to any one item of a group. *The* is a **definite article.** It indicates that the noun it precedes is a specific person, place or thing.

Audience. The person(s) who reads or listens to what the writer or speaker says.

Auxiliary verb. *See* Phrase.

B

Base form. *See* Verb tense.

Bias. A tendency to think a certain way. Bias may affect the way a writer or speaker presents his or her ideas.

Bibliography. A list of the books, articles, and other sources used as reference sources in a research paper.

Body. The central part of a composition that communicates the main idea identified in the introduction.

Bookmarks/favorites. The feature on many Web browsers that allows the user to save addresses of Internet sites so that sites can be accessed quickly.

Brainstorming. A group activity in which people generate as many ideas as possible without stopping to judge them.

C

Case. The form of a noun or pronoun that is determined by its use in a sentence. A noun or pronoun is in the **nominative** case when it is used as a subject, in the **objective** case when it is used as an object, and in the **possessive** case when it is used to show possession.

Cause-and-effect chain. A series of events in which one cause leads to an effect that in turn leads to another effect, and so on.

Characterization. The methods a writer uses to develop the personality of the character. A writer may make direct statements about a character's personality or reveal it through the character's words and actions or through what other characters think and say about the character.

Chronological order. The arrangement of details according to when events or actions take place.

Clarity. The quality of a piece of writing that makes it easy to understand.

Clause. A group of words that has a subject and a predicate and that is used as part of a sentence.

> An **independent clause,** also called a **main clause,** has a subject and a predicate and can stand alone as a sentence.
> A **dependent clause,** also called a **subordinate clause,** has a subject and a predicate, but it makes sense only when attached to a main clause.

Cliché. An overused expression. *(white as snow)*

Clustering. The grouping together of related items as a way of organizing information.

Coherence. A quality of logical connection between the parts of a paragraph or composition.

Cohesive writing. A type of writing in which sentences and paragraphs are logically connected to one another.

Collaboration. The process of working with others on writing or other projects.

Colloquialism. A casual, colorful expression used in everyday conversation.

Comparative degree. *See* Adjective; Adverb.

Comparison-and-contrast. A way of organizing ideas by illustrating their similarities and differences.

Complement. A word or phrase that completes the meaning of a verb. Three kinds of complements are **direct objects, indirect objects,** and **subject complements.**

Conceptual map. A graphic device that develops a central concept by surrounding it with examples or related ideas in a weblike arrangement.

Conclusion. A restatement or summing up of the ideas in a composition that brings it to a definite close.

Conflict. The struggle between two opposing forces that lies at the center of the plot in a story or drama.

Conjunction. A word that joins single words or groups of words.

> A **coordinating conjunction** (*and, but, or, nor, for, yet*) joins words or groups of words that are equal in grammatical importance.
> **Correlative conjunctions** (*both . . . and, just as . . . so, not only . . . but also, either . . . or, neither . . . nor*) are pairs of words used to connect words or phrases in a sentence.

Connotation. The thoughts and feelings associated with a word, rather than its dictionary definition.

Constructive criticism. Comments on another person's writing made with the intention of helping the writer improve a particular draft.

Context. The words and sentences that come before and after a specific word and help to explain its meaning.

Coordinating conjunction. *See* Conjunction.

Conventions. Correct spelling, grammar, usage, and mechanics.

Correlative conjunction. *See* Conjunction.

Credibility. The quality of a speaker or writer that makes that person's words believable.

D

Declarative sentence. A sentence that makes a statement.

Deductive reasoning. A way of thinking or explaining that begins with a general statement or principle and applies that principle to specific instances.

Definite article. *See* Article.

Demonstrative adjective. *See* Adjective.

Denotation. The dictionary definition of a word.

Dependent clause. *See* Clause.

Descriptive writing. Writing that uses sensory detail to convey an impression of a setting, a person, an animal, and so on.

Desktop publishing. The use of computer programs to format and produce a document that may include written text, graphics, and/or images.

Dialect. A variety of a language spoken by a particular group of people. A dialect may be regional (based on location) or ethnic (based on cultural heritage).

Dialogue. The conversation between characters in a written work.

Diction. A writer's choice of words and the arrangement of those words in phrases, sentences, or lines of a poem.

Direct object. *See* Complement.

Documentation. Identification of the sources used in writing research or other informative papers; usually in the form of endnotes or footnotes, or using parenthetical documentation.

Drafting. One of the steps in the writing process; the transforming of thoughts, words, and phrases into sentences and paragraphs.

E

Editing. One of the steps of the writing process in which a revised draft is checked for standard usage, varied sentence structure, and appropriate word choice.

Editorial. An article in a newspaper or other form of media that expresses an opinion about a topic of general interest.

Elaboration. The support or development of a main idea with facts, statistics, sensory details, incidents, anecdotes, examples, or quotations.

Ellipsis. A mark of punctuation consisting of three spaced periods, that shows the omission of a word or words.

E-mail. Short for electronic mail. Messages, usually text, sent from one person to another by way of computer.

Evaluating. Making a judgment about the strengths and weaknesses of a draft in content, organization, and style.

Evidence. Facts or examples from reliable sources that can be used to support statements made in speaking or writing.

Exclamatory sentence. A sentence that expresses strong or sudden emotion.

Explanatory writing. *See* Expository writing.

Expository writing. A kind of writing that aims at informing and explaining. Examples of expository writing are news articles, how-to instructions, and research papers.

Expressive writing. Writing that emphasizes and conveys the writer's feelings.

F

Fact. A piece of information that can be verified.

Feedback. The response a listener or reader gives to a speaker or writer about his or her work.

Figurative language. Words used for descriptive effect that express some truth beyond the literal level. Figures of speech such as similes, metaphors, or personification are examples of figurative language.

Formal language. Language that uses correct grammar and omits slang expressions and contractions. It is especially common in non-fiction writing that is not personal.

Fragment. An incomplete sentence punctuated as if it were complete.

Freewriting. A way of finding ideas by writing freely, without stopping or limiting the flow of ideas, for a specific length of time.

Future tense. *See* Verb tense.

G–H

Generalization. A statement that presents a conclusion about a subject without going into details or specifics.

Genre. A division of literature or some other medium. The main literary genres are prose, poetry, and drama. Each of these is further divided into subgenres.

Graphic organizer. A visual way of organizing information; types of graphic organizers are charts, graphs, clusters, and idea trees.

Home page. The location on a Web site by which a user normally enters the site. A typical home page may explain the site, summarize the content, and provide links to other sites.

Hyperlink. Highlighted or underlined phrases or words on a Web page that, when clicked, move the user to another part of the page or to another Web page.

Hypertext. Links in some electronic text that take the user to another document or to a different section in the same document.

I–J

Ideas. In writing, the message or theme and the details that elaborate upon that message or theme.

Idiom. A word or phrase that has a special meaning different from its standard or dictionary meaning. (*Burning the midnight oil* is an idiom that means "staying up late.")

Imagery. Language that emphasizes sensory impressions that can help the reader of a literary work to see, hear, feel, smell, and taste the scenes described in the work.

Imperative sentence. A sentence that makes a request or gives a command.

Indefinite article. *See* Article.

Independent clause. *See* Clause.

Inductive reasoning. A way of thinking or explaining that begins with a series of examples and uses them to arrive at a general statement.

Informative writing. A kind of writing that explains something, such as a process or an idea. *See also* Expository writing.

Intensifier. An adverb that emphasizes an adjective or another adverb. (*very* important; *quite* easily)

Interjection. A word or phrase that expresses strong feeling. An interjection has no grammatical connection to other words in the sentence.

Internet. A worldwide computer network that allows users to link to any computer on the network electronically for social, commercial, research, and other purposes.

Interpretation. An explanation of the meaning of a piece of writing, a visual representation, or any other type of communication.

Interview. A question-and-answer dialogue that has the specific purpose of gathering up-to-date or expert information.

Introduction. The beginning part of a piece of writing in which a writer identifies the subject and gives a general idea of what the body of the composition will contain.

Inverted order. The placement of a predicate before the subject in a sentence. In most sentences in English, the subject comes before the predicate.

Irregular verb. *See* Verb tense.

Jargon. Special words and phrases used by a particular group of people.

Journal. A personal notebook in which a person can freewrite, collect ideas, and record thoughts and experiences.

L

Learning log. A journal used for clarifying ideas about concepts covered in various classes.

Listing. A technique used for finding ideas for writing.

Literary analysis. The act of examining the different elements of a piece of literature in order to evaluate it.

Logical fallacy. An error in reasoning often found in advertising or persuasive writing. Either-or reasoning and glittering generalities are types of logical fallacies.

M

Main clause. *See* Clause.

Main idea. *See* Thesis statement.

Main verb. The most important word in a verb phrase.

Media. The forms of communication used to reach an audience; forms such as newspapers, radio, TV, and the Internet reach large audiences and so are known as mass media.

Memoir. A type of narrative nonfiction that presents an account of an event or period in history, emphasizing the narrator's personal experience.

Metaphor. A figure of speech that compares seemingly unlike things without using words such as *like* or *as*. (*He is a rock.*)

Mood. The feeling or atmosphere of a piece of writing.

Multimedia presentation. The use of a variety of media, such as video, sound, written text, and visual art to present ideas or information.

N

Narrative writing. A type of writing that tells about events or actions as they change over a period of time and often includes story elements such as character, setting, and plot.

Nonfiction. Prose writing about real people, places, and events.

Noun. A word that names a person, a place, a thing, an idea, a quality, or a characteristic.

Number. The form of a noun, pronoun, or verb that indicates whether it refers to one (**singular**) or more than one (**plural**).

O

Object. *See* Complement.

Onomatopoeia. The use of a word or phrase that imitates or suggests the sound of what it describes. (*rattle, boom*)

Opinion. A belief or attitude that cannot be proven true or false.

Oral tradition. Literature that passes by word of mouth from one generation to the next. The tradition of a culture may reflect the cultural values of the people.

Order of importance. A way of arranging details in a paragraph or other piece of writing according to their importance.

Organization. The arrangement of main points and supporting details in a piece of writing.

Outline. A systematic arrangement of main and supporting ideas, using Roman numerals, letters, and numbers, for a written or an oral presentation.

P

Paragraph. A unit of writing that consists of related sentences.

Parallelism. The use of a series of words, phrases, or sentences that have similar grammatical form.

Paraphrase. A restatement of someone's ideas in words that are different from the original passage but retain its ideas, tone, and general length.

Parenthetical documentation. A specific reference to the source of a piece of information; placed in parentheses directly after the information appears in a piece of writing.

Peer response. Suggestions and comments provided by peers, or classmates, about a piece of writing or another type of presentation.

Personal pronoun. *See* Pronoun.

Personal writing. Writing that expresses the writer's own thoughts and feelings.

Personification. A figure of speech that gives human qualities to an animal, object, or idea.

Perspective. *See* Point of view.

Persuasion. A type of writing that aims at convincing people to think or act in a certain way.

Phrase. A group of words that acts in a sentence as a single part of speech.
A **prepositional phrase** begins with a preposition and ends with a noun or a pronoun. A **verb phrase** consists of one or more **auxiliary verbs** followed by a main verb.

Plagiarism. The dishonest presentation of another's words or ideas as one's own.

Plot. The series of events that follow one another in a story, novel, or play.

Plural. *See* Number.

Poetry. A form of literary expression that emphasizes the line as the unit of composition. Traditional poetry contains emotional, imaginative language and a regular rhythm.

Point of view. The angle, or perspective, from which a story is told, such as first- or third-person.

Portfolio. A collection of various pieces of writing, which may include finished pieces and works in progress.

Predicate. The verb or verb phrase and any modifiers that make an essential statement about the subject of a sentence.

Predicate adjective. *See* Adjective.

Preposition. A word that shows the relationship of a noun or pronoun to some other word in the sentence.

Prepositional phrase. *See* Phrase.

Presentation. The way words and design elements look on the page.

Presenting/Publishing. The last step in the writing process; involves sharing the final writing product with others in some way.

Prewriting. The first stage in the writing process; includes deciding what to write about, collecting ideas and details, and making an outline or a plan. Prewriting strategies include brainstorming, and using graphic organizers, notes, and logs.

Prior knowledge. The facts, ideas, and experiences that a writer, reader, or viewer brings to a new activity.

Progressive form. *See* Verb tense.

Pronoun. A word that takes the place of a noun, a group of words acting as a noun, or another pronoun. The word or group of words that a pronoun refers to is called its **antecedent**.
   A **personal pronoun** refers to a specific person or thing.

Pronoun case. *See* Case.

Proofreading. The final part of the editing process that involves checking work to discover typographical and other errors.

Propaganda. Information aimed at influencing thoughts and actions; it is usually of a political nature and may contain distortions of truth.

Proper adjective. *See* Adjective.

Prose. Writing that is similar to everyday speech and written language, as opposed to poetry and drama.

Publishing. The preparation of a finished piece of writing, often involving available technology, so that it can be presented to a larger audience.

Purpose. The aim of writing, which may be to express, discover, record, develop, reflect on ideas, problem solve, entertain, influence, inform, or describe.

R

Regular verb. *See* Verb tense.

Representation. A way in which information or ideas are presented to an audience.

Research. The search for information on a topic.

Review. The analysis and interpretation of a subject, often presented through the mass media.

Revising. The stage of the writing process in which a writer goes over a draft, making changes in its content, organization, and style in order to improve it. Revision techniques include adding, elaborating, deleting, combining, and rearranging text.

Root. The part of a word that carries the main meaning.

Run-on sentence. Two or more sentences or clauses run together without appropriate punctuation.

S

Sensory details. Language that appeals to the senses; sensory details are important elements of descriptive writing, especially of poetry.

Sentence. A group of words expressing a complete thought. Every sentence has a **subject** and a **predicate.** *See also* Subject; Predicate; Clause.

A **simple sentence** has only one main clause and no subordinate clauses.

A **compound sentence** has two or more main clauses. Each main clause of a compound sentence has its own subject and predicate, and these main clauses are usually joined by a comma and a coordinating conjunction. A semicolon can also be used to join the main clauses in a compound sentence. A **complex sentence** has one main clause and one or more subordinate clauses.

Sentence fluency. The smooth rhythm and flow of sentences that vary in length and style.

Sentence variety. The use of different types of sentences to add interest to writing.

Setting. The time and place in which the events of a story, novel, or play takes place.

Simile. A figure of speech that compares two basically unlike things, using words such as *like* or *as.* (*Her hair was like fine wire.*)

Simple predicate. *See* Predicate; Sentence; Subject.

Simple sentence. *See* Sentence.

Spatial order. A way of presenting the details of a setting according to their location—from left to right or from top to bottom.

Standard English. The most widely used and accepted form of the English language.

Style. The writer's choice and arrangement of words and sentences.

Subject. The noun or pronoun that tells who or what the sentence is about.

Subordinate clause. *See* Clause.

Summary. A brief statement of the main idea of a composition.

Supporting evidence. *See* Evidence.

Suspense. A literary device that creates growing interest and excitement leading up to the climax and resolution of a story. A writer creates suspense by providing clues to the resolution without revealing too much information.

Symbol. An object, a person, a place, or an experience that represents something else, usually something abstract.

T

Tense. *See* Verb tense.

Theme. The main idea or message of a piece of writing.

Thesis statement. A one- or two-sentence statement of the **main idea** or purpose of a piece of writing.

Time order. The arrangement of details in a piece of writing based on when they occurred.

Tone. A reflection of a writer's or speaker's attitude toward a subject.

Topic sentence. A sentence that expresses the main idea of a paragraph.

Transition. A connecting word or phrase that clarifies relationships between details, sentences, or paragraphs.

U–V

Unity. A quality of oneness in a paragraph or composition that exists when all the sentences or paragraphs work together to express or support one main idea.

URL. The standard form of an Internet address; Stands for Uniform Resource Locator.

Venn diagram. A graphic organizer consisting of two overlapping circles; used to compare two items that have both similar and different traits.

Verb. A word that expresses an action or a state of being and is necessary to make a statement.

Verb phrase. *See* Phrase.

Verb tense. The form a verb takes to show when an action takes place. The **present tense** names an action that happens regularly. The **past tense** names an action that has happened, and the **future tense** names an action that will take place in the future. All the verb tenses are formed from the four principal parts of a verb: a **base form** (*freeze*), a **present participle** (*freezing*), a **simple past form** (*froze*), and a **past participle** (*frozen*).

A **regular verb** forms its simple past and past participle by adding *-ed* to the base form. Verbs that form their past and past participle in some other way are called **irregular verbs.**

In addition to present, past, and future tenses, there are three perfect tenses— **present perfect, past perfect,** and **future perfect.**

Each of the six tenses has a **progressive** form that expresses a continuing action.

Voice. A writer's unique way of using tone and style to communicate with the audience.

W

Web site. A location on the World Wide Web that can be reached through links or by accessing a Web address, or URL. *See also* URL; World Wide Web.

Word choice. The vocabulary a writer chooses to convey meaning.

Word processing. The use of a computer for the writing and editing of written text.

World Wide Web. A global system that uses the Internet and allows users to create, link, and access fields of information. *See also* Internet.

Writing process. The series of stages or steps that a writer goes through to develop ideas and to communicate them.

GLOSARIO
DE ESCRITURA Y LENGUAJE

Este glosario te ayudará a encontrar fácilmente las definiciones utilizadas en escritura y en la gramática del inglés.

A

Adjective/Adjetivo. Palabra que modifica, o describe, un nombre (*noun*) o pronombre (*pronoun*). Un adjetivo *indica qué tipo, cuál, cuántos* o *cuánto*.

> **Comparative degree/Grado comparativo.** Adjetivo que compara a dos personas, lugares, cosas o ideas (*worse, sadder;* en español: *peor, más triste*).

> **Superlative degree/Grado superlativo.** Adjetivo que compara más de dos personas, lugares, cosas o ideas (*worst, saddest;* en español: *el peor, la más triste*).

> **Possessive adjective/Adjetivo posesivo.** Pronombre posesivo que va antes del nombre.

> **Predicative adjective/Adjetivo predicativo.** Siempre va después de un verbo copulativo y modifica al sujeto de la oración.

> **Proper adjective/Adjetivo propio*.** Adjetivo que se deriva de un nombre propio; en inglés siempre se escribe con mayúscula.

> **Demonstrative adjective/Adjetivo demostrativo.** Se usa antes del nombre: *this, that, these, those (este, ese, aquel, estos, esos, aquellos)*.

Adverb/Adverbio. Palabra que modifica a un verbo, adjetivo u otro adverbio. Los adverbios indican *cómo, cuándo, dónde, de qué manera* y *qué tan seguido* sucede algo.

Algunos adverbios tienen diferentes formas para indicar los grados **comparativo** (*comparative*) y **superlativo** (*superlative*) (*loud, louder, loudest; sweetly, more sweetly, most sweetly;* en español: *fuerte, más fuerte, lo más fuerte; dulcemente, más dulcemente, lo más dulcemente*).

Allusion/Alusión. Referencia en un texto escrito a un personaje, lugar o situación muy conocidos de una obra literaria, musical, artística o histórica.

Analysis/Análisis. Acción de descomponer un tema o escrito en distintas partes para encontrar su significado.

Anecdote/Anécdota. Narración breve o incidente que se presenta como parte de una narrativa más larga.

Antecedent/Antecedente. *Ver Pronoun.*

Appositive/Apositivo. Nombre colocado junto a otro para identificarlo o agregar información sobre él. (Mi entrenadora de baloncesto, *Ms. Lopes,* pidió tiempo fuera.)

Argument/Argumento. Afirmación, razón o hecho en favor o en contra de algún comentario; texto escrito que trata de persuadir.

Article/Artículo. Nombre dado a las palabras *a, an* y *the* (en español: *un, uno/a, el, la*). *A* y *an* son artículos **indefinidos** (*indefinite articles*), que se refieren a cualquier cosa de un grupo. *The* es un artículo **definido** (*definite article*);

indica que el nombre al que precede es una persona, lugar o cosa específicos.

Audience/Público. Persona (o personas) que lee o escucha lo que dicen un escritor o un hablante.

Auxiliary verb/Verbo auxiliar. *Ver Phrase.*

B

Base form/Base derivativa. *Ver Verb tense.*

Bias/Tendencia. Inclinación a pensar de cierta manera. La tendencia influye en la manera en que un escritor o hablante presenta sus ideas.

Bibliography/Bibliografía. Lista de los libros, artículos y otras fuentes que se utilizan como referencia en una investigación.

Body/Cuerpo. Parte central de una composición que comunica la idea principal identificada en la introducción.

Bookmarks/favorites/Marcadores/favoritos. Característica de muchos buscadores de red que permiten guardar direcciones de Internet para entrar a ellas rápidamente.

Brainstorming/Lluvia de ideas. Actividad de grupo en que se generan tantas ideas como sea posible sin detenerse a analizarlas.

C

Case/Caso. Forma de un nombre o pronombre que está determinado por su uso en la oración. El nombre o pronombre está en caso **nominativo** (*nominative case*) cuando se utiliza como sujeto; en caso **acusativo** y **dativo** (*objective case*) cuando recibe la acción del verbo, y en caso **posesivo*** (*possessive case*) cuando se utiliza para indicar posesión o propiedad.

Cause-and-effect chain/Cadena de causa y efecto. Serie de acontecimientos en que una causa lleva a un efecto que, a su vez, lleva a otro efecto, y así sucesivamente.

Characterization/Caracterización. Métodos que utiliza un escritor para crear sus personajes. Puede ser describiendo directamente su personalidad, o revelándola con sus palabras y acciones, o bien a partir de lo que otros personajes piensan y dicen de él.

Chronological order/Orden cronológico. Organización de detalles de acuerdo con el tiempo en que sucedieron los acontecimientos o acciones.

Clarity/Claridad. Cualidad de un escrito que lo hace fácil de entender.

Clause/Proposición. Grupo de palabras que consta de sujeto y predicado, y que se usa como parte de una oración compuesta.

> **Independent clause/Proposición independiente.** También llamada **proposición principal** (*main clause*); tiene sujeto y predicado y hace sentido por sí misma.
> **Dependent clause/Proposición dependiente.** También llamada **proposición subordinada** (*subordinate clause*); tiene sujeto y predicado pero depende de la proposición principal.

Cliché/Cliché. Expresión usada con demasiada frecuencia (*blanco como la nieve*).

Clustering/Agrupamiento. Reunión de temas relacionados para organizar la información.

Coherence/Coherencia. Relación lógica entre las partes de un párrafo o composición.

Cohesive writing/Escritura coherente. Tipo de escritura en que las oraciones y párrafos están lógicamente relacionados entre sí.

Collaboration/Colaboración. Proceso de trabajar en equipo para escribir un texto o realizar un proyecto.

Colloquialism/Expresión coloquial. Expresión informal y pintoresca que se utiliza en la conversación diaria.

Comparative degree/Grado comparativo. *Ver Adjective; Adverb.*

Comparison-and-contrast/Comparación y contraste. Manera de organizar ideas, señalando sus similitudes y diferencias.

Complement/Complemento (u objeto). Palabra o frase que complementa el significado de un verbo. Tres complementos son: **directo** (*direct object*), **indirecto** (*indirect object*) y **predicativo** (**atributo**) (*subject complement*).

Conceptual map/Mapa conceptual. Recurso gráfico que desarrolla un concepto central rodeándolo con ejemplos o ideas relacionadas a manera de red.

Conclusion/Conclusión. Afirmación que resume las ideas de una composición, antes de ponerle punto final.

Conflict/Conflicto. Lucha entre dos fuerzas opuestas que constituye el elemento central de la trama en un cuento u obra de teatro.

Conjunction/Conjunción. Palabra que une palabras o grupos de palabras.

> **Coordinating conjunction/Conjunción coordinante.** Las palabras *and, but, or, nor, for, yet* (*y, pero, o, no, para, aun*) unen palabras o grupos de palabras que tienen igual importancia gramatical.
> **Correlative conjunction/Conjunción correlativa*.** Las palabras *both . . . and, just as . . . so, not only . . . but also, either . . . or, neither . . . nor* (*tanto . . . como, así como, no sólo . . . sino, o . . . o*) son palabras en pares que vinculan palabras o frases en una oración.

Connotation/Connotación. Pensamientos y sentimientos relacionados con una palabra, más que con su definición de diccionario.

Constructive criticism/Crítica constructiva. Comentario sobre lo que escribe otra persona, con la intención de ayudar a que mejore el borrador.

Context/Contexto. Palabras y oraciones que vienen antes y después de una palabra y ayudan a explicar su significado.

Conventions/Reglas de escritura. Normas que regulan la ortografía, la gramática, el uso y la puntuación de un escrito.

Coordinating conjunction/Conjunción coordinante. *Ver Conjunction.*

Correlative conjunction/Conjunción correlativa*. *Ver Conjuntion.*

Credibility/Credibilidad. Cualidad de un hablante o escritor que hace creer sus palabras.

D

Declarative sentence/Oración afirmativa. Oración que declara algo.

Deductive reasoning/Razonamiento deductivo. Pensamiento o explicación que parte de una afirmación o principio generales y los aplica a casos específicos.

Definite article/Artículo definido. *Ver Article.*

Demonstrative adjective/Adjetivo demostrativo. *Ver Adjective.*

Denotation/Denotación. Definición de una palabra que da el diccionario.

Dependent clause/Proposición dependiente. *Ver Clause.*

Descriptive writing/Escritura descriptiva. Tipo de escritura que ofrece detalles sensoriales para comunicar la impresión de un escenario, persona, animal, etcétera.

Desktop publishing/Edición por computadora. Uso de programas de computadora para formar un documento con texto escrito, gráficas y/o imágenes.

Dialect/Dialecto. Variedad de lenguaje hablado que usa un grupo particular. Un dialecto puede ser regional (de un lugar) o étnico (de un grupo cultural).

Dialogue/Diálogo. Conversación entre personajes en un escrito.

Diction/Dicción. Palabras que escoge un escritor y cómo las utiliza en frases, oraciones o versos.

Direct object/Complemento directo. *Ver Complement.*

Documentation/Documentación. Identificación de las fuentes que se emplean para escribir un artículo u otros textos informativos; generalmente se ponen como notas al pie, al final del texto o entre paréntesis.

Drafting/Borrador. Paso del proceso de escritura; transformación de ideas, palabras y frases a oraciones y párrafos.

E

Editing/Edición. Paso del proceso de escritura en que se revisa que el borrador corregido tenga un lenguaje estándar, una estructura sintáctica variada y la elección adecuada de palabras.

Editorial/Editorial. Artículo en un periódico u otro medio que expresa una opinión sobre un tema de interés general.

Elaboration/Elaboración. Sustento o desarrollo de una idea principal con hechos, estadísticas, detalles sensoriales, incidentes, anécdotas, ejemplos o citas.

Ellipsis/Puntos suspensivos. Signo de puntuación que consiste en dejar tres puntos para indicar que se están suprimiendo una o varias palabras.

E-mail/Correo electrónico. Mensajes, generalmente textos, que se envían por computadora.

Evaluating/Evaluación. Juicio sobre las fallas y aciertos de un borrador en cuanto a contenido, organización y estilo.

Evidence/Evidencia. Datos o ejemplos de fuentes confiables que sirven para sustentar afirmaciones escritas o habladas.

Exclamatory sentence/Oración exclamativa. Oración que expresa una emoción fuerte o repentina.

Explanatory writing/Texto explicativo. *Ver Descriptive text.*

Expository writing/Texto descriptivo. Tipo de escritura que informa o explica, como artículos periodísticos, instrucciones y artículos de investigación.

Expressive writing/Texto expresivo. Texto que realza y transmite los sentimientos del escritor.

F

Fact/Hecho. Información que puede comprobarse.

Feedback/Retroalimentación. Respuesta del escucha o lector al mensaje de un hablante o escritor.

Figurative language/Lenguaje figurado. Palabras usadas con un efecto descriptivo que expresa una verdad más allá del nivel literal. Los tropos, como el símil, la metáfora y la personificación, son ejemplos de lenguaje figurado.

Formal language/Lenguaje formal. Lenguaje que utiliza una gramática correcta y omite contracciones y expresiones coloquiales. Es común en textos de no ficción, que no son de carácter personal.

Fragment/Fragmento. Oración incompleta con puntuación de oración completa.

Freewriting/Escritura libre. Búsqueda de ideas escribiendo durante un tiempo determinado, sin detenerse ni limitar el flujo de ideas.

Future tense/Tiempo futuro. *Ver Verb tense.*

G–H

Generalization/Generalización. Afirmación que presenta una conclusión sobre un tema sin dar detalles específicos.

Genre/Género. Clasificación literaria o de otro medio. Los principales géneros literarios son la prosa, la poesía y el drama. Cada uno se divide en subgéneros.

Graphic organizer/Organizador gráfico. Manera visual de organizar la información, como las tablas, las gráficas, las redes y los árboles de ideas.

Home page/Página principal. Página por medio de la cual un usuario entra normalmente a un sitio de Web. Por lo general, explica el sitio, resume el contenido y proporciona vínculos con otros sitios.

Hyperlink/Hipervínculo. Oraciones o palabras sombreadas o subrayadas en una página en red que al activarse con un clic conectan con otra parte de la página o con otra página de la red.

Hypertext/Hipertexto. Vínculos en textos electrónicos que llevan a otro documento o a una sección distinta del mismo documento.

I-J

Ideas/Ideas. En composición, el mensaje o tema y los detalles que lo elaboran.

Idiom/Modismo. Palabra o frase cuyo significado es diferente del significado estándar o de diccionario. (*Se le pegaron las sábanas* es un modismo que significa "se levantó muy tarde").

Imagery/Imaginería. Lenguaje que describe impresiones sensoriales para que el lector de un texto literario pueda ver, oír, sentir, oler y gustar las escenas descritas.

Imperative sentence/Oración imperativa. Oración que exige u ordena algo.

Indefinite article/Artículo indefinido. *Ver Article.*

Independent clause/Proposición independiente. *Ver Clause.*

Inductive reasoning/Razonamiento inductivo. Pensamiento o explicación que parte de varios ejemplos para llegar a una afirmación general.

Informative writing/Texto informativo. Texto que explica un proceso o una idea. *Ver también Descriptive text.*

Intensifier/Intensificador. Adverbio que refuerza un adjetivo u otro adverbio (*very* important, *quite* easily; *muy* importante, *bastante* fácil).

Interjection/Interjección. Palabra o frase que expresa un sentimiento muy fuerte. La interjección no tiene relación gramatical con las demás palabras de la oración.

Internet/Internet. Red mundial computarizada que permite comunicarse electrónicamente con cualquier computadora de la red para buscar información social, comercial, de investigación y de otro tipo.

Interpretation/Interpretación. Explicación del significado de un texto, de una representación visual o de cualquier otro tipo de comunicación.

Interview/Entrevista. Diálogo a base de preguntas y respuestas cuyo propósito es obtener información actualizada o de expertos.

Introduction/Introducción. Sección inicial de un texto en la que el escritor identifica el tema y da la idea general de lo que contendrá el cuerpo del mismo.

Inverted order/Orden invertido. Colocación del predicado antes del sujeto. En la mayoría de las oraciones en inglés, el sujeto va antes del predicado.

Irregular verb/Verbo irregular. *Ver Verb tense.*

Jargon/Jerga. Palabras y frases que usa un determinado grupo.

Journal/Diario. Libreta personal en la que con toda libertad se anotan ideas, pensamientos y experiencias.

L

Learning log/Registro de aprendizaje. Diario para aclarar ideas sobre conceptos tratados en varias clases.

Listing/Lista. Técnica para generar ideas a partir de las cuales se escribe un texto.

Literary analysis/Análisis literario. Examen de las diferentes partes de una obra literaria a fin de evaluarla.

Logical fallacy/Falacia lógica. Error de razonamiento que se encuentra con frecuencia en publicidad o en escritos persuasivos, como razonamientos con dos alternativas opuestas o generalidades muy llamativas.

M

Main clause/Proposición principal. *Ver Clause.*

Main idea/Idea principal. *Ver Thesis statement.*

Main verb/Verbo principal. La palabra más importante de una frase verbal.

Media/Medios. Formas de comunicación usadas para llegar a un público. Los periódicos, la radio, la televisión y la Internet llegan a públicos muy grandes, por lo que se conocen como medios de comunicación masiva.

Memoir/Memoria. Tipo de narrativa de no ficción que presenta el relato de un hecho o período de la historia, resaltando la experiencia personal del narrador.

Metaphor/Metáfora. Tropo que compara dos cosas aparentemente distintas sin usar las palabra *like* o *as (como). (Él es una roca.)*

Mood/Atmósfera. Sentimiento o ambiente de un texto escrito.

Multimedia presentation/Presentación multimedia. Uso de una variedad de medios como video, sonido, texto escrito y artes visuales para presentar ideas e información.

N

Narrative writing/Narrativa. Tipo de escritura que narra sucesos o acciones que cambian con el paso del tiempo; por lo general tiene personajes, escenario y trama.

Nonfiction/No ficción. Texto en prosa acerca de personas, lugares y sucesos reales.

Noun/Nombre (o sustantivo). Palabra que nombra a una persona, lugar, cosa, o a una idea, cualidad o característica.

Number/Número. Forma del nombre, pronombre o verbo que indica si se refiere a uno (**singular**) o a más de uno (**plural**).

O

Object/Objeto. *Ver Complement.*

Onomatopoeia/Onomatopeya. Palabra o frase que imita o sugiere el sonido que describe (*rattle, boom;* en español: *pum, zas*).

Opinion/Opinión. Creencia o actitud; no puede comprobarse si es falsa o verdadera.

Oral tradition/Tradición oral. Literatura que se transmite de boca en boca de una generación a otra. Puede representar los valores culturales de un pueblo.

Order of importance/Orden de importancia. Forma de acomodar los detalles en un párrafo o en otro texto escrito según su importancia.

Organization/Organización. La disposición y el orden de los puntos principales y los detalles de apoyo en un escrito.

Outline/Esquema. Organización sistemática de ideas principales y secundarias con números romanos, letras y números arábigos para una presentación oral o escrita.

P

Paragraph/Párrafo. Una unidad de un texto que consta de oraciones relacionadas.

Parallelism/Paralelismo. Serie de palabras, frases y oraciones que tienen una forma gramatical similar.

Paraphrase/Parafrasear. Repetir las ideas de otro con palabras diferentes del original pero conservando las ideas, el tono y la longitud general.

Parenthetical documentation/Documentación parentética. Referencia específica a la fuente de la información que se pone entre paréntesis directamente después de ésta.

Peer response/Respuesta de compañeros. Sugerencias y comentarios que dan los compañeros de clase sobre un texto escrito u otro tipo de presentación.

Personal pronoun/Pronombre personal. *Ver Pronoun.*

Personal writing/Escritura personal. Texto que expresa los pensamientos y sentimientos del autor.

Personification/Personificación. Tropo que da cualidades humanas a un animal, objeto o idea.

Perspective/Perspectiva. *Ver Point of view.*

Persuasion/Persuasión. Tipo de escritura encaminado a convencer a pensar o actuar de cierta manera.

Phrase/Frase. Grupo de palabras que forma una unidad en una oración.
> **Prepositional phrase/Frase preposicional.** Comienza con una preposición y termina con un nombre o un pronombre.
> **Verb phrase/Frase verbal.** Consta de uno o más **verbos auxiliares** (*auxiliary verbs*) seguidos del verbo principal.

Plagiarism/Plagio. Presentación deshonesta de palabras o ideas ajenas como si fueran propias.

Plot/Trama. Serie de sucesos en secuencia en un cuento, novela u obra de teatro.

Plural/Plural. *Ver Number.*

Poetry/Poesía. Forma de expresión literaria compuesta por versos. La poesía tradicional contiene un lenguaje emotivo e imaginativo y un ritmo regular.

Point of view/Punto de vista. Ángulo o perspectiva desde el cual se cuenta una historia; por ejemplo, primera o tercera persona.

Portfolio/Portafolio. Colección de varias obras escritas de un estudiante, que puede tener obras terminadas y otras en proceso.

Predicate/Predicado. Verbo o frase verbal y sus modificadores que hacen una afirmación esencial sobre el sujeto de la oración.

Predicate adjective/Adjetivo predicativo. *Ver Adjective.*

Preposition/Preposición. Palabra que muestra la relación de un nombre o pronombre con otra palabra en la oración.

Prepositional phrase/Frase preposicional. *Ver Phrase.*

Presentation/Presentación. La forma en que se ven en una página las palabras y los elementos de diseño.

Presenting/Publishing Presentación/ Publicación. Ultimo paso del proceso de escritura que implica compartir con otros lo que se ha escrito.

Prewriting/Preescritura. Primer paso del proceso de escritura: decidir sobre qué se va a escribir, reunir ideas y detalles, y elaborar un plan para presentar las ideas; usa estrategias como lluvia de ideas, organizadores gráficos, notas y registros.

Prior knowledge/Conocimiento previo. Hechos, ideas y experiencias que un escritor, lector u observador lleva a una nueva actividad.

Progressive form/Durativo. *Ver Verb tense.*

Pronoun/Pronombre. Palabra que va en lugar del nombre; grupo de palabras que funcionan como un nombre u otro pronombre. La palabra o grupo de palabras a que se refiere un pronombre se llama **antecedente** (*antecedent*).

> **Personal pronoun/Pronombre personal.** Se refiere a una persona o cosa específica.

Pronoun case/Caso del pronombre. *Ver Case.*

Proofreading/Corrección de pruebas. Último paso del proceso editorial en que se revisa el texto en busca de errores tipográficos y de otra naturaleza.

Propaganda/Propaganda. Información encaminada a influir en los pensamientos o acciones; en general es de naturaleza política y puede distorsionar la verdad.

Proper adjective/Adjetivo propio*. *Ver Adjective.*

Prose/Prosa. Escritura similar al lenguaje cotidiano tanto oral como escrito, a diferencia de la poesía y el teatro.

Publishing/Publicación. Presentación de una obra escrita terminada mediante el uso de la tecnología, para darla a conocer a un público amplio.

Purpose/Finalidad. Objetivo de la escritura: expresar, descubrir, registrar, desarrollar o reflexionar sobre ideas, resolver problemas, entretener, influir, informar o describir.

R

Regular verb/Verbo regular. *Ver Verb tense.*

Representation/Representación. Forma en que se presenta información o ideas al público.

Research/Investigación. Proceso de localizar información sobre un tema.

Review/Reseña. Análisis e interpretación de un tema presentado por lo general a través de los medios de comunicación masiva.

Revising/Revisión. Paso del proceso de escritura en que el autor repasa el borrador, cambia el contenido, la organización y el estilo para mejorar el texto. Las técnicas de revisión son agregar, elaborar, eliminar, combinar y reacomodar el texto.

Root/Raíz. Parte de una palabra que contiene el significado principal.

Run-on sentence/Oración mal puntuada. Dos o más oraciones o proposiciones seguidas, cuyo significado es confuso debido a su inadecuada puntuación.

S

Sensory details/Detalles sensoriales. Lenguaje que apela a los sentidos; los detalles sensoriales son elementos importantes de la escritura descriptiva, sobre todo en la poesía.

Sentence/Oración. Grupo de palabras que expresa un pensamiento completo. Cada oración tiene **sujeto** (*subject*) y **predicado** (*predicate*). *Ver también Subject; Predicate; Clause.*

> **Simple sentence/Oración simple.** Consta de una proposición principal y no tiene proposiciones subordinadas.
>
> **Compound sentence/Oración compuesta.** Tiene dos o más proposiciones principales, cada una con su propio sujeto y predicado; por lo general van unidas por una coma y una conjunción coordinante, o por un punto y coma.
>
> **Complex sentence/Oración compleja.** Tiene una proposición principal y una o más proposiciones subordinadas.

Sentence fluency/Fluidez oracional. El ritmo suave y suelto de las oraciones que varían en longitud y estilo.

Sentence variety/Variedad de oraciones. Uso de diferentes tipos de oraciones para agregar interés al texto.

Setting/Escenario. Tiempo y lugar en que ocurren los sucesos de un cuento, novela u obra de teatro.

Simile/Símil. Tropo que compara dos cosas esencialmente distintas, usando las palabras *like* o *as* (*como*). (*Su pelo era como hilo de seda.*)

Simple predicate/Predicado simple. *Ver Predicate; Sentence; Subject.*

Simple sentence/Oración simple. *Ver Sentence.*

Spatial order/Orden espacial. Forma de presentar los detalles de un escenario según su ubicación: de izquierda a derecha o de arriba hacia abajo.

Standard English/Inglés estándar. La forma más ampliamente usada y aceptada del idioma inglés.

Style/Estilo. Forma en que un escritor elige y organiza las palabras y oraciones.

Subject/Sujeto. Nombre o pronombre principal que informa sobre quién o sobre qué trata la oración.

Subordinate clause/Proposición subordinada. *Ver Clause.*

Summary/Resumen. Breve explicación de la idea principal de una composición.

Supporting evidence/Sustento. *Ver Evidence.*

Suspense/Suspenso. Recurso literario que genera interés y emoción para llegar al clímax o desenlace de una historia. Un escritor crea suspenso al proporcionar pistas sobre el desenlace pero sin revelar demasiada información.

Symbol/Símbolo. Objeto, persona, lugar o experiencia que representa algo más, por lo general, abstracto.

T

Tense/Tiempo. *Ver Verb tense.*

Theme/Tema. Idea o mensaje principal de una obra escrita.

Thesis statement/Exposición de tesis. Exposición de la **idea principal** o finalidad de una obra en una o dos oraciones.

Time order/Orden temporal. Organización de detalles en un texto escrito según el momento en que ocurrieron.

Tone/Tono. Reflejo de la actitud del escritor o hablante hacia un sujeto.

Topic sentence/Oración temática. Oración que expresa la idea principal de un párrafo.

Transition/Transición. Palabra o frase de enlace que aclara las relaciones entre los detalles, oraciones o párrafos.

U–V

Unity/Unidad. Integridad de un párrafo o composición; coherencia entre todas las oraciones o párrafos para expresar o sustentar una idea principal.

URL/URL. Forma estándar de una dirección de Internet. (Son iniciales de *Uniform Resource Locator*.)

Venn diagram/Diagrama de Venn. Organizador gráfico que consta de dos círculos que se traslapan, usado para comparar dos cosas con características comunes y diferentes.

Verb/Verbo. Palabra que expresa acción o estado y que es necesaria para hacer una afirmación.

Verb phrase/Frase verbal. *Ver Phrase.*

Verb tense/Tiempo verbal. El tiempo de un verbo indica cuándo ocurre la acción.

> **Present tense/Presente.** Indica una acción que sucede regularmente.
>
> **Past tense/Pasado.** Indica una acción que ya sucedió.
>
> **Future tense/Futuro.** Indica una acción que va a suceder.
>
> En inglés todos los tiempos verbales están formados por las cuatro partes principales del verbo: **base derivativa** (*base form*) (*freeze, congelar*), **participio presente** (*present participle*) (*freezing, congelando*), **pretérito simple** (*simple past form*) (*froze, congeló*) y **participio pasado** (*past participle*) (*frozen, congelado*).
>
> Un **verbo regular** (*regular verb*) forma su pretérito simple y su participio pasado agregando la terminación *ed* al infinitivo. Los verbos que forman su pretérito y participio pasado de otra forma se llaman **verbos irregulares** (*irregular verbs*).
>
> Además de los tiempos presente, pasado y futuro hay tres tiempos perfectos: **presente perfecto** (*present perfect*), **pretérito perfecto** (*past perfect*) y **futuro perfecto** (*future perfect*).
>
> Cada uno de los seis tiempos tiene una forma **durativa** (*progressive form*) que expresa acción continua.

Voice/Voz. La forma única que tiene un escritor o escritora de usar el tono y el estilo para comunicarse con los lectores.

W

Web site/Sitio Web. Sitio de World Wide Web que puede ser alcanzado mediante vínculos o una dirección Web o URL. *Ver también URL; World Wide Web.*

Word choice/Léxico. El vocabulario que selecciona una escritora o escritor para presentar un significado.

Word processing/Procesador de palabras. Programa de computadora para escribir y editar un texto.

World Wide Web/World Wide Web. Sistema global que usa Internet y permite a los usuarios crear, vincularse y entrar a campos de información. *Ver también Internet.*

Writing process/Proceso de escritura. Serie de pasos o etapas por los que atraviesa un escritor para desarrollar sus ideas y comunicarlas.

---

*Este término o explicación solamente se aplica a la gramática inglesa.

*W*hat are the basic tools for building strong sentences, paragraphs, compositions, and research papers? You'll find them in this handbook—an easy-to-use "tool kit" for writers like you. Check out the helpful explanations, examples, and tips as you complete your writing assignments.

Writing Good Sentences

A sentence is a group of words that expresses a complete thought. Every sentence has a subject and a predicate.

Using Various Types of Sentences

How you craft a sentence—as a statement, question, command, or exclamation—depends on the job you want the sentence to do.

Type	Job It Does	Ways to Use It
Declarative	Makes a statement	Report information *October is National Pizza Month.*
Interrogative	Asks a question	Make your readers curious *Why is pizza so popular?*
Imperative	Gives a command or makes a request	Tell how to do something *Spread the toppings on the pizza dough.*
Exclamatory	Expresses strong feeling	Emphasize a surprising fact *Every second, Americans eat about 350 slices of pizza!*

Varying Sentence Structure and Length

Many sentences in a row that look and sound alike can be boring. Vary your sentence openers to make your writing interesting.

- **Start a sentence with an adjective or an adverb.**
  Suddenly the sky turned dark.

- **Start a sentence with a phrase.**
  Like a fireworks show, lightning streaked across the sky.

- **Start a sentence with a clause.**
  As the thunderstorm began, people ran for cover.

Many short sentences in a row make writing sound choppy and dull. To make your writing sound pleasing, vary the sentence length.

- **Combine short sentences into longer ones.**

   Tornadoes are also called twisters. They are spinning clouds. The clouds are funnel shaped.

   Tornadoes, also called twisters, are spinning funnel-shaped clouds.

- **Alternate shorter sentences with longer sentences.**

   Tornado winds are powerful. They can hurl cows into the air, tear trees from their roots, and turn cars upside down.

Using Parallelism

Parallelism is the use of a pair or a series of words, phrases, or sentences that have the same grammatical structure. Use parallelism to call attention to the items in the series and to create unity in writing.

Not Parallel Gymnasts are strong, flexible, and move gracefully.
Parallel Gymnasts are strong, flexible, and graceful.

Not Parallel Do warm-up exercises to prevent sports injuries and for stretching your muscles.
Parallel Do warm-up exercises to prevent sports injuries and to stretch your muscles.

Not Parallel Stand on one leg, bend the other leg, and you should pull your heel.
Parallel Stand on one leg, bend the other leg, and pull your heel.

Revising Wordy Sentences

Revise wordy sentences to make every word count.

- **Cut needless words.**

   Wordy We need to have bike lanes in streets due to the fact that people like to ride their bikes to work and school, and it's not safe otherwise.
   Concise We need bike lanes in streets so that people can safely ride to work and school.

- **Rewrite sentences opening with the word *there*.**

   Wordy There are many kids riding their bikes in the street.
   Concise Many kids ride their bikes in the street.

- **Change verbs in passive voice to active voice.**

   Wordy Bikes are also ridden by grown-ups who want to keep fit.
   Concise Grown-ups who want to keep fit also ride bikes.

✓ **Check It Out**

For more about how to vary sentence length and structure, review Unit 20, Sentence Combining, pages 516–523.

TRY IT OUT

Write four sentences, one of each type—declarative, interrogative, imperative, and exclamatory—about food, sports, or another topic that interests you.

Writing Good Paragraphs

A paragraph is a group of sentences that relate to one main idea. A good paragraph develops a single idea and brings that idea into sharp focus. All the sentences flow smoothly from the beginning to the end of the paragraph.

Writing Unified Paragraphs

A paragraph has **unity** when the sentences belong together and center on a single main idea. One way to build a unified paragraph is to state the main idea in a topic sentence and then add related details.

Writing Topic Sentences A **topic sentence** gives your readers the "big picture"—a clear view of the most important idea you want them to know. Many effective expository paragraphs (paragraphs that convey information) start with a topic sentence that tells the key point right away.

Elaborating Topic Sentences Elaboration gives your readers a specific, more detailed picture of the main idea stated in your topic sentence. Elaboration is a technique you can use to include details that develop, support, or explain the main idea. The following chart shows various kinds of elaboration you might try.

Revising Tip

To make a paragraph unified, leave out details that do not relate to the topic sentence.

Topic Sentence: The state of Florida is known for its alligators.	
Descriptions	Alligators look like dinosaurs from millions of years ago.
Facts and statistics	Alligators can weigh as much as six hundred pounds.
Examples	Alligators eat a wide variety of foods, such as fish, insects, turtles, frogs, and small mammals.
Anecdotes	Silvia almost fainted when she came home to find an alligator paddling around in her swimming pool.
Reasons	Face-to-face encounters with alligators are now common because people have built golf courses over the animals' habitat.

Writing & Research Handbook

Writing Coherent Paragraphs

A paragraph has **coherence** when all the sentences flow smoothly and logically from one to the next. All the sentences in a paragraph *cohere*, or "stick together," in a way that makes sense. To be sure your writing is coherent, choose a pattern of organization that fits your topic and use transition words and phrases to link ideas.

Organizing Paragraphs A few basic patterns of organization are listed below. Choose the pattern that helps you meet your specific writing goal.

- Use **chronological order,** or time order, to tell a story or to explain the steps in a process.
- Use **spatial order** to order your description of places, people, and things. You might describe the details in the order you see them—for example, from top to bottom or from near to far.
- Use **order of importance** to show how you rank opinions, facts, or details from the most to least important or the reverse.

Using Transitions Linking words and phrases, called **transitions,** act like bridges between sentences or between paragraphs. Transitions, such as the ones shown below, can make the organization of your paragraphs stronger by showing how ideas are logically related.

To show time order or sequence
after, at the beginning, before, finally, first, last year, later, meanwhile, next, now, second, sometimes, soon, yesterday

To show spatial relationships
above, ahead, around, at the top, below, beyond, down, here, inside, near, on top of, opposite, outside, over, there, under, within

To show importance or degree
above all, first, furthermore, in addition, mainly, most important, second

✓ **Check It Out**
For more about transitions, see page 120.

TRY IT OUT

Copy the following paragraph on your paper. Underline the topic sentence. Cross out the sentence that is unrelated to the topic sentence. Add a transition to make a clear connection between two of the sentences.

A local artist creates weird and funny sculptures from fruits and vegetables. First he uses a sharp knife to carve faces that look like animals, such as bears and pigs. He glues on tiny beans to make eyes. Finally he uses beet juice to paint the mouth. Although the process sounds easy, it requires great imagination. The octopus sculpted from a banana is the silliest work of art I've ever seen.

Writing Good Compositions

A composition is a short paper made up of several paragraphs, with a clear introduction, body, and conclusion. A good composition presents a clear, complete message about a specific topic. Ideas flow logically from one sentence to the next and from one paragraph to the next.

Making a Plan

The suggestions in the chart below can help you shape the information in each part of your composition to suit your writing purpose.

Introductory Paragraph

Your introduction should interest readers in your topic and capture their attention. You may

- give background
- use a quotation
- ask a question
- tell an anecdote, or brief story

Include a **thesis statement,** a sentence or two stating the main idea you will develop in the composition.

Body Paragraphs

Elaborate on your thesis statement in the body paragraphs. You may

- offer proof
- give examples
- explain ideas

Stay focused and keep your body paragraphs on track. Remember to

- develop a single idea in each body paragraph
- arrange the paragraphs in a logical order
- use transitions to link one paragraph to the next

Concluding Paragraph

Your conclusion should bring your composition to a satisfying close. You may

- sum up main points
- tie the ending to the beginning by restating the main idea or thesis in different words
- make a call to action if your goal is to persuade readers

Drafting Tip

Sometimes you'll need two paragraphs to introduce your topic. For example, the first paragraph can tell an anecdote; the second can include your thesis statement.

Drafting Tip

A good conclusion follows logically from the rest of the piece of writing and leaves the reader with something to think about. Make sure that you do not introduce new or unrelated material in a conclusion.

Using the 6+1 Trait® Model

What are some basic terms you can use to discuss your writing with your teacher or classmates? What should you focus on as you revise and edit your compositions? Check out the following seven terms, or traits, that describe the qualities of strong writing. Learn the meaning of each trait and find out how using the traits can improve your writing.

Ideas The message or the theme and the details that develop it

Writing is clear when readers can grasp the meaning of your ideas right away. Check to see whether you're getting your message across.

✔ Does the title suggest the theme of the composition?

✔ Does the composition focus on a single narrow topic?

✔ Is the thesis, or main idea, clearly stated?

✔ Do well-chosen details elaborate the main idea?

Organization The arrangement of main points and supporting details

A good plan of organization steers your readers in the right direction and guides them easily through your composition—from start to finish. Find a structure, or order, that best suits your topic and writing purpose. Check to see whether you've ordered your key ideas and details in a way that keeps your readers on track.

✔ Are the beginning, middle, and end clearly linked?

✔ Is the order of ideas easy to follow?

✔ Does the introduction capture your readers' attention?

✔ Do sentences and paragraphs flow from one to the next in a way that makes sense?

✔ Does the conclusion wrap up the composition?

Voice A writer's unique way of using tone and style

Your writing voice comes through when your readers sense that a real person is communicating with them. Readers will respond to the **tone,** or the attitude, that you express toward a topic and to the **style,** the way that you use language and write sentences. Read your work aloud to see whether your writing voice comes through.

✔ Does your writing sound interesting when you read it aloud?

✔ Does your writing show what you think about your topic?

✔ Does your writing sound like you—or does it sound like you're imitating someone else?

Revising Tip

Use the cut-and-paste features of your word processing program to experiment with the structure—the arrangement of sentences or paragraphs. Choose the clearest, most logical order for your final draft.

6+1 Trait® is a registered trademark of Northwest Regional Educational Laboratory, which does not endorse this product.

Word Choice The vocabulary a writer uses to convey meaning

Words work hard. They carry the weight of your meaning, so make sure you choose them carefully. Check to see whether the words you choose are doing their jobs well.

- ✔ Do you use lively verbs to show action?
- ✔ Do you use vivid words to create word pictures in your readers' minds?
- ✔ Do you use precise words to explain your ideas simply and clearly?

Sentence Fluency The smooth rhythm and flow of sentences that vary in length and style

The best writing is made up of sentences that flow smoothly from one sentence to the next. Writing that is graceful also sounds musical—rhythmical rather than choppy. Check for sentence fluency by reading your writing aloud.

- ✔ Do your sentences vary in length and structure?
- ✔ Do transition words and phrases show connections between ideas and sentences?
- ✔ Does parallelism help balance and unify related ideas?

Conventions Correct spelling, grammar, usage, and mechanics

A composition free of errors makes a good impression on your readers. Mistakes can be distracting, and they can blur your message. Try working with a partner to spot errors and correct them. Use this checklist to help you.

- ✔ Are all words spelled correctly?
- ✔ Are all proper nouns—as well as the first word of every sentence—capitalized?
- ✔ Is your composition free of sentence fragments?
- ✔ Is your composition free of run-on sentences?
- ✔ Are punctuation marks—such as apostrophes, commas, and end marks—inserted in the right places?

Presentation The way words and design elements look on a page

Appearance matters, so make your compositions inviting to read. Handwritten papers should be neat and legible. If you're using a word processor, double-space the lines of text and choose a readable font. Other design elements—such as boldfaced headings, bulleted lists, pictures, and charts—can help you present information effectively as well as make your papers look good.

Revising Tip

Listen carefully to the way your sentences sound when someone else reads them aloud. If you don't like what you hear, revise for sentence fluency. You might try adding variety to your sentence openers or combining sentences to make them sound less choppy.

✔ Check It Out

See the Troubleshooter, pages 248–267, for help in correcting common errors in your writing.

Writing & Research Handbook

Evaluating a Composition Read this sample composition, which has been evaluated using the 6+1 Trait® model.

Ideas The introduction hooks readers by connecting to their experience. It includes a thesis statement, which is developed in the following paragraphs with an example.

Organization The body paragraphs are arranged in order of importance.

Sentence Fluency A variety of sentence types helps the writing flow smoothly.

Organization Transitions effectively link ideas within and between paragraphs. Ideas flow naturally from one to the next.

Word Choice Nouns and verbs are strong and precise.

Voice The personal voice reveals something about the writer's personality.

Conventions The composition is free of errors in grammar, spelling, usage, and mechanics.

Joining the Team

It's not always easy to take a risk and try something new. It's much easier to play it safe and to keep doing the same things you always do. But sometimes having just a little curiosity about something is all you need to make a decision that can change your life for the better.

Last fall I made such a decision, and I haven't regretted it for a moment. I decided to join the school track team, even though I've never competed in any sport before. I like to run with my dog in the park, and I wondered what it would be like to run as part of a team. So how do I know I made the right decision? I made a list of three questions—from the least important to the most important—to help me think through my decision. Did becoming a member of the track team give me a sense of pride? Did I improve my physical fitness? Did I find running competitively enjoyable? Here's what I discovered as I answered these questions.

First, I feel proud of what I have contributed to the team. I haven't finished first or second or even third in a race yet. But I like and admire my teammates, and cheering them on at track meets makes them feel good. And that makes me feel good about myself too.

Second, joining the track team has made me more physically fit. I used to hate running laps and doing crunches. After a while, though, I started to see the results of doing my exercises, and now I don't mind. My strength and endurance have increased, and my time is improving in every event. Better physical fitness is giving me more energy for other activities, such as babysitting for my little brother.

Above all, I know I made a wise decision to join the track team because I enjoy running more than I ever imagined I could. I've discovered that I have a competitive streak in me. I want to win, and I know I can win if I keep practicing. My dog definitely appreciates the fact that I can keep up with him now, and we run together in the park nearly every day. That's fun for both of us!

All kinds of benefits can come with trying something new. So if there's something you're curious about—learning to cook like a gourmet, performing in a school play, or raising money for charity, for example—I strongly recommend that you give it a try!

Writing Good Research Papers

A research paper reports facts and ideas gathered from various sources about a specific topic. A good research paper blends information from reliable sources with the writer's original thoughts and ideas. The final draft follows a standard format for presenting information and citing sources.

Exploring a Variety of Sources

Once you've narrowed the topic of your research paper, you'll need to hunt for the best information. You might start by reading an encyclopedia article on your topic to learn some basic information. Then widen your search to include both primary and secondary sources.

- **Primary sources** are records of events by the people who witnessed them. Examples include diaries, letters, speeches, photos, posters, interviews, and radio and TV news broadcasts that include eyewitness interviews.
- **Secondary sources** contain information that is often based on primary sources. The creators of secondary sources conduct original research and then report their findings. Examples include encyclopedias, textbooks, biographies, magazine articles, Web site articles, and educational films.

When you find a secondary source that you can use for your report, check to see whether the author has given credit to his or her sources of information in **footnotes, endnotes,** or a **bibliography.** Tracking down such sources can lead you to more information you can use.

If you're exploring your topic on the Internet, look for Web sites that are sponsored by government institutions, famous museums, and reliable organizations. If you find a helpful site, check to see whether it contains links to other Web sites you can use.

Evaluating Sources

As you conduct your research, do a little detective work and investigate the sources you find. Begin by asking some key questions so you can decide whether you've tracked down reliable resources that are suitable for your purpose. Some important questions to ask about your sources are listed in the box on the next page.

> **Research Tip**
>
> Look for footnotes at the bottom of a page. Look for endnotes at the end of a chapter or a book. Look for a bibliography at the end of a book.

Ask Questions About Your Sources

✔ **Is the information useful?**
Find sources that are closely related to your research topic.

✔ **Is the information easy to understand?**
Look for sources that are geared toward readers your age.

✔ **Is the information new enough?**
Look for sources that were recently published if you need the most current facts and figures.

✔ **Is the information trustworthy and true?**
Check to see whether the author documents the source of facts and supports opinions with reasons and evidence. Also check out the background of the authors. They should be well-known experts on the topic that you're researching.

✔ **Is the information balanced and fair?**
Read with a critical eye. Does the source try to persuade readers with a one-sided presentation of information? Or is the source balanced, approaching a topic from various perspectives? Be on the lookout for **propaganda** and for sources that reflect an author's **bias,** or prejudice. Make sure that you learn about a topic from more than one angle by reviewing several sources of information.

Giving Credit Where Credit Is Due

When you write a research paper, you support your own ideas with information that you've gleaned from your primary and secondary sources. But presenting someone else's ideas as if they were your own is **plagiarism,** a form of cheating. You can avoid plagiarism by citing, or identifying, the sources of your information within the text of your paper. The chart below tells what kinds of information you do and don't need to cite in your paper.

DO credit the source of . . .	DON'T credit the source of . . .
• direct quotations	• information that can be found in many places—dates, facts, ideas, and concepts that are considered common knowledge
• summaries and paraphrases, or restatements, of someone else's viewpoints, original ideas, and conclusions	
• photos, art, charts, and other visuals	• your own unique ideas
• little-known facts or statistics	

Citing Sources Within Your Paper The most common method of crediting sources is with parenthetical documentation within the text. Generally a reference to the source and page number is included in parentheses at the end of each quotation, paraphrase, or summary of information borrowed from a source. An in-text citation points readers to a corresponding entry in your **works-cited list**—a list of all your sources, complete with publication information, that will appear as the final page of your paper. The Modern Language Association (MLA) recommends the following guidelines for crediting sources in text.

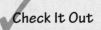
Check It Out

To see the relationship between parenthetical documentation and a works-cited list, study the sample research paper on pages 689–690.

- **Put in parentheses the author's last name and the page number where you found the information.**

  Sundiata would later be known by such titles as "Lord Lion," "Lion of Mali," and "Father of the Bright Country" (Koslow 12).

- **If the author's name is mentioned in the sentence, put only the page number in parentheses.**

  According to Philip Koslow, Sundiata would be known by such titles as "Lord Lion," "Lion of Mali," and "Father of the Bright Country" (12).

- **If no author is listed, put the title or a shortened version of the title in parentheses. Include a page number if you have one.**

  The facts of his life as a king are known, but many details about his early life are uncertain ("Sundiata").

Preparing the Final Draft

Ask your teacher how to format the final draft. Most English teachers will ask you to follow the MLA guidelines listed below.

- Put a heading in the upper left-hand corner of the first page with your name, your teacher's name, and the date on separate lines.
- Center the title on the line below the heading.
- Number the pages one-half inch from the top in the right-hand corner. After page one, put your last name before the page number.
- Set one-inch margins on all sides of every page; double-space the lines of text.
- Include an alphabetized, double-spaced works-cited list as the last page of your final draft. All sources noted in parenthetical citations in the paper must be listed.

On the next page, you'll find examples of how the sources you use for your research paper should be written and punctuated in a works-cited list, the final page of your paper.

MLA Style

MLA style is most often used in English and social studies classes. Center the title *Works Cited* at the top of your list.

Source	Style
Book with one author	Price-Groff, Claire. *The Manatee*. Farmington Hills: Lucent, 1999.
Book with two or three authors	Tennant, Alan, Gerard T. Salmon, and Richard B. King. *Snakes of North America*. Lanham: Lone Star Books, 2003. [If a book has more than three authors, name only the first author and then write "et al." (Latin abbreviation for "and others").]
Book with an editor	Follett, C. B., ed. *Grrrrr: A Collection of Poems About Bears*. Sausalito: Arctos, 2000.
Book with organization or group as author or editor	National Air and Space Museum. *The Official Guide to the Smithsonian Air and Space Museum*. Washington: Smithsonian Institution Press, 2002.
Work from an anthology	Soto, Gary. "To Be a Man." *Hispanic American Literature: An Anthology*. Ed. Rodolfo Cortina. Lincolnwood: NTC, 1998. 340–341.
Introduction in a published book	Weintraub, Stanley. Introduction. *Great Expectations*. By Charles Dickens. New York: Signet, 1998. v–xii.
Encyclopedia article	"Whales." *World Book Encyclopedia*. 2003.
Weekly magazine article	Trillin, Calvin. "Newshound." *New Yorker* 29 Sept. 2003: 70–81.
Monthly magazine article	Knott, Cheryl. "Code Red." *National Geographic* Oct. 2003: 76–81.
Online magazine article	Rauch, Jonathan. "Will Frankenfood Save the Planet?" *Atlantic Online* 292.3 (Oct. 2003). 15 Dec. 2003 <http://www.theatlantic.com/issues/2003/10/rauch.htm>.
Newspaper article	Bertram, Jeffrey. "African Bees: Fact or Myth?" *Orlando Sentinel* 18 Aug. 1999: D2.
Unsigned article	"Party-Line Snoops." *Washington Post* 24 Sept. 2003: A28.
Internet	"Manatees." *SeaWorld/Busch Gardens Animal Information Database*. 2002. Busch Entertainment Corp. 3 Oct. 2003 <http://www.seaworld.org/infobooks/Manatee/home.html>.
Radio or TV program	"Orcas." *Champions of the Wild*. Animal Planet. Discovery Channel. 21 Oct. 2003.
Videotape or DVD	*Living with Tigers*. DVD. Discovery, 2003. [For a videotape (VHS) version, replace "DVD" with "Videocassette."]
Interview	Salinas, Antonia. E-mail interview. 23–24 Oct. 2003. [If an interview takes place in person, replace "E-mail" with "Personal"; if it takes place on the telephone, use "Telephone."]

Evaluating a Research Paper Read this sample research paper, which has been evaluated using the 6+1 Trait® model.

The Early Life of King Sundiata of Mali

In the beginning of the thirteenth century, a boy named Sundiata Keita was born near the kingdom of Kangaba, a region of West Africa. Sundiata was no ordinary boy. In fact, he grew up to become the founder and first king of the West African empire of Mali. The facts of his life as a king are known, but many details about his early life are uncertain ("Sundiata"). To find out more about Sundiata as a boy, historians have had to play the role of detectives searching for clues.

Some historians have had to get their information about Africa's past from storytellers, called *griots*. Griots are like living history books, because they tell stories about things that happened a long time ago. These stories are passed down from generation to generation. In the 1960s, West African historian D. T. Niana wrote down Sundiata's story. This story was told to him by Djeli Mamoudou Kouyata, a griot from the nation of Guinea (Koslow 12). Kouyata's version of Sundiata's life as a child may be based on fact, but no one knows for sure if the events he described really happened.

Kouyata said that Sundiata's father was named Maghan Kon Fatta and his mother was named Sogolon. Maghan Kon Fatta was king of the Mandingo people, who lived in and near present-day Mali. Sogolon was one of his many wives. When Sundiata was born, a prediction was made that he would rise to greatness someday. However, many obstacles stood in his way.

Sundiata faced one of his biggest challenges when he was a young child. He had been born with a disability. He crawled around like a baby until he was seven years old (McKissack and McKissack 49). People teased him and called him names, but Sundiata showed incredible courage. One day Sundiata announced to his mother that he was going to walk. According to the griot Kouyata's story, "Sundiata then told a blacksmith to make him the heaviest possible iron rod, and then, with trembling legs and a sweaty brow, he proceeded to lift himself up, bending the rod into a bow in the process" ("Mali," Part I, 3). People were amazed that Sundiata had accomplished such an incredible feat.

However, Sundiata's troubles were not over. Kouyata tells that Sundiata and his mother were in danger after Maghan Kon Fatta died. Sundiata's half-brother had become the king of Kangaba, and he thought that Sundiata would be a threat to him. To escape certain death, Sundiata and his mother went into exile. *(continued)*

Ideas The title suggests the paper's theme. The central idea is clearly expressed in the introduction.

Word Choice Special terms are defined. Carefully chosen words show that the truth of the story is not certain.

Sentence Fluency A variety of sentence lengths and structures helps the writing flow smoothly.

Ideas Parenthetical citations (using MLA style) give credit to the source of ideas.

Conventions Writing is free of errors in spelling, grammar, usage, and mechanics.

Organization Information is organized in chronological order.

The story goes that over the next few years, Sundiata grew stronger and wiser. He became an excellent hunter and warrior. By the time he was fifteen years old, Sundiata had fought his first major battle. His heroism and leadership in battle caught the attention of Mansa Tankura, king of Mema. When Sundiata was eighteen years old, he became an adviser to this king. Kouyata describes the teenage Sundiata this way: "He was a tall young man with a fat neck and a powerful chest. Nobody could bend his bow. Everyone bowed before him and he was greatly loved" (Koslow 14).

Organization The conclusion sums up the information and ties the ending to the beginning.

Voice The writer sounds curious and fascinated about the topic.

Sundiata would grow up to be the founder and first king of the empire of Mali. He would be known by such titles as "Lord Lion," "Lion of Mali," and "Father of the Bright Country" (Koslow 12). These are facts about Sundiata's adult life. However, the legends about his early life are more interesting than the facts. As a young boy, did Sundiata really overcome a disability and miraculously learn to walk? As a teenager, did Sundiata really become a military hero and a royal adviser? The answers to these questions remain a mystery.

Presentation Like every good research paper, this one ends with a properly formatted list of works cited. There's an entry for every work used as a source of information. Remember to put your works-cited list on a separate sheet of paper.

Works Cited

Koslow, Philip. *Mali: Crossroads of Africa*. New York: Chelsea, 1995.

"Mali: Africa's Empire of Empires." *Kennedy Center African Odyssey Interactive*. John F. Kennedy Center for the Performing Arts. 2 Nov. 2000 <http://artsed.kennedycenter.org/aoi/events/theater/empire.html>.

McKissack, Patricia, and Fredrick McKissack. *The Royal Kingdoms of Ghana, Mali, and Songhay*. New York: Holt, 1994.

"Sundiata Keita." *Encyclopedia of World Biography*. Detroit: Gale Research, 1998.

INDEX

Compound subjects, 305, 306, 307, 443
  diagraming, 471
  subject pronoun in, 363
  and subject-verb agreement, 443
Compound words, 501
Computer catalog, 532–533
Computers, 645–657
  CD-ROM, 656
  diskettes, 656–657
  DVD, 656
  e-mail, 654–655
  history, 645
  hyperlinks, 649
  for multimedia presentations, 292
  removable storage, 657
Conceptual map, 659
Conclusion of narrative, 162, 659
Conflict, 659
Conjunctions
  in compound sentences, 305
  coordinating, 425, 659
  correlative, 425, 659
  definition of, 425, 659
  Troubleshooter for, 253
Connotation, 660
Constructive criticism, 660
Context clues, 544–545, 660
Contexts for writing. *See* Writing prompts
Contractions, apostrophes in, 501
  distinguished from possessive pronouns, 501
  double negatives and, 403
Conventions, 34, 133, 660, 683–684, 690
Cooperative Learning, 49, 61, 65, 69, 73, 109, 117, 121, 151, 163, 167, 193, 205, 233
Coordinating conjunctions, 425, 659
Correlative conjunctions, 425, 659
Creative writing, 11, 22, 23, 49, 57, 73, 78–81, 159, 167, 221
Credibility, 635–636, 660
Critical listening, 617–620
Critical thinking

drawing conclusions, 178, 214, 246
evaluating characters, 87
interpreting, 140
making inferences, 34
Cross-curricular writing
  in architecture, 23
  in art, 57, 65, 141
  in geography, 11, 117, 247
  in history, 189, 215
  in mathematics, 35, 197
  in music, 155
  in science 88, 113
  in social studies, 53, 179
Cryptograms, 564

D

Dates
  capitalizing of, 479
  commas in, 495
  numbers in, 505
Declarative sentences, 297, 489, 660
  diagraming, 466
Deductive reasoning, 660
Definite article, 658
Definition
  as context clue, 544
  in dictionary, 539
Demonstrative adjectives, 381, 658
Demonstrative pronouns, 381
Denotation, 660
Dependent clause, 659
Descriptive writing, 100–141
  describing place in, 122–125
  details in, 110–113, 117
  drafting, 104, 108, 112, 119, 124, 131, 132
  editing, 116, 120, 123, 128, 133
  exploring places in, 126–129
  focusing on details in, 114–117
  literature models in, 106, 107, 110, 114, 118, 124, 126, 134–139
  note taking for, 109, 110–113
  ordering details in, 118–121
  organization in, 119
  presenting, 124, 133

prewriting, 103, 105, 131
revising, 112, 132
transitions in, 120, 121
uses of, 108
word choice in, 106–109
Desert, dessert, 566
Desktop publishing, 660
Details
  checking, in editing, 70–73
  choosing, 56, 116, 153
  in descriptive writing, 102–103, 110–121, 123, 127
  listening for, 617–618
  in narrative writing, 153
  order of importance, 52, 118, 153
  organizing, 50, 52, 153
  in personal writing, 25
Dewey decimal system, 530–531, 532
Diagraming sentences, 465–471
  adjectives, 468
  adverbs, 468
  direct objects, 467
  indirect objects, 467
  predicate adjectives, 469
  predicate nouns, 469
  predicates, compound, 471
  predicates, simple, 465
  prepositional phrases, 470
  sentences, compound, 471
  sentences, four kinds of, 466
  subjects, compound, 471
  subjects, simple, 465
Dialect, 660
Dialogue, in narrative, 660
  punctuating, 473
  writing, 156–159
Diction, 660
Dictionary, 536
  definition in, 539
  entry word in, 539
  guide words, 537
  organization of entry, 537, 539–540
  illustrations in, 537
  parts of speech labels, 540
  pronunciation key, 537, 540
  sample entry, 537, 540
  synonyms, 540
  types of, 536
  usage information in, 540

L

Languages, capitalizing
  names of, 479
Lay, lie, 457
Learn, teach, 457
Learning log, 662
Leave, let, 457
Legibility, 75, 247
Letter writing, 99
  business, 497
  capitalization in, 473
  commas in, 493
  friendly, 16–19, 224
Library
  card catalog, 528, 533
  computer catalog, 528,
    532–533
  finding books in, 533
  obtaining information at,
    198–199, 239, 527
  organization of books in,
    530–531
  references in, 534–535
  sections in, 527–529
Lie, lay, 457
Line graphs, 580
Linking verbs, 337
  as action verbs, 337
  defined, 337
  list of, 337
  and predicate adjective, 337
Listening
  analyzing persuasive tech-
    niques and propaganda,
    619–620
  evaluating commercials, 619
  following instructions, 617
  organizing spoken ideas, 618
  to persuasive speech, 618
  purpose for, 618
  taking notes, 618
  See also Speaking
Listening and speaking, 11, 19,
    45, 49, 61, 73, 109, 113, 121,
    129, 151, 155, 159, 163, 167,
    193, 197, 201, 205, 225, 233
Listing, 47, 49, 53, 61, 71, 107,
    109, 111, 121, 127, 151,
    187, 191, 203, 215, 662
Lists
  colons to introduce, 497
  commas with, 491

Literary analysis, 662
Literature. For a complete list-
  ing of the literature in the
  book, *see* p. xxv
Literature, responding to, 34,
    87, 140, 178, 214, 246
  See also Writing about
    literature
Logical fallacy, 662

M

Magazine writing, 90–99
Main clause, 659
Main idea and supporting
    details
  organization of, 50–53
  in paragraphs, 62–65
Main verbs, 341, 662
Maps, 127
  keys for, 582
  scales for, 582
Mass media, 629–634
Matching tests, 586–587
Measure, abbreviations for
    units of, 503
Mechanics. *See* Capitalization;
    Punctuation
Media, 662
  critical listening, 222–223
Media messages, 635–643
  analyzing, 635
  producing, 640
Memoir, 662
Memory
  devices, using, to learn prob-
    lem words, 567
Memos, 274–277
  format, 277
  model, 274, 276
  parts, 276, 277
  purpose, 275
  style, 276
  tone, 274, 275
  types, 275
  word processing template,
    276
Metaphor, 662
Misreading, commas to
    prevent, 493
Modifiers
  adjectives, 379
  adverbs, 395, 397

articles, 381
  good and *well,* 401
  predicate adjectives, 337
  See also Adjectives; Adverbs
Months, capitalization of, 479
Mood, 662
Movies, 633, 634
Multimedia presentation,
    290–293, 662
  creating with computer soft-
    ware, 292
  example, 290, 292
  parts, 293
  to persuade, 291
  style, 292
  types, 291
Multiple-choice tests, 586
Music, writing topics in, 155

N

Names, capitalization of, 473
Narrative writing, 142–179, 662
  conclusion for, 162
  details in, 153
  developing real-life story in,
    148–151
  dialogue in, 156–159
  drafting, 145–146, 154, 158,
    169–170
  editing, 149, 162, 171
  keeping story on track in,
    152–155
  literature models in, 149, 156,
    172–178
  organizing, 152–155
  presenting, 158, 171
  prewriting, 145, 161, 165, 169
  revising, 146, 153, 166, 170
  writing about real events in,
    160–163
Nationalities, capitalizing
    names of, 479
Negatives, double, 403
Nominative case, 361–362, 659
Nonessential elements,
    commas with, 491
Nonfiction, 662
  classification of, 533
Note cards for report, 576
Notes
  in descriptive writing, 109,
    110–113

commas with, 499
direct, 473
indirect, 473
in note taking, 576, 577
punctuating, 499

R

Real-life story, developing, 148–149
Reference works
atlas, 535
dictionary, 536–537, 539–540
encyclopedias, 534–535
thesaurus, 538
Reflecting, 27, 81, 133, 171, 209, 241
Regular verb, 341, 666
Representation, 664
See also Viewing and Representing
Research, 664
Research reports
drafting, 200
editing, 199
prewriting, 198–199
sources, 685–687
Responding to literature. *See* Literature, responding to
Review, 664
Revising, 664
checklist for, 27, 59, 80, 132, 170, 208, 240
compare-and-contrast essay, 192
descriptive writing, 112, 132
expository writing, 184, 192, 208
narrative writing, 146, 153, 166, 170
oral reports, 624
personal writing, 24
persuasive writing, 220, 231, 232, 240
thesaurus in, 112
TIME Facing the Blank Page, 91, 96–97
wordy sentences, 678
in writing process, 40, 44, 58–61, 62–65, 66–69
Root words, 547, 664
Run-on sentences, 307, 664
Troubleshooter for, 252–253

S

Salutation, capitalization of, 473
Science, writing topics in, 113
Search engine, 649
Semicolons, 497–498
Sensory details, 20, 110–113, 122–124, 126, 664
Sentence combining
compound sentences, 517
compound elements, 519
prepositional phrases, 521
Sentence fluency, 66, 87, 665, 683–684, 690
Sentence fragments, 299
Troubleshooter for, 250–251
Sentence variety, 517–522, 665
Sentences
capitalization of, 473
clear sentences, 307
complex, 664–665
compound, 307, 517, 664–665
declarative, 297, 489, 660
definition of, 297, 664–665
diagraming, 466–471
exclamatory, 297, 489, 661
imperative, 297, 489, 661
interrogative, 297, 489
predicate in, 299, 301, 303, 305
run-on, 252–253, 307
simple, 307, 664–665
subject in, 299, 301, 303, 305
topic, 63–64
types of, 677
varying, 66–68, 677
word order in, 303
Series, commas in, 116, 491
Setting, 122–125, 665
Silent *e*, spelling and, 557
Simile, 665
Simple predicates, 301, 465
Simple sentences, 307, 664–665
Simple subjects, 301, 465
Singular indefinite pronouns, 369
Singular nouns, 321
6+1 Trait® writing, 682
Social studies, writing topics in, 11, 69, 189
Spatial order, 665

Speaking
giving directions, 622
giving oral reports, 75, 624–627
taking part in informal discussion, 622–623
using telephones, 621
in writing conference, 26, 59, 88, 141, 247
Spelling
building skills in, 563
changes in, 557–562
compound words, 560
dictionary used for, 539
doubling the final consonant and, 559
of easily confused words, 566
of foreign words, 546
forming plurals and, 561–562
ie and *ei,* 558
problem words in, 565–567
roots, 547–550
suffixes and the final *y* and, 558
suffixes and the silent *e* and, 557
syllable boundaries, 559–560
syllables and, 539
words commonly misspelled, 565
SQ3R study method, 573–575
Standard English, 665
Standardized tests, 588–590
Stanzas, 22
States, abbreviations for, 503
Story writing. *See* Narrative writing
Storytelling, 625–627
Student models, 9, 22, 122, 160, 165, 236
Study skills
book parts, 569–570
graphic aids, 579–582
outlining, 577–578
setting study goals, 571
SQ3R study method, 573–575
taking notes, 576–577
time management, 572
Style sheet MLA, 668
Style, 665

Subject complement, 659
Subject pronouns, 361, 363
  subject-verb agreement with,
    439
Subjects, 299, 664, 665
  complete, 301
  compound, 305, 307, 443
  defined, 299
  diagraming, 465, 466
  finding, 303
  in complete sentence versus
    fragment, 250–251
  position in sentence of, 303,
    441
  simple, 301
  understood, 303, 466
Subject-verb agreement
  with compound subjects, 443
  with interrupting words and
    phrases, 441
  with noun subjects, 439
  with subject pronouns, 439
  Troubleshooter for,
    254–255
Subordinate clause, 659
Suffixes, 547, 548–550
  and the final *y*, 558
  and the silent *e*, 557
Summary, 162, 233, 665
Superlative form of an adjec-
    tive, 383, 385, 658
Superlative form of an adverb,
    399, 658
Support, for argument
    See Evidence
Suspense, 665
Symbol, 665
Symbols, for revising and
    proofreading, 72
Synonyms, 538, 540, 552, 590

T

Table of contents, 569, 570
Tables, 579
Teach, learn, 457
Technical writing, 269–289
Technology presentations,
    290–293
Telephones, using, 621
Television program, Case study
    of, 218–221
Tenses, of verbs, 339

using, 339
Tests
  grammar usage, and
    mechanics on, 590
  matching items in, 586–587
  multiple-choice items in, 586
  preparing for, 584–585
  standardized, 588–590
  time management for, 585
  true-false items in, 586
  See also Study skills
Than, then, 457
Their, they're, 457, 556
Theme, 665
Then, than, 457
There, beginning sentence with,
    441
There, their, they're, 556
Thesaurus, 538
  electronic, 125
  in revising, 112
Thesis statement, 665, 681
They're, their, 457, 556
Thinking skills, *See* Critical
    thinking
Third-person pronoun, 361
Time expressions
  abbreviations in, 503
  colons in, 497
  numbers in, 505
TIME Facing the Blank Page,
    90–99
Time lines, 581
Time management
  as study skill, 572
  for tests, 585
Time order, 665
Titles of persons
  abbreviations in, 503
  commas with, 495
Titles of works
  capitalizing, 479
  italics with, 499
  quotation marks with, 499
Tone, 665
Too, comma with, 495
Topic, finding, 46–49
Topic sentences, 63, 65, 95, 665
  elaborating, 679
  and main idea, 63
  placement, 63
Transitions
  in descriptive writing, 120,

121, 132
  in expository writing, 196
  list of, 120
  in paragraphs, 64, 680
Transitive verbs, 333
Travel brochures, creating, 128,
    129
True-false tests, 586
TV reviews, 234–237
  drafting, 236
  editing, 235
  prewriting, 235
Two, to, too, 457, 556, 566

U

Underlining. *See* Italics
Understood subject, 303, 466
Unity, 665
URL, 647, 665
Usage
  glossary of problem words,
    455, 457
  glossary of special usage
    problems, 459–462
Using Computers
  copy function, 61
  comparing Web sites, 193
  composing paragraphs on,
    69, 109
  creating charts on, 45, 237
  creating graphic organizers,
    121
  desktop publishing, 201
  drawing program, 49
  electronic thesaurus, 125
  e-mail, 229
  grammar checker, 73, 77
  line-spacing function, 163
  modems, 647
  page-layout option, 129
  researching famous people,
    167
  secured files, 15
  spelling checker, 73
  word processing program,
    69
  writing poetry on, 23
  See also Computers; Word
    processing